Systems, Stability, and Statecraft: Essays on the International History of Modern Europe

Paul W. Schroeder
Edited and with an Introduction by
David Wetzel, Robert Jervis, and
Jack S. Levy

SYSTEMS, STABILITY, AND STATECRAFT
© Paul W. Schroeder, 2004

First published 2004 by
PALGRAVE MACMILLAN™
175 Fifth Avenue, New York, N.Y. 10010 and
Houndmills, Basingstoke, Hampshire, England RG21 6XS
Companies and representatives throughout the world

PALGRAVE MACMILLAN is the global academic imprint of the Palgrave Macmillan division of St. Martin's Press, LLC and of Palgrave Macmillan Ltd. Macmillan® is a registered trademark in the United States, United Kingdom and other countries. Palgrave is a registered trademark in the European Union and other countries.

ISBN 1–4039–6357–6 hardback   ISBN 978-1-4039-6358-1
ISBN 1–4039–6358–4 paperback

Library of Congress Cataloging-in-Publication Data
Schroeder, Paul W.
    Systems, stability, and statecraft: essays on the international history of modern Europe / Paul W. Schroeder ; edited and with an introduction by David Wetzel, Robert Jervis, and Jack Levy.
        p. cm.
    Includes bibliographical references and index.
    ISBN 1–4039–6357–6 (alk. paper) – ISBN 1-4039-6358-4 (pbk : alk paper)
        1. Europe–History–1789–1900. 2. Europe–History–20th century.
3. Europe–Foreign relations–1815–1871. 4. Europe–Foreign relations–1871–1918. 5. Europe–Foreign relations–1918–1945. 6. Europe–Foreign relations–1945– 7. State, The. 8. Balance of power. 9. International relations. I. Wetzel, David. II. Jervis, Robert, 1940– III. Levy, Jack S., 1948– IV. Title.

D308.S37 2004
940.2'8–dc22   2003067187

A catalogue record for this book is available from the British Library.

Design by Newgen Imaging Systems (P) Ltd., Chennai, India.

First edition: August 2004
10 9 8 7 6 5 4 3 2 1

Printed in the United States of America.

Transferred to Digital Printing 2008

Systems, Stability, and Statecraft

CONTENTS

ACKNOWLEDGMENT

Normally the author of a scholarly work has many persons and institutions to thank for assistance and advice in carrying through his project. In this case, I have just one debt to acknowledge, but it is a major one: to the coeditors, without whose time, energy, scholarly acumen, and enterprise this book would never have been published.

Paul W. Schroeder
Champaign, Illinois

INTRODUCTION

David Wetzel, Robert Jervis, and Jack S. Levy

There has been no historian in the field of international relations in our time whose approach to his subject has been more richly innovative, more imaginative, or more erudite than Paul W. Schroeder. There doubtless have been many specialists who have been more prolific in their publications. Schroeder has published only four books—each of them substantial, two of them seminal, all of them more than enough, to be sure, to give a picture of the qualities that so awe his pupils, his colleagues, and his friends.[1] What is less well known, however, is that these same qualities are also reflected in the fifty essays more than he has published during the course of his career. These essays are now scattered in the various learned journals and thus inaccessible to the lay reader. This makes it all the more necessary that those who have the privilege of knowing him should seek to bring together the most significant of these contributions in one place and between two covers. With this purpose in mind, we have selected fourteen of Paul Schroeder's essays—twelve published, two unpublished—from the past four decades. These essays deal with the great topics and themes of the international history of Europe from the end of eighteenth century down to the present day.

Although Schroeder, like most historians, does not generalize the way political scientists do,[2] his essays are of great interest to political scientists as well as to historians, not only through his compelling analysis of specific events and eras, but also because he develops certain theoretical themes and emphasizes important processes and patterns that challenge standard propositions in the field. He argues that many students of international politics, be they political scientists or historians, have overlooked important tools of statecraft, placed excessive weight on the material structure of international politics at the expense of prevailing worldviews, and, partly as a consequence, have missed the crucial if unsteady progress of international affairs.

Paul Schroeder's historical essays are scholarly discourse at its finest. But they are more than that—much more. They constitute a ceaseless explosion of ideas—brilliant, original, forcefully and carefully argued. They heighten resistance to the superstitions of the profession, the flood of conventional knowledge—all of it plausibly wrong—that the surrounding sources of information have spread like a sterile sort of gloss over contemporary historical thought. To believe that until Napoleon the states of Germany were medieval backwaters and that only because of him did they break through to modernity; that the coalitions against Napoleon failed for lack of a common purpose; that the Congress of Vienna was not a transition, but a throwback to the world order of the eighteenth century; that the Holy Alliance was a cloak for the pursuit of Russia's interests instead of an instrument for the preservation of peace; that intermediary states are simply subjects and objects of the international political system with no intrinsic role to play of their own; that the Crimean War was caused by Russia's threat to the independence of Turkey but that its real purpose, once the war got under way, was to free Central Europe from her domination; that Metternich was the architect of the Vienna system, Bismarck the consummate *Realpolitiker*, and Gladstone the champion of enlightened diplomatic moderation; that Prussia secured freedom of action by her triumph over Austria in 1866 and Germany by her victory over France in 1870; that Great Britain wanted a balance of power in nineteenth century Europe and did pursue one; that Turkey, not Austria-Hungary, was the Sick Man of Europe in the pre-1914 years; that the recklessness of *Weltpolitik* forced the Entente Cordial of 1904 and the Triple Entente of 1907 upon the British government; that World War I was really the third Balkan war; that the history of international relations is the history of ceaseless spasms of embittered antagonisms between sovereign states—to believe these and a hundred other pieces of common knowledge causes error and blindness in current discussions about history and international politics. In the struggle against such conventional ideas, Paul Schroeder is the leader of the opposition, and these fourteen articles, all richly informed by his masterly command of the sources and literature on which they are based, constitute a series of resilient and seminal challenges to many of the reigning orthodoxies and standard views of our professions.

On more than one occasion Paul Schroeder has expressed the view that international politics is a system that is dynamic, not static; directional, not linear or circular; and that a critical turning point in international history came during the Napoleonic wars. It seems only fitting, therefore, to begin this collection of essays with one addressed to Schroeder's view of Napoleon. Napoleon's career is the greatest of modern legends. Schroeder gives the legend a good showing in order to demonstrate that it was a legend and that it overreached itself by its own authority. The entire system that Napoleon devised was nothing less than a criminal enterprise. Schroeder's essay, despite its cool tone and sobering scholarship, is an anti-Napoleon tract, one of the most damning ever composed.

It is worth pointing out, though Schroeder does not emphasize it, that Napoleon the man exemplified some nasty, even evil, qualities, including an unshakable self-righteousness, a thoroughgoing hatred of everything not French, and a high degree of bloody-mindedness with relation to anyone who disagreed with him or questioned his aspirations to the mastery of Europe. But it was in international politics that his whole unconscionable ambition found its fullest and most virulent expression. His system was one of incredible criminality, of a criminality effectively without limits. Here, as the outlines of his actions begin to emerge, through the fog of confusion and irrelevance with which he loved to surround them during his lifetime, we are confronted with a record beside which the wildest murder mystery seems banal. He was, to begin with, a man devoid of principle. To have a principle, Martin Wight once wrote, necessarily involves the exercise of restraint whenever action threatens to contradict that principle.[3] Thus, all the great powers in Napoleon's time could point to specific ambitions that they would like to satisfy—Britain to the defense of the seas and her empire, Russia to Constantinople, Austria to holding the ring in Germany and keeping ahead of Prussia, Prussia to supremacy in North Germany and the region northeast of the Rhine. Napoleon could point to everything and to nothing. Nothing could satisfy Napoleon because he had no aims to satisfy and nothing could satisfy the principles he stood for because he did not stand for any.

Thus diplomacy could not solve Napoleon's problems because he had no problems that could be solved. Far from being the forerunner of European unity that a writer has recently found in him,[4] he was a throwback to the six-teenth century, a *condottiere* who could not understand or even admit as possible the world that his opponents represented. In such a character, no grain of subtlety is discernible. Even down to his last days, Napoleon saw himself as the greatest teacher of humankind and, thanks to a vast hierarchy of obe-dient yes-men beneath him, his lightest observations became infallible truths before which inconvenient evidence must bow and retire.

Napoleon's one great contribution was negative. His rapaciousness, his inordinate and unscrupulous ambition, managed to convince the statesmen of Europe that things could not go on as they had; that the kind of politics they had practiced during the eighteenth century had made possible Napoleon's rise and that to protect the international order on which they had depended from being overwhelmed there could be no peace with him. He had to be replaced, but so too did the system that had allowed him to come into existence.

How they did so and what motives and causes prompted their action is a theme to which Schroeder turns in his essay on the Vienna settlement. Anyone who has ever seen the Schönbrunn Palace on outskirts of Vienna may recall the Prince de Ligne's apt remark: "*Le Congres danse, et ne marché-pas.*"[5] Schroeder has no sympathy with such a view. To be sure, an extraor-dinary amount of money was spent on balls, dances, symphonies, and the like, but the gravity of the tasks by which the men of 1815 were faced was daunting in the extreme. Now that Napoleon's imperium had been broken, how much it would if France be allowed to keep? If new frontiers between states were to be delineated, how was this to be carried out? In an area of the world as devastated as Central Europe, what did legitimacy mean and what did it require? This was the dilemma that the statesmen of 1815 had to con-front. They meant to fashion a new international system to replace the one that had been in vogue since the eighteenth century.

That the international system of the eighteenth century was a witches' brew, nothing more than a thoroughly regrettable expedient, tiding the powers over dangerous moments in European affairs, is a point Schroeder never ceases to emphasize. Efforts toward resolution of major political differences between the powers were practically abandoned. Belief in the inevitability of war—itself the greatest disservice to peace—had grown unchecked. In Europe many situations had arisen that required only the slightest disturbance to draw the powers into a major war. The complete uncertainty as to the adversary's intentions and the premium that rested on the element of surprise in the eighteenth century easily led statesmen to take, under the pressure of fear or misunderstanding, actions the effects of which were irreparable.[6]

Belief in the efficiency of war as an instrument of policy was underlined by its results. During the eighteenth century, two empires, the French and the Ottoman, fell into a decline and indeed, by the end of it, seemed on the verge of collapse; another, Sweden, lay decimated and a third, Polish Lithuania, had the life squeezed out of it altogether. Two others—Prussia and Russia—came into their own and an ancient fourth, the Habsburg monarchy, acquired something of a fresh start. It was war—and only war—by which changes of this scope were carried through. Even the bloodless partitions of Poland were direct by-products of the Russo-Prussian struggle.[7]

It is this fact and others like it that lead Schroeder to encourage a different attitude toward the Congress of Vienna, and to do so he adopts three lines of approach. First, he denies that the Vienna settlement rested on a balance of power in any meaningful sense. For a balance of power to exist, A. J. P. Taylor once observed, "no one state must be strong enough to eat up the rest, and any tendency toward domination by one is thwarted by a combination of checks and balances of the others."[8] Schroeder compares the respective strengths of the powers of Europe at the end of the Napoleonic wars and finds that two of them, Russia and Great Britain, which he calls the flanking powers, were decisively stronger than the other three, France, Austria, and Prussia—so much so that they dominated the Continent and could press upon it their will if they wished. The system of Vienna was not, then, one of balances, but one that rested on the shared hegemony of these two flanking powers.[9]

Second, throughout his account of the Congress of Vienna, Schroeder stresses the deep emphasis placed on equilibrium and legitimacy, and he denies that these concepts had anything in common with the balance of power as it is generally understood. The men of the Congress of Vienna left a substantial body of memoranda and writings backed up by numerous records of private opinions of intimates like Gentz, confidant of Metternich and secretary of the Congress, who reflected the terminology of his generation in calling the postwar system the "federation of Europe." Alternative terms used by him were the "general union" and the "European league." The group of principled powers he referred to was as "the great alliance," "the union of the great powers," or the "union of sovereigns."[10] Schroeder concedes that phrases like "balance du pouvoir" or "Gleichgewicht der

Kräfte" were part of the vocabulary of the Vienna statesmen, but he argues that balance of power was only part of their overall system and not its main component and perhaps not even an important one.

Third, Schroeder asks why, given the apparent disparity between the balance of power and the settlement that was actually devised, so many scholars have persisted in using the former to describe the events of 1814–15. That the Congress of Vienna represented a great achievement has been recognized at least since 1925 with the publication of the great works of Heinrich von Srbik and C. K. Webster.[11] Yet, what these writers, and later ones—of whom Henry Kissinger is the most conspicuous but by no means the only example[12]—have failed to appreciate is how truly revolutionary the Vienna system was. Instead, they speak of a restoration, a return to stability, a reestablishment of a balance of power, even an age of reaction and repression of revolution and change.

Schroeder will have none of it. Eighteen fifteen represented a revolution, if ever one is entitled to speak of a revolution; it inaugurated systemic change so far-reaching, so revolutionary, so fundamental in norms, rules, expectations, and collective assumptions that it laid the foundations of the world that has followed ever since. Standard interpretations of the Vienna system fail to comprehend the nature of these changes, and indeed much of nineteenth century European politics, because they continue to view that system through the lenses of traditional conceptions of balance of power.[13]

Schroeder analyzes this new conception of balance and equilibrium in his essay on "The Nineteenth Century System: Balance of Power or Political Equilibrium?" In contrast to eighteenth century Europe, in which power—calculated in terms of territory, population, and revenues, and leveraged by alliances—was used to balance and restrain power, Schroeder argues that it was a fundamentally different system that emerged after the Congress of Vienna. What made it different, and what explains the far greater stability of the nineteenth century, was primarily a "transformation of political thinking," in which political leaders had come to conceive of balance and equilibrium in new ways. Schroeder argues that this was a "predominantly moral, legal, and social-communal model of balance in which equilibrium required first and foremost the maintenance of the political and social order as a whole and the unity of all powers in defense of the legally established order." It was a "balance of satisfactions, a balance of rights and obligations and a balance of performance and payoffs, rather than a balance of power."[14]

Thus the men at Vienna cast out onto the surface of international life a host of new, and for the most part, historic methods and functions. They demonstrated, first of all, that political equilibrium is possible in international affairs without a balance of power, and that traditional balance of power politics often works against international stability. Second, they showed that international systems, though chaotic, can be restrained and moderated through the cooperative efforts of the great powers. Third, the Vienna statesmen left behind a host of other accomplishments that identified them, as George Kennan once observed, as gardeners not mechanics:[15] the creation of (1) international intermediary bodies—especially a defensively-oriented European center; (2) restraining alliances, understandings, and ententes; (3) a whole series of treaties that settled territorial disputes from 1787 to 1815. The historic task of the Vienna statesmen was to sever the international system from its roots and launch it on a path of movement. This was the task that was accomplished in 1815.

Schroeder extends his argument about the revolutionary changes of 1815 and the inauguration of a new international order to Russian behavior throughout the nineteenth century. In his essay on "Containment Nineteenth Century Style: The Case of Russia," Schroeder contrasts the ruthless and domineering behavior of Russia since the time of Peter the Great with the "conservative, legalistic, antirevolutionary" policy that aimed for peace and great power cooperation after the Congress of Vienna. This was a time when many Europeans feared that Russia would use its enormous gains in territory and influence from the eighteenth century to make a bid for a broader position of hegemony. Schroeder concedes that Russia was expansionist in Asia, but argues that it knew when to stop so as to avoid wars with other European powers over non-European conflicts, and that in any case expansionist behavior outside of Europe did not threaten the stability of the European system.

Scholars who acknowledge Russian restraint in the first half of the nineteenth century generally attribute it to the effective functioning of a balance of power system and Russia's fear that its pursuit of expansionist policies would trigger a hostile balancing coalition. Schroeder dissents from this view. He argues that Russian leaders were restrained primarily by the new international order and sense of European community that they themselves had helped to construct. They believed in the new treaty system, in the principle of monarchial solidarity, and in the desirability and feasibility of collective great power management of European politics, and they sought the prestige, national and individual, that would come from Russia's playing a central role in that system. The other leading statesmen of Europe responded to their fears of Russian power and ambition not by seeking to form a *cordon sanitaire* around it, but by attempting to influence Russia by bringing her into their system of alliances. They believed that each country's vital interests could be preserved while at the same time subjecting the parochial perspectives of each to the broadening understanding of the interests of others.

Schroeder ends this chapter with the generalization that "any government is restrained better and more safely by friends and allies than by opponents or enemies." This is a key theme in Schroeder's worldview, and one he develops more fully in his essay on "Allies, 1815–1945: Weapons of Power and Tools of Management." This essay has been particularly influential among political scientists because it departs from the conventional interpretation of alliances in terms of an implicit "capability aggregation model," in which states join together, usually for specific and short-run purposes, in order to deploy greater resources than either could do alone.

Schroeder does not deny that this occurs, but he shows that alliances can serve other, less obvious, functions. They can be instruments by which one ally can influence or control another or a way in which all of the members can restrain and guide each other. Countries give up some autonomy by entering into an alliance, and in parallel gain some ability to shape what their partners will do. There is no contradiction between fearing another state and seeking to develop close ties with it; indeed, the latter policy is often the best way to influence a potentially threatening state and ensure that frictions do not escalate to overt conflict. The use of alliances as a tool of influence and control has often been associated with Bismarck, but Schroeder provides a more general conceptualization and applies it to a wide range of historical cases.

As Schroeder emphasizes in many of his essays, diplomacy often works through grouping, bringing states together in a way that makes it difficult for any of them to undertake unilateral adventures. Inclusion can be a potent instrument in part because states fear being excluded. We can of course interpret this in pure power terms and argue that in international politics as in social life, isolation is almost always dangerous, not splendid. But there is more to it than this. While unusual domestic imperatives may drive a state to cut itself off from the outside world as much as possible (e.g., Tokugawa Japan), most states seek broad acceptance. One reason South Africa finally rejected Apartheid was the steady toll exacted on leaders and the white elite by prolonged exclusion from most forms of international contact. Even North Korea today, with its ideological commitment to self-sufficiency, strongly desires acceptance as a normal state.

The desire for inclusion and acceptance stems in part from straightforward security concerns; being part of the society of nations is a sign that others are likely to respect the state's independence, an implicit form of nonaggression pact. But being included also has intrinsic value. It is taken by all as an indication that despite whatever important differences in policy and interest exist, there are important commonalities as well, that the state is not inferior to the others, and that it is a member in good standing of a highly valued club. Schroeder is not equating political leaders with teenagers in their desire for approval, but he sees that most national leaders seek genuine recognition by their opposite numbers and that citizens and elites identify with their states and find validation in others' acceptance of them.

Groupings of states do not operate in a vacuum, of course, but require at least a modicum of common interest and purpose. But the converse is true as well; interests and purposes do not form by themselves, but are shaped by the groupings that exist and are possible. On some occasions, of course, states may be so inner-directed and committed to values antithetical to others that only containment and war will work. The sort of containment that was effective against—or rather with—Russia in the nineteenth century could not work with Nazi Germany. Indeed, as Schroeder argues with respect to World War I, by 1914 states had developed worldviews that saw others as conspiring enemies and framed their own interests in so narrowly nationalistic a fashion that armed conflict had become inevitable. But this was not a product of international anarchy and domestic instability, but came instead from the way the states treated each other. National goals can be more or less moderate, more or less compatible with the goals of others, and more or less informed by an understanding that the states form a system and that national actions have important if difficult-to-discern implications for the health and stability of the system.[16] States cannot fully determine others' goals, but they can influence them.

Conventional scholars understand this, and point to the role of superior force and hostile alliances in curbing the ambitions of the great disturbers of the international system, of enforcing moderation from the outside. This of course is part of the picture, but Schroeder realizes that it misses the more important part. States can go a significant way toward inducing moderation by recognizing others' vital interests. "Recognizing" has two meanings, both of which apply here. One is recognizing in the sense of understanding, of seeing interests of others that may not be easy to discern. The state must seek to understand what it is that others need to maintain their roles in the international system. Perhaps the cardinal sin in international politics—and Schroeder sees this as a moral as well as a political failing—is to be blind to others' contributions and needs. The failure of Great Britain to understand the position, value, and fragility of Austria-Hungary and the implications this had for the entire international system, for example, was a root cause of World War I.[17]

Acting on an appreciation of others' needs can lead to granting it what is required for it to be willing to continue to work with others and abstain from the unilateral use of force, to abide by international agreements and understandings. Sometimes, of course, states will not settle for anything less than the domination if not the destruction of their neighbors. Hitler again provides the obvious example. But it also is an unusual case. More frequently, states are willing or can be brought around to being willing to live with arrangements that are at least minimally satisfactory to others.[18]

For Schroeder, normal diplomatic arrangements, agreements, and institutions, important as they are, are shaped by deeper impulses. In a well-functioning international system, such as that which characterized most of the nineteenth century, political elites develop a set of values and perspectives that support grouping, moderation, and respect for others. They learn from experience—almost always bitter experience—that the alternative of unregulated competition for power and short-run interest leads to bloody wars that tear the system and the member states apart.[19] This is not learning in the sense of getting a better idea of what instruments can reach a standard goal, but rather what sociologists and political scientists refer to as socialization, the learning (or relearning) of basic attitudes and values, of appropriate ways of constructing a broader system. Central to the evolution of international politics and behavior in specific circumstances are the ways in which leaders have been socialized to view the world and their own interests in it, and how they think others can be best influenced and accommodated.

Socialization by necessity is a process that is both individual and collective. Individual leaders and states are socialized, but not in isolation from each other. They are moved by events that they share, and each state helps socialize the others. The best example, and the one with greatest consequences for

European history, was the resocialization that grew out of the Napoleonic wars. The leaders were able to form a coalition, bring down Napoleon, and, even more impressively, drastically alter the way international politics had been conducted because they shared the experience of a generation of incredibly destructive warfare. The leaders then came to realize that whatever they did, it would be insanity to return to the old ways of conducting international business. They not only learned new mechanisms of cooperation, but they came to understand that routinely seeking security at the expense of others would end in mutual destruction. They came to appreciate that moving alone in a highly interactive system was likely to harm others and bring down their wrath, and that they could best flourish by working together.

Power was not absent, of course, but it was joined by a new sense of responsibility, and a conception of living in a world in which no state could afford to entirely neglect broader interests. It was not, or not only, that states moderated their demands in the anticipation that others would oppose them, but that they saw themselves as part of a larger system, and that their conceptions of self-interest and how to further it changed.

This conception of international order is epitomized, in Schroeder's view, by the Vienna system. The tragedy of that system, for Schroeder, was that political leaders of the mid-nineteenth century missed a great opportunity to consolidate the new international order and instead found themselves locked into the disastrous road to the Crimean War. In the crisis leading up to the war, and throughout its three-year course, there was one power that worked persistently to avoid being dragged into the war and to bring that war to an end as swiftly as possible. The power in question was Austria, and the statesman who guided the Austrian ship of state during this terrible time was Buol, the foreign minister. For years Buol was viewed as a dark figure. Metternich, for instance, called his policy "idiotic," and even so detached a historian as M. S. Anderson, writing in 1966, labeled him the "architect of disaster."[20] In a series of remarkable essays, one of which is reproduced here, Schroeder found a wholly different character. He argues that while Buol took many paths that proved dead ends, he believed in them for the purest of motives. And when Schroeder, as a historian, tries to chart the course of the decisions he took, his sympathies are often with him, if not always, with them.

Many of these decisions ran into vigorous opposition from his opponents at home. Of these, Bruck, an economist, minister of commerce under Prince Schwarzenberg, and Buol's predecessor, was by far the most formidable. From his position in Constantinople, Bruck bickered fiercely with Buol over the course of Austrian policy. Bruck was a diplomat of severely limited vision and ability, and he pined for a policy based on tradition, on alliance with Russia, a new Holy Alliance. But it is clear from Schroeder's essay that it was Buol, not Bruck, who was the traditionalist and who tried to apply Metternich's principles to the crisis at hand. Like Metternich, Buol wanted to check Russia without humiliating her. Like Metternich, he knew that the issue was not whether Russia should be contained, but how; like Metternich, he saw the specter of revolution on the horizon if the Eastern question broke away from diplomatic control. Both Metternich and Buol knew that their policy would not be tolerated by their opponents at home unless it made Austria and hence Europe more secure; therefore, they sometimes seemed to the diplomatic community at Vienna to be shifty and not above cheating their allies. Their ultimate object, a general settlement of the Eastern question through Concert diplomacy, did not alter.

Schroeder's concern, as he says at the outset, is more to draw attention to the defects of Bruck's policy than to point out the advantages of Buol's.[21] Yet his preference for Buol's policy is clear, and it is not hard to see why. That Buol did not want a violent solution to the Eastern question; that he wished to end the conflict as rapidly as possible; that he shrank from grandiose slogans; that he blenched from picturing the war as a crusade; that he wished to keep open the channels of communications to all sides; that he was incredulous at schemes that would pull Russia down from the ranks of the great powers; that he skillfully used his diplomatic prowess carefully and with an eye toward bringing its full force to bear at critical moments; that he wanted to end the war with a minimum of prejudice to the future stability of the Continent—is clear. The main answer to the Eastern crisis that Buol envisaged was simple and straight out of Metternich's book: a five-power Concert including Russia. Turkey would be preserved and peace saved, not by building Turkey up or by pulling Russia down, but by compelling Russia to deal with Turkey only in concert through the four other great powers.

In the end, Buol's efforts failed, and Austria emerged from the Crimean War worse off than anyone else—worse off, even than Russia, who had met defeat on the battlefield and humiliation at the peace table. Indeed, Russia, though defeated, reformed herself vigorously and within 20 years was stronger than ever. As for the French and especially for British, victory in the war was superficial, for they too would soon reap a bitter harvest from the Concert's destruction. The transmogrification of Russia from a conservative power into a revisionist one and the withdrawal of Russian support for the Concert system opened the door to the unification of Italy and Germany that was to prove inimical, indeed catastrophic, to the interests of Britain. None of Britain's political leaders understood then or until many years later the full import to their country of a united, powerful, militarized, conservative Prussia-Germany. In that lack of understanding surely, as Norman Rich has pointed out, are to be found some of the roots of the fatal Anglo-German antagonism of the twentieth century.[22]

In another essay, not published in this book, Schroeder begins by recounting a story of the American humorist, Robert Benchley, who faced an examination at Harvard that included the question: "Discuss the Canadian-American fisheries treaty from the standpoint of the Canadians or the Americans." Benchley retorted that he could not bring himself to discuss it from either the standpoint of the Canadians or the Americans and would instead discuss it from the standpoint of the fish.[23] Schroeder may well have used this same lead to open his piece on "The Lost Intermediaries."

Schroeder begins his essay with a general formulation. All intermediary bodies have, he points out, some function in helping states mitigate conflicts: "Where they exist," he writes, "Great Power competition stands a good chance of being limited to primacy. Where they do not, Great Power rivalry tends powerfully toward struggles for mastery."[24] Here he is at pains to stress that, of all such regions, the four South Germany states constituted one of the richest, most fertile zones of Europe for flexibility, moderation, and restraint in the ordering and management of international relations, and that their disappearance into Germany in 1871 had consequences "almost as important as the so-called unification of Germany itself."[25]

The core of Schroeder's essay deals with the consequences of the Franco-Prussian War, in particular the disappearance of the four states of South Germany—Bavaria, Württemberg, Hesse-Darmstadt, and Baden—and with the implications of this for the European international system. His central contention is that by absorbing the states of South Germany in 1871, Bismarck displayed a certain unusual ineptness and actually made Germany's position with respect to the other great powers—France, Austria, and, most of all, Russia—immeasurably, not to say irremediably, worse than it had been before.

Schroeder recognizes that there are objections to this view, two of them particularly forceful, but he disposes of them in characteristic exemplary fashion. One is that the states of South Germany had been conquered as much as the states that Prussia had absorbed in 1866, and that all were tied to her by treaties of alliance. The second objection is that the Treaty of Prague, which ended the Austro-Prussian War of 1866, was ephemeral and transitional, a stopgap settlement that no one really cared about and whose arrangements were so obviously provisional and tenuous that the union of Germany in some form or another was inevitable.

The first objection, he notes, errs in the facts. Though these four southern states were in Prussia's orbit prior to 1870, they clearly acted independently of her in significant ways, developing as they did domestic, military, and even foreign policy that were independent of Bismarck and even downright worrying to him. Consider Bavaria: the victory, in the elections of May and November 1869, of the anti-Patriot Party; the overthrow, in February 1870, of the prime minister, Hohenlohe; and the notorious unreliability of King Ludwig II.

The second objection dissolves as well, for it underestimates what Schroeder sees to be the real strength of the peace of 1866. That the peace did not provide a lasting basis for Germans' national existence is clear enough; that it could not have done so is much more debatable. As Lothar Gall has argued, the settlement had in it the three elements that are essential for any settlement of the German question. It was, first of all, an international settlement accepted by all the major actors—by Austria, by France, and even by Russia. It could function, therefore, as an intermediary body that ordered Central European affairs and at the same time hamstrung great power interference. In addition, its organization balanced great powers' need for independence with smaller states' requirement for security and stability. Finally, its transitory nature was paradoxically a source of its strength.[26] All attempts to undermine the settlement of 1866 ran into the sand—Napoleon III's schemes to block Prussia at the Main through a maze of intricate alliances; Bismarck's schemes to bring the south German states into the North German Confederation; Austria's schemes to throw her net over the same states by sham pretense of liberal reform; and Baden's scheme to get into the confederation voluntarily.

Schroeder does not, it should be noted, deny the role of the settlement of 1866 in advancing the great changes that came over Europe in the years that followed. After 1866, he notes, the powers outside Germany lost interest in the south German states. Austria, Russia, and Italy had, he argues, some interest in keeping the star of Prussian power from rising in the German political sky, but for each, for different reasons, this interest was more apparent than real. By 1870, most Austrians had forgotten about south German independence; they were dismayed by the seeming instability of the anti-Prussian cause; the woeful disunity among its various components, the confusing, kaleidoscopic quality of the changes in the political and military fortunes of the various groups. In any case, Austria, in a pinch, had always opted for a deal with Prussia over south German heads; Russian ambitions were fixated on the Black Sea, Italian ones on Rome. For each, indifference was preferable to intervention.

One power, however, could not afford such indifference: France. For her, the fate of South Germany, with whom she was connected by reasons of history and geography, was a life-and-death matter. After 1866, France saw the Prussian threat clearly and attempted to do what she could—acquiring Luxemburg and Belgium, forging a maze of alliances, and so on—to block Prussia. These attempts represented a clear effort to confront the Prussian danger, but as Schroeder points out, with respect to the south German states, they represented no change at all. Indeed, they made an already bad situation much worse. Especially was this the case after 1867 when the French determined that a crossing of the Main by Prussia would constitute a *casus belli*. This could only make a Franco-Prussian War more likely and with it, the possibility that the states who had the most to fear from such a war—Bavaria, Württemberg, Baden, and Hesse-Darmstadt—would disappear.

Schroeder's argument has some important implications for the origins of the Franco-Prussian War. If the picture he paints is accurate, traditional views of its outbreak—what Bismarck was after in trying to promote a crisis of relations with France in the Hohenzollern candidacy—lose much of their force.[27] The real question becomes: What danger was so great for him in 1870 as to make him adopt a scheme that was so uncharacteristic of him, one that could easily backfire, blow up in his face, and quite possibly cost him his job? Schroeder's essay suggests a possible answer: not a desire to provoke war with France, but the need to counteract the multiplex simultaneity of the debacles described at the end of his essay: the founding in Baden of a particularist and anti-Prussian *Volkspartei*; the unleashing in Württemberg of a campaign by Bismarck's opponents to tear up the military budget, and, worst of all, the overthrow, just alluded to, of the Hohenlohe ministry and its replacement in Munich by a ministry of the pro-Austrian Patriot Party. From the force of the evidence Schroeder presents, one might well conclude that Bismarck was in no hurry to annex the states of south Germany and that he was driven into action only because events in Bavaria and elsewhere had upset the status quo. A considerable piece of historical revision, to say the least.

In 1887 Bismarck sent this malicious comment to William Ewart Gladstone, the British prime minister. "Tell him that while he is busy chopping down trees, I am busy planting them"[28]—a remark that reveals as much about Bismarck's caustic tongue as it does about Gladstone's gardening habits. They were wildly different men—Bismarck and Gladstone. Their dislike for each other was intense, and yet there was, as Schroeder points out, more between the two of them than meets the eye.

The standard view of Gladstone runs something like this. He was, or became, the People's William. He knew perfectly well that the people were wholeheartedly on his side. He promoted moderation and caution in political judgment. The essence of Gladstone's foreign policy was his belief in the public law of Europe. The rulers of Central Europe, especially Austria-Hungary, having proved untrue to public law, were powers with whom Great Britain should have nothing to do. Their policy toiled after events, accumulating errors, without discovering in them a solution for Europe's troubles. Gladstone's vision was entirely different. He wanted to combine progress and Christianity. He advocated economy and peace, but managed to take a step that led inevitably to modern British imperialism. With John Bright, he believed that moral law is intended not only for individual life, but for the life and practice of states in their dealings with each other. He personified, in short, righteousness, a moral fervor, that swelled as he took up, reluctantly, international questions. He wanted to ignore the Continent and to discharge the British mission in the rest of the world. The British, calling upon those qualities of mind and spirit that had made their country the center of the highest form of civilization the modern world had ever known, would teach everyone else to follow their example.[29]

The champion of moderation and enlightenment is, Schroeder notes, a long way from the Gladstone of history—a man essentially no different from the general run of human agents who find themselves in places of authority, subject to the same limitations, affected by the same restrictions of vision, tainted by the same original sin and, one may add, by the same inner conflicts between flesh and spirit, between self-love and charity. It is easy to make fun of Gladstone. Schroeder resists the temptation. He lets Gladstone make fun of himself. Gladstone, Schroeder shows, was a man of daring improvisation. He made lightning decisions and then presented them as the result of some long-term policy. He could really judge a situation as it existed at the moment without worrying about the Concert of Europe or what he said the day before. He lived with an intensity that would have exhausted any lesser man. His intense personal vision led him to ignore others or to push them out of the way. Whatever he did, in Africa, in the Balkans, or in Egypt, was in Britain's strategic interest, and it is difficult to resist the feeling that Gladstone was on God's side because God had so arranged things to be on Gladstone's.

These observations will suffice to give some idea of the many points of this essay—richly informed by Schroeder's familiarity with British international history, interesting, carefully argued, and deserving of a detailed critical comment that could not be given within this space. But one or two of them speak to the heart of the essay's central concern.

Schroeder rejects, to begin with, the suggestion that Bismarck tricked Gladstone into intervening in Egypt in the hope of ruining Anglo-French relations. He recognizes the multitudinous aspects of Gladstone's policy, and shows how changes to it resulted in a policy torn asunder by moral, legal, and practical shortcomings. He disagrees with those who believe that Gladstone's moral principles overrode his practical limitations. He rejects, on balance, the view that Gladstone's policy represented an alternative to Bismarck's *Realpolitik*. He favors an explanation that sees them as sides of the same coin. Finally, he rejects an orientation that gives primacy to motives in the analysis of international politics. Results, he believes, often count more than motives in international affairs.

Despite his pious pretenses, Gladstone was, in Schroeder's view, devoid of moral earnestness. His policy is best characterized as one that presaged that of Sir Edward Grey, as "realist" a foreign minister who ever held office. Like Grey, he speculated on friendship with France; like Grey, he wanted to detach Italy from the Triple Alliance and destroy the Three Emperors' League; like every British minister, except conservatives like Disraeli, he despised Austria; like Grey, he was willing to make concessions to Germany outside Europe as long as she remained restrained within it.

Schroeder's discussion is not without contemporary relevance. It gains in significance by virtue of the pervasive bewilderment that prevails today in academic, journalistic, and governmental circles on the question addressed to the respective roles of moral absolutes and national interest in foreign policy. It shows, among other things, how readily a genuine subjective idealism can be turned to the service of *Realpolitik* and imperialist expansion; how easily double standards and an ethics of success triumph over principle; and how easily victories lure the victor into unmanageable tangles and ironic unintended consequences. Such tangles and consequences played a significant role in the drift of the system toward war in 1914. This was the tragic result, in Schroeder's view, of a breakdown in political equilibrium in Europe, an end to the observance of the values of prudence, of proportionality, and of international law, and the return of the competitive zero–sum politics of an earlier era.

The instability of early twentieth century Europe was pronounced and deeply rooted. Never since 1871—in fact, never since the breakup of the Concert of Europe in 1854—was Europe, and particularly Central Europe, fully stable. The framework prevailing in Eastern and Central Europe in the period in the early years of the century was so deeply impregnated with hostile and uncompromising assumptions that it was becoming difficult to keep control of a number of potentially explosive situations.

The British entente with Russia in 1907 completed the formation of the Triple Entente of Britain, France, and Russia, which stood opposed to the Triple Alliance or, more accurately, the Dual Alliance of Germany and Austria-Hungary, since Italy had, by a series of agreements with France, long since parted company with her Central European allies. Competition between the states of Europe, once confined to the areas overseas, now centered on the European fault lines—the Rhine and the Balkans.

For one vital actor a deep-seated pessimism and an extreme militarization not only of her thought but also of her life had become the hallmark of the prewar age, and that was Austria-Hungary. By 1914, exhausted and weakened, she had all but washed her hands of the Concert system; become unshakably unconvinced that the Concert was broken and bankrupt; and determined that only by taking up arms could she maintain her status and interests as a great power against potentially fatal threats. Why Austria-Hungary decided to push over the established system from which she had once benefitted and from the fall of which she alone could not gain is the topic Schroeder addresses in "World War I as Galloping Gertie."

There was one power that added immeasurably to the problems Austria faced and turned her from a stabilizing member of the system into a destabilizing and vengeful one, and that was Britain. Almost every aspect of Britain's policy from 1890 to 1914, if not intentionally anti-Austrian, had consequences that made it so. The alliances of Britain with France in 1904 and with Russia in 1907, though concerned with areas outside Europe, vitally affected Austria in the most negative of ways, for they impelled Britain's partners into actions that were, to say the least, inimical to Habsburg interests. Who, Schroeder asks, was threatened by France's success in consolidating her alliance with Russia after Germany's defeat at the conference at Algeciras in 1906? Did this not have the effect of reviving Russian interests in the Balkans and Russia's policy directed against Austria-Hungary? Similarly, who was jolted by France's attempts to lure Italy out of the Triple Alliance? Was not the result of this the unchaining of *Italia irredenta* on the same Balkans, adding immeasurably to the perennial Austrian–Italian differences over an area where Austria had life-and-death interests? It was Austria, not Germany, Schroeder shows, who was, or became, the real target of Entente diplomacy; Austria, not Germany, who was in danger of becoming, in the years before 1914, hopelessly encircled by the powers hostile to her. All the disturbing elements in the relations between Austria and the Entente Powers proceeded, he notes, almost overwhelmingly from the Entente side.

One might object, as a responsible critic has, that the central problem from which Schroeder has averted his eyes was the nationalities question; that the monarchy was disintegrating because the peoples within it were detaching themselves from its control; and that this made impossible any solution by Britain or anyone else to preserve the status quo.[30] But this misses the point and misunderstands his argument on several fronts. No other power was called upon to save the Habsburg Monarchy, any more than anyone was called upon to save Imperial Russia in its far worse crises of 1905–06. That was not necessary. The Habsburg Monarchy was capable of indefinitely soldiering on or muddling through in 1914, as she had done recurrently throughout her long life in many worse crises.

What a sane international policy called for, and what everyone including the Central Powers did in 1905–06, was not to take advantage of an indispensable great power's internal troubles to bring her down, and not to support or encourage external attacks or subversion against her. The nationalist outbursts in the Balkans had continued more or less regularly since 1821 (or better, 1804) and had never caused a great war (though they had come close on some occasions) precisely because they were in the end not allowed to destroy the indispensable foundation of nineteenth century European peace, which was the fragile restraining alliance and balance between Germany, Austria-Hungary, and Russia. The plain fact is that Britain (especially) and France, which had often tried to break up this restraining alliance throughout the nineteenth century for their own selfish purposes (in 1825–27, the 1830s, 1848–49, Crimean War, Polish Crisis of 1863, Eastern Crisis of 1875–78, Bulgarian Crisis 1884–87, etc.), now quite deliberately took advantage of the alienation of Russia and Austria to advance their own security and imperialist purposes. Particularly after 1907, they simply refused to restrain Russia and even encouraged her in supporting and defending Serbian and Rumanian nationalist aspirations against the Monarchy. Thus Schroeder charges Britain not with treachery but instead with long-range stupidity and irresponsibility in failing to see and prepare for the systemic consequences of what she was doing.

Schroeder develops many of these themes regarding the outbreak of World War I in another essay, written more than three decades later and focused around the analytic theme of contingency and counterfactual analysis in history. In "Embedded Counterfactuals and World War I as an Unavoidable War," Schroeder argues that counterfactuals are inherent in historical analysis and potentially quite useful, but he questions conventional approaches to counterfactual analysis and argues that the most useful counterfactuals to investigate are those that were actually perceived and debated by the historical actors themselves.

Schroeder illustrates his methodological orientation to counterfactual analysis through an inquiry on the outbreak of World War I. While he accepts the argument that in the absence of the German–Austro-Hungarian initiative (after the assassination) that aimed at a local war and accepted the risk of a general war, World War I would not have happened, at least at that time, Schroeder criticizes a number of propositions commonly associated with that view.[31] He argues, contrary to the conventional wisdom, that the security challenges facing Germany and Austria-Hungary in 1914 were not primarily of their own making and that they were responding to a system that was being controlled by others; that German and Austro-Hungarian policies and actions (as opposed to their rhetoric) were in fact more moderate than those of the other great powers; that the leaders of the Central Powers had few viable alternatives in 1914; and that the war was basically inevitable.

This failure of the great powers to restrain each other is a significant step back from the new international order of the Concert period where statesmen believed that a defeated France and a potentially threatening Russia were each best influenced by bringing them into the system of restraining alliances of the Concert. However, this return to earlier ways of behavior does not lead Schroeder to conclude that history is essentially circular or repetitive. In contrast to such a nondirectional conception of history, and in contrast to the view of realist international theory that anarchic international structures generate patterns of competitive politics that vary relatively little over time, Schroeder argues that the history of international relations demonstrates a clear sense of progress, of unidirectional, upward movement. From this he derives a "certain amount of rational hope and emancipatory power in facing the future of international politics,"[32] exuding an optimism that would have daunted even Macaulay.

The recognition of the European states system in 1648, the replacement of a crisis-prone and destabilizing system of dynastic legitimacy with a system of balance of power in the eighteenth century, and, most significantly of all, the transformation of political thinking and the emergence of a new collective mentality of rules and procedures toward the end of the Napoleonic wars—all these significantly stabilized international politics and reduced the frequency of war.

The nineteenth century transformation was conceived in the 1780s when the British economy was the first to achieve self-sustaining growth, and the French Revolution began the process of clearing away the *ancien régime*, but it could gather strength only when peace came and the immense new resources in finance, management, and science could be put to constructive use. That, in turn, could not have been accomplished without the diplomatic revolution that Schroeder describes, one that transformed international politics in a manner it had never been transformed before or since.[33] It was just as essential as the birth of a new concept of domestic politics that grew out of the French Revolution,[34] and in Schroeder's opinion surpassed the French Revolution in significance and long-range importance. With Harold Nicolson, he argues that the post-Napoleonic revolution endured beyond the Vienna system and the mid-century crisis marked by the revolutions of 1848 and the Crimean War.[35] This long-term progress in international politics led, in the nineteenth century, to the rise of the trading state, the emergence of growing numbers of international organizations and, more recently, to international integration, heralding an accelerating, irreversible evolution (or revolution) that possibly constitutes the deepest and most fundamental transformation ever.

Schroeder's conception of modern diplomatic history differs from the traditional "event history," as the French *Annalistes* so contemptuously characterized political and diplomatic history of the Rankean tradition, because he subsumes individual events within a *histoire de longue durée* and adopts a systemic perspective.[36] But Schroeder's history also differs from the systemic perspective advanced by the historian Paul Kennedy in *The Rise and Fall of the Great Powers* (1988) or by political scientists like Kenneth Waltz in his structural realist *Theory of International Politics* (1979). While those systemic perspectives focus primarily on material structures and posit, implicitly or explicitly, that similar structures tend to recur in international politics and generate similar behaviors and outcomes at different points, Schroeder emphasizes ideational structures that change over time, so that similar material structures generate different behaviors and outcomes at different points.

Schroeder rejects any assumption of "an essentially unchanging cyclical struggle for power or the shifting play of the balance of power," and focuses instead on the "fundamental changes in the rules, norms, expectations, and collective assumptions."[37] He shares with M. S. Anderson a great respect for the increasingly complex network of classical diplomacy which, with all its faults, was one of Europe's greatest gifts to the world.[38] But he sees the different stages in the evolution of international politics not so much as reflections of changing cultural assumptions of the eras of faith, the Enlightenment, of industrialization, and so on, as Anderson does, but as an autonomous process with its own internal dynamics of progress. European statesmen ultimately learned from their defeats, setbacks, and disastrous experiences in the Napoleonic wars and set out to create a system that, in turn, shaped and limited the culture of international political interaction.[39]

Schroeder further refines his theory of historical development in his essay on "The Cold War and Its Ending in 'Long-Duration' International History." He argues that European international politics has progressed through certain identifiable stages of historical development, and that the Cold War can be interpreted as a continuation of that pattern. More specifically, Schroeder argues that the periods 1643–1715 and 1811–20 each mark definitive transformations in European politics which broke with the past in ways that were evident to contemporaries as well as to later historians. Each transformation marked the emergence of a new order, a new set of assumptions and collective mentalities of political leaders, and a growing consensus of a conception of peace that facilitated a relatively stable operation of the new system. Each system went through a stage of crisis, partial breakdown, and partial transformation which led in turn to the next stage of renewed stabilization but then gradual deterioration. The last phase of development involved the final breakdown of the old order and the earliest stage of the emergence of a new one. Schroeder argues that the Cold War and its end fit this pattern and constitute the final breakdown of the old order and a breakthrough to new system, comparable to the new orders of 1643–1715 and 1811–20. Each new order, he argues, is superior to the previous one, at least in terms of the degree of normative consensus and the prospects for peace.

The fact that we can discern meaningful progress suggests that the absence of world government and the persistence of structural anarchy do not doom the world to perpetual warfare or preclude a trend toward a more humane international politics, one built on learning and benign socialization. Despite occasional regression to older patterns of behavior, political leaders are not trapped in a merciless game whose rules they cannot influence, but instead, collectively, and for the most powerful of them individually, they can build a better world. Countries and leaders often have a significant range of choice, and, contrary to many students of international politics, Schroeder thinks that states can behave morally or immorally and that scholars have the right and the duty to judge their choices and to make moral judgments.

Schroeder develops this theme in "International History: Why Historians Do It Differently than Political Scientists." He argues that one of the prime responsibilities of a historian is to render justice to states and their leaders. Few are villains; fewer still are heroes. But some not only do a better job than others of advancing their own interests, but even more importantly do a better job of building a well-regulated system, of carrying out their responsibilities, of developing, living by, and enforcing the principles that permit as many states as possible to thrive. Although in some cases indignation and condemnation on the part of the historian reflect mere hindsight and fleeting contemporary values, when appropriately developed, these sentiments can set the record straight and pay due honor—and dishonor—to people for their vision, values, and choices. Furthermore, these evaluations can educate and guide citizens and future leaders, thereby enhancing, if only modestly, the prospects for progress.

It is in this context that Schroeder judges current American foreign policy so severely in "The Mirage of Empire Versus the Promise of Hegemony." The policies of George W. Bush are not merely an adaptation to the dangers and opportunities posed by the current international environment, but reflect a choice to revert to an older way of trying to rule rather than to manage the international system. Contrary to the argument of some analysts, including one of us, who see the overthrow of Saddam and the broader policy that this behavior represents as typical of a dominant state,[40] Schroeder stresses the large role of choice involved in the decisions to pursue an empire rather than a more consultative and benign hegemony. This can be condemned not only as likely to bring grief to many countries, including the United States, but more deeply as a step backward that calls for a moral as well as pragmatic criticism. As the entire corpus of his work demonstrates, detailed understanding of historical events, far from being antithetical to analysis of contemporary problems and judgments about the wisdom of current policies, can provide an informed basis for them.

I

War, Peace, and the Concert

1

NAPOLEON'S FOREIGN POLICY:
A CRIMINAL ENTERPRISE

Napoleon's decision to invade Russia against the almost unanimous advice of his closest counselors presents an intriguing and important puzzle to which Harold Parker provides a persuasive psychological explanation.[1] I would propose not a different causal explanation of Napoleon's decision, but instead a different characterization and understanding of Napoleon's foreign policy in the context of the international system.

My text, or pretext, comes from one of G. K. Chesterton's Father Brown detective stories. In it, Father Brown, asked whether he did not accept the science of criminology, replies that he would gladly accept the science of criminology if his interlocutor would accept the science of hagiology. I take Chesterton's point to be that hagiology and criminology concern themselves with two poles in the range of human conduct, both of which require more in the way of explanation than does that of the ordinary sinner. Both saintly and criminal behavior can to a degree be explained, or at least dealt with, in a "scientific" or scholarly manner, that is, regarded as phenomena on which empirical data can be gathered and theories and generalizations developed and tested. Whether or not one attempts so to explain criminality and saintliness, however, one needs at least to recognize that they exist, not ignore them where they appear, and not try to explain them away or obscure their essential differences.

This is the context within which I wish to place my discussion of Napoleon's foreign policy. I accept Professor Parker's explanation of Napoleon's psychological makeup, suggesting only that Napoleon's psychology and political outlook, however explained, should be regarded or classified as criminal. I join Napoleon's admirers in recognizing his genius in various areas—military, administrative, organizational, political, even literary. I accept that he had an extraordinary capacity for planning, decision making, memory, work, mastery of detail, and leadership. My sole concern here is to argue that these remarkable qualities, amounting undeniably to genius, were turned in international politics to the service of an undertaking that can properly be labeled as "criminal."

The Journal of Military History, 54, 2 (April, 1990), 147–62. Copyright © (1990).

This demands a definition of terms. A criminal in politics by my definition is someone who understands the concept of law and recognizes that organized society is based upon it and cannot dispense with it. He/she knows further that ideas of law and lawful conduct play a role, though a more marginal and contested one, also in international politics. Governments conduct diplomacy, engage in negotiations, conclude treaties and conventions, and even wage wars within a broad context of law and an understanding of lawful and unlawful conduct. They generally expect and demand that treaties be observed, promises kept, and recognized rights respected, appealing for international sanctions or resorting to self-help against putative lawbreakers. A political criminal is one who, knowing this, turns the devices, concepts, and uses of law in international politics to his own ends, not merely selectively and partially as statesmen normally do, but in a regular, principal fashion. Repudiating the claims and applicability of law for himself and his own actions, he at the same time asserts and usurps its authority *vis-à-vis* others, demanding not only that other international actors meet their putative lawful obligations to him but that they also regard and obey him as the source of law. Thus a political criminal reverses Kant's Categorical Imperative, treating everything in politics—other men, groups, states, institutions—never as ends in themselves, always as means to his ends. He equally reverses Clausewitz by making politics a continuation of war by other means. My contention is that this definition of a criminal outlook in politics characterizes the essence of Napoleon's foreign policy.

How to show this, or at least back it up, in a short essay? Two methods would seem available. One would be to compile a catalogue of various alleged criminal acts by Napoleon in international politics. This would not be difficult to do. One could readily show that he repeatedly and deliberately violated the neutrality of small states; that he resorted to judicial arrests and murders against foreign subjects; that he ordered his generals and satraps to use preventive terror to control their domains; that he not only conquered and suppressed other states in war, but also used tactics of bullying, manipulation, and extortion on them in times of peace, almost without regard to whether they were hostile or friendly; that he frequently violated understandings, promises, and treaty commitments; that on principle he ruthlessly subordinated the interests of all the states and peoples he ruled to those of France and ultimately of himself personally; that he declined to accept responsibility or show regret for the enormous human costs of his ventures, even, for example, the destruction of the Grand Army in Russia; that he blamed the French people and his allies for his downfall, accusing them of betrayal and insufficient support; that while displaying indifference and contempt for the rights and honor of other men and states, he felt genuine rage if (in his perception) he was betrayed or frustrated by anyone else; that this rage frequently fueled in him a search for vengeance (e.g., his treatment of Pope Pius VII or of Venice, his execution of the Duc d'Enghien, the Nuremburg bookseller Palm, and others, his constant vows and efforts to humiliate and destroy England, his attempt to blow up the Kremlin on leaving Moscow in 1812, his cry in 1813 after Bavaria's defection, "Munich must burn! and burn it shall!"). Such acts, it could be argued, demonstrate a pattern of lawless conduct in international affairs, and show in Napoleon an outlook characteristic of the sociopath in civil society.

A second method would be to choose one important chapter of Napoleon's foreign policy for analysis as a sample or model of underlying criminal principles and presuppositions in the whole. A good choice might be Napoleon's dealings with Pope Pius VII. Here one would note Napoleon's insistence that the Pope obey him not merely on political issues, but on vital matters of church doctrine and polity (the Organic Articles, the Napoleonic Catechism, marriage and divorce, nomination and control of bishops); his insistence that Pius's refusal to do so had nothing to do with religious faith, principles, or higher loyalty but demonstrated the Pope's will-ful and criminal obstinacy; Napoleon's genuine belief, even while he himself was a thoroughgoing skeptic and opportunist in matters of religion, that the Catholic Church from its head to its lowest members, like all other religions and churches, had an overriding moral and religious obligation to serve him; his argument, on ordering the seizure and imprisonment of the pope and the annexation of his lands, that he was carrying out the punishment of God on the papacy because the popes had chosen to rule as princes while Jesus had died on the cross. One might see in this evidence of the consummate ego-centricity, the simultaneous rebellion against all law and usurpation of its authority, characteristic of the true criminal.

Yet neither of these is in my view a satisfactory way to establish the thesis, though both have plenty of substance to them. The difficulty is that no mat-ter how many instances of supposed criminal conduct one induces from Napoleon's career or any particular section of it to argue for the criminal character of the whole, critics will offer counterexamples to show that Napoleon also could and did often behave in rational and generous fashion, that he showed affection toward his family, wives, associates, soldiers, fellow officers, and others; or they will argue that his political behavior was not criminal, or no more so than necessary and usual in international politics, or that his allegedly criminal actions were forced upon him by circumstances and the higher law of *raison d'etat*. Most basic of all, they may claim that since international politics by definition is not governed by law, according to the old Roman principle of *nullum crimen sine lege* ("no crime without a law") there can by definition be no criminal action in international politics. Therefore neither method is likely to convince skeptics. More important, both tend to distort the real point I wish to make and distract attention from it. The thrust of my argument is not that any decent person ought on moral grounds to condemn Napoleon as a criminal. Though I do not disguise my own estimate of his moral character, my opinion or anyone else's on that score is relatively unimportant for historical analysis. The historian is con-cerned not to reach the most satisfactory moral judgment of his character but to make the best historical judgment on his foreign policy, so as to increase our historical understanding of it. My thesis is simply that no mat-ter how one may react to Napoleon's actions and personality on moral grounds, in order to properly understand his foreign policy and its impact on the European system one needs to see it as a criminal enterprise.

This is required, I contend, in order to understand the origins of Napoleon's wars. With all of them—beginning with Britain in 1803 and continuing through Austria and Russia in 1805, Prussia in 1806, Spain in 1808, Austria in 1809, and Russia in 1812—one is struck by a common feature: while it cannot be said that Napoleon went out of his way to avoid any of them, neither can it be said that he went out of his way deliberately to start them. Each of these wars, at least at the time it broke out, was in some respect unwelcome to him. This fact has helped lead many historians, especially the biographers and other historians who rely chiefly on Napoleon's correspondence and on French sources for their evidence, to blame his opponents for starting at least some of the wars, especially 1803, 1806, and 1809. It also helps account for the wide disagreement among historians on the general question of Napoleon's responsibility for them. A few largely exonerate him and blame his enemies; others explain them mainly as the result of various "objective" forces beyond Napoleon's or anyone's control—France's commitment to the security of its "natural" frontiers as a goal it could not surrender and Europe could not accept, the Continental System, the stalemated war with Britain, and so on. Still others, while recognizing the large role played by Napoleon's imperialist ambitions, lust for glory, and despotic spirit, also find considerable greed and ambition in other powers and assign them part of the responsibility. Professor Parker's explanation of Napoleon's decision to invade Russia belongs apparently in this latter category. Like many of its kind, it is plausible, moderate, and fair, and rests on considerable evidence. Nonetheless, I think it misses something in failing to see and account for another feature of these wars, often ignored but equally striking.

If it is true Napoleon did not exactly welcome his wars at the time they began, it is even more true that Napoleon's opponents, even on those occasions when they technically were the aggressors in starting the wars, were basically far more reluctant than he to fight. The same European powers who accepted, prepared for, and sometimes launched war with Napoleon, whether under apparently favorable or obviously unfavorable military and diplomatic circumstances, had all without exception earlier, sometimes just shortly before, pursued policies of making peace with Napoleonic France and seeking coexistence on the basis of French hegemony in Europe. A persistent legend about the Napoleonic era holds that the main European response to Napoleon's conquest was one of stubborn resistance; that the conquered peoples and states of Europe continued to harbor hopes of liberation and independence despite their defeat and subjugation, that they resisted assimilation into the Napoleonic Empire, and that finally, when the back of Napoleon's military power was broken in Russia, they rose to overthrow his yoke.

This Resistance-War of Liberation myth is often combined with its twin, the legend of the liberating and regenerating ideals of the French Revolution as spread abroad by the Revolutionary and Napoleonic armies. European governments and peoples, we are told even by some great historians like Georges Lefebvre, adapted the ideals of the French Revolution to the purpose of defeating Napoleonic France. Both these ideas are about as wrong as broad historical interpretations can be. In fact, the normal, natural, and almost universal response in Europe to the experience of Napoleon's military power and conquest was submission, appeasement, and efforts at accommodation in various forms. Between 1801 and 1812 every major power that collided with Napoleon, to say nothing of the lesser ones, tried in this way to come to terms with Napoleon, often time and again—Britain in 1802 and again in 1806–07, Austria in 1801–04, 1806–08, and 1809–12, Prussia for the whole decade before 1806 and even more desperately after 1807, Russia in 1801–03 and again in 1807–10. One American historian has seen a marked parallel between the Addington government's appeasement of Napoleon in 1802–03 and Chamberlain's appeasement of Hitler in 1938–39![2] The problem with this analogy is not merely that it breaks down at certain points, as historical analogies always do, but that it is too restricted.

Between 1800 and 1812 almost every government in Europe, and most statesmen in Europe, went much further in trying to appease Napoleon than Chamberlain did with Hitler. The apparent exceptions to this rule—the heroic resistance of Spain from 1808, Russia in 1812, and Prussia in 1813—actually help prove the rule that the standard response to Napoleon's power was appeasement. Both Spain and Russia decided to resist only after enduring years of exploitation and humiliation as Napoleon's allies; their national resistance occurred only after they were actually invaded, and persisted because they were never fully conquered. In Prussia, it was the provinces of East Prussia and Silesia, which were never fully occupied by the French before 1812, which rose in 1813, and this only after the French had fled; Berlin and the Mark of Brandenburg, occupied since 1806, did not. Everywhere in Europe during the War of Liberation in 1813–14 governments and peoples, however much they groaned under Napoleonic tyranny, preferred not to rise at all or waited to rise until after they were liberated by allied armies, or the French had fled, or their own governments had decided to switch sides. Holland, Switzerland, and most of Germany and Italy are all examples.

The failure of Germany to rise in support of the Russians and Prussians in the spring of 1813, after Napoleon's defeat in Russia, again proves the point. As for the defection of Napoleon's satellites, he did more to drive Bavaria, Württemberg, and other states into the enemy camp than the allies did to lure them over. By continuing to demand more money and men from states he had already exhausted while flatly refusing to protect them, he made defection their only way to survive. As for the most important ally to defect, Austria, it did so only after Metternich's desperate efforts to mediate a negotiated peace favorable to France had foundered on Napoleon's flat refusal to negotiate.

There is no problem in explaining this virtually universal resort to appeasement. The experience of Napoleon's power was enough to make every European power try some form or other of accommodation—joining him if possible to get a share of the imperial spoils, buying him off, or making an arrangement to stay out of his way. Some states like Bavaria did this fairly eagerly and trustingly, others like Austria only with reservations or in desperation. Only Britain, which Napoleon could not destroy, continued to fight doggedly, and this only because it concluded in 1803 that an actual peace with Napoleon was humiliating and intolerable and in 1806–07 that any peace was impossible. What demands explanation is not Europe's repeated recourse to appeasement, but its consistent failure. The only satisfactory answer is the simple and obvious one: Napoleon could not be appeased. Each war was the outcome of the uniform experience of one European state after another that it was impossible to do business with Napoleon, that peace with him on his terms was more dangerous and humiliating than war. It is most striking of all that the appeasers themselves, the very men who had advocated accommodation and coexistence with France, regularly abandoned their own policies, admitting, even though they still dreaded war and feared defeat, that accommodation would not restrain Napoleon. This was true of Austria's Count Cobenzl and Archduke Carl in 1805, of Emperor Francis and Carl again by 1809, of Prussia's Counts Lombard and Haugwitz, the Duke of Brunswick, and King Frederick William III by 1806, of Prussia's Baron von Stein in 1807, of Prince Hardenberg in 1808–12, of Count Rumiantsev and Tsar Alexander by 1812, of Count Metternich in 1813.

Thus to pose the question in its usual form, why European states, despite earlier defeats, continued to form new coalitions against France, is to miss the point. (It is also historically inaccurate—Napoleon forged bigger and more effective coalitions between 1800 and 1813 than his opponents did—but leave that aside.) It is equally irrelevant to dwell on the immediate or proximate causes and occasions for the various wars in explaining them. For if one pays serious attention to documents and testimony from other states rather than France alone, one quickly sees that the central problem is not how wars broke out, but why peace constantly failed, why efforts at accommodating France broke down, why monarchs and statesmen who genuinely did not want to fight France came to the conclusion that they had to do so. I find it inexplicable that good historians can simply assert what is technically true, that Prussia started the war of 1806 or Austria that of 1809, and not ask themselves what could have induced so timorous and irresolute a king as Frederick William III, eager only to enjoy further peace and neutrality, to gamble everything on war against the French? Or what could make so narrow-minded and fearful a sovereign as Emperor Francis, whose highest ambition was to hang onto his hereditary estates in peace and who had been thoroughly beaten by France in three great wars, throw the iron dice again alone and unsupported in 1809? *That* demands explanation.

While no explanation of individual cases can be attempted here, once again the heart of the matter is simple. European statesmen of all kinds believed—wanted and needed to believe—that Napoleon, though an extraordinarily powerful and effective leader, was nonetheless a normal statesman operating somewhere within the normal rules, with whom normal international politics was possible. He was not. He was a criminal leader of a criminal enterprise, with whom normal transactions and relations designed to achieve their normal aims of equality, security, and independence were not possible. They were accustomed to the unscrupulous, semipiratical politics of the late eighteenth century; in most instances they wanted to continue it to their own benefit, in collaboration with France. But their previous experience, far from preparing them for dealing with Napoleon, misled them. Constantly they found themselves playing half a corsair to his corsair and a half, driven into a corner where the only way out was a *Flucht nach vorne*, desperate resistance. The analogy with Europe's reaction to Hitler is obvious. To adapt Paul Reynaud's famous remark in June 1940: They thought they were dealing with Louis XIV, but they learned that Napoleon was not Louis XIV; he was Genghis Khan.

This schema applies precisely to the war in 1812. The central cause of Russo-French alienation was the central issue for Russia's security, the fate of Poland. The real turning point from alliance toward eventual war was Napoleon's rejection of the agreement reached in February 1810 between the Russian chancellor Rumiantsev and the French ambassador Caulaincourt guaranteeing Russia against a revival of a Kingdom of Poland. Further, what emerges most clearly in the Russian documents and literature is that Tsar Alexander and Rumiantsev really tried in 1807–10, if with growing skepticism and pessimism, to lay the basis for a durable junior partnership of Russia with France, so as to force Britain to peace and thereby pacify Europe. That the Russians had their own ambitions and interests (Finland, Sweden, the Balkans, Turkey, the Straits) was obvious; that they saw certain areas which they must not concede outright but somehow preserve as buffer zones or share with France (Silesia, Poland, Austria) was also plain; but that Russia ceded full control of most of Europe to France, recognizing all the French vassals and satrapies even in Spain, and that the tsar, genuinely anti-British and eager to force Britain to the peace table and exclude it from Europe, had declared war and cut off British trade to Russia at considerable economic cost to Russia, is equally undeniable.

What the Russians learned was that no compromise they suggested ever was attainable, no security pledge honored (the refusal to guarantee Russia against a revived Polish Kingdom being the worst blow); that Napoleon treated not only old established Russian interests in North Germany but also direct treaty provisions like that of Tilsit guaranteeing the territory of the Grand Duke of Oldenburg as scraps of paper, not even worth consulting Russia about; and that Napoleon, while demanding that Russia close its ports to neutral goods as well as British and to open them wide to French goods, himself had launched trade openly on a massive scale with the British for the benefit of France. The issue in 1810–12 concerning the Continental System was not whether Russia would fulfill its promises to help force Britain to peace; it had fulfilled those promises already by the end of 1807 and never broke them. It was whether Napoleon, who had perverted the Continental System into a weapon for the economic subjugation of his Continental empire rather than of Britain, could subjugate Russia in this fashion also.

This lawless, criminal character of Napoleon's policy explains Russia's decision to accept war. No sane leader or nation goes to war against such odds as Russia faced unless it believes it has no choice. It also illuminates Napoleon's decision. Professor Parker, like almost everyone, concentrates on explaining what drove Napoleon into this venture—what forces working from behind pushed him into it, so to speak. Well and good; but one also needs to ask, as few do, what positive goals led him into it, drew him on. Napoleon was a man characterized by constant, intense, purposive calculation. This capacity more than anything else made him a great military leader. One must always ask about him even more than about most statesmen what end he had in mind, what exactly he hoped to accomplish. We are accustomed, with Georges Lefebvre, to deny that there was any final aim or coherent overarching scheme of empire behind his imperialism. I quite agree. He had no final goal, because he often pursued any and all goals and none in particular; because his imagination and ambition could be captured by anything and his loyalty secured by nothing. But the lack of a final political goal surely need not have meant the absence of intermediate ones.

One would suppose that for so great a venture as this he must have had a set of war aims, a concept of how and where the fighting ought to end. One seeks it in vain in his correspondence. The Foreign Office and its activity provide no clue; by 1812 it was functioning as little more than an auxiliary commissariat for the Grand Army and a wing of French military intelligence.[3] Nor does the diplomacy by which Napoleon put together his great coalition reveal his aims. His vassals and satellites were simply commanded into line, Prussia bludgeoned, Austria bullied and bribed, all with no notion or promises of where it would end. The one state in Europe that enjoyed a little room for choice, Sweden, escaped Napoleon precisely because he would not say where he was going or make payoffs to secure its help. Why was there no set of war aims, no political program for this massive venture on which the fate of the Empire and Europe would ride? Napoleon could not state his final goals to his allies or foes because he had none. Nothing is more revealing and pitiful than his efforts, after reaching Moscow, to get Alexander to talk to him, to induce the tsar to admit defeat and make peace. Not only did Napoleon, the back of his own army broken, have no means to make Alexander admit defeat or even persuade him to talk; had the tsar against his interests and at the risk of assassination agreed to negotiate, Napoleon would have had nothing to say to him. What terms did he have in mind? What could he possibly have proposed?

But surely Napoleon's concrete war aims can be inferred from the reasons that drove him into war. Was he not fighting to close the hole in the Continental System, which Alexander's ukaz of December 31, 1810 had opened up, and thereby to discourage Britain and force it to the peace table? Very well—how? How, by invading and beating Russia, would he close the alleged hole in the Continental System? Would this mean that French customs agents would be stationed in Russian ports as they already had been all over Europe? Would they prove more effective there than they had everywhere else? Would this mean French annexation of Reval and Tallinn and Petersburg as it had of Hamburg and Bremen and Lübeck? And how exactly would even this, if effected, bring Britain to its knees? Britain had been at war with the whole Continent including Russia since 1807. For most of that time it had given up any serious hope of regaining Russia as an ally. The Russian and Baltic market was not critical to the survival of the British economy; the worst blow to British trade in 1811 and 1812, the result of Napoleon's cunning, American ingenuousness, and British clumsiness and stubbornness, was Britain's break and war with the United States. The British had given way just too late in 1812 to prevent this war; in real desperation, they could always come to terms with America, more than making good any economic losses the defeat of Russia would have caused them. And anyway, suppose the British had decided in 1812 or whenever to sue for peace, what could Napoleon have replied to them? What peace terms could or would he have offered? What peace terms had not been tried? What peace terms, offered and agreed on, would he not soon have found intolerable and overthrown or subverted?

This emptiness, this lack of any real political goal in Napoleon's ventures, is by no means special to his invasion of Russia. It characterizes his foreign policy as a whole. In reading Napoleon's correspondence from 1806–09 to determine just what he wanted of Austria, what role he expected Austria to fill in his system, I noted that his main complaint about Austria from 1806 on was that everywhere—in Germany, in the Near East, with Poland and Russia—Austria was in his way. His most common and persistent demand was not that Austria stop arming and menacing him—that became dominant only in 1808—but that Austria cease to obstruct his purposes, that Austria leave him alone. Ponder for a moment the concept of a European states system that this implies: an ancient great power located in the heart of Europe, with roots and ties everywhere to North, West, East, and South, is assigned the duty, on pain of destruction if it fails to obey, of leaving Napoleon alone, getting out of his way wherever his way might take him.

Everyone knows how much the problem of what to do with Austria preoccupied Talleyrand, how hard and often he tried to persuade Napoleon, especially in 1805, to find some permanent place for Austria in his system. All too often schemes like Talleyrand's Strasbourg Memorandum have been judged on whether or not they were practical solutions to France's problems, which misses the main point. What the Strasbourg Memorandum and similar proposals illustrate is the fundamental difference between Talleyrand and Napoleon. Talleyrand, a normal, venal, unscrupulous, opportunistic European statesman, took it for granted that one had to find a permanent place and role for a country like Austria within the international system, and tried to devise one that Napoleon would accept. Napoleon, a criminal in international politics, took it for granted that he need not assign Austria any role at all if he chose not to. This Napoleonic concept of international politics did not apply uniquely or specially to Austria. The whole of his policy toward Prussia or Poland is exactly the same—a prolonged cat-and-mouse game in which he put off the decision as to what, if anything, he would choose to do with these states. Above all, it applies to 1812. France and all of Europe were mobilized to invade Russia—hundreds of thousands of men killed, endless suffering caused—in the last analysis for no better reason than that Russia and Britain were in Napoleon's way, would not leave him alone, obstructed what he wanted to do, whatever that was.

This is why I say that one cannot understand Napoleon's foreign policy without reckoning with its essential criminality, recognizing the dark void at its center. It is not true that Napoleon merely continued or somewhat extended the normal amoral lawlessness of eighteenth century international politics. Certainly there was a great deal of that lawlessness, especially toward the end of the century, and outstanding exemplars of aggressive and piratical politics, perhaps the best or worst being Frederick II of Prussia and Catherine II of Russia. No eighteenth century leader over his or her whole career, however, consistently broke all the rules in the Napoleonic style. There were plenty of semicriminals, demicorsairs, but none on the Napoleonic scale. And to repeat, the scale of the crimes is not the correct or decisive criterion. All the eighteenth century international crimes, including the partitions of Poland, had some system of rules, some notion of European order, however brutal and defective, in mind. Napoleon did not; that is why he could lie so freely about it on St. Helena. One can say what Frederick II wanted—equality with Austria now, the potential for superiority and domination in Germany later; what Catherine wanted—superiority *vis-à-vis* the German powers, arbitership in Europe, control of Poland, the lion's share of the Ottoman Empire. One can make these goals, however danger- ous and aggressive, compatible with some notion of a European system, an international order. One cannot do so with Napoleon. The only thing that one can confidently say he wanted was more.

Nor without this understanding of Napoleon's nonconception of a European and world order (a void that it might take a Joseph Conrad ade- quately to portray) can one understand the impact of Napoleon on Europe and the European states system. The main task for the international historian in this period is to relate and to explain how the character of European pol- itics came to be transformed between the eighteenth and the nineteenth cen- turies. This transformation can neither be described nor explained without bringing into the picture the criminal character of Napoleon's policy and the effects of having it beaten into Europe by fifteen years of French conquest, domination, and exploitation, any more than one can account for the changed nature of European and world politics since 1945 without reference to the policies of Hitler's Germany and their effects. This is not to claim an essential likeness in the phenomena; it is to assert that they are both essen- tial ingredients in the transformation. Until Napoleon, despite the Eastern War and the wars of the French Revolution from 1787 to 1801, Europe had continued to follow the prevailing eighteenth century rules of international politics—a wholly competitive balance of power game, operating through compensations, indemnities, and beggar-my-neighbor rivalries. Destructive and unstable though this system had proved to be, nothing else was believed to be possible; somehow, the reigning assumption ran in the early years of the French Revolution and ensuing wars, if France could only be curbed and its revolution crushed, the old system could still be made to work. That belief was a major reason Europe at first greeted Napoleon's accession to power mainly with relief and anticipation. He looked like a normal, calculable statesman, a monarch without as yet a crown, someone who would play the usual game by the known rules, if more ruthlessly and successfully than most.

Then came the rude awakening. Napoleon's great service to European international politics was to be a very efficient scourge of God. He convinced European princes and statesmen that an alternative to eighteenth century politics had to be found because playing the old game with him was intolerable. They were used to high-stakes poker among heavily armed players ready at intervals to tip the table over and shoot it out; but now they discovered that the game was run by someone who always cheated, held the biggest guns as well as the high cards, made his own rules, always won, and never paid off. And so they had to end this game of poker and invent a new post-1815 game of contract bridge. Napoleon contributed nothing positive to this outcome. Nevertheless, lawless to the end, a law unto himself, he drove Europe into a new system of international politics bounded by law.

I recognize that in advancing this thesis I open myself to the charge, dreaded by historians, of being a moralizer, a prosecuting attorney. But the charge, for one thing, strikes me as shouting "Fire, fire!" in time of flood. For every historian who distorts the record by moralizing, ten do so by excessive coyness, calling things by any other name—mistakes, errors, blunders, miscalculations, aberrations, irrationality, stupidity, sickness—so as to avoid the word "crime." Not to see the criminal side of Napoleon, to deny his demonic dimension, is to deny something quintessential to him personally and vital to our historic understanding, to make him less great and less interesting than he was. How many explanations have not been attempted to show just where Napoleon went wrong, who or what corrupted him and was responsible for his final defeat and downfall? Is any of them convincing? Is it clearer with Napoleon than almost anyone else in history that character was destiny? Who can really believe that Napoleon somewhere changed, went wrong, got off the track at Amiens, or Austerlitz, or Tilsit, or (least convincing of all) with the Austrian connection and in the arms of Marie Louise? This diminishes Napoleon. Let him be Lucifer, not Samson. We do him more historic justice by recognizing in him the soul of a corsair, a *condottiere*, a capo mafioso, but arguably the greatest corsair, condottiere, and capo mafioso in history.

Besides, as I have argued, this verdict is not a moral judgment on Napoleon, though certainly it implies one. It is instead the key, the prerequisite, to an understanding of his policy and its impact upon European international politics. And anyway, what I am saying is not new, but old and conventional. Most historians have not to my knowledge called Napoleon a criminal in so many words (though contemporaries did, and worse); but they have said the same thing in more subtle ways. Albert-Leon Guerard called him a true scoundrel ("un vrai scélérat"). Tocqueville's verdict was that he was as great as any man could be without virtue; Marshal Foch's, that he forgot that a man cannot be God; Madame de Staël's, that for him no man existed but himself. Perhaps Professor Parker agrees in calling him an imperial madman. I sense myself that I have here contributed truisms and cliche's to the debate, rediscovering America. By way of excuse, sometimes the obvious needs stating; repeatedly, in reading even newer works on Napoleon, I feel that someone needs to say again that morally this emperor had no clothes. My conclusion, however, is a modest one: on Napoleon's foreign policy, including the invasion of Russia in 1812, the famous verdict on his judicial murder of the Due d'Enghien should be reversed to read: "It was worse than a blunder, it was a crime."

Bibliographic Note

The origins of this essay, as a commentary on Harold T. Parker's paper, and its nature as a broad interpretation of Napoleon's foreign policy, preclude the citation of detailed footnotes. I merely want to indicate some of the principal documentary sources I have relied on and give a very few references to the massive secondary literature. For Napoleon himself the most important source is the official *Correspondance de Napoléon ler; publiée par ordre de l'Empereur Napoléon III*, ed. A. du Casse, 32 vols. (Paris, 1858–70). In the voluminous memoir literature, the most important work for 1812 and after is Armand Augustin Louis Caulaincourt, *Mémoires du Général de Caulaincourt*, 3 vols. (Paris, 1933). For Talleyrand's role, the best source is his *Lettres de Talleyrand à Napoléon, d'après les originaux conservés aux Archives des Affaires Étrangères* (Paris, 1967).

On the origins of the war of 1812, the two fundamental works are Grand Prince Nikolai Mikhailovich Romanov, *Diplomaticheskie snosheniia Rossii v Frantsii po donesian poslov Aleksandra i Napoleona 1808–1812*, 7 vols. (St. Petersburg, 1905–14) and Albert Vandal, *Napoléon et Alexandre ler*, 3 vols. (Paris, 1891–96). For Russian foreign policy in general in this period, the fundamental source is the documentary collection *Vneshnaia Politika Rossii xix i nachala xx veka*, 1st ser., 1801–1815, 8 vols. (Moscow, 1960–67). However, many volumes in the *Sbornik Imperatorskogo Russkogo Istorichestkogo Obshchestvo*, 148 vols. (St. Petersburg, 1867–1917) also contain vital material. For Prussia, Paul Bailleu, ed., *Preussen und Frankreich von 1795 bis 1807*, 2 vols. (Leipzig, 1881–87) is essential.

There is a great deal of published correspondence from Austrian archives for the earlier period in Alfred Vivenot and Heinrich Zeissberg, eds., *Quellen zur Geschichte der deutschen Kaiserpolitik Österreichs während der französischen Revolutionskriege 1790–1801*, 5 vols. (Vienna, 1873–90) and various collections edited by Hermann Hüffer. For 1812–14 Wilhelm Oncken, *Öesterreich und Preussen im Befreiungskriege*, 2 vols. (Berlin, 1876) remains fundamental.

For Britain in the earlier period the Grenville papers (William Wyndham Grenville, Baron Grenville, *The Manuscripts of J. B. Fortescue, esq., Preserved at Dropmore . . .*, 10 vols. [London, 1892–1927]) are indispensable. For 1812 and after the papers of Castlereagh (*Memoirs and Correspondence of Viscount Castlereagh*, 12 vols. [London, 1850–53]) and the works of Charles K. Webster, especially his *The Foreign Policy of Castlereagh 1812–1815* (London, 1931) are equally so. The best biography of Napoleon remains that of J. M. Thompson, *Napoleon Bonaparte* (London, 1952; reprinted Oxford, 1988); the best survey of the period is that of Georges Lefebvre, *Napoléon*, English translation, 2 vols. (New York, 1969).

Did the Vienna Settlement
Rest on a Balance of Power?

The question posed by the title of this essay must appear a bit unreal. However much historians have differed in interpreting various aspects of the Vienna settlement and the nineteenth century international system founded upon it, they have never doubted that these included a balance of power as an essential ingredient.[1] Irrefutable evidence seems to come directly from the peacemakers at Vienna themselves; in everything from official treaties to private letters and diaries, they spoke of peace and stability in terms of a proper balance ("juste équilibre") achieved by a redistribution of forces ("répartition des forces"), or in similar balance of power phrases.[2] Not only did their language seem to make the balance of power a vital goal and working principle of the settlement but so did their conduct and the outcome of their efforts. What else were the statesmen at Vienna doing if not restoring a balance of power in Europe by redistributing territories and peoples? What can account for international peace and stability after 1815 if not that the European balance of power was restored after a generation of French revolutionary expansion and Napoleonic imperialism, this time supported and strengthened through a system of alliances, treaty guarantees, and Concert diplomacy?

The balance of power interpretation of the Vienna settlement appears so obvious that a challenge to it is likely to be understood as merely a call to redefine or reclassify it, involving a taxonomic dispute of the sort familiar to historians. A scholar may deny, for example, that there was a Renaissance in the thirteenth century and mean by the denial only that conditions prevailing in the thirteenth century do not fit his or her definition and taxonomic requirements for a "genuine" Renaissance. This essay is not that kind of challenge to the balance of power interpretation of the Vienna settlement. It may seem so at times, simply because the case to be made here, necessarily a prima facie one, involves some definition and interpretation of balance language and ideas. It will always remain possible to argue that a different definition

The American Historical Review, 97, 3 (June, 1992), 683–706. Copyright © (1992), American Historical Association. All rights reserved. Used by permission of the publisher.

of balance of power would meet the objections to be raised in regard to 1815. Nonetheless, the thesis is not that the 1815 balance of power needs to be defined or understood differently, or that the settlement represented a particular, modified kind of balance of power,[3] but rather that any balance of power interpretation of the Vienna settlement is misleading and wrong. Its essential power relations were hegemonic, not balanced, and a hegemonic distribution of power, along with other factors, made the system work. A move away from eighteenth century balance of power politics to a different kind of politics was an essential element in the revolutionary transformation of European international politics achieved in 1813–15.

Let us turn first to what actually happened in 1813–15—whether power was distributed in a "balanced" way and if balanced, in what sense, and whether the system operated and sustained itself by a recognizable balance of power mechanism.

These questions call for a definition of the balance of power—a notoriously slippery, vague, and protean term, repeatedly debated and variously defined. One political scientist has identified nine different meanings of the phrase in the literature, including one in which "balance of power" means hegemony. I have found eleven different meanings of the term, some contradictory to others, in the working language of nineteenth century diplomacy.[4] Moreover, even if the literal meaning or denotation of the phrase were clear, that would not end the difficulty. For what the term connotes and involves in the form of necessary conditions, component elements, and corollaries is also controversial. Balance of power analysts, for example, have long broken lances over whether or not a balance of power system presupposes or requires such things as an even distribution of power, the absence of dominant coalitions, the presence or permanent possibility of blocking coalitions, flexibility in alliances, a holder or manager of the balance, and the existence of independent smaller states.[5]

Yet the confusion and flexibility attending the term do not preclude stating a reasonable minimum definition of it, identifying certain features and conditions as *sine qua non*.[6] A "balance of power system" must mean one in which the power possessed and exercised by states within the system is checked and balanced by the power of others. All the major actors in the system must be subject to this kind of restraint, at least potentially having to fear the countervailing power of a blocking coalition or other deterrent action by other states, should they upset the balance by aggression, threat, or an inordinate growth in capability. The requirements usually cited for a balance of power system— alliance flexibility, the existence of at least two or more actors of relatively equal power, the desire of all states to survive and maintain their independence, and the possibility of the use of force—are all corollaries of this basic requirement. The goals of balance of power, whether they be peace and stability or simply the preservation of the independence of the system's member states, are supposedly reached by maintaining this kind of countervailing balance.

This definition fits not only ordinary usage but also the way the Vienna system has been conceived. The allied statesmen, it is supposed, reduced

France nearly to its ancient limits, restored Austria and Prussia to their size and status of 1805–06, strengthened the states bordering France as a barrier against the renewal of French aggression, guaranteed the independence and integrity of all European states, especially the smaller ones, and united Germany in a defensive confederation, all in order to restore a balance of power that would deter any great power from endangering the integrity, essential interests, or independence of any other state, as France had done for a generation.[7]

The same power-balancing mechanism is also supposed to have worked after 1815 to ward off such threats to the balance as French revisionism, Russia's potential menace to the Ottoman Empire and its aspirations to world leadership, Prussian ambitions in Germany, or Austrian and Prussian rivalry. The blocking alignments naturally changed with changing conditions. After the original Quadruple Alliance against France became obsolete and the initial Anglo-Austrian combination to check France and Russia broke down in the early 1820s, a liberal-constitutional camp emerged in the West in the 1820s and 1830s to counterbalance the Eastern Holy Alliance. British statesmen such as George Canning and Lord Palmerston, manipulating the balance and exploiting various rivalries within and between the blocs, successfully managed crises (the Greek revolt in the 1820s, the Belgian problem of 1830–39, and the Near Eastern crisis of 1839–41) in ways that preserved peace, maintained the balance system, and promoted British interests.[8]

The balance of power interpretation of the 1815 settlement seems so obvious and coherent that certain basic factual questions are sometimes overlooked. Did the actual distribution of power in 1815 meet the minimal requirements for a working balance of power? Was power apportioned so that all the major actors and actual or potential power blocs were subject to countervailing power from others?

Here it is important to remember that power in international politics does not derive solely, or often mainly, from capability aggregation—growth in territory and population, resources, number of men under arms, industrial and technological development, fiscal and economic strength, and other factors affecting state power. Effective power is inextricably related to security, which in political terms is determined largely by the relationship between capabilities and vulnerability, the resources available to the state and the actual and potential demands on those resources in the international arena.[9] Eighteenth and early-nineteenth century statesmen knew this, of course, and calculated power along precisely these lines. The factors they normally used to measure power and to calculate gains and losses were often fairly crude— population, revenues, size of armed forces, and size of territory; but their evaluations of their own power and security and that of other states regularly involved comparing capabilities against vulnerabilities or threats.[10]

Even on the basis of raw power, resources, and capabilities, one can hardly speak of a balance of power in 1815. Prussia, for example, never achieved more than marginal status as a great power under Frederick II in the eighteenth century and had to strain to maintain that nominal rank while hoping someday to become a truly great power by means of expansion.[11] Having barely survived in the Napoleonic period, Prussia emerged in 1815 as even less a real, independent great power than in 1789. Its fifteen million people and limited resources in no way compared with those of Russia, the British Empire, or France. Austria was somewhat better off than Prussia but not decisively so.

Yet the imbalance in the great powers' intrinsic capabilities in 1815 and after pales in comparison to the imbalance in terms of their capabilities versus their vulnerability.[12] The so-called balance of power included five great powers, two on the flanks and three in the center. Each of the two flanking powers commanded more intrinsic resources than any of the other three. Russia had by far the largest territory, the greatest population, and the largest standing army; Britain dominated the seas while leading the world in industry, commerce, colonies, and financial power (indeed, if one takes India into account, as Edward Ingram and others have taught us we must, even in respect to land forces Britain was a great power).[13] At the same time, each of these flanking powers enjoyed virtual impregnability by virtue of geography, as Napoleon's failure to bring either of them down had proved. Geography also presented the three central powers, France, Austria, and Prussia—each of them markedly weaker than either of the flanking powers—with permanent, unavoidable strategic threats from their various neighbors. Thus Britain and Russia were so powerful and invulnerable that even a (highly unlikely) alliance of the three other powers against them would not seriously threaten the basic security of either, while such a (hypothetical) alliance would likewise not give France, Austria, and Prussia security comparable to that which Britain or Russia enjoyed on their own.

The system was just as imbalanced in regard to alliance capability, for the same reasons. Britain and Russia, not dependent on alliances for their basic security, could always make them when they wished and, from 1815 to 1848, regularly did. France, Austria, and Prussia, which were dependent on alliances for security, never gained alliances that made them truly secure militarily. (This is not to say that they lived in constant insecurity. All three of the major central states enjoyed more security from external threats in 1815–48 than they ever enjoyed before or since. It is only to deny that this security derived from military alliances or a balance of power.) France constantly sought military allies after 1815 (mainly Britain, sometimes Russia), but its quest always ended in frustration. Even Austria and Prussia, closely allied and usually linked with one of the flanking powers, could not always count on their help. Britain, for example, was not available to meet a possible French attack on Austria in Italy in 1830–32, and even Russian help was doubtful at that time, given the Polish insurrection. In any case, the German powers would always have had to bear the main brunt of a French attack themselves, as the Near Eastern crisis of 1840 illustrates.[14] Russia, to be sure, proved a loyal ally for both the German powers, especially after 1820, but this loyalty derived not from their military alliance or the balance of power but from their ideological solidarity in the Holy Alliance. Russia used its

THE VIENNA SETTLEMENT 41

military alliances with Austria and Prussia under Catherine II (1762–96) to keep both German powers insecure, dependent on Russia, and locked in rivalry with each other.[15] This was a normal balance of power policy; had Russia played a balance of power game after 1815, it would have done the same thing again, as its diplomats sometimes advised.

The disparities in power and security among the five powers in 1815 and after are great enough to challenge the notion that the "Directory of Europe" or "Concert of Europe" derived from a European pentarchy of great powers. Certainly, the Concert existed, and it exercised a real, powerful influence on international politics;[16] but the idea that it rested on any sort of comparable power status among the five members is very doubtful. The usual definition of a great power is a country that can rely primarily on its own resources for the defense of its interests and existence. Both flanking powers undoubtedly qualify under this definition; France probably does also, though less clearly. But Austria, although qualified in terms of size, population, and potential resources, suffered from so many external and internal weaknesses and vulnerabilities that it could not possibly meet the most likely external threats it faced (a war against France or a major revolution in Austria's sphere of influence or within Austria itself) without getting immediate help from allies such as Russia, Prussia, and the German Confederation. A number of incidents illustrate the point—the revolutions of 1820–21, the war scares of 1830–32, the crisis of 1840–41.[17] These were not solely, or mainly, a matter of Austria's internal weaknesses and rigidity. Before and after 1815, the Habsburg Monarchy exemplified what John Herz, Robert Jervis, and others have discussed as the "security dilemma": the inability of a state to meet external threats by increasing its capability, because every such exertion serves only to arouse its opponents to like or greater exertions, thus increasing its insecurity.[18] As for Prussia, it had the most slender resources among the five great powers, by far the most exposed and vulnerable frontiers, and the most extensive military obligations; there was no serious threat that it could have met without major allied assistance. Thus the balance of power in 1815 consisted of a pentarchy composed of two superpowers, one authentic but vulnerable great power, one highly marginal and even more vulnerable great power, and one power called great by courtesy only.

Still more imbalance prevailed in an aspect of international politics important to Europe since the fifteenth century and vital since the seventeenth, repeatedly a central issue in great wars, including the recent revolutionary and Napoleonic ones: the world outside Europe. Eighteen fifteen left the two flanking powers with expanded and strengthened world positions—Russia in the Caucasus and Persia, Central Asia, the Far East, and North America, and Britain all over the globe. They could pursue these interests and try to expand their influence in various spheres almost without regard to the actions or reactions of the other powers. Likewise, neither was yet seriously constrained by imperial competition or conflict with the other. Their main world interests hardly touched in 1815. France was left meanwhile in a position essentially like Spain, Portugal, or the Netherlands, with residual colonies surviving on British sufferance,[19] and the other two "great powers" had hardly begun to think about playing an active role in the world outside Europe.[20]

On the reverse side of the coin, Britain and Russia, while effectively reserving world politics for themselves, also retained a dominant influence in areas adjacent to Continental Europe, long important in international politics, and often contested among European states—the Mediterranean, North Africa, the Levant, the Balkans and the Ottoman Empire, and the Baltic—even where other powers had interests in these areas as important as Britain's and Russia's or more so. France could not expand its influence or activity in the Mediterranean or North Africa, or Austria in the Balkans or the Adriatic, or Austria and France in the Levant, or Prussia in the Baltic, without at least tacit permission from Britain or Russia or both. Russia generally had more to say about the fate of Serbia, the Danubian Principalities, Greece, and the Ottoman Empire after 1815 than did Austria, and it enjoyed more influence in Denmark, Sweden, and the Baltic than Prussia. The Levant, in which historically French influence and trade had predominated and to which the British were relative newcomers, was dominated after 1815 by Britain; it controlled the western Mediterranean from Gibraltar and Malta. For decades, the British were able to block French plans to construct the Suez Canal in Egypt. The balance of power established in 1815, in other words, enabled two great powers to say to the others, "Our world spheres of influence are strictly ours; yours are European and therefore must be shared with us."

These imbalances were no accident. Broadly speaking, they represented the goals Britain and Russia had pursued throughout the Napoleonic wars and were the fruits of their victory. Not balance of power but hegemony—who would enjoy it and what forms it would take—had always been the focus of the wars of 1787–1815. By concentrating on the issues disputed at Vienna and the problems that later arose out of the settlement (Germany, Italy, Poland, Belgium, revolution and counterrevolution, liberal constitutionalism and nationalism versus monarchial conservatism), historians have obscured what was uncontested in the outcome, British and Russian ascendancy, and the fact that this was what British and Russian statesmen intended to achieve. Both powers constantly proclaimed their aim as the restoration of a balance of power on the Continent, but this means nothing—or rather, shows that their respective definitions of the European balance of power were hegemonic, as they had always been. For British statesmen, the European balance meant a weakened France restrained by other Continental powers and barriers, giving Britain a free hand to intervene or not in European affairs as its interests required and freeing it from serious rivalry on the seas or overseas. The British concept of Britain as the necessary disinterested holder of the balance was a good way of rationalizing its hegemonic role and reconciling it with balance of power theory and propaganda.[21]

The Russian understanding of the European balance was equally hegemonic. The balance in Europe was something Russia should hold and control, not something that would check Russia. "Balance of power" meant

Russian predominance in Poland and a vague Russian paramountcy in the Baltic and Near East, with Germany not united but confederated under joint Austro-Prussian leadership, and both German powers, especially Prussia, closely allied to Russia and dependent on Russian support against dangers from France in Germany and Italy. These post-1815 ideas were simply a new, conservative version of Russia's traditional glacis policy, involving territorial and political arrangements designed to restrain the other powers and give Russia security to the west and south as well as influence and prestige.

Britain's and Russia's pursuit of hegemony under the guise of balance of power was thus normal and traditional, merely less obvious after 1815 than it had been in the late eighteenth century, when it had been pursued overtly, aggressively, and by the early 1790s apparently with entire success. Britain in 1792 was dominant in Western Europe and overseas, the Dutch Patriot Revolt having been crushed, French influence routed, the United Provinces and Prussia allied to London, and France left mired in revolution. This enabled Britain to do what it wanted in India and to force the Spanish to diplomatic surrender at Nootka Sound. Russia, having defeated the Ottoman Empire in 1768-74 and 1787–92, dominated the Black Sea and was on the march toward the Mediterranean, had reasserted its control over Poland and played the leading role in its partitions, and could exploit the rivalry between Austria and Prussia in Germany and the new tensions between revolutionary France and its neighbors. To cap these British and Russian bids for hegemony under the guise of balance, most Britons and many Russians considered their two governments natural allies, destined to be joint arbiters of Europe.

The pattern of emerging Anglo-Russian hegemony was neatly illustrated in the Anglo-Russian Ochakov crisis of 1791. The confrontation came about because each had expanded its sphere of influence so far that they briefly collided, immediately in the Ottoman Empire, less directly over Central and Eastern Europe. Yet the crisis arose not from real rivalry but from an attempt by the British Prime Minister William Pitt to define the terms of their potential partnership in running Europe. Pitt, like most Britons, considered Russia Britain's natural ally but saw Russia getting out of hand and needing to be curbed into partnership. Catherine was not averse to partnership with Britain but only on her terms. Pitt started the confrontation; Catherine won it.[22]

Britain and Russia were not alone in saying "balance" while meaning "hegemony." Almost everyone did. Austria's idea of a balance in Germany meant Austrian control of the Reich and supremacy over Prussia; Prussia's idea of a German balance meant an Austro-Prussian stalemate in the Reich, Prussian superiority in North Germany, and overall Prussian equality with Austria. Even the most moderate eighteenth century program for the balance of great powers, that of Louis XVI's Foreign Minister Count Vergennes, involved elements of French hegemony—and Vergennes' moderation was one reason why his program ended in disastrous failure.[23]

The pattern in which balance of power slogans and rules served hegemonic aims persisted through most of the wars of the French Revolution and

Napoleon. Far from these being wars unleashed by French hegemony and imperialism and fought by the allies to restore a balance of power, they represented for at least the first fifteen years (1792–1807) a great contest between three bids for hegemony, British, Russian, and French, with the rest of Europe, small and former great powers—Prussia as well as Austria—trying to survive the contest and where possible profit from it. French statesmen naturally used balance of power arguments and slogans to justify their hegemonic aims just as the British and Russians did, probably with the same mixture of disingenuousness and sincerity, and the French arguments were at least as objectively valid as those of their opponents.[24]

Had France, before or during Napoleon's reign, ever been willing and able to consolidate its control of Western Europe (it had chances to do so, but the revolutionary governments did not pursue them seriously or consistently and Napoleon never considered them at all), a genuine system of balance of power could conceivably have arisen in Europe, with French power balancing the obvious geographic advantages of Britain and Russia. It would not have been a stable or peaceful system, but it would have been in some real sense balanced in terms of power. Instead, Napoleon's boundless ambition and egotism compelled the allies to carry the war to the point of defeat for France and the reduction of its power. With that, Europe fortunately lost any chance of establishing a working balance of power and was left with the power imbalances of 1815.

It was on the basis of these imbalances that the system worked after 1815. Historians may talk all they wish about checks and balances, rival alliances and ideological camps in the West and East, and the interpenetration of alliances and alignments in certain areas like the Low Countries or the Near East. This cannot disguise or obscure the most decisive fact about the system: nothing prevented Britain and Russia, whenever they chose, from combining to impose their will on the rest of Europe, regardless of the feelings, the interests, and even, in certain instances, the independence and integrity of other members. This happened twice after 1815, in 1826–29 over the Greek question and in 1839–41 over the second Muhammad Ali crisis in the Near East. In both cases, the other great powers, though dismayed by this Anglo-Russian coalition, could not stop it or break it up. In 1827, France had felt impelled to join it, and Austria watched helplessly while the allied intervention in Greece led to exactly what Austria had feared and predicted, a Russo-Turkish war and the threatened destruction of the Ottoman Empire.[25] In 1840, the French premier Adolphe Thiers, fearing political defeat, goaded by French nationalist feeling, and outraged that Britain (actually, Lord Palmerston) should choose Russia over France as a partner in the Near East and exclude France from the Concert, resorted to a threat of war in Europe. Significantly, Thiers could not threaten war against France's opponents in the current crisis, Britain and Russia, but only against the powers France could get at militarily—Austria, Prussia, and the German Confederation. The crisis came to a close when Louis-Philippe backed down and replaced Thiers; the episode ended only months later with a chastened

France's readmission into the Concert.[26] These episodes represent as good evidence of the hegemonic pattern of post-1815 European politics as one could ask for. Even when Russia and Britain were not in alliance, no combination of other Continental states could coerce or control them; and, when they joined forces, no state or coalition could effectively resist them.

It may be argued that these circumstances only modify the character and working principle of the balance of power system after 1815, rather than disprove its existence. The 1815 balance of power may simply have been bipolar rather than multipolar, like the world balance after 1945, with Britain and its partners balancing against Russia and its allies. This explanation will not do either. It makes sense to speak of a bipolar balance of power when, as during the Cold War, there were two well-defined blocs with clear-cut power alliances checking and restraining one another. But Britain and Russia did not operate in this fashion in the pre-1848 era. No arms race or competition for power set them at odds; they did not even compete very much for influence or colonies. They were leaders but not leaders of clear-cut rival blocs. They sometimes worked in close partnership, as in 1826–29 and 1839–41. Usually, despite their ideological differences and the beginnings after 1828 of a perceived rivalry between them in the Middle East and Central Asia, they left each other alone in their respective spheres.[27] Britain stood by while Russia crushed the Polish Revolt in 1830–31 and helped extinguish the Free City of Cracow in 1846. Russia did not try to get in Britain's way in the Low Countries or the Iberian Peninsula. Not until Britain, joined by France, attempted in 1853–54 to unite all of Europe against Russia were Anglo-Russian relations truly put on a balance of power basis—which led to the Crimean War and wrecked the Vienna system.[28]

The shared British and Russian hegemony prevailing after 1815 is only the most obvious reason for insisting that the settlement was not based on a balance of power. It was also permeated with sub-hegemonies. The German "balance" involved an Austro-Prussian partnership that managed the German Confederation and dominated the other German states. Austria's hegemony in Italy was virtually unchecked. For most of the post-1815 period, France had three Continental great powers allied against it, and it never gained reliable allies against this potential hegemonic threat. For decades, Central and Eastern Europe were dominated by the so-called Holy Alliance of the Eastern Powers. All these aspects of the settlement, as prominent in it and important to it as the hegemony and invulnerability enjoyed by Russia and Britain, represent additional problems for the standard view.

One should not expect too much precision and consistency in the use of political terminology, of course, especially with a term like "balance of power." Nonetheless, to describe an international system like that of 1815, in which such great disparities existed between the major actors (to say nothing of the many lesser ones) in terms of raw power, alliance capability, security, influence, and opportunities and freedom for action, as one of a "balance of power," is to block understanding and scholarly progress rather than advance it.

This essay could stop here, claiming to have shown that whatever the 1815 system might have been, it was not one of balance of power. But a purely negative case such as this is rarely convincing, first because it seems to leave some important concerns and arguments for the prevailing view unanswered, second because it does not indicate why the prevailing and allegedly misleading view came to seem so convincing, and finally because it offers no plausible alternative. In other words, one needs somehow to anticipate the obvious objections to this revisionist view and answer, at least provisionally, some pertinent questions about it.

There are, it would seem, at least three plausible reasons for continuing to interpret the settlement of 1815 as based on a balance of power, despite the evidence to the contrary visible in the actual distribution of power and the operation of the system. The first objection is, "How can one otherwise account for all the balance of power language of the era, the repeated testimony of European statesmen that the settlement needed to rest and operate on a balance of power, or explain all the bargaining and haggling they did over territories before, during, and even after the Congress in order to achieve a workable balance?" The second is, "How, except on the assumption that a working, stable balance of power existed, can one explain the success of the Vienna system, the fact that for several decades peace was preserved and most governments chose to accept and operate within the system, believing that their interests were at least minimally protected by it—in short, that Europe was in balance?" The third is, "How could a system based on Anglo-Russian hegemony and on various sub-hegemonies produce a peaceful, stable Europe between 1815 and 1848, when, as this essay itself argues, earlier bids for hegemony, especially Britain's and Russia's at the end of the eighteenth century and France's under Napoleon, destroyed the system and produced a generation of war from 1792 to 1815? How could hegemony after 1815 suddenly come to be a recipe for peace and stability?"

These are serious objections. To indicate the broad answers: First, the language of the Vienna era certainly demonstrates that the international system required and rested on political equilibrium—but not that there was a balance of power. The same point applies to the bargaining that went on: it was necessary for producing equilibrium, not balance of power. Second, the stable, peaceful political equilibrium Europe enjoyed from 1815 to 1848 rose not from a balance of power but from a mutual consensus on norms and rules, respect for law, and an overall balance among the various actors in terms of rights, security, status, claims, duties, and satisfactions rather than power. Third, the difference between the nascent or emergent Anglo-Russian hegemony in late-eighteenth century Europe that helped wreck the European system and the shared Anglo-Russian hegemony in Europe in 1815 and after that helped make the system work is the difference between a predatory and a benign hegemony. The same applies, *mutatis mutandis*, to other sub-hegemonies in the Vienna settlement.

These bare-bones assertions cannot be demonstrated here, but they can at least be fleshed out somewhat. Having tried at some length elsewhere to establish the first point, that the language of the Vienna era reflected a search for political equilibrium rather than balance of power,[29] I will only briefly summarize it here. Statesmen in the Vienna era used a variety of different words and phrases in referring to the European balance. The most common are generic terms: "equilibrium," "European equilibrium," and "political equilibrium." What these meant or referred to was often vague, and their denotation and connotation can only be determined, if at all, by the context. Careful study makes clear, however, that two distinct though inextricably intertwined core meanings are involved in balance language. The one is legal and moral rather than political. "European equilibrium" means a condition of international stability, peace, respect for rights and law, the preservation of order, the supervision of international affairs and legitimation of change through the European Concert. This core meaning is unmistakably indicated in the frequent direct association of "equilibrium" with peace, the status quo, the maintenance of treaties, the preservation of the honor and rights of individual states, and similar desirable conditions. A phrase such as "équilibre des droits" marks this kind of meaning clearly. The other core meaning is the political one of "balance of power" in the ordinary restricted sense—an even distribution of power and policies of checking dangerous uses or accumulations of power by means of countervailing power. Such phrases as "equilibrium of states," "equilibrium of powers (*puissances*)," and "balance" often have a balance of power meaning, though not necessarily so. Others such as "équilibre de pouvoir" or "des pouvoirs," "balance du pouvoir," "Gleichgewicht der Kräfte" (I cannot recall any instances of "balance de force" or "des forces") and related phrases such as "répartition des forces," "contrebalancer," or "jeter un poids dans la balance" indicate clearly enough a process of balancing forces or power. Phrases such as these, though encountered less frequently than the others in this era, prove that checking and balancing power was one element in the process of achieving an overall balance in the system. But they also indicate that the two things were not seen as identical, that a balance of power was implicitly recognized to be part of a larger whole. In other words, the idea of redistributing power among states so that one power would in particular instances be balanced against another power was only one limited aspect of a balanced political order as European statesmen conceived it and represented only one partial means for achieving it. Labeling the whole settlement a balance of power is unacceptably reductionist.

I am not here twisting the language and meaning of the time to fit a particular theory, as some might think. It is rather the proponents of the balance of power view, especially British and American ones, who do this, doubtless unwittingly, when they routinely render terms such as "équilibre européen" or "politisches Gleichgewicht" into English as "balance of power." This mistranslation requires one to devote considerable scholarly effort and persistent argument to convey the simple fact that when European statesmen said "political equilibrium," they *meant* political equilibrium, no more and no less—and that political equilibrium was both broader than balance of power and different from it.

An important instance of the use of balance concepts and language at the Congress of Vienna will illustrate the point. Prince Talleyrand argued that there could be no European equilibrium unless the legitimacy of all thrones was recognized, in particular that of the king of Saxony. As usual in politics, Talleyrand's contention was freighted with hidden purposes and connected with French and Bourbon interests. But Talleyrand also presented an argument in which he genuinely believed, which many shared with him, and which fits much thinking and practice at the Congress. One element in his argument—that the European equilibrium demanded the preservation of the throne and territories of the king of Saxony—fits the ordinary balance of power paradigm. To give Prussia all or most of Saxony, he contended, would make Prussia too powerful in northern Germany, threatening Austria and undermining the balance in Germany as a whole. But the main elements in Talleyrand's argument go far beyond questions of power, territory, and population, stressing the broad psychological and political implications of the question and making clear that he was principally concerned in his defense of legitimacy with upholding the moral and legal bases of the European equilibrium. Despoiling the king of Saxony, he insisted, would render every other German and European prince insecure on his throne and would revive the old politics of aggrandizement, force, and deceit born of fear and insecurity that Europe was trying to end and replace with a better system. The Napoleonic wars, he maintained, had not only destroyed the balance of power by making France too powerful but had destroyed all equilibrium ("tout équilibre") by undermining all rights, rendering all titles to any kind of property insecure, and substituting everywhere "l'empire de force" for the rule of law. The European equilibrium therefore had to be based on a restoration of the rule of law, beginning with its foundation, the security and legitimacy of all thrones—a principle as vital for the rights and security of the peoples of Europe as of their rulers.[30]

No one, I think, can study this period without concluding that Talleyrand here reflected the convictions of the great majority of European statesmen at Vienna. Like him, they used equilibrist arguments one-sidedly and self-interestedly, trying to extract advantages and promote particular interests; but they also genuinely understood and believed this notion of "legitimacy" to lie at the heart of European equilibrium and to constitute its central requirement. In a crunch, they would rather compromise or yield on their particular demands than destroy the foundation of the new system: respect for rights and the rule of law. In other words, the words "European equilibrium" implied a variety of things at Vienna. But they meant "rule of law" more centrally than "balance of power," and it was the consensus that existed among European governments on the moral and legal nature and requirements of the European equilibrium far more than any agreement about the necessary distribution of power that made the innumerable delicate transactions and compromises of the Vienna settlement possible.

This general framework indicates the answer to the second half of the question, the connection between the apparently ethereal, idealistic concept of the European balance and the practical business transacted at Vienna—the hard bargaining, changes of boundaries and rulers, and transfers of territories and peoples that unmistakably added up to a redistribution of power. There is no contradiction; a legal and moral balance, an *équilibre des droits*, was a major aim in the bargaining and required prolonged, intense bargaining to be achieved. The very term "balance of rights" implies this; the Vienna statesmen knew, as sensible ones must, that most quarrels in international politics do not pit right against wrong but rights against other rights. Consider the phrase commonly used to describe the allies' overall aim: "un juste équilibre par une sage répartition des forces." The adjectives mean something. The equilibrium must be just, correct; the redistribution of forces wise, suiting not merely the disputants but also the broader needs of Europe as a whole. This was a clear break with the competitive eighteenth century code for balance of power transactions, in which everyone sought all possible compensations and indemnities simply in order to keep up with or get ahead of its neighbor and rival.

In addition, the needs of Europe were understood more in legal, moral, and sociopolitical terms than in terms of simple power. The way in which this *répartition des forces* was applied to its most important and immediate target, France, illustrates the point. Everyone, including most Frenchmen once they faced defeat, agreed that French power had to be reduced to limits compatible with the independence and security of its neighbors in Europe. It should then have been easy for the allies to agree on this goal and solve the problem in political terms, imposing the necessary reduction in power on France by force. Yet nothing like this happened. The allies in 1813–14 did not approach the central and apparently simple problem of reducing France to manageable size mainly on the basis of calculations of power, as they so often had in previous coalitions. They seriously divided over how far France's power had to be reduced, with most of them ready during much of the period to let France keep its so-called natural frontiers and Napoleon retain his throne, which would have left France still very powerful and capable of aggression. More important, the main aim of all the allies in dealing with the French problem was to persuade the French government and people to *agree* with their proposed solution and accept it as good for France and Europe alike, with as little coercion by war as possible. Not only did the allies constantly, from early 1813 until about two weeks before the final surrender, bargain with France for a negotiated peace but they always intended that France should if possible emerge from the war relatively strong, not weak; united, not partitioned; secure, not threatened; and thereby satisfied, not discontented and restless. The constant allied appeals to France to make peace on a basis that would leave France stronger and greater than it had ever been under its kings were not mere propaganda: the commitment was amply fulfilled in the actual peace. Thus, even with France (indeed, especially with France), the statesmen of Vienna understood that a European balance required at least as much assurance as deterrence;[31] that a *sage répartition des forces* was needed for moral, political, and psychological equilibrium rather than merely for balance of power.

The determination to prevent French power from threatening the independence or security of other states by setting up barriers to French expansion—an unavoidable concern given France's recent record—had few if any counterparts in the rest of the settlement. All the other great powers remained capable of menacing their small neighbors. Britain could threaten any state vulnerable by sea and was expected to dominate the Netherlands; Russia was in a position to bully Sweden and Turkey if it chose; Austria could do so with the smaller states in Italy and Austria and Prussia with the lesser German powers. Only a few Frenchmen or representatives of smaller powers suggested erecting balance of power restraints to prevent the victorious great powers from abusing their power, and even these suggestions were not serious. This does not mean that statesmen at Vienna were unaware of or indifferent to the danger that the great powers would threaten or destroy the independence of smaller states. On the contrary, statesmen at Vienna were remarkably sensitive to the problem of small-power independence and security. It merely means that the allies chose moral, legal, and political means rather than balance of power measures to maintain a balance in this vital respect.

The main reason for redistributing territories, peoples, and thrones in Europe in 1814–15 was not really to balance power against other power but, except for France to some degree, to reconcile claims among different states, to fulfill promises, to balance conflicting demands and requirements, to meet specifically-felt needs, to protect the independence and security of all states, and thereby to achieve a general equilibrium in which all the members of the European family of states would share in certain balanced advantages and duties. The process involved adjudication, mediation, and reconciliation more than weighing power; the balance sought in redistributing forces was mainly a balance of rights, that is, a balance between conflicting claims based on various rights. The Vienna equilibrium represented ideally a balance between what each state needed or claimed to need in order to fulfill its proper role and function within the European family and what that family as a whole considered necessary and proper. The redistribution was intended to produce a genuinely equal and fair balance in legal rights. Every state was to have its rights and territories recognized and sanctioned internationally. Rank, status, and privileges were also to be balanced, distributed according to each state's role and duties in the international system. The *répartition des forces* at Vienna was designed to bring many other vital elements of international relations into balance, even and especially, where power was not balanced and could not be.[32]

The second question concerned how the Vienna system could have preserved peace so long and well without the restraining and deterrent effects of the balance of power—the knowledge that any state attempting aggression or a violation of the treaties would provoke an overwhelming coalition against itself. This plus the general post-1815 mood of war weariness and satiation, monarchial solidarity, and fear of revolution are supposed to account for the general peace after 1815.

Far too many axioms and assumptions are hidden in this apparently innocuous explanation of the post-1815 peace and stability to discuss in this essay. There is, for example, the assumption or implication that war weariness in 1815 accounts for the durability of peace but without an explanation of why a similar or greater war weariness after other great world wars (1648, 1713–14, 1763, 1919, 1945) failed to have that salutary effect. Something of the same could be said for the notion that ideological solidarity and fear of revolution produced a peaceful international system. Why here and not elsewhere? There is the apparent question-begging assumption that successful deterrence of aggression and treaty violations must be due to a balance of power—as if deterrence is not a very tricky and unpredictable process, often serving to provoke aggressive behavior and produce spiraling conflict rather than curb or prevent it.[33] There is, finally, the tacit assumption that states fear isolation or confrontation by a hostile coalition in international politics essentially for reasons of power politics and security, when it clearly can be as much or more a matter of prestige or concern for the state's or the regime's honor and reputation.

At the heart of this objection, however, is the belief that aggression and unlawful behavior under the Vienna settlement were successfully deterred by balance of power means, by potential or actual threats of a blocking coalition, and this notion can be checked against the facts. Part of the answer has already been given. The two strongest states in the system, Britain and Russia, never faced even the threat of a hostile coalition to deter them by force from taking action. Nothing like this was ever contemplated against Britain, and the means proposed on various occasions to constrain Russia in the Near East involved diplomatic combinations designed to persuade it in friendly fashion to coordinate its policy toward the Ottoman Empire with the other powers. Under the Vienna system, deterrence of Britain or Russia by balance of power means was not possible, not attempted, and, as things turned out, not necessary. As for the other so-called great powers, they could be deterred by either of the superpowers, France by Britain, Austria and Prussia by Russia, merely by the withdrawal of support rather than the application of pressure. A blocking coalition was never necessary and therefore never tried. Even France in 1840 was not really an exception to this rule.

Yet one should not conclude that the Vienna settlement offered no effective means of deterrence—quite the contrary. Deterrence under the Vienna system took the form of moral and legal political pressure, the threat that reckless or unlawful behavior would cost the offending state its status and voice within the system, leading to its isolation from it and the attendant loss of systemic rewards and benefits. This kind of deterrence was highly effective. It helped keep Russia from going to war with the Ottoman Empire in 1821–23, France from trying to exploit the Belgian revolution in 1830–32, Austria and Italy from clashing over Italy, France from saber-rattling its way into war in 1840, and everyone from generally upsetting the peace.

Another point is not strictly related to the balance of power argument but is worth adding here. It is commonly supposed that the ruling monarchs and elites in 1815 accepted the compromises necessary to a stable peace mainly in order to avoid internal revolution. They needed international peace and solidarity to help them preserve the existing sociopolitical order and their privileged positions within it; to manage and, where necessary, to suppress the popular discontents created by war, postwar depression, and the spread of the ideas of the French Revolution and the popular liberal and national demands raised in the course of the War of Liberation. This view contains a kernel of truth but much more distortion. Of course rulers everywhere longed for peace, quiet, and a return to normalcy; so did their peoples. But just as it is incorrect to believe that the balance of power compelled governments to follow peaceful policies in 1815 and after, so it is wrong to suppose that the fear of revolution or of the popular pressures created by French revolutionary ideas or Napoleonic reforms motivated them to construct a more peaceful international system. This mistakes the reigning spirit of the era and stands the thinking and priorities of Europe's leaders on their heads. No major European government was ever threatened with overthrow by the ideas, propaganda, and subversion of the French Revolution, nor were many minor ones. What did destroy many minor thrones and sent those in Berlin, Vienna, and St. Petersburg reeling was war—not merely military defeat and the loss of territory and wealth but the stripping of their resources, the destruction of their armies, the danger that their soldiers, public servants, and peoples would rebel simply in order to have peace. The princes of Europe had little to fear from popular uprisings, certainly not from any inspired by the French Revolution. All the actual uprisings in Europe from 1798 through 1814, in Belgium, Switzerland, Sicily and Calabria, Spain, the Tyrol, Russia, and Germany, were traditional ones, mainly peasant in character and led by local notables and religious leaders, directed against the foreigner and driven by traditional loyalties to God, king, and country. The pressures for reforms and constitutions in 1815 and after came by and large not from the masses of people but from bureaucrats, government ministers, some members of the middle classes, and occasionally from centralizing princes themselves. Other segments of the elites opposed them. What the peoples overwhelmingly wanted in 1815 was much the same as what rulers wanted—an end to the strains, taxes, conscription, and sufferings of war. In short, European leaders were not driven to seek lasting peace in 1815 because they feared revolution. They did so because they feared war, had learned that war *was* revolution, and wanted no more of it.

Thus, however much the bargaining at Vienna may look like a revival of the old competitive eighteenth century balance of power politics, it was different. A continuation of the process by which the final coalition of 1813–14 had been built, the Vienna settlement involved achieving a consensus more than competing or fighting. The disputes were sometimes prolonged and difficult to settle precisely because typical eighteenth century devices—the use of force and the violation of other states' rights and independence—had been ruled out, and only negotiation and compromise were left. The territorial quarrels between Austria and Bavaria in 1814–16, for example, lasted as long as they did simply because Metternich would not and could not use the methods that Joseph II or Baron Thugut had used with Bavaria and other small German states before him (or, for that matter, the tactics that Count Montgelas, the Bavarian premier, had used under Napoleon against Austria). And, while most of the settlements and treaties of previous decades, especially those during Napoleon's reign, were never expected to last, those reached at Vienna were supposed to be permanent and therefore had to be negotiated with greater care.

As for the question of how hegemony, a factor in undermining the international system before 1815, became a stabilizing element then and thereafter, the answer is easy: the character and spirit of post-1815 hegemonies, both the main ones and the subordinate ones, were drastically different—selfish and predatory before, relatively benign, inactive, and tolerable thereafter. The transformation is most dramatic in the case of Russia. If one surveys Russian policy toward the Ottoman Empire, Austria and Prussia, and the German empire during Catherine's reign and to some extent under Paul I and Alexander I until about 1812, and then compares it with Russian policy in the Vienna era, it is hard to believe the two policies belong to the same country. Pre-Vienna Russia was bent on destroying the Ottoman Empire or at least gobbling up large tracts of its territory and exploiting its internal problems and weaknesses; post-Vienna Russia was bent on saving the Ottoman Empire from collapse. Pre-Vienna Russia encouraged and exploited the rivalry between Austria and Prussia to paralyze them both and promote Russian ascendancy over Central Europe and Russian influence in the German empire; post-Vienna Russia encouraged a close partnership between Austria and Prussia, allowed them to manage the German Confederation on their own, and repeatedly told smaller German states pleading for Russian protection that they had to look to Austria and Prussia.

The change is only somewhat less startling in Britain. The British government before the wars and during much of their course cold-bloodedly exploited the weaknesses of its rivals France and Spain in order to expand its empire, especially in India and the West Indies but also in South Africa, the Indian Ocean, the South Seas, and Latin America. After the wars, Britain restored some of its colonial conquests, allowed its former rivals to maintain their empires and practice their mercantilist policies, and exercised its control of the seas mainly in a mutually beneficial policing fashion (against piracy and the slave trade). France before 1815 was Britain's natural and necessary enemy, to be reduced and constrained as much as possible. France after 1815, though still an object of suspicion, was Britain's normal partner in European affairs, to be restrained through watchful partnership. Britain under William Pitt and William Grenville in the 1790s treated the United Provinces as a British satellite that was supposed to follow British policy in Europe and pay for British support with commercial and colonial concessions. Britain under the earl of Liverpool and Viscount Castlereagh in 1813 and after not only helped create an expanded Kingdom of the United Netherlands but also allowed it to pursue an independent role in Europe and a mercantilist colonial and commercial policy in the Far East.

Similar turnarounds took place in the sub-hegemonies in Europe. The contrast between Austro-Prussian rivalry in Germany and exploitation of the Reich estates before 1800 and Austro-Prussian cooperation in creating and managing the Confederation thereafter is dramatic. True, their leadership, especially Austria's, was politically repressive after 1819, but Prussia's creation and leadership of the German *Zollverein* is a perfect example of benign hegemony.[34] The main reason Metternich could turn the Confederation into an instrument of political standstill is that most governments feared revolution and wanted Austria's support against it. Austrian hegemony in Italy was too exclusive and politically conservative, but it was legal, unaggressive, and nonexpansionist, in stark contrast to Austria's Italian ambitions during much of the war. On the whole, Austrian support was welcomed by Italian regimes as a barrier against revolution and war. In the one instance in which a post-1815 hegemony cannot be termed benign, Poland, we can still cite a failed attempt to create one—the failure of the Congress effectively to guarantee the special position of the Polish territories within the three partitioning powers, and the failure of these three powers' measures, especially Russia's, to satisfy the Poles with cultural and administrative autonomy.

One more aspect of the hegemonic Vienna system must be mentioned: the fact that while Britain and Russia each exercised a certain hegemony in their respective spheres, they did not usually combine their forces to dominate Europe, nor did they try to exploit the states between them in a rivalry with the other. Thus the twin nightmares of Continental Europe—Anglo-Russian intimacy and Anglo-Russian enmity—both of which had menaced and oppressed Europeans in the pre-Vienna era, were avoided. Eighteenth century balance of power rules and practices produced predatory, destabilizing hegemony. The Vienna era's equilibrist rules and practices promoted benign, stabilizing kinds of hegemony.

What about the Polish–Saxon crisis at the Congress of Vienna? It certainly looks like a classic balance of power confrontation—Russia insisting on taking the lion's share of Poland, thereby threatening Austria, Prussia, and Germany; Russia's partner Prussia demanding all of Saxony; Austria, France, and Britain resisting in the name of balance of power; Russia and Prussia threatening the use of force; the other three powers concluding a secret defensive alliance on January 3, 1815; and, finally, after a crisis and threat of war, Russia and Prussia accepting a compromise. Appearances, however, are deceptive. The case is far too complex to discuss thoroughly here, but a brief mention of the high points suffices to show that the Polish–Saxon crisis does not represent a case in which balancing tactics preserved a balance of power in Europe. It was instead the occasion when the old eighteenth century balance of power politics flared up most dangerously at Vienna but failed in the end to prevail. The balance of power contest ended with a hands-down victory for the hegemonic power threatening the balance, Russia. But, after winning, Russia shrank back from the cost of its victory in terms of the general European balance and helped promote a compromise that, far from establishing a new balance of power, confirmed and strengthened both Anglo-Russian hegemony and European political equilibrium.

A few basic points drawn from any standard account will help make this interpretation at least plausible.[35] First, for Austria, the state most threatened by the Russo-Prussian plans for Poland and Saxony, the critical issue was not balance of power but political equilibrium. Metternich always knew, and made clear to Russia, that while Austria disliked and feared the great expansion of Russia militarily and territorially in Poland, it could live with it. What Austria could not accept was Alexander I's intent to create a constitutional, autonomous Kingdom of Poland out of Russia's share, raising a permanent revolutionary threat and making both Austria's and Prussia's Polish territories ungovernable.[36] Thus the contest was more about political equilibrium, the terms on which the Eastern powers would cooperate in governing their respective Polish populations, than balance of power. On this score, Austria simply had to accept defeat. Alexander went ahead with his constitutional plans for Poland and, as Metternich predicted, thereby helped create a revolutionary problem that recoiled on Russia more than on Austria and Prussia.

Second, Austria, it is true, at first attempted to meet the Russian threat by balance of power tactics, notably the Metternich-Hardenberg agreement of October 22, 1814, which granted to Prussia all of Saxony if it would join Austria in a strong anti-Russian stand over Poland. But this strategy collapsed within two weeks when Alexander pressured Prussian King Frederick William III into denouncing the Metternich-Hardenberg agreement and lining up solidly behind Russia. Alexander also successfully defied all the balance of power arguments and pressure of Castlereagh. By late November, Metternich accepted his defeat and sought a rapprochement with Russia to prevent both Russia and Prussia from winning at Austria's expense. Thus Russia easily won the balance of power contest in the Polish-Saxon affair by early December 1814. Moreover, Russia never surrendered this victory or compromised it away. Alexander went ahead with his Kingdom of Poland; in the final settlement, Russia retained most of the territory it had earlier claimed; and Russian Poland remained territorially and strategically a threat to Austria, Prussia, and the later German Reich until World War I.

Third, the real crisis and threat of war in Europe arose after Russia's balance of power victory, because of its effects on Europe's emerging and still fragile political equilibrium. Austria, accepting defeat by Russia, now withdrew its promise to let Prussia have Saxony and abandoned its cooperation with Prussia in a general German settlement. Prussia, facing heavy losses, threatened to annex Saxony with or without the consent of the other powers, and this rash threat created some danger of war. Alexander, dismayed at the side effects of his victory (he had driven Britain and France together into opposition, made Austria defect to the West, put Prussia in serious danger, promoted a breakdown of the German settlement, and put the entire European alliance he aspired to lead at enormous risk), intervened to save the situation, not so much by backing down himself but by compelling his own junior partner Prussia to accept major sacrifices in Saxony. While the tsar forced Prussia to pay the main costs of a compromise, sweetening the pill with some concessions to Prussia in Poland, Castlereagh kept France and Austria in line through the Triple Alliance of January 1815 and helped reconcile Prussia to defeat through concessions in Saxony and the Rhineland. As Castlereagh's and Liverpool's correspondence makes clear, the Triple Alliance, which was directed against Prussia rather than Russia and only concluded after the worst crisis was over, was never intended for purposes of war. Liverpool was convinced that the British public and Parliament would not stand for it, and he approved of the alliance as a way of avoiding war and particularly of controlling Austria.[37]

In other words, balance of power politics was tried in the Polish–Saxon crisis, and it led, as it usually does, to a victory for the hegemonic power. When the participants saw what balance of power politics was leading to, they backed off and, under the lead of the hegemonic powers, returned to the practices of political equilibrium.

This essay has covered much ground already, inevitably hastily and superficially, and it may be foolish to break more. Critics will surely find enough to object to. Yet one more question is bound to occur even to a receptive reader: If the case against the balance of power interpretation is so clear, why have many excellent scholars adopted it? The question need not be answered to sustain the case, but it is a natural and legitimate one, and there are possible answers.

Among the factors that would seem to help account for the persistence of the balance of power paradigm are the extraordinary flexibility and protean character of the concept (not even democracy, socialism, or Christianity match it in ability to be all things to all people), the weight of tradition and conventional usage, and especially the hold that so-called realist notions about international politics have over scholars in the field, political scientists and historians alike. It seems axiomatic to many persons that, although rules, norms, and mutually accepted practices can modify and influence the conduct of international affairs to some extent, ultimately international politics must rest on power and reduce to relations of power. Thus they find a fundamental challenge to this notion, a denial of the sway of balance of power in a particular era, hard to take seriously.[38]

To this general observation can be added a specific one: the persistence of the balance of power interpretation of the Vienna settlement is part of a larger historiographical problem—the failure or refusal of historians to recognize this settlement's truly revolutionary character, its uniqueness among all the peace settlements of European history. Time and again, leading scholars concede its virtues of moderation and durability, frequently noting at the same time that these virtues were purchased at a high price in terms of liberty, reform, and progress, and then pass on. The Vienna settlement is thus assigned a normal place in the series of international settlements, all of which are supposed to have worked for a time because of war weariness and temporary ideological solidarity but sooner or later to have decayed and broken down. In this way, historians are free to concentrate on the really important revolutions and sources of change in the early nineteenth century—domestic-political, social, economic, intellectual, and cultural. But the most obvious fact about the Vienna settlement, plain to everyone willing to look at it, is elided and obscured: 1815 is the one and only time in European history when statesmen sat down to construct a peaceful international system after a great war and succeeded; the only settlement, unlike 1648, 1713–14, 1763, 1919, 1945, and many others, that was not accompanied or quickly followed by renewed or continued conflict, revived tensions, arms races, and competitive balance of power politics. This astonishing accomplishment in international politics, moreover, this uniquely non-utopian revolution, made possible much of the structural change and progress in nineteenth century European society. It is high time that this extraordinary accomplishment be squarely recognized, high time that an answer be given to those who insist that international politics never really changes, that it always must remain in the old cycles of balance of power and systemic breakdown and conflict, high time to point to the Vienna era and say with Galileo, "Eppur, si muove" ("and yet, it moves").

The alternative interpretation of the Vienna system offered here, that it rested not on balance of power but on hegemony, also has implications for historians of international politics. It may be time to give the concept of balance of power a rest. The term is doubtless unavoidable and can serve useful purposes, but it has been so abused and become so misleading that it would benefit from a period on the shelf. Spend the time instead on hegemony—its importance as an organizing principle in international politics, its legitimate and fruitful uses as well as its dangers, the possibilities of peace through the right organization and use of hegemonies, and the dangers of attempting to erect artificial balances of power in situations of natural hegemony. There is plenty of political science theory to apply, if one wants it: hegemony theory, regime theory, cognitive theory, deterrence theory.[39] There are plenty of eras besides that of Vienna to which to apply it. In discussions of the origins of World War I, for example, compare the amount of attention paid to Imperial Germany's growth in power and its supposed threat to the balance of power with that paid to the decline or disappearance of British and Russian hegemony, phenomena at least as obvious, far more easily demonstrable, and at least as clearly connected with the breakdown of the system. Paying more attention to hegemony (a neutral word, after all, simply denoting a factual condition of leadership or primacy, without the inescapable pejorative connotations of colonialism or imperialism) might not only be profitable for the study of history but have useful implications for the international world of the late twentieth century.

3

BRUCK VERSUS BUOL: THE DISPUTE
OVER AUSTRIAN EASTERN
POLICY, 1853–55*

Karl Ludwig Baron Bruck is famous in Austrian history as one of her greatest economic statesmen.[1] His solid accomplishments as Austrian minister of trade and of finance, founder of the Austrian Lloyd and of Austrian chambers of commerce, and developer of Trieste, demonstrate an uncommon degree of energy and administrative ability,[2] while the breadth and daring of his politico-economic ideas justify the verdict that he was one of the most original thinkers among the statesmen of his era.[3] Certainly his dream of a central European customs union leading to a political union of Austria and Germany in an empire of seventy millions exercised a powerful influence on his own and later generations of historians and publicists, especially those of a pan-German persuasion.[4]

Yet it is not with Bruck the economic statesman or the advocate of Mitteleuropa that this essay is concerned, but with Bruck the diplomat and would-be shaper of Austrian foreign policy. While all of Bruck's great economic conceptions and aims imply a certain foreign policy stance, and his various efforts for trade treaties and customs unification involved him in considerable negotiation, especially with Prussia, his basic outlook in foreign policy is best revealed in his activity as Austrian Internuncio to the Porte in 1853–55. Bruck did not come to this post as a novice in diplomacy—in 1849 he had negotiated the Peace of Milan with Sardinia-Piedmont.[5] His service at Constantinople, however, was vastly more important for Austria and revealing as to Bruck's ideas, not only because of the crucial issues raised by the Crimean War and the strategic position he occupied, but because, almost from the beginning, Bruck waged from Constantinople a running battle with Count Buol, the Austrian foreign minister, over the conduct and aims of Austrian policy. Many other leading Austrians ranged with Bruck in opposition, so that the internal straggle over Austrian policy can be seen, without great distortion, as a contest between Bruck and Buol.

The Journal of Modern History, 40, 2 (June, 1968), 193–217. Copyright © (1968), The University of Chicago Press. All rights reserved. Used by permission of the publisher.

Most historians who have dealt with this contest have sympathized with Bruck's position, seeing in it a viable alternative to the alleged vacillations and blunders of Buol that brought Austria to disastrous diplomatic defeat in the Crimean War.[6] This essay will argue a contrary point of view. It will contend that whether or not Buol was right (a good case can be made for his policy, but not here), Bruck was wrong—wrong not merely technically, as insubordinate to his superior, or accidentally, in that his opposition embarrassed Austria in her relations with other nations, but fundamentally. Bruck really had no consistent, practical policy to offer as an alternative. His goals in foreign policy, moreover, were bad goals, both unattainable and undesirable, based on false premises, and springing from dangerous impulses and instincts.

No signs of the later rift between Bruck and Buol were apparent at the time of Bruck's appointment in late May 1853. Bruck was Buol's personal choice for this post and enjoyed his respect and admiration; and, though Bruck would have preferred being sent to Frankfurt as envoy to the German Confederation, he readily accepted the assignment.[7] The task confronting Austria in the Near East was difficult enough, and the situation sufficiently critical, to justify sending someone of Bruck's great reputation and energetic personality. The failure of the Menshikov mission to Turkey, Menshikov's departure and the rupture of Russo-Turk relations, and the Russian threat to occupy the Danubian Principalities had raised an acute danger of war. Austria's prime goal always was to prevent war. At the same time, as Buol said repeatedly throughout the crisis, Austria could not tolerate Russia's claim to an exclusive supremacy in the East, treating Turkey as her own private preserve. Nor could she allow Russia to entrench herself on the lower Danube, or to extend her influence in the Balkans generally. Therefore, Austria had not fully supported Menshikov's demands on Turkey, and Russia was already resentful because of it.[8] Yet, openly to support Turkey and oppose Russia was obviously dangerous. Hence, Buol's strategy (like Metternich's in the 1820s) was to browbeat the Turks into granting at least a nominal satisfaction to Russia's demands and to persuade the Russian bear that, having thrown a good fright into Turkey with its growls, it could now with honor return peacefully to its den. Bruck seemed an admirable choice for overawing the Turks, gaining the necessary concessions, and convincing them that Austria was their one real, disinterested friend.[9]

Bruck entered heartily into the spirit of his instructions. His vigorous arguments to the Porte on the political and financial dangers of its present position, and the absolute necessity of a quick settlement with Russia, his urging of a compromise between the last Turkish and Russian notes, and his insistence that Turkey must trust Austria to protect her independence were all in line with Buol's thinking.[10] Buol had no complaints on Bruck's performance in the first month, and hoped for favorable results.[11]

In July, however, an incident came to a head which, while it did not directly affect the Eastern question, demonstrated some of the personal qualities in Bruck, an acute sense of personal and national honor and a penchant for strong action, which were to lead to trouble with Buol later. Basically, the affair, involving a Hungarian revolutionary refugee named Martin Koszta, was trivial enough, one of many minor quarrels between the United States and Austria in the mid-nineteenth century. The legal and diplomatic issue was whether Koszta, who had fled to America and declared his intent to become a citizen, could claim American protection when he returned to Europe and fell into Austrian hands. The complicating factor was that Koszta had been arrested on Turkish soil, at Smyrna, and, acting under orders from the American chargé d'affaires in Turkey, an American corvette had stopped an Austrian brig in the harbor of Smyrna and compelled Austrian officials to surrender Koszta. Koszta's fate was settled peaceably through French mediation by allowing him to return to America permanently. Bruck, however, believed that Austria's honor had been outrageously insulted by this action and demanded satisfaction, not from the Americans, but from the hapless Turks who had failed to stop it. (This is, incidentally, another good example of how Turkey was repeatedly pushed around by other powers in quarrels in which she was entirely uninterested.) The satisfaction Bruck demanded, and obtained, was the resignation of the Turk minister of the interior. Bruck insisted that this represented a major gain for Austrian prestige and influence in Turkey.[12] It is far more likely that it tended to make Turkey resist Austrian and European pressure on matters of far greater moment than the Koszta affair, and certain that it caused Buol trouble with the Western powers, who protested against Bruck's violent tactics and his implied threats to Turkish sovereignty.[13]

Austria did, in fact, encounter stiff Turkish resistance to her advice on the great issue of policy toward Russia. Buol, as noted above, wanted Turkey to accept a compromise between the last Turkish note and the final Russian one.[14] Bruck, supported by the French and Prussian envoys, LaCour and Wildenbruck, tried hard to bring the Turkish foreign minister, Reshid Pasha, to accept the so-called amalgamated note. The Turks, however, stubbornly refused. They were greatly aroused by the Russian occupation of the Danubian Principalities, and their resistance was secretly encouraged by the powerful British ambassador, Stratford Canning, Lord Redcliffe.[15] Not a patient man when thwarted, Bruck now joined with Redcliffe in a new demarche. With the support of the other ministers, he proposed that Reshid should protest to Russia against the occupation of the Principalities, but at the same time offer to send a special ambassador to the tsar for negotiations. Reshid complied, drawing up a letter to Russian Chancellor Count Nesselrode on July 20, to be transmitted to Petersburg through Vienna.[16]

This move was not only unauthorized but also imprudent and inopportune. For one thing, it encouraged a direct Russo-Turk confrontation which at this time Buol wanted to avoid, desiring as he did to interpose a European mediation between Russia and Turkey and (as Metternich had always done) to substitute a general European protectorate over Turkey for an exclusive Russian one. In addition, Buol considered Reshid's language to Russia so provocative that it would compromise Austria, and he refused to transmit the letter to Petersburg. Yet this demarche in itself need not have caused serious disagreement between Bruck and Buol. If ill-advised, it was nonetheless well intentioned, and Buol had encouraged Bruck to use his initiative. More serious were early hints that Bruck differed sharply in spirit and outlook from Buol. While Buol's tactics were wholly those of persuasion, Bruck began calling for stronger measures. On July 14 he requested authorization to go directly to the sultan, demanding a definite answer on the "amalgamated" note within one week or Austria would give up her mediation and leave Turkey to her fate.[17] Again, while Buol regarded Anglo-French cooperation with Austria as essential and was quite willing to support any proposal from any quarter that would actually settle the Russo-Turk quarrel, Bruck was strongly anglophobe from the beginning and laid great stress on breaking English influence and establishing Austrian supremacy at the Porte.[18]

But most important, where Buol's will to preserve peace was virtually unconditional, Bruck, by late July 1853, was already developing ideas on how Austria should exploit the opportunities that a war, now probable, would bring. If Russia went to war, he wrote Buol on July 23, Austria should conclude "a secret agreement with Russia, that at the moment the Russians cross the Danube, Austria will immediately occupy Serbia, Bosnia, and Hercegovina and will give this movement the appearance of a diversion against Russia." Such a move would give Austria a concrete pledge in hand for the ultimate peace negotiations.[19]

Five days later Bruck sent Buol a long analysis of the probable course of military operations in the coming war. He foresaw a Russian advance over the Danube, an easy Russian victory over the Turks, no effective participation in the war by England and France, and by winter a willingness on the part of Turkey and the sea powers to buy peace by ceding the Danubian Principalities to Russia. This cession would of course endanger Austria more than any other state. Since, however, Austria could not order Russia to stop, and to join openly in the Russian attack on Turkey would invite general war, the only recourse for Austria must be a move into the western Balkans, designed apparently to check Russia but actually undertaken "in order not to come out empty-handed in the ensuing peace negotiations" and "to see what Russia thinks about the Austrian claims to the Turk inheritance."[20]

Buol ignored these suggestions for an underhanded Austrian participation in the partition of Turkey, as he did similar ones from other quarters.[21] Reproving Bruck for exceeding his instructions in the demarche to Reshid, Buol abruptly changed his own tactical approach. No longer urging that the Porte draw up a compromise note on the advice of the four ambassadors, Buol now insisted that Turkey accept a European proposal, the famed Vienna Note, drawn up by representatives of the four powers at Vienna and accepted by the tsar. Even before its formal adoption by the powers, Buol ordered Bruck to press the note strongly on Turkey, and to abstain from any more collective demarches at Constantinople.[22]

Bruck was understandably very irritated by this rebuke, as well as by the transfer of the fulcrum of mediatory action from Constantinople to Vienna, and he let Buol know it. In his official dispatches he disparaged the content of the Vienna Note as clearly inferior to what had been worked out in Constantinople and made other thinly veiled criticisms of Buol's whole handling of the crisis. A private letter contained the first of his many offers, or threats, to resign.[23]

Yet, outwardly, Bruck conformed to the new line and (unlike Redcliffe) loyally attempted to sell the Vienna Note to the Turks. But the Turks, as Bruck expected, refused to accept the note without alterations. Again Austrian mediation efforts faced an impasse. Buol hoped, without real conviction, that Russia might be persuaded to accept the Turk alterations in the note, but also wanted to continue efforts to frighten Turkey into yielding.[24] Bruck, at first also hopeful that Turkey might not remain adamant, soon gave up on Buol's despairing expedients and returned to urging Buol to start planning Austria's role in the coming war. Indeed, he felt, Austria should act before actual fighting broke out. An Austrian occupation of Little Wallachia, in secret agreement with Russia, would cause Slav insurrections in Bosnia and Herzegovina which Austria could exploit to her advantage. Or, if Prussian and German support were assured, all of Central Europe could rise up en masse as an armed mediator, exacting the necessary commitments from Russia, imposing terms on Turkey, and excluding England and France entirely from the affair.[25]

This advice seemed clear and drastic enough—yet Bruck could change his mind with mercurial swiftness. Two weeks later he proposed a new combination, in cooperation with Redcliffe, for assuaging Turkey's fears: Turkey might be brought to accept the unaltered Vienna Note if she received in exchange a declaration by Russia and the four powers that they understood the note in the sense of Turkey's reservations.[26] This suggestion was much closer to Buol's cautious way of thinking; indeed, he had already anticipated it. In late September, he and Emperor Francis Joseph met Tsar Nicholas and Nesselrode at Olmütz. There Nicholas formally declared that Russia understood the Vienna Note as simply confirming her old treaty rights, narrowly interpreted. This Olmütz Project was, as H. W. V. Temperley says, a very serious effort for peace.[27] It repudiated Nesselrode's so-called violent interpretation of the Vienna Note in early September, which had so angered Turkey and the West. If Nicholas' word was accepted, there would be no more ground for conflict. But with Buol's typical bad luck, his project grew rotten before it was ripe. England and France were no longer willing to accept Nicholas' *bona fides*, and no longer able to hold back Turkey. The arrival of British and French steamers at Constantinople, in addition to the earlier arrival of the Egyptian fleet, encouraged the Turks to take the bit in their teeth, presenting Russia first with an ultimatum to evacuate the Principalities and then, in early October, with a declaration of war.[28]

Buol was disheartened by this new setback; not so Bruck. Nothing was lost, he insisted, by the failure of Austria's peace efforts. In fact, the affair was only now beginning to be interesting. England and France were helpless to intervene effectively, and if Turkey were soundly beaten and had to pay an indemnity, so much the better—"otherwise the Muslims could become unbearably arrogant." The important thing was to insure that Austria mediated the peace and advanced her interests in the process.[29] The best means of doing this, in turn, was by joining with Russia to erect an Austro-Russian condominium over Turkey, by "bringing that minority of the older Turkish statesmen to the helm, who recognize that the real salvation of Turkey lies in a close union with Austria and Russia."[30] The final rejection of the Olmütz Project by Turkey,[31] after England had already repudiated it and had led France to do likewise, spurred on Bruck in urging Buol not to try now to stop the conflict, but to let it take its course. The war, he now insisted, would remain localized and limited in scope, and represented no great danger to Austria. The English were only bluffing and would back out of a real conflict.[32] Far from seeking Anglo-French help in settling the issue now (which would only deliver Turkey into the hands of the West, that is, the camp of the revolution), Austria ought to forbid the sea powers to undertake any land action in Turkey's behalf. She should then remain calm and wait until spring, when a good blow by the Russians would bring the Turks to their senses and pave the way for an Austrian settlement. "By a solution of the question in an Austrian sense," he explained, "I mean that the *dominating* influence of the Western powers be broken and the *proper* Austro-Russian influence prevail."[33]

Buol continued to follow exactly the opposite policy, trying, now that hostilities had broken out, to promote direct Russo-Turk peace negotiations, but also working for a new four-power plan for mediation between the belligerents. While he refused to yield to all the Western demands and proposals,[34] Buol felt compelled to go some distance to meet the English point of view and achieve four-power unity. Thus the new European Note of December 5 to Turkey, proposing peace negotiations, was more pro-Turk and anti-Russian than Buol would have liked it, to say nothing of Bruck.[35] In his defense and in answer to Bruck's repeated calls for an Austro-Russian entente, Buol argued that Austria could not simply trust in Russia's promises and allow events to take their course. A Near Eastern war, no matter who was responsible, meant too many grave dangers for Austria—among them, the possible breakup of Turkey and the certain armed intervention of the sea powers. Austria, therefore, had to mediate between the belligerents, and as mediator she could not consider Russian interests alone. An Austro-Russian entente against the West at Constantinople was theoretically very desirable; but, through no fault of Austria's, it had now become impossible, at least for the present.[36]

Despite the divergence in their viewpoints,[37] Bruck received Buol's instructions on the new demarche to Turkey with apparent enthusiasm, promising the most energetic pressure on the Turks in its behalf. Perhaps he reasoned that the plan, in calling upon Turkey to propose peace negotiations to Russia, built a golden bridge for the Russians, whose lethargy in failing to trounce the Turks in the field Bruck found "maddening and incomprehensible."[38]

By failing actually to carry out these instructions, however, Bruck precipitated the first sharp and open clash with Buol. Despite clear directives from

Vienna not to initiate new moves or collective demarches at Constantinople, on December 15 Bruck joined with Redcliffe and the other envoys in sending identical notes to the Porte, laying down the terms on which Turkey should negotiate with Russia.[39] Buol accepted this action mildly enough as "in the sense of our instructions of 11 November," though it clearly violated their letter.[40] But then a few days later Bruck joined the other envoys in declining even to deliver the Vienna Conference Note of December 5 to the sultan. He argued that no other envoys would have supported him in presenting the note and that its vague contents would have encouraged the Turks to demand unreasonable conditions for negotiations (which was true). It was, nevertheless, Redcliffe's lead, and not his government's orders, which Bruck had followed.[41]

The response from Vienna was a stiff official rebuke from the emperor (inspired, of course, by Buol), telling Bruck in the future to follow orders and to avoid even the appearance of solidarity with the insubordination of his colleagues.[42] Privately, Buol took a milder tone. Laying the chief blame on Redcliffe, he regretted only that Bruck had not condemned the latter's conduct and had failed to realize that the proposal of the ambassadors could be useful only if it clearly represented the united will of their governments. He had wanted Turkey to respond to an official move by Europe; now Turkey would respond, if at all, to the unofficial opinion of the envoys. In addition, Redcliffe was now in command of the situation, and he was more concerned with his own prestige and the humiliation of Russia than with peace.[43]

This reprimand brought Bruck to the point of a formal revolt against Buol's authority. Already before this he had begun to complain bitterly of the manner in which he was treated—his proposals were ignored, decisions necessary to his work were neglected, persons incompatible with him were kept on in the service. If Vienna persisted in overriding him, he would have to resign.[44] His response to the rebuke was an explosion of wounded pride. Officially, he denied every charge against him, including that of insubordination.[45] Privately, to Buol, he denounced his condemnation without a hearing as utterly unfair and unprecedented, and demanded as satisfaction a direct vote of confidence from the emperor himself.[46]

Here was obviously the point at which Bruck should have been recalled, if only for the good of the service. A stronger man than Buol, and one more secure in his own position, would surely have done so. Yet, without any apparent apology or backing down on either side, the crisis passed over, and Bruck stayed on at Constantinople. The particular dispute between Vienna and Constantinople, moreover, had no perceptible effect on the negotiations, chiefly because both Buol's move for mediation and Redcliffe's were overtaken and ruined by the course of events. In this case, it was the Russian destruction of a Turkish fleet at Sinope, and the consequent entry of English and French fleets into the Black Sea to protect Turkey, which made mediation virtually hopeless.

The action of the Western fleets, however, occasioned new disagreement between Buol and Bruck. Initially, Bruck proposed sending an Austrian frigate into the Black Sea also, in order to maintain Austria's influence and prestige. The proposal was rejected. Bruck then took it upon himself, with the Prussian envoy, Wildenbruck, not only to protest to Redcliffe and the French envoy, Baraguey d'Hilliers, against the Anglo-French naval movement, but also formally to denounce it before the sultan. Faced with British and French protests, Buol had to disavow Bruck, pointing out to him that, however regrettable the Anglo-French action, Austria could not dispense with Western support in the Eastern question.[47]

This disagreement was symptomatic of the deepening rift between Buol and Bruck as general war approached. Buol, unwilling to leave any expedient for peace untried, pushed through still another four-power summons for peace negotiations at the Vienna Conference on January 13, but, realistically, he expected little to come of it.[48] Having failed to prevent a war dangerous to Austria, he now had to plan how to limit it and to protect Austrian interests. His policy was simple. If Russia would unequivocally bind herself, come what may, to nonrevolutionary conduct and goals in the war, then Austria would promise to remain neutral. If not, Austria would have to join Turkey and the West, at least diplomatically, in order to check Russian expansion by forcing Russia out of the Danubian Principalities.[49]

Such a policy was, of course, abhorrent to Bruck. Yet all the bases for the Austro-Russian entente against the West that he had previously advocated were shattered. The general war he had once believed averted was at hand. England and France, far from bluffing, showed themselves determined to fight. Russia, by transforming her occupation of the Principalities into virtual annexation, appealing to Orthodox believers everywhere for a crusade against the infidel, and, preparing to cross the Danube, showed how little her promises were to be trusted in a crisis. Finally, to replace the present pro-Western Turk ministry with one favorable to Austria and Russia was manifestly impossible. Bruck, therefore, fell back on the second policy he had previously urged. Austria, backed by Prussia and Germany, must simply call a halt to the war on all sides.[50] As for the failure of his predictions, he had a simple explanation—Vienna was to blame. It was Buol who had played into Redcliffe's hands, who had by an imprudent declaration of neutrality in October 1853 struck out of Bruck's hand the weapon with which to fight him. Moreover, how could he be expected, in a few months, with inadequate support, to make good what years of Austrian weakness and blundering at Constantinople had ruined?[51]

Buol pursued his policy undeterred by this advice and criticism. In January, Nicholas I sent Count Orlov to Vienna on a special mission to persuade Austria to pledge neutrality in the war. The tsar refused, however, to pay the Austrian price for neutrality, a promise not to cross the Danube, not to raise the Balkan peoples in revolt, and not to take any Turk territory even if Russia won the war. Unanimously, the Austrian conference of ministers rejected neutrality on Russia's terms, and Buol set out in February and March to create a united front of the West, Austria, and Prussia to force Russia away from the Danube.

During these months, Bruck complained sharply that he was being deliberately kept in the dark on Austrian policy.[52] The complaint was justified—even such a vital step as Austria's support of the Anglo-French summons to Russia to evacuate the Principalities was communicated to Bruck with only the most general and colorless explanation.[53] Yet, there was an obvious reason for the lack of communication—Bruck was actively working against Buol's policy at Constantinople. Not only did he declaim night and day against an entente with the West, but he was also trying to break up the entente between England and France—an unnatural and dangerous alliance, which, he characteristically argued, was Buol's fault in the first place. Relations between Baraguey and Redcliffe at Constantinople, he said, were so tense that a few shrewd moves by Austria, which Russia would gladly support, would suffice to separate France from England. This would bring on "the day of reckoning with England . . . the true, conscious, deliberate bearer of the Revolution."[54]

This last was no mere rhetorical phrase for Bruck. His letters are one long anti-English tirade.[55] Behind every disturbance in the East—the Greek risings in Epirus and Athens, the unrest in Serbia, the spread of revolutionary Graeco-Slavic propaganda in the Balkans—he saw the hand of English agents, led by Redcliffe. And England's motives were never idealistic, even of the revolutionary sort, but simply selfish and imperialist. Domination of the whole Mediterranean, trade monopolies, colonies, territory, satellites—this was what the English were after.[56] "A weak Greece, a weak Turkey, entirely surrendered to the influence and practically to the rule of England, that is what they want; as in India, so in Europe."[57] To gain this empire, England had to weaken Russia and destroy her maritime position. There could be but one response to such a policy: a Continental league of Russia, Austria, and France against England, to expose her for the paper tiger that she was.[58]

If this league against Great Britain could not be achieved, however, at least Austria could avoid joining with the West. This is the main point of Bruck's oft-cited plea for an Austrian armed neutrality in league with Prussia and Germany—it was a *pis aller*, a substitute for the openly anti-English orientation he would have preferred and an alternative to the entente with the West he abhorred. There are, moreover, two other significant points about this proposal. First, Bruck wanted a Central Europe united, not for defensive neutrality or nonintervention, but rather for a decisive intervention in the conflict at a favorable moment, when the combined armed forces of Austria, Prussia, and Germany, a million men, could dictate the terms of settlement.[59] Second, Bruck's argument for the maintenance of neutrality rested in part on Russian promises that had already become invalid. He contended as late as March 20 that Austria could safely remain neutral as long as Russia did not cross the Danube, the Russian promise to restore the Danubian Principalities to their previous condition held good, and no insurrections broke out in Serbia and Bosnia.[60] Now, doubtless, Buol did not keep Bruck fully informed. Yet Bruck knew that the Orlov mission in January had broken down precisely on the tsar's refusal to confirm the very promises that Bruck here cites as still valid. He must have known of Nicholas's determination not to return Christian peoples once "liberated" to the Turkish yoke. In close touch with Austrian consuls at Bucharest and Jassy, Bruck could not have been ignorant of what was going on in the Principalities, where occupation was becoming indistinguishable from annexation and where the Russians were preparing for the campaign across the Danube, which they were to launch the next month. Finally, he could hardly have been unaware that Nicholas now more than ever regarded the war as a religious crusade and that only the fear of Austria's reaction kept Russia from openly playing the revolutionary card and arming Bosnians and Serbs against the Turks. Bruck, in other words, was ignoring all the factors that had driven Buol reluctantly to abandon neutrality and move into opposition to Russia.

Though Bruck's arguments failed to shake Buol, they were sufficiently shared by other members of the government to throw a temporary road-block in the path of Buol's policy. In ministerial conferences of March 22 and 25, Buol presented his case for openly aligning with the West to compel Russia to evacuate the Principalities. The emperor, however, strongly influenced by Bruck's good friend and admirer Baron Hess, the Austrian Chief of Staff, rejected Buol's arguments on the ground that the risks of war were too great. The conference decided that Austria must first conclude a defensive alliance with Prussia before intervening in the conflict.[61] Moreover, it was Hess, whose views were close to Bruck's, who was sent to negotiate the alliance with Prussia, concluded on April 20—and he did so in a manner not wholly in accord with Buol's wishes.

This temporary reverse brought no change in the Western orientation of Austrian policy, however. By the end of April, even Hess agreed that the time had come for Austrian intervention.[62] Buol at this point tried again, in one of his now infrequent private letters, to win Bruck's cooperation. Assuring Bruck that he was being given all the information possible, Buol begged him to understand the imperative necessities of Austria's position. While Austria would do everything possible to avoid an open break with Russia, by far the greatest and most immediate danger Austria faced was that of Russian preponderance in the East. Against this, Austria had to erect a barrier. English and French efforts in the same direction needed to be encouraged and guided, not rebuffed or frustrated.[63]

The plea was lost on Bruck, for whom, as he confessed, the very thought of Austrian cooperation with England made the blood rush to his head in rage.[64] He responded by ringing new changes on the theme of the English menace[65] and denouncing Austria's self-degradation in collaborating with the sea powers to quell anti-Turk uprisings in Epirus.[66] Above all, he insisted that Austria had no need of any help to protect her interests. With a solid German bloc behind her, he argued, "the Imperial government could dictate its conditions to both sides."[67] His reasons for dismissing Buol's nightmare of hostile coalitions is significant: "Austria and Germany solidly united... have no need of either Russia or England or France, since all three together

will never stand against Austria and Germany and we will always be a match
for any two of them, since we are bound to get in addition the help of the
third."[68] That third power whose help Austria–Germany could always command could only in this instance, of course, be Russia. The question of why
Buol continued to permit Bruck to express his opposition so openly and to
violate his orders for so long,[69] rather than end the anomalous situation with
Bruck's recall or his own resignation, cries out for an answer. In the absence
of clear-cut documentary evidence, one can only reasonably conjecture that
Buol, who was not a fighter, preferred to tolerate Bruck at Constantinople
rather than risk a confrontation at Vienna, where Bruck had powerful influence and friends. As for Bruck, he probably stayed on in the hope of restraining a policy hateful to him.[70] The latent dispute, however, flared up in the
summer and fall of 1854 into an open conflict that made some sort of
settlement unavoidable.

The occasion was an apparently brilliant triumph for Austrian diplomacy:
the Austrian occupation of the Danubian Principalities. On June 3 Austria
summoned Russia to evacuate the Principalities or face conflict with entering
Austrian troops. She followed this with the June 14 Convention with
Turkey, which Bruck signed, providing for joint Austro-Turkish occupation
of these provinces. The tsar's military advisers, especially General Paskevich,
had long been conscious of the acute dangers of Russia's exposed strategic
position. At their pleas, Nicholas yielded, grinding his teeth, and withdrew
his army behind the Pruth, while Austria moved in. Though the Russians
presented their withdrawal as merely a strategic move, Buol had achieved a
major political victory—the occupation of the Principalities without war.

As an advocate of an economic and political union of Central Europe and
of Austrian expansion to the southeast, Bruck was wholly in favor of Austrian
occupation of the Principalities. His quarrel with Buol concerned the legal
basis, mode, and purposes of the occupation. For Buol, the expulsion of Russia
was the first essential step toward the speedy reestablishment of peace and legal
order both in the Principalities and in Europe. While he did not want to provoke Russia needlessly, and resisted strong English and French pressure to
enter the war before the means of persuasion were exhausted, he would have
used force had Russia refused to leave.[71] Once in occupation, Buol believed
that Austria had to act on a legal basis, in cooperation with the suzerain power,
Turkey, and Turkey's allies, neither claiming an exclusive occupation for herself nor using her forces to restrict the military operations of the allies.[72]

Bruck saw the matter wholly differently. A main object of Austrian occupation, he believed, was to interpose the Austrian army between Russia and
the Allies, so as to give Russia security on her Bessarabian frontier. In his
view, Turkey and the Allies possessed no military or political rights in
Moldavia and Wallachia. The June 14 Convention gave Austria the right to
an exclusive occupation if Russia withdrew from the Principalities without
fighting, and Austria unquestionably had the deciding voice in all matters of
administration.[73] In short, Bruck wanted the Principalities occupied solely by
Austria, in behalf of Austro-Russian interests, against Turkey and the Allies.

These differences emerged in the question of the reinstatement of the former hospodars, Prince Stirbei and Prince Ghika, both championed by Austria but opposed on various grounds by the Turks and Redcliffe. Bruck insisted that Austria should demand their reinstallation and recognition from Turkey as a matter of right, and acted accordingly at the Porte without waiting for orders.[74] On July 31 Buol wrote Bruck setting forth his policy of cooperation with the Allies and instructing him to advance the cause of Stirbei, the more controversial of the two hospodars, by persuasion rather than peremptory demands. Bruck responded with a violent dispatch, rejecting his instructions, refusing to abandon his position, and again threatening resignation. This was 1848 all over again, he said, except that now Vienna was promoting the revolution.[75]

Bruck's letter elicited a cold, stiff reply from Buol ordering Bruck not only to accept the July 31 dispatch as his guideline but also to communicate it to the Porte and his colleagues in Constantinople.[76]

This storm was by no means settled when another issue heightened it. Bruck learned first from Redcliffe and then from Buol that Austria was negotiating with the Western powers on a joint basis for peace, which led to their agreement on the Four Points in early August. Again Bruck issued an impassioned warning against this policy, pleading for union with Prussia and Germany, and insisting that only the West, not Russia, was Austria's rival and a menace to her. With Austria at the head of Central Europe, Russia would grant anything Austria desired in the Principalities; indeed, Russia would be forced to become Austria–Germany's ally. Cooperation with England and France would lead to nothing but the revolutionizing of the Principalities.[77] In fact, Turkey herself would rather have an exclusive Austrian protectorate over the Principalities, or an Austro-Russian one, instead of the joint European one that Buol proposed. The Four Points actually contravened Austrian interests and threatened to pull Austria into a disastrous war that would destroy Russia, ruin the hopes for a Central European union, and undermine Austria's own power position in the East and in Europe.[78] Indeed, the whole policy of trying to secure Austrian interests by inspiring the confidence and sympathy of other powers was fundamentally wrong. Where vital interests were at stake, as in the Principalities, the only course was to act first and negotiate later ("Erst handeln, dann verhandeln").[79]

As these arguments remained without effect, Bruck increasingly discarded all restraints, even those of polite form, in his polemic against Buol. He accused Buol to his face of desiring war with Russia, of deliberately fomenting an open break with her, and of encouraging the wanton lies of the anti-Russian press in Vienna.[80] He further took the lead in an anti-Buol Austrian fronde through correspondence with Hess and Field Marshal Lieutenant Count Coronini, commander of the Austrian army in the Principalities, both of whom shared Bruck's views about the occupation. He promoted and encouraged their resistance to orders from Vienna, contravened Buol's views on policy toward the allies and Turkey, and supplied the military commanders with arguments to use in their running dispute with both the Turks and

Buol over the administration of the provinces, the reinstatement of Stirbei, and Turkey's right, if she wished, to go through Moldavia to get at Russia in Bessarabia.[81] According to reports reaching Buol, Bruck even threatened the Turks with withdrawal of Austria's occupation forces if Austria did not get her way.[82] All this activity he carried on without any attempt to conceal it from Buol.

Buol's repeated explanations of his policy and his arguments that Austria had no right to do or demand what Bruck wanted were useless.[83] Buol had no other recourse but to secure a formal decision of the emperor in his favor and to take decisions in disputes over occupation policy out of the hands of Bruck and the military commanders, with an ambassadorial conference in Vienna now set up as the final authority. Bruck received an announcement of the new arrangement, together with a catalogue of his errors,[84] while Coronini was flatly told that Bruck was wrong and that he should take his further instructions strictly from Vienna.[85] Formally interpellated by the Ottoman government on the activities of the fronde, Buol firmly rejected Turk insinuations that Austria was following a double policy. He also assured Turkey, however, that the new instructions to Hess and Bruck settled all the outstanding differences.[86]

At this same time, Buol sent a long private letter to Bruck that clearly indicated his desire, despite everything, to avoid an irreparable breach. The time had come for complete frankness, said Buol; Paris and London were constantly bombarding him with protests over Bruck's language and conduct. The Allied complaints were twofold: that Bruck claimed an exclusive protectorate for Austria in the Principalities, and sought it by intimidation of the highest Turk authorities; and that he displayed an open sympathy for Russia, while obstructing good relations with the West and trying to hinder the operations of Turkish forces in the Principalities. While defending Bruck on the first score, Buol could not deny that, if Bruck held the same language at Constantinople as he did in his dispatches, then it was no wonder that the Allies had taken offense, or even that they believed Austria was playing fast and loose with them and only waiting for a chance to go over to Russia's side. Buol literally begged Bruck to consider the difficulties that Bruck's insubordination daily created for him and to conform to his instructions for the sake of duty and the good of the whole cause. He concluded with a statement of his policy so clear and (I believe) honest that it merits quotation:

> We want to obtain a good peace from Russia, and, if necessary, gain it by force. As long as she has not accepted the four points as a basis for negotiation, we are Russia's *opponents*. We can achieve this peace *only* in accord with the sea powers. Therefore the *first* concern is that nothing disturb this accord. A great union with Germany in order to decide the issue *vis-à-vis* both East and West is a beautiful but empty dream. Prussia feels nothing but hatred and envy toward us and the small states can only at best be compelled to do what they feel like doing. To rely on such allies would be simply too naive ....It is not a question at this moment of gaining the *entire influence* which *cannot fail* to be ours once the great struggle is ended ....At present it is a matter of upholding

the alliance at any cost, of getting us *forgiven* for the fact that we, although we are *not belligerents,* still actually enjoy a more influential position than those who are already in the war.[87]

Bruck answered Buol's plea once again by not merely denying all the complaints against him but also taking the offensive with a categoric denunciation of Buol's policy from 1848 on, both as foreign minister and as ambassador. The record, according to Bruck, was one of unalloyed blunders, weakness, indecision, and lost opportunities leading straight to disaster. Again his main theme was that only in union with Prussia and Germany could Austria maintain her interests against the West; only from Russia, in exchange for protecting Russia's southwestern frontier, could Austria gain her rightful exclusive protectorate in the Principalities. Bruck flatly refused to conform to Austrian policy except on one condition: should Russia accept the Four Points, Austria and Germany would join in imposing them on the West, thereby demonstrating Austria's independence in policy.[88]

This reply at long last made Bruck impossible as Internuncio. From then on until his recall, he received only routine information and tasks of secondary importance from Buol, although Buol preserved an outwardly correct and even friendly tone in their correspondence.[89] As for Bruck, he maintained his former line of argument to the end,[90] but he also obviously gave up hope of influencing Buol. Austria's alliance with England and France on December 2 elicited from Bruck only a cold, terse expression of his disapproval, combined with the hope that at least Prussia and Germany might be brought into the alliance. The news that Prussia and Germany supported the coming negotiations for peace cheered him somewhat, though the alliance, in his eyes, still ruined Austria's correct position as arbiter of the struggle.[91] In January 1855 the emperor, undoubtedly at Buol's suggestion, invited Bruck to return to Vienna and his old post as minister of finance. After some hesitation, Bruck accepted, though not without complaining that he would have to repair the financial chaos others had created, and demanding full powers for the task.[92] From February 1855 until his death by suicide in 1860, Bruck served as finance minister, with considerable success. His opposition to Buol from within the Cabinet continued, but his preoccupation with foreign policy ended with his recall.[93]

From the practical standpoint, Bruck's mission to Constantinople was certainly a failure. He was able to stir up a good deal of dust, to create the appearance of two different Austrian policies, to embarrass Buol, and perhaps to assist in slowing down the trend toward rapprochement with the West in the spring of 1854. Yet, neither in Constantinople nor at Vienna was Bruck able decisively to influence the negotiations or policy decisions. The fault was in part in Bruck's own shortcomings as ambassador (and I can see no ground for the favorable verdict on his diplomacy in the literature).[94] An invincible insubordination, a penchant for violent action, an extreme sensibility on questions of personal and national honor, and an impatient inclination to force decisions through by ultimatum and bluff are not the hallmarks of the good diplomat.

Yet does not the greater fault lie with Buol, who turned a deaf ear to Bruck's advice and persisted in a hopeless and ultimately disastrous policy? I think not. Buol was right in rejecting Bruck's advice, although this does not necessarily make his own alternative the best one. Bruck's policy can be made persuasive only by seriously misinterpreting it. He did not, as is claimed and as some of his phrases suggest, advocate a genuinely independent neutral policy directed equally against encroachments from both East and West.[95] As the whole previous narrative shows, the thrust and purpose of Bruck's policy was pro-Russian and anti-West, in the sense that Bruck always wanted Austria to advance her interests in the Near East *with* Russia and *against* England and France. Russia, even when she had to be checked and guided, was a potential ally and partner; England, the permanent enemy. Hess's views, incidentally, were much the same[96] and were shared in general by the whole anti-Buol military coterie. The chief difference is that Hess, fearful of Russian military might, tended to regard Russia as the senior partner in the combination, while Bruck envisioned Russia as the junior partner of an Austrian-controlled Central European union.

It is equally misleading to lump Bruck together with Metternich as advocates of an Austro-Prussian union for neutrality.[97] While it is impossible to analyze Metternich's views on the Crimean War thoroughly here, two points are clear: first, Metternich, like Buol and unlike Bruck, blamed Russia chiefly for starting the war, saw Russian preponderance in the Near East as the great and immediate danger for Austria, and insisted that Russia must return to conservative principles before the Austro-Russian entente could be restored. Second, Metternich advocated neutrality primarily out of his profoundly realistic and pessimistic conviction that the war could bring nothing but harm and danger to Austria, that there were simply no gains possible or desirable for her in the Near East. Austria's best course, therefore, was to stay out of the war, defend her interests, and wait until war weariness on both sides enabled Austria to mediate a peace without victory. He favored an entente with Prussia because she seemed to have the same pacific, unambitious policy in the Near East.[98] There is an enormous difference between this policy of nonintervention and virtual abnegation and the soaring ambitions of Bruck, who saw the whole crisis as a great opportunity for political, economic, and even territorial gains and who wished to forge in the Central European union a new instrument of power with which to dictate a solution according to Austria's interests.

It cannot even be said that Bruck genuinely appreciated the value of an Austrian partnership with Prussia and Germany,[99] if by "partnership" is meant a genuine cooperation based on equality and mutual interests and desires. Bruck, like almost all Austrians, took for granted the primacy of Austria in Central Europe, as well as the identity of Germany's interests with those of Austria. In the union he envisioned, Austria would lead and make the decisions, and Prussia and Germany would follow. That Prussia and Germany might have interests conflicting with Austria's, especially in the East, and that they had a right to an independent policy, never entered into his calculations.

The main point, however, is not that Bruck's policy has been misinterpreted. It is that his policy was wrong, and his policy was wrong because his ideas and ways of thinking were wrong. He lacked the prime requisite for foreign policy, the sense of limits, the feeling, schooled by history and experience, for the reactions of other powers and the consequences of one's actions. For example, his proposal to check the Russian drive into the Balkans by a preventive occupation of Bosnia, Serbia, and Little Wallachia (whether or not this was its real purpose) would have been highly dangerous. Bruck could hardly have been unaware that Russia had for months been urging this course on Austria, for obvious reasons.[100] It would have encouraged the Russian advance, made Austria Russia's partner in crime, threatened to involve Austria in war with Turkey, England, and France, and, incidentally, raised the specter of revolution in Italy and Hungary. Bruck's whole thought on Russia is basically naive. He did not see that, while Russia and Austria could be friends everywhere else, in the East they were rivals, and they could stay friends only if both carefully observed the *noli me tangere* here. His sometime confidence in Tsar Nicholas' promises lacked the realistic insight that such promises, however sincere, must be swept away by the course of a great war—that in foreign policy necessities, capabilities, and opportunities tend to take precedence over intentions. He showed no understanding of how dangerous a nationalist, religious, and Slavophile hubris would be aroused within Russia by the good beating he hoped Russia would administer to the Turks. His proposal of an Austro-Russian condominium over Turkey paid no attention to the immense advantages that race, language, religion, and historic traditions would give to Russia in this partnership. On this score, Francis Joseph, at twenty-four, saw far more clearly than Bruck.[101]

His thought on the balance of power and the European Concert is equally defective. One looks in vain for any serious consideration, in all his proposals for a Central European union, of what countercoalitions might be called into being against Austria by the creation of his union of seventy millions in the heart of Europe. The belief that England and France could simply be excluded from the settlement of the Eastern question, and made to swallow an Austro-Russian hegemony, is shockingly unhistorical. As bad or worse is his notion that England would be helpless to do anything about a Continental league against her—this at the very height of England's industrial, commercial, and maritime supremacy.

Even Bruck's central conception of a powerful Central European union was devoid of all basis of reality. Prussian and German support for Austria, as Buol knew well, was available only for one purpose: to keep Austria and Germany out of the conflict at any cost.[102] This was a perfectly legitimate policy for Prussia and the German states to follow, but it had no relation to Bruck's grandiose power-political plans. Knowing as he did the caution, suspicion, and anti-Austrian ambitions of Prussia, and the intractable particularism of the other German states, Buol was right in characterizing Bruck's scheme as naïve, as a beautiful but empty dream.[103]

One must add, it was not even a beautiful dream. Finally, the spirit behind Bruck's ideas and the tendency they represent are at once the worst and most significant aspects of his policy. Bruck's language breathes the spirit of *Machtpolitik*. He enormously overestimated Austria's power and capabilities, greatly underestimated the dangers confronting her, and repeatedly advocated force as the answer to any opposition. His advice really called upon Austria to abandon legality, moderation, and consensus and to seek her salvation in the pure, unprincipled exercise of power. It is this spirit, and not mere naïveté, which accounts for the dangerous misconceptions and startling recklessness of Bruck's policy.[104] The perils Austria faced, and the restraints under which she operated, were not merely ignored by him, but despised. The dangers of such an outlook as Bruck's in foreign policy—romantic, right radical, exclusively Austrian with a pan-German cast—can hardly be exaggerated, especially for a hard-pressed conservative state like Austria, possessing very little margin for error.

As for Buol and his policy, a general reappraisal is clearly out of place here. One point, however, can be made: the fairly common charge that Buol deliberately exploited the Near Eastern crisis for the sake of Austrian gains, that he courted isolation and saw force as the final answer to all questions, is not merely false—it is grotesque. His contest with Bruck alone, quite apart from a mass of other evidence, demonstrates the opposite—that he was struggling to avert the degeneration of conservative policy into *Machtpolitik*, trying to solve Austria's new problems and dangers through the old diplomacy, through a moderate, European solution. For this effort, at least, he deserves some credit.

4

THE LOST INTERMEDIARIES: THE IMPACT OF 1870 ON THE EUROPEAN SYSTEM

There is something odd about the way historians deal with the events of 1870–71. We remember 1866 in part for the expulsion of Austria from Germany and the annexation of Hanover, Nassau, and Frankfurt. We are aware that Italian unification ended Austrian rule in Lombardy-Venetia and independent governments at Florence, Naples, and Rome.[1] We know that 1806 saw not only the creation of a Confederation of the Rhine, but also the end of the Holy Roman Empire.[2] We agree, at least in the West, that the right term for what happened between 1772 and 1795 is not the gathering in of the Russian lands, but the partition of Poland.

In other words, historians regularly pay close attention not only to what emerges or is created in international politics, but also to what is ended or destroyed. Eighteen seventy-seventy one is an exception. The historical debate, an extensive one, centers entirely on the character of what emerged in those years—united Germany, Prussian Germany, Bismarckian Germany, a Great-Prussian military monarchy, whatever–and the impact of that new creation upon the international system.[3] If what disappeared in 1870–71 is considered important at all, we think of the downfall of Napoleon III's regime, the overthrow of the Paris Commune, or the temporary end of French rule in Alsace-Lorraine. No one seems to think it important that in 1870–71 four states, Bavaria, Württemberg, Baden, and Hesse-Darmstadt, ended their independent existence.[4]

If this observation served only to point out a historiographical anomaly, it would be trivial. It intends rather to introduce a wider theme, the impact of the disappearance of these independent states upon the international system, and to sketch out a prima facie case (no more) that the end of South Germany's independence was a development almost as important for that system as the so-called unification of Germany.

The International History Review, 6 (February, 1984), 1–27. Copyright © (1984), The International History Review.

The distinction between German unification and the disappearance of South German independence, and the attempt to distinguish between their respective effects, may seem meaningless. Clearly the two phenomena are different sides of the same coin. Must not the consequences of one automatically accrue to the other? No, not really. The main reason historians have for paying attention to what disappears from history is not merely the desire to give a fair and complete account of events, or to pay a decent respect to lost causes and unrealized historical potentialities. It is the recognition that the passing of old forces *per se* makes a difference in history. For example, even though the Holy Roman Empire had ceased to be a major force in Europe long before its demise, and the immediate effects on international politics of its abolition in 1806 were almost nil, nevertheless its disappearance meant and symbolized the end of one historical way to conceive of Germany and organize it, namely, as a *Rechtsordnung*. Its demise therefore simultaneously paved the way for other modes of organization, and created a gap to be filled, a desire for something else to replace the functions and values of the historic Empire.[5] If this point holds of so shadowy an entity as the Empire in its final decades, it applies *a fortiori* to the existence of independent states. There is little doubt that in nineteenth century Europe certain states, though relatively small and weak, had an importance for the nineteenth century system far transcending the power they possessed. Had they disappeared, annexed by some greater power or partitioned among several, their disappearance would have tended to destabilize the system not merely or mainly by its effects on the general distribution of power, but by the removal of their presence, the absence of their functions. Belgium, Holland, Switzerland, and the Ottoman Empire belonged to this category throughout the century; Serbia, Rumania, Bulgaria, Sardinia-Piedmont, and Denmark could plausibly be named for some periods. The disappearance of Poland in the late eighteenth century is a good example of the destabilizing effects indicated here. This essay proposes to add the South German states to the list. It will try to indicate in a general way how smaller states, often referred to in the eighteenth and early nineteenth centuries as *corps, états*, or *puissances intermédiaires*, are important to the system, and to show more specifically how and why the disappearance of independent states in South Germany, especially Bavaria and Württemberg, deeply affected the international system.

To do so even in a rudimentary way requires some discussion of practical and symbolic roles and functions of intermediary states in an international system. The subject is one to which historians have paid little attention.[6] True, there are many careful studies of the international politics and diplomacy of small powers. They tend, however, either to treat intermediary states as the objects and targets of the policies and actions of great powers, or to show how these smaller states tried actively to protect and advance their own interests as players in the great game of international politics. Valuable as both perspectives are, they do not exhaust the possibilities. A little reflection suggests that intermediary states are not simply objects and subjects of an international political system shaped and operated by the competition between great powers. By their existence, by being present, they also help to shape international politics and limit its possibilities.

Some of these functions and effects are obvious, often talked about in the eighteenth and nineteenth centuries as now; others largely go unremarked. The most familiar are the geographical and strategic functions.[7] Intermediary states are by definition intermediary between great powers. To call them "buffer states" or "buffer zones" expresses only part of what they do. They may act as buffers between great powers; they also, by occupying strategic areas, can serve either as foci of international competition or remove these areas from international competition. Sometimes they may do something of both (e.g., the Ottoman Empire both prevented international conflict over the Straits, and was the focus of competition at the same time). They may separate great powers, keeping them from interacting, or link them, facilitating interaction—again, sometimes both at the same time. The Low Countries, Denmark, Switzerland, the Ottoman Empire, Sardinia-Piedmont, and the smaller states of the German Confederation were intermediary in this geographic and strategic sense from 1815 on. Other states less critically located could become so in special situations. Sweden became an important geographic intermediary power in the Crimean War. Had Austria and France come to blows over Naples, the states of Central Italy would have become so.

Other less tangible functions are important. An inertial or flywheel effect can be produced by intermediary powers, a drag on great power conflicts exerted by their desire not to get involved or to do so only on their own terms. The effect of German small and middle state policies in the crises of 1830–32 or in the Crimean War illustrates this. Intermediary states also exert what might be called a distraction effect in international politics. The necessity for great powers to pay attention to intermediary powers in a crisis, and worry about what they may do, can serve as a deterrent. Austria and France, for example, were distracted and deterred from direct conflict after 1815 by the question of what the lesser German and Italian states might do.

The most important role of intermediary bodies, however, is not a single assignable function, but a kind of cumulative effect of their presence. By multiplying and complicating the possible modes of great power interaction, they tend to render international politics more flexible and increase the possibilities for managing relations without overt conflict. While the principle involved is easier to illustrate than to define specifically, a reasonably clear statement of it is possible. Great powers interacting in the presence of intermediary bodies, and partly through them, enjoy a broad range of modes for their interaction. In respect to the intermediary states and each other, they can variously try to cooperate to maintain the status quo, share influence, neutralize the area, pledge mutual nonaggrandizement and noninterference, compete for dominant influence, partition the area into spheres, or seek some combination of these. None of these modes intrinsically tends toward overt great power conflict; some lead away from it. Great powers that face each other directly, in the absence of intermediary states, enjoy fewer choices of relations. Though there are always gradations and variations, basically the choices reduce to four: (1) an equal partnership or alliance; (2) dependence by one power on the other one; (3) a hostile alliance, in which two rival great powers agree to be allied solely or mainly because without alliance ties they are likely to get into war; and (4) direct competition and rivalry. None of these inherently promises a stable or satisfactory relationship. A partnership of great power equals (e.g., the oft-proposed Anglo-German alliance at the turn of the twentieth century) is difficult to achieve and even harder to sustain. Power relations change; so do the burdens of the alliance, breeding mistrust and resentment. The inferior partner in a dominant–dependent relationship will accept that status only out of hard necessity, and will constantly try both to assert its own independence and to use its partner's power for its own purposes. The dominant power will be equally tempted to drag the dependent one along—witness Austro-German relations from 1879 on. A hostile alliance is still more a *pis aller*, and usually requires a third partner to impose, control, sustain the alliance (Germany for Austria and Italy after 1882, or and Rumania after 1883). The dangers of overt, unmediated rivalry are too obvious to discuss. In sum: where intermediate states exist, great power rivalry stands a good chance of being limited to competition for primacy. Where they do not, great power rivalry tends powerfully toward struggle for mastery.

The point is easy to illustrate in nineteenth century politics. Relations between Britain and France, which actually centered mainly on intermediary states (the Low Countries, Switzerland, Spain, Portugal, Sardinia-Piedmont and other Italian states, Greece, Turkey), usually involved a combination of competition and cooperation. Serious confrontations between France and Britain arose only when one power feared the other would gain full sway over some intermediary state—that France might control Spain, Belgium, or Italy, or Britain, Greece, or Turkey. The most serious rivalry between them, culminating in open confrontation in 1898, resulted mainly from Britain's unilateral occupation of an intermediary body, Egypt, which they had agreed to share. Much less cooperation and far sharper rivalry marked France's competition for primacy in Italy with Austria after 1815. Yet so long as intermediary states like Sardinia-Piedmont, the Papal States, and the Two Sicilies remained intact and independent, even if they leaned to one side, the competition remained bloodless, and there were instances (over the Papal States, for example) where Austria and France could work together.[8] Once Napoleon III and Cavour agreed on a policy of eliminating these intermediary states, creating an Italy that almost everyone in Europe was sure would be a French satellite, an all-out Austro-French struggle for mastery was virtually assured. The same principle applies to Austro-Prussian relations in Germany and Austro-Russian relations in the Near East. A combination of competition and cooperation was possible so long as the intermediary bodies remained intact; their disappearance promoted a struggle for supremacy. Poland in the late eighteenth and nineteenth centuries seems to contradict this thesis, but actually provides only a variant of it. The partitions of Poland (1772–95) did create a bitter three-way rivalry, especially between Austria and Prussia, already enemies in Germany. The Polish issue, which more than anything else wrecked the Austro-Prussian alliance of 1792, also came close to wrecking the anti-French Eastern coalition in 1814–15. Only the conviction that Poland could not be restored as an intermediary state, that it would always be a center of liberal and revolutionary conspiracy and a satellite of France, forced the three Eastern powers into a mutual alliance of restraint (the so-called Holy Alliance and its later variants) designed, among other things, to keep Poland from being restored. In a sense, the Polish nation remained a *corps intermédiaire* linking Austria, Prussia, and Russia even when there was no Polish state. When the Three Emperors' Alliance finally broke down in the 1880s, however, Poland once again became the focus of a three-way rivalry, especially during World War I.

This is not to suggest that intermediary states serve solely to promote restraint, flexibility, and peace in international relations. They are also obviously sources of trouble, conflict, and war. Nor does this mean that small states themselves generally pursue less selfish, aggressive policies than great ones. At best, such a generalization would be very hard to prove. What is at issue is less the conscious policies and actions of intermediary states than the functions and roles resulting naturally, largely unwilled, from their existence. The concern here is not with driving forces in history, elements making for change (e.g., industrialization, scientific and technological change, population growth, changes in ideology and belief systems, ambitious and charismatic leaders), but with inhibitors in history, elements controlling, limiting, and directing change. These are subtler, harder to detect (in nature and science, I am told, as well as in history), and hence easily overlooked. But no historical explanation is complete or sound without them. Two analogies may help illustrate the role of intermediary states in the international system. One involves seeing the international system as a kind of ecosystem in which smaller states, though never dominant, contribute enough to the ecology that their disappearance destabilizes it. The other pictures them as working in international politics somewhat as inhibitors do in nature and society—for example, as inhibiting factors control cell activity in the human body, or as unarticulated social and cultural restraints limit and direct societal change. All the functions of intermediary states discussed so far belong to this inhibitory, controlling, switch-throwing variety.

The question this essay raises, then, is whether eliminating the South German states as independent actors in 1870 did not substantially alter the international system by eliminating them as important inhibiting factors in international politics.

The first requirement of a plausible prima facie case is some evidence that these states filled that inhibiting function before their demise. In the geographic-strategic sense, there can be no doubt about it. They certainly controlled a vital area lying between great powers, too dangerous to allow any of them exclusively to control. Since the sixteenth century, South and Southwest Germany had been a key prize, continuously fought over, as vital as the Low Countries, more important than Switzerland and Northern Italy. The upper Rhine and Danube valleys represented classic military highways for France, Germany, and Austria, and were no less important for trade and cultural exchange. The greatest threat to Prussia and lesser princes of the German empire to arise in the late eighteenth century was Austria's attempt to annex Bavaria, which would have given her command of Germany. French control of South Germany, reaching its climax under Napoleon, proved intolerable not only to Austria but ultimately to Prussia as well. In 1813, the fate of Germany and the whole Napoleonic Empire hung in good measure on what South Germany would do. How to organize the "third Germany," especially South Germany, was in important respects the key issue of Central European reorganization in 1813–20, 1848–51, and, of course, 1863–70. No intermediary zone in Europe was more important geographically and strategically than South Germany.

The South German states also plainly exerted an inertial, flywheel effect on the European policies of the German great powers. From 1814 to 1820, the stubborn defense waged particularly by Bavaria and Württemberg of their territory and sovereign independence gained under Napoleon decisively affected the constitution of the German Confederation.[9] After 1820, though Austria and Prussia together could lead or drag the other states with them, it always took effort, and had definite limits. When the two powers were divided, any effort by either of them to force other states, especially the South German ones, wholly into their camp proved counterproductive— witness Prussia's discomfiture in 1849–50, and Austria's in 1853–56. As for the *Zollverein*, important as was the economic leadership Prussia gained through it in South Germany, more remarkable is the caution, moderation, and attention to South German interests the Prussians had to display in order to achieve it and maintain it, and the limited degree to which the customs union could be used for political gains, right down to 1870.[10]

Most obvious is the flexibility introduced into great power politics by the existence of independent German states after 1815, South Germany in particular. Austro-Prussian cooperation after 1815, in stark contrast to the enmity of the previous three generations, plainly grew out of the need to manage a confederation of states guaranteed their independence. Without this, one cannot believe that simple monarchical solidarity would have kept the two powers from open rivalry very long. Prussia was never a meek follower of Metternich's system. During the 1830 revolutions, it threatened to go its own way entirely;[11] from the 1820s on, it consciously sought economic and political primacy in the Bund through the *Zollverein*. What kept Austro-Prussian rivalry confined for so long to a covert competition for primacy was above all the need to manage the Bund, especially South Germany (Prussian leadership of North Germany had long been tacitly conceded). On the other hand, the attempt to end the independence of the middle and smaller states, either by revolutionary action in 1848–49 or by Prussian action in 1849–50, necessarily created an open Austro-Prussian contest for mastery, no matter how liberals or Prussian leaders tried to link Austria to it or conciliate her. When Austria itself drew back from war with Prussia over Germany in 1850, a main reason was the conviction of Prince Schwarzenberg and other

Austrian leaders that Germany was not manageable without Prussian cooperation. Despite their open rivalry after 1850, Austria and Prussia remained unwilling partners in Germany until Bismarck's revolutionary policy of destroying the Confederation revived the all-out struggle for mastery.[12]

As for France, while the French government never seriously exploited the opportunities for securing and improving France's international position which the existence of the German Confederation and independent South German states provided her, every French government after 1815 recognized their value, at least in principle, as a protection against a united Germany and as an opportunity for the expansion of French trade and cultural and political influence. Of this, more later. Russia, as is well known, considered the German Confederation and Austro-Prussian dualism an important element in its security, and tried to keep up its influence in South Germany, especially in Württemberg, as one aspect of Russia's system of buffers against war, revolution, and liberalism. Even Italy found the existence of independent German states useful in its struggle to gain international recognition after 1860, and an independent South Germany certainly was more comfortable for Italian security than one incorporated into either Prussia or Austria.[13]

But merely to show that independent German states, especially in South Germany, were important intermediary bodies in the European system after 1815 is not to prove that their disappearance in 1870 seriously affected it. After all, nature and society evolve. Systems of all kinds—ecological, human, international—come and go. Since the Bismarckian system of 1871 endured, after a fashion, for forty-three years, the first decade or so with apparent stability, it seems audacious to link its ultimate collapse to the demise of certain states at its creation. That is, however, the argument. The absence of intermediary states especially in South Germany between the new German Reich and its neighbors, I contend, removed vital inhibiting and modifying factors in their relations, narrowing available choices and possibilities and promoting problems that in time proved unmanageable. Three such problems, commonly reckoned among the basic causes of the Bismarckian system's downfall, emerged quickly after the disappearance of independent German states and are plainly linked to it. They are: (1) Austria-Hungary's growing dependence upon Germany for its existence as a great power, leading to Germany's entanglement in Austria's internal problems and external rivalries; (2) an enduring enmity between France and Germany; and (3) the evolution of Russo-German friendship into rivalry and hostility. The end of South German independence did not directly create or cause these problems. Many other forces did that. But once there was no independent South Germany to inhibit and deflect the developments, they became far less manageable.

The connection is clearest with Austria-Hungary's unhealthy dependence upon Germany. One indispensable condition for Austria's maintaining an independent stand *vis-à-vis* Prussia after 1866 was an independent South Germany. Austria could have decided before 1870 to accept its inferiority and base its future existence on "*Anlehnung an Preussen*" (Bismarck's phrase). Up to November 1870, however, so long as rational hope remained for an independent South Germany, Austria under Chancellor Count Beust pursued an independent policy in Germany and elsewhere. When this hope disappeared, Beust, a longtime opponent of Bismarck and of Prussian domination of Germany, promptly became an advocate of an Austro-Prussian alliance.[14] Naturally, Beust and his successor in late 1871, Count Andrássy, used various arguments for the new policy, citing various Austrian purposes that a Prussian alliance could serve.[15] One can take their arguments seriously, without ignoring the underlying logic of Austria's position and the absence of plausible alternatives that were clearly decisive for Beust. Militarily, 1870 made Austria's position fundamentally worse. Not only had France, Austria's only serious possibility as a great power ally, been put out of action for a long time, but also Austria's frontier with Prussia–Germany, already long and vulnerable, was doubled in length. How that frontier could possibly be fortified and defended, at a time when Austria faced pressing military needs all along her frontiers (Galicia, Transylvania, Croatia-Slavonia, Italy)[16] and her finances were chronically strained,[17] is an unanswerable question. Historically, religiously, and culturally, the area of Germany to which Austria was most closely tied disappeared in 1870 into the Reich. From the nationality standpoint, so long as independent South German states existed, the position of Austria's German minority remained more or less normal within Germandom as a whole. German identity, German culture, Germany's mission were not routinely identified with the new Reich. After 1871, the Austro-German position became abnormal, objectively and in their own eyes. This intensified the need for the Austrian government to preserve the loyalty of Austro-Germans by concessions, lest they turn from the strongest centripetal to the most dangerous centrifugal force in the monarchy—which in turn made it difficult if not impossible to deal with the demands of other nationalities, especially the Czechs. This result showed up as well in 1871 in decisive form.[18]

In other words, 1870–71 affected Austria profoundly in more ways than can be mentioned here, much less discussed. But they need no discussion, nor need anyone try to decide which particular impact—military-strategic, inner-political, national—was most important. Basically, 1871 left Austria no alternatives. With the demise of independent South German states went the old balance in Austrian policy between Central European and Near Eastern interests, her *raison d'être* as a great power. From this balanced, if precarious, position Austria had even after 1866 been able to negotiate with France and Italy for alliances and to play a general European great power role. Now the one overriding issue was relations with the German Reich, and here Austria had no real choice. A genuinely equal partnership was desirable but wholly unrealistic, given existing power relationships and Bismarck's and William I's known predilections for Russia. All-out competition with Germany would be suicidal. There were none of the requirements present for a restraining alliance between rivals. Austria's one option was to accept dependence upon Germany, and try through a German alliance to be a great power in the one area left to her, the Near East, against the one rival she could stand up to with German backing, Russia. By great skill and ingenuity Bismarck succeeded in controlling this problem for a good while, but it never went away, tended always to get worse, and grew beyond his managerial powers even before his fall. In this instance, an apparently determinist formula is not too strong: no independent South Germany, no really independent Austria-Hungary.

The case is less clear-cut with France, but plain enough. Since the French Provisional Government that took over in September 1870 protested not against the unification of Germany, but only against the annexation of French territory, a stand maintained by the Third Republic's later governments, this makes it appear as if only the German annexation of Alsace-Lorraine stood in the way of ultimate Franco-German reconciliation.[19] It has even been suggested that France would not have been alienated from Germany had unification been achieved by less illiberal, authoritarian, militarist means.[20] Both contentions overlook fundamental elements in the logic of the situation. When Bismarck later expressed the wish that the French would forgive Germany Sedan as they had forgiven Britain Waterloo, he ignored, doubtless deliberately, the different politico-strategic determinants. No British army threatened France with invasion after 1815; the annexation of South Germany made a greatly expanded German army a permanent threat along an enormously lengthened Franco-German frontier. Now the classic route for French invasion of Germany was the base for a German invasion of France. The loss of Alsace-Lorraine made this security problem even worse, to be sure, and gave it a highly emotional, patriotic cast. But the annexation of South Germany was far more important in creating it and making it insoluble. In fact, the annexation of Alsace-Lorraine was to some degree a consequence and integral part of the annexation of South Germany.[21] To assume that France could be genuinely reconciled to Germany simply if Germany returned the lost provinces, or became a liberal parliamentary state, before France had achieved security on its northeast frontier, the main goal of French policy for two centuries,[22] is a remarkable supposition. After achieving security through some alliance like the Franco-Russian alliance of 1891–94, France might have sought German friendship; surely not before.

Once again, however, one should not concentrate on any single issue, Alsace-Lorraine or German militarism or French insecurity, as the root cause of Franco-German enmity, but ask the more basic question: what patterns in Franco-Prussian relations were possible before and after an independent South Germany disappeared? Empirical answers emerge from the record of French policy. After Königgrätz, the French government still sought an alliance and partnership with Prussia, until disillusioned by its failure to get compensations and by the Luxembourg fiasco. After 1867, France viewed Prussia as a dangerous rival and sought allies against it. Still, so long as the South German states stayed out of the North German Confederation, France found the situation tolerable. No one would any longer contend that Napoleon III deliberately aimed for war, or believed that Prussia had to be greatly weakened for France's security.[23] In fact, the existence of South German states which, though allied to Prussia, were still capable of some independent decision and action provided some incentive to both great powers not to seek a violent confrontation—Prussia because it might alienate them, France because it might drive them wholly into Prussia's arms. (Why both sides decided in 1870 to defy the risks and ignore the possible South German reactions to a confrontation remains the most interesting and important question about the origins of the war.) In short, the South German states as a geographic, military, and political *corps intermédiaire*, made the rivalry between France and Prussia potentially manageable, even while they were the focus of that rivalry.

Once South Germany was in the Reich, France had few choices, if any. Even without the Alsace-Lorraine issue, French feelings of humiliation and fear were too strong to admit any kind of partnership—certainly not before France had recovered equal strength and status with Germany. Unfortunately, the passage of time that could have tempered French feelings also served to widen German industrial, demographic, and military superiority, so that even had France by the 1880s or 1890s wanted an alliance with Germany, it would have required a third partner, perhaps Russia or Britain, to balance Germany (in the way that Prussia, which seriously considered a French alliance in the 1850s and early 1860s, would only enter it with Russia as a partner). Britain was not available for such an arrangement; a Franco-German–Russian alliance would have given Russia the role of arbiter between France and Germany, which Germany was too strong to accept, while Austria and Britain would have reacted strongly against it. In other words, no Franco-German partnership was possible except for limited, temporary purposes (this actually came about at times). A rival alliance of restraint was even more out of the question. Yet France remained too strong and too *bündnisfähig* to reconcile itself to a dominant–dependent relation like Austria. What remained was what actually developed—long-term Franco-German rivalry, for which Alsace-Lorraine was primarily a symbol and the end of South German independence a cause. It was, moreover, an inherently unstable, dangerous rivalry not simply because of the national passions and the arms race involved, but basically because given Germany's central position, with no intermediary bodies between her and her great power neighbors, the equality and security France naturally sought necessarily meant inferiority and danger for Germany.

Russo-German antagonism seems different. Certainly Russia's leaders wanted South Germany to remain independent of Prussia. For a moment in 1870, Russia entertained the idea of intervening diplomatically along with Austria to save that independence. But Prussia's victories and the opportunity for Russia to overthrow the Black Sea clause soon ended this impulse. Russia apparently reconciled itself to the 1871 settlement, as it had to that of 1866. In any case, the actual issues and developments behind Russo-German estrangement in 1871–90—economic quarrels, Near Eastern policy, German military power, nationalist and cultural antagonism, and so on—appear to have no connection with the demise of South German independence.[24]

A connection is nonetheless there. Russia's grievances against Germany after 1871 converged in the growing belief that Germany, far from proving a grateful friend, was manipulating Russia, obstructing her policy, restricting her freedom, undermining her prestige, and even threatening her security.[25] The end of South German independence, to be sure, did not itself produce this conviction, except in the sense of increasing the power and resources directly at Berlin's disposal. Instead, South Germany's independence ceased to inhibit such feelings after 1870 as it had done before.

Showing this is not simple, but it can be done. Even if one accepts the feelings of Russian leaders about Germany after 1871 as subjectively genuine, and takes their complaints about German conduct seriously, it is difficult to see Russian antagonism as simply a reaction to German actions and policies toward Russia, that changed objectively for the worse. The economic rivalries and tariff questions of the late 1870s and 1880s of which so much has been made by historians clearly arose after the onset of serious estrangement.[26] Besides, it can be shown that whatever Germany and Russia did to each other in economic competition (and it was not a one-way conflict), their overall economic relationship continued to flourish, and benefited Russia at least as much as Germany. No one doubts that Bismarck and William I wanted to retain a Russian alliance and Russian friendship after 1871. It is more plausible to conclude that it was Russian expectations of Germany, Russian standards for judging German conduct, which above all changed after 1871.

A good way to illustrate this is to compare Prussia's policy toward Russia during the Crimean War (1854–56) and Germany's policy toward Russia in the next great Eastern crisis of 1875–78, and to note their respective effects on Russo-German relations. Objectively viewed, leaving aside Prussia's excuses, the former policy was anti-Russian.[27] Prussia made an alliance with Russia's renegade ally Austria, supported Austria in forcing Russia to evacuate the Danubian Principalities, joined Austria and the Western powers in exacting concessions and sacrifices from Russia, and even joined, however reluctantly, in supporting Austria's ultimatum of December 1855 compelling Russia to accept Western terms. Of course the Prussians pleaded that they were doing all this out of friendship, to prevent still worse calamities for Russia. But Prussia also made similar excuses for not fully joining the West. Nicholas I could have said far better what France's Foreign Minister Drouyn de Lhuys once did, that the Prussian king offered nothing but his tears.[28] Yet this policy, in effect unfriendly and in intent at best lukewarm, not only did not ruin Russo-Prussian relations; it inaugurated a close relationship after 1856 very useful to Prussia.

In 1875–78, however, with Russia facing dangers equally as menacing (a war with Austria and Britain in the spring of 1878 would surely have been as disastrous to Russia as the Crimean conflict), Bismarck not only genuinely tried to stay friends with Russia, but to support Russia to the limit of German abilities and interests as he saw them. Up to the Congress of Berlin at least, his policy was clearly pro-Russian in this sense. Whether it was so during the congress is still a controversial point, but it is hard to see that he did anything to harm Russia's permanent interests, and objectively German meditation served to rescue Russia from an extremely dangerous position of her own making.[29] Yet this policy earned Germany the bitter resentment of the tsar and other Russian leaders, and spawned a serious crisis in Russo-German relations. It oversimplifies the situation, but does not seriously distort it, to conclude that Russia was not estranged from Prussia by the latter's taking sides against Russia in 1854–56, but was estranged from Germany by Germany's refusal to take sides for Russia in 1875–78.

Naturally, the Russians had immediate reasons for their attitudes in each case. As always, one can explain the difference in demands and expectations by the normal empirically based historicist narrative. For a more general explanation, one is tempted to say that Russians were indulgent toward the Prussia of the 1850s because it was relatively weak and vulnerable and made Russia feel superior, and were demanding of the Germany of the 1870s because it was powerful and made Russia feel inferior. But the answer remains far from complete. One important reason for the change in Russian attitudes, easily overlooked, is the disappearance of the South German states. So long as Prussia was Austria's rival for influence over independent smaller states in Germany, Prussia could plausibly argue that her support for Russia in the Near East was limited by her German policy. If Prussia became involved in Near Eastern problems when German interests did not clearly demand it, particularly if this involved a danger of war or meant trouble for Austria, the other German states would turn against Prussia. The argument continued to hold good even after 1866, and helped Bismarck deal with Russia's quest for support against Austria in the 1868–69 Cretan crisis.[30] After 1870, Bismarck wanted to continue the old Prussian policy of not being involved in the Near East unless Prusso-German interests called for it, but now the old ground and excuse, Prussia's necessary preoccupation with her position within Germany, was gone. Bismarck could now only claim reasons of general policy for withholding support—a desire for good relations with all powers, no special German interest in the area, the desire to support both Russia and Austria-Hungary. However plausible in terms of normal *Realpolitik*, such arguments were not good enough for Russia. Not only were they poor recompense for Russia's supposedly generous support of Prussia in 1863–70, but they were also another humiliating proof of German strength and Russian weakness. Germany could now afford to deny Russia the kind of support Russia had not dared deny Prussia in the 1860s. They were also transparent; anyone could see that Bismarck, even if he played the honest broker, also benefited greatly from Russia's quarrels with other powers. And they proved to Russians how the leadership role and a free hand within the monarchical camp had passed from Russia to Germany.

To put this in general terms: Prussia-Germany's meteoric rise in power and wealth had already before 1870 altered the old dominant–dependent relation Russia had enjoyed with Prussia since 1813. After 1871 as after 1866, Bismarck hoped and believed that Germany and Russia could live as

equal partners and friends, with no conflicts of interests. But such a relationship, difficult to achieve and tenuous under the best of circumstances,
requires not merely approximate equality of power and status within the system, but also approximate equality of burdens and commitments. It could
work only if Prussia-Germany remained to some degree tied down within
Germany, concerned about the other German states and Austria, as Russia
was tied down by Austrian and British rivalry in the Near East and by British
rivalry elsewhere. The annexation of South Germany destroyed this possibility, putting an end to Prussia's concern about independent German states
and by the same token, as any Russian could see, ending any concern about
Austria as well. It was idle to expect Russia to accept an "equal" friendship
so patently unequal. Still less than France would Russia tolerate a dominant-
dependent relation. A rival alliance of constraint, which the Three Emperors'
League of the 1880s was to a considerable degree, was plainly a *pis aller*. The
obvious Russian choice was to try by alliances, military reform, and economic development to regain real equality with Germany. Then, perhaps,
they could be real friends again. Once again, it oversimplifies but does not
seriously distort things to see Russian policy as one long effort at this, including, from the "War-in-Sight" crisis of 1875 on, the desire to see Germany
pinned down in Western Europe.[31] With the annexation of the South
German states, Bismarck ruined his own best device for fending off Russian
fears and jealousy, escaping agonizing choices for Germany between Austria,
Britain, and Russia in the Near East, and establishing a stable, friendly relation with Russia.

There are, of course, obvious objections to this whole argument. Were the
South German states really independent before 1870 in a meaningful sense?
One of them, Baden, was bent on joining the North German Confederation;
another, Hesse-Darmstadt, already had part of its territory in it. All were tied
to North Germany, economically by the *Zollverein*, militarily and politically
by offensive–defensive alliances. How could they any longer be called independent states?

The answer is that independence in international politics is not a matter
so much of a precisely defined status and attributes as of the actual role and
functions a state performs. Even if Bavaria and Württemberg were effectively
in Prussia's orbit prior to 1870, they clearly acted independently in significant
ways, developing domestic policies, military policies, and even to some extent
foreign policies that were different from Prussia's and very worrisome to
Bismarck. To get an idea of the difference such a degree of independence can
make in the international system, imagine what Europe would be like today
if the Soviet Union's East European satellites, nominally independent sovereign states, were free to act as independently of the Soviet Union as Bavaria
and Württemberg did *vis-à-vis* Prussia in 1868–70.

But was this South German independence, even if real enough, doomed
to be ephemeral? Were not the arrangements made in 1866 on both sides of
the Main so obviously provisional; the force of German nationalism and the
economic inducements and pressures toward final unification so strong in

South Germany; and the strain involved in the unresolved situation so wearing, that sooner or later, and probably sooner rather than later, a North–South union of some kind was inevitable? Besides, it is odd to have South German independence presented as a solution to international problems, when it was plainly perceived in 1866–70 as a problem itself, loaded with danger of war.

Time is lacking to deal adequately with these plausible arguments. Some of the premises can be challenged. Not all economic trends in Germany led toward unification.[32] In any case, Bismarck's attempt to use the economic weapon to force the political pace in 1868 through the *Zollparlament* had backfired, and any threat on his part to dissolve the *Zollverein* was a two-edged sword.[33] Furthermore, had unification been delayed just a few more years, the crash of 1873 and the resultant depression would have made union with North Germany less attractive to South Germany economically,[34] as it already was unacceptable to many on political, social, and religious grounds. German nationalism was far from a dominant force; it was clearly in decline from 1868 to 1870 in Bavaria and Württemberg, and challenged seriously even in Baden. And even if one were to concede that some kind of North–South union was inevitable, this really does not affect the case made here, which is not that the South German states could necessarily have remained independent indefinitely, but that their disappearance made an important difference in the international system.

The most straightforward reply, however, is to concede the provisional nature of the 1866 settlement, insisting at the same time that by 1870, barring a Franco-Prussian war or some similar cataclysm, it enjoyed fair prospects for durability. In fact, the very unfinished, provisional nature of the 1866 settlement, and the fact that it really satisfied none of the parties involved, made it more likely to last, barring a solution imposed by violence.

Even those who like paradoxes may find it excessive to have the 1866 settlement described as durable because provisional, satisfactory in that it satisfied no one. But the claim makes sense, and fits what happened. From 1866 to 1870, the various efforts made and programs launched to alter or overthrow the 1866 settlement all had one thing in common: failure. Bismarck's attempts to make South Germany ripe for annexation; Beust's program to recoup Austria's influence in Germany by liberal reform; France's various efforts to stop Prussia at the Main by a European coalition, or an Austrian-led South German Confederation, or international guarantees; the Bavarian Minister-President Hohenlohe's proposal to replace the North German Confederation with a wider, looser union embracing South Germany and German Austria; Baden's attempts to go into North Germany by itself, or drag the other South German states with her—all these initiatives and more were stalled, dead in the water.

Such a stalemate can be resolved by violence, as this one was. But another outcome is also common enough in history—witness West Berlin, the current division of Germany, the Third French Republic—in which a provisional settlement gradually becomes, for practical purposes, permanent. That outcome was the more possible in 1870 because the 1866 settlement, while satisfying no one, also directly challenged and threatened no one. All Prussia's former grievances were now met, and even Bismarck in his audacious mendacity could not claim that Prussia had a right and need to absorb South Germany. France could have lived with the 1866 settlement; Napoleon III was responsible for helping to promote it. Austria, Russia, and Italy did endorse it; even the British, indifferent to the German question *per se*, preferred the status quo to a violent overthrow. Above all, this settlement, because it was provisional, preserved the right of the peoples and governments of South Germany to stay independent if they wished, without denying the right of nationalists in North and South Germany to work peacefully for unification.

Thus, the 1866 settlement has much to recommend it. The fact that it was quickly and decisively overthrown does not prove its inherent instability or unsatisfactory nature. It fell victim, on the positive side, to the failure of the international actors who had an interest in seeing South Germany remain independent to do anything serious to insure its survival. This failure to act, or indifference to the fate of the South German states, must of course count as a weakness of the 1866 settlement. But it is something that needs to be noted and explained as a cause of that settlement's demise, not proof of its inherent fragility or worthlessness.

Of all the parties involved, the governments of Bavaria and Württemberg, and in particular the leaders of the Bavarian Patriot Party and the Württemberg democrats and *Grossdeutsche*, bear the least responsibility for the outcome. They were clearly overwhelmed by the rapid pace of events, a wave of Francophobe German nationalism, and Bismarck's manipulation. Nonetheless, there is a sharp contrast between the determination with which Bavaria and Württemberg sought and defended their sovereign independence in 1800–20, and the ease with which they surrendered its most important attributes in 1870. One is equally inclined to absolve Beust of responsibility; he tried in 1870 both to prevent the war and to save South German independence even once it began. But he was a Saxon, an old German trialist. Austria's record as a whole in supporting South German independence, or the smaller states and the confederation in general, is very different. From Metternich through Schwarzenberg, Buol, Rechberg, and Mensdorff, Austrian statesmen had always, in a pinch, preferred a deal with Prussia to coalition with the middle states. By 1870, most Austrian Germans cared little for South German independence, and non-Germans still less. Many Austrian leaders from 1866 on saw a chance to enlist Prussia-Germany in support of particular Austrian interests. Russia and Italy also had some idea of what the disappearance of South Germany could mean to them, but more immediate gains (Rome, the Black Sea clause) were more important. As for Britain, its indifference by the 1860s to the survival of the South German states was total. The only thing that mattered was that their disappearance into Prussia-Germany not cause a war with France, and even that contingency would not call for any British action.[35]

None of this surprises. Even if there were abstract advantages for most states in South German independence, for all of them letting Prussia have its way (or letting German nationalism take its course, as the misleading phrase went) was far safer than intervention, and might bring concrete advantages. For one vital actor, however, this was not true: France. From 1815 on, France had had a central, vital stake in South German independence. That independence was, after all, largely Napoleon's creation, and if he had ruined much of France's natural influence in South and Southwest Germany by his exploitative policies, both the need for France to keep these areas from falling under the power of Austria or Prussia, and the means to do so, were still there.[36] As one expert says, French policy toward Germany after 1815, especially toward the confederation, has been studied only piecemeal and inadequately.[37] This applies strongly to French policy toward South Germany, a modern version of the classic tale of the Sibylline books. Every French regime (Bourbons, Orleanists, the Second Republic, even the Second Empire) recognized at least in principle the great value for France of a federally organized Germany. Everyone saw the danger of a united Germany, or one dominated by one or the other German great power. Everyone again, at least in principle, viewed South and Southwest Germany as the natural field for French political influence and economic and cultural activity. Yet no regime was ever willing to pay the price of gaining or maintaining what France wanted, with the result that one after another France's opportunities slipped away.[38] After 1815, France had a chance to exploit Bavaria's old and new resentments against Austria and what remained of Francophile sentiment in the South German states to make them consider France, as in the past, the natural patron of South Germany's independence and territorial and political aims. In the 1820s and early 1830s, France had the chance to support South German resistance to the *Zollverein* by offering South and West Germany a French-led alternative. During and after the 1830 revolutions, France had the chance to promote the German constitutional movement and widen the gap between the constitutional states and Austria and Prussia. During the late 1830s and 1840s, France at least could have tried to slow down the tide of German nationalist sentiment and divert it from France as its target. In the 1848 revolutions and their aftermath, France again had the opportunity, if it wished, to encourage and support the middle states in their desire for a trialist, federalist reorganization of Germany. In the Crimean and Italian Wars, the negotiations with Prussia for a trade treaty, the Polish and Schleswig-Holstein crises, and the crisis leading up to the War of 1866, France need not either have ignored and pushed aside the South German states, or joined Prussia or Austria at various times in forcing them into line, as it regularly did.

This is not to suggest that French statesmen always had clear, easy choices to make. Obviously, from 1815 on, any French role in German politics had to be an indirect one, played with skill and prudence. Memories of the *Rheinbund* and growing German nationalist sentiment made any too-direct intervention likely to be counterproductive. Nevertheless, what Douglas Johnson says of Guizot, that he recognized the importance of the secondary states of Germany to France, and detected early a threat to France in Prussian preponderance over them, but that he "does not seem to have done much to consolidate the French position with the lesser German states,"[39] applies broadly to France's whole German policy from 1815 to 1870.

It can be claimed that this changed after 1866. No doubt France tried to preserve the independence of the South German states in the 1866 settlement, and made a guarantee of the Main frontier the key point in her running contest with Prussia after the Luxemburg Crisis of 1867. But in the most important respects this was no change at all. France continued in 1866 to seek territorial compensations in Germany precisely at the expense of South German states (a key factor in driving them into alliance with Prussia). France maintained her normal procedure of dealing with South German questions over the heads of the South German states themselves, recklessly disregarding their particular interests and independence, trying first for alliance with Prussia, then with Austria and Italy, and finally for some kind of European great power settlement.[40] France's determination after 1867, moreover, to make Prussia's crossing the Main the *casus belli* for a general European war threatened South Germany far more directly and powerfully than it protected it, and undermined and tended to discredit the very forces resisting union with Prussia. It is no accident, but the result of French policy, that in what had once been the most pro-French and anti-Austrian parts of Germany (Baden, Württemberg, Bavaria), there were still important *Grossdeutsch* and pro-Austrian groups left in 1870, but no French party at all.[41]

A final opportunity nevertheless arose for France to defend its vital interests in South Germany in 1870. It too was thrown away. The gravest criticism of French policy in July is not the obvious one that it served to unite South and North Germans in war against France. It is rather that France could well have used this crisis to strengthen South German independence while avoiding war, and evidently failed even to consider the possibility. At that very time the military alliances tying Bavaria and Württemberg to Prussia were undergoing severe scrutiny, even attack. Bavaria's *Landtag*, controlled by the anti-Prussian Patriot Party, had just drastically reduced the military budget, hampering the planned reorganization of the army along Prussian lines. In the hot public debate over the nature and extent of Bavaria's obligations, the Patriots, including Bavaria's Minister-President Count Bray-Steinburg, maintained that the alliance of 1866 imposed only the same defensive obligations as the old pre-1866 confederation—an argument attacked and feared by Bismarck. Württemberg's democrats campaigned for replacing the army with a Swiss-style citizens' militia, and while this program was unlikely to succeed and alienated many moderates, it was certainly dangerous to those wanting closer ties to Prussia.[42] In the middle of this internal South German debate, a war crisis arose between Prussia and France, neither of which was at the moment popular with most South Germans. In the opinion of almost all European observers, moreover, the crisis had originated in a Prussian initiative clearly provocative toward France, launched for purely Prussian dynastic rather than German national interests.

The question irresistibly arises: what might France have done with this opportunity? A plausible answer is: having once secured Prince Leopold of Hohenzollern-Sigmaringen's renunciation of the Spanish throne; having, if the French wished, underlined their diplomatic victory over Bismarck by securing a confirmation of the renunciation and international guarantees against renewal of the candidacy; France then, the danger of war passed, could have tactfully pointed out to the South German states, perhaps best through the medium of Austria, how narrow an escape they had had. Only France's moderation and restraint, plus some good luck, Frenchmen could argue, had kept Prussia from starting a war for purely Prussian and frivolous reasons which would in all likelihood have engulfed them. Surely it was time for the South German states to reconsider those ties to Prussia which so clearly endangered South Germany's security and independence. France for her part was ready, in consultation with the South German states themselves, Austria, and the rest of Europe, to consider international measures to protect the South German states in their critical geographic position from the dangers of future great power rivalries.

One can imagine no more powerful diplomatic weapon against Bismarck and in favor of France's essential interests than such a policy. The idea, moreover, is not speculation, but precisely what Beust in Austria wanted to do, and was suggesting to his old friend Bray-Steinburg in Bavaria.[43] There is no sign, however, that French leaders ever entertained this idea. The fact that they supposed that the South German states were indifferent to the Hohenzollern candidacy *per se* only encouraged the illusion that the South German states therefore would stay neutral while France and Prussia fought it out over their fate—another reason for the duc de Gramont, French foreign minister, to want to settle France's score with Prussia now rather than later.

Naturally, any theorizing as to the longer-range results of a different French stance in 1870 is bound to be speculative to some degree, and rapidly becomes otiose. One can confidently affirm that a different policy was from an objective standpoint entirely possible, that it certainly would have been wiser than the one followed, and that it could have had dramatically different immediate and long-range results—nothing more. The value of counterfactual reasoning, however, is not to establish what might have happened, but to render clearer what really did happen. What really did happen in 1870–71, to return to the main theme of this essay, is that South German independence was ended. This is not merely what the long-range results of the war were about, but also what the origins of the war were about. It is misleading and distorting (as the century-old controversy over the war guilt of 1870, now happily exhausted, has always done) to debate which of the two great powers, Prussia or France, was more aggressive toward the other, when the most obvious fact is that this was first and foremost a war of aggression by both great powers against the independence of the South German states.[44] It is equally misleading, though less obviously so, to examine the impact of 1870–71 upon the European system solely from the standpoint of what forces it unleashed, what problems it created or worsened, and what resentments it left behind; to ask solely whether Europe could be stable and peaceful under the leadership of a united Germany, and how, and with what kind of Germany—all without first asking whether the system in the long run could operate entirely without the existence and the mediating, inhibitory functions of the *corps intermédiaires* present in Central Europe from 1815 to 1870. It has taken a surprisingly long time to raise this kind of question. But then wars, like hell, usually mean truth seen too late.

5

GLADSTONE AS BISMARCK

Some years ago Professor Denis Mack Smith read a paper entitled "Cavour in 1859" at the American Historical Association convention. The discussant, Professor R. John Rath, commented that the essay had made Cavour look more like Bismarck than Gladstone. Mack Smith replied that this was true, but not very significant, since Gladstone was more like Bismarck than Gladstone.[1]

This was a witty riposte, but not an original idea and not necessarily profound. The charge that Gladstone was a hypocrite who used moral appeals to his own political advantage was common in his lifetime. The well-known quip of Henry Labouchere comes to mind, that it did not bother him to discover that the Grand Old Man always had the ace of trumps up his sleeve, but that it did irritate him continually to be told that the Lord God Almighty had put it there.[2] Historians like R. T. Shannon,[3] P. A. Hamer,[4] and John P. Rossi[5] have demonstrated connections between Gladstone's keen sense of political timing and party needs and some of his moral stands in foreign policy.

Nonetheless, Mack Smith's dictum is useful as the ground or occasion for another look at Gladstone's policy, the main aim being not to decide whether Gladstone and Bismarck were similar as personalities, or whether they pursued similar courses in foreign policy, but whether the Gladstonian system of foreign policy represents a genuine alternative to the Bismarckian system. The case for seeing these two men at opposite poles in the history of European international relations, a case made by such historians as Paul Knaplund[6] and W. N. Medlicott,[7] does not rest mainly on the idea that Gladstone acted consistently on the basis of moral principles while Bismarck acted steadily on the basis of Realpolitik, that is, amoral state interest. The contention is rather that even if both men as practical politicians strove to defend their country's interests, Gladstone's ends ultimately differed substantially from Bismarck's. He envisioned and tried to create a European order based on cooperation rather than conflict, mutual trust instead of

Canadian Journal of History/Annales canadiennes d'histoire, 15, 2 (1980), 163–95. Copyright © (1980), Canadian Journal of History. All rights reserved. Used by permission of the publisher.

rivalry and suspicion; the rule of law was to supplant the reign of force and self-interest. This concept of a harmonious Gladstonian Concert of Europe being opposed to, and ultimately defeated by, a Bismarckian system of manipulated alliances and antagonisms, remains a prevalent interpretation of late nineteenth century European history.[8]

This essay rejects their view. It argues that Gladstone's foreign policy represents no idealistic alternative to Bismarckian Realpolitik, either functionally, in terms of its actual results and impact on the European system, or ideally, in terms of its basic conceptions and purposes.

Both Bismarck and Gladstone, we may be sure, would have been outraged at Mack Smith's remark. As everyone knows, Bismarck despised Gladstone, considering him incompetent, reckless, a tactless blunderer, a captive of his own demagogic oratory, a mad professor, and, along with Gambetta, Gorchakov, and Garibaldi, a member of the European revolutionary quartet on the G string.[9] Less often noted is Gladstone's aversion to Bismarck. He once called him "the incarnation of evil"[10]—not for Gladstone a rhetorical phrase, but a precise characterization in moral and religious terms. Not only had Bismarck committed great crimes, like the annexation of Alsace-Lorraine,[11] but even when he pursued moderate or peaceful policies, he did so for selfish, insidious reasons.[12]

Most historians would agree with the principal characters in denying the similarity Mack Smith alleges. They seem clearly to represent antithetical principles of morality and Realpolitik in foreign policy. For Bismarck, at least as he is regularly viewed, international politics was strictly a game of power, interests, alliances, and alignments. Peace and stability were the tenuous result of balanced antagonisms and managed rivalries. For Gladstone, international politics was a field for the application of moral principles. Peace and order should be the permanent result of subordinating selfish interests to the higher goals of national liberty, justice, and European public law.[13] Whether historians have in various degrees approved of Gladstone's foreign policy principles,[14] or disagreed or reserved judgment,[15] they have seen the wellsprings of his policy as moral rather than realpolitical[16]—thus apparently rejecting Mack Smith's contention.

It is easy to choose the best period in Gladstone's career in which to test Gladstone's foreign policy principles: his second ministry, 1880–85. Although Gladstone developed strong moral ideas about foreign policy early in his career and changed them little afterward,[17] only in this period were foreign policy issues as important to him as domestic ones. Moreover, the international questions he dealt with in 1880–85 combined clear moral and realpolitical aspects, and the issues are particularly suitable for contrasting Gladstone's policy to Bismarck's, since during much of this period the two men were rivals for the leadership of Europe.

The method for appraising the moral basis of Gladstone's policy is more debatable. An obvious way would be to examine his policy for inconsistencies, a double standard, and evidences of political or personal interests concealed behind its moral claims. But this procedure, even if it yielded some interesting results, has severe limitations. Barring a demonstration (which I think impossible) that Gladstone's moral claims were the product simply of systematic hypocrisy and/or massive self-delusion, all such an approach could do at best is to show that his moral principles had certain limits and inconsistencies to them—hardly a surprising outcome. Furthermore, the procedure involves the slippery business of trying to read Gladstone's mind and to determine the genuineness and significance of feelings and motives he probably only partly recognized and understood himself—using literary evidence that for these purposes is bound to be indirect, incomplete, and tendentious.[18] Most important, this approach, concentrating on Gladstone's motives and mental processes, easily loses sight of what is objectively more important in international politics, the broader, more impersonal grounds and results of his actions.

This essay therefore will concentrate on analyzing Gladstone's actions in terms of the European system, seeing what impact they had upon other countries, what alignments and ententes they promoted, and what ends or outcomes they tended actually to serve, relegating to second place the questions of whether Gladstone consciously recognized and intended these, and what his ostensible moral motives were.

Since a brief essay cannot deal in detail with five years of complicated foreign policy, only three developments from this period will be given close attention (even here considerable compression will be necessary). The three particularly useful for analyzing elements of morality and Realpolitik are Gladstone's quarrel with Austria[19] in his 1880 election campaign, his diplomatic campaign on behalf of Montenegro, and the Egyptian question. Other issues will be dealt with mainly in terms of whether they conform to the main pattern or diverge from it.

The story of Gladstone's verbal attack on Austria is simple, at least at first glance. Claiming that the Austrian Emperor Francis Joseph and the Viennese press had interfered in the impending British elections in favor of the Conservatives, Gladstone in a speech on March 17 strongly denounced Austria, saying among other things that there was no spot on the map where one could put his finger and say that there Austria had done good. The public attack on a friendly power by a prospective prime minister caused some stir in Britain and elicited a sharp protest from the Austrian Ambassador Count Karolyi. After his election, however, Gladstone smoothed over the rift between the two countries by a letter to Karolyi regretting the language he had used.[20] On the surface, the incident looks like an instance of Gladstone's being carried away by moral indignation into committing an impolitic act, requiring him to execute a rather embarrassing retreat thereafter.

More closely examined, the story looks different. While accepting as genuine Gladstone's belief that the Austrian government and press had interfered in the British elections, one has difficulty seeing what valid ground he had for this belief. The Austrian government certainly sympathized with the Conservatives, not out of aversion to Gladstone's liberal principles or his notorious Austrophobia, but simply out of fear that a Gladstone ministry would return Britain to isolationism, wrecking the cooperation Austria enjoyed with Disraeli's government in the Balkans and leaving Austria without support against Russia.[21] After Gladstone's election Austria was just as eager to work with Britain as before.[22] In any case, Francis Joseph's words, as reported by British Ambassador Sir Henry Elliot, clearly represented no attempt to influence the British elections.[23] As for the alleged attacks by the Viennese press, Gladstone relied upon a report in a none too reliable English paper, later claiming that Elliot should have contradicted the report if it were not true.[24] In any case, Gladstone's outburst on March 17 was not the result of a particular provocation, but part of his pattern of denunciations of Austria both earlier and later in the Midlothian campaign (as well as prior to it).[25] These attacks served to support his general campaign against the wicked foreign policy of Disraeli and Salisbury. Neither the March 17 speech nor others like it caused Gladstone any real embarrassment or political damage. Liberals paid scant attention to the incident,[26] while the Conservatives gained no useful campaign material from it.[27]

The important point, however, is that Gladstone's postelection "apology" was not really an apology or retraction, either in fact or in Gladstone's perception. The Austrian government took the lead in healing the breach, while Gladstone declined to say anything until Austria disavowed the aggressive aims he had ascribed to her. His actual apology amounted to saying that he would not have referred to Austria's past sins had he then had what he now possessed, Austria's promise not to commit them in the future.[28] As Gladstone's private secretary Edward Hamilton noted, and as Gladstone maintained then and later, his statement of regret served to pin Austria down to a pledge of non-aggrandizement and noninterference in the Balkans.[29]

The way in which Gladstone used the restoration of normal relations with Austria is also significant. While the Austrian government accepted Gladstone's letter and quickly put the affair behind them, Gladstone immediately asked the foreign secretary, Lord Granville, to get Austria to propose a solution to the pending question of the Montenegrin frontier.[30] Granville complied by urging Vienna to cede to Montenegro a slice of the Herzegovina, which Austria had occupied under the Berlin Treaty. This proposal was accompanied by a warning that if the Montenegrin question led to complications, Austria would be the power most endangered by them. At the same time, a strongly pro-Slav and anti-Austrian English writer was appointed as British consul at Ragusa in Austrian Dalmatia, in order to represent, in Gladstone's words, an "official channel...as to feeling on the Slavonian side."[31] Also at this time Gladstone was assuring a Liberal supporter that Britain intended to support Serbia in the current Austro-Serbian negotiations for a railway convention.[32] Gladstone concurrently worked out a plan for a general British rapprochement with Russia, and, along with his Cabinet colleague the Duke of Argyll, entertained ideas for "reforms" in European and Asiatic Turkey that clearly would have promoted the breakup of the Ottoman Empire.[33]

If, then, one analyzed Gladstone's policy in this affair in terms of the real functions and impact of his actions, the result could be summed up as follows. He first took advantage of an unproved allegation that an unpopular foreign government had intervened in the British elections as a means to enhance his own reputation as the defender of liberty and to identify his opponents with this hated foreign regime. He next required this foreign government, which needed good relations with Britain far more than Britain did with it, formally to disavow the aggressive aims with which he, Gladstone, had charged it, thereby gaining a pledge of good conduct to be used against that government in the future. He then tried to follow up the liquidation of the incident by demanding concrete concessions from this government at the same time as he was hoping to achieve a working partnership with her major rival, and entertaining plans deleterious to the interests and stability of another neighboring state with whom she had important ties. Had such a policy been executed by someone else—say, Canning or Palmerston—few historians would have any difficulty detecting the kind of hard-boiled, realistic politics being played.

This incident was only a prelude to the Montenegrin question, a much more important initiative in Gladstone's foreign policy, and one impossible to describe in detail here.[34] Suffice it to say that the question of delineating the Turkish–Montenegrin frontier was left over from the Treaty of Berlin in 1878. Though a European decision on the frontier had been reached in April 1880, it broke down over the organized resistance of Albanian tribes to being transferred to Montenegrin rule. From May to October 1880, Gladstone's and Granville's policy was to organize the powers into a Concert that would compel Turkey to break the resistance of her Albanian subjects and to turn over the disputed territory to Montenegro. Turkey's delays and resistance to European pressure, combined with European worries about the increasingly drastic measures urged by the British, led in October to a breakdown of Concert action, with France and Austria, backed by Germany, refusing to go the length of armed occupation and bombardment of Turkish territory, as demanded by Gladstone. Gladstone, however, determined to act forcefully against Turkey, with or without united European cooperation. Fortunately for him, the Porte yielded just in time, so that Montenegro actually gained all the territories he wanted her to have.

Gladstone's words and actions throughout this affair appear moralistic through and through. He cast whole peoples and regimes in the role of moral heroes and villains, seeing the Montenegrins as an unspoiled race of Homeric stature, and the Turks as barbaric oppressors.[35] He expressed constant outrage at the Sultan's perfidy, persistent suspicions of the ulterior motives of other powers, especially Austria and Germany, and an unshakeable conviction of the righteousness of his cause. His frequent appeals to the powers to subordinate their selfish interests in order to vindicate the public law of Europe and promote the liberty and progress of Balkan peoples seemed to many recklessly to ignore the concrete results and dangers of intervention. All these, one could argue, were typical signs of a morally-based policy.

But once again if this policy is viewed from the standpoint of its actual impact on European politics, other aspects begin to emerge. For this purpose one needs briefly to note what other powers were doing, especially Germany and Austria. Since late 1879 Bismarck had been primarily working to get Austria-Hungary, allied with Germany in October 1879, to join a revived Three Emperors' League with Russia, so that Germany could appease Russia, prevent an Anglo-Russian or Franco-Russian entente, and manage the Austro-Russian rivalry in the Balkans. Naturally, Bismarck used Gladstone's anti-Turkish, anti-Austrian, and pro-Russian tendencies as ammunition in this campaign, trying to get Austria to abandon hope of support from England.[36] But Austria clung to the idea of an English connection as some insurance against Russo-German intimacy at her expense.[37] For this reason she was always in principle eager to cooperate with England over Montenegro and other Balkan questions; in fact, the government at Vienna had earlier irritated Salisbury by being too eager to take up Montenegro's cause.[38] Through the summer and early fall of 1880, Austria's Foreign Minister Baron Haymerlé remained cooperative, despite his growing dismay at Gladstone's policies and the strong German and domestic pressure put on him to turn away from England.[39]

Aware of Austria's eagerness to cooperate, Gladstone, as already noted, hoped to gain from Austria not just diplomatic help, but concrete sacrifices for Montenegro.[40] Simultaneously he developed for Cabinet discussion a scheme for a general settlement with Russia over Central Asia, delimiting their spheres of influence and providing for Anglo-Russian cooperation in maintaining Persia's independence—a plan similar to the Anglo-Russian Convention eventually concluded in 1907.[41] Austria's cooperation was thus used to help Britain try to gain an entente with Russia in Central Asia and Russia's cooperation in the Balkans.[42]

This plan also suited Gladstone's general desire, in relations with Russia, to replace tactics of confrontation with those of gentle persuasion and trust.[43] But these were not the tactics he generally used in the Montenegrin question. Turkey was subjected to a steady diet of denunciation, pressure, and threats; Gladstone began planning for military coercion of her already in mid-July. Other outcomes considered possible if Turkey remained stubborn were a union of Bulgaria and Eastern Rumelia (separated by the Treaty of Berlin), and independence for Albania. Britain, he believed, should declare the entry of Turkish troops into Montenegro a *casus belli*.[44] Austria's role in Gladstone's scheme was to help supply the means and forces to coerce Turkey, without being able to influence the ends of coercion. Gladstone's answer to Austria's fears that revolution and war would arise out of European action against Turkey was that these dangers should spur Austria to make Turkey yield before the Balkan peninsula exploded. Austria's eventual retreat from armed coercion was termed shabby by Gladstone.[45]

Though he worked ardently to organize and lead the Concert, Gladstone had no intention of binding Britain to its collective decisions. Britain had instead a right and duty to denounce laggards and defectors among the powers, and then to enforce the public law of Europe herself, with the aid of any powers willing to help her. At different times he envisioned France, Russia, and Italy, Russia and Italy, or Italy alone as executors of the mandate of

Europe along with Britain. Thus functionally the European Concert consisted for Gladstone of Britain and whichever powers followed her lead.[46] In addition, though he often appealed to the Treaty of Berlin as the legal basis for his policy, he actually was willing to enforce only the anti-Turkish, pro-Montenegrin features of it. When Russian, Bulgarian, and Montenegrin evasions or violations of the treaty were called to his attention, he pleaded that in these cases Britain and Europe had no jurisdiction, or claimed that these violations were a result of Turkish violations, or even argued in one case that since only Turkey as the suzerain power over Bulgaria had the right to punish illegal Bulgarian actions in Eastern Rumelia, and since she chose not to, the powers could not intervene.[47] Clearly Gladstone's public law of Europe operated in a selective fashion.

These anomalies can doubtless be explained as the sort of inconsistencies likely to arise in a policy based on moral principles and fueled by righteous indignation. They do not show by themselves that his supposedly morally based policy was actually realpolitical. But again, if one concentrates upon the effects that Gladstone's policy in regard to Montenegro tended to have upon European international politics, the verdict might be that it promoted the following purposes:

(1) Preventing or breaking up the nascent Three Emperors' League[48] by sowing trouble between Russia and Austria over Montenegro, an area of long-standing suspicion and rivalry between them.

(2) Asserting British leadership over the European Concert, at the same time preserving Britain's independence from its control; and using the idea of European Concert and collective action as a means not only to spread the responsibility and cost of action, but also to defuse domestic opposition to British foreign policy in this area.[49]

(3) Through support for a liberal nationalist cause in Montenegro, elevating the prestige of the British government at home and abroad and fulfilling promises Gladstone had made to the electorate,[50] without thereby threatening any direct British interest or risking any reprisal against Britain (neither Turkey nor Austria being able to arouse the Irish, India, or the Boers).

(4) Promoting a liberal entente with France and Italy in the Balkans, where (unlike Egypt) no strong French interests were involved, and Italy was already a rival to Austria.

(5) Establishing a basis for cooperation and entente with Russia in Central Asia, where Britain's position was vulnerable, at the same time using British cooperation with Russia in the Balkans to restrain any dangerous ambitions she might have there.

(6) Advancing British influence among the independent states and subject peoples of the Balkans in anticipation of the final downfall of Turkey, now considered incurably corrupt and Anglophobe.

This is not an argument, of course, that Gladstone's moral claims were simply a cover for these hidden purposes. Individual motives and aims cannot be deduced from the functions or results of actions in a general system. But it does indicate a functional pattern to Gladstone's policy of a standard realpolitical character.

Another question left over from the Berlin Congress, the delineation of the frontier between Turkey and Greece, interested Gladstone almost as much as the Montenegrin question. But here a combination of prudential considerations led to a more restrained British policy. Gladstone later claimed credit for the settlement of 1881, which was favorable to Greece,[51] but really Bismarck's leadership was mainly responsible for it. Of interest here is merely the similarity, moral and functional, between Gladstone's pro-Greek policy and his pro-Montenegrin stance. Once again his zeal for Europe's honor was connected with a concern for Britain's prestige—in particular, a fear lest Britain appear to be backing down before Turkey.[52] Here again he contemplated, if not actually promoted, the use of violent means in behalf of good ends, contending that only if the Greeks first attacked the Turks could Europe effectively take up their cause.[53] Once again Gladstone leaned toward the same European alignments. Despite the bad conduct France had shown over Montenegro, he desired an entente with her, and sought cooperation with Italy and Russia. (In the case of Russia, his concern over Russian moves in Central Asia was again a factor.)[54] At the same time he remained suspicious of Austria,[55] and distrusted Bismarck's motives even while he acknowledged his services to the cause of Greece.[56] Even Gladstone's suggestion that Britain could help promote a peaceful settlement by awarding Cyprus,[57] which Britain had occupied in 1878 under the Cyprus Convention with Turkey, to Greece, turned out to have some practical advantages for Britain. Gladstone and his Cabinet hated the Cyprus Convention, wanted to get rid of the commitments it involved to Turkey, and regarded Cyprus as a useless and compromising acquisition.[58] Ceding the island to Greece would solve these problems, while also tending to annul the bargain Salisbury had made in 1878 with France, in which he promised France a free hand in Tunis in exchange for Cyprus and British primacy in the Anglo-French Dual Control over Egypt.[59] Thus by the cession of Cyprus Britain and the Greeks would gain in every way, while only Turkey, the legal owner of Cyprus, would lose.

The Bulgarian question produced even less concrete British action than the Greek one. Though wholly sympathetic to Bulgarian nationalism, Gladstone, hoped that a policy of British nonintervention would discourage any interference in Bulgaria by Turkey, Austria, Russia, or Germany. By the time the Bulgarian crisis became acute in 1884–85, Britain was too distracted by other issues to have acted effectively even had Gladstone wanted to. Hence the Bulgarian question is important for our purposes only in illustrating Gladstone's attitude toward certain larger European issues, namely, the final disposition of Turkey's European territories, and the role and destiny of the Austrian Empire in the Balkans and Europe.

Though Gladstone often claimed that he wanted to preserve the Ottoman Empire, he had long wanted to end Turkish rule in Europe. The emancipated

Balkan peoples themselves, in his view, would then provide stability for the region, ideally through uniting them in a Balkan league or a single large state. To quote Edward Hamilton, a "union of Slaves and 'Roumans' and perhaps Greeks, so as to have one large Graeco-Slav country, . . . would more than anything stay the hands of Russia and put an end to Austria's sinister designs."[60] As for Austria and her efforts to maintain a sphere of influence in the Balkans as the last region where she could play a great power role, Gladstone offered the standard British Liberal advice. Austria should concentrate on her own internal reforms, and in the Balkans seek solely to win the goodwill of the Balkan peoples by a policy of benevolent noninterference.[61]

By late 1883, however, Austria protested despairingly that no amount of restraint on her part would curb Russia's drive to dominate Bulgaria. Elliot and Granville agreed that Austria's present policy was peaceful and Russia's aggressive.[62] Gladstone, explaining why he nonetheless still considered Austria somewhat more dangerous than Russia to Balkan liberties, indicated clearly that the problem lay less in Austria's actions than in her makeup. Russia, though governed despotically, was a Slavic state whose people could sympathize with the Balkan Slavs. She therefore possessed a basis for a popular Balkan policy. Austria, though now governed more liberally than Russia, was not a Slavic state and could not become one. Therefore every attempt made by Austria to compete with Russia in the Balkans was bound to fail, harming herself and others.[63]

In other words, Gladstone knew that his own advice for Austria on how to check her declining great power status and influence was hopeless. The nationality principles he espoused would oust her from the Balkans as surely as they already had from Italy and Germany—a process of expulsion that Gladstone had applauded. Nor was he oblivious to the implications of the nationality principle for the very existence of the Monarchy. After condemning as futile and mischievous any attempt by Austria to make herself over into a Slavic power, and after suggesting that Britain seek an entente with France to cooperate in countering any such Austrian moves, Gladstone remarked, "Is it not strange to see how largely the *mot* of Metternich that Italy was a geographical expression is becoming applicable to Austria."[64]

One may thus conclude that Gladstone recognized that his Balkan policy and principles condemned Austria to further decline and eventual demise, and that the only action he contemplated was cooperation with France to check Austria from doing anything important in the Balkans to reverse the trend.[65] The point here is not to judge the wisdom and realism of Gladstone's attitude toward Austria and of his more general Balkan views. It matters here only to see that functionally this attitude and policy had some powerful realpolitical aspects and implications.

But all the Balkan questions in Gladstone's second ministry pale in importance alongside that of Egypt. Here, moreover, there is a particular problem involved in portraying Gladstone as any kind of Realpolitiker—namely, the difficulty of ascribing to him a real policy on Egypt. Historians seem to agree that circumstances, accident, and blunder, rather than moral principles or realpolitical design, brought England into Egypt, and that in Egypt the dif-ferences between Liberal and Conservative principles and policy that Gladstone had tried to maintain in the Balkans and elsewhere disappeared.[66]

One must concede the force of this argument. Still, the mere fact that a policy proves to be hastily improvised and inept does not prove that it had no basis in Realpolitik. In one respect, moreover, Egypt affords a better test of Mack Smith's thesis than Balkan issues do. The fate of Egypt, unlike that of Montenegro or Greece, directly involved a prime British interest, the security of the Suez Canal. Therefore rather than having to infer possible British realpolitical interests and aims from the results and tendencies of Gladstone's actions, one can look directly in Egypt for a connection between British interests and Gladstone's policy. Such a connection is readily found: throughout the various phases of the Egyptian question, Gladstone's moral principles and attitudes regularly tended to support British needs and inter-ests as he conceived them. As usual, his stance toward Turkey, the various European powers, and the European Concert shows this connection espe-cially well.

An attempt fully to demonstrate this thesis would involve recounting the whole story of British involvement in Egypt, far too big a task.[67] All that can be done here is to indicate how Gladstone conceived of British needs and interests during various phases of the question, and to illustrate, rather than prove, the claim that his moral attitudes served to meet these needs. The first phase of his policy runs from early 1881, when Gladstone's Cabinet first became aware of the revolutionary situation developing in Egypt, to July 1882, when the British bombardment of Alexandria in effect ended Dual Control and joint action with France and propelled England into unilateral intervention. During this period the British government's aims and interests were: while maintaining the entente with France, to retain the British lead in the Dual Control that Salisbury had established;[68] to keep other European powers from interfering; and to avoid an armed occupation of Egypt because, if this were done with France, it would jeopardize British para-mountcy, and if done without her, it would ruin the entente. In addition, Gladstone and Granville had to contend with a Cabinet, Parliament, and public deeply divided over whether strong action was needed to protect British interests or whether such action would waste the taxpayers' money and violate Liberal principles.

Gladstone undoubtedly entertained strong moral feelings about the Egyptian question, feelings that had no obvious realpolitical ground or aim. There is ample evidence of them: his belief in "Egypt for the Egyptians," his wish not to ignore the Egyptian Chamber of Notables, his concern over the French Premier Gambetta's lack of liberal spirit, and his repugnance at the thought of Bismarck and the Turks advocating a more liberal policy than England.[69] But the important question for the kind of analysis being attempted here is whether these feelings had much real impact on British policy. More important still is the question of how some of Gladstone's moral claims—in particular, his insistence that Britain represented the interests of the entire civilized world in Egypt and that the European Concert must support her there—actually served British interests and strategy. An example: When the Anglo-French Joint Note of January 8, 1882 failed to curb the incipient revolution in Egypt, and in fact actually worsened it, a split developed within the British Cabinet over possible intervention by force—whether it was necessary to protect European life and property, and whether, if done at all, it should be strictly an Anglo-French move, or be carried out by the Turks as suzerains over Egypt, with the consent or participation of Europe.[70] Gladstone liked the idea of "bringing in the other powers" both to avert dangers in Egypt and also to pave the way for European backing for Britain in her current dispute with the United States over America's proposed revision of the Clayton-Bulwer Treaty governing the building of a Panama canal.[71] But he told Granville,

> I quite agree in your view that this concert would not be applicable to the executive part of the business, requiring as it does sharp consideration from day to day: while there might be great advantage in having Europe pledged as to the general basis, were it only to prevent the Turk from intriguing.[72]

A fortnight later, though still opposed to intervention at the present time, Gladstone wanted Turkey to be a party to it if it became necessary, and wanted it to "represent the united action & authority of Europe."[73]

One can easily see the functional purposes in calling for Turkish participation and European support on the basis that Britain was upholding Turkish, European, and general world interests in Egypt. Europe would give its moral support and authority, and Turkey supply the legal sanction and material forces, to an intervention Britain and France would be free to control from day-to-day. A precedent would be set for European support for Britain in her Panama dispute with the United States; the Turks would be kept from "intriguing" in Egypt; European sanction would help keep an intervention in Egypt from setting a bad example for the Central Powers or Russia in the Balkans; and Concert approval might even ease the qualms of some of Gladstone's followers who feared the party was abandoning the noninterventionist stand on Egypt proclaimed before the election.[74] In functional terms, Gladstone's moral appeal to the European Concert over Egypt was every bit as self-interested as, say, Metternich's moral appeal to the European alliance over Italy in 1820–22.

To be sure, during the long crisis from late May to mid-July, culminating in the British bombardment of Alexandria and the dispatch of troops to Egypt, appeals to the European Concert and attempts to use the Turks failed to help Gladstone much. He continued to be torn between powerful legal, moral, and practical arguments against intervention[75] and equally compelling reasons for it,[76] and in the end was dragged along by events. But the point remains valid that he still hoped to solve his dilemma through using Europe and the Turks, thus enabling Britain to achieve the purposes of intervention while escaping or sharing its costs and onus. His memorandum of

June 21, urging that Britain propose a Turkish intervention to the Ambassadors' Conference at Constantinople, and if the Turks declined, call upon the Conference to invite the powers "to provide for or sanction a military intervention other than Turkish under their authority,"[77] indicates his thinking clearly.

Though the same general thesis holds good also for the period from mid-July to mid-September, during which Britain gradually proceeded to conquer and occupy Egypt alone, the relation between Gladstone's morally-based attitudes and claims *vis-à-vis* Turkey and Europe and the shifting aims of British policy underwent a series of interesting developments. For example: his first step, following the bombardment of Alexandria was to claim the moral endorsement of all of Europe—for it was a step toward peace. The claim occasioned private protests from both Austria and Germany on the ground that it distorted their position. Gladstone's main intent in making the claim, however, was clearly domestic-political more than international—to stop defections from the Liberal party, exemplified by John Bright's resignation from the Cabinet.[78] When the bombardment and the subsequent landing of British troops served further to accelerate the Egyptian revolution under Colonel Arabi, Gladstone proposed getting the Sultan to send troops to subdue Arabi while Britain and France jointly occupied the Canal. Europe, acting through the Constantinople Conference, was supposed to endorse the Anglo-French move while controlling the actions of Turkey.[79] But quickly Gladstone came to detect more Ottoman perfidy in the Sultan's delays and more German bad faith in Bismarck's failure to put strong pressure on Turkey. Hence, just as Gladstone had done in the case of Montenegro, he set out to mold a Europe more responsive to British purposes. On July 22 he urged that if the Sultan failed to respond immediately to a European summons to send troops to Egypt, France and England should propose to the Conference that they and Italy end the anarchy and bloodshed in Egypt by military intervention. He further suggested: "Germany and Austria being hopeless, should we nevertheless, in the interests of international law & order, endeavour to obtain the countenance of Russia?"[80] This is an interesting example of how to mobilize the European Concert in the interests of "international law and order": England and France, disregarding the rights of the suzerain power Turkey, would seek the active support of Italy and the consent of Russia for a military intervention in Egypt and occupation of the Suez Canal, while leaving Germany and Austria out of the picture.

With France remaining stubbornly unwilling to join in armed intervention, Gladstone, though he continued to urge getting Italy to participate and Russia to give its consent,[81] now began to see advantages for Britain in unilateral action,[82] and to find moral arguments for it. By late July he felt that since the Sultan was forcing England to act alone in defense of the cause of civilization, England had the right and duty to impose strict conditions on any Turkish participation in an Egyptian intervention.[83] Sir Garnet Wolseley's initial victories over the Egyptians in August made the British

more confident of the outcome and more convinced that the French and
Turkish hesitations were useful to Britain.[84] Granville heartily approved the
news that Lord Dufferin, ambassador at Constantinople, had canceled the
assurances previously given Turkey about Egypt, while Gladstone wanted to
make sure that Salisbury's secret agreement with France for cooperation in
Egypt was equally void.[85] By early September Gladstone had come to believe
that Britain would actually do Turkey a favor by not concluding a convention with her for military cooperation in Egypt, for the absence of such a
convention would help preserve Turkey from the greed of other powers. As
he saw it, a joint occupation of Egypt might lead to an Anglo-Turkish quarrel, thus "reopening the whole Eastern Question and giving an opening to
the 'land-hunger' of some, if not all, of the Powers."[86] Gladstone now began
to worry that the Turks, having perfidiously declined earlier to occupy
Egypt, might now perfidiously change their minds, sign a convention, and
come in. Granville, though unsure how to defend it, on the whole favored
Wolseley's idea that if the Egyptians surrendered to the British before the
Turkish troops arrived, they should be prevented from landing.[87] Gladstone
continued to promise that Britain would work out with Europe the bases of
the new order in Egypt, but once again he had no intention of allowing this
to restrict Britain's freedom of action:

> I observe [he wrote Granville] that attempts are still being made to tighten
> upon us the language of the proposed closing Protocol of the Conference upon
> its adjournment. And without doubt it is well to be in agreement with every-
> body. Still, I hope you will not agree to any words which would make us
> dependent upon all and each of the powers for our eventual settlement in
> Egypt. Is not the following a possible combination: that Russia and perhaps
> Austria should sell Egyptian interests to the Sultan against some boon to them-
> selves? Each has selfish aims to prosecute, and neither can be supposed to care
> much for Egyptian liberties.
>
> Happily the question of the Protocol, or of any Protocol, does not *burn*—
> for us at any rate.[88]

This is an example of a fairly common heads-I-win, tails-you-lose aspect
to Gladstone's arguments. Where, as in the Balkans, Russia and Austria had
direct interests and Britain none, Gladstone would argue that Britain, the
sole disinterested great power, had therefore the right and duty to defend the
rights of local populations. Where, as in Egypt, British interests were more
immediate than those of Russia and Austria (though both powers, especially
Austria, had interests there), Gladstone would contend that it was selfish of
them to want any say in the matter. The apparent inconsistency, however,
disappears in the face of Gladstone's conviction that even where British interests were involved, Britain was a friend to liberty—which Russia seldom was
and Austria never. The main point remains that Gladstone's moral attitudes
went hand-in-hand with practical moves designed to give Britain freedom of
action while limiting other powers. Gladstone indeed recognized that
Britain's new position in Egypt would rest on a combination of military

conquest and moral claims. Victory, he told Granville, would make Britain's place in Egypt like Russia's in Bulgaria—"not the result of stipulation, but of effort and sacrifice crowned by success."[89]

Gladstone therefore shared in the general enthusiasm over Wolseley's decisive triumph at Tel-el-Kebir and joined in optimistic plans for exploiting it. He assured his Eastern European admirers that Britain's work in Egypt would emulate that of Russia in Bulgaria, thus helping to stimulate further emancipation of the South Slavs.[90] But the concrete aims of Britain, even in the afterglow of victory, remained as divergent and difficult to harmonize as ever: (1) to reduce Turkish suzerainty in Egypt to a pure formality without breaking with Turkey, undermining the Ottoman Empire, or promoting revolution; (2) to end the system of Dual Control formally and ease France entirely out of Egypt, without destroying the general Anglo-French entente; (3) to secure European endorsement and support for British control of Egypt while limiting European interference; (4) to control Egypt without burdening the British taxpayer; and (5) in general to minimize British responsibilities and commitments in Egypt while assuring Britain paramountcy. Little insight or exposition is needed to see how these concrete ends were served by Gladstone's moral arguments, such as these: that Britain was serving Egypt's, Europe's, and the civilized world's needs in Egypt more than her own; that Dual Control had enslaved Egypt and forced Britain to bear the burdens of armed intervention, while the British occupation had now liberated Egypt; that Britain had a right to the support of the powers because only she was determined to preserve the Ottoman Empire and promote Egypt's welfare and liberties; and that India ought to pay a major share of the costs of the war and occupation, because India had long imposed great military and financial burdens on Britain and benefited from the security of the Canal more than Britain did.[91] Sometimes realpolitical calculations reinforced the moral arguments. For instance, Gladstone opposed abolishing the sultan's rights in Egypt outright, because it might encourage Austrian designs on Ottoman territory in the Balkans; and he hoped to reconcile France to the abolition of Dual Control with some concessions elsewhere.[92]

In early 1883, however, the time of troubles that Robinson and Gallagher call "Gladstone's Bondage in Egypt" set in.[93] It ended for Gladstone only with his resignation in mid-1885, and shattered all his hopes in regard to Egypt. Britain's policy of supporting the Khedive and preparing Egypt for self-rule came to mean ruling Egypt. Putting Egyptian finances in order required either burdening the British taxpayer or angering and defying Europe by reducing Egypt's obligations to European bondholders. The idea of neutralizing Egypt under the aegis of the powers, instead of providing a convenient means of protecting British paramountcy while limiting her commitments, raised the dangers of renewed French intervention and of Bismarck's manipulation of the Concert against Britain. These insoluble basic problems were heightened by a series of humiliating disasters in the Sudan, culminating in Gordon's death in early 1885. Challenged from both right and left in Parliament, his Cabinet deeply divided over the Egyptian question, and unable to reach a satisfactory arrangement with France and Europe over Egyptian finances, Gladstone by late 1884 was looking for a way out of the Egyptian imbroglio. By spring 1885 a host of other foreign, colonial, and domestic challenges in the Balkans, Central Asia, various parts of Africa, and Ireland made him yearn for a graceful exit from power.[94]

It is impossible here either to deal with these developments in detail or to describe fully the role of Gladstone's moral principles in his efforts to cope with them. But the pattern is the familiar one of moral claims and attitudes functioning to further the aims of policy or, increasingly with time, to cover its retreat. Into this pattern fits a whole series of British initiatives: the efforts to reach an agreement with France, giving the rest of Europe no choice but to accept it, without, however, conceding to France a return to Dual Control; Britain's quest for a European endorsement for her occupation and administration of Egypt (useful both in order to quiet domestic dissent over Egypt and to avoid too exclusive a cooperation with France on financial affairs), without allowing Europe actively to interfere in Egypt; then, after Europe as a whole had proved difficult to deal with, the idea of seeking a European sanction for the occupation from certain select powers (once more, these were supposed to be France, Italy, and Russia); the effort to get Turkey to assume the main burdens of the military occupation of Egypt and, later, of the defense of the Sudan, at the same time as the British were excusing themselves from any obligations to Turkey under the Cyprus Convention on the grounds that Turkish persecution of the Armenians made this impossible; and finally, the general policy of avoiding giving Russia, Austria, or Germany any excuse for armed intervention in the Balkans during the Bulgarian crisis by insisting that there was no parallel at all between the two situations, and that British actions in Egypt had been and remained entirely legal, peaceful, conservative, and unselfishly European.[95]

All this shows how readily one can detect normal realpolitical functions and effects in Gladstone's moral stands on the Egyptian question. But another element of Gladstone's policy in 1884–85, closely connected with Egypt, proves harder to integrate into this scheme. It not only complicates the picture, but indicates certain limits to the functional explanation of Gladstone's policy given thus far.

That element is the Anglo-German colonial dispute of 1884–85, arising initially over Angra Pequeña in Southwest Africa. So far as its origins are concerned, the dispute can no longer be explained as one deliberately provoked by Bismarck as a move in his domestic and European policy.[96] The proximate cause, as G. N. Sanderson remarks, was "the provocative incompetence, and worse" with which the British treated Bismarck's correct and reasonable initial claim to a protectorate, using delays and evasions in an attempt to maintain a British Monroe Doctrine in Africa.[97]

However, our concern is neither with the origins and course of the quarrel itself, nor the question of why a government already beset by many other problems should have caused itself further grief as Britain did. The sole purpose here is to connect Gladstone's attitude toward Germany in this colonial dispute with his feelings about Germany and Austria on the Egyptian question. As one might expect, throughout this period Gladstone remained suspicious of Austria's aims in the Balkans, dissatisfied with her support in Egypt, and contemptuous of Austria as a mere German satellite.[98] As to Bismarck, Gladstone remained highly distrustful of him even while he steadily supported Britain over Egypt,[99] and when the colonial dispute turned Bismarck into an opponent over Egypt, Gladstone angrily accused him of having lured Britain into Egypt in order to entangle her there so as to create an Anglo-French quarrel Germany could exploit. Gladstone now blamed Bismarck for the failure of Anglo-French negotiations in June 1884, and saw him as the main source of Britain's difficulties.[100]

Gladstone's suspicions of Austria had little justification, as Granville recognized. Much as Austria disliked many aspects of British policy in Egypt, especially its treatment of Turkey, she was too vulnerable in Europe and too fearful of an Anglo-Russian rapprochement or a British abandonment of the Balkans to Russia to oppose Britain over Egypt.[101]

The case in regard to Bismarck is more complicated. He had begun urging Britain to take Egypt as early as 1876. When Gladstone took office, Bismarck hoped that Egypt would help distract him from what Bismarck regarded as his dangerous meddling in Europe, especially the Balkans. Whatever his reasons were, Bismarck steadily supported British policy in Egypt up to June 1884, as Granville conceded. His anti-British campaign in Egypt and Africa thereafter was bewildering and painful to the British, but stayed within tolerable limits. For example, at the Congo Conference in Berlin the German and British positions actually proved closer than those of Germany and France, with whom Bismarck had been trying to form a coalition, so that Britain emerged from the conference on balance a winner.[102]

As to the main charge, that Bismarck lured the British into Egypt so as to entangle her there and create an Anglo-French quarrel he could exploit: first of all, the evidence is at best ambiguous. Bismarck urged the British to move into Egypt long before any Anglo-French rift developed. He urged an intervention in partnership with France as well as without her. When Britain finally did intervene alone, Bismarck urged the government to conciliate French feelings over the move.[103] He seems then to have anticipated either an Anglo-French quarrel over Egypt or a durable Anglo-French partnership, and to have expected to take advantage of either one.

More important, the fact that Gladstone and other contemporary statesmen (as well as many historians since) should concentrate on Bismarck's supposed Machiavellian intrigues in the Egyptian question says more about them than about Bismarck. Putting the blame for Britain's troubles in Egypt on Bismarck is like putting the blame for someone's broken leg on the person who lent him a pair of skis. Obviously Bismarck encouraged other powers to satisfy their various ambitions outside of Europe with an eye toward gaining Germany more security and a freer hand within Europe. Equally obviously, he was aware that if and when these powers acquired the gains they sought, whether it be Bulgaria or Constantinople for Russia, Bosnia for

Austria, Tunis for France, or Egypt for Britain, they might find their acquisitions a source of trouble and of disputes with other powers. But it was not
his duty to warn other statesmen, grown men all, of the risks they were taking.
And in this particular case, the British, not Bismarck, *caused* Britain to go
into Egypt. France and England, not Bismarck, *caused* the Anglo-French
quarrel over Egypt.

The purpose here is not to defend Bismarck against Gladstone's charges,
but to point out a contrast between Gladstone's somewhat unreasonable
attitude toward Bismarck over Egypt and the reasonable, even generous
stance he took toward what became a strongly anti-English campaign by
Germany in Africa and the Southwest Pacific. On colonial questions, there
were important anti-German voices in the Cabinet—the Lord Chancellor,
Lord Selborne, and the Colonial Secretary, Lord Derby, in particular.
Granville, to say the least, was careless about German claims.[104] But Gladstone,
as soon as he recognized that Bismarck really wanted protectorates, sincerely
welcomed Germany to the ranks of civilizing colonial powers. His sweet rea-
sonableness on this score, however, coincided with denunciations of
Germany's actions and aims not only in regard to Egypt, where the German
use of the Egyptian stick did hurt Britain, but also in the Balkans and elsewhere where British interests were not involved.[105] The problem is not that
one can find no good practical reasons for Gladstone to accommodate
Bismarck on colonial issues. The reasons are clearly expressed by Gladstone:
the need for German goodwill in Egypt, the fact that Britain had all the
colonies she wanted and would not benefit from preemptive expansion,
the further fact that having Germans as neighbors would tend to make
obstreperous British colonials at the Cape Colony or in Australia more
dependent on the homeland and thus more manageable, and even the realization (as Bismarck's son Herbert frankly told Gladstone) that German
colonies would always be vulnerable to the British navy and hostage to
Britain's goodwill.[106] The difficulty is that the same prudential considerations that justified a policy of accommodating Germany in Africa not only
would, if applied earlier, have avoided the whole quarrel, but would have justified a different attitude toward Germany and Bismarck generally throughout the period. Plainly Gladstone's moral aversion to Bismarck stood in the
way of this, which suggests that a functional explanation of his policy in
terms of Realpolitik does not solve all its problems.

Nonetheless, this difficulty does not overthrow the general pattern that
both the Egyptian question and other questions display—that of Gladstone's
moral stands having the effect of promoting normal realpolitical aims and
strategies for Britain. One could even argue by a parallel with later British
policy that Gladstone's attitude toward Germany on colonial questions conforms to Gladstone's overall approach to the European system as a whole.
Here a consistent pattern of Gladstonian attitudes and desiderata emerges.
He regularly wanted a liberal entente with France; hoped to detach Italy
from the Central Powers, *de facto* if not *de jure*; wanted to end Britain's
rivalry with Russia; viewed Austria with suspicion as a tool for German

expansion; and felt a strong aversion to German leadership of the Continent, including the Three Emperors' Alliances or other combinations promoting it. What this describes, as historians will recognize, is not merely a normal realpolitical British outlook, but more precisely, the general views of the Foreign Office under Sir Edward Grey in the decade before World War I— surely a period when Britain pursued a "realistic" foreign policy. Like Gladstone, Grey was willing to have Germany reasonably satisfied in the colonial sphere so long as she was checked in Europe.

Here is where a critic may explode in protest against this whole approach as reductionist. It virtually ignores Gladstone's driving moral passion, thus obscuring the most distinctive characteristic of his policy.[107] It stresses only ways and instances in which his moral principles failed to make a clear difference in his actions, slighting clear counterinstances. It fails to recognize that foreign policy decisions fulfill a variety of functions in national and international life besides power-political ones. Therefore it overlooks the moral functions of Gladstone's foreign policy—the ways in which it served to promote the values, satisfy the consciences, and reinforce the self-esteem of Gladstone, his party, and the British public. In its concentration upon the supposed realities of European politics, that is, rival alignments and conflicts of interests, it pays no attention to how moral values influence the perception and definition of interests, and the ways in which statesmen and peoples conceive their goals in international affairs. In the end, this approach gives us a portrait of Gladstonian foreign policy with Gladstone left out. It tells us, unsurprisingly, that he worked to advance British interests, but not that he genuinely identified British interests with the advance of Christian civilization, international justice, and national liberty. It points out that he favored a certain pattern of European alignments, but not what "Europe" meant to him, namely, the ideas of Christian and classical civilization.

There is force to this objection, and it can be supported by considerable evidence. It points to the kind of stand-off that often results when historians using different approaches and presuppositions arrive at divergent conclusions. Each side can concede much of what the other side claims, while insisting that what it emphasizes is really decisive. The historian taking the systemic approach to foreign policy will argue that it does not finally matter what Gladstone aimed to do and believed he was doing. If one looks at his actions in the context of the international system, and appraises their actual effects, his policy becomes a normal kind of Realpolitik. A scholar in the historicist tradition will contend that to understand Gladstone's policy, one must take full account of his aims, motives, and aspirations, which were very different from the usual realpolitical ones. Since the choice between these approaches (and others as well, for that matter) rests finally not on which intrinsically makes better sense of all the available evidence, but on which leads to the most satisfying overall view of history, there can be no clear-cut decision between them.

This seems to lead to a rather limp conclusion: Gladstone's policy did represent an alternative to Bismarckian Realpolitik, from the standpoint of

Gladstone's ideals and motives, but did not, from the standpoint of its actual implementation and effects—a reasonable outcome, perhaps, but hardly exciting. It may be, however, that by looking again at points on which both sides agree, one might be able to get beyond the deadlock.

Both would agree that Gladstone really wanted to transform international politics along moral lines, and that his efforts failed. (There would be disagreement, of course, on why they failed—whether it was mainly Bismarck's opposition, or Gladstone's blunders, or the inherent impracticality of his schemes, or something else.) Implicitly, then, both would agree that Gladstone's ideals in foreign policy, considered as ideals, were not realpolitical; that had these ideals somehow been put into practice, this would have meant a break with the usual competitive, conflictual, state-interest–based international politics.

This is the question to be addressed: Did Gladstone's *ideals* in foreign policy, *per se*, constitute an alternative to Realpolitik? To answer this it will help to look at a fairly typical expression of Gladstone's principles: an essay "Germany, France, and England," published in October 1870 at the height of the Franco-German War.[108] The article mainly discussed the danger of further German conquest and possible future wars, but the principal lesson Gladstone wished to point out was the meaning of current events for England:

> Happy England! Happy, not because any Immaculate Conception exempted her from that original sin of nations, the desire to erect Will into Right, and the lust of territorial aggrandisement.... But happy with a special reference to the present subject, in this, that the wise dispensation of Providence has cut her off, by that streak of silver sea . . . though in no way from the duties and the honours, yet partly from the dangers, absolutely from the temptations, which attend upon the neighborhood of the Continental nations.

The great advantage of England's insular position, Gladstone insisted, was not that it had helped make her rich, strong and secure (though it had), but that

> It marks out England as the appropriate object of the general confidence, as the sole, comparatively, unsuspected Power. In every quarrel, in every difficulty, it is her aid that is most courted; it is by her agency that parties, if they seek a mediator, prefer to come together; it is under her leadership that neutrals most desire to move. And this, not because she is believed to be exempt from infirmity, but because she is known not to be exposed to temptation. All that is wanted is that she should discharge the functions, which are likely more and more to accrue to her, modestly, kindly, and impartially....
>
> One accomplishment yet remains needful to enable us to hold without envy our free and eminent position. It is that we should do as we would be done by; that we should seek to found a moral empire upon the confidence of the nations, not upon their fears, their passions or their antipathies. Certain it is that a new law of nations is gradually taking hold of the mind, and coming to sway the practice, of the world; a law which recognizes independence, which frowns upon aggression, which favours the pacific, not the bloody settlement of disputes,

which aims at permanent and not temporary adjustments; above all, which recognises as a tribunal of paramount authority, the general judgment of civilised mankind. It has censured the aggression of France; it will censure, if need arise, the greed of Germany.... The greatest triumph of our time—a triumph in a region higher than that of electricity and steam—will be the enthronement of this idea of Public Right, as the governing idea of European policy; as the common and precious inheritance of all lands, but superior to the opinion of any. The foremost among the nations will be that one, which by its conduct shall gradually engender in the mind of the others a fixed belief that it is just. In the competition for this prize, the bounty of Providence has given us a place of vantage: and nothing save our fault or folly can wrest it from our grasp.

Gladstone in this passage, as in many others, does apparently call for an international politics based on law, morality, and human rights rather than on power and state interests. Such a transformation, however, demands two basic changes in the international system: first, in place of the existing system of self-help, in which every sovereign state is finally defender and judge of its own cause, substituting some system of international law, to recognize and harmonize national rights and to adjudicate disputed claims; and second, replacing the existing competition for security, power, influence, and prestige with a cooperative pursuit by all nations of joint ends.

Gladstone's ideals, even as he expressed them, clearly do not call for either of these basic transformations. There is no trace here, or elsewhere in his writings, of any institutional arrangement—a world government or world court—to establish international law and adjudicate international disputes. The European Concert was certainly not this—not, that is, a judicial or deliberative body whose decisions were to be binding on all members. For Gladstone, the European Concert was an abstract moral ideal; it meant roughly the same thing as European public law, or enlightened opinion. As has been repeatedly shown, he believed and acted on the belief that powers whose attitudes and policies were not enlightened had abandoned the Concert, and that powers like Britain which were enlightened had the right and duty to speak and act in the name of Europe regardless of what the majority of powers believed. When he spoke of a "new law of nations" ruling over the minds of men and Public Right being enthroned, not only was he talking about moral, ideological, and intellectual changes rather than institutional ones; he was also describing not a switch from power to justice as the basis of international relations, but a stage in that struggle between conflicting rights and competing legitimating principles which has always been a central element in normal international competition. All Gladstone wanted, all he here called for, was that one set of rights be recognized (like the right of small nations and peoples to independence), while another set of rights were denied or downgraded (like the right, of states such as Austria and Turkey to rule over their alien subjects, or the right of a great power to preserve its vital interests in adjoining areas). To call this kind of appeal an alternative to Realpolitik is mere conceptual confusion. It would make as much sense to speak of Cavour as abandoning Realpolitik when he appealed to the nationality principle, or Lenin as doing so when he called for proletarian revolution. These are not alternatives to Realpolitik, but ways of practicing it.

As for substituting international cooperation for the competition for security, power, and prestige among nations, no one could make it clearer than Gladstone here that his new system was based upon Britain's superior, invulnerable power-political position and designed to enhance Britain's leadership, prestige, and influence without increasing her burdens. Instead of eliminating competition, this system in its very ideal was competitive at the core. No doubt Gladstone believed that British leadership was safe and benign, and wanted it exercised in nonmilitary ways. Nonetheless, he wanted and expected Britain and other states who followed her principles to win under the system, and states who opposed it to lose. And the stakes were not negligible; security, prosperity, and even survival were among them.

This is not an abstract theoretical point. It conforms to, and makes sense of, the whole functional pattern of Realpolitik in Gladstone's policy discussed earlier. It fits into his favored pattern of European alignments like a glove. All the states he sought to associate with Britain were ones he believed capable of sharing in British principles and profiting from them—Italy, France, the Balkan states, even Russia to some extent. Those he opposed were governments—Turkey, Austria, Germany—whose contrary principles and selfish interests made them a threat to the new system and Britain's leadership of it.

Above all, the recognition that Gladstone's moral system represented a form of Realpolitik yields a further insight into his hostility to Bismarck—a hostility directed less at what Bismarck actually did, most of which was helpful to Britain and to causes Gladstone favored, than at the motives Gladstone believed Bismarck entertained. To be sure, Gladstone hated what Bismarck represented—the politics of *do ut des*, might makes right—and the entangling alliances that robbed Britain of her natural friends and partners in Europe. But most of all he hated and feared what Bismarck was trying to do to Britain, precisely by cooperating with her. Like the tempter in the wilderness, Bismarck used his wiles to try to destroy Britain's unique moral position and authority. By luring her into a military occupation of Egypt, alienating her from her friends, provoking her into actions harmful to her reputation, and ensnaring her in commitments and entangling alliances, Bismarck was trying to make Britain an ordinary country. He had to be shown that this would not work. As Edward Hamilton wrote,

> Mr. G. thinks it is a good thing that Bismarck's eyes should be opened to what is likely to occur in this country politically [i.e., that Liberalism would remain the dominant political force] and that he should be made to face the inevitable and to feel that England's position in the world is an independent one and that she can afford to be exempted from many necessities incumbent upon other European Powers.[109]

Gladstone clearly misjudged Bismarck in some respects, but on the score of Bismarck's aims toward Britain, especially under Gladstone's leadership, he was basically correct. Bismarck was in principle neither an enemy nor a friend of Britain. He claimed, to be sure, that he had repeatedly tried to be a close ally of England and had always been rebuffed, but he often adopted this pose of the disappointed suitor with various countries for tactical reasons. Bismarck knew that Britain's position was virtually invulnerable, and even in 1884–85 never seriously thought of challenging it, despite his use of the *baton égyptien* against Britain and his passing references to a possible maritime league with France. But Bismarck's diplomacy, whether cooperative or antagonistic, was clearly intended to bring Britain, and Gladstone in particular, down into the real world. He did want to break what he considered the arrogant English attitude of "Quod licet Iovi non licet bovi," to bring Britain to recognize and operate within the usual rules, to make her act like a wealthy, secure, powerful, but nonetheless ordinary European great power. It was a source of pride to Gladstone till the end of his life that he had frustrated this effort.[110]

Thus the rivalry between Gladstone and Bismarck is best viewed not as a clash between different principles and systems, but, as a normal contest over political leadership and alignments, for the normal rewards of prestige, influence, and (ultimately) security and power. It belongs in the same category as the rivalries between Canning and Metternich or Palmerston and Metternich, which also involved major differences of principle and worldview, but which no one would seriously argue were on that account outside the range of normal Realpolitik.

A final objection can be made to this thesis—one too important to ignore, though too sweeping and fundamental fully to discuss here. It is that in attempting to prove that Gladstone's system of foreign policy was basically another form of Realpolitik, this essay has simply defined international politics as Realpolitik, excluding any other kind by definition. Everyone who engages international politics, whatever his aims and principles, engages willy-nilly, knowing it or not, in a game in which all his actions are perforce translated into realpolitical moves, and in which the outcome inevitably must be viewed in terms of power, security, influence, prestige, and state interest. The only way to eliminate Realpolitik from international politics would therefore be to eliminate international politics, that is, to make international affairs no longer international, but world-governmental, and no longer political but religious or ideological. If this is the case, then the distinction between idealism and Realpolitik in foreign policy becomes meaningless.

Without pursuing the point thoroughly as a problem in the theory of international politics, one must recognize an important, relevant truth here. Every effort to change the nature of international politics by proscribing Realpolitik and enlisting governments instead in the pursuit of higher goals or supposedly universal ideals is an illusion, and always results either in failure or in a new level and kind of power struggle, often more violent and dangerous than the old. This is true whatever the source and character of the ideals. In the realm of international politics, far more than personal or social affairs, Lord Acton's famous dictum holds good: power tends to corrupt, and the more absolute the ideals that try to use power for their purposes, the more absolutely those ideals will be corrupted.

But if law and moral ideals cannot ban Realpolitik, they can to an extent limit, control, and even transcend it. This happens all the time, and is just as much a part of international politics as power struggles are. Not even in wartime are international affairs conducted simply on the basis of Realpolitik, and there have been times and places where one could say that law was a more important basis for the ordinary conduct of international relations than the egoistic calculation of state interests. This came about not where realpolitical competition was banned or denounced, but where it was transcended in an Hegelian sense; where a particular status quo founded upon power became the basis for a general system of law and justice. In this sense, historians can speak of the Holy Roman Empire in its last centuries as being a *Rechtsordnung* rather than a power structure,[111] and can claim that an informal reign of law helped account for European peace between 1815 and 1848.

The distinction between an idealistic and realpolitical foreign policy is therefore not vacuous.[112] But the rule of law and the promotion of moral ideals have to proceed out of Realpolitik. This, we have seen, did not happen with Gladstone. Instead, both in terms of the functions and effects of his policy, and finally in terms of his very ideals, Realpolitik emerged from morality. It would be wrong and unfair to agree with Carlyle that both Disraeli and Gladstone were charlatans, but that only Disraeli knew it. Even Disraeli was no charlatan, and Gladstone certainly was not, consciously or unconsciously. But it is neither wrong nor unfair to conclude that both Bismarck and Gladstone were Realpolitiker, even if only Bismarck knew it.

Or was Bismarck simply that? Could one outdo Mack Smith by contending that Bismarck was more like Gladstone than Bismarck? I do not mean pointing out, as some historians have, that important elements of moral and religious ethos were bound up in his statecraft, or that his struggle to preserve peace after 1871 made him a genuine defender of a conservative European order.[113] Rather, even if one admitted what most contemporary scholars emphasize, the narrow political, social, and personal bases of his policy, and the unattractive sides of his personality and principles,[114] could one still argue that just as Gladstone was a Realpolitiker *malgré lui*, so the functions and tendency of Bismarck's policy of peace after 1871, regardless of his intentions, was to promote a certain kind of morality, justice, and rule of law to limit and control the Realpolitik he himself had preached and practiced? The ironical possibilities of an essay on "Bismarck as Gladstone" are intriguing. But it would require another argument as long and paradoxical as this one.

6

Containment Nineteenth Century Style: How Russia was Restrained

Inspector Gregory: "Is there any other point to which you would wish to draw
my attention?"
Sherlock Holmes: "To the curious incident of the dog in the night-time."
Gregory: "The dog did nothing in the night-time."
Holmes: "That was the curious incident."
Arthur Conan Doyle, "Silver Blaze," in *The Annotated
Sherlock Holmes*, ed. W. S. Baring-Gould
(New York, 1967), 2, 277

Historians, as well as detectives, must take into account not only the occurrence of the expected, but also the nonoccurrence of the expected. This essay argues that a nonevent, the failure of an unexpected development to take place, became very important in the nineteenth century European states system and, further, that this nonevent may be interesting and instructive for present and future international politics as well.

The nonevent in question is the failure of Imperial Russia, in the years from 1815 to 1890, to become a hegemonic world power. In 1813–15, it was commonplace for European statesmen and publicists to predict that Tsarist Russia, endowed with enormous size, a large population, vast resources, a huge army, centralized despotic power, and an invulnerability to attack derived from climate and distance, would succeed Napoleonic France as the dominant power on the Continent, competing with Britain for world supremacy. This fear repeatedly surfaced throughout the century. The feared and expected Russian hegemony never developed. To say that Russia did not become a hegemonic world power dominant over Europe is not to say that she tried and failed; she did not ever really try. Instead, Russia was restrained, playing the role, by and large, of a normal great power, acting to stabilize and maintain the European system and community rather than to undermine or dominate it. The fact of Russian restraint and the explanation of how Russia was restrained are what this essay will briefly examine.

But first this alleged fact needs to be established against a different view held by many historians, plausible enough on its face: that nineteenth century Russia was a dangerously aggressive, expansionist power. Undoubtedly, Russia expanded a good deal territorially between 1815 and 1890, completing her conquest of the Caucasus and Transcaucasus, taking over the whole of Central Asia, and wresting large areas in Asia from China. The process involved considerable use of force—and some overt war. Besides this imperialist expansion in Asia, Russia also fought three wars with the Ottoman Empire and, it is claimed, threatened Turkey's integrity and independence throughout the century. She held most of Poland in subjection, suppressing two Polish revolutions with massive force. In alliance with Prussia and Austria, Russia acted as the gendarme of Europe, not only holding down her own restive nationalities, but also encouraging and aiding her allies to crush revolts in Germany, Italy, and Spain. Russian agents, it is said, constantly kept the Balkans astir, and Russian ideologies—Pan-Orthodoxy, Panslavism— were a standing menace to other countries in Central Europe. This hardly looks like the picture of a normal, responsible great power.

The reply is simple. The arguments made about Russia's imperialist expansion in Asia are true enough, but largely irrelevant. The ones about Russia's policy and actions in Europe are relevant, but largely false.

To the first point: Russia's expansion in Asia, extensive and forcible though it was, did not threaten the European system or world balance of power because the prevailing system and balance permitted, even encouraged, it. The period in question, remember, was one in which Britain expanded her empire to include almost one-fourth the world's area and population; in which France revived a nearly vanished empire, colonizing huge territories in Africa and Southeast Asia; in which the United States expanded from the Atlantic to the Pacific, came to dominate the whole Western hemisphere, and gained colonies in the Caribbean and the Pacific; in which old, decaying colonial powers like Spain, Portugal, and Holland began to revive and consolidate their empires, and newcomers like Germany, Italy, Japan, and even Belgium joined in the scramble. Not only would it be unrealistic to expect Russia, already a world power in 1815, not to participate in this expansion, but to accuse Russia of undermining the international system by being imperialistic in Asia is even more unhistorical—like charging a nineteenth century businessman with undermining the economic system by being a capitalist. Imperialism was the international system, to a considerable degree, as capitalism was an integral part of the economic system.

As for the violence and military conquest involved, again one simply cannot make Russia worse than normal. French imperialism involved at least as much conquest and was fostered at least as much by military and naval lobbies. As for Britain, in the halcyon reign of Queen Victoria (1837–1901), that so-called *Pax Britannica*, hardly a year went by without British colonial wars or punitive expeditions all over the globe.

This way of supporting the case for Russia's moderation might seem to ruin it by making it trivial. Russia was restrained, it seems to prove, only in the sense that she was no worse an imperialist than others. She upheld the European system—meaning that like other European powers she did whatever she wanted with non-European peoples. As a comment about nineteenth century European attitudes toward the non-European world, this has some force. As a criticism of Russia's foreign policy overall, however, it misses a point very important in international politics, even though it gave little comfort then to the victims of European imperialism. The nineteenth century international system, it is true, did not stop European powers from expanding at the expense of the non-European world; it did stop them from fighting one another in the process, and this involved real restraints. From the days of Vasco da Gama to Napoleon, European history is studded with wars fought between European powers to control the trade and territory of various parts of the non-European world. Between 1815 and 1914, with more states involved in an even more intense scramble providing ample occasions for war, not one such conflict occurred. (Even the apparent exceptions prove the rule. The Boer War, 1899–1902, was fought between peoples of European stock; but the Boer Republics were not European states or, in the British view, independent ones. Russia's chief imperialist rivals in East Asia were Britain and, to a lesser degree, Germany; but the only state she fought, in 1904–05, was Japan. As for the Leninist view that World War I was an imperialist war, the issue is too complex and controversial to discuss here. Clearly, however, the imperialist issue, if any, was the control of Europe, not Asia or Africa.) In avoiding wars with other European powers over non-European prizes, Russia showed as much restraint and obedience to the rules as did other states, even in her competition with Britain in Asia. The notion that in the nineteenth century Russia was constantly trying to encroach on the British Empire and threaten the approaches to India is largely a myth, as British historians increasingly recognize. Americans, moreover, ought to be aware of the readiness of nineteenth century Russia to drop her once lively interest in Latin America, abandon her outposts on the West Coast, and ultimately sell Alaska, in part out of a desire for good relations with the United States.

Thus, Russia's imperialist expansion in the nineteenth century, whatever its intrinsic character, did not constitute, in the context of that time, reckless or aggressive international behavior, nor did it undermine international peace and stability. Nor was it seen to do so. No European states worried more about the Russian menace, or had more reason to, than Russia's western neighbors, Austria and Prussia-Germany. Yet far from worrying about the growth of Russian power through eastward expansion, Austrian and German statesman often encouraged Russia to look eastward—it was a welcome distraction from Central Europe and the Balkans. Even the British, who frequently perceived Russia as a menace to their empire, especially in India, could not claim that Russian gains in Central Asia upset the international system or the European balance. When the British did claim that Russia was disturbing the balance, they pointed to something else—the size of the Russian army, or Russia's actions in Poland, the Balkans, or Central Europe—as the source of the problem.

As for Russia's European policy in general from 1815 to 1890, rather than being restless, domineering, and eager for hegemony, after 1815, and still more after 1820, it can better be described as conservative, legalistic, anti-revolutionary, and oriented toward peace and great power cooperation. This represents a decisive change from the general character of Russian foreign policy ever since Peter the Great (1696–1725). Sweeping generalizations like this are always too simple and should be carefully qualified and backed by evidence in a way that is impossible in this essay. Nevertheless, the real contrast between Russian foreign policy in the nineteenth century and in earlier eras can be outlined here, if not fully portrayed or proved.

Before 1815, Russia's consistent aims toward the Ottoman Empire were to wrest away its northern territories (the Ukraine, the Crimea, the whole northern and eastern Black Sea coast, Bessarabia, the Rumanian Principalities) and to maintain an exclusive domination over the Turkish government, so as to be ready to control any division of the spoils if the Ottoman Empire collapsed. For many Russians, including Catherine the Great, Russian rule at Constantinople was the final goal. After 1815, while Russians continued to claim a special position *vis-à-vis* Turkey and the Balkans based on geography, ethnicity, religion, and treaty claims, the Russian government nevertheless genuinely preferred to keep the Ottoman Empire alive and intact. Russia not only more than once passed up good opportunities for war with Turkey, but she also more than once came to Turkey's aid to save it from other enemies, retroceded territory seized from Turkey in the course of conflict, and cooperated in international arrangements and agreements to sustain the Ottoman Empire.

Before 1815, Russia's basic policy in Germany was to promote and exploit the divisions between the major German states and within the Holy Roman Empire for Russian ends. After 1815, Russia willingly accepted the creation of a German Confederation that limited Russia's influence in Germany and united Germany for possible defense against Russia as well as other states, and Russia encouraged Austria and Prussia to cooperate in leading the Confederation.

Before 1815, Russia was bent on political and military domination of the Baltic—witness her organization of the Leagues of Armed Neutrality in 1780 and 1801, her conquest of Finland and the Aland Islands from Sweden in 1809, and her constant efforts to control North Germany. She also made considerable efforts to maintain both a naval and a territorial presence in the Mediterranean and to enjoy special rights of passage through the Turkish Straits. After 1815, Russia relied for her security in the north on good relations with her neighbors and made no protest when Prussia—and later the German Reich—became a rival Baltic naval power. Russia abandoned the idea of bases in the Mediterranean, along with the right to send her warships through the Straits, and contented herself with closing the Black Sea defensively against other navies.

In the eighteenth century, Russia had practiced a particularly ruthless brand of power politics, participating in the planned extinction of various states (Poland, Turkey, Sweden, and Prussia) by war and partition. The ambition of Catherine was to make Russia the equal of the other great powers of the Continent combined, and capable of competing with Britain in the outside world. After 1815, Russia accepted a normal role within the European Concert, supported the treaty system with its guarantees for large and small states alike, advocated the right of all the great powers acting in concert to supervise European politics, and sought cooperation rather than rivalry with Britain.

On one major issue, Poland, Russian nineteenth century policy looks like a simple continuation of the eighteenth century. First dominated by Russia and then partitioned by Russia, Austria, and Prussia in the eighteenth century, Poland remained after 1815 divided among the three Eastern monarchies, with Russia, having the lion's share, repressing all attempts at Polish revolt. But even here there are differences between eighteenth century greed and nineteenth century defensive anxiety. In 1815, Alexander I really hoped to reconcile the Poles with a constitution and autonomy; in 1861, in abolishing serfdom Alexander II actually gave Polish peasants a better deal than he gave the Russians. Some European observers (Bismarck, for one) felt that during the 1863 revolt Russia was willing to liberate the Poles if she could find a way to do it without danger. And nothing makes clearer the difference in attitudes of all three partitioning powers than the question, confronted at different times, of who should have the key city and territory of Cracow. In 1795, Austria and Prussia nearly went to war over it; in 1814–15 Russia tried her best to gain it and, failing, reluctantly agreed to give it free-city status in order to prevent Austria from getting it. But in 1846, after another Polish rising had convinced the three powers that Cracow's shadow independence had to be extinguished, Prussia and Russia proposed that Austria annex it, and Austria reluctantly agreed. Whatever one thinks of the oppression of Polish nationality, that kind of conservative cooperation simply could not have happened in the eighteenth century.

Are these differences really significant? One could claim that comparing Russia's action in the eighteenth and nineteenth centuries is like comparing a man's appetite before and after a huge meal, or the actions of an industrial robber baron before and after he has captured control of the industry. It was the huge gains in territory, power, and influence that Russia made in Europe before 1815 which satiated her after 1815; it was the problems of absorbing, administering, and developing her vast territories, plus the fear of losing her gains by more war and revolution, plus her persistent economic and fiscal weaknesses that made her conservative.

To a large degree, this is obviously true. But it does not undermine the case at all. It simply proves that the Russian government was inherently satiable, knew when and how to stop—not a quality universally encountered in international politics. Governments can always want more—insatiable ones like Napoleonic France and also normal ones like those of eighteenth century Russia. Insecurity at home, fear of revolution, the inability to solve domestic problems—all these factors, far from working automatically to produce pacific restraint in foreign policy, often work in just the opposite way, spurring a regime to foreign policy adventure. Catherine had more cause to fear peasant revolt than Nicholas I did, and Nicholas II was more threatened by general revolution than Alexander II or Alexander III. But Catherine and Nicholas II did not, on that account, become peaceful conservatives in foreign policy.

Besides, it would be wrong in principle to locate the main source of Russia's new moderation in foreign policy in the changed mood of her leaders. The wish to settle down, a genuine desire to enjoy peace and stability, is no doubt one necessary condition for a moderate foreign policy, but it is nowhere near a sufficient condition. The wars of the French Revolution and Napoleon certainly prove this. It is safe to say that by 1801—or at the latest by 1807—all the governments of Europe, including the French, were desperately eager for peace and stability, yet they were not to have it until after many more years of war on an unprecedented scale. It is too easy to blame this outcome solely on the blind ambition of Napoleon. He was indeed insatiable; but even had he been willing to stop, he had already gone too far by 1807 to allow any system of peace, any viable international order, to develop. The main source of international peace and stability is and always must be systemic rather than dispositional; what counts is less the disposition of leaders and peoples to seek peace than the existence and operation of a system—a stable network of rules and relationships between states—that enables statesmen effectively to seek peace and, even in a sense, compels them to promote it whether they want to or not. The primary difference between the pre-1815 and the post-1815 eras lies in the absence of a working international system in the former and its existence in the latter. Russia was restrained not mainly by her own moderate impulses, but by a viable international order she herself had helped to create.

Within that nineteenth century system, the chief restraints upon Russia came from her friends and allies. This is not a self-evident proposition; most British statesmen of the time, many historians since, would hold that a balance of power and the fear of a hostile coalition held Russia back. This view also is superficially plausible but misleading. A balance of power of sorts was established in 1814–15; Russia, like other states, recognized and endorsed the principle of peace based upon a just equilibrium among nations. However, the direct use of balance of power politics against Russia and the explicit attempts to create a hostile coalition against her (as Metternich tried without success to do in 1828–29, and England and France did with greater success in the Crimean War) always proved counterproductive in that these moves tended to break down the restraints on Russia, encouraging her to strike back in one of the many areas of Europe or Asia vulnerable to her pressure. Russia was restrained after 1815 less by the fear of arousing a hostile coalition against her than by the desire to gain and retain useful friends.

One can see this illustrated in the Polish–Saxon question at the Vienna Congress, the crisis that best marks the gradual change from expansionism to conservatism in Russian policy. What made Alexander decide in late December 1814, to compromise on his demand that Russia gain most of

Poland and Prussia all of Saxony was not really the fear of creating a hostile coalition; still less was it the threat of war. Alexander clearly began to yield even before he heard reports of a possible Austrian and British alliance with his former enemy France against Russia and Prussia (as actually happened on January 3, 1815), and he never did believe that Austria and Britain would really go to war over Poland and Saxony. What changed his mind was the potential loss of Austria and other German states as friends and allies, as the price Russia would pay for getting her maximum terms. This loss would destroy Alexander's hope of a general European alliance he could lead and of a settlement in Germany favorable to Russian interests. Thus, Alexander accepted a compromise, primarily at Prussia's expense, mainly to retain potential friends and allies and to sustain a general European alliance.

This compromise also identifies for us the most important institution of the nineteenth century system promoting Russian moderation. It was not the balance of power, nor the Vienna system of treaties, nor even the European Concert and its rules—though these all helped—but rather the so-called Holy Alliance. Popular history sees this partnership between Russia, Austria, and Prussia as a reactionary league against liberalism and revolution, which it was. But it was also—and most important—an instrument for managing the mutual dependence and rivalry existing among the allies themselves. Simply put, Russia, Prussia, and Austria were all simultaneously rivals and friends (a "friend" in international politics, meaning not a state that one likes, but a state that one needs, which is intimately involved with one's own welfare and with which one therefore wants to deal and get along on a permanent basis). Russia needed Austria and Prussia as friends and allies to provide her a military barrier to the West, to help defend the conservative political and social order, and to help manage the problems of Poland and Turkey. However, both Austria and Prussia had been Russia's enemies in the recent past; there was an existing Austro-Russian rivalry in the Balkans, and a potential Russo-Prussian one in the Baltic. If either German power, especially Prussia, defected to the British or French camp, Russia would be in trouble. Hence, Russia needed the alliance both to secure the help of these powers and manage their rivalry with her. Moreover, she needed to manage Austria's and Prussia's mutual friendship and rivalry with each other just as much as her direct relations with them. Simply put, Russia wanted Austria and Prussia, old enemies now forced to sleep in the same German bed, to be reasonably cooperative in running Germany—not too united, or Russia might be faced with the menace of a united Germany, but also not too hostile, or Germany would split up, becoming a prey to liberal and revolutionary impulses, and a Prusso-Austrian war might arise that would confront Russia with grave dangers. The best outcome was just enough tension to keep both powers needing Russia and soliciting her friendship. Thus, the Holy Alliance served and constrained Russia and her partners in various ways, locking them in mutual support and restraint.

This was not a routine choice or automatic development. Russia, like all powers, would have preferred to have the advantages of the Holy Alliance without its constraints. Bismarck once said with his typical cynicism that in every alliance there must be one horse and one rider, and he intended that Germany always be the rider. The crux of the Polish–Saxon crisis was Russia's attempt to make Austria, Prussia, and the rest of Germany the horses Russia would ride. After this experiment failed, however, Russia never repeated it, even though there were opportunities (in 1848–50 or in the 1860s) for her to try to recreate the situation in Germany so favorable to her in the eighteenth century—Prussia and Austria locked in bitter enmity, Germany torn apart between them, and Russia the *tertius gaudens*, the arbiter courted by all sides. Russia's policy was neither glorious nor successful in the eras of the 1848 revolutions and Bismarck's wars. Russian statesmen soon came to regret having been too pro-Austrian in the first and far too easily manipulated by Bismarck in the second. Nonetheless, Russia cannot be accused of trying to exploit the breakdown of the European order for selfish purposes; more than any other European power (Austria possibly excepted), she then stood for a European solution to the German question. Even after Bismarck's creation of a Prussian-dominated Germany, Russia was willing to restore the Holy Alliance in a new form, the so-called Three Emperors' League. This stance was not abandoned until Russia was convinced, with fair reason, that Holy Alliance ideas were only tools to be used against her by Austria, with German backing. The contribution the Holy Alliance in its various forms made to European peace is most apparent after its demise in the 1880s. It is no accident that World War I broke out as a quarrel between Russia and Austria, backed by Germany, over the Balkans. Once they could no longer coexist within an alliance, as distrustful friends, these three powers were virtually bound to become mortal enemies.

Besides the Holy Alliance, Russia was also restrained to some degree by her own ideology and the use that other powers could make of it. Russian ideology means here neither the official nationalism of Nicholas I nor Slavophil ideas and Panslav doctrines. None of these ever determined Russian foreign policy in this period, though they did exert influence at times. The central ideology of Russian foreign policy was a set of conservative internationalist beliefs shared by every tsar and Russian foreign minister from Alexander I and Nesselrode to Alexander III and Giers: monarchical solidarity, the sanctity of treaties, the right of the European Concert to supervise changes in them, and the existence of Europe as a community, a family of nations. Of course, Russia sometimes violated her own principles. But it is fair to say that no one clung to them longer or more faithfully than Russia, and that time and again other states were able to restrain Russia by appealing to and manipulating these principles.

Such an argument as this—that nineteenth century Russia was restrained mainly by her friends through a constraining alliance and through appeals to her conservative internationalist principles—would seem to make this historical theme utterly irrelevant to twentieth century conditions. Would anyone today hope to restrain the Soviet Union within a new Holy Alliance or manage it by appealing to its conservative internationalist principles?

No, not exactly. Obviously, the differences between the nineteenth and late-twentieth centuries are enormous, both in terms of Russia's power and position and in the nature of the prevailing international systems. Nor does any sensible historian suppose that history can supply exact analogies or direct prescriptions for current policy. He knows rather, as Carl Becker once said, that one of the main purposes of history is to free one from the tyranny of misleading historical analogies. To discard all historical analogies as inexact, however, is as foolish as to cling slavishly to a particular comparison.

The right objective is discriminating comparison, taking both similarities and differences equally seriously and looking for elements of general truth and applicability. There are such elements to be found in a comparison between nineteenth century and twentieth century Russia. Moreover, the analogy need not be useful solely in suggesting how one should deal with the Soviet Union now. Its main use might consist in showing us how the methods now in vogue for dealing with Russia have worked in the past and what problems and dangers may be associated with them. The analogy could also suggest ideas on how to prepare for the future—what methods of restraint might work with the Soviet Union at a time when present conditions have changed.

One major power in the nineteenth century was particularly unhappy with the Holy Alliance—Great Britain. (So was France much of the time, but her attitude was not so critical.) Some British leaders recognized the Alliance's stabilizing functions, but more commonly Britain denounced it and frequently tried to break it up. The reasons for this stand were entirely normal in international politics. The British reasoned that the Holy Alliance gave Russia too much security and influence, threatened the balance of power, endangered Turkey and other small states, and held back peaceful progress in Europe. In addition, if the Alliance were broken up, Britain could hope to extract concessions from one or more of its members or to form her own partnership with one of them, especially Russia herself. Finally, many British believed that the Holy Alliance encouraged Russia to expand outside Europe, a tendency that menaced the British Empire.

Thus, Britain's attitude is understandable. Nevertheless, in the long run the British policy was unwise. The restraints imposed on Russia and the German powers by the Holy Alliance served basic British interests in peace and stability as well as general European ones. Once the Holy Alliance disappeared, Britain proved quite incapable of managing European and Balkan affairs without it, and the war that started in Eastern Europe in 1914 immediately engulfed her also. Even in the shorter run, the British strategy of trying to break up the Alliance proved counterproductive. Each time the Holy Alliance broke down in the nineteenth century (1828–29, 1853–56, the 1860s, 1877–78, 1890 and after), its fall actually spurred Russian expansion in the Near and Middle East, Central Asia, and the Far East, mostly at Britain's expense.

This suggests a point so simple and familiar that it should be commonplace; but it needs emphasizing in an age of international politics dominated by ideas of balance of power, deterrence, and the reinforcement of antago-nistic alliances. Some sort of balance of power is necessary in any system of mutual restraints; it may have to be the main device if other restraints are not working. But pure balance of power policies never work safely or well and can easily make problems worse, destroying mutual restraints rather than promoting them. Hence, balance of power strategy and tactics must never be allowed to replace or suppress the superior method of international restraint through alliances between friends for the management of mutual interests and conflicts. Any government is restrained better and more safely by friends and allies than by opponents or enemies—the United States by its NATO allies and other friends, Israel by the United States and/or Egypt, radical Arab or Islamic states by watchful friends within the Arab and Islamic worlds.

BIBLIOGRAPHICAL NOTES

A wide-ranging interpretive essay like this cannot hope to demonstrate its argument point by point. What follows, therefore, is only an indication of some sources and suggestions for further reading, especially more recent books in Western languages.

Some works illustrating the character of Russian foreign policy before the Seven Years' War (1756–63) are: B. H. Sumner, *Peter the Great and the Ottoman Empire* (London, 1949); A. S. Donnelly, *The Russian Conquest of Bashkiria, 1552–1740* (New Haven, 1968); and Herbert Kaplan, *Russia and the Outbreak of the Seven Years' War* (Berkeley, 1968). Evidence of how difficult an ally eighteenth century Russia was is given by L. Jay Oliva, *Misalliance: A Study of French Policy in Russia during the Seven Years War* (New York, 1964). The best overall survey of Catherine II's for-eign policy (1762–96) is in Isabel de Madariaga, *Russia in the Age of Catherine the Great* (New Haven, 1981). There are useful essays in Marc Raeff, ed., *Catherine the Great. A Profile* (New York, 1975); important for special aspects are Isabel de Madariaga, *Britain, Russia, and the Armed Neutrality of 1780* (New Haven, 1962); Herbert Kaplan, *The First Partition of Poland* (New York, 1962); and Alan W. Fisher, *The Russian Annexation of the Crimea, 1772–1783* (Cambridge, 1970). Dietrich Gerhard, *England und der Aufstieg Russlands* (Munich, 1933), describes the vital economic aspects of Russia's expansionist drive in the eighteenth century, whereas David Ransel analyzes the domestic political background in *The Politics of Catherinian Russia* (New Haven, 1975).

The foreign policy of Catherine's successor, Tsar Paul, is now undergoing reinter-pretation; two recent works carrying over into the early reign of Alexander I are Norman E. Saul, *Russia and the Mediterranean, 1797–1807* (Chicago, 1970) and Hugh Ragsdale, *Detente in the Napoleonic Era* (Lawrence, KS., 1980). The best over-all view of Alexander's foreign policy is Patricia K. Grimsted, *The Foreign Ministers of Alexander* I (Berkeley, 1969). An unusually objective as well as scholarly Soviet treat-ment of one aspect of his policy is A. M. Stanislavskaia, *Rossiia i Gretsiia v kontse XVIII—nachale xix veka* (Moscow, 1976). George F. Jewsbury details Russia's trou-bles in annexing and administering Bessarabia, acquired in 1812, in *The Russian Annexation of Bessarabia, 1774–1828* (New York, 1977). For the absorption of Georgia, see David M. Lang, *The Last Years of the Georgian Monarchy, 1658–1832* (New York, 1957).

Many works deal with Alexander's religious conversion and his philanthropic ideals for a new European order. Francis Ley overstresses the religious-mystical elements in *Alexander ler et sa Sainte-Alliance 1811–1825* (Paris, 1975), whereas Jacques-Henri Pirenne overemphasizes the power-political aspects in *La Sainte Alliance*, 2 vols. (Neuchatel, 1946–49). The best overall treatment is Maurice Bourquin, *Histoire de la Sainte-Alliance* (Geneva, 1954). The basic change in Russian policy, which I claim occurred between 1812 and 1820, climaxing in the Polish–Saxon crisis, is best traced in the great Russian documentary collection *Vneshnaia Politika Rossii XIX i nachala XX veka*, published by the Soviet Ministry of Foreign Affairs (Ser. 1, 1801–17, 9 vols.; Moscow, 1960–74). Other vital sources are the *Sbornik* of the Imperial Russian Historical Society 148 vols. (St. Petersburg, 1867–1916), and A. A. Polovtsov, ed., *Corréspondance diplomatique des ambassadeurs et ministres de Russie en France . . . de 1814 à 1830*, 3 vols. (St. Petersburg, 1902–07). The Polish–Saxon issue itself is dealt with in E. V. Gulick, *Europe's Classical Balance of Power* (Ithaca, 1955). C. K. Webster, *The Foreign Policy of Castlereagh*, 2 vols. (London, 1925), Henry Kissinger, *A World Restored* (Boston, 1957), and Enno E. Kraehe, *Metternich's German Policy*, (Vol. 1; Princeton, 1963) deal with various reactions to the threat of Russian hegemony in Europe. For evidence of how Metternich managed Alexander in 1820–23, see Paul W. Schroeder, *Metternich's Diplomacy at Its Zenith, 1820–1823* (Austin, 1962). Russell H. Bartley shows the persistence, but also the decline and failure, of Russian activity in the Western Hemisphere in *Imperial Russia and the Struggle for Latin American Independence, 1808–1828* (Austin, TX., 1978).

Many recent works deal with various aspects of Nicholas Is domestic policies, but there is no comprehensive survey of his foreign policy. The most important development overall was the emergence of Anglo-Russian rivalry. Soviet historians blame Britain for it; British historians, although rightly rejecting Soviet charges of a British conspiratorial offensive, now recognize that Russia also had essentially defensive aims. See, for example, M. E. Yapp, *Strategies of British India* (Oxford, 1980); David Gillard, *The Struggle for Asia, 1828–1914* (London, 1977); and F. R. Bridge and Roger Bullen, *The Great Powers and the European State System 1815–1914* (London, 1980). Two works that together explain the change in British attitudes toward Russia are M. S. Anderson, *Britain's Discovery of Russia, 1553–1815* (New York, 1959) and J. H. Gleason, *The Genesis of Russophobia in England* (Cambridge, MA., 1950). Harold N. Ingle demonstrates the genuine pacific conservatism of Nicholas's foreign minister in his *Nesselrode and the Russian Rapprochment with Britain, 1836–1843* (Berkeley, 1976). Two works by R. F. Leslie deal with the Polish revolts of 1830 and 1863—*Polish Politics and the Revolution of November 1830* (London 1955), and *Reform and Insurrection in Russian Poland 1856–1865* (London, 1963).

Recent works on the diplomacy of the Crimean war (John S. Curtiss, *Russia's Crimean War* (Durham, NC, 1979); Paul W. Schroeder, *Austria, Great Britain and the Crimean War* (Ithaca, 1972); and Winfried Baumgart, *Der Friede von Paris* (Munich, 1972) show that Russia's blunders and miscalculations, rather than clear aggressive intent, got her into the war. Equally agreed is that her defeat sharply altered Russian policy in Europe and Asia. On Russia's policy in Europe, especially toward Germany, two works by W. E. Mosse, *The European Powers and the German Question, 1848–1871* (Cambridge, 1958) and *The Rise and Fall of the Crimean System, 1855–1871* (London, 1963) are useful, and Dietrich Beyrau, *Russische Orientpolitik und die Entstehung des Deutschen Kaiserreiches 1866 bis 1870/71* (Munich, 1974) is outstanding. On Russian imperialism, the best general work is

Dietrich Geyer, *Der russische Imperialisms* (Göttingen, 1977). Valuable individual studies are R. K. L. Quested, *The Expansion of Russia in East Asia, 1857–1860* (Kuala Lumpur, 1968); Firuz Kazemzadeh, *Russia and Britain in Persia, 1864–1914* (New Haven, 1968); N. A. Khalfin, *Russia's Policy in Central Asia, 1857–1868* (translated and abridged from the Russian original) (London, 1964); Richard A. Pierce, *Russian Central Asia, 1867–1917* (Berkeley, 1960); and Seymour Becker, *Russia's Protectorates in Central Asia: Bukhara and Khiva, 1865–1924* (Cambridge, MA., 1968). Two valuable interpretive essays are B. H. Sumner, "Tsardom and Imperialism in the Far East and Middle East, 1880–1914," *Proceedings of the British Academy*, 27 (1941), 25–65, and Peter Morris, "The Russians in Central Asia, 1870–1885," *Slavonic and East European Review*, 53 (1975), 521–38.

On Russian policy in Europe after 1871, besides Geyer, William L. Langer's classic studies, *European Alliances and Alignments, 1871–1890* (New York, 1939), and *The Diplomacy of Imperialism, 1890–1902*, 2 vols. 2nd ed. (New York, 1956) remain useful, as does A. J. P. Taylor, *The Struggle for Mastery in Europe 1848–1918* (Oxford, 1954). Werner Markert, ed., *Deutsch-russische Beziehungen von Bismarck bis zur Gegenwart* (Stuttgart, 1964) discusses German–Russian relations in general, whereas George F. Kennan, *The Decline of Bismarck's European Order* (Princeton, 1979) discloses the micro-history of Russia's alienation from Germany and rapprochement with France. On Russia in the Eastern Crisis of 1875–79, the best work remains B. H. Sumner, *Russia and the Balkans 1870–1880* (Oxford, 1937), but G. H. Rupp, *A Wavering Friendship: Russia and Austria, 1876–1878* (Cambridge, MA., 1941) and Bruce Waller, *Bismarck at the Crossroads* (London, 1974) are also helpful. On the ideology and internal development of Pan-Slavism, see Michael B. Petrovich, *The Emergence of Russian Panslavism, 1856–1870* (New York, 1956); for its impact on Russian policy, such as it was, see David Mackenzie, *The Serbs and Russian Panslavism, 1875–1878* (Ithaca, 1967), and T. A. Meininger, *Ignatiev and the Establishment of the Bulgarian Exarchate 1864–1872* (Madison, 1970). Charles Jelavich's *Tsarist Russia and Balkan Nationalism* (Berkeley, 1958) details the heavy-handed blunders that got Russia into trouble over Bulgaria in the 1880s.

On the Russo-Japanese War of 1904–05, which most clearly marks a turn to reckless imperialism, the background is described by George A. Lensen, *The Russian Push toward Japan* (Princeton, 1959), and in his edited work, *Russia's Eastward Expansion* (Englewood Cliffs, 1964). The origins of the war are best discussed in A. M. Malozemoff, *Russian Far Eastern Policy, 1881–1904* (Berkeley, 1958), and Shumpei Okamoto, *The Japanese Oligarchy and the Russo-Japanese War* (New York, 1970). For the outcome, see John A. White, *The Diplomacy of the Russo-Japanese War* (Princeton, 1964).

Though twentieth century Russian and Soviet policy is beyond our purview, let me recommend three works: Adam Ulam, *Expansion and Coexistence: Soviet Foreign Policy, 1917–73* (2nd ed., New York, 1973) for a general history; Vojtech Mastny, *Russia's Road to the Cold War, 1941–1945* (New York, 1979) for the impact of World War II; and Hélène Carrère d'Encausse, *L'Empire Eclaté* (Paris, 1978), on the internal and imperial problems of the USSR today.

Finally, a few surveys and interpretations. Barbara Jelavich, *A Century of Russian Foreign Policy 1814–1914* (Philadelphia, 1964) is a good compact overview, stronger on Europe than elsewhere. The official Soviet history of international relations is V. P. Potemkin, ed., *Histoire de la diplomatic* 3 vols. (Paris, 1946–47). On the

Eastern Question, usually the central aspect of Russian foreign policy, see M. S. Anderson, *The Eastern Question 1774–1923* (London, 1966). Two stimulating attempts to interpret the overall character of the Russian Empire are Reinhard Wittram, "Das russische Imperium und sein Gestaltwandel," *Historische Zeitschrift*, 187 (1959), 568–93, and Alain Besancon, "L'empire russe et la domination sovie-tique," in Maurice Duverger, ed., *Le Concept d'Empire* (Paris, 1980), 365–78. For a collection of essays comparing Imperial Russian and Soviet policy (though they tend to stress too much the continuity of expansion), see Ivo J. Lederer, ed., *Russian Foreign Policy* (New Haven, 1962).

II

WORLD WAR I

World War I as Galloping Gertie:
A Reply to Joachim Remak

In a recent article, Joachim Remak argues that modern research on the origins of World War I, led by Fritz Fischer and his students, has distorted our view while expanding our knowledge. The search for more profound causes of the war has tended, in Remak's phrase, to make us miss the forest for the roots. World War I was really the Third Balkan War. It arose from the last of a long series of local Austro-Serbian quarrels, none of which had led to war before; it involved a series of political maneuvers and gambles typical of the great power politics of that time, maneuvers that previously had not issued in general conflict. Only the particular events of 1914 caused this particular quarrel and this diplomatic gamble to end in world war.[1]

There is much truth in this familiar view, and considerable point to Remak's criticism of an overly determinist interpretation of 1914. Yet his version appears to me as unsatisfactory as those he criticizes. This essay, without claiming to exhaust the literature or to say anything brand new,[2] will suggest another way to look at the origins of the war, and propose a view different from Remak's, Fischer's,[3] Arno Mayer's,[4] and others now current.

To start with Fischer: most of what he says about Germany and her bid for world power is true. Many of his formulations and emphases are open to challenge. He is too hard on Bethmann-Hollweg and misinterprets the motives of his crucial decision in 1914.[5] He often underestimates the importance and persistence of concerns other than *Weltpolitik* in German policy, and he tends to blur the difference between Germany's prewar and wartime goals in emphasizing their continuity. But these points do not destroy his main argument. From 1890 on, Germany did pursue world power. This bid arose from deep roots within Germany's economic, political, and social structures. Once the war broke out, world power became Germany's essential goal. Fischer and his students have made the old apologias for German policy impossible.

The Journal of Modern History, 44, 2 (September, 1972), 319–44. Copyright © (1972), The University of Chicago Press. All rights reserved. Used by permission of the publisher.

The difficulty arises in accepting the notion, implicit in all of Fischer's work and explicitly drawn by many historians as the chief lesson of it, that Germany's bid for world power was the *causa causans*, the central driving force behind the war. Fischer never demonstrates this convincingly. His case is far more informative, compelling, and reliable on Germany's policy and national character than on the origins of the war. He may be able to tell us what Germany was like without worrying much about the policies of other powers (although even here the comparative dimension is lacking). But he cannot assume, as he constantly does, that German policy was decisive for other powers without a great deal more investigation than he has done. Moreover, Fischer's own principle of *der Primat der Innenpolitik* should have led him to assume that other powers would, like Germany, act mainly from their own indigenous drives, rather than mainly react to what Germany did, as he depicts them doing.

More important, the whole attempt to find a *causa causans* behind the multiplicity of contributing factors is misconceived. It is like looking for *the* driving force behind the French or Russian Revolutions, or the Reformation, or the American Civil War. Immediately, one encounters a plethora of "causes" far more than sufficient to account for the phenomenon one wishes to explain, clearly connected with it, and yet not "sufficient" in the sense that any set of them logically implies what occurred. The fact that so many plausible explanations for the outbreak of the war have been advanced over the years indicates on the one hand that it was massively overdetermined, and on the other that no effort to analyze the causal factors involved can ever fully succeed. When on top of earlier valid arguments Fischer and his disciples insist that Germany's bid for world power was really behind it all, when Marxist historians insist that the war was the inevitable outcome of monopolistic capitalist imperialism, when Arno Mayer proposes domestic political and social unrest and the dynamics of counterrevolution as decisive, and when Peter Loewenberg argues in reply that this role belongs to the fundamental drives revealed by psychodynamic theory,[6] one begins to suspect that all these approaches, however much valuable information and insight they may provide, cannot deliver what they promise. Not only is an attempt to reduce or subordinate the various contributing factors to some fundamental cause methodologically very dubious,[7] but also, even if it worked—even if one managed to fit all the contributing factors into a scheme of causal priority through factor analysis—this would still not give the *causa causans*. For in the breakdown of a system of relations such as occurred in 1914 as a result of various intertwined and interacting forces, the system itself enters into the work of destruction. In the process wittily described by Hexter as "Galloping Gertie,"[8] the very devices built into a system to keep it stable and operative under stress, subjected to intolerable pressures, generate forces of their own that cause the system to destroy itself. World War I seems to me clearly a case of "Galloping Gertie." Witness how statesmen and military leaders everywhere in 1914, especially in the Central Powers, felt themselves to be in the grip of uncontrollable forces. They sensed that their calculations were all

futile and that what their actions would finally produce lay beyond all calcu-
lation. Remak, appreciating this fact and rejecting the search for a *causa causans*, rightly insists that the answer must lie in the narrative and in analysis within it. But his particular answer to the question, "Why World War I?"
is similarly misleading. True, it required certain contingent events to start a
war in 1914; but this does not mean the whole development was purely
contingent, with nothing inevitable about it. Europe's frequent escapes from
crises before 1914 do not indicate the possibility that she could have continued
to avoid war indefinitely; they rather indicate a general systemic crisis, an
approaching breakdown. Remak's view of July 1914 as the one gamble that
did not succeed overlooks the fact that those who gambled in Germany and
Austria did not expect to succeed in avoiding general war.

Thus the search for the fundamental cause of World War I is futile, while
the argument that the war simply happened is unhelpful. Is there no exit
from the cul-de-sac? A different question may help: not "Why World I?" but
"Why not?" War was still the *ultima ratio regum*. World War I was a normal
development in international relations; events had been building toward it
for a long time. There is no need to explain it as a deviation from the norm.
In this sense, the question "Why not?" answers the question "Why?"

More important, it points to what is unexpected about the war and needs
explanation: its long postponement. Why not until 1914? This question
clearly needs answering in regard to Austria. Historians continue to exercise
themselves over why the Austrian Monarchy risked its own destruction by
insisting on punishing Serbia. The favorite (and very unsatisfactory) answer
is that this was the kind of futile, absurd action to be expected from so decrepit
an empire with so inept a ruling class. In fact, the problem is nonexistent.
Preventive wars, even risky preventive wars, are not extreme anomalies
in politics, the sign of the bankruptcy of policy. They are a normal, even
common, tool of statecraft, right down to our own day. British history, for
example, is full of them; the British Empire was founded and sustained in
great part by a series of preventive and preemptive wars and conquests. As
for the particular decision of June 1914, the evidence is plain that Berchtold,
although often wavering, resisted the idea of a punitive war on Serbia until
the assassination. With the death of Francis Ferdinand, leader of the peace
party, Berchtold simultaneously ran out of alternatives, arguments, and support for any other policy, and gave in.[9] The real problem is to explain why
Austria waited so long and tried so many other futile devices to stop the
steady deterioration of her Balkan and great power position before resorting
to force. The idea of eliminating Serbia as a political factor by conquest,
occupation, or preventive war was at least sixty years old, and constantly
advanced. For over two centuries Austria had lived under the brooding
threat of Russian encirclement in the south.[10] Why did she act only in the
desperate situation of 1914, with all alternatives exhausted?

A similar question arises with Germany. Why, with her powerful impulse
toward *Weltpolitik*, did she fail to resort to war under favorable circumstances
in 1905, or 1908–09, or even 1911, and try it only in 1914, when military

and political leaders alike recognized the gambling nature of the enterprise? The same question, What held her back? applies to Europe in general. Fischer, Mayer, and the Marxists insist that the war did not just happen, but was caused. This is true, but so is the converse. Until 1914 peace did not just happen, but was caused. The wars that did not occur seem to me harder to explain than the one that did. Arno Mayer contends that we know all we need to about the European system; we lack an adequate analysis of the domestic sources of the violence that destroyed it. I disagree. We know more than we need to (although more knowledge of course is always possible and valuable) to understand in general what was impelling Europe to destruction. We neither fully understand nor appreciate the restraints holding her back, and why these gave way only in 1914.

This essay therefore deals with the question, Why not until 1914? It proposes to account for the critical difference between the system's surviving the challenges facing it and its failing to do so, by pointing to a vital element of stability within the system which in 1914 finally became destructive and generated the collapse of the system. That element, it will surprise no one to hear, was Austria-Hungary. The essay will also, briefly and sketchily, make a case for a point less trite and obvious: that a chief source of the pressures turning Austria from a stabilizing into a destructive member of the system, besides her own internal debility and Germany's policy for becoming a world power, was Britain's policy for remaining one.

The most important change in European politics after 1890, as everyone knows, was that Germany lost control of the system. Who gained the initiative she lost? For a short time, Britain seemed to; but the long-range gainers were France and Russia. Their alliance, giving them greater security in Europe, freed them to pursue world policy. Manchuria, China, Indochina and Siam, Persia, Central Asia, the Mediterranean, the Senegal, the Niger, the Congo, and the Upper Nile were the areas where Russian and French pressures were brought to bear. In every case, Britain was made to feel it.

The challenge to Britain's world leadership, coinciding with Germany's loss of control of the European system, helped conceal the latter phenomenon from the Germans themselves and contributed to their persistent belief that they could play the game of two irons in the fire and that eventually Britain would have to seek German help. Part of the challenge to Britain came from German and American industrial and commercial competition, but there was not much to be done about this. Countermeasures like imperial tariffs and economic union were likely to hurt Britain and anger the dominions rather than hamper her rivals. Besides, the main threat was to the security of the empire, not to trade, and this danger stemmed from France and Russia. Far from threatening the British Empire in the 1890s, Germany hovered about Britain like an opportunistic moneylender, ready to offer her services at exorbitant rates and hoping for a favorable chance to buy into the firm. France and Russia competed directly with Britain and tried to drive her out of key positions. Isolated and foolish challenges like Fashoda could be faced down, but the fundamental vulnerability of Britain's position in Egypt,

South Africa, the Straits, Persia, the Persian Gulf, the Far East, India, and India's Northwest Frontier oppressed the British daily. Added to this was the rise of the United States to world power and the danger of native unrest and risings in Egypt, South Africa, Ireland, and above all India. The challenges could doubtless be met, but not by the old policy, and also not by great new expenditures or tests of strength. The empire had always been acquired and maintained on the cheap, and Parliament required that it be kept so, especially now that new demands for welfare measures were being added to the old Liberal and Radical calls for cuts in military spending. As for tests of strength, the Boer War convinced most Englishmen of the dangers of isolation and the severe limits to British resources for overseas ventures.

It was therefore inevitable that Britain would meet her new problems mainly by trying to devolve some of her imperial burdens on others (the dominions or other friendly powers), and by trying to come to terms with her opponents. Bowing out gracefully in favor of the United States in the Western Hemisphere was easy and relatively painless; equally natural was the limited alliance with Japan.[12] But the main answer to Britain's difficulties would have to be a deal with her chief opponents, France and Russia. Far from representing a great break in British tradition, such a rapprochement was the obvious step for Britain, a move for which there was ample precedent and tradition throughout the nineteenth century. What held it up was not British reluctance to break with splendid isolation—Salisbury, the great defender of this tradition, had been looking for chances to come to terms with France and Russia all through the 1890s.[13] It was the refusal of France and Russia to make a deal on terms acceptable to Britain, counting as they did on British vulnerability to make her ultimately come to them. It took more than a year after Fashoda fully to convince Delcassé that there was no way to get Britain out of Egypt, and five years to be ready to admit it openly. Even then the British made concessions to France over Morocco which her business community there did not like at all.[14] As for Russia, only military defeat and revolution in 1904–05, plus an expanded Anglo-Japanese alliance, finally convinced her that she must forget about putting pressure on Britain in Afghanistan. Even then, the Russians proved difficult to deal with in Persia before and after 1907.[15]

This suggests that there is no need to bring in the German menace to explain Britain's rapprochement with France and Russia. The Triple Entente was a natural development explicable purely in terms of the needs and aims of the three powers—especially Britain. Her friendships with France and Russia were ends in themselves, vital for her imperial interests, and not means of checking Germany, and remained so. Rather than seeking friendly agreements with France and Russia because of the German threat, Britain tended to see Germany as a threat because of the agreements she sought and obtained from France and Russia. Repeatedly, before the war British spokesmen's main complaint against Germany was that she resented British agreements with other powers and tried to break them up. The great British fear was that Germany might lure France and Russia into her camp, leaving Britain isolated.[16]

"But you forget three things," one might reply. "Britain did not approach France and Russia until she had first attempted an alliance with Germany and failed. The agreements with France and Russia were strictly extra-European and colonial in nature, and not directed against Germany; only Germany's dangerous conduct made them into a coalition against Germany. Above all, it was Germany's direct, overt, and formidable naval challenge which forced Britain to draw close to France and cooperate with Russia in Europe."

The first point errs on the facts. The story of a missed opportunity for an Anglo-German alliance in 1898–1901 is a myth, as Gerhard Ritter argued long ago.[17] Britain never really tried for it or wanted it. Naturally she would have liked to get Germany to defend British interests for nothing, but a mutual tie was never seriously in question. There was no basis for an alliance. Lord Curzon pointed out in 1901 that the German navy was too weak to be of much help to Britain and the army was not available where Britain needed it.[18] Frances Bertie put the general political case against an alliance: it would be useful only in the extreme case of a losing British war against France and Russia, but such a war would compel Germany in her own interests to help Britain, alliance or no. Tied to Germany, Britain would lose her freedom to conduct world policy and to hold and exploit the balance between rival Continental powers.[19] Even Lansdowne quickly saw that a German alliance would draw French and Russian antagonism onto Britain, costing her the desired rapprochement with the Dual Alliance.[20]

As for British cooperation with Germany, the only possible basis for this was the one laboriously erected by Bismarck and grudgingly accepted by Salisbury in the Near Eastern Triplice of 1887: British cooperation with Austria and Italy to uphold the Near Eastern status quo.[21] This was undermined in 1893 by the Admiralty's conclusion that the fleet could no longer defend Constantinople against Russia while a French fleet operated from Toulon in Britain's rear. Once the British government accepted this conclusion, it eliminated any possibility of serious support for Austria in the Balkans, and thus of cooperation between Germany and Britain on the Continent. The only way now open for Britain in the long run to defend her Near Eastern interests, and the only one seriously pursued, was a deal with Russia.[22] It took somewhat longer for Britain to conclude that Italy was no real help in the contest with France over East Africa, but after 1898 she also became largely superfluous.

What happened in China, where Britain and Germany supposedly came closest to real partnership only to have Germany back out, again illustrates the impossibility of an alliance. Salisbury never designed or intended the Anglo-German agreement of October 1900 to stop Russia in China. He wanted it to hold Germany back, keeping her out of the British sphere in the Yangtze, which she hoped to penetrate, while Salisbury negotiated what he really desired, an agreement over spheres of influence with Russia. When Prince Bülow told the *Reichstag* in March 1901 that Germany was not obliged to oppose Russia in Manchuria and would not do so, he merely expressed bluntly the letter and spirit of the 1900 agreement. Naturally and typically, when Lansdowne's and Chamberlain's illusions were pricked, Lansdowne promptly turned to Japan, while Chamberlain became not long after the most strident Germanophobe in the Cabinet.[23]

The second point, that Britain's colonial agreements were not directed against Germany, but only became so because of Germany's conduct, is true in the sense that Britain did not want to encircle Germany but to protect her empire; this is precisely my contention. It also touches on an important truth, that Germany was not in fact the prime target of Entente diplomacy—of which more later. But what about France's and Russia's purposes in these colonial agreements? Whether Delcassé's policy of trying to encircle and isolate Germany was mainly a reaction to German moves[24] or the product of his own ambitions for France (undoubtedly it was both), his whole program, especially as it reached a climax in Morocco, was so overtly and rashly anti-German that most of his colleagues, including some ardent colonialists, warned him against it.[25] The British knew quite well about this aspect of French policy. They chose to accept the agreement with France for their own reasons and to let Germany worry about the European consequences. As for the Anglo-Russian Convention of 1907, its fundamental presumption was that Britain would pay Russia for cooperation in Central Asia by helping the Russians improve their position in Europe, especially in the Balkans and the Straits—directly at Turkey's and Austria's expense, indirectly at Germany's. The British knew that Russia had been exerting pressure on India in great part in order to make Britain subservient to Russian policy in Europe, and they had long been contemplating using the Balkans and the Straits as lures for Russia.[26]

It becomes even more disingenuous to claim that Britain's ententes were not intended to apply to Europe or to hurt Germany when one sees how they were used. From 1904 on, the British understood perfectly that the price of their friendships with France and Russia was diplomatic and moral support for these powers in their disputes with Germany and Austria. They gave that support even when, as often happened, they strongly disapproved of French or Russian policy. Germany and Austria, and France and Russia, respectively, being tied by firm alliances, could afford sometimes to restrain their partners and deny them diplomatic support. Britain, refusing all military commitments, had to give her friends moral support more unstintingly or risk seeing them go into the other camp.

Furthermore, even if Germany's encirclement was not a British aim, the "circling out" of Germany, her exclusion from world politics and empire, *was* Britain's goal in good measure. Grey and others made it clear time and again that the purpose of Britain's ententes, next to keeping France and Russia friendly, was to deter Germany from "interfering" and "bullying" in Asia or Africa, to keep her out of areas like Persia where she had no real business, to stop the Baghdad Railway, to neutralize the *baton égyptien*, and to teach Germany that she had to settle all imperial questions *à quatre*, before a united front of Entente powers. The *Auskreisung*, which Fischer portrays as the result of German aggressiveness and blunders, was precisely the outcome British diplomacy was bent on achieving.

As to Germany's naval challenge, all the facts, old and new, can be freely acknowledged.[27] There was a great German naval program aimed directly at Britain and designed to promote *Weltpolitik*. It undoubtedly became ultimately Britain's greatest naval danger (after the Franco-Russian danger faded away) and the foremost element in Anglo-German rivalry. No improvement could come in Anglo-German relations without some naval settlement. But it is one thing to see the naval challenge as a real, serious issue, sufficient to itself to compel Britain to be on guard against Germany. It is quite another to argue that it primarily shaped British policy toward Germany, or that an end to the naval race would have significantly changed British policy. The latter assumptions remain unproved. The German naval challenge did not cause the revolution in Britain's political alignments, and an end to the naval race would not overturn them. The German Navy was not really taken seriously by either the government or the Admiralty until 1906–07, by which time the Entente Cordiale was a fixture in British policy and the search for an agreement with Russia had long been under way. Nor will the naval challenge do to explain the rise of Germanophobia in Britain. The anti-Germans were clearly gaining control of the Foreign Office by 1901; popular hatred of Germany was ripe with the Kruger Telegram and the Boer War. Anti-German spokesmen in the government and the press did not need the German Navy for their propaganda, though they exploited it fully. They centered their fire on the general danger of German power, the evil of Prussian militarism, and the German bullying and blackmail of Britain since the 1880s.[28]

Nor should one ignore the fact that Germany's naval challenge was the only one among the many threats facing Britain which the British always knew they could beat. The realignment of British foreign policy came at a time when she enjoyed almost unprecedented naval superiority. The recognition in 1906–07 that Germany was now the only possible naval foe greatly improved, not worsened, Britain's strategic position; it facilitated the concentration of the fleet in home waters more than it forced it. Even the Tories, always alert for any sign of naval unpreparedness, agreed in 1905–06 that naval spending could be reduced.[29] British publicists and a hysterical public might dream of a German invasion; Sir John Fischer dreamed of Copenhagening the German fleet and, like his successor, wanted to land 100,000 men on Germany's Baltic coast in case of war.[30] Contrast the British confidence that they would be able to drive Germany from the high seas, destroy her commerce, and conquer her colonies with relative ease, with British pessimism on other scores—the knowledge that they could not hope to match American naval strength in the western Atlantic or Japanese in the Far East, and that the only long-range answers to the problems of Egypt and India were deals with France and Russia. Of course the British were angered by Germany's naval challenge; it was expensive, gratuitous, and worrisome. But they never doubted they could meet it; it had its domestic and foreign policy uses; it was much easier to get money voted for ships than for men and supplies to defend the Northwest Frontier. All in all, it was a price Britain was willing to pay for the friendship of Russia and France, although she would have preferred not to pay at all.

Above all, no naval agreement would have ended Anglo-German rivalry or caused Britain to abandon the anti-German coalition. To be sure, Germany demanded an unacceptable price for a naval agreement, Britain's promise of neutrality in Continental war. But then Britain was never willing to pay for a naval agreement, except possibly with the poisoned fruit of a colonial agreement at Portugal's or Belgium's expense.[31] If a naval agreement were concluded, the British would say, the improved atmosphere and friendly feelings it would produce would facilitate future amicable agreements on subjects of mutual interest—which is diplomatic language for "No concessions." In fact, Nicolson, Hardinge, Crowe, and other influential foreign policy leaders were deathly afraid of a naval agreement. As Hardinge argued, the Russians "must not think for a moment that we want to improve our relations with Germany at their expense. We have no pending questions with Germany, except that of naval construction, while our whole future in Asia is bound up with the necessity of maintaining the best and most friendly relations with Russia. We cannot afford to sacrifice in any way our entente with Russia—even for the sake of a reduced naval programme."[32] Grey constantly reassured France and Russia that no agreement with Germany, naval or other, would disturb Britain's existing friendships, and he meant it.

If one needs further evidence that an end to the naval threat would not change Britain's basic policy toward Germany, the secret Anglo-Russian naval talks of June 1914 over cooperation in the Baltic and the Mediterranean supply it. Perhaps Egmont Zechlin makes too much of the impact of these talks on German policy in 1914,[33] but the point here is what they show of British policy. Britain agreed to these talks, it must be remembered, after the naval race had ended on terms favorable to her, after Germany had cooperated with her during the Balkan Wars, and while agreements with Germany over the Portuguese colonies and the Baghdad Railway were in their final stages. British writers argue that the talks meant nothing to Britain. Since her naval authorities had recently concluded that the Royal Navy would not be able to penetrate into the Baltic in case of war anyway, the conversations would lead to nothing, and were merely a political sop to Russia.[34] But that is precisely the point. At a moment when better relations with Germany seemed uniquely possible, and when Grey believed such relations would be vital to prevent war over the Balkans, Britain was willing to destroy this hope (for these talks, like the similar ones with France, had little chance to remain secret and did not), to risk creating a grave new strain with Germany, to promote Russo-French hopes and German fears of a full Anglo-French-Russian alliance, and to deliver the best possible propaganda to navalists in Germany for resuming the naval race—all in order to avoid disappointing the Russians. This marks a high point in the British appeasement of Russia that had been going on for fifteen years, and proves further that the *raison d'etre* of British policy was her ententes with France and Russia, regardless of what Germany did, just as Germany was determined to try for world power regardless of what Britain did, and that rivalry with Germany was a price Britain was willing to pay for the sake of these ententes.

"Very well," someone will say, "what of it? Britain was simply playing the game by the normal rules. Was she supposed to have appeased Germany instead? What possible concession would have done any good? In any case the anti-German coalition Britain joined was a loose, defensive one which never would have caused war unless Germany tried to break it by force, which she did. Far from refuting the Fischer thesis, you have made it more plausible. Faced with the impossibility of achieving world power and standing by peaceful means, Germany chose war. Rather than condemning British policy, you vindicate it. For whatever her motives (and what power ever acts for motives other than self-interest?), Britain was preserving the European balance of power against the unmistakable threat of German domination. That this defense was desperately needed, two world wars would seem to give adequate proof."

The argument is tenable, provided its basic premises are accepted. If Germany's main activity was her pursuit of world power; if, further, the great problem for Europe was how to cope with Germany's growing power; if the main aim of British policy, whatever its ulterior motives, was to preserve a balance of power in Europe, and the chief effect of British policy was to restrain German ambitions, then British policy was justified regardless of its motives and even of its outcome. In pursuing her own interests, Britain was also upholding the best interests of Europe as a whole, and of peace.

But in fact the premises are unsound. Of course Germany played world policy; so did every other power that could, and some that could not. The point is how Germany played it. Somehow Fischer never quite succeeds in explaining the contrast between the remarkable growth of Germany's power and wealth and her uniform failure to translate that power into corresponding diplomatic, political, and territorial gains. Even a small power like Belgium, or a would-be great power like Italy, could emerge from the imperialist scramble with impressive gains; Portugal and Holland could consolidate their possessions while hungry great powers looked on. But Germany ended up with little more than Bismarck had already gained in 1884–85, and this at the cost of weakened alliances and a ruined European position. It will not do to explain this failure simply by German aggressiveness and blunders. Who could be more aggressive and commit more blunders than Imperial Russia? Yet she survived a disastrous war, revolution, and bankruptcy, and emerged by 1914 with her alliances stronger than ever and her expansion once again under way. Nor will it do to cite Germany's inconsistency, her repeated failure to know what she really wanted.[35] For the point is that no matter what Germany tried, she lost. She lost ground in Morocco when she remained passive and waited for France to come to her; she lost ground when she tried standing up for the principle of the open door; and she lost further ground when she tried to pound her fist on the table and demand compensations. Whether she tried to challenge Britain or France or Russia, or (as she did repeatedly) tried to win their friendship, she always finally succeeded in tightening the Entente against her.

The main reason for Germany's failure is not ineptness and aggressiveness, or her late start in *Weltpolitik*, or even unfavorable geography, although these are involved. It is that Germany could not pursue *Weltpolitik* all out. Each of the Entente powers could carry on a world policy without directly overthrowing the European system (although their imperialism indirectly undermined it). They could even, as the British did, indulge in the flattering belief that *their* world policy sustained the European system and made it work. But an unrestrained *Weltpolitik* by Germany, as the Germans were forced to recognize, was bound to isolate her and destroy the system upon which she had to rely for security as much as upon her army. Thus the exigencies of Continental policy repeatedly imposed themselves upon Germany and restrained her.

This explains what most needs explaining about prewar German policy. The problem is not, as is often imagined, one of accounting for her reckless conduct in terms of her aggressive, imperialist character and aims. It is one of accounting for the surprising moderation of German policy until 1914, in view of her aggressive character and aims. It is clear that the Entente powers were counting upon Germany's desire for peace and exploiting it; even Germanophobes like Eyre Crowe insisted that she would back down before a firm front. The restraints lay, of course, not in Germany's policy or character or the supposed peace party at Berlin, but in the position and role the system forced upon her—which made it all the more important for the Entente not to overstrain the system holding her back.

The contradiction between what Germany wanted to do and what she dared do and was obliged to do accounts in turn for the erratic, uncoordinated character of German world policy, its inability to settle on clear goals and carry them through, the constant initiatives leading nowhere, the frequent changes in mid-course. It is commonly said that after 1890 Germany played the game of international politics like a plunger on the stock market, always looking for quick short-term gains. The truth is worse than this. Germany played it like a plunger looking for quick gains without making any investments, a gambler trying to win without betting. The Germans were always hoping to be paid for doing nothing, merely for being where they were; expecting to be feared and to have their interests respected because of the power they possessed but dared not exert. They wanted Britain to pay them in Africa for the trouble Germany refrained from causing Britain with the Boers. They wanted Russia to pay for benevolent German neutrality during the Russo-Japanese war, and Britain and Japan to pay for plain German neutrality during the same war. Russia and Britain were supposed to do something for Germany on account of her not penetrating Persia, and France likewise if Germany did not cause more difficulty over Morocco. The British ought to concede Germany something if she stopped building more ships. Disappointed, the Germans wondered with querulous self-pity why everyone was against them—the same mood they had often expressed before unification,[36] and which would become the national disease after 1918.

Of course German restraint was not worthless to other powers; often it was invaluable. Russia was extremely lucky to have Germany and Austria-Hungary covering her rear in 1904–05, and the Russians knew it. But no one pays for such services when they can be had for nothing, especially since it was not too hard to see that the real reason why Germany refrained from causing more trouble was that she dared not do so. Like it or not, she was bound to her alliances and to her central European position. Even Italy had more freedom for *Weltpolitik* than she, and used it. For the Entente powers and Italy, alliances were primarily associations for profit; for Germany and Austria, they were necessarily associations for security.[37]

Nor can one agree without serious reservations even to the universal assumption that British policy was directed toward maintaining a European balance of power. Of course it was in one sense: Britain wanted to keep Germany from dominating the Continent by either overpowering France and Russia or luring them into her camp. This was entirely legitimate and necessary, but it alone is not enough to make Britain's a real balance of power policy. For, quite apart from some general reservations one may have about the whole character of British equilibrist thought,[38] the important point is that the British neither recognized nor did anything about the most critical threat to the European balance after 1900, but helped make it much worse. The immediate threat to the balance in 1914 was not German power. That danger existed, but it was under control, so far as it could be by peaceful means. The impression everywhere in Europe was that the Entente powers, especially Russia, were gaining the upper hand.[39] The greater danger stemmed not from German or Russian power but from Austrian weakness. One of the few incontestable points in balance of power theory is that preserving the system means preserving all the essential actors in it. Equally obvious, nothing is more likely to occasion a major war than a threat to the existence or great power status of an essential actor. Whatever the underlying causes of the nineteenth century European wars may have been, they were all touched off by a violent reaction from some declining or threatened essential actor to a menace to its existence, essential interests, or prestige. This was true of Turkey in 1853, Austria in 1859 and 1866, France in 1870, and Austria in 1914. Long before 1914 it was obvious that Austria's existence was threatened. Everyone saw her as the next sick man of Europe after Turkey. The British virtually wrote off Austria as a great power by the mid-1890s. In 1899 Delcassé tried to reach agreements with Russia and Italy in the expectation of her impending demise. From 1908 on almost everyone anticipated that the long-awaited general war would probably arise over a Russo-Austrian quarrel involving Serbia. From 1912 on the Russians and Serbs repeatedly told their Western friends that Austria's collapse was imminent, and that they intended to have the lion's share of the remains.[40]

Yet Britain's "balance of power" policy entirely ignored this immediate danger, and served actually to increase the threat from Germany as well. Germany ultimately might well have gone to war for world power (although she passed up chances earlier); but she was virtually bound to accept war, even provoke it, rather than let Austria go under and thus lose her last reliable ally. This was not a matter of Germany's ambitions, but of her vital interests, as the British well knew.

Once again, even if this trite contention is true, what of it? Was Britain to blame if Austria in 1914 decided to commit suicide out of fear of death, and Germany decided to join her, or rather pushed her into it? Were the Entente Powers supposed to sacrifice their interests to save a rival power from suc-cumbing to its own internal weaknesses?

As it happens, the theoretical answer to both these rhetorical questions is yes. A real balance of power policy would have required from the Entente precisely such a policy of restraint for themselves and controlled support for Austria, just as maintaining the Near Eastern balance had always required the powers to support Turkey, not exploiting her weaknesses or seeking individ-ual gains. It indicates the inherent contradictions of balance of power poli-tics that the actions it promotes, which its proponents consider normal and natural, actually serve to undermine the balance rather than maintain it. But there is a practical answer more important than the theoretical one. The threat to Austria's existence, which I would argue was primarily international rather than internal in character, was a product in great part of Entente pol-icy. As a result of the preoccupation of diplomatic historians with motives and aims instead of effects, both German and Entente policies have always been discussed almost exclusively in terms of the German problem, when in fact their effects were far greater on the Austrian problem. The best answer to the German encirclement myth is not that Entente policy was really mod-erate and unprovocative; there has been too much whitewashing of British, French, and especially Russian policy in this whole debate.[41] The answer is rather that the Entente really encircled Austria rather than Germany. Of course Germany was hemmed in and constrained. But she still had allies she controlled or strongly influenced, neutral states still leaned her way (Denmark, Sweden, Holland, Switzerland, Turkey), and she was still inher-ently so strong that no one wished to challenge her directly. If her bid for world power was frustrated, the more modest aim of eventually loosening the rival coalition and insinuating herself into Britain's favor was not fore-closed. Grey resisted all pressures from France, Russia, and the Foreign Office to turn the ententes into alliances, and may even have entertained the hope ultimately of bringing a chastened and more moderate Germany into the Triple Entente, as the Radicals urged.[42]

Austria, in contrast, was hopelessly encircled by 1914 and knew it.[43] Russia, supported by France, was forming a new Balkan League around Russia's protégé and Austria's worst enemy, Serbia. Rumania was defecting, Bulgaria was exhausted and wavering under strong Russo-French pressure, Turkey was leaning toward Russia, Italy was cooperating with Russia in the Balkans; even Germany was a wholly unreliable support politically, and Austria's chief competitor economically in the Balkans.

This isolation and encirclement resulted, moreover, principally from Entente moves and policies, always discussed as if they had nothing to do with Austria. Delcassé's policy, for example, was obviously aimed against Germany (and for a good while against Britain). But is there no significance to the fact that virtually his first move in strengthening and transforming the

Dual Alliance was to seek an agreement with Russia over the spoils of the Austrian Empire, and that even after his fears of a German seizure of Austrian Adriatic ports proved groundless, he still hoped Austria's demise might give France the chance to recover Alsace-Lorraine?[44] Who was menaced by French efforts to lure Italy out of the Triple Alliance and to get her to concentrate her attention on the Balkans and *Italia irredenta?* Not Germany; Austria. Whose vital interests and security were ultimately threatened by France's move to take over Morocco? Not Germany's; only the pan-Germans and some ardent colonialists claimed Morocco as a question of vital interest. The Kaiser, the Foreign Office, and the bulk of Germany's military, naval, and business leaders saw it as a question primarily of prestige and honor. What the French protectorate in Morocco actually did was to pave the way for Italy to attack Turkey over Tripoli and to spread the war into the eastern Mediterranean, to encourage Russia to advance her plans for the Straits, and to promote the assault of the Balkan states upon Turkey, thus raising life-and-death questions for Austria. This was not merely what happened in the event; it was what sensible leaders foresaw and planned for, what was in good part provided for in written agreements.

It is true that Austria did not oppose either France's move on Morocco or Italy's ambitions for Tripoli. This was because, knowing that she could not stop them, she pursued the forlorn hope that, distracted by these gains, they might lessen the pressure on her, or that by supporting them she might persuade France and Italy to keep these Mediterranean moves from having dangerous repercussions for Austria in the Balkans, and to recognize her vital interests there. This policy, which had never worked for Austria throughout the nineteenth century, suffered absolute shipwreck in 1912–14, when it became apparent that all the powers, grateful though they were for Austria's restraint, intended to make her pay for everyone else's gains, and pay precisely in the only area where she had vital interests, the Balkans.

Whom (besides Persia) did the Anglo-Russian Convention of 1907 endanger? Not Germany, whose role and interests in Persia were secondary. The agreement, as intended and promoted by Britain, served to turn Russia's attention toward the Straits, the Macedonian question, and her Balkan rivalry with Austria. France's and Britain's loans to Russia, French economic penetration of the Balkans, France's arms deliveries to Serbia and Greece, and her closing her money markets to Vienna while opening them to Austria's enemies were all intended to hit Germany, insofar as they had a political purpose; but Austria was much more directly hurt. The same is true of Russia's policy, fully backed by France, of uniting the Balkan states into a league under her direction, pulling Rumania and Turkey also into her camp. Intended supposedly to protect the Straits and Turkey from German influence, it served above all to destroy Austria's position. Even the Anglo-French and Anglo-Russian naval talks were directed as much against Austria in the Mediterranean as against Germany in the North and Baltic Seas. From 1912 on France was determined not to allow an Austro-Serb or Austro-Russian rapprochement, so as not to lose a valuable third front in the Balkans against the Central Powers in case of war.[45]

Austria was therefore the actual target of Entente diplomacy. Results count more than motives. To a surprising degree, moreover, Entente statesmen knew what the effects of their policies would be and accepted them. But how was Britain responsible for this? It is easy to see why Russia, France, and Italy might want Austria weakened, but why should Britain, her old friend and natural ally, help undermine her position?

In fact, one can argue that Britain's policy (like Russia's and even, in certain respects, France's) was more anti-Austrian than anti-German. Although opposing German ambitions, the British took Germany seriously and were careful not to push her too far or trample her interests underfoot. They never took Austria seriously and were regularly ready to let her pay, or make her pay. Britain never encouraged France or Russia to provoke Germany; firmness and moderation were the watchwords. But from the mid-1890s on, she urged Russia to concentrate her power and attention on Europe, telling her that with time and patience she could become the arbiter of Europe—the worst possible threat to Austria. The British never liked Delcassé's anti-German stance over Morocco. But they worked to break up the long-standing Austro-Russian cooperation in Macedonia, valuable though they knew it to be for European peace, exploiting the Austro-Russian rift to promote a separate Anglo-Russian program for the Balkans and Turkey. Macedonia became the birthplace of the Triple Entente; it was supposed to cement the Anglo-Russian entente at Austria's expense as the first Moroccan crisis had consolidated the Anglo-French accord at Germany's.[46]

The British did not encourage France to try to recover Alsace-Lorraine; they did drop repeated hints to Russia about how cooperation in Asia would eventually help her in Turkey and the Straits. Britain welcomed the Franco-German agreement over Morocco in 1909 and showed little concern as the French first strained and then broke the Act of Algeciras so recently concluded. When Austria annexed Bosnia, legalizing a situation long existing de facto and giving up her hold on the Sanjak of Novi-Pazar in the process, Britain helped promote an international crisis over the violation of a treaty thirty years old, whose relevant provision had never been intended by Britain herself to remain long in force. The British sometimes tried to calm French suspicions of Germany. During the Bosnian Crisis and after, they impressed upon Russia that she had suffered a humiliating defeat at the hands of Austria backed by Germany—this regardless of the consequences for the balance of power and future Austro-Russian relations,[47] and despite the fact that the British knew of the prior Austro-Russian bargain over Bosnia and considered Isvolski himself largely to blame for Russia's discomfiture.[48]

While Britain in 1911 urged France to compensate Germany generously for her protectorate in Morocco, she simultaneously encouraged Russia to form a Balkan League, including Turkey, to stop Austria in southeastern Europe. Grey rejected the idea of pulling Italy entirely out of the Triple

Alliance, for fear of provoking Germany; but he welcomed Italy's cooperation with Russia and her concentration on the Adriatic,[49] and he tried to
quell anti-Italian press sentiment in Britain over Italy's aggression in the
Tripolitan War. While Grey cooperated with Germany during the Balkan
Wars, it was often at Austria's expense, and always with great care not to
offend Russia.[50] Although the outcome of these wars fatally tipped the
Balkan balance against Austria, the frantic cries from Vienna for some consideration of Austria's position went unheeded as before. To Austria, the
Foreign Office preached abnegation and restraint; among themselves, British
leaders agreed that it would be better not to become entangled at all in
Balkan questions and Austria's selfish intrigues, were it not that friendship
for France and Russia required it.[51] Meanwhile the British envoys at Sofia
and Petersburg encouraged a Serbo-Bulgarian rapprochement under Russian
sponsorship that would seal Austria's isolation and compel her to remain
quiet. If a partition of Turkey became unavoidable, the British recognized
that German interests would have to be taken into account. Austria, on the
other hand, had good reason to fear that Britain would join with France,
Germany, and Russia to cut her out.[52]

On the eve of the war, the Foreign Office was aware of the fear prevalent
in both Berlin and Vienna that Austria might collapse. Far from viewing this
eventuality as a danger *per se*, Nicolson feared only that Russia and Germany
might come together over the spoils, and urged preventing this by a close
Anglo-Russian alliance. Grey feared rather what actually happened: a preventive war launched by Germany out of fear of Russia's growing strength
and Austria's decline. His only answer to this was to work with the supposed
German peace party under Bethmann, so as to conciliate Germany and get
her to put still more restraining pressure on Austria. No thought of any
action to help maintain Austria's independence and integrity was entertained. If Austria and Russia actually got into war, Grey hoped to keep
Germany and France out of it—thus holding the ring for Russia, giving her
the opportunity she had wanted ever since the Crimean War.[53]

Finally, if one agrees with Fischer (as I do) that something can be learned
of the general character and direction of a nation's policy before 1914 by
seeing what it does and plans immediately upon the outbreak of war, then it
is significant that Britain's contribution to the breakup of the Austrian
Monarchy, the promises and concessions to Italy, Rumania, Serbia, and
Russia that soon rendered it inevitable, began already on August 5, 1914, a
week before Britain's declaration of war on Austria.[54] Equally significant,
while Britain always expected and even wanted a united Germany to survive
World War I, to serve both as a balance against Russia and France and as a
market for British goods, they considered Austria dispensable, reckoning
freely from 1916 on breaking her up (even if Germany absorbed the
German-speaking territories!) or on using a drastically reduced, federated,
and Slav-dominated Austria in some kind of anti-German combination.[55]

Of course there was no great anti-Austrian plot. The British did not think
of Austria as their enemy; they tried not to think of her at all. They did not

plan to isolate and destroy her; they simply did not concern themselves (as they never had earlier in the nineteenth century) with the question of whether the concessions and defeats forced upon Austria before the war, and the territorial sacrifices to be imposed on her during and after it, would leave her viable. Britain undermined Austria's position before the war—indeed, throughout the nineteenth century—and assisted in her destruction during it, in a fit of absence of mind, a state from which many British historians on this subject have not yet emerged.[56] Austria was not Britain's concern, as Grey repeatedly told his ambassador at Vienna, Sir Fairfax Cartwright; Britain wished to be cordial to her without entangling herself. She was like China or Persia. The British had nothing against her, but she could do nothing for them, they in turn could not save her, and certainly no British interests would be sacrificed for her sake, including the only important British interest in the Balkans, keeping on good terms with Russia.

What makes Britain's responsibility for Austria's plight a heavy one, although less direct than Russia's or France's, is that Britain alone was in a position to manage the European Concert so as to control the Balkan situation. Russia was bound to be Austria's rival, Serbia and Rumania bound to have territorial aspirations at Austria's expense, Italy bound at least to watch Austria jealously. These problems were there and could not be solved or spirited away. But they could have been controlled. Russia was not bound to be Austria's enemy; throughout the nineteenth century she had always found it profitable to seek a modus vivendi with Austria whenever it was plain that an aggressive course would get her into trouble. The danger regularly arose when Russia got tacit or open Western support for a forward policy, as she did before 1914. Serbia would try all she could get away with, but would not commit suicide by fighting Austria alone; Rumania was entirely opportunistic, Italy not really vitally engaged in the Balkans. As for Austria, all through the century she had lived with international and internal problems that were insoluble but not fatal. There were so many dangers that her only hope was to outlive the threats and outlast her enemies; she always tried this course, and only abandoned it when it seemed too hopeless or humiliating, and violence appeared to be the only recourse. Right up to June 1914 all Austrian leaders, including those aggressively inclined toward Serbia and Italy, wanted an entente with Russia. Hence the situation was not inherently out of control, but only Britain could have exercised that control. France could not have checked Russia's diplomatic offensive, even had she wanted to; she was too dependent on Russian aid. Britain did not try, not so much because she feared losing Russia to Germany, or feared renewed trouble for India, as because she saw no reason to make the effort.

Instead, she expected Germany to do the whole job both of sustaining Austria and restraining her. It is strange that the Germans have not made more of this. Most German charges against England were baseless or highly exaggerated, most German expectations and demands from Britain absurd or dangerous. But the old, long-standing German and Austrian efforts to get Britain to bear her European responsibilities by upholding Austria have a good deal to be said for them. Never mind that Germany had selfish reasons for wanting to involve Britain, that Germany herself helped greatly to create the Austrian problem, and that German support for Austria was anything but loyal and disinterested. The fact remains that German support for Austria and restraint of her and Russia helped prevent several likely general wars, and that Austria by her very existence and her policy was restraining Germany, preventing her from playing world policy with a free hand. Moreover, only the presence of the Habsburg Monarchy holding down the Danube basin kept Germany or Russia from achieving mastery over Europe. With Austria there and determined to remain an independent great power, it was very difficult for either of them to fight each other, or dominate the other, or combine for aggressive purposes. Let Austria go under, and a great war for the mastery of Europe became almost mathematically predictable. The Germans, William II in particular, had many irrational beliefs, including the apocalyptic vision of an inevitable fight to the death between Teutons and Slavs.[57] But their fear of this contest, and the belief that Austria's impending dissolution must bring it on, were entirely rational.[58]

The main trouble with leaving the task of supporting Austria to Germany alone was not that it was unfair or exceeded Germany's resources, but that it was counterproductive for peace. The more the Germans alone supported Austria, the more she became and was considered a German satellite, against her will; the more she and Germany, instead of restraining each other, became involved in each other's largely individual quarrels, the more Austria, despairing of finding help from Britain, France, or the Concert, would be prone to seek her salvation in violence, and the more Germany, fearful of Austria's demise or defection, would be tempted to push her into it—the scenario of 1914.

Only a commitment by Britain to use her influence with France to help keep Austria in existence by maintaining a balance of power in the Balkans and restraining Austria, Russia, and the Balkan states alike could have prevented this.[59] Such a policy had worked with Turkey for a long time, and she was far more vulnerable, weak, backward, despised, and dispensable than Austria. But the whole British tradition went against this. Despite many fine phrases, the British never understood what Austria's function really was in Europe, and how valuable she was to Britain. At best, Austria was for Britain a useful means to check France or Russia or to help Turkey; more often she was considered a menace to Turkey and a reactionary satellite of Russia or Germany, endangering the balance by her subservience and the peace by her reckless repressive policies. When France and Russia loomed as the chief dangers, Britain saw a united Italy and a united Germany under Prussia as the best answers. When Germany then became the chief danger, friendship with Russia and France was the solution. In both cases, Austria was forgotten or considered useless. As for the critical problem of east–central and southeastern Europe, the British knew little and cared less, but supposed that Austria was an anachronism and that a liberal nationalist solution would be best all round if achieved by peaceful means. Even had they better understood what was at stake, they would not have changed their policy. For to support Austria, however cautiously, would be to abandon Britain's coveted freedom from commitments, to give up that policy of a free hand toward the Continent which accounted for Britain's greatness and which, only slightly modified, had worked brilliantly since 1900. By 1914, all the challenges to Britain were under control. The empire and the home islands had not been so secure in two generations, all without war, great expense, or binding alliances. To this day, the thought that Britain's prewar successes in foreign policy might be connected with the final catastrophe, that in the struggle for peace, unlike her usual record in war, Britain this time won all the battles and lost the war, has not penetrated British historiography.

Yet it would be wrong to end on this note, as if Britain were especially to blame—as misleading as the current excessive concentration on Germany, and far more unfair. The basic point is that everyone saw the central threat to the European system in the decline of Austria, and no one would do anything about it. Russians, Serbs, Rumanians, Greeks, and Italians all exploited it; the French thought only of their security. Even Germany made the problem worse, by promoting Austria's survival not as a European independent great power, but as a German state and Germany's satellite, and by insisting against Austrian protests that war, if it came, must be fought as a great duel to the death between Germans and Slavs. The British, meanwhile, did not want Austria to die, but hoped that if she must, she would at least do it quietly. In 1914 Austria decided not to die quietly, and once this long-postponed decision to recover her position by violence was taken, there was no stopping short of a general holocaust.[60]

The only reason for laying greater stress on Britain's role here is that objectively (although not psychologically) she had greater freedom to act otherwise and greater ability to change the outcome. The attitudes behind it all, in any case, were universal—the same short-sighted selfishness and lack of imagination, the same exclusive concentration on one's own interests at the expense of the community. Everyone wanted a payoff; no one wanted to pay. Everyone expected the system to work for him; no one would work for it. All were playing the same game—imperialism, world policy, *Realpolitik*, call it what you will—all save Austria, and she also would have played it had she been able.[61] All believed, as many historians still do, that *sacro egoismo* is the only rational rule for high politics, that it even represents a higher realism and a higher morality, when it really is only a higher stupidity. And so the system was bent and twisted until it broke; its burdens were distributed not according to the ability to bear them, but the inability to resist. Inevitably the collapse came where all the weight was concentrated—at the weakest point. Two titles from Nietzsche and Nestroy sum the whole process up: "Menschlich, allzu menschlich," and "Gegen Torheit gibt es kein Mittel."

EMBEDDED COUNTERFACTUALS
AND WORLD WAR I
AS AN UNAVOIDABLE WAR

This essay, though it may seem to do so, does not take a determinist stand either on counterfactual reasoning and contingency in history in general or on the origins of World War I. On the war, though its conclusions differ from R. N. Lebow's argument that it could readily have been avoided,[1] it agrees with Lebow's views on many points and concedes a large causal role in all great events in history, including World War I, to contingency, chance, and particular choices. It even argues that in a certain objective sense the war remained avoidable up to its very outbreak, and presents other grounds for considering it unavoidable.

It also broadly agrees with Philip Tetlock's and Aaron Belkin's views on the necessity, unavoidability, and potential utility of counterfactual reasoning in historical study.[2] The difference between my views and theirs lies in the practical rather than the theoretical realm. While in general accepting the Tetlock–Belkin analysis of the various types of counterfactual reasoning and the basic tests to use for them, I will suggest a different notion about how and where to apply counterfactual reasoning concretely to historical expla-nation, as a better way of showing historians the value of counterfactual rea-soning for accomplishing their task. That task (here I agree with the historians who are skeptical about it) is not to speculate on what might have happened in history, but to shed light on what actually did happen, why it did, and what it means.

As for whether World War I ever became unavoidable, and if so, when and why, once again the point I wish to make is a practical more than theoretical one. Clearly there were contingent events and developments occurring and important choices being made in 1914 right up to end of the July Crisis. One can undoubtedly make a case, as Lebow has done, that some vital events in the causal chain, such as the assassination of Franz Ferdinand, could eas-ily not have happened. It is more difficult, but not impossible, to argue that vital decisions could have been made differently. But this fact in itself does not make the war avoidable, because it does not cancel the practical limits to the avoidability of outcomes in human affairs. To term an outcome inevitable often means no more than to say that the time when it could have been avoided is past—that the kinds of decisions, actions, or chance developments required to avert it, though possible earlier, have become so unlikely or unthinkable as to rule out any plausible scenario for avoiding it.[3] This is an obvious point, yet it is not easy or commonplace to apply it to particular developments in history, especially major ones like the outbreak of great wars or revolutions. My hope is to use a particular application of counterfactual reasoning to history to show one specific way in which World War I by 1914 had become unavoidable.

THE CASE FOR "EMBEDDED" COUNTERFACTUAL REASONING

The Tetlock–Belkin theses seem to assume that the way for historians or other scholars to apply counterfactual reasoning to historical exposition and explanation is to pose the question, "What if ?"—that is, to imagine or conceive of a way in which a particular event or development could have unfolded differently, and to ask, "What if this had happened? What further changes would have resulted?"[4]

A working historian, however—even if, like me, he agrees that counterfactual elements are logically implied in all explanation, including historical explanation—may have serious qualms about this procedure. The reason is that though it is logically defensible to think up counterfactual questions with which to confront the historical record, the exercise seems pointless or at best of limited value from a practical standpoint because even so-called easily imagined variations introduced into the complex matrix of historical developments can change so many variables in so many unpredictable or incalculable ways, leading to so many varied and indeterminate consequences, that the procedure quickly becomes useless for helping us deduce or predict an alternative outcome. Tetlock and Belkin of course see the problem and deal with it in terms of abstract logic. Yet my feeling is that the procedure's practical limits and problems sensed by the working historian are not sufficiently grasped.

The difficulty, as noted, is that if the variation is really important, involving a central component or variable in the historical equation, introducing it will alter so much of the complex web of history that the results of omitting or altering that crucial variable become incalculable. If the variation introduced, however, is minor, sufficiently precise and limited enough that its immediate consequences can be calculated with confidence, its implications for general historical explanation or for suggesting any important alternative outcome are unlikely to be important. A major counterfactual, in other words, will change too much, and a minor one too little, to help us explain what really did happen and why, and why alternative scenarios failed to emerge, the only sound reasons for using counterfactual reasoning. Thus using this kind of "What if?" counterfactual procedure might well have the perverse and ironic effect of confirming ordinary historians in their resistance to counterfactual reasoning and strengthening their tendency to see history as the result of pure contingency and chance.

One might of course reply that if historians cannot or will not recognize the presuppositions and assumptions involved in the explanations they offer, other scholars will have to identify and analyze them, and subject them to various tests, including those of counterfactual reasoning. Again I agree, up to a point. The alternative kind of counterfactual reasoning I will suggest might help historians get over the tendency toward a naïve pragmatic empiricism. Yet it would be rash of scholars in other fields to suppose that because a particular historian fails to give compelling theoretical grounds for being dissatisfied with a particular counterfactual procedure, his or her concerns can be safely ignored. Practitioners may well sense from experience and schooled intuition that a plausible idea or theory will not work in their field, even if they have difficulty articulating theoretical reasons why. Moreover, the principal contention here, that some major easily imagined counterfactual variations in particular sections of history change so much that the entire subsequent development becomes incalculable, while other variations, just as easily imagined, make no significant difference at all, can readily be illustrated in any period of history.[5]

One can get around the difficulty, I suggest, by a different concept and method of counterfactual reasoning. It starts by conceiving of counterfactuals not as non-history (that is, imagined or virtual as opposed to real history, what might have happened rather than what did), but rather as *real* history, an integral part of history, embedded in history both in the actual experience of historical actors and in those constructions or reconstructions of history constantly made not only by scholars but also by everyone who reflects on the past. History, like life itself, is lived, acted, made, and relived and reconstructed in the face and presence of counterfactuals. Historical actors in all arenas of life constantly think, calculate, decide, and act in the face of uncertainty; they repeatedly ask the question, "What if?" try to answer it, and make decisions and act on that basis. Historians take this for granted. They know instinctively (or are quickly taught) that historical actors regularly face an uncertain, open future. Recognizing this, they must portray and analyze that situation and show why and how actors responded to the questions, choices, and alternatives they faced as they did. If they are at all sophisticated, they also realize that carrying out this task requires not merely trying to discover and analyze the actors' thought worlds and the role played by their counterfactual questions and calculations, but also framing and posing their own counterfactual questions as to what might have happened had the actors answered their counterfactual questions differently. Thus in seeking to discover the real nature and results of the actual choices made by actors in the face of their uncertainty and their counterfactual questions, historians must use their advantages of hindsight and historical evidence to ask counterfactual questions of their own, such as: What other decisions and actions could the historical actors have made under the existing circumstances? To what extent did they recognize and consider these? What circumstances made these choices or alternative courses genuinely possible or merely specious and actually unreal? What might the alternative results of these choices have been? The real justification for the use of counterfactual reasoning in history and the best answer to those who reject it is the fact that historians cannot faithfully convey the real nature and results of historical decisions and actions simply by constructing a factual narrative of "what happened" without confronting the various counterfactuals, both those faced by the actors and those necessarily posed by the historian, integrally embedded in that story.[6]

This understanding of counterfactual reasoning not only justifies its use but also suggests how it ought to proceed. The first task is to discover and analyze the counterfactual questions actually seen and faced by the historical actors themselves. This part is so obvious, normal, and ubiquitous an element of historical research that it needs no discussion here. The second step, less obvious but no less necessary, involves looking carefully at the reconstructions and explanations of historical events and outcomes offered by historians (especially oneself) with the specific aim of discovering and analyzing the implicit and explicit counterfactual questions and assumptions they contain. The next assignment is to test rigorously these counterfactual assumptions and scenarios that historians wittingly or unwittingly pose, by means of the kinds of tests and criteria Tetlock and Belkin suggest and the same types of historical evidence as are employed to construct the "factual" story. By ferreting out and analyzing the overt or concealed counterfactuals embedded in historians' reconstructions and explanations of history, I contend, we can both better explain the actual course of historical events and better judge whether the counterfactual possibilities envisioned by the actors and those constructed and used by historians were sound or illusory. In short, it can help us better understand both what did happen in history and why this particular thing rather than some other possible thing occurred.[7]

This kind of counterfactual reasoning has other advantages as well. It represents something historians regularly do, whether or not they are fully aware of it, and thus is a method that, once understood, they can hardly reject. Most important, it seems to me to fit the nature of history, recognizing its openness and uncertainty for the actors themselves while insisting at the same time that history's outcomes, though not predetermined, can and must be explained by causes. It thereby takes seriously both the contingent and the determinate character of the past; respects both the extent and the limits of its range of possibilities. It depicts history as unfolding in an indeterminate way, the product of unpredictable human conduct and material circumstances, but not as kaleidoscopic chaos. It offers a way of distinguishing between genuine and specious counterfactual scenarios, showing that while much could have happened differently, not everything, including many of the things historical actors and later historians have thought were possible, could have happened. It fits our sense, learned from life as well as history, that at some point some things once indeterminate do become inevitable.

Embedded Counterfactuals and World War I as an Unavoidable War

I now need to illustrate how a certain degree and kind of inevitability in history applies to the origins of World War I (not demonstrate it, which might be impossible and would certainly take too long).[8] The topic suits the purpose for several reasons. First, the story is very well known and does not need to be expounded in detail. Second, though the scholarly debate over the origins of the war which raged for decades after 1914 has not completely died out, a clear consensus view has emerged which denies that the war was inevitable and ascribes its origins to specific avoidable choices and actions taken by particular actors. Hence it represents a good challenge. Third, it illustrates particularly well the potential value of detecting and analyzing embedded counterfactuals, the surprising results it can lead to, and the dangers of failing to do so. Finally, in asking whether this world war, a major source and cause of Europe's subsequent relative decline, was avoidable, it suggests further major counterfactual questions it will not attempt to answer, namely, whether absent World War I European world supremacy would have lasted a considerable while longer and World War II have been avoided.

My treatment of this huge subject must be brief and sketchy, little more than an outline, and is bound to seem dogmatic in some places and trite in others. It will start by discussing the current prevailing view of the origins of the war, analyze and criticize the counterfactuals embedded in it, and from this develop a divergent view.

The Standard Explanation and Its Counterfactuals

By common agreement, the direct proximate cause of World War I was the German and Austro-Hungarian decision that Austria-Hungary issue an ultimatum to Serbia in July 1914 following the assassination of Archduke Franz Ferdinand by Bosnian nationalists with connections to Serbia. The German powers intended by this ultimatum to provoke a local war against Serbia and eliminate it as a political factor in the Balkans, thus shifting the balance there and in Europe generally in favor of themselves. Without necessarily intending to start a general war, the German powers consciously risked provoking one by this initiative, as actually happened.

Disagreement persists over the motives and attitudes prompting this go-for-broke gamble, with some historians emphasizing the fear and desperation felt by leaders in Germany and Austria-Hungary, others stressing their aggressive aims and their hopes that they could either get away with a successful local war or win a wider one. This disagreement makes little difference in deciding whether this war was avoidable, however, because everyone agrees that Germany and Austria-Hungary, whatever their reasons, *chose* to take this gamble; they were not forced into it. This belief implies a counterfactual: they had viable alternatives, could have chosen other ways to protect their interests without risking a great war. A similar consensus prevails that the other great powers, Russia, France, and Britain, reacted essentially defensively to the German–Austrian move and had little choice other than to do so in self-defense, given their vital interests and the unmistakable challenge presented them. The counterfactual scenario embedded in the consensus explanation thus ascribes to Germany and Austria-Hungary a choice of alternate strategy or strategies by which they could reasonably have hoped to protect their vital interests by peaceful means, while denying that the other major actors had practical alternatives for saving peace once the Central Powers launched their initiative.

To be sure, few attribute the German–Austro-Hungarian gamble purely to aggressive expansionism, militarism, and paranoia, or deny that the international situation was becoming increasingly unfavorable and dangerous for the Dual Alliance in 1914. The consensus view, in fact, uses this to help explain the Austro-German action, while denying that this justifies it or renders it necessary, claiming among other things that Germany and Austria-Hungary had themselves largely created the dangers threatening them by failing to reform internally while pursuing unrealistic, aggressive policies abroad. Again this involves an implied or stated counterfactual: even as late as 1914 the Central Powers could have changed their policies and thereby made themselves more secure within the existing international system without overthrowing it.

Consensus historians recognize further that Germany, already in 1914 largely isolated diplomatically and threatened with encirclement by the Triple Entente, faced an imminent future threat, that once Russia had completed its announced plans for military expansion, scheduled for completion by 1917, the German army would be numerically as decisively inferior to those of its opponents as the German navy already was on the sea. But the consensus view claims that Germany had largely created this perilous situation for itself by the aggressive world policy it had followed ever since Bismarck's fall in 1890. Its naval race with Britain, its restless quest for colonies, bases, and spheres of influence around the globe, and its frequent resort to bullying and threats, all designed to give Germany hegemony over Europe and a world position competitive with those of Britain, Russia, and the United States, provoked the alliances, ententes, and armaments races, first at sea and then on land, by which Germany now felt encircled and threatened. Since these dangers arose primarily from Germany's policies and actions (here comes another important counterfactual), different German policies could over time have reduced or eliminated them. Even as late as 1914, had Germany realized that none of its neighbors intended to attack it or violate its rights and had it decided to give up its drive for world power, pursuing instead a sensible, moderate policy focused on economic expansion, it had good chances to enjoy a reasonably secure, prosperous, and honorable place in the European and world international system. In fact, prominent historians have argued that Germany's economic dynamism was so great that it needed only a prolonged period of peace to achieve mastery in Europe.[9]

Almost everyone also recognizes that Austria-Hungary faced even graver dangers than Germany, and that these were less obviously the result of its own actions, at least in the international arena. The Habsburg Monarchy before 1914 was growing steadily more isolated politically and diplomatically and losing its great power status and reputation. Two allies, Italy and Rumania, were unreliable and hostile, the latter to the point of open defection. Its most important ally, Germany, was the Monarchy's most serious economic rival, especially in the Balkans where Austro-Hungarian interests were concentrated, and the Germans tended both to dominate Austria-Hungary politically and strategically and to ignore its vital interests. Austria-Hungary's military security against a host of possible or probable enemies (Serbia, Russia, Italy, Russia's ally France, and even Rumania) depended totally on receiving major, timely help from Germany in case of war. Yet given Germany's own threatened military position facing a likely two-front war, Germany's gambling offensive strategy for fighting it (the Schlieffen Plan), and the fact that the Dual Alliance lacked a military convention or an agreed and coordinated military strategy, how much actual military help Germany would provide its ally was anyone's guess. Meanwhile Austria-Hungary's long-standing security problem had been further worsened by the disastrous outcome of the two Balkan Wars in 1912–13. The Peace of Bucharest in August 1913 left Austria-Hungary with no reliable partner in the last region, the Balkans, where it still counted as a great power and had its most vital interests. The Ottoman Empire was virtually expelled from Europe, while Bulgaria, which the Austrians counted on to check Serbia, was defeated and exhausted, Rumania alienated, the new Kingdom of Albania a basket case and albatross around Austria-Hungary's neck, and Italy an active rival in Albania and the Adriatic with irredentist claims on Austrian territory. Even Germany had not given its ally steady support during the prolonged crisis, but had held Austria-Hungary back in order to preserve general peace and pursue its own particular aims. Meanwhile Austria-Hungary's worst rivals and enemies, Russia, Serbia, and Montenegro, had emerged from the Balkan Wars stronger, more confident, and more hostile, and Russia, aided by its ally France, seemed poised to consolidate its dominance over the entire region by expanding the Balkan League it had earlier sponsored and thereby promoted the Balkan Wars in the first place. The decline in Austria-Hungary's strength and status, obvious to everyone, enabled other powers to ignore its interests, to exploit its internal problems, especially the nationalities conflicts, to raise irredentist claims on the Monarchy's territory, and in Serbia's case, to wage a cold war of propaganda and a guerilla war of terrorist subversion against it. They further spurred dissatisfied nationalities and groups within Austria-Hungary to demand concessions from the Austrian and Hungarian governments, sometimes soliciting foreign support for them, thus exacerbating the already grave problems of governance in both halves of the Monarchy and inducing anger and hopelessness in those who remained *Habsburgtreu*. Most important, Austria-Hungary, far more than Germany, had fallen hopelessly behind in the land arms race then reaching a crucial stage among the great powers in Europe (only Italy was worse off, and Italy was only a would-be great power). Given Austria-Hungary's limited economic and fiscal resources and the restrictions imposed on its military exertions by the parliamentary system in both halves of the Monarchy and the autonomous position enjoyed by Hungary, there was simply no hope for it to catch up. It thus faced the prospect of fighting a great war against several foes with only doubtful German support and under conditions of hopeless inferiority.[10]

No historian to my knowledge denies the gravity of Austria-Hungary's situation; various factors in it are regularly invoked to explain its go-for-broke gamble in 1914. Yet many also contend, as they do with Germany, that Austria-Hungary had largely brought this on itself. For decades or generations it had failed or refused to solve its own internal problems, especially the nationalities conflicts, and thus exposed itself to irredentist subversion and external threats. It had made this worse by a stubborn, aggressive defense of outworn positions and untenable claims in foreign policy (its so-called Pig War against Serbia before 1908, its annexation of Bosnia in 1908, the subsequent humiliation of Russia in 1909, its refusal to reach reasonable compromises with Serbia, Montenegro, and Italy during the Balkan Wars of 1912–13, the hopeless attempt in 1913–14 to create a viable new Balkan satellite in Albania). Once more the consensus verdict, by implication more than explicitly, posits a major counterfactual: though by 1914 the hour was late, the Monarchy's one remaining chance to survive its crisis was not the use of force, either internal or external, but reform in the direction of federalism, turning itself into a more free and democratic union of peoples and recognizing the interests of the other nationalities besides those of the master races, the Germans, Hungarians, and Italians.[11]

Thus in both cases the supposedly counterproductive and dangerous foreign policies of Germany and Austria-Hungary culminating in their gamble in 1914 are linked to a wider problem and at least partly explained by it: the failure or refusal of their regimes to reform and modernize in order to meet their internal political and social problems. Instead these regimes chose to stay in power, preserve their existing social order and the interests of their respective elites, and manage their internal social and political divisions and problems through an assertive, expansionist foreign policy (a resort to so-called secondary integration and social imperialism).

These explanations, in assigning Germany and Austria-Hungary the primary responsibility for causing the threats against which they decided to act in 1914 and explaining their policies as directed as much against internal problems as external dangers, add (as noted) further counterfactuals to the original counterfactual thesis, that these two powers had means and choices for protecting their legitimate interests in 1914 other than aiming for a local war and risking a general one. To lay these out for Germany: (a) Had Germany not conducted a reckless, aggressive pursuit of world power for decades before 1914, its general interests and position in world politics would not have been threatened as they were or were perceived to be in 1914. (b) Had Germany pursued political reform and social integration rather than manipulated social imperialism and secondary integration at home, its government would not have needed to pursue a reckless, aggressive foreign policy for domestic-political reasons. (c) A more democratic, liberal, and well-integrated Germany using peaceful, normal ways of protecting its legitimate interests would not have encountered enmity and opposition from the other great powers, especially from Britain and France as fellow democracies, but would have been welcomed as a partner for peace and prosperity in Europe and the world.[12] Somewhat similar counterfactuals apply to Austria-Hungary. A reformed, more progressive and democratic Monarchy pursuing wiser policies toward its nationalities and a more conciliatory foreign policy could have solved or managed its internal and external problems to such an extent that it would have both been less vulnerable to pressures and threats from its opponents and have encountered fewer such threats, thus eliminating the need for the suicidal gamble of 1914.[13]

The Counterargument and Its Counterfactuals

First, a logical and methodological point: If, as I claim, these counterfactuals are embedded in the consensus scenario and logically implied by it, then those who advance this view have an obligation to back them up, showing by research, analysis, and evidence that these counterfactual propositions are at least reasonable, more probable than not. The burden of proof lies on them to do this, not on others to disprove them. By and large this has not been done. Historians have usually devoted close attention first to determining the facts on the origins of the war, both immediate and long term, and then to linking the outbreak of the war to the German–Austro-Hungarian initiative in July 1914, both by connecting that initiative to their particular situation and aims in 1914 and by trying to show how their general situation and aims derived from their previous foreign and domestic policies and actions. In other words, starting from a correct initial premise that the German powers' initiative was the immediate proximate cause of the war, they have then constructed a plausible case that this initiative derived from and was caused by a general situation which also primarily resulted from German and Austro-Hungarian actions and policies over a much longer term. The null hypothesis stated or implied in this argument, however, has not been systematically laid out and examined, nor have the counterfactuals embedded in it been analyzed and researched in detail. No serious attempt has been made to back up the (hidden, implied, unarticulated, but real and logically necessary) claim that absent those supposedly decisive German and Austro-Hungarian policies and actions, the general situation in 1914 would have been different in the ways the consensus view contends.

Whatever the reasons for this disparity, so long as the counterfactuals clearly, logically, and necessarily implied in the consensus argument have not been researched and analyzed with the same care as the other so-called facts in the case, both the argument making the German–Austro-Hungarian initiative the main cause rather than merely the occasion for war and thus making these powers primarily responsible for it, and the argument that the war was inherently avoidable, the result of particular decisions that could have been made differently, remain unproved. Absent this analysis of the embedded counterfactuals, we do not know whether in fact the leaders of Germany and Austria-Hungary had any real freedom to act otherwise than they did, or what difference it would have made (*ex hypothesi*) had they done so.

The argument could stop here, with a claim that the consensus case for World War I as an avoidable conflict remains unproved and with a call for more research. While this might be prudent, it would be inconclusive and not very interesting or helpful. Instead I will attempt three things. The first is to show that the counterfactual assumptions and implications of the consensus view are not only largely unexamined and unproved, but also improbable and in some instances untenable. The second is to lay out an alternate set of counterfactual conditions and performances necessary if war were to be averted both in 1914 and for some indefinite but significant period thereafter. The last is to argue that this (counterfactual) set of conditions and actions required *ex hypothesi* for avoidance of a general war in that era not only was not recognized, accepted, or carried out by the various actors at this time, but also that the existing international system, that is, the circumstances, political culture, and rules and practices that then prevailed in international power politics, worked to make it highly unlikely that these necessary steps would or could have been taken. This makes it in turn almost impossible to construct any plausible counterfactual historical scenario by which the war could have been avoided, and thus justifies terming the war inevitable.[14]

Obviously this is a tall order. The counterargument against the consensus view will have to be as bare-boned as the previous exposition of that view, or more so. It starts with conceding (in fact, insisting) on several points basically correct in the standard view concerning the immediate origins of the war—that the German–Austro-Hungarian initiative of July 1914 aimed at a local war and risked a general war with the aim of reversing the prevailing trends in international politics by violence, that this launched the great power crisis resulting in general war, that during the July Crisis the other great powers were primarily reacting to the Central Powers' initiative, and that without this particular Austro-German initiative no local or general war would have developed *at this particular time*. But these points have long been obvious. The key question regarding both responsibility for the war and its avoidability is the counterfactual one implicit in the consensus case: the question of whether other choices were available to the Central Powers at that time which, under the existing rules and conditions of the game, offered them an opportunity to satisfy their security needs reasonably without risking a major war. If so, they chose war when it was avoidable—if not, then not.

The related question, whether they were also responsible for creating the insecurity that prompted them to gamble, is not strictly speaking relevant to the question of inevitability of the war, though it is to that of ultimate responsibility for it. If they themselves largely created the general situation that made a desperate gamble their only hope for survival, one might argue that this made war in 1914 in a sense unavoidable—they were bound soon to do something desperate that would touch it off—but also that they were responsible for it even if they had no better choice at that time. Yet though this question of responsibility is less central for our purposes than the first, the two are so closely related that even a *prima facie* case against the consensus argument, to be coherent, must deal with both. Therefore I will deny both sets of counterfactuals. That is, in addition to denying that Germany and Austria-Hungary had viable alternatives in 1914, I will also briefly state some reasons why they were not chiefly responsible for creating the critical security challenges they faced in 1914, why different policies on their part would not have substantially changed their situation, and why the existing international system precluded other reasonable peaceful alternatives for meeting the threats they faced.

I start with an assertion that will sound deliberately provocative, even outrageous, but that in my view represents a reasonable, almost self-evident interpretation of historical evidence. In the whole period from about 1890 to 1914, the international *policies* and *actions* of Germany and Austria-Hungary, as distinct from their aims, attitudes, gestures, language, and ambitions (especially those of Germany) were actually more restrained and moderate than those of any other great power. One cannot point to specific German or Austro-Hungarian *actions* between 1890 and July 1914 that were as aggressive, expansionist, imperialist, law-and-precedent-breaking, and belligerent as many of those taken during this same period by every other major power—Russia in East Asia and Central Asia, Britain in East and South Africa, Southeast Asia, and Central Asia, France in West, Central, and North Africa and Southeast Asia, Italy in North and East Africa and the Eastern Mediterranean, the United States in Central America, the Caribbean and the Western Pacific, and Japan in East Asia. The same point holds, *mutatis mutandis*, for a number of small powers, notably Serbia, Greece, Bulgaria, and Montenegro.

This of course does not make Germany and Austria-Hungary, especially the former, peace-loving defensive status quo powers. Germany was as active a participant in the colonialist-imperialist scramble of the era as it could be, while Austria-Hungary would have liked to participate, tried to do so on an informal basis, and did join halfheartedly in the open imperialist scramble toward the end, but never had the means to pursue it seriously. Both powers had active foreign policies and pursued aims by no means limited to preserving the status quo. Germany in particular constantly sought gains and repeatedly made attempts at achieving them—seldom, however, pursuing its initiatives consistently or very far or succeeding in doing more than arouse fear, resentment, and opposition from other states. Behind its various restless impulses lay the overall goals of *Weltpolitik*. This meant for Germany essentially a policy of maintaining its security in continental Europe (which, given Germany's central location, required at least half-hegemony there) while simultaneously making gains in world power and position (colonies, bases, markets, a formidable navy, and alliances) that would make it competitive in the twentieth century with Britain, Russia, and the United States. Both goals were to be achieved with the aid of Germany's military and economic power, but mainly by means of shrewd diplomacy and power politics—using Germany's key position in Europe and the free hand it supposedly gave her to exploit what Germans supposed were irreconcilable rivalries between Britain, Russia, and France, so that Germany could reach favorable deals and arrangements especially with Britain. Austria-Hungary's main aims were necessarily more defensive—to preserve its territorial integrity, independence, and great power status against many serious challenges and threats, particularly in the one area where it still had vital great power interests and some imperialist ambitions, the Balkans and Near East. Its policies, toward the other great powers if not lesser ones, were correspondingly more conciliatory.

Yet to dwell, as most historians do in explaining the origins of World War I, on what the Central Powers wanted and tried to do is largely beside the point. The salient fact is that throughout 1890–1914 their various initiatives, regardless of their nature and intent, regularly failed—failed either relatively in the sense of yielding them only limited gains at high long-term costs (for example, Austria-Hungary's annexation of Bosnia in 1908 or Germany's Berlin-to-Baghdad Railway project), or absolutely in the sense of ending in defeat and greater insecurity for one or both (for example, the two Moroccan Crises and the two Balkan Wars).

Equally striking is the contrast in this regard between their experience here and that of the other great powers. The latter were able to gamble, commit serious blunders, provoke wars, experience serious setbacks and defeats, and not only survive their gambles and failures but often reap long-term profit from them. The French, though they were humiliated by Britain at Fashoda, escaped unscathed from this foolish gamble and eventually gained the colonial deal and entente with Britain they wanted. Two overt, dangerous French challenges to Germany in Morocco launched serious crises, but ended by improving France's colonial and European positions. Britain used the threat of war successfully to compel France to back down over the Sudan and Egypt, got away with an aggressive, badly run war in South Africa, and forced the Germans to accept their terms in Persia and Mesopotamia. The Russian government pursued an especially reckless imperialist policy almost everywhere, especially in the Far East, and yet not only survived the disastrous war and the crippling revolution in 1904–06 its policies had brought upon it, but by 1914 was not only pursuing its old imperialist goals in the Balkans and the Turkish Straits more boldly than ever, but also exploiting its new accord with Britain to encroach on Persia, and even laying the foundations for a revival of Far Eastern expansion. Italy's reckless adventure in Ethiopia in 1896 led it to a humiliating defeat—and subsequently to a rapprochement with France that enabled Italy thereafter to play off both sides in the European alliance system for the benefit of Italian interests in Africa, the Mediterranean, and the Balkans. Eventually this policy emboldened Italy to commit what was arguably the most cynical and dangerous act of imperialist aggression in the whole prewar period, condemned by everyone—its attack on the Ottoman Empire in Libya and the Dodecanese in 1911–12, an act directly linked with the two Balkan wars and World War I itself. Yet Italy emerged from this adventure with no concrete losses and handsome territorial gains. Japan's risky, all-out gamble in 1904–05 in launching a preventive war against Russia paid off handsomely. The U.S. war against Spain in 1898, a war against a state that posed no threat to the United States and was thus surely avoidable even if in some respects justified, paid off even more handsomely at almost no risk.

This will doubtless be seen as an argument drawn from a familiar exculpatory tradition: the contention that Germany and Austria-Hungary were not as imperialist, reckless, or aggressive in the prewar era as other powers—to which the obvious answer is that they were imperialist, reckless, and aggressive where and when it really counted, in Europe in 1914. Let me say emphatically (I have the impression that this is an instance where one must shout in order to be heard) that this is not my point. The argument has nothing whatsoever to do with the character of German and Austro-Hungarian policy as compared to those of other powers. It has to do with who was really controlling the system, making the rules, and running the show, and thereby directly challenges the consensus case making the German powers primarily responsible for the security threats they faced in 1914 and contending that they could have warded off these threats by peaceful means. For it establishes that Germany and Austria-Hungary were not in control of the international system, but being restrained and controlled by it. The initiative and leadership in European politics from 1890 to 1914 always lay with their opponents, increasingly so as time went on. The standard reply, that the Central Powers lost control because of their own blunders and provocative acts, breaks down in numerous ways. It is a circular argument; it begs the question; it smacks of the ethic of success; it ignores the patent evidence that Germany's and Austria-Hungary's policies and initiatives regularly failed regardless of their character, whether aggressive and provocative or moderate and conciliatory;[15] it fails to specify concretely what different policies could have led to success, or explain how and why they could have. In more theoretical terms, it ignores a fundamental argument advanced by realists in international relations theory, an argument not always valid but here supported by strong evidence: that systemic factors, the distribution of power, vulnerability, and opportunities within the system, account for the major power-political patterns and outcomes of international politics more than do the character and aims of the individual actors. Logically and methodologically it errs in applying its principle of the primacy of domestic influences and interests not only to explain *decisions* in foreign policy (which is always in principle legitimate), but also to account for *outcomes* in international relations, where systemic factors must be taken into account. Finally, it errs by applying this dubious principle of the primacy of domestic politics one-sidedly, to the Central Powers far more than to the Entente.

The moral of all this is simple: to understand international outcomes from 1890 to 1914, one must stop looking first and foremost at what Germany and Austria-Hungary were doing, and concentrate on the powers who held the initiative in world affairs, basically running the system and making it work for them. One must further assume, barring evidence to the contrary, that their policies were primarily internally motivated, driven essentially by their own needs, purposes, and interests, and that Germany and Austria-Hungary, who could not and did not control events, were reacting to what the other powers were doing more than the other way around. Research on the policy of the various Entente powers done from this standpoint serves to confirm this judgment and produces a picture very different from the standard one.[16]

The distortions produced by focusing on Germany and Austria-Hungary as the prime movers in the international system are not remedied but made worse by stressing the domestic pressures and unsolved internal problems supposedly driving their foreign policies. Regardless of the extent to which this explanation may be justified (obviously their foreign and domestic policies were inextricably interwoven; in the case of Austria-Hungary, the distinction between foreign and domestic policy virtually breaks down), such a concentration on their internal problems in explaining their policies and motives simply reinforces the fundamental error of making these powers the prime movers within the system. The key to explaining the German powers' policies lies not in what their governments and their constituent interest groups and elites would have liked to do, but what they found themselves compelled to do. It makes better sense to analyze British, French, Russian, American, Italian, and Japanese policy in terms of domestic pressures and influences, for each of these governments had more effective choices and room to translate its desires into some kind of action.[17] It also bears remembering that the foreign policy/domestic politics nexus works both ways. Domestic pressures influence and shape foreign policy, but success or failure in international politics and foreign policy also strongly influence domestic politics. This was obviously the case in prewar Germany, where the government's perceived failures in foreign policy promoted dissatisfaction throughout the political spectrum, with right-radical groups and special interests especially calling for strong action to defend the country's interests.[18] If the danger to the regime and governing elites arising from foreign policy failure was serious for Germany, it was life threatening for Austria-Hungary. The steady erosion of the state's independence and international prestige not only encouraged dissident elements to press their claims and weakened the attachment of the loyal and dominant ones, but at the same time encouraged foreign governments to advance irredentist territorial claims and to promote internal discontent and subversion within Austria-Hungary and, in the Serbian case, to support terrorist resistance within it,[19] and encouraged almost every government to ignore or oppose its interests in international crises. To contend that the internal problems allegedly motivating the Central Powers' aggressive, dangerous foreign policies should have been handled instead by internal reforms is to ignore the extent to which, especially for Austria-Hungary, developments in the international arena contributed to those internal problems and made them unmanageable without foreign policy success.

This is (to repeat) not an attempt to blame their opponents for the failure of German and Austro-Hungarian statecraft that terminated in their July 1914 gamble.[20] It is instead an attempt to get beyond the old, tired blame game by showing that the root cause lies deeper than the policies of either the Central Powers or their rivals. It derives from the overall character of the international game being waged and the fundamentally unfavorable geopolitical position Germany and Austria-Hungary occupied within it.

That game requires at least a thumbnail description here. It comprised two simultaneous contests, inextricably intertwined and interdependent but with differing characteristics, stakes, and rules. The first was that of the old European balance of power. By 1914 this had evolved into an extremely competitive, zero–sum contest played for very high stakes (national survival) and at great risk (general war among populous industrialized states possessing mass armies); yet until just before 1914 certain minimal restraints or norms of international conduct left over from the Vienna era still prevailed. These norms, combined with prudence derived above all from fear of a general war, served to restrict the competition in Europe between individual powers and rival alliance systems to one waged for relative advantage rather than decisive victory; the powers aimed to ensure themselves victory in case of war and an upper hand in imperialist competition, but not to conquer or eliminate one's rivals. The notion of preserving a balance of power, still widely held as an ideal though each power defined the desired balance differently and pursued it in opposed, incompatible ways, rested on a general recognition that even a victorious great war would be terribly risky and costly and might prove counterproductive, creating new international dangers by destroying the existing balance or eliminating essential actors. Thus the game resembled high-stakes poker played by heavily armed men bent on winning but reluctant to raise the stakes too high, both to avoid losing themselves and to avoid provoking others facing impending bankruptcy into kicking over the table and starting a gunfight. As a result, there was a certain unspoken, consensual limit on the size of the bets and a general assumption that over major issues some compromise involving a minimal level of satisfaction for everyone, or at least all the great powers, should emerge. This last remnant of the old European Concert principle remained alive, though barely so, in the two Moroccan Crises, the Bosnian Crisis, and the diplomacy of the Balkan Wars.[21]

Another game was being played alongside European balance of power politics, however, called imperialism or world politics (different names for the same thing). Its stakes were shares in the economic, military, political, and territorial control and exploitation of the non-European world; its goals and rules resembled the board game Monopoly; and it evolved differently from its companion game. The nineteenth century European balance game began in 1814–15 with conservative monarchical cooperation against war, revolution, and territorial change and gradually evolved by 1914 into almost unrestrained zero–sum competition. Imperialism, always present throughout the nineteenth century but only taking center stage after about 1870, started out then as an individualistic scramble, carried on initially more by individuals and firms than governments, for goods supposedly free for the taking. This made imperialism at first a win-win contest for governments, less dangerous and more cooperative than the European balance game, in some ways a safe outlet for drives and energies too dangerous to be employed in Europe. Hence late-nineteenth and early-twentieth century imperialism sometimes led to confrontations but seldom to wars between European states (even the wars that occurred between European powers and the colonized peoples and states were usually small-scale affairs)[22] and often to deals dividing the spoils between certain claimants.[23]

Yet in the end European imperialism was more rapacious than ordinary balance of power politics, quite apart from the rapacity it showed to colonized peoples and territories. Unlike the European game, its primary aim was not security and relative advantage, but clear gains and acquisitions, which as time went on increasingly drove states to seek unchallenged control of particular areas, shutting others out. To be sure, sharing-out agreements continued to be made up to and through the Great War—consortia to build railways, carry on commercial activities, or exploit mineral resources in China or the Ottoman Empire, agreements to permit other powers commercial access to one's own colonies, international or bilateral deals over Egyptian, Ottoman, or Chinese customs, and others. Yet not only were these agreements often a *pis aller* necessary to avoid dangerous conflicts or to share prizes too expensive or troublesome to exploit exclusively. They were also usually monopolistic or semi-monopolistic in character, dividing up regions so as to exclude others and enable each partner to monopolize its own sphere. Moreover, even this element of cooperation tended increasingly to break down into confrontation or open conflict. New Imperialism, in short, tended inexorably toward exclusive paramountcy and control. Witness the aggressive extension of the American Monroe Doctrine in the Western Hemisphere (Cuba and the Caribbean, the Panama Canal, Venezuela, Brazil) and the Pacific, extending even to the Philippines; the British version of their own Monroe Doctrine, informal but effective, in much of Africa, India, and elsewhere; France's preemptive extension of its exclusive control from Algeria to Tunisia and Morocco; Russia's version of exclusive empire in Central Asia, tried less successfully in Manchuria, North China, and Korea, where Japan countered this with its own program. The Anglo-Russian Convention of 1907, which tried to avoid conflict and ensure cooperation by dividing Persia and Central and South Asia into clear-cut spheres, led to far more friction than cooperation between the two imperialist partners.

This points to further crucial differences. European balance of power politics before 1914, even at its most competitive as in its rival security alliances, was supposed to keep all the necessary players in the game and to last indefinitely with no decisive end-point. The players had established, relatively fixed, legally recognized positions and well-known, comparable assets and opportunities, making the idea of regulating competition among them by an equilibrium of forces thinkable, though not necessarily feasible. European imperialist politics, in contrast, was designed to keep some players in the game while driving others out. Its conclusion, with final winners and losers, would come when all the available world spoils were divided up, promoting a dominant spirit of *Torschlusspanik*—panic at the closing of the gates—from early on. Finally, the players started from very different starting points with vastly different, almost incommensurable and noncomparable assets, liabilities, and opportunities. When the serious game began after 1870, Great Britain began with a vast empire and many opportunities for further expansion, but at the same time with a new formidable challenge facing it. Its vast, far-flung possessions and the informal character of its paramount position in much of Africa and Asia, both stemming from a period in which it had no serious rival in naval, industrial, and commercial terms, made the British Empire now vulnerable and hard to defend against new competitors at a time when Britain was gradually losing its industrial supremacy, and the efforts necessary to defend it might undermine the very commercial strength and prosperity on which the Empire ultimately depended and which it was supposed to promote. Two other powers, Russia and the United States, had extensive empires that were mainly continental and hence less vulnerable, giving them both considerable security and potential for further expansion. France had a substantial colonial empire and numerous opportunities for expansion, but relatively little power and capital to expend on them. Other actors (Spain, Portugal, and the Netherlands) had residual empires they were determined to retain and exploit but could not defend against serious challenge. Finally, new players having no prior stake and widely varying capacities nonetheless entered determined to play (Germany, Japan, Italy, the King of Belgium, and toward the end Austria-Hungary). Even this does not exhaust the roster of players. Those who became targets of imperialism—China, the Ottoman Empire, various African states and empires—did not simply react passively, but developed their own programs, sometimes expansionist-imperialist ones (Great Serbia, Great Bulgaria, the Greek *Megale Idea*, Pan-Turanianism, and the like).

All this ensured that the imperialist game, unlike the European one, could not be played according to more or less rational rules and calculations leading to some sort of balanced power and satisfactions, but would end in clear winners and losers. Moreover, while the high stakes of the European balance game, the fact that the survival of the nation was at risk in any general war, made for caution, the high stakes in imperialist politics, based on the general conviction that a nation's future survival and prosperity in the coming century depended on acquiring world power and position, had an opposite effect. Since the immediate danger of a great war breaking out over imperialist quarrels seemed small, imperialist competition encouraged strategic and tactical boldness, going for broke.

This relates to our main question, because in order to judge whether Germany and Austria-Hungary had alternative policies available by which they might have averted the threats they faced in 1914 and eliminated any need to gamble, one must appraise how much intrinsic chance they had to succeed in these two interlocking games from an earlier point—say, 1890—at which both games became more seriously competitive. In the European balance game, in my judgment, their basic starting positions, strengths, and liabilities gave neither much chance for significant gains and assured Austria-Hungary in particular of difficulty in holding its own regardless of what it did. The most fundamental miscalculation German leaders made was their expectation that Germany's central position in Europe would help it exploit rivalries between other powers and make itself indispensable to both sides, at a profit. That geographical position (as Bismarck had recognized—it gave him his nightmare of coalitions) was instead mainly a handicap, forcing both powers always to reckon with the likelihood of a two-front war (in Austria-Hungary's case a multi-front one), increasing their vulnerability and limiting their freedom of maneuver and alliance capability. Centrally located as they were, they could make firm commitments only to each other or to weaker states needing their support, such as Italy and Rumania. They also had an additional liability often ignored in the literature: unlike all the other important powers save the Ottoman Empire, they had territories other states and/or peoples coveted and in certain instances claimed by right. In Germany's case, this meant France (Alsace-Lorraine), Denmark (North Schleswig), and the Poles (Polish Prussia). Austria's case was far worse: Italian nationalists claimed the Veneto and Trentino, Istria, and parts of Dalmatia; Russian nationalists and leaders, including the Tsar, wanted to solve the Ukrainian problem by annexing East Galicia and the Bukovina; Serbia claimed all the Austro-Hungarian territories populated by Serbs or Croats; and Rumania had its eyes on Transylvania.

To be sure, these claims and velleites did not immediately threaten Germany's and Austria-Hungary's territorial integrity. Like other notions some Russians had about the Turkish Straits or East Prussia and Prussian Poland or some British and French had about Germany's colonies, these aims were likely to come into play, and did, once war broke out, but no one save radical Serbian nationalists and their backers in the Serbian military and in extreme Panslav circles in Russia wanted a war to achieve them. Throughout the prewar period the Central Powers, especially Germany, remained too strong for other powers to challenge them too directly in Europe. In other words, their basic situation was unfavorable but not disastrous; it was likely that they would lose in terms of relative security and advantage, but unlikely that they would forfeit their positions as European great powers. This pretty much sums up the outcome of European great power politics from 1890 to 1910. Given their basic situation at the outset, its unfavorable course for them was natural and normal if not strictly predictable, readily understandable without invoking particular blunders or provocations on their part as explanations. Nor is there ground to suppose that other policies on their part would necessarily have changed this result very much.

If the question is what basic chances for success they had in the imperialist-world politics game from about 1890 on, the answer could well be the familiar bon mot about their wartime situations in 1917: in Berlin it was serious but not hopeless; in Vienna it was hopeless but not serious. Almost everything in their geopolitical situation worked against them for success in imperialist expansion: no initial foundation in terms of colonies, overseas trade, bases, and readily projected naval or military power; an unfavorable geographic location with only limited access to one ocean, easily blocked by rivals in case of war; an exposed position in Europe which forced them to limit their commitments and be risk-averse in the world game, making them unattractive as imperialist partners and tempting as targets; and internal divisions and weaknesses hampering both, especially Austria-Hungary. Germany had only one of the requirements for success in the imperialist world game, a vibrant growing economy, and Austria–Hungary, though growing economically, did not enjoy even that.

Just as important as these liabilities in insuring their defeat were the rules of the imperialist game and the way the other powers played it. The dominant fact—obvious yet somehow frequently overlooked or, if noticed, not taken seriously—is that the other imperialist great powers, Britain above all, but also Russia, France, Italy, and to some extent the United States and later Japan, played the imperialist game to make Germany and Austria-Hungary lose, as part of their strategy to win. The common German charge that the Triple Entente deliberately encircled Germany in Europe was false, at least so far as Britain was concerned, but another charge, that Germany and Austria-Hungary were deliberately circled out of world politics as much as possible, is obviously true. The Anglo-French Entente Cordiale in 1904 was intended to keep Germany from interfering with exclusive British and French control in Egypt and Morocco. British efforts from 1890 on to reach an agreement with Russia over the Middle East, culminating in their 1907 convention on Persia and Central Asia, were designed to prevent German penetration of this region—an aim Russia shared. Much of British foreign policy on South Africa was directed at keeping Germany from interfering there at all, whether as a partner or as an opponent. France deliberately set out to do the same *vis-à-vis* Germany in both Moroccan Crises, violating international agreements of 1880, 1906, and 1909 in the process. The United States worked with Britain in Latin America, the South Seas, and the Far East to limit German influence. The British and Russians collaborated against Germany on the Baghdad Railway and fought especially hard against German influence at Constantinople and in Mesopotamia. Russia, encouraged by Britain and aided by France, worked from 1907 on to check Austro-Hungarian influence in the Balkans and especially after 1911 to eliminate that influence entirely. Russia, Britain, Japan, and the United States all tried to check German economic and political expansion in China and the Far East. In the prewar scramble for concessions in Asiatic Turkey, all the other powers, including Italy and Germany, worked against Austria-Hungary.

Of course this is not evidence of a sinister anti-German or anti-Austro-Hungarian conspiracy. These tactics broke no rules because these *were* the rules, the way to play the imperialist game for fun and profit. One no more needs to invoke an anti-German or anti-Austro-Hungarian conspiracy to account for this pattern than one needs to talk of conspiracies to account for monopolistic and oligopolistic combinations and strategies in the business world, or to explain how these often target particular firms and sometimes drive them out of business. Everyone recognizes these tactics as part of the game.[24] The pattern, however, does further undermine the view that German and Austro-Hungarian policies were primarily responsible for the threats to their interests and security, and that Germany could have achieved its needed place in the sun had it followed less aggressive and provocative policies. This is like arguing that firms being deliberately driven out of business by others could have saved themselves by following less aggressive and provocative policies toward their competitors. It ignores both the concrete evidence to the contrary and the basic rules and nature of the game.

A similar unrealism afflicts the related argument that Germany, even if it lost the contest in power politics, would nonetheless have survived and prospered simply by continuing its current rate of economic growth, becoming in a few more years of peace an economic hegemon in Europe too powerful for the others to challenge. This argument, on the surface plausible, seems to ignore certain facts, such as the precarious nature of Germany's economic achievements and prosperity in an age of intense competition and frequent booms and busts (German economic growth was being surpassed by the United States at the same time and at much the same rate as Germany was surpassing Great Britain, and Russia had the fastest rate of industrial growth before 1914); or the fact that the more German trade and exports grew, the more dependent the German economy became on external markets and imports for further growth and survival, and the more vulnerable it became to military threats to these. Since British leaders calculated that they could destroy German overseas commerce and ruin Germany's economy by a naval blockade and made this their primary strategy in case of war, it was reasonable for Germans to feel vulnerable to this threat regardless of how much economic power and wealth they amassed. Indeed, the wealthier they became, the more that sense of threat would grow. Fear of loss, as psychologists have long established, is a more powerful motivator than hope of gain. But even apart from these considerations, obvious yet inexplicably widely ignored, the most important thing here is to understand the counterfactual question. It is not, "How would the European and world economies have developed had peace lasted for some years after 1914?" That question is both too loaded with indeterminate contingent variables to be answered, and not relevant here. The question is rather, "In the real world of 1914, could Germany's leaders and public reasonably have been expected to rely for their security against foes already superior to Germany on the sea and expected shortly to achieve superiority also on land on the prospect or possibility that if peace lasted long enough, Germany's economic dynamism would protect it against these strategic and military threats?"

The answer to this question seems self-evident to me, but it is apparently not so to others, and so one needs to look at its underlying assumptions and implications. To rely on this expectation, German leaders would have had to be confident not merely that Germany would win the current economic competition, but also that a generally free, liberal world economic order with open access for everyone to international trade, especially overseas, would endure indefinitely, regardless of developments on the European and world strategic and military stage and regardless of whether Germany could if necessary support its economic interests with political and military weapons. This assumption simply flies in the face of the facts. It assumes that Smithian free-market liberalism by 1914 had decisively triumphed over neo-mercantilism, protectionism, and economic imperialism, when in fact all the major powers save Britain believed in protectionism and mercantilism rather than free trade. Even Britain practiced a form of imperialist protectionism, and most states were more protectionist than Germany. It assumes that Germany's rivals would have peacefully come to terms with Germany's economic domination, when in fact they were already worried by Germany's economic progress and took active measures before the war, especially in Russia and France, to avoid becoming economically dependent on Germany.[25] It assumes that the prewar international economic system operated largely independently of European high politics and military strategy and would continue to do so, when in fact everyone believed that a strong state and a strong economy required each other and that it was the government's duty to bring the nation's political, military, and economic resources together to promote its national interests. Tariff wars, discrimination against foreign goods and enterprises, and attempts by governments to promote their nationals' economic interests or to use these interests to promote their political and strategic ends were central to the age of imperialism. Even the British, who still adhered to free-trade principles, relied on their naval supremacy and empire as a hedge against dangerous competition or decline.

In other words, this counterfactual holds that the Germans, of all people, should have believed and trusted in the message of Norman Angell's prewar book *The Great Illusion*: that growing interdependence in the modern capitalist economy had rendered war obsolete, counterproductive, and unthinkable. True, Angell was right in criticizing the reigning neo-mercantilist, protectionist, and militarist doctrines of his day, but he also ignored power political realities and their connection to economics then and since.[26] The counterfactual argument that Germany could have broken up or loosened the alliances or quasi-alliances against it by more moderate, patient policies and conduct has similar problems. Granted, Germany's opponents genuinely perceived Germany as unpredictable and dangerous, and were acting partly to counter that threat. But this does not mean that Germany could have removed that perception and changed its opponents' policies simply by becoming somehow more moderate and conciliatory in its behavior. Germany posed a threat particularly to Russia and France mainly because of where it was located and the power it possessed rather than by its policies, and their alliances and ententes were intended to meet this objective, structural threat by giving the Entente powers a margin of military preponderance over Germany. Any signs of German restraint would and did serve as proof that these alignments were working and should be continued. Besides, as already noted, these combinations had important uses in world politics. Their central value for Britain was to help preserve the British Empire by maintaining Britain's good relations with France and Russia so as to curb both their colonial rivalries with Britain and German competition. Preserving the so-called balance of power in Europe was part and parcel of this policy. In other words, the anti-German alliances and ententes were so intrinsically valuable for the Entente powers for both their security in Europe and their world-imperialist purposes that German good behavior would not have made them give them up, and that German attempts to undermine or loosen them, or even join them, served as more proof that Germany was treacherous and dangerous. The history of prewar politics shows this. The cognitive biases apparent in the consensus view—the ascription of more freedom of choice to one side (in this case Germany) than to the other, and the belief that it could easily have changed its policy and thereby have induced the other side to change too—are familiar to political psychologists.

All this concerns only the German side of the problem, on which most historians concentrate, ignoring thereby the more immediate and pressing half, the Austro-Hungarian problem.[27] The counterfactuals embedded in the consensus view involving Austria-Hungary are even stranger than those for Germany, and receive less scrutiny. But in a way this is not surprising, for in regard to Austria-Hungary the consensus case with its embedded counterfactuals rests on assumptions so unwarranted as hardly to deserve discussion. A good example is the notion that internal reforms could have solved the nationalities disputes within Austria-Hungary and thus given it the needed power and cohesion to survive the ruthless competition of European and world politics. This assumes two things: that nationalities conflicts of the kind that have troubled the Habsburg Monarchy and other multinational states in modern times are soluble by any means,[28] and that internal reforms, if they succeed in promoting greater domestic harmony, also make a state stronger for foreign policy purposes. No support is offered in theory, argument, or evidence for either assumption, and none is available. In fact, the Austrian government launched many reforms between 1867 and 1914 that helped make the Monarchy a progressive, modernizing state in important respects— a thriving culture, a growing economy, an advanced educational system, and a political system that, though riddled with conflict and tensions, respected civil rights and included democratic features. But these reforms also, inevitably, hampered rather than aided the Monarchy's efforts to conduct a strong foreign policy. The more freedom its many peoples, factions, and parties enjoyed to contend for their particular rights, status, and share of power within the Monarchy, and the more parliamentary (and thereby more chaotic) its politics became, the less chance there was to unite everyone on a single foreign policy agenda, or to raise the taxes needed to keep Austria-Hungary competitive in the European arms race, or to prevent foreign governments and groups from intervening in the Monarchy's nationalities conflicts, and the nationalities themselves from exploiting this.

Even more implausible is the suggestion that successful internal reforms, whatever these might have been, would have lessened the hostility or changed the aims of its opponents abroad. Russian nationalists and the Russian government were not interested in protecting the rights of Ukrainians (so-called Ruthenes) in East Galicia; their concern was to prevent Ukrainian nationalism from spreading from East Galicia and the Bukovina to Imperial Russia, and the ideal solution was to annex these territories to Russia. Much the same holds for Italian nationalists and their irredentist claims, as well as Rumanian nationalists, to say nothing of the Serbs. This has nothing to do with the question of whether Austria-Hungary should have done something more or different to meet its internal problems; it means only that meeting its internal problems would not have significantly changed the attitudes or actions of its opponents.

The central weakness in the counterfactual case on Austria-Hungary, however, parallels the one in regard to Germany: it ignores the basic rules and nature of the game. Austria-Hungary's competitors and opponents were acting with regard to the Monarchy essentially in behalf of their own interests and aims, not in reaction to what it did. Austria-Hungary could have prevented this only by changing the nature and stakes of the game to make this unprofitable—which was what it finally tried to do by its July 1914 gamble. One more feature of the standard counterfactual scenario deserves mention: that it leaves the two sides of its case, the German and Austro-Hungarian aspects, unconnected when they are in fact tightly interwoven. It suggests a counterfactual solution for Germany's security problem, namely, that it show greater restraint, moderation, and patience toward its opponents and accept some temporary military and strategic insecurity while seeking its future security through the relaxation of tensions in Europe and German economic growth. For Austria-Hungary it suggests domestic reforms to strengthen it politically and militarily so that it could better defend its interests against external challenges. Leave aside for the moment the inherent flaws in these proposals, already discussed, and ask simply how they fit and work together. The answer is: They do not—they contradict each other. Suppose *per impossibile* that Austria-Hungary could before 1914 have achieved the internal cohesion and economic strength to keep up with the others in the arms race; how would that have fit in with a simultaneous effort by Germany to try to cool the arms race? It would have been obviously and directly contrary to it—the main reason being that the fixed policy of all three Entente powers was to consider Austria-Hungary as simply Germany's subordinate ally, no matter how desperately the Austrians pleaded that they were pursuing an independent policy, so that a stronger, more confident and assertive Austria-Hungary automatically meant in St. Petersburg, Paris, and London a stronger, more dangerous Germany.[29] Or consider the impact of German efforts to conciliate its opponents on Austria-Hungary's security problem. The historical evidence is clear: such efforts by Germany made Austria-Hungary's problems worse. What Russia wanted as proof of German moderation and cooperation, also demanded by Britain, was that Germany restrain Austria-Hungary in the Balkans. Germany's refusal in Russia's eyes to restrain Austria-Hungary in 1909 was the source of massive, permanent Russian resentment. When Germany did restrain its ally from 1910 to 1913, thereby helping prevent a general war and temporarily improving Russo-German and Anglo-German relations, that also contributed hugely to undermining Austria-Hungary's position and fuelling frustration and despair among its decision-makers. Or consider the suggestion that Germany should have relied on peaceful economic expansion for its future security. One of Germany's most important economic targets before 1914 was the Balkans and the Ottoman Empire. German economic expansion there directly threatened Austria-Hungary's trade, prosperity and independence more than those of any other state, serving to encourage Austria-Hungary's opponents, Serbia in particular, and push Austria-Hungary toward violent countermeasures.

These points are important not just as further instances of the internal contradictions in the consensus scenario and the ways it neglects the Austro-Hungarian problem, but as evidence of a profound misunderstanding of the German problem as well. Those who insist that Germany was mainly responsible for the Central Powers' gambling strategy in 1914, even though Austria-Hungary conceived that strategy, demanded German support for it, and finally launched it, argue that Austria-Hungary could not possibly have acted without German help, and that since Germany gave its ally a blank check, subsequently pressed Austria-Hungary forward, and never really tried to restrain it, Germany was chiefly responsible. Once again the embedded counterfactual assumptions demand examination. There are at least two, closely related: first, that the German government, if it genuinely wanted peace, could have rejected Vienna's demand for support, regardless of Austro-Hungarian warnings that a denial of support would critically affect the alliance, future Austrian policy, and the survival of the Monarchy as a great power; second, that Germany, in the interest of general peace, could and should have detached its security and great power status from Austria-Hungary's survival as a great power—a survival that Germans, like everyone in Europe, including especially the Austrians, considered genuinely threatened.

It is hard to conceive how these assumptions could be defended. They seem to contradict everything known about the history of German and Austrian relations in Central Europe, the connection between this problem and the wider problems of relations with Russia over Eastern Europe and the Balkans, and the nature of European international politics, both political and military. Above all they strike one as an impossible way to promote durable European peace. In a more peaceful and stable earlier era, Bismarck recognized and acted upon an insight fully confirmed by history since 1914: that breaking up the Habsburg Monarchy or eliminating it as a great power, regardless of how this happened and whether or not Austria deserved it, would have revolutionary consequences for Germany and Europe as a whole. That insight is here ignored. The surprise is not that Germany recognized this community of fate in July 1914 and backed Austria-Hungary's desperate gamble; the decision to do so had essentially been taken earlier in 1914.

The surprise is rather that the German government earlier tried for a long time to ignore its ally's problems or to sweep them under the rug, even in various ways helping make them worse, and that only now it seriously reckoned with the consequences for Germany of Austria-Hungary's continued decline and potential collapse or defection as an ally.

The crowning anomaly in the consensus view and its counterfactuals lies thus in its ignoring precisely what the July Crisis most clearly proves: that Germany could not ignore the Austro-Hungarian problem even though it wished to, because the German and Austro-Hungarian problems were Siamese twins, and part of still wider and more complex Central and East European and Near Eastern problems, so that an attempt to solve or manage the German question and the question of European peace without seriously dealing with the Austro-Hungarian problem was an attempt to play Hamlet without the Prince of Denmark.

An Account of the Origins of the War with Different Embedded Counterfactuals

The argument thus far seems to suggest that the war was inevitable for the following reasons:

(a) The nature of the European power game and of Germany's and Austria-Hungary's respective positions within it made its actual outcome by 1914, namely, relative loss, frustration, and looming danger for Germany and even worse decline and immediate peril for Austria– Hungary, likely from the outset.

(b) Similarly, the nature of the imperialist game and of Germany's and Austria's positions in it made its actual outcome, that Germany would lose relative to its rivals, but not absolutely or fatally, while Austria– Hungary risked losing completely, even more likely.

(c) Yet these unfavorable outcomes and trends were probably not enough individually and by themselves to make the two powers risk a general war in order to reverse them. This is suggested by the fact that on several occasions previously (1904–05, 1908–09, and 1912–13) they passed up opportunities for war when their chances for success were better than they were in 1914. Nevertheless, given the facts that these two games were tied together both objectively and in their perception, and that the Central Powers, like others, believed that both contests were critical to their ultimate survival, security, and prosperity as great powers, their belief that they were losing and declining in both made it likely that at some point they would take some risky action to reverse the trend. Any immediate, overt challenge and threat to the independence, integrity, and great power status of one or both of them, such as arose on June 28, 1914, would increase that likelihood dramatically.

(d) Since their rivals shared their assumptions regarding the nature, rules, and stakes of the combined European-world politics game and were therefore equally determined to maintain their favorable positions or improve them, any German–Austro-Hungarian initiative to reverse the existing trends of the game was almost certain to meet strong resistance and produce a direct collision between the two sides. The tense, crisis-laden atmosphere of prewar politics, with many vital issues unresolved and major developments in flux, made it virtually certain that occasions for confrontations and clashes of interest would arise. These facts, plus the high stakes on both sides and the absence of any mutually acceptable compromise of their irreconcilable purposes, entitle one to consider a general war as inevitable sooner or later.

This view comes close, but it is too determinist or determinist in the wrong way. It makes the decisive element the nature, rules, and stakes of the prevailing game of international politics and the objective conditions under which the various actors entered it and played it out. The version I propose locates the determining element elsewhere—not in the international game itself, which still could conceivably have continued for some time without general war and without radical changes in its rules, but in the political culture of the era and in certain dominant beliefs about the prevailing game.

Let me try to show the subtle difference by an analogy, inevitably inexact but perhaps useful for illustration. Compare World War I to a train collision involving five trains, all in a race to reach the station first or at least to avoid coming in last. The strict determinist view just outlined holds that they collided because all five were on intersecting tracks, the only way to avoid an accident was for at least one or two of them to give way to the others and thereby lose the race, and all considered this action with its predictable outcome unacceptable. An indeterminist view would hold that the trains, though running on unsafe tracks at dangerously high speeds with obsolete equipment operated in certain instances by reckless engineers, were not running on intersecting tracks but parallel ones set dangerously close together. Hence a collision was not inevitable but could only arise by accident (say, if one of the trains left the tracks or swayed into another one) or by deliberate recklessness. My version holds that while all five trains involved in the race were running together closely enough that all would be involved in any accident, only three of the five were on a potential collision course. These three, however, had been in similar races over this same terrain a number of times before, and knew how an accident could be avoided—when to slow down, what signals to give, what switches or side-tracks to take, and so on—actions that involved some active coordination between themselves and at least passive cooperation from the other two trains in the race. What caused the collision in this instance was a refusal by the engineers on all five trains at critical moments to take the steps their experience told them were needed to avoid an accident. They failed to act out of a shared conviction that the game no longer allowed for such actions—that they had become futile and counterproductive, would cause them to lose the race, and were in any case not their particular responsibility. This collective mentality and fixed attitude made the collision unavoidable.

Notice that this last version shifts the focus from, "Who or what caused the train wreck?" to "Who or what caused the failure to avoid it?" Applied to World War I, the focus is changed from, "Who or what caused the outbreak of war?" to "Who or what caused the breakdown of peace?" For many reasons impossible to discuss here, I contend that explaining peace rather than war should be the prime emphasis in studying war and international politics in general. But regardless of this claim as a broad principle, the aim here is solely to show in a prima facie way that the distinction makes sense and that World War I is better explained as the breakdown of peace than the outbreak of war. The analysis intends to show how the war had become unavoidable not because the forces and impulses driving the different powers toward it had become irresistible, but because the actions needed to avoid it had become unthinkable. Consistent with the theme of this essay, the argument involves counterfactual reasoning.

The strict determinist argument sketched out earlier holds that under the circumstances prevailing by 1914 the German powers were virtually certain sooner or later to try to reverse the prevailing trends pointing toward an outcome unacceptable to them through violent means that would risk general war, and that the others were equally certain to resist this strongly, resulting in war. To see why this comes close but misses the target, one needs to ask two closely related counterfactual questions. First, what plausible circumstances might have led Germany and Austria-Hungary in 1914 to decide once again, as they had done several times before, to try other less provocative and dangerous ways of defending their security and vital interests? Second, what actions, plausible under the circumstances, might the other powers have decided to take before or during the July Crisis suitable to deter and/or dissuade the German powers from a course risking war?

These counterfactual questions seem to give the game away to the indeterminists, opening the door wide to many suggestions and alternative scenarios commonly encountered in the literature. Things would have been different had the assassination attempt failed, or had the Austro-Hungarians agreed to stop their attack on Serbia at Belgrade, or had Russia given the Serbian government different advice, or had Britain given Germany a clear warning that it would enter the war on France's side, and so on. However, the argument made earlier, that all the major actors were fundamentally driven by long term concerns based on shared assumptions about the nature, rules, and stakes of the game and a shared understanding of where that game was headed, closes the door against that kind of general speculation about contingencies. If one side by 1914 was determined to reverse the prevailing trend and avert the predicted ultimate outcome even at the grave risk of war, and the other side was equally ready to accept war rather than let that happen, then different individual events and actions at the time of the July Crisis would only have altered the occasion, timing, and form of the final collision, not averted it, *unless the different events and actions also changed these shared assumptions, beliefs, and expectations.* The real questions therefore are, first, whether such a change in these reigning collective European mindsets and understandings about international politics was possible at all before or during the July Crisis, and second, what alternative policies, decisions, and actions conceivable in terms of the minimal-rewrite rule and compatible with historical evidence might have effected this change, that is, might have altered the reigning perceptions of current and future trends sufficiently on both sides, especially on the Central Powers, to change their views of what could and must be done. The strong determinist position denies that any such shift was possible; the indeterminist one denies that any was necessary. The view advanced here is between and beyond both. It is that, objectively and historically speaking, strategies and tactics were still available to the great powers that might have averted a collision by changing crucial prevailing mindsets, but that subjectively, in terms of what the actors considered conceivable and feasible, they were not—and therefore war was inevitable.

    The first step in testing this is establishing just what needed to change in the mindsets of what particular actors. The consensus view holds that only German and Austro-Hungarian attitudes needed to change; that view, as we have seen, will not do. But did virtually everything in the whole situation have to change? The determinist view fits the common impression that Europe by 1914 was a tinderbox filled with explosive material waiting for a spark, so that war could have broken out over any one or any combination of many issues or causes. That picture is also misleading. Actually, Europe in June 1914 was near general war, as it had been repeatedly since 1908, but it was not yet at the brink or certain to go over it, and most of the conflicts that divided the great powers were not such as to set off a war. In fact (here again comes counterfactual reasoning) no convincing scenario can be constructed by which most of the issues in dispute could have caused a general war, either alone or even in combination. One could compile a long list of issues—Anglo-German naval rivalry, Alsace-Lorraine and other irredentist territorial claims, military threats, colonial and commercial rivalries, historic national hatreds, ethnic and racial animosities—that were serious, sufficient to create hostility and tension, but not matters over which any great power wanted or intended to fight, or for which it could plausibly start a war. Instead, only three great powers contemplated starting a general war under any circumstances—Russia, Germany, and Austria-Hungary—and their respective grounds for doing so were limited and specific. Russia was willing, though not eager, to fight for two reasons: to prevent any other power from gaining control of the Turkish Straits (witness its willingness to use force to prevent its own allies and associates, Bulgaria and Greece, from seizing Constantinople in the first Balkan War, and its strong stand over the Liman von Sanders affair in early 1914); and to prevent what the Russian government, driven by a nationalist press and so-called public opinion, viewed as another humiliation like that of 1908–09 in the Balkans at the hands of the German powers. Germany was willing to go to war rather than allow its army to become decisively inferior to those of its foes, either through Russia's successful completion of its armaments program or by Austria-Hungary's collapse or defection, or both. Austria-Hungary's will for war was the most desperate and dangerous of all. Although with good reason it feared general war more than any other great power, its leaders had already concluded by early 1914 that it could not tolerate any further deterioration of its great power status and its Balkan position, particularly through more challenges and provocations from Serbia. These were the only issues that could have caused general war in 1914, and they did cause it. The question of the avoidability of war therefore rests neither on whether some impossible set of sweeping changes in the whole international situation occurred, nor on whether certain particular contingent events involved in the outbreak of war in July 1914 could have gone differently, but on the specific question of whether these particular great powers could have been deterred and/or dissuaded from risking general war for these particular reasons.

The answer is "Yes." It arises not from theory or speculation, but solid historical evidence. The first thing to recognize is that these problems were not new to these powers, but old and familiar, almost standard; they had repeatedly caused wars or threatened to cause them before.[30] Twice in the previous century (1809 and 1859) Austria had gone to war rather than accept a further decline in its great power status and position and more threats to its prestige and rights. In 1756 Prussia had deliberately launched a preventive war against Austria and Russia rather than wait for an overwhelming coalition to jell against it.[31] Russia had been ready in the Bulgarian Crisis of 1884–87 to fight Austria rather than accept another supposed humiliation at its hands. Not only were the essential dangers in 1914 familiar, almost commonplace; so were the theater, the terrain, and the three players. Ever since 1763 at the end of the Seven Years War, when Russia and Prussia had fully emerged as recognized great powers, these three states had dominated Central and Eastern Europe, competing over territory, interests, influence, leadership, and security. This area, even during the Napoleonic wars, had been constantly the main focus and center of European politics. The issues that dominated the Austro-German–Russian relationship and threatened the peace in 1914 had *mutatis mutandis* been vital for them the whole time.

But if the issues and dangers were familiar, so were the remedies. The astonishing fact (astonishing both in itself and in its being so widely ignored) is that the 150 years of Austro-German–Russian relations after 1763 represent a story not of constant rivalry, conflicts of interests, struggles for power and influence, and frequent tensions and crises leading to war, but of constant rivalry, conflicts of interests, struggles for power and influence, and frequent tensions and crises resulting in *peace*. Between 1740 and 1914, Austria and Russia, always rivals in the Balkans, often rivals elsewhere as well, frequently at swords' points, *never* fought each other, except for two occasions in 1809 and 1812 when they were dragged by Napoleon into half-hearted campaigns that they would never have entered on their own. The same is true between 1762 and 1914 for Prussia–Germany and Russia. Austria and Prussia fought two short wars over Germany, to be sure—one indecisive in 1778–79, the other decisive in 1866. Yet within thirteen years of the latter they were again allies, as they had been most of the fifty years before 1866—without ever ceasing to be rivals. In the same way Austria and Russia and Germany and Russia were frequently allies though always rivals.

Thus the central story in European international history from 1763 to 1914 is this remarkable Austro-German–Russian *peace*. Nineteen fourteen must be seen first and foremost not simply and generically as the outbreak of general European war, but as the breakdown of that specific long peace. To explain the war, scholars must first explain it, understand what maintained and revived it so long, often against improbable odds, and then, having done this, ask themselves whether the measures and devices that had previously served to maintain this Austro-German–Russian peace no longer would work in 1914, or whether (as I believe) they simply were not tried.

To attempt any such serious analysis here would stretch the already elastic bounds of this essay beyond the breaking point. I will therefore merely make some general points, more by assertion than by argument. First, the procedures and principles of European diplomacy used for dealing with such problems as these, especially those of the European Concert, were well known. Where seriously tried, they still worked even in 1914. One vital issue capable of causing war in 1914, that of the Turkish Straits, was actually handled successfully in this way. Russia's warnings to Bulgaria and Greece to stay away from the Straits and its success (with British and French support and restraint) in inducing Germany and the Ottoman Empire to back down on the Liman affair under cover of a face-saving formula without using force against the Turks were examples, if risky ones, of traditional Concert diplomacy on the Eastern question. The underlying principles behind both were traditional: that Russia had special interests in the Straits and could not allow others besides Turkey to control them, but could rely on diplomacy and the Concert to defend its interests and was not allowed to act unilaterally or by force. True, the other fighting issue for Russia, that it would not tolerate another humiliation in the Balkans at the hands of Austria-Hungary and Germany, and the corresponding fighting issue for Austria-Hungary, that it could not endure any further undermining of its great power position in the Balkans or challenges from Russia and its client Serbia, were far more difficult to handle, not merely because of the mutually incompatible perceptions and enflamed public opinion on all sides, but also because (in my view) Russian perceptions were one-sided and unjustified. The widespread belief that Russia's rights had repeatedly been violated, its prestige and honor challenged, and its security and historic mission in the Balkans threatened ever since 1908 by the German powers simply does not square with undeniable facts. In 1908–09, as even more in 1904–06, Russia had been lucky to escape dangers of its own making, that the Central Powers could have exploited but did not. Since then Russia had been mainly winning in the Balkans and getting away with a very bold offensive policy. Yet this was far from the first time that Russia had blamed difficulties largely of its own making on Germany and Austria (witness the Eastern Crisis of 1875–78 and the Bulgarian Crisis of 1884–87) or that Austria had seen Russian pressure as an alp that it had to shake off at almost any cost (the Crimean War). Historically, there were tested ways of handling such problems short of war.[32]

As for Germany's fear of Russia, here again one must distinguish between the irrational fear of being overrun by barbarian hordes from the East and the concomitant belief in a great, inevitable Teuton–Slav struggle for mastery in Europe, and the concrete and rational fear of being hopelessly outmanned by 1917 by the combined Russo-French armies and those of their allies. Diplomacy could not directly combat the former fear, but it could have done something to manage the latter, even within the existing alliance structure. For instance, there could have been some informal equivalent for Germany of Bismarck's Reinsurance Treaty with Russia in 1887, assuring Germany that France and Britain would not support a Russian attack on Germany, as Bismarck had reassured Russia that Germany would not support a British–Austrian offensive against it.

The other requirement for simultaneously deterring and reassuring Germany concerns Austria-Hungary, and brings us to the heart of the problem. One can hardly overemphasize the destabilizing effect of the conviction among German leaders by 1914, one promoted by the Austrians themselves, that Germany must now use its ally or lose it—stand by it now at any risk and cost, or expect shortly to have to fight without it because of Austria-Hungary's defection, paralysis, or breakup. It is difficult enough to imagine a counterfactual scenario in which Germany with its powerful, irresponsible military, its erratic, impulsive monarch, and its semi-authoritarian, deeply divided government and society would have calmly stood by while Russia and France completed their efforts to achieve military superiority over it. It is quite impossible to imagine Germany doing so while it simultaneously was losing its last remaining useful ally. The implication is clear: one indispensable key to restraining Germany and in general to preventing a major war was stabilizing Austria-Hungary's international status by doing something serious about the Austro-Hungarian problem.

The common reply to this assertion, or rather, dismissal of it, is that Austria-Hungary's decline and eventual collapse were irreversible, the result of its internal decay and impossible to solve or arrest by international politics and diplomacy. As already indicated, I deny the premise, as do other scholars more expert on Austro-Hungarian internal affairs than I. Austria-Hungary's problems and weaknesses were real and would not go away or be cured, but they were not of themselves destroying it or even keeping it from being a working political entity, functioning far more soundly in most respects, for example, than Russia or its Balkan neighbors or Italy. It was the combination within the cauldron of European international competition of internal and external pressures on Austria-Hungary and the purposeful exploitation of these by other states that was ruining its international position. It is simply not true—in fact, nonsense—to say that European international politics could do nothing about this or about preventing a war that might arise out of it. Were this principle true, the Habsburg Monarchy would not have survived a number of crises in its long, crisis-riddled existence. It had repeat-edly been saved in the past by support, usually passive but sometimes active, from various members of the European family of states including Russia who recognized that its disappearance would bring with it incalculable consequences and insoluble problems.

Yet making this simple historical observation, or citing the traditional balance of power principle of the need to preserve in order to maintain a viable international system, risks confusing the central issue to the advantage of those whose interest it is to confuse it. The question is not whether the Habsburg Monarchy could have been saved in 1914, or should have been, or whether other powers including its rivals should have done something concrete to save it. My own view, indicated earlier, is that the Monarchy did not need active intervention by anyone in its internal problems in order to survive and continue to muddle through, as it had done for most of its existence with fair success. Quite the contrary—it needed less intervention and pressure from outside. But regardless of this, the real question is whether, in the face of mounting evidence of the possibility or likelihood of the collapse or paralysis of so essential an actor as Austria-Hungary, the members of the European international system had reasons, incentives, precedents, and devices for taking some kind of action to manage and control the process and international consequences of so mammoth a change, or whether they were bound simply to let it happen and see what emerged from the wreckage.

Thus correctly posed, the question answers itself, and not on the basis of any moral considerations, but on those of history and elementary state self-interest. The Austro-Hungarian problem in its *international* dimensions and repercussions was precisely the sort of question with which the international system was supposed to deal, and could have dealt. Historical precedents abounded in 1914 for the systemic European management of the problems and dangers presented by declining and threatened vital units. They varied widely, of course, from brutal measures like planned partitions of the declining units with more or less balanced compensations to the more powerful ones (Poland and the German Empire in the late-eighteenth and early-nineteenth centuries) through less brutal, more controlled management (the Ottoman Empire in the Balkans and North Africa) through measures of joint guarantee and protection (Belgium, Switzerland, Denmark, and for a considerable period the Papal State). What was unprecedented was what actually happened before and during 1914—the ignoring of this issue, the absence of any collective European response to the prospective downfall or disappearance of a central actor like Austria-Hungary, a contingency long and widely foreseen and predicted. That was a great, astonishing departure from tradition.

What could and should have been done to manage the international aspects and consequences of the Austro-Hungarian problem over the longer term is of course controversial, as is whether any feasible international action would have been effective. But it is not hard to propose measures, plausible on their face, for short-term action in 1914, that is, for a European intervention following the assassination of Franz Ferdinand to stop the incident from escalating into a dangerous confrontation and war. Something certainly could have been attempted to satisfy Austria-Hungary's prestige and honor and to compel Serbia to conform at least outwardly to its international commitments to act as a good neighbor.[33] Since the particular steps Austria-Hungary demanded—a serious investigation of the ties between the assassination plot and Serbia's government, its nationalist organizations, and its military intelligence, followed by concrete measures to prevent future provocations, would not and probably could not be carried out by Serbia no matter what its government promised, and since Russia's attitude meant that they also could not be undertaken by Austria-Hungary without provoking an international crisis, the obvious conclusion, based on historical precedents, would be that Europe acting in concert would ask Austria-Hungary to turn its cause and demands over to them, and then carry through seriously an investigation of the terrorist attack and any required sanctions on Serbia. The nineteenth century provided ample precedent for international action to compel smaller states, however innocent they might claim to be and however righteous their cause, to stop challenging great powers and causing international crises, just as there were precedents for requiring great powers to act through the international community and not take the law into their own hands. Greece and other Balkan states, for example, had repeatedly been compelled by joint great power intervention to stop irredentist campaigns against the Ottoman Empire, and the Ottomans prevented from taking revenge on their rebels and enemies. Russia was more than once required in the nineteenth century to turn its cause and national honor in the Balkans over to the European Concert to defend. The fact that this procedure did not always work or was not always tried makes no difference. It was there, it could and did sometimes work, and in some instances like this one it was the only thing that could have worked (the only means, for example, that could have prevented the Crimean War, and almost did).

Yet in a way this discussion too, however necessary it is to clear the ground, is irrelevant and distracting, for the obvious, overriding fact is that before and during 1914 no action of this sort was tried, seriously considered, or even entertained. The danger of war steadily increased, the European powers were quite aware of the crucial specific source of that danger in the Austro-Hungarian problem, they knew about the kinds of measures used in the past and still available to meet such dangers, and collectively they did nothing. This inaction is the most important development in prewar diplomacy and in the July Crisis. It also strikingly illustrates both how counterfactual reasoning can serve the vital historical purpose not of telling us what might have happened, but of illuminating what really did happen, and why one needs to see 1914 not as the outbreak of war but as the breakdown of peace. Every account of the July Crisis discusses the crucial delay between July 5, when Austria-Hungary received Germany's support for its ultimatum to Serbia, and July 23 when the ultimatum was actually delivered. Some have speculated that the delay was fateful in allowing the initial shock of the assassination to wear off (which is doubtful—the Serbian and Russian reactions, the decisive ones, would have been the same earlier). But another delay, far more fateful and inexplicable, is hardly mentioned or discussed in the vast literature. For a full month after the assassination, the powers did absolutely nothing in concert to prepare for or deal with the possible or likely consequences of this sensational event. Everyone knew that Austria-Hungary and Serbia were mortal enemies, that they had gone to the brink of war at least four times in the past five years, three of them in the past year, and that Russia was Serbia's ally and protector and Austria-Hungary's main enemy. Yet when something occurred that anyone could see might set off this long-envisioned war, the Entente powers averted their eyes, went about their other business, waited for whatever Austria-Hungary and Germany might do, and insofar as they thought about the incident at all, shrugged their shoulders and hoped for the best. Meanwhile Austria-Hungary and Germany took actions that set off the war.

This argument seems paradoxically to prove the precise opposite of what was promised and intended—to show that the war was not inevitable. For if the means for a serious attempt at avoiding it were known and available, as I have just argued, then the root cause of the war must have been contingent, have lain in a collective failure to apply them.

But of course that collective inaction in 1914 is neither inexplicable nor really contingent. Behind the failure to act lay precisely those shared assumptions and convictions about the nature, stakes, and reigning course of the international contest earlier cited as the reasons why determinists consider the war objectively unavoidable, by virtue of the *force des choses*. I contend only that the pressure of events did not make war objectively unavoidable by making peaceful choices impossible in the face of hard realities like security threats, alliance commitments, and arms races, but made it subjectively unavoidable by fatally constricting what all the actors would entertain as a conceivable, rational course of action in the face of this crisis or any other like it. The particular reasons why the various powers did not even consider taking any of the steps mentioned above to anticipate a crisis and manage it collectively are familiar and obvious. Austria-Hungary and Germany were determined to reverse the existing trend in international politics they considered fatal to them, and saw in this crisis a final chance to do so. The Entente powers equally saw in this crisis a danger to the existing trend favorable to them and were equally determined not to allow it to be reversed. Russian policy, seen by Russians as a defense against German and Austro-Hungarian aggression, was resolutely bent on maintaining and extending Russia's control over the Balkans. French policy was rigidly fixed on maintaining the existing alliances and therefore doing nothing to weaken the Franco-Russian one.[34] Britain's was fixed on maintaining its ententes, both in order to check Germany in Europe and avoid threats to the British Empire—the latter aim, the primary one, requiring maintaining the entente with Russia at all cost.[35] But behind these familiar positive reasons for failure to act collectively, there was a still more fundamental negative one. No one believed that a sane, rational policy allowed any longer for this kind of collective response. Anyone who tried to suspend the rules of power politics, of "every man and every alliance for himself, and the devil take the hindmost," was a fool and would earn the fool's reward. Hence to ask any British, French, Russian, Italian, or even German leader to sacrifice or subordinate particular interests and opportunities of theirs for the sake of some sort of collective action to stabilize the international position of Austria-Hungary so as to lessen the chances of a general war was to ask the impossible and absurd—to ask them to commit political suicide at home and to be laughed at and swindled abroad. Stabilizing Austria-Hungary's position was really not anyone's business except that of Austrians and Hungarians, or perhaps Germans if they wished to do so for their own power-political reasons. This profound practical indifference to the survival of a vital actor such as the Habsburg Monarchy was, to repeat, a break with tradition. It did not represent normal Realpolitik, but constituted a different concrete definition of it, a different collective attitude toward international politics.[36] The power whose final break with the Concert principle proved decisive, Austria-Hungary, was also the last and most reluctant to abandon it, because it was the one most dependent on it and on collective international support and restraint to survive. This outlook was evident before 1914. One of Foreign Minister Aehrenthal's chief aims in 1908 had been to revive the old Three-Emperors' League and the moribund Austro-Russian entente in the Balkans by a deal with Russia over Bosnia and the Straits. Even in 1914 this idea was far from dead. The original Austrian proposal for reversing the current disastrous trends in the Balkans called for political rather than military action and was changed only in the wake of the assassination (though how much difference this would have made is debatable).[37] During the July Crisis itself Austro-Hungarian leaders hoped against hope that Russia might let it get away with a local war against Serbia, and if Russia did, they intended to use the opportunity to seek a fundamental rapprochement with Russia through negotiations for a joint solution to both the Balkan and the Ukrainian problems.[38] There is a tragic appropriateness about Austria-Hungary's breaking at last with the Concert principle and thereby destroying itself and Europe with it, like the blinded Samson pulling down the pillars of the temple, just as there is about Tsarist Russia's acting upon the shibboleths of its honor and its alleged historic mission of protecting the Balkan Slavs rather than its true state interests, thereby signing its own death warrant.[39]

To argue for the inevitability of World War I on this ground is, to repeat, *not* to blame Britain, Russia, and France for it while exonerating Germany and Austria-Hungary, or to characterize the former as more blind and reckless than the latter. It is an attempt to root the disaster deep in a political culture that all shared, which all had helped to develop, and upon which all acted in 1914, Germany and Austria-Hungary precipitating the final descent into the maelstrom. It is to see the origins of the war as finally a tragedy more than a crime, though crimes were surely involved; as inevitable by reason of wrong beliefs, hubris, and folly too broadly and deeply anchored in the reigning political culture to be recognized, much less examined and changed. The tragedy of its origins thus connects with the tragedy of the war itself in its hyperbolic protraction and destruction, evoking, like Shakespeare's *Romeo and Juliet*, the verdict, "All are punished."

III

TOOLS OF INTERNATIONAL STATECRAFT

9

ALLIANCES, 1815–1945: WEAPONS OF POWER AND TOOLS OF MANAGEMENT

Though the term "alliance" has often been used loosely to mean simply "friendship" or "working partnership,"[1] jurists and theorists have long insisted on a narrower definition, according to which an alliance is a treaty binding two or more independent states to come to each other's aid with armed force under circumstances specified in the *casus foederis* article of the treaty. Whether offensive or defensive, limited or unlimited, equal or unequal, bilateral or multilateral, alliances must involve some measure of commitment to use force to achieve a common goal.[2]

Political scientists by and large adopt this definition as describing not only what technically constitutes an alliance, but also how alliances work and what functions they fulfill. "In concept and in practice," writes one authority, "alliance combines the capabilities of nation-states not simply for the sake of forming associations but essentially to preserve, magnify, or create positions of strength for diplomacy or war."[3] "The purpose of the alliance (treaty of mutual assistance)," writes another, "is to combine the power of the allies against their common enemy."[4] The basic idea of an alliance, another states, "is to assure a preponderance of strength should it come to a contest of capabilities."[5] Alliances, to quote a classic work, are "a necessary function of the balance of power operating within a multiple-state system."[6] Similar statements could be cited almost at will, defining alliances as means of capability-aggregation, collective defense, war, security, and power diplomacy.

The discussion of alliances is not confined to their power-political uses, to be sure. Some political scientists view them as designed only for situations of conflict,[7] or as serving only minor purposes other than capability-aggregation.[8] But most recognize additional purposes of alliance as well—those of legitimating one's own regime or that of an ally, preventing revolution or internal disturbances, spreading an ideology, or enhancing a state's influence and status, for example.[9] Alliances, we know, play a role not only in the balance of power, but also in collective-security or concert systems.[10] The internal rivalries and cross-purposes that all alliances contain are no secret; neither are the negotiations and maneuvering that go on almost constantly between partners in an alliance. None of this, however, invalidates the consensus that alliances are instruments of power politics. The additional purposes and uses of alliances are almost always interpreted as ancillary to those of power and security, and intra-alliance politics are explained as a product of these main purposes, as the result of differing perceptions of the goals, the payoffs, the distribution of burdens, and the strategy and tactics of the alliance.

Despite this consensus, some of the ideas advanced in international-relations theory might lead one to question whether alliances need be primarily instruments of power. Most political scientists do not consider international politics as simply an arena of power conflict; some would even deny that power is the most fundamental reality in it.[11] The central problem for international-relations theory, one often hears, is understanding order rather than power, devising a viable principle of international order for the control and management of conflict.[12] The balance of power doctrines with which alliances are generally connected have been challenged on various grounds: whether balance of power politics constitutes a real system with identifiable rules and practices,[13] whether that system is stable or tends inherently toward disequilibrium and conflict,[14] and whether historically the balance of power really governed international relations and helped to preserve peace in previous centuries.[15] Everyone knows that alliances in practice do not always serve to increase a nation's power and security, and that allies often clash with each other more than they unite in a common cause.[16] All this might lead one to wonder whether alliances really need to function primarily as weapons of power.

A few writers have in fact gone beyond the power-and-security view of alliances in pointing to their functions as tools of management and control. Richard A. Falk, for example, argues that international violence has been held within tolerable limits in recent decades, partly through the control exercised by the great powers—the United States and the USSR—over the smaller powers within their alliance systems.[17] Robert E. Osgood writes: "Next to accretion, the most prominent function of alliances has been to restrain and control allies, particularly in order to safeguard one ally against actions of another that might endanger its security or otherwise jeopardize its interests." He further remarks: "Primarily his [Bismarck's] alliances were intended to limit the options of allies while keeping Germany's commitments to them equally limited."[18] Most interesting is the concept of the functions of alliance expounded in the writings of George Liska. In 1962, though still regarding alliances mainly as means of capability-aggregation, he described their goals as: "Always to restrain the adversary and, if and when desirable, also each other and the scope of a conflict."[19] By 1967 he looked on alliances as general means of management in both interstate and imperial systems,[20] and in 1968 he listed a whole series of purposes for forming alliances, the main ones being "aggregation of power, interallied control, and international order or government."[21] Here the power purposes of alliances are not ignored or denied, but they are dethroned, and other functions are emphasized as being equally important.

Compared to political scientists, historians by the nature of their work must pay more attention in detail to the diverse purposes and uses of alliances. Absorbed in digging out the complex motives and calculations behind alliances and in tracing the intricate maneuvers of intra-alliance politics, the diplomatic historian learns very quickly that the unintended functions and results of alliances are often more important than the intended ones. Yet despite the close attention given to the details of forming alliances and to politics, most historians conceive of alliances much as political scientists do—basically as weapons of national security and power, instruments in balance of power politics. Normally, historians do not try to account theoretically for the diversity of purposes of alliances or the phenomena of antagonistic intra-alliance politics. If they do, their answers are likely to resemble those of most political scientists.

Because this essay will argue that a great deal of evidence about alliance politics from 1815 to 1945 suggests a different interpretation of functions of alliances, the question naturally arises, if such evidence exists, why have most historians as well as political theorists missed it or failed to draw the right conclusions from it? Obviously, no very confident answer can be given; the reason could be simply that the majority view is correct. But assuming that this divergent interpretation can be upheld, the answer might lie first in the fact that almost all historians, like political scientists, assume that international relations in modern times have rested fundamentally upon a balance of power. Although there has been debate over whether the balance of power should be the basis for international relations, few have disputed that it actually has been; the notion of balance of power is usually taken for granted. This assumption fairly well determines one's conception of the function of alliances also. If all international relations rest on a balance of power, alliances naturally operate as power instruments in the balance.

Another factor, which is more intangible, may also be fundamental. Both historians and political scientists have concentrated on explaining war and conflict in international relations—historians dwelling generally on the particular causes of particular crises and wars; political scientists, on the general conditions and reasons for international conflict. This emphasis, however natural and understandable, may introduce an insensible bias into the inquiry. The danger is not so much, as some suggest, that power and conflict come to be overrated in international relations, whereas the elements of cooperation, interdependence, and common interests are neglected. It is, rather, that the stress on accounting for war suggests that war is a deviation from the norm, requiring explanation, whereas peace is not. But this assumption is eminently open to challenge. Let us accept what seems quite evident: the fundamental, overriding fact of international politics continues to be the existence of enormous power at the disposal of rival, independent states, with only weak and tenuous restraints upon its use. This very fact means that war is more normal than peace, and that peace (that is, the restraint of violent international conflict within narrow limits) needs explanation more than war does. This is not merely a theoretical point. It is often more difficult for the historian to explain why war did not break out at a particular time than to explain why it did at another; theorists seem to have more difficulty discerning and defining the general causes of peace than the general causes of war.

Yet, in fact, peace prevails more generally in international relations than does war. Thus the main problem that students have is to account for the theoretically unexpected relative prevalence of peace. This involves determining how various devices of control and management work to keep conflicting national aims and uncontrolled national power from causing more wars than actually happen. The point applies to alliances very directly. One may well assume that their original, normal purposes were and are power oriented—security, capability-aggregation, gains of various kinds. Yet these purposes serve better to explain why violent conflicts occur rather than how they are avoided. If the latter question comes to be seen as the main one, it leads one immediately to suspect that alliances have perhaps been fulfilling other functions than their original or "normal" ones—functions of the control and management of conflict.

In any case, this essay will attempt, in a rapid overview of the European international system from 1815 to 1945, to illustrate the management and control functions of alliances.[22] It may help to set down here some of the main points that will emerge:

(1) The desire for capability-aggregation against an outside threat has not always played a vital role in the formation of alliances. Sometimes powers entered into alliances even though one party or the other (occasionally both) had no need or desire for capability-aggregation. In certain cases, the formation of alliances served to weaken a power's military position rather than to strengthen it.

(2) Some alliances, though directed nominally or partly against a particular threat or opponent indicated in the *casus foederis*, had primary aims or targets that were quite separate from those specified in the treaty.

(3) All alliances in some measure functioned as pacts of restraint (*pacta de contrahendo*), restraining or controlling the actions of the partners in the alliance themselves. Frequently the desire to exercise such control over an ally's policy was the main reason that one power, or both, entered into the alliance. In every case, the way in which the alliance functioned as a *pactum de contrahendo* had an important effect upon the success and durability of the alliance, and on its impact upon the general system.

(4) Although alliances were commonly used to try to isolate and intimidate an opponent, alliances were frequently also employed in order to group and conciliate an opponent, in the interest of managing the system and avoiding overt conflict. For example, a group of powers might form an alliance in order to compel an opponent to come into the alliance in

order to avoid isolation; or one power might form an alliance with another, in order to compel that ally to become reconciled with its opponent, so that the opponent could in turn be drawn into a wider alliance or a further combination.

(5) The perception of a threat from another power might lead a state to try either to form an alliance against that power, in order to meet the threat by capability-aggregation, or to ally with that power, in order to manage the threat through a *pactum de contrahendo*.

The fundamental European alliance after the Congress of Vienna in 1814–15 was the Quadruple Alliance of November 1815 which united Austria, Britain, Prussia, and Russia in defense of the peace settlement. Obviously this alliance served the purpose of mutual security against a revival of French aggression and imperialism or against any other threat to the newly established status quo. But no less important for these powers was their general desire to remain allied in order to manage the international system and to solve new problems as they arose. Not only the cataclysms of the previous quarter-century, but also the strains and problems of the final coalition against Napoleon in the period 1812–14, the conflicts among the great powers that arose during the peace congress, and Napoleon's return from Elba—all combined to convince the great powers that it was vitally necessary for them to make a durable alliance of mutual cooperation and restraint. Significantly, it was Lord Castlereagh, foreign secretary of the least threatened and "European" of the powers, who sponsored a specific provision for postwar conferences of the great powers in Article VI of the treaty. The same concern for cooperation among the great powers led the allies in 1818 to bring France into the alliance, so that there now existed a Quintuple Alliance to run Europe.[23]

The Holy Alliance of September 1815, which was sponsored by Tsar Alexander I of Russia, also aimed at European concert and mutual restraint on a still loftier plane. The actual treaty was virtually meaningless as an operative instrument, because it contained no *casus foederis* and only a vague statement of aims. Nevertheless, the term "Holy Alliance" denotes a real alliance, one of the most important mutual-security arrangements of the nineteenth century. For the three original signatories—Austria, Prussia, and Russia—formed in fact a very effective union against liberalism, revolution, and territorial and political change. Several times the Holy Alliance sanctioned or helped to execute armed intervention against revolutions (1821 in Italy, 1830–32 in Italy and Poland, 1846 in Cracow, 1849 in Hungary). In other ways as well, the alliance of these Eastern powers served as a powerful deterrent to war or revolt.

Important as the Holy Alliance was for security purposes, however, it was even more significant and effective as a mutual pact of restraint upon these three powers themselves. Each of them was a jealous rival of the other two at the same time that it shared in a common conservative cause. Each needed and used this alliance to control its partners and to manage intra-alliance rivalries in Germany, Italy, Poland, and the Near East so as to avoid war. Prince Metternich, the Austrian chancellor, demonstrated especially well how the Holy Alliance could be used as a pact of restraint. He recognized that Alexander's original mystical, vaguely liberal dream of a Holy Alliance as a fraternal Christian union among monarchs and peoples might well serve as a cover for expanded Russian influence in Europe, with Russia taking up the cause of moderate political reform. Metternich therefore recast the Holy Alliance treaty into a safe, absolutist form, and then he spent the next decade using his archconservative Holy Alliance principles to restrain and manage Alexander I. Much of the diplomacy of the Italian, Greek, and Spanish revolutions from 1820 to 1823 consists of Metternich's efforts to control Russian policy through and within the alliance of the Eastern powers.[24]

The German Confederation of 1815, which was basically a permanent defense league of all the German states, led by Austria and Prussia, similarly served both for mutual security for Germany, especially against France, and as a pact of mutual restraint for controlling the German problem from within. The confederation worked to harmonize the rival claims of Austria and Prussia to leadership and to reconcile these claims of the great powers with the demands for independence of the middle-sized and small states, as well as to protect Germany from outside threats. During the 1820s and 1830s, Metternich used the confederation much more for controlling the internal policies of member states and for managing Austria's junior partner Prussia than he used it for European high politics. His favorite ploy was to insist that Austria could take care of her European interests quite easily without the confederation. Therefore, if the other states did not cooperate with Austria in confederate policy, Austria would pull out and leave them to their fate. This was obviously a bluff, but it was often an effective one.[25]

Metternich never succeeded, despite repeated efforts, in establishing an Italian league that would enable Austria to tie down and manage Italy in similar fashion. Nonetheless, Austria's alliances and dynastic connections in Italy served the same combined security and managerial purposes. The Austro-Neapolitan secret alliance of June 1815 is a good example of an alliance that gave security to the weaker state and control to the stronger (Naples was forbidden by the treaty to change her form of government without Austria's permission).

In July 1827 the existing combinations of Quadruple, Quintuple, and Holy (that is, Eastern) alliances were partly broken up by a new partnership when Britain, Russia, and France concluded a convention for joint intervention in the six-year-old Greek revolution against Turkey. Although technically this was not a treaty of alliance, the partners always termed themselves allies, and so they were. Their convention provided for the combined use of force, if necessary, to impose a settlement on Turkey, and it quickly led to a three-power armed intervention, allied destruction of the Turco-Egyptian fleet, a Russian war against Turkey, French occupation of southern Greece, and finally by allied imposition on Turkey of peace terms, which included an independent Greece under an allied protectorate. From our standpoint, the most interesting thing about this significant and powerful alliance is that capability-aggregation and mutual security against a threat that was perceived in common had nothing to do with it. Each of these three powers alone was strong enough to coerce Turkey; each professed (more or less sincerely) to be Turkey's friend and defender and to want to preserve and help her. The alliance, it is obvious, was intended for purposes of management, not power. It grew out of an attempt by the British foreign secretary, George Canning, to form a pact of restraint with Russia in 1826. Fearing that Russia, Britain's chief rival, would eventually, on its own, intervene in Greece, Canning decided to go partners with Russia in order to manage her, to solve the Greek problem, and to advance British interests and prestige in the Levant. The French joined in because they dared not allow Russia and Britain to act without them and thought that France could gain status and influence by participating. The results belied these purposes, to be sure. Instead of a peaceful settlement, the alliance resulted in a war from which Russia, which was supposed to be constrained, made important gains, and which exposed the European system to grave dangers (the collapse of the Ottoman Empire, permanent enmity between Austria and Russia, and the revival of French expansionism). Nonetheless, the alliance still demonstrates the importance—even, in certain instances, the primacy—of management motives in the formation of alliances.[26]

The Russo-Turkish alliance that was signed at Unkiar-Skelessi in July 1833 also demonstrates this. For Turkey, of course, an alliance with its most powerful enemy was purely a desperate security measure to meet the immediate threat of the invading army of Mehemet Ali, khedive of Egypt. As the Turks said, a drowning man will seize hold even of a snake. But the alliance brought security, in the usual sense, to Russia. The Egyptian army posed no threat to Russia, and from a military standpoint, a Turkish alliance was a distinct liability. Had the Western powers chosen to challenge Russia over this treaty (as the British foreign secretary, Lord Palmerston, was strongly inclined to do), Russia would have found it impossible to defend the Turkish Straits against the navies of the Western powers. The only way this alliance contributed to Russia's security was in helping Russia to preserve and control Turkey, thereby keeping the vital straits from falling into other, more dangerous, hands. The treaty thus gave Turkey free protection (a secret protocol expressly excused her from any military obligation) in exchange for Russian influence at Constantinople and an assurance that the Black Sea would be closed against invaders. Russia had other long-range ambitions in mind as well—gaining more privileges for Orthodox Christians in Turkey and strengthening Russia's special position in the Danubian Principalities (later Rumania). But expansionist aims notwithstanding, this was basically a pact of management and control.

The way in which Russia's main rivals in the Near East—Britain and Austria—reacted to Unkiar-Skelessi and the danger of Russian predominance at Constantinople again illustrates in how many different ways alliances can function. Metternich immediately sought to control Russia through a *pactum de contrahendo*. This was his normal method; besides, Austria needed Russia's support too much elsewhere to challenge Russia openly in the Near East. In the Münchengratz Agreement of September 1833, Russia and Austria promised to cooperate to preserve the Ottoman Empire and, should it collapse despite their efforts, to act only in concert to meet the problem. Prussia joined this agreement a month later. Having thus enlisted Russia, Metternich tried to bring the Western powers as well into his alliance, in order to control Russia.

Palmerston refused to join. Distrusting Russia and Austria equally, and preferring balance of power and confrontation tactics, he promoted a quadruple alliance among Britain, France, Spain, and Portugal in 1834, which was supposed to overawe the Eastern powers and deter them from their supposedly aggressive designs. In reality, for Palmerston's purpose the alliance was both unnecessary and useless. What it actually did was to function as a pact for restraint and management in Western Europe, especially in the Iberian Peninsula. It gave British friendship and support to the insecure regime of King Louis Philippe of France in exchange for considerable British control over French policy in the Spanish and Portuguese civil wars.[27]

The successful settlement of the Belgian question from 1830 to 1839, which culminated in an international guarantee of an independent, neutral Belgium, was more the product of ordinary diplomacy than of alliance politics. One chapter in the story, however, admirably illustrates the principle of allying with one's rival to control his policy. Britain was the power that was most interested in establishing Belgian independence and neutrality; then and later, Britain considered France the great threat to Belgium. Yet when it became necessary to impose a settlement upon the king of Holland by armed force, Britain signed a convention for this purpose in October 1832 with France. Left alone or allied against, France would cause trouble; within an alliance, France could be used and controlled.[28]

Another alliance over the Eastern Question, the Austro-British–Russian agreement of July 1840, shows another way in which alliances are used for management and restraint. Militarily the alliance was directed against a renewed menace to Turkey from Mehemet Ali, and it succeeded brilliantly in meeting it. By November 1840 Mehemet had been driven back to Egypt and had been forced to submit. But from the more important standpoint of European politics, France, not Mehemet, was the target of this alliance; and its aim (for Austria and Russia, if not for Palmerston) was to bring France back into the Concert of Europe and to force it to conform. Initially, in July 1839, France had joined the other powers in promising help to the sultan and in demanding European control over the peace terms that he would offer to Mehemet. But thereafter France began trying to manage the policy of the concert for its own ends, attempting to save some of Mehemet's gains for him so as to promote French influence in Egypt. The Triple Alliance of July 1840 served as formal notice to France that, unless France got back into line, the other powers would act against Mehemet without France. The European war scare that followed in October/November 1840 derived from

French resentment of their own isolation, and their hope to bluff the other powers into allowing France back into the concert without full conformity on France's part. France's joining in the five-power Straits Convention of July 1841 represented France's formal readmission to the concert, as well as a success for alliances as tools of management.[29]

The revolutions of 1848 ended the European stability that had generally prevailed since 1815, producing not only internal upheavals but also international tensions and wars (in Italy, Hungary, and Schleswig-Holstein), which threatened to destroy the existing alliance systems. France became a republic, potentially radical and expansionist, while Italy was swept by revolution and joined in a nationalist war against Austria. This wrecked the conservative entente between France and Austria that had begun to develop before 1848; it also revived their ancient, bitter rivalry over Italy. Both the Holy Alliance and the German Confederation were paralyzed by the revolutions in Central Europe, the German nationalist unification movement, the open rivalry between Austria and Prussia for leadership in Germany, and Prussia's temporary turn to liberalism and an anti-Russian policy.

What is surprising, therefore, is that the main prerevolutionary alliance systems by and large survived the revolutions. Not only did they survive; they actually continued to function for both security and management, indicating how vitally both functions were needed. It was not accidental that when by 1850–51 all the various efforts to create a more united Germany had run aground, the German governments revived the fallen 1815 confederation. Prince Schwarzenberg, the Austrian premier, expressed the prevailing attitude accurately and without cynicism in remarking that a threadbare cloak was better than none. All the unification efforts, in fact, had been constrained by the fear of destroying Germany's existing bonds and of replacing them with nothing, leaving Germany a prey to Austro-Prussian enmity, French or Russian domination, and internal revolution and civil war. In essence, Holy Alliance principles and restraints had held everyone back from drastic steps from 1848 to 1850—not merely conservatives, but also German nationalists, liberals, and romantics, even the supposedly modern *Realpolitiker* Schwarzenberg (who had taken control in Austria in late 1848) and the new Emperor Francis Joseph. They had had a golden opportunity to confront Prussia and to solve the German question by force in 1850, but they had passed it by—above all because Prussia, though a dangerous rival, was also an indispensable ally against the revolution. Not until Bismarck came to power in Prussia in 1862 would such restraints finally be swept aside.[30]

Holy Alliance principles, as well as fears for Poland, likewise led Tsar Nicholas I to send an army to help Austria crush the Hungarian revolution in 1849. In similar traditional fashion, Nicholas used his mediating position between Austria and Prussia in order to control their policy and manage the German problem, both the general Austro-Prussian rivalry and the conflict between Germany and Denmark over Schleswig-Holstein. His aims were the typical mixture of security, management, and control—preventing war, returning Prussia to conservative paths, and avoiding any unification or strengthening of Germany. Russia, as Nicholas and other statesmen knew, drew great advantages from a confederated Germany and a controlled Austro-Prussian rivalry. The trouble with Russian management in this case was that it was pushed too far, with too arrogant and superior an air. Schwarzenberg, in particular, resented Russian domination and Nicholas' assumption that Austria must follow his lead in the Near East out of gratitude over what he had done for Hungary, and he resolved from the outset to prove himself ungrateful to Russia if the occasion should arise.[31] As for Austria and Prussia, each returned after 1850 to using the unreformed confederation to restrain and manage the other. Prussia even conceded Austria a special three-year defensive alliance in 1851, mainly as a pact of restraint.

Italy in 1849–50 provides more instances of control and management through alliances. The treaties that Austria concluded with its client states in central Italy in 1849 gave them security against either invasion or externally supported revolt and gave Austria control, thus making sure that the rulers of Tuscany, Modena, and Parma could not again surrender to revolutionary movements. Austria even considered using her control to try to replace Leopold II of Tuscany with a more reliable ruler. The Roman question in 1849–50 illustrates well the diplomacy of rivals in an alliance. Pope Pius IX, after fleeing from Rome in the face of revolution, appealed to the Catholic powers of Europe, especially Austria, to restore him to power. Schwarzenberg, precisely because he feared French rivalry and ambitions in Italy, resisted Pius' pleas for unilateral Austrian intervention and insisted instead on drawing France into a working partnership in Italy. The French, seeing that such a partnership would strengthen Austria's position, which France wanted to undermine, tried instead to accept the principle of Austro-French partnership in Italy, but to use it in order to prevent any action that would favor the pope. When this policy proved unworkable and some intervention at Rome seemed inescapable, France attempted suddenly to intervene alone, on its own initiative. Austria, however, promptly endorsed France's action, supported the action with Austria's own parallel occupation of other papal territories, and thereby more or less snared France into a partnership against her will.[32]

The Crimean War (1853–56), which pitted Turkey, Britain, France, and, finally, Sardinia against Russia, tended naturally to promote alliances primarily as instruments of war, security, and capability-aggregation. Yet even in this major conflict, the largest since Napoleon's time, alliances continued to operate in a very important way for control and management. For example, the Anglo-French alliance for war—which was formalized in April 1854, after war had already been declared—actually developed from an entente formed by Britain with France in early 1853 for the purpose of restraining France and managing the Eastern crisis, then in its early stages. France's ambitions at first seemed more dangerous to the British than did Russia's; both powers expected to use their partnership so as to control the other and to better manage the international situation. But as in the period 1825–27, an alliance that was intended for control resulted in loss of control and war.

In a series of moves and developments that is too complicated to relate here, the Western powers—who were struggling to preserve their partnership, to manage one another, and to force Russia to retreat—finally succeeded only in pushing Russia into war and pulling themselves in afterwards. Yet even in wartime, their alliance, which was carefully fitted out with a mutual self-denying clause against territorial aggrandizement, continued to function for control as well as for military victory. Disputes between the allies over war aims and peace terms went on almost continuously. Most French leaders and the French public favored a negotiated peace in the spring of 1855, which Austria was promoting at the Vienna peace conference. Britain opposed a negotiated peace and succeeded in frustrating it. But the next winter, France convinced Britain that the existence of the alliance depended upon reaching peace and, with Austria's help, got Britain to agree to a moderate settlement in March 1856.

An even better example of a *pactum de contrahendo* that was concluded during the Crimean War is the Austro-Prussian alliance of April 1854. Austria sought this alliance partly to get Prussian and German support for Austria's position with regard to the Near East and for Austria's policy against Russia (under the German Confederation, the member states were only bound to defend the Austrian territory that was within the confederation against attack so that Austria's southeastern lands were not protected). In addition, Austria wanted through this alliance to force Prussia and the German states to accept and acknowledge Austria's leadership both in Germany and in European affairs. Thus, from Austria's standpoint, the alliance served both for capability-aggregation and for management. Prussia and the German states, however, agreed to assume further obligations to defend Austria solely in order to restrain it, to prevent Austria, if possible, from allying with the Western powers and either going to war against Russia or provoking Russia to attack Austria. Both Prussia and the rest of Germany assumed that if Austria became involved in the war, they also would be dragged in. The same motives of control and restraint led these states to extend their alliance with Austria in November 1854 and reluctantly to support Austria's peace terms to Russia in 1855 and 1856.

Prussia and Germany managed to escape involvement themselves, but they were not successful in keeping Austria from joining the West. The Anglo-French–Austrian alliance of December 2, 1854, derived from a very complicated mixture of motives, yet it is safe to say that once again the purposes of management and control predominated. The British wanted only an alliance that would get Austria into the war (in fact, they would have preferred simply to hire the Austrian army as mercenaries). Since it seemed unlikely that Austria would actually fight, Britain opposed an alliance with Austria, fearing that it might drag the West into an unsatisfactory peace settlement. The only reason, therefore, that the British reluctantly accepted this alliance was in order to retain control over France; if Britain refused to join, France might, on its own, ally with Austria and thus escape British control. France sought the Austrian alliance in order to produce an irreparable breach between Austria and Russia, destroying the old Holy Alliance once and for all. If this happened, then whether or not Austria actually entered the war against Russia, France would be in a controlling position after the war, able to exploit Austro-Russian hostility and play one off against the other. Austria's motives for this alliance were purely those of management. Only by joining with the Western powers could it hope to both control and end the war before it became revolutionary in its extent and effects. Through this alliance, Austria hoped to force Russia to admit defeat, to moderate Western war aims, to bring both sides to the peace table, and to bring about a negotiated settlement that would check Russia in the Near East, guarantee Turkey, and protect Austrian interests.[33]

One more alliance during the Crimean War illustrates how even a clearly offensive alliance can also serve management functions—Sardinia's alliance with Britain and France in January 1855. For the Western powers, this was simply a means of getting a Sardinian contingent to fight on their side in the Crimea (though an Anglo-French rivalry for control and influence in Sardinia quickly arose from this alliance). Sardinia's entrance into this alliance was not really a matter of free choice; Western and domestic pressures, combined with a general fear of what would happen to Sardinia if it did not act, more or less forced Sardinia into it. Insofar as the Sardinian premier Count Cavour chose to join the West, however, his purposes were those of management rather than security. He wanted to counteract the Austro-French alliance, which threatened to reduce Sardinia to political impotence, to insinuate Sardinia into the West's good graces ahead of Austria, and, if possible, to gain Western support for Sardinia's ambitions in Italy during and after the war.[34]

The final alliance that derived from the Crimean War was the pact of April 1856, which allied Britain, France, and Austria against Russia in defense of Turkey and the recently concluded Peace of Paris. This was clearly an instrument of power and mutual security, yet of the three allies, only Austria took it very seriously in this regard, and the Austrians did so mainly because they had long-range management purposes in mind. Austria's foreign minister, Count Buol, calculated that an alliance guaranteeing Turkey against Russia would compel Britain and France to give general support to Austria, for only with Austrian aid could they protect Turkey. With British and French backing, Austria could afford to brave Russia's and Prussia's anger over Austria's recent policy, and could manage the Italian, German, and Near Eastern problems. As it turned out, this alliance did little for Turkey and nothing at all for Austria.[35]

The Italian crises and wars of 1858–61, which united Italy, showed again how varied alliance purposes can be. The Franco-Sardinian alliance of January 1859—ostensibly a defensive alignment—really formed part of an elaborate plan concocted by Cavour and Napoleon III in July 1858 to provoke war with Austria and expel Austria from Italy. The co-conspirators, however, had quite separate and divergent plans for Italy, each intending to use and control the other. When their plot against Austria began to break down, menacing France with a wider war than Napoleon had bargained for, the emperor used his superior power in the alliance to restrain Cavour and even to force him to postpone or abandon the plan. Only Austria's imprudent ultimatum to Sardinia in April 1859, which touched off the war, kept this basically aggressive alliance from working out to be a pact of restraint, against the wishes of both allies.[36]

The Anglo-French partnership over Italy, which was formed after the Whigs returned to power in mid-1859, was another example of an informal alliance that was formed for control rather than capability-aggregation. Though the British were pro-Italian and anti-Austrian, the main reason the government insisted upon joining with France in support of Sardinia was to control France and thus prevent Napoleon from making territorial gains or acquiring a dominant influence in Italy. In January 1860 Palmerston, now prime minister, and John Russell, the foreign secretary, proposed a formal alliance with France and Sardinia for a final settlement of the Italian question. The three powers would impose terms on Austria (which had just lost half its Italian territory in the 1859 war), and Britain could keep France from taking anything for itself. In other words, in order to curb a dangerous aggressor, avert a threat to the balance of power, and manage an international problem, Palmerston proposed allying with the aggressor states against their weakened and vulnerable opponent.[37] The cabinet rejected the proposal out of the usual British aversion to commitments, and soon Napoleon's annexation of Nice and Savoy turned Palmerston violently against France, leading him in turn to seek an Austrian and Prussian alliance against her. Nonetheless, joining with France in order to control France remained a common, almost a standard, British policy, which was followed in connection with France's intervention in Syria in 1861, and even more with regard to the Polish Revolution of 1863. The main reason that Britain did not try harder for joint action with France in 1863–64 to save Denmark from Prussia and Austria was the British conviction that in this instance France was too likely to escape British control. It was safer to let Prussia aggrandize itself at the expense of Denmark than to risk French aggrandizement on the Rhine.[38]

Although Bismarck's alliances from 1863 to 1870 are mainly examples of capability-aggregation for purposes of expansion, he also devoted much attention and skill to managing his allies. It was not military or security needs that led him to draw Austria into alliance in 1863 against Denmark. The Prussian army was perfectly capable of dealing by itself with both the forces of the German Confederation and the Danish army in Schleswig-Holstein, and Bismarck seems to have had no real fear of foreign intervention. His main reason for drawing in Austria was to commit and compromise the empire, thus ruining its reputation with the Western powers (especially Britain), with the German nationalists, and with the smaller German states, and entangling Austria in a complicated question over which Bismarck might later pick a quarrel with that country. Bismarck's Austrian counterpart, Count Rechberg, also desired control and management. Joint intervention, he hoped, would pin Prussia down to a conservative settlement of the

Schleswig-Holstein issue and might serve to restore the old Holy Alliance partnership in Germany. Bismarck easily won the contest for control in this alliance.[39]

The alliance that Bismarck concluded with Italy in April 1866 is an exception to the general rule. It was a purely offensive device, with no other purpose than to wage a joint war on Austria. But this fact also accounts for other unusual aspects of the alliance. Although Italy was eager for war against Austria, the alliance took months to negotiate, because Italy feared betrayal and would not sign until it was reasonably sure that Prussia would actually fight. For the same reasons, Italy agreed to an alliance of only three months' duration, and the alliance lasted even less than that, with Bismarck letting Italy fend for itself once Prussia had defeated Austria.[40] The alliances that Prussia concluded, immediately after this victory, with the South German states of Bavaria, Württemberg, and Baden displayed the more normal mixture of motives. These states gained security, especially against France, while Bismarck sought and gained, mainly, management and control. He expected that these alliances, combined with the German nationalist movement and the economic union of North and South Germany in the *Zollverein*, would serve to unite these states eventually with the new Prussian-led North German Confederation. For the present the alliances would keep South Germany from gravitating into France's or Austria's orbit, or from forming an independent South German Confederation.[41] The alliances, despite powerful opposition in South Germany to union with Prussia, helped in 1870–71 to bring these states both into the war against France and into a new German Reich.[42]

In contrast to the shifting and volatile pattern of European alliance politics from 1848 to 1871, the European system and its alliances appear to have been stable during the Bismarckian era, 1871–90. This stability can be seen equally well as genuine or as deceptive. That is, some scholars have credited the alliances with preserving peace, maintaining a balance of power, and giving Europe a long period of relative calm; but others have interpreted the alliances as both a product and a cause of repeated crises and growing antagonisms in Europe and as the beginning of its division into armed camps.

Both views are partly true. To oversimplify a complicated point: Bismarck's alliances were genuine efforts to give Germany security and to make Europe stable and peaceful, aims that Bismarck recognized to be inseparable. His alliances were therefore both weapons of security and instruments of management. Bismarck was particularly skillful in the latter function, checking opponents, controlling allies, associating antagonistic powers with Germany and thereby with each other, diverting ambitions away from Europe, restraining conflicts within it, and generally managing the system. It is difficult to believe that any other device would have worked as well as his did; it is still harder to believe, as some scholars suggest, that in the absence of Bismarck's intrigues and domineering management, the European powers would naturally have settled down to peaceful coexistence without serious crises or tensions.

But at the same time, Germany's recent record of aggression and lawlessness, its central geographic location, its unstable, half-hegemonic power position in Europe, and its meteoric rise to that position—all caused strains and fears throughout Europe and raised the constant danger of a hostile coalition against Germany. These fears and strains, added to the normal conflicts and crises of European politics, forced Bismarck into increasingly complex alliance combinations and into expedients that, over the long run, tended to promote tensions and antagonisms rather than to allay them. In short, Bismarck, through his alliances, skillfully managed the European system for peace; but that system was probably unmanageable in the long run, and Bismarck's creation of a powerful Prussia–Germany was partly (though only partly) responsible for this condition of inherent unmanageability.

This interpretation applies well to Germany's first and most basic alliance, the Dual Alliance of 1879 with Austria-Hungary. Capability-aggregation for security undoubtedly was one reason for this alliance, especially for Austria, which gained security against Russia and could hope to attach Germany to Austrian policy in the Balkans. Bismarck, too, had some security concerns, chiefly over the hostility toward Germany that Russia had displayed in 1878–79 (though plainly Bismarck exaggerated this hostility and even provoked it somewhat in order to sell an Austrian alliance to the pro-Russian Emperor William I). Security considerations were also involved in his desire to tie Austria down, which would prevent Austria from ever joining a coalition against Germany and thus help to keep France isolated. Moreover, geographical and military considerations made this alliance a virtual necessity for both powers. The German–Austrian frontier was so long and exposed that they would either have to be allies or else enemies, constantly armed against each other.[43]

All the same, Bismarck mainly wanted and used this alliance for management and control, of Austria first of all. Bismarck's maxim that every alliance must have one horse and one rider, and that Germany must be the rider, here came into play. He wanted to manage not only Austria's foreign policy, but even Austria's internal policy and constitution. Austria-Hungary must remain the Dual Monarchy, run by Germans and Magyars, with no experiments in Slav-dominated federalism that would make her an unsafe ally or an incalculable factor in Europe. The reasons for Bismarck's letting Germany assume an unequal share of the burdens of the alliance and for his trying in vain to make the alliance public and permanent under parliamentary sanction were to make any independent policy by Austria more difficult.[44]

The Dual Alliance, moreover, immediately became a tool for managing a power that was even more important to Germany than Austria—namely, Russia. The Eastern crisis of 1875–78, which had wrecked the revived Holy Alliance of 1872–73 and had brought Austria and Russia close to war, had presented Bismarck with a dread alternative: either a break with Russia, leaving Russia free to ally with France, or a dangerous, one-sided German alliance with Russia, which would involve the eventual sacrifice of Austria-Hungary, with all the revolutionary consequences that its demise would have, and which would draw the hostility of Britain upon Germany. The Dual Alliance was Bismarck's means of avoiding this impossible choice. By allying with Austria, encouraging an Anglo-French entente, and harassing Russia diplomatically and in the press, Bismarck forced Russia to seek a return to a Holy Alliance relationship as Russia's only escape from isolation. The Dual Alliance also enabled Bismarck to compel Austria to accept a revival of the Three Emperors' Alliance with Russia in 1881, and to recognize Russia's interests in the eastern Balkans. In short, Bismarck forced Austria and Russia once again to become allies, because otherwise they were likely to go to war. (Conceivably, though less probably, they might also have worked out their differences and become partners without Germany—which would have represented another kind of danger for Bismarck.) The Dual Alliance thus served directly as a pact of restraint upon Austria; it also became a step toward a wider pact of restraint that would include Russia, with Germany as the manager.[45]

Bismarck's ancillary alliances with Italy (the Triple Alliance, 1882), Rumania (1883), and Serbia (through an Austro-Serb treaty of 1881) fit the same pattern. Security counted most for these states (security for the ruling dynasty from internal dangers as much as state security against foreign threats). Control counted most for Germany. Bismarck never counted on much Italian help in case of war with France; he once remarked that he would be satisfied if one Italian corporal and one drummer boy appeared on the French frontier in response to the *casus foederis*. The Triple Alliance served mainly to control Franco-Italian rivalry, which at this time was acute over Tunisia, and even more to manage the more deep-rooted rivalry of Italy and Austria, which was still more dangerous for Germany. This was why Bismarck insisted upon the Triple Alliance, compelling Italy to pass through Vienna on the way to Berlin. The Austro-Italian alliance from 1882 to 1914 not only worked as a pact of restraint on both sides; it is also the clearest instance of two enemies becoming allies mainly in order to avoid going to war with each other.[46]

Although Bismarck's alliances were the most obvious *pacta de contra-hendo* in this period, they were not the only ones. The unwritten "liberal alliance" between France and Britain over Egypt (1876–82), like the other Anglo-French ententes, was a partnership for mutual restraint and control, especially for Britain. When the Egyptian government began to break down through bankruptcy, the British did not wish to monopolize Egypt; they could not renounce it because of the Suez Canal; therefore, they chose to share with France in dual control. The Egyptian story unfortunately illustrates what may happen when a partnership of mutual restraint breaks down and one partner emerges with the prize. When, through fortuitous events, Britain became sole occupier of Egypt in 1882, this set off a colonial and world rivalry between the erstwhile partners that lasted two decades and brought them close to war more than once, despite repeated sincere attempts on both sides to get back to the "liberal alliance".[47]

The complicated alliance and quasi-alliance arrangements of Bismarck's last years in power illustrate the primacy of control and management in his system, as well as the increasing complexity and fragility of the means that he had to devise for it. He relied more heavily than ever on managing balanced antagonisms in order to preserve peace, even promoting them (for example, encouraging Russian policy in the Near East by the Reinsurance Treaty of 1887, while he also encouraged Britain, Austria, and Italy to conclude the Mediterranean Agreements to oppose Russia). But these tactics need not be interpreted either as good, skillful, balance of power politics or as dangerous and deceptive intrigues. They simply indicate that Bismarck's policy of using alliances for control and management was breaking down, forcing him to think of alliances mainly for security. For years he had struggled to avoid choosing between Britain and Russia. But in early 1889 he sought in vain a defensive alliance with Britain, and before his fall in March 1890 he was evidently maneuvering in a complicated and secretive fashion toward a simultaneous coup d'état within Germany and a closer tie with Russia, possibly sacrificing his alliance with Austria. These were desperate expedients; a direct alliance of Germany with either Britain or Russia would have imposed the chief burden of the alliance on Germany and given the other partner more control. The fact that Bismarck not only contemplated these moves but actually began to try them indicates the impending breakdown of his system.[48]

Bismarck was so ingenious, however, that one cannot be certain that he could not have managed Germany's alliance problems at least for a while longer. They quickly proved unmanageable for his successors, and the transformation of European alliances from instruments of management into weapons of security and power proceeded apace. The Franco-Russian alliance that Bismarck had struggled to prevent arose in the period 1891–94 as a defensive treaty directed against the Dual Alliance and tied to its existence. Neither Russia nor France originally had aggressive purposes in the alliance; from a balance of power standpoint it was a normal, healthy development. But unlike the Dual Alliance, it was intended only for mutual security, not for the management either of the allies' policies or of general European questions. Equally unlike the Dual Alliance, it contained a military convention and a *casus foederis*, which was supposed to apply automatically in case of an attack or mobilization by Germany or Austria.

Nonetheless, even this alliance worked to some extent as a pact of restraint. Russia made clear that it would not support France in a war of revenge for Alsace-Lorraine; France declined to support Russia against Britain in the Near East or the Far East. Thus the alliance served in practice to keep both partners from adventures in Europe, while freeing them for their individual imperial ambitions in Africa and Asia, which were directed much more against Britain than Germany.[49] In 1899, however, the *casus foederis* was changed to apply, not only to an Austro-German attack or mobilization, but also to any threat to the European balance of power. The French foreign minister, Delcassé, who sponsored the change, expected Austria-Hungary to break up soon, and he wished to use the alliance to keep Germany away from the Adriatic Sea and, if possible, to recover Alsace–Lorraine by diplomacy in the ensuing shuffle. The alliance might thus have been turned more to purposes of general management and control. But actually, Delcassé's basic purpose was to strengthen the alliance as an instrument of French power and security, thus altering the existing balance of power. He hoped to bring Britain gradually into the alliance, to wean Italy away from the Triple Alliance, and to open the way, by the isolation of Germany, to a reversal of 1871—all by peaceful means if possible.[50]

Meanwhile the Triple and the Dual alliances tended to become weaker both as security instruments and as tools of control. Sensing Germany's loss of leadership in the European system, Italy began to demand more support from its own allies for its colonial policy as the price for adhering to the alliance, and at the same time Italy began to loosen its alliance ties. By 1902 it had become clear that Italy would not fight on the side of its allies in a general war. In a paradoxical way, Italy's infidelity made the Triple Alliance even more a *pactum de contrahendo*. The British before 1914 vetoed all proposals for making Italy switch alliances, arguing that Italy's presence in the Triple Alliance served only to restrain Germany, while it constituted no threat to Germany's opponents.

After Bismarck's fall, Germany's turn to world policy led Germany to try to use its alliances more for purposes of extra-European gains, thereby weakening the Dual Alliance as a pact of restraint and as a tool for managing European problems. But there was a countervailing trend that derived from Austria-Hungary's eagerness to avoid war in order to have some chance of solving her critical domestic problems. In order to hold Germany back, Austrian statesmen strove for independence from German control within the alliance; they also dissociated themselves from German *Weltpolitik* and tried to discourage it, especially where it involved such challenges to Britain as the German navy and in particular, they sought and gained a measure of entente with Russia. Thus the same weakness, vulnerability, and unsolved domestic and foreign problems that, in 1914, finally drove Austria completely into Germany's arms and promoted their joint plunge into war made Austria one of the most important forces for peace, one of the most important bridges between alliances, and one of the most important restraints on Germany during an earlier period, especially from about 1895 to 1907. Austro-Russian cooperation in the agreements of 1897 and 1903 put the most dangerous area in Europe—namely the Balkans—on ice. An Austro-Russian treaty of neutrality in 1904 gave Russia invaluable security in her rear during the Russo-Japanese War and the abortive revolution of 1905. During the first Moroccan crisis of 1905–06, Austria tried to restrain Germany, ultimately contributing significantly to a peaceful outcome. All this proves that under certain circumstances even a weaker power can exercise some control and influence over a stronger partner within an alliance.[51]

With the Anglo-Japanese Alliance of 1902, Britain left her "splendid isolation" and entered the alliance system. Her alliances and ententes also served primarily to manage problems—not, however, those of running the European system or of preserving general peace, but those of meeting new challenges to the British Empire. Japan's basic purpose in the initial limited alliance of 1902 was capability-aggregation: If Japan went to war with Russia over the Manchurian–Korean issues, Britain would at least keep France neutral. Britain's alliance goal was to save its Far Eastern commercial, naval, and imperial position—which was threatened by Russia and secondarily by Germany—by devolving some of the burden on Japan. The British had already tried several expedients without success—an Open Door policy, together with the United States; proposals to Russia for a direct understanding; cooperation with Germany. Now the British hoped that Japan would constrain Russia and that the alliance might even make Russia amenable to a direct agreement with Britain.[52]

As it turned out, it required a Russo-Japanese War in 1904–05, which the British did not desire, and a Russian defeat and revolution, which they did not expect, to bring Britain an unexpected harvest. In 1905 Britain expanded its pact with Japan into a direct defensive alliance protecting India. This wider alliance helped to make Russia, whose government now needed Western financial support in order to survive, amenable to the direct understanding that Britain had sought for a decade. In 1907 the two powers concluded a convention dividing their spheres of influence in Persia and Central Asia. Both this agreement and the Japanese alliance served Britain as pacts of restraint. The British consciously used the alliance for the purpose of restraining Japanese commercial and naval competition in East Asia, which was now the most formidable for British interests. As for Persia, by conceding Russia a sphere in the north, Britain protected her exclusive control of the Persian Gulf, curbed Russian penetration of central Persia and Afghanistan, and gained some Russian help in dealing with Germany over the Baghdad Railway. In addition, this entente enabled the British consciously to divert Russia's attention and ambitions toward the Balkans, where Russia would collide with Germany and Austria, rather than with Britain.[53]

The same motive of managing the problems of the British Empire accounts, on Britain's side, for the Entente Cordiale—the Anglo-French agreement of 1904 over Morocco and Egypt, which eventually by 1914 had developed into a quasi alliance. While the French, especially Delcassé, had a long-range aim in mind—that of lining Britain up with France and Russia against Germany—the British foreign secretary, Lord Lansdowne, saw the entente as a simple colonial deal exchanging French concessions in Egypt for British cooperation in Morocco.[54] The common view that the main reason for Britain's ending her rivalries with France and Russia and forming ententes with them was to meet Germany's naval challenge and to save the European balance of power is at least very one-sided.[55] This may have been what the British ended up doing, or believed they were doing; it was hardly what they set out to do. As with Lansdowne, the goal of his Liberal successor, Lord Grey, in strengthening the entente with France and in reaching the 1907 agreement with Russia was to protect Britain's world position by supplanting overseas rivalries with cooperation and partnership, just as Britain had done earlier with the United States. The British knew about Germany's naval program in 1904, of course, but they did not need this entente to meet the challenge. Although eventually the German naval menace came to seem

214 SYSTEMS, STABILITY, AND STATECRAFT

formidable, Germany initially became Britain's main naval rival more through the decline or disappearance of other rivals than through Germany's own efforts.

As for the possibility of German hegemony on the Continent, this certainly worried the British, who never ceased reiterating before 1914 that the existing line-up of powers had to be preserved in order to maintain peace and the balance of power. But the great danger that Britain sought to avert by upholding her friendships with France and Russia was not a Continental war in which Germany would defeat them and emerge predominant. Britain's ententes with France and Russia were not designed to meet this danger; Britain steadily refused to expand them into alliances, and never expected, even if it went to war with Germany alongside France and Russia, to send large land forces to fight at their side. The real danger against which the ententes protected Britain was Franco-German or Russo-German friendship— the chance that Germany might break up the Franco-Russian alliance or the Entente Cordiale, that Germany might win Russia over, or that Germany might insinuate itself into the Franco-Russian alliance, thus isolating Britain and exposing her empire anew to French, Russian, and German pressure.[56] This prospect most frightened the British before 1914 and mainly determined Britain's policy in all the prewar crises. Britain used and valued its ententes, not as weapons of power for maintaining the European balance, but as tools for managing imperial problems. They came to have a vital impact on the European system, not simply because Germany tried unsuccessfully to break them up, or because France and Russia tried constantly to exploit them in European power politics but also because the British themselves, in order to preserve their friendships, sought to maintain a certain salutary rivalry between the Continental blocs. There is nothing intrinsically wrong with such a policy. Britain's resort to balanced antagonisms in 1908–09 or from 1912 to 1914 was no more reprehensible *per se* than Bismarck's policy of balanced antagonisms in the periods 1879–81 and 1885–87. The difference is that Bismarck saw that the antagonisms had to be managed if they were to remain balanced, and he therefore undertook to manage them. The British insisted that this was not their problem. In that failure of insight and action lies a certain British responsibility (but their only one) for what happened in 1914.[57]

The final alliance system that was erected before 1914 was the Balkan League of Bulgaria, Serbia, and Greece, which was promoted by Russia in 1912. For the Balkan states, this was strictly an offensive alliance for conquest of Turkish territory and for security from Austrian intervention. Like many alliances for aggrandizement, it held together well in war, and then fell apart over the division of the spoils. But St. Petersburg had promoted this alliance for different purposes—uniting the Balkan states under Russian control, excluding Austria, and managing Balkan affairs to Russia's own advantage. Russian hopes of using this Balkan alliance as a pact of restraint and management were entirely unrealistic, as Russia's friends saw immediately. Even with help from other great powers, Russia could not hold its clients back from war against Turkey in November 1912, and Russia proved equally unsuccessful in trying to settle the Bulgarian–Serbian dispute after the first Balkan War. It was really only Russia's good luck that its bungling attempt to manage Balkan affairs through this alliance ended in a political defeat for rival Austria-Hungary rather than in embarrassment and danger for Russia itself.[58]

The role played by alliances in the origins of World War I has been examined repeatedly, with the verdict often being that the excessive rigidity of the alliance system was an important factor. Had the powers not been bound together in rigid alliances, it is charged, a quarrel between one great power and its small, troublesome neighbor would never have led to war among five great powers. This argument about the excessive rigidity of the alliances needs modification at least. Britain was not rigidly committed to France in 1914 and was not committed at all to Russia. In 1912–13, Germany was not committed to Austria's Balkan policy, and held Austria back from war against Serbia. Italy was basically uncommitted, despite the Triple Alliance; Rumania had just escaped into neutrality from her alliance with the Central Powers; Balkan alignments were still fluid. One could more easily argue that too much fluidity in alliances, rather than excessive rigidity, helped to bring on the war by raising dangerous fears and hopes in the different camps. Austria was frightened at losing Rumania as an ally and at facing a new Balkan League, whereas France and Russia were encouraged to cap their triumph by creating such a league. Germany feared that Britain might openly ally with France and Russia; yet Germany also hoped that Britain might remain neutral in a Continental war. Germany was afraid that its ally Austria-Hungary might either break up internally or turn to neutrality. Austrian and German leaders hoped that Russia, out of monarchical sentiment, would not actually support Serbia if Austria punished it for the assassination of Archduke Francis Ferdinand.

A more valid connection between alliance developments and the origins of the war lay in the long-term changes that were developing in alliance purposes and functions. The functions of management and restraint had not yet disappeared (Austria and Italy in 1914 were still giving a classic exhibition of allies that were locked in mutual support and rivalry, especially in Albania), but they had receded far into the background. By then, allies usually did not dare to try to control their partners, for fear of undermining the alliances as indispensable weapons of security. Only if this is what is meant by the increasing rigidity of alliances is the charge correct. In 1909 the Austrian general staff (though not the Austrian government) accepted the German Schlieffen Plan, with all its disastrous political implications, in order to commit Germany to support Austria against Russia. In 1912 France stopped trying to hold Russia back in the Balkans and began urging Russia forward instead. Britain did not encourage her friends into forward moves; but neither dared she alienate Russia by trying to restrain her. Most decisive of all, Germany stopped holding Austria back in early 1914, and actually pushed her forward in July; finally, Austria gave up trying to save herself by staying out of Germany's quarrels and by refusing to join in a struggle for the supremacy of Teuton over Slav. Instead, she decided, in desperation, to gamble her existence on an all-out alliance with Germany and on a joint political and military move to restore her tottering position by a resort-to violence.

The story of alliances during World War I is too complicated to allow more than a brief summary here. As one would expect, short-range capability-aggregation for purposes of military victory almost always won out over long-term political management. Yet, even in the furnace of battle, statesmen still paid some attention to how they could manage political problems and to how they could control their allies during the war and after it. Austria negotiated stubbornly with Germany over the fate of conquered Poland and other Eastern territories, mainly in the hope of remaining a great power independent of Germany after the war. Austria and Germany, as rival partners, both tried to control the policy and strategy of their ally Turkey, but they failed.[59] Russia concocted her war aims in Europe not so much for security against a future German threat (this she expected to eliminate) as against a future Anglo-French challenge. Britain and France agreed to Russia's aims in the Straits and in the Near East only after assuring themselves of new gains in that area—new positions of strength from which they could confront each other and Russia and from which they could cooperate with each other after the war.[60] Anglo-French relations in the Near East during and after the war represent a long story of rivals in alliance who were working to restrain and use each other.[61] The United States, once it was in the war, tried to control the war aims of its associates.

Postwar alliances continued this pattern. For France, the Anglo-French unwritten alliance in Europe was mainly a means of security against Germany; but Britain used it, as she had used the "liberal alliance" of the nineteenth century, for control, for limiting the alliance to Western Europe, for curbing France's supposed desire for European hegemony, and for trying to keep France from treating Germany too harshly. Britain's policy during the French occupation of the Ruhr, as well as Britain's promotion of the Locarno treaties, clearly illustrates this tendency.[62]

In a similar way, French alliances with Poland and Czechoslovakia combined France's search for security with its desire to manage Polish and Czech policy in the supposed common interest. While hoping to tie Poland and Czechoslovakia tightly to France, the French hoped to remain free in order to promote some sort of Danubian confederation, which would include Hungary and Austria, to strengthen the *cordon sanitaire* against Germany and Russia. The scheme suited neither Poland nor Czechoslovakia, and Czech foreign minister Eduard Benes countered it with his own alliances with other anti-Hungarian states, namely Rumania and Yugoslavia (the Little Entente). As for Poland, it was far too independent and ambitious to be controlled by France—witness its quarrels with Czechoslovakia, the Polish offensive against Soviet Russia in May 1920, or the nonaggression treaty with Nazi Germany in 1934.[63]

The alliance network that France, Czechoslovakia, and the Soviet Union erected in 1935–36 was purely a security weapon against Germany; no other motive could have brought these three states together. Yet the very absence of intra-alliance control and management proved important in this alliance system. Many of its weaknesses were obvious even before it broke down in 1938: the geographical obstacles hindering the stronger powers, especially Russia, from effectively aiding Czechoslovakia, the weakest and most exposed partner; the lack of military conventions or agreements; France's defensive strategy; and internal opposition to the alliance, as well as mutual distrust on all sides. But a major weakness that has gone largely unremarked was the fact that none of these allies could exercise effective influence over its partners on policies that decisively affected the alliance. Both France and the USSR tried repeatedly and unsuccessfully to push the other one forward against Germany. France could do nothing to stop Russia from drastically weakening her army in the Great Purge of 1936–38. Russia and Czechoslovakia could not change France's military strategy. Neither great power could help Czechoslovakia meet her minorities problems, especially the Sudeten German one, which threatened to cripple her in a crisis. The allies could not achieve a common policy even on so elementally important a question as how to react to a German Anschluss with Austria.[64]

As for the Anglo-French alliance from 1935 to 1938, the point relevant to our theme is that Britain's appeasement policy toward Germany was in the last analysis an attempt to use this alliance for control and management in the interests of peace, rather than for power and military security.[65] Knowing France's dependence on Britain and France's willingness to have Britain take the lead, British statesmen, especially Chamberlain, tried to solve the Czech crisis and to avert war with Germany by leading their ally France into an agreement and into a wider partnership with the very powers against whom Britain and France were allied—namely Germany and, to a lesser extent, Italy. Chamberlain hoped to render peace secure, once the Czech–German crisis had been settled at Munich through four-power agreement, by supplementing the Anglo-French alliance with an informal Anglo-German partnership and Anglo-Italian friendship. It is not too fanciful to see this as an attempt to widen a particular alliance into a general European concert (excluding the Soviet Union, to be sure) like that of the nineteenth century. Unfortunately, Hitler was not Alexander I, and Chamberlain was not Castlereagh or Metternich.[66]

After the German occupation of Prague in March 1939 made this form of appeasement impossible, the Western allies turned to security and capability-aggregation against Germany as their prime goal. The German threat now led Britain to extend its commitments in unprecedented fashion—to guarantee the independence of Poland, Rumania, and Greece and to seek an alliance with the Soviet Union. Yet even in these frantic alliance efforts the British were still trying to manage the international problem and to control their allies. A major reason for giving a guarantee to Warsaw was to get Poland to defend Rumania, which the British considered to be more threatened initially than Poland and which they could not protect. Moreover, the Anglo-French alliance with Poland was not really intended to stop Hitler and to preserve the status quo of 1939 at any cost (Poland's independence was guaranteed, but not her existing borders), but to create conditions under which Germany and Poland might reach a negotiated settlement. With Poland making some concessions Germany's domination of East-Central Europe was not supposed to be ended or prevented, but controlled, kept within bounds that were compatible with British and French honor. Germany might still make gains, but not by any more brutal surprises like the takeover of rump Czechoslovakia in March.[67]

The matter of intra-alliance control and management, moreover, helps to explain why no Western–Soviet alliance was formed. One reason, though not the most important one, that neither side tried as hard for an alliance as it might have is that both sides knew that they could not control their partners' actions under the alliance. The Western powers not only had to worry about what the USSR would do once it intervened to aid Poland and the Baltic states; they also could not be sure how long and hard the Soviet Union would fight and whether, having got the Western powers involved, it might not make a separate peace with the Germans. The Soviet Union naturally had a similar distrust of the West, especially after Munich; and no assurances or control devices could have removed the distrust on either side. This bolsters the view that a genuine Soviet–Western united front against Germany was never a real possibility in 1939.[68]

Hitler's alliances were mainly intended for capability-aggregation, though he usually ended up exercising a brutal control over those who sided with him. (Franco, an exception, was careful to avoid any real alliance with Hitler.) The Italo-German alliance of May 1939 (the Pact of Steel) was an overtly offensive treaty in which Mussolini frivolously and fatalistically threw Italy into Germany's arms. Yet even Mussolini attempted to some extent to hold Hitler back through this alliance in August 1939, as he had done earlier, in September 1938. Moreover, Mussolini's determination to keep Italy a great power in the alliance rather than a satellite explains much of Italian policy—the unnecessary seizure of Albania, the attack on France in June 1940, and the disastrous invasion of Greece in October 1940, which ended by reducing Italy to satellite status.[69]

The Axis Alliance that linked Japan to Germany and Italy in September 1940 was, to an even greater degree than the Pact of Steel, exclusively an alliance for capability-aggregation and gain. Ideological ties and sympathies were much less important here than they were between Hitler and Mussolini; Germany and Italy at least had geographical propinquity and some mutual interests, while Germany and Japan had little to offer each other except mutual permission for each to expand at the expense of the other nations. The one area where the two powers might have cooperated, against the Soviet Union, was where political and military coordination was most strikingly absent. There was then hardly any cooperation, management, or control within the Axis Alliance—not much besides cross-purposes, betrayals, and attempts to exploit one's partner. But this explains in good part why the alliance failed so completely both diplomatically and militarily.[70]

The Grand Alliance among Britain, the United States, and the USSR in World War II also served primarily as an instrument of power. Victory being the overriding goal of each power, military considerations dominated alliance politics, at least until late in the war. Even questions of great, long-range political significance—such as the time and location of a second front, or how much aid to give to which resistance movements, or whether the Western allies should try to land in southeast Europe—were decided mainly on immediate military grounds. The chief strains and problems in the alliance concerned military issues—the delay in the second front, fears of a Soviet separate peace with Germany, the question of Soviet participation in the war against Japan.[71]

Yet long-range concerns over the control and management of problems and allies were always present and active. The vital question for Britain was that of remaining a great power and defending her interests in the company of giants like the United States and the USSR, particularly after another world war had drained her resources and undermined her empire. Her only hope was successfully to manage the United States, which involved a number of tasks—such as preserving a special Anglo-American partnership and preventing a Soviet–American one at Britain's expense; securing American long-term military and economic help; curbing the anti-imperialist, anti-British tendencies in American policy; and preserving British economic interests against American encroachment. Rather late in the war, the desire to preserve some sort of balance in Europe by managing the Soviet Union and checking Soviet expansion also became important. Churchill's proposal to Stalin in October 1944 that the Balkans be divided into spheres of influence may be seen as a not very skillful effort to manage a rival within an alliance.[72]

Stalin, although he profoundly distrusted the West, doubtless wanted to maintain the wartime alliance after victory, both for security reasons and in order to get the economic aid that his devastated country needed. But precisely because Stalin preferred that the alliance continue, he was determined to establish positions of strength such that Soviet relations with the West could be based on old-fashioned realpolitik, on principles of *do ut des* [I give so that you give] and nothing for nothing, with each power free to act as it wished in its own sphere. Stalin, in other words, was determined not to be managed or influenced by the West in this alliance, especially in any way that might affect his power or style of rule in Russia. The Soviet Union had to be given security not so much through the alliance as against the alliance; the security Stalin needed was not so much external and military as internal and ideological. This required, along with great new purges and repressive measures within Russia, the establishment of friendly, democratic governments in East–Central Europe, as Stalin understood those terms. The Sovietization of east–central and southeastern Europe was neither a case of revolutionary Soviet expansionism, as the orthodox American view used to have it, nor mainly a Soviet response to an American challenge in Russia's sphere, as American revisionist critics contend. It was basically a logical and indispensable requirement for Soviet security as Stalin defined it—the sealing off of Russia from any subversive influences that might undermine his regime. Theoretically speaking, the Western powers could have preserved the wartime alliance with the USSR, had they resolved from the outset to accept without challenge whatever the Soviet Union did at home or to its neighbors. Stalin would have doubtless given America and Britain the equal freedom to run their countries and control their satellites as they saw fit. But this was incompatible with any conception of a postwar alliance that was entertained in the West, and indeed it was incompatible with any durable alliance relationship at all.[73]

As for the United States, without even trying to summarize the wide-ranging controversy over American policy in the alliance, one can say that it was riddled with contradictions and paradoxes, most of all precisely on whether the Grand Alliance was to be used as a military instrument or as a tool for long-range management and control. On the one hand, the United States, even more than the other two great powers, fought the war simply for total victory. Although less threatened by invasion than either the USSR or Britain, the United States was, if anything, even more determined than they to end German and Japanese militarism forever through total victory, occupation, drastic control, and sweeping remodeling of their societies. Hence no power was more inclined than the United States to see the Grand Alliance as a military instrument for total victory, to sacrifice or subordinate political to military considerations, and to put off decisions that might jeopardize the military effectiveness of the alliance.

At the same time, no great power fought the war for more grandiose (if inconsistent and confused) aims and ideals for the postwar world. It seems impossible to make a consistent program out of these, either as a liberal democratic program for lasting peace and cooperation or as a sinister imperialist plan to make the world safe for American capitalism.[74] There is no way to harmonize Roosevelt's idea of Four Policemen (policing the world for peace and dividing it into spheres of great power control) with other American ideas about national liberation, disimperialism, and international control of vital areas, or to harmonize these, in turn, with notions of world peace through capitalist-based economic recovery and development via the Open Door policy. But the point is not whether American ideals were consistent or inconsistent, sensible or unrealistic, noble or sinister. The point is that whether American leaders liked it or not, any hope of achieving such sweeping aims required not merely the total defeat of the enemy but also (among other things), first and foremost, a massive effort by the United States to manage and control its great power allies while the war was still going on. The United States therefore followed the peculiar policy of refusing in principle to use the Grand Alliance for purposes of intra-alliance management, for fear of ruining it as a military instrument, while entertaining war aims that required that it be used for management purposes on a massive scale. Moreover, despite the American preoccupation with total victory, American leaders did begin fairly early to consider using American economic, political, and military power to manage and control their allies; they increasingly attempted to do so, especially after the development of the atomic bomb. Much of what the United States did in the earlier stages of the Cold War, which is usually interpreted either as an effort to check Soviet revolutionary expansionism or as an American attempt to deprive the Soviet Union of its legitimate wartime gains, is better seen as a belated American attempt to manage the Soviet Union and to bring it back to the American conception of the goals of their alliance.

This survey suggests certain conclusions. The first has already often been mentioned. Technically, alliances are mutual security pacts with a *casus foederis*; for various reasons, this technical definition is useful and should be retained. But functionally, alliances serve many diverse purposes and are best considered as general tools for management and control in international affairs.

If this be so, then analyzing and categorizing alliances according to their types or provisions (defensive or offensive, limited or unlimited, consultative or automatic, with or without military conventions, bilateral or multilateral) are not likely to be very fruitful in describing what alliances really do; nor are attempts to establish statistical correlations between the numbers and types of alliances existing at various times and the corresponding levels of international conflict and tension likely to be very fruitful.[75] Nothing can substitute for the painfully empirical task of functional analysis of particular alliances.

Such analysis should look for other motives and purposes besides the standard ones of mutual security and capability-aggregation—in particular, for the desire to control one's ally, the aim of managing an international problem, and even the hope of avoiding conflict by allying oneself with a rival. In any case, the way in which mutual control or influence is exercised is always important for the durability and effectiveness of an alliance.

Some commonly held ideas about alliances may need to be revised or discarded if these points are valid. For instance, alliance flexibility may not be as useful for peace and stability as balance of power theorists generally hold, and alliance rigidity *per se* may not be as productive of confrontation and war. If an alliance functions as a pact of mutual restraint, it may promote peace to have powers locked tightly into it. It also need not be true, as is often supposed, that powers must have generally harmonious aims and outlooks if they are to become allies and then stay together. In the past, fairly durable alliances and partnerships have been formed that were based on little more than the realization that there was no other means available for managing a dangerous problem and that the likely alternative to an alliance was war. One may fervently hope that this principle continues to work—for example, for the United States and the USSR in the Middle East.

There is no magic formula for using alliances as tools of management for the purpose of promoting international peace and stability. Just as the deceptively simple formulas of balance of power and collective security have often proved inapplicable or counterproductive, so, as our survey illustrates, many efforts to use alliances as instruments of management and control have proved futile, foolish, and even disastrous. Moreover, statesmen can just as well employ alliances as management devices to promote war as use them to preserve peace—witness Palmerston during the Crimean War or Bismarck in the 1860s. Nonetheless, one can make a case that the management potential of alliances offers certain hopeful possibilities for durable peace. Traditionally, the quest for a viable principle of international order has oscillated between two poles—the balance of power versus the integration of nations into an international community. So-called realists see the basic, inescapable reality of international politics as the dispersal of power among essentially independent centers of decision with inherently divergent and potentially conflicting interests and purposes, so that the only way to achieve stability and peace is through balance, checking power with countervailing power. "Idealists," seeing this game either as futile and counterproductive *per se* or else as having become intolerably dangerous in the present state of arms development, look to various processes and devices of international integration—economic interdependence, world organization, international law, federal and regional movements, and so on—to supplant international conflicts with international community.[76] Neither approach seems to be very hopeful. To put it simply, balance of power politics does not seem to be able to create the needed durable restraints and cooperation among nations; indeed, it may often undermine them, whereas movements for integration cannot face or overcome the hard reality of conflicting power and purposes.

It may therefore be more hopeful to seek something in the middle, to search for models in associative–antagonistic relationships in nature and society, to look for devices that specifically unite rivals. Alliances and quasi alliances in international relations are precisely such associative–antagonistic relationships. They normally contain large elements of rivalry as well as cooperation, conflict as well as mutuality of purpose. A knowledge of how they work and survive, therefore, might help in the search for a viable principle of international order. Certainly there is plenty of contemporary material for study. The Western alliance system has been riddled with rivalries and conflicts over intra-alliance control and management, not only between France and the United States, but also between France and Germany, Britain and France, and other members. Yet the alliance has survived till now. In the Warsaw Pact, the struggles over how control is exercised, and by whom, have been less obvious (except where they have broken into the open and been settled by brute force) but no less real. One can conceive of the détente between the United States and the USSR some day developing into a rival alliance, a *pactum de contrahendo* covering at least certain areas of the world and designed to keep peace there in a way that is not too different from that in which the Austro-Russian pact of restraint once kept peace in the Balkans. It is not impossible that Russia and China, once close allies and now enemies, could return to being hostile allies. But to speculate thus is to open up themes even vaster than the subject of this essay.

THE NINETEENTH CENTURY SYSTEM: BALANCE OF POWER OR POLITICAL EQUILIBRIUM?

Students of international politics do not need to be told of the unsatisfactory state of balance of power theory.[1] The problems are well known: the ambiguous nature of the concept and the numerous ways it has been defined,[2] the various distinct and partly contradictory meanings given to it in practice and the divergent purposes it serves (description, analysis, prescription, and propaganda);[3] and the apparent failure of attempts clearly to define balance of power as a system and specify its operating rules.[4] Not surprisingly, some scholars have become skeptical about the balance of power "system"[5] and a few have even denied that balance of power politics prevailed in the nineteenth century.[6] None of the methods generally used seems to promise much help. These have included studying the views and theories of balance of power held by individual publicists, theorists, and statesmen,[7] making case studies of the balance of power in certain limited periods,[8] analyzing events and policies within an assumed balance of power framework,[9] or constructing theoretical analyses comparing the supposed system of balance of power to other systems.[10] Undoubtedly a method for operationalizing the study of the balance of power would be very valuable, and efforts to do this have yielded useful information. But the obstacles to establishing reliable indices of power and status and the problems of quantifying alignments and cooperation–conflict ratios in international affairs are formidable indeed.[11]

At the same time, the concept of balance of power seems indispensable. There is hardly a discussion of current international politics in serious journals or newspapers that does not use it or rest on it, and it seems equally unavoidable in making sense of the nineteenth century European state system.

This essay in suggesting a solution may make the problem worse. For "balance of power" it will advocate substituting a phrase apparently just as vague

Review of International Studies, 15 (April, 1989), 135–53. Copyright © (1989), Cambridge University Press. Printed in Great Britain. All rights reserved. Reprinted with the permission of Cambridge University Press.

and subject to misunderstanding and manipulation, namely "political equilibrium." The argument to be sketched out is that the nineteenth century international system, as any stable international system must do in the twentieth
century as well, depended mainly not on balancing power against other power
but on balancing other vital factors in international politics, and that pure balance of power politics destroys political equilibrium rather than sustains it.

    The argument rests mainly on a study of the language of nineteenth cen-
tury international politics. The research has consisted simply of reading carefully through an extensive selection of diplomatic correspondence and
political writings from leaders of all the major powers between 1815 and
1914 (for details see the appendix), trying to ascertain how often statesmen
used balance of power language; in what contexts, to what apparent ends,
and with what meanings they employed it; and how balance of power language related to other expressions, ideas, and slogans. The methods used
were traditional historical ones, with counting used only to control subjective impressions and qualitative judgments rather than to lay the basis for statistical correlations or formal content analysis. This approach was chosen
partly because the main purpose of the study was historical rather than "scientific," that is, to write a history of balance of power thought in the nineteenth century rather than to attempt to develop a systematic balance of
power theory. But more important, while it proved possible to gain some
useful information from analyzing the incidence of balance language, the
patterns of usage, and the overt meanings applied to various terms, the most
important questions to be asked and answers to be gained from the material
were irreducibly qualitative—what purposes balance language served in various instances, what tactics and strategies were involved, what meanings it
held, and what roles it played within different policies, contexts, and systems
of thought. Even counting instances of balance language turned out often to
involve subjective interpretation; one could not decide whether a word or
phrase represented balance language without deciding what it meant in context and what aim it was supposed to serve. But even if the research lacks the
rigor desired in social science or the material does not permit it, its results
clearly render even more dubious the idea of the balance of power as a
doctrine, principle, or mechanism governing nineteenth century European
politics, while at the same time it may indicate ways in which the concept of
balance remained important in the nineteenth century system.

RESULTS OF SURVEYING THE DOCUMENTS

My first point is a low-level one: explicit balance language was not used very
much in nineteenth century diplomacy.[12] While statesmen sometimes
referred to the European balance and showed apparent concern over it, most
of the time it seems to have been ignored. The explanation can hardly lie in
a selective bias in the sample, for the research was deliberately focused on
periods of change and crisis where balance of power questions seemed most
likely to arise. Nor is it the explanation that statesmen seldom referred to

general principles, concentrating instead on immediate practical questions. To the contrary, statesmen constantly explained and justified their policies and actions in terms of general principles. But the preservation of peace, the maintenance of treaties and legal rights, the preservation of the social order (or the status quo, the monarchical order, the political order, existing territorial boundaries, and the like), the prevention of revolution, the satisfaction of national interests, honor, or public opinion, upholding international law, maintaining the unity of the powers or the Concert—all these were more frequently mentioned. Of course, the term "equilibrium" is protean enough to allow the possibility that some of these slogans imply a concern for the balance of power. (I will later argue that they did indeed show a concern for equilibrium, but not balance of power.) The fact remains that explicit references to the balance of power are relatively scarce.[13]

Another obvious finding is a wide fluctuation in the incidence of balance language. More often than not one can find no serious discussion of the balance of power on issues that one supposed vitally affected it.[14] Questions that at one time were seen as central to the balance at another evoked no such concern. Certain aspects of a single issue might be seen in terms of balance of power while its other aspects would be separated from it.[15] Colonial and imperial disputes were normally not considered as affecting the European balance, but at any time some power could make a particular colonial question a balance of power issue, only to drop it again later.[16] No question seems to have been so minor or special that it could not somehow be presented as a general question of the European balance; but also no question was so universal or central that its connection with it could not at times be ignored.

The terminology used reveals further problems. There is nothing surprising in the fact that statesmen used a wide variety of words and phrases in connection with the concept of balance, or that they connected it with many elements in international relations besides power (they spoke of balance of influences, races, rights, opinions, rank, status, and so on), or that they might detect or call for a balance in almost any limited geographic area (for example, in the Gulf of Chih-Li or the upper Adriatic).[17] Serious problems arise only when one tries to coordinate and harmonize the diverse meanings that the term "European equilibrium" and its equivalents bore. These include (the list is not exhaustive):

1. An even or balanced distribution of power.
2. Any existing distribution of power.[18]
3. Any existing general situation or status quo, with no particular regard to power relations.[19]
4. The European system or order, the general framework of European politics.[20]
5. Some indeterminate meaning involving some combination of the above.[21]
6. As a verb, to play the role of a balancer, which can mean (a) oscillating between two sides,[22] or (b) being an arbiter between two sides, each of which roles may require either being within the balance or standing outside it.[23]

7. Stability, peace, and repose.
8. A labile, shifting condition in international affairs, tending toward resolution by conflict.[24]
9. The rule of law and guaranteed rights.
10. The general struggle for power, influence, and advantage—power politics according to the rules of raison d'état.
11. Hegemony.[25]

No doubt some combinations and reconciliations of these diverse meanings are possible. They seem, however, not to be variations on one central theme, but involve at least two, intertwined yet divergent and tending to clash. One central meaning, most prominent in the first half of the century but persisting as a minor note in the second, is that of equilibrium as stability, peace, the rule of law, the mutual guarantee of rights under treaties, and the supervision of all major changes in the system by the great powers. Space forbids piling up instances of this usage, but it clearly dominated the meaning of "balance" for four or five decades after 1815 in Central and Eastern Europe, and was prominent also in France and Britain. Even after the mid-century revolutions and triumphs of *realpolitik* had largely discredited such conservative international principles and enthroned the idea of reason of state, one still finds occasional instances of this definition. The other theme is that of "equilibrium" as balance of power in the ordinary or restricted sense—an even distribution of power and the policy of checking and containing dangerous uses or accumulations of power by countervailing power. No neat dichotomy is possible between the two meanings or uses. Equilibrium can mean either "stability and the rule of law" or "balance of power" interchangeably. One can find statesmen (for example, Metternich or Talleyrand) using the term in one sense in one sentence and in the other in the next. Nevertheless, the difference between equilibrium understood as harmony and stability under law and as balance of power can be detected not merely contextually but also in the actual terminology employed. Often when statesmen wanted to make clear that by equilibrium they meant a balance of power, they chose to express this through particular variants of the generic term equilibrium, for example, "équilibre des forces," "équilibre entre les forces européennes," "équilibre par une juste partition des forces," or more occasionally, "balance du pouvoir" or "balance des puissances." They also used phrases and terms unmistakably denoting a power balance—"counterweight," "counterbalance," "weighing of forces," "balancing of forces," and so on. Only when these terms are present—and they are not in most cases—is it safe to assume that balance of power in the strict sense is actually meant.

The distinction between equilibrium in a legal and moral sense and as strict balance of power shows up in the two divergent political vocabularies connected with balance terminology. The moral–legal definition of equilibrium tends to merge with the general slogans and ideas of conservative politics, so that the phrase "European equilibrium" often becomes almost interchangeable with such phrases as the unity of the powers, the Concert of Europe, order and peace, and the independence of Europe—all terms that have no necessary balance of power connotation and are in express opposition to power politics. Balance of power terminology, meanwhile, flows into the language of *realpolitik*, politics governed only by state interests rather than principles or moral rules, the science or game of checking one's opponents so as to gain the upper hand or a free hand. Often one cannot tell whether a word like "counterweight" or "counterbalance" has the connotation of maintaining a balance, or simply denotes some power-political move.

CONTRADICTIONS IN EQUILIBRIST THOUGHT

Were this diversity in the meanings and central themes of equilibrist language combined with a general consensus on the rules or practices needed to achieve and maintain equilibrium, the different meanings and definitions might not be troublesome. In fact, however, there seems to be no rule or principle proposed for equilibrist politics that cannot be countered by a contrary principle from within equilibrist thought. Some nineteenth century statesmen, like many scholars today, believed that the balance of power required states to be flexible and non-ideological in their foreign policies, forming and changing alliances and alignments on the basis of their interests and balance requirements. But many others insisted on a particular ideology and principles, usually conservative ones, as absolutely vital to the European equilibrium, and one can easily see how pure balance of power concepts could and did lead to the idea of Europe as divided into ideological or racial blocs in standing competition with each other (constitutional versus absolutist states, Latins versus Anglo-Saxons, or Teutons versus Slavs, etc.).[26] It is often assumed that balance requires a fairly even distribution of power, but statesmen as different as Prince Metternich, Prince Talleyrand, and Lord Balfour doubted or denied it,[27] and the term "equilibrium" was often used for situations in which the distribution of power was anything but even or balanced. Does equilibrium at least require that in actual practice different powers or blocs balance each other, as the Franco-Russian alliance supposedly balanced the Triple Alliance after 1891? Again this is often claimed, but many nineteenth century statesmen insisted that the very existence of rival alliances undermined the European equilibrium. Moreover, at times the working definition for equilibrium meant a dominant coalition set up against a supposed aggressor (witness the French and English concept of a European balance against Russia during and after the Crimean War, or the Russo-French-Serbian concept of a Balkan equilibrium against Austria before World War I). Indeed, I have yet to find one convincing instance in the nineteenth century of any power willingly relying for peace on the existence of two equal blocking coalitions or genuinely consenting to have the balance of power constrain it as well as its rivals, as Edmund Burke once advocated. W. H. Riker's thesis that the logic of coalitions leads inexorably to the formation of winning rather than merely blocking coalitions seems borne out in practice.

The raison d'etre of a balance of power system is often said to be the protection of the independence of smaller states, and over the course of the nineteenth century many small states were designated as essential to the equilibrium (Denmark, Switzerland, Belgium, Holland, Sardinia, Serbia, etc.). But a balance of power can also operate, as in the eighteenth century, on the basis of the balanced partitioning of small states (a point which Bismarck reminded the British in 1869 when they tried balance of power arguments to persuade Prussia to defend Belgium against France).[28] Moreover, balance of power arguments were actually employed in the nineteenth century to justify the extinction of a number of small states (for example, in the course of Italian and German unification).

Even the apparently most obvious and necessary balance of power rule—that the independence and integrity of all actors must be preserved—was often violated. On the one hand, all the major states were almost routinely described as essential to the European balance, especially vulnerable, threatened states like Austria and Turkey.[29] On the other, there were many proposals and some actual campaigns to save the European balance or to erect a new and better one by attacks on major states. Some examples: the plans Palmerston, Stratford de Redcliffe, and some other Britons entertained to preserve the European balance by throwing Russia back into Asia;[30] the arguments of Italian nationalists and Italophiles in the 1850s and 1860s that Austria had to be destroyed or transformed before a true European equilibrium could exist;[31] and France's aim in the war of 1870 to restore the European balance by eliminating Prussia as a major power.[32] Even the total disappearance of a major state could be fitted into an equilibrist scheme. Russia, Prussia, and Austria argued that the equilibrium would be destroyed if Poland were restored. Polignac and Charles X of France wanted to improve the European balance by a general partition of Turkey in 1829, and Tsar Nicholas I briefly contemplated the same idea in 1853. Austria's defeat in 1866 caused widespread expectation of her complete collapse and fear for the general equilibrium as a result, though no one did anything about the danger. But when, between 1899 and 1901 Austria again was thought to be on the verge of breakup, the remedy France, Russia, and even Austria's ally Italy contemplated to save the balance of power was to plan the partition of Austria and apportion the various shares in advance.[33]

Finally, the most important goal of a system of equilibrium is supposedly to protect the independence of states by compelling each power to recognize the independence of others as the price of its own.[34] Yet balance of power policies can and sometimes do lead or even require states to deny the de facto independence of other states, and to treat them solely as members of a coalition regardless of their individual intentions, needs, and policies. Prior to World War I, British statesmen knew that Austria was trying desperately to retain its independence *vis-à-vis* Germany and that it often acted independently, sometimes even against German wishes. Yet the British persisted in viewing and treating Austria as Germany's satellite (for example, they counted the Austrian army and navy simply as adjuncts to Germany's), because the existing balance of power consigned Austria to the role of Germany's junior partner, regardless of what she wanted or tried to do.[35]

To all these irreconcilable contradictions in meanings, core themes, principles, and practices in balance language and thought must be added another: the basic conception of how a European balance should be constituted or structured. Again one must distinguish between normal, untroublesome, epistemological and definitional problems and those presenting real difficulties. It does not constitute any grave problem for balance of power theory that in practice the ideas of what constituted a proper balance constantly changed and clashed. For example, what Britain and Italy in the 1880s termed an equilibrium in the Mediterranean was exactly what France called British imperial domination.[36] Instances of this are very common, but they may prove no more than that different powers interpret the requirements of balance in different, self-serving ways. A more serious difficulty lies deeper, in the notion of what structure and broad arrangements were required for any durable European balance to exist. Here there were fundamental divergences of view. For example, German statesmen and publicists after 1815 viewed the German and European balance as a complex one, involving at least three main elements in a kind of hierarchical relationship. The first requisite element was that the two great powers Austria and Prussia be balanced in power and status within Germany. The second was that Germany have a federative structure binding the rival great powers in permanent partnership both with each other and with the smaller German states, guaranteeing all parties their rights, security, territories, and independence. Third was the recognition and guarantee of the German Confederation by the other European great powers. What Germans meant by equilibrium, then, was a complicated balancing of power, status, and rights within Germany, contained and controlled within a German Confederation and guaranteed by a united Europe. Compare this with the standard British conception of the European equilibrium throughout the century, especially from the 1860s on: a united Germany, perhaps allied with Austria and Italy, watching and checking Russia and France so that Britain would be arbiter of Europe and have a free hand for its extra-European concerns. These basic conceptions of the European balance have nothing in common but the name. When Germans and Britons said "European equilibrium" in the nineteenth century, they not only did not define the term similarly; they were not even thinking in similar categories.[37] Other almost equally glaring divergences could be cited.

To state clearly what the argument is not: it is not a claim that the confusion and contradictions within balance of power language are so pervasive that they render the concept useless. Historians and political scientists constantly deal with elastic concepts that have come in practice to have highly charged and very divergent meanings—democracy, socialism, Christianity, populism, and the like. So long as one can identify a central conceptual core or a standard working definition, one can usually show how the various divergent strains relate to them, and/or one may choose to rule out some meanings and usages as abuses of the term rather than uses of it. It can happen, however, that a term, usually a value-loaded one, comes to contain such manifest internal contradictions that it can no longer serve usefully to contain and unify its various meanings. This may have happened, for example, to the term "democracy." When the same term is applied to states and systems as diverse as the United States and the Soviet Union or Sweden and North Korea, and when scholars like J. L. Talmon argue that all these divergent uses are in a certain sense equally historically legitimate, and when such phrases as "economic democracy" become common parlance, then one may conclude that the term, at least in its unqualified form, has ceased to function as a useful scholarly tool. One must, to give it any clear content, specify what one means by it, that is, must say "Soviet-style democracy" or "liberal democracy," or the like. This was and is the case, I contend, with nineteenth century language of the balance of power. The contradiction between core meanings and practices is such that when one says "European equilibrium" one ought to specify whether one means equilibrium as stability and peace through the rule of law and great power unity, or equilibrium through balance of power. Both meanings were and are widely used; both are legitimate; and they contradict each other.

Or one might conclude that there was nothing to either core; that balance of power language was and is empty phraseology—to paraphrase Talleyrand, a gift of God enabling men to conceal their thoughts. One could make a case of this sort, and I for one would be hard-pressed decisively to refute it. Yet it would be, in my view, as mistaken as the opposite one of making balance of power the reigning principle and mechanism governing European politics. There is less balance language in the documents than one would expect, but more than can be dismissed or explained away. Equilibrist language plainly meant many contradictory things to different people, but it did not mean nothing at all. The self-interest, opportunism, cant, propaganda, and hypocrisy clearly associated with balance language do not exhaust its meaning and significance. A consistently unprincipled and opportunistic use of language in politics is as difficult and improbable as a consistently principled one; to use phrases regularly without attaching any meaning to them is as hard as to use them regularly with their full, consistent meaning. The rest of this essay, therefore, will contend that balance of power language and thought in the nineteenth century, despite its lack of unified content, was still significant, and even suggests a certain limited way in which a common core to equilibrist conceptions existed after all.

THE SIGNIFICANCE OF THE BALANCE OF POWER IDEA

The balance of power idea is significant, for one thing, because it has a history. It was not a lodestar to guide the ships of state, but it was also not a kaleidoscope of random and meaningless shifts and contradictions. Balance of power thought has a history, tricky but not impossible to trace and explain, in which changes in language and meaning about the European equilibrium are connected with (though not necessarily or strictly derived from) other changes in European political and social life. Changing interests, needs, opportunities, and policies on the part of the various states and their elites and changes in the rules of the game of high politics are reflected in changes in the concept of balance of power. This makes it at least partly a dependent variable. Instead of the balance of power explaining what happened in European politics, what happened in European politics largely explains what happened to the idea of balance of power. But even dependent variables exert an influence on events by way of the normal interpenetration between effect and cause. Furthermore, the concept of balance of power can provide valuable clues about changes within the European system precisely in its role of dependent variable.

Only a full history of balance of power thought in the nineteenth century or the citing of many examples would adequately back up this claim. Both are impossible here, but a couple of instances in which changes in balance of power thought illuminate developments in European politics will serve to illustrate the point. For example, one can trace how the central concept of equilibrium changed and evolved in 1813–17. The period began with Europe still adhering to the old competitive eighteenth century model, stressing balance through compensations and indemnities, the calculation of forces on the basis of territory, population, and revenues, and the management of threats and crises through hostile alliances and coalitions. It ended with a predominantly moral, legal, and social-communal model of balance in which equilibrium required first and foremost the maintenance of the political and social order as a whole and the unity of all powers in defense of the legally established order.[38] The development was not simply a reflection of the transition from war to peace—indeed, peace became possible only because of this change in thinking—but indicated a profound change in the accepted rules of European statecraft. Even more dramatic is the way Prussian statesmen almost overnight changed the way they conceived the European equilibrium in 1859. On June 24, France and Sardinia won the Italian war over Austria at the Battle of Solferino. After this battle, the conservative-equilibrist model of equilibrium that Prussian statesmen had consistently adhered to was tacitly abandoned and they switched to a liberal-nationalist balance of power model.[39] In the Prussian documents of 1859–63 one can see the struggle between old conservative principles and the new Bismarckian *realpolitik* reflected in the ways balance of power language is used.[40] The debate in France over Italian and German policy, especially in 1865–70, is better understood if one sees that Frenchmen were not simply arguing over what organization for Italy and Germany would most favor French power and security, but were debating fundamental differences over the structure of a stable equilibrium in Europe. The question, put briefly and too simply, was whether, as Napoleon III and his liberal advisers believed, a stable equilibrium could be best secured by the triumph of nationalism and by an alliance between the nationally satisfied and progressive powers (France, Prussia, and Italy); or whether, as opponents like Adolphe Thiers and Jules Favre insisted, the European equilibrium was incompatible with nationalism and required that Italy and Germany remain divided.[41]

Most scholars, while wanting further proof, would probably not be greatly disturbed by the notion that the concept of the balance of power was in many respects a dependent variable in the nineteenth century, reflecting broader changes in international politics. It may seem inconsistent to make further claims that a central core in equilibrist language and thought exists and played a significant role in the nineteenth century. This essay nonetheless claims this and will try to make sense of the claim, if not demonstrate it. The argument goes like this: throughout the nineteenth century, most statesmen believed, correctly, that the European system had to be balanced for purposes of stability, peace, and a tolerable international atmosphere. This recognition influenced their behavior to a considerable degree; even aggressive and unscrupulous politicians like Cavour and Bismarck, once they had achieved their goals, wanted to help achieve a European balance to preserve their gains. The balance statesmen usually envisioned and sought, however, was not mainly a balance in power or based on power, operating by using the power of certain states to check others and keep anyone from growing too powerful or aggressive. It was instead a broader balance in general political conditions and goods, a political equilibrium. (That term, incidentally, is a far better rendering of the most common phrases used in balance language, namely "équilibre de l'Europe," "équilibre europeen," and "équilibre politique" and their equivalents in other languages, than the inaccurate and misleading "balance of power.") I contend, in short, that when European statesmen said "European equilibrium" or "political equilibrium," they meant precisely that, and did not usually mean "balance of power."

THE IDEA OF POLITICAL EQUILIBRIUM

Obviously, the problem is to give specific content to the idea of political equilibrium, which may seem more nebulous than the concept of balance of power. One might, as I formerly did, conceive of international political equilibrium as a form of homeostatic balance, that is, a self-adjusting equilibrium akin to the ecological balance in nature between the animal population of a territory and the available food supply; between bodily processes in human physiology; and between personal needs and fulfillment, drives and satisfactions in psychology. But this idea, while not wrong and possibly suggestive, is not very helpful, because it is both artificial (no statesman ever said explicitly that his idea of equilibrium involved homeostasis) and otiose. All equilibria in social organizations work by homeostasis in one form or another; the term says nothing about what is specifically required for equilibrium in international politics.

It would seem better to try to specify directly what goals or goods the members of the nineteenth century family of states (a common but not meaningless phrase) sought in international politics—goals or goods that they believed a political equilibrium would provide them. In a general way it is possible to identify these. Subjectively political equilibrium meant the enjoyment of stability, peace, and guaranteed rights; freedom from threats and isolation; the recognition of one's legitimate interests, sphere of influence, and the right to a voice in general affairs; and especially for the great powers, assurance of equality in rank, status, and dignity, even if not in power. Whenever these conditions were believed not to prevail, statesmen would claim that the balance was upset. In objective terms, political equilibrium required that (1) the rights, influence, and vital interests claimed by individual states in the international system be somehow balanced against the rights, influence, and vital interests claimed by other states and the general community, and (2) that a balance or harmony exist between the goals pursued by individual states, the requirements of the system, and the means used to promote one's interests. Oversimplified, political equilibrium meant a balance of satisfactions, a balance of rights and obligations, and a balance of performance and payoffs, rather than a balance of power.

This does not of course eliminate the vagueness and ambiguities attaching to the term; to do so would fly in the face of the evidence and the nature of international politics. Nevertheless, an understanding of political equilibrium along these lines is both more faithful to the nineteenth century record and closer to the realities of international politics generally. It recognizes the power of an ideal to which almost everyone had to pay lip service no matter how much it was distorted for individual purposes. It avoids the logical trap of supposing that because the balance of power understanding of equilibrium is too narrow and reductionist, the concept itself was wholly vacuous. It recognizes and takes seriously the other goods sought in international politics—peace, security, independence, honor, dignity, status, community, law, even morality—all too often submerged in the common and simplistic belief that the bottom line always was and is power and concrete advantage. Above all, it seems to me to meet the very problems in balance language and thought that this essay has tried to bring out.

First, this idea of political equilibrium seems to comprehend most of the meanings and uses of the term equilibrium and to represent a kind of meeting ground and common goal for its divergent strands. Both legalist-moralist and *realpolitik* interpretations of the European balance agreed, if only in theory, on the importance of a balance of satisfactions. The most rigidly conservative Austrian statesmen, in arguing that the European balance required that every letter of existing treaties be preserved, also insisted that this served to protect and harmonize all legitimate interests. At the same time an advocate of pure balance of power politics like Sir Eyre Crowe, even while contending that power and state interests alone counted in international relations and that only superior power would check Germany, also claimed that the purpose of the balance of power policy he advocated was, having tamed Germany's aggressive instincts, to bring her into an honorable and profitable role in the European community. Both implicitly envisioned a balance of satisfactions as the goal and essence of political equilibrium.

Second, the concept of political equilibrium takes account of a fact overwhelmingly apparent from this survey: nineteenth century Europeans judged whether an international balance existed and whether or not it was satisfactory on the basis of factors and conditions that had nothing directly to do with the distribution of power. A good European equilibrium depended upon having one's honor and dignity recognized, one's national rights satisfied, treaties maintained, the great powers united, all the great powers equally represented in the Concert, and other such criteria. Two concrete examples: in the turbulent 1860s, Russian leaders repeatedly proclaimed that the European equilibrium was being destroyed not by the territorial changes taking place in Italy and Germany or even the fact that these changes were being brought about by war and the destruction of treaties, but by the fact that these changes were not being submitted to the great powers for their review and sanction.[42] In other words, the political equilibrium was being undermined not by shifts in power *per se*, or even by certain states' aggressive use of power, but by their rejection of the method established to preserve the international order by giving legal sanction to such changes. Gladstone's government in Britain would take much the same stand in 1870–71 over the unilateral Russian denunciation of the Black Sea clauses of the Peace of Paris in 1856. Another example is the frequent complaints of French diplomats after 1870 that the European equilibrium no longer existed. The French argument was not simply that Germany and its allies had become too strong and France too weak and insecure. French spokesmen meant also, often primarily, that the equilibrium was destroyed because France was denied her rightful role and status in Europe (exactly what many Frenchmen had said after 1815). A great power's honor demanded that it have alliance capability, that is, possess friends and allies; Bismarck's success in isolating France in Europe *per se* destroyed the equilibrium. Clearly what the French, like many others, were concerned about was not simply balance of power, but balance of status and satisfactions.

This view of political equilibrium further helps account for the many instances where issues became overt questions of the European balance even though little or no change in power relations occurred and no serious case could be made that the power balance was involved. Once again, two quick examples: France's annexation of Nice and Savoy in 1860. Superficially, this appears a classic instance of a shift in the balance of power—the aggrandizement of a supposedly dangerous potential hegemon at the expense of a smaller threatened state. In fact, as both Prussian and Russian statesmen agreed, the annexation of Nice and Savoy weakened rather than strengthened France's relative power position both in Italy and in Europe. The cession of Nice and Savoy by Sardinia–Piedmont, engineered by Cavour, was a small price to pay for France's consent and help in expanding Sardinia into a Kingdom of Northern Italy. The annexations had the further effect of turning Britain, hitherto a partner with France in Italy, into an opponent, and roused the rest of Europe against France. There is no question that from a power standpoint the annexations hurt France; opponents of Napoleon III constantly stressed that his Italian policy had created grave new threats for her. Yet the Prussians and Russians insisted nevertheless that the annexations threatened the equilibrium by the precedent they set. A great power could now get away with going to war, gaining territory as a result, and refusing to submit the gains to the sanction of the other powers.[43] Their argument, in other words, was that the weakening of the network of mutual restraints and obligations among the great powers, not the change in their power relations, ruined the European balance. The way in which Prussia soon followed the French example on a far grander scale proved that they were right.

Another good example is the second Mehemet Ali Crisis in 1840. When Britain, Russia, Austria, and Prussia allied for joint diplomatic and military action against the Pasha of Egypt Mehemet Ali without France's participation, the French contended that this undermined the European equilibrium; a fairly serious war scare arose in Europe out of the issue. This crisis, like all Near Eastern crises, certainly involved a major question of the balance of power—the preservation of the Ottoman Empire. But there was no disagreement on this goal between France and Britain, the chief rivals in this crisis, or any other power. Both the Western powers in fact agreed that Russia, Britain's chief partner against France at this juncture, represented the major long-range threat to Turkey's independence and the Near Eastern balance. The Anglo-French dispute arose not over ends but means—the best way to save Turkey and check Russia. Nor did the French government see the four-power alliance formed to act in the Near East as a power threat to France in Europe. The French knew that Austria and Prussia were desperately eager to avoid any quarrel in Europe, much less armed conflict; this was why when the French government under Thiers made preparations for war, it did so on the Rhine, intending to fight not her real opponents, Britain and Russia, who were not accessible, but the vulnerable German states. The whole issue was really not about power and security, but prestige and honor. As Guizot, then ambassador to Britain and later premier, frankly said, the powers had not threatened French security or attacked her interests, but had paid too little attention to her voice.[44] Britain in choosing Russia as a partner against France had humiliated France, and this had destroyed the European equilibrium. Clearly it was an equilibrium of rights, status, and prestige, rather than power, that the French were talking about.

The concept of political equilibrium also fits better with the principal devices used to maintain stability and peace in Europe—invoking the Concert of Europe, appealing to international law and the sanctity of treaties, and restraining a potential aggressor or hegemon not by forming a blocking coalition against it but by bringing the dangerous power within a restraining alliance or partnership. It seems artificial to consider these techniques, very often used and frequently successful, simply as variants or refinements of balance of power politics. In particular, the attempt to restrain a dangerous power by allying with it rather than against it seems directly to violate standard balance of power practice, with its reliance on blocking coalitions and countervailing power to deter aggression. But as methods for achieving a political equilibrium conceived as a kind of communal balance based on adherence to group norms and enforced more by persuasion and warning from friends than threats from opponents, these techniques make good sense.[45]

Through the notion of political equilibrium one can also recognize real meaning in certain uses of the term equilibrium, which otherwise would have to be regarded as meaningless or pure propaganda. Take, for example, the argument by Cavour and other Italian nationalists in the 1850s that Austria was upsetting the balance established in 1815 by extending its hold over Italy and dominating Europe through a simultaneous Austrian hegemony over Italy, Germany, and the Balkans.[46] As an analysis of actual power relations and trends, this was nonsense and no one knew it better than Cavour. His game was to exploit Austria's isolation, weakness, and vulnerability, and his claim to want to restore equilibrium to Italy was as disingenuous as Hitler's claim to want to defend the oppressed German minority in Czechoslovakia. He aimed to bring all of Italy directly or indirectly under Sardinian rule, specifically wanted to destroy the 1815 system, would have preferred to see Austria destroyed along with it, repeatedly attempted to bring about general or revolutionary wars to accomplish this, and was eager to join any coalition to achieve his aims, the stronger and more dominant the better. In one sense therefore his talk about the European equilibrium was pure propaganda. But from another angle it was not. Austrians and other conservatives constantly attacked Italian nationalists for destroying European peace and equilibrium for the sake of their revolutionary ambitions. The main Italian reply was not that Austria was really destroying the balance by its growth in power—that convinced only the already converted—but that no genuine balance or lasting peace was possible in Europe until the Italian people gained their legitimate rights and Italy her proper place alongside the other states of Europe. The Italian argument based on balance of power was bogus; the one based on political equilibrium was genuine and plausible. Against the concept of balance and peace as depending on the guarantee of legitimate rights through the strict observance of treaties, the Italians opposed a concept of balance and peace depending upon the satisfaction of the legitimate needs of oppressed nationalities. Both sides were really talking about an equilibrium of rights and satisfactions rather than power. Certain Prussian and Russian statesmen, moreover, suggested a method for reconciling the two concepts in a higher equilibrium: the conflicts between treaty rights and national demands should be balanced by the great powers in international conferences, with their decisions established in new general treaties.[47]

THE CASE OF 1914

Finally, the concept of nineteenth century balance as one based on political equilibrium rather than power suggests an answer to the most obvious challenge to be raised against the thesis: If the system embodied all the vital legal, political, and even moral bonds and restraints you claim, why did it collapse in total war in 1914? The most common explanation traces the breakdown of the system primarily to a threat to the balance of power—Germany's inordinate growth in power and ambition. This is not the place to discuss the questions and problems facing this view, which appear to me to be cumulatively disabling. Was German power really growing relative to that of its rivals before 1914, or in relative decline, as many of its leading generals and politicians believed? Was not power fairly evenly distributed between the two blocs, with each checking the other in standard balance of power fashion? Was either side interested in maintaining only a blocking coalition, or were both trying for a dominant one? Did either side have a concept of the balance of power remotely acceptable to the other in terms of general security and status? How, if at all, does the German threat to the balance account for the focal point of the pre-1914 crises and the actual war—the nationalities, conflicts, and Austro-Russian rivalries in the Balkans? Why, if Germany was determined to bid for world power, did it postpone doing so until 1914 when its chances for victory had been much better in earlier crises?

The case against a balance of power interpretation of 1914 cannot be pursued here, but the case for interpreting World War I as a result of the disappearance of political equilibrium in Europe, both as a condition and as an ideal, and the consequent reversion to pure balance of power competition, can be outlined briefly. It is not a question of deciding whether the Central Powers or Entente Powers were more to blame. One could easily argue that Germany and Austria primarily ruined the political equilibrium in Europe: Germany by the ambitions, unpredictable moves, and dangerous ideas of many of her leaders and pressure groups, Austria-Hungary by her efforts to restore her eroded great power position through pressure, threats, and overt violence against her smaller neighbors. Both powers, it could be claimed, lacked the necessary domestic political balance to conduct a steady foreign policy; both tried to solve their unsolved domestic problems by foreign policy victories; both made it impossible for the rest of Europe to enjoy peace and stability and forced other countries into hostile alliances; and both together touched off the final conflagration.

But the actions of Germany and Austria-Hungary in destroying political equilibrium are only part of a wider picture—the virtual disappearance of the ideal of political equilibrium in European international politics. The general evidence for this is familiar: the way in which, especially from 1908 on, every issue involved a crucial test of strength between the rival alliances; the widespread belief that a great conflict was inevitable and even desirable as the only way problems could be resolved; the deterioration and degradation for partisan purposes of every device previously used to maintain peace and equilibrium (Concert diplomacy, international conferences, great power supervision of small power conflicts); the increasing inability or unwillingness of great powers to restrain their allies and partners for fear of weakening their alliances or ententes in case of war; the transformation of ordinary quarrels between states into aspects of great world-historical struggles between peoples, races, and ways of life; the attempts to achieve an equilibrium in critical areas, like the high seas or the Balkans, which clearly meant the domination of one side over the other.[48] All these pre-1914 developments familiar to every historian show how far the ideal of political equilibrium as a balance of rights and satisfactions had disappeared.

Another manifestation of this decline, less well known, is even clearer. Repeatedly before World War I, as the documents show, various statesmen from all the different countries discussed the fate of Austria-Hungary, predicted the Empire's demise, and remarked upon its probable effects. Never was Austria's fate taken up as a question vital to the European equilibrium. Only one power made any suggestion as to how the powers might fend off the troubles Austria's collapse would create and thus help preserve the system and peace. In 1905 Germany twice suggested to Russia that they sign a mutual nonaggrandizement pact binding each not to profit territorially from Austria's demise—a typical *pactum de contrahendo* or restraining agreement common earlier in the nineteenth century. Russia, though in serious trouble at the time as a result of defeat by Japan and revolution at home, studiously ignored the suggestion.[49] Russia, like Serbia, Italy, and Rumania in varying degrees, looked on Austria's coming collapse as its own opportunity, even if it might cause some dangers as well. France did perceive a serious danger in Austria's coming collapse—not, however, that of chaos and upheaval in East, Central, and southeastern Europe leading to a general war, but that of a Russo-German agreement over the Habsburg spoils, which would wreck the Franco-Russian alliance.[50] Britain viewed Austria's impending breakup with regret, but without concern, having no interests herself in Central and Eastern Europe.

This was not a question of what if anything to do about some future eventuality, but one that vitally concerned current policy. Prior to World War I, especially in 1913 and 1914, Austria was no longer treated as a great power whose interests, rights, sphere of influence, and dignity demanded consideration. Britain, France, and Russia, though regarding Germany as their main foe, continued to respect her as a great power, worried about her reactions, and avoided trying things that they knew she would not tolerate. Their main concern with Austria was how to prevent her from violently resisting what was obviously happening to her, and the usual suggestion, made especially by the British, was that Germany must restrain her ally. Various European developments affecting Austria were repeatedly discussed. Among these were a future union of Serbia and Montenegro giving Serbia access to the Adriatic, a reconciliation between Bulgaria and Serbia, the further defection of Austria's ally Rumania to the side of the Entente, the final forging of a Balkan league putting all the Balkan states under Russian protection, and closer links between Russia and Italy to check Austria in the Balkans. Statesmen recognized that these measures would further undermine Austria's position, so that she would be bound to react against them. But the conclusion was never drawn that these plans therefore should be avoided or these developments prevented, but only that things must be taken slowly, step by step, in line with Austria's growing debility and inability to react.[51]

It is useless and irrelevant to condemn these attitudes. In an age of rampant nationalism and imperialism, why should Russia, Serbia, Rumania, and Italy not have irredentist aims at Austria's expense? In a time of constant crisis and threat of war, why should France and Britain not be wholly preoccupied with their own security and particular interests? Both Austria and the international system were arguably hopelessly decayed and impossible to preserve. All this proves is that the idea of a political equilibrium in Europe, a balance of satisfactions and rights among all important actors, had disappeared in favor of all-out competitive balance of power politics in which all states, even essential actors, were fair game. The eighteenth century system had been destroyed in the same way, though there was then no steep decline from a previous higher standard of international behavior. Not even Germany wanted to keep Austria alive because she was an essential actor in the system, or because her disappearance would create chaos and almost certain war, but because whether Austria liked it or not she was a vital ally for Germany in the coming struggle between Teuton and Slav for mastery in Europe. It is not easy to draw the line beyond which normal interstate rivalry and conflict becomes destructive for a system of political equilibrium. But it is usually not too difficult to see when that equilibrium is gone, when a minimal balance of rights, status, security, and satisfaction among the participants in the system no longer exists and no one does anything about it. It is too pointed a formulation, but the essential truth is that the nineteenth century European system collapsed when it finally ceased to rest upon political equilibrium and operated solely as a balance of power system. The point is worth keeping in mind also in the late twentieth century.

APPENDIX

The following is a list of the volumes perused for this study. It contains only works read through in their entirety; many others were consulted but appeared to offer little likelihood of significant results. The abbreviation that is used in the notes precedes each item. The numbers in parentheses after each volume number represent the clear and doubtful instances of balance language found.

APP: *Die Auswärtige Politik Preussens 1858–1871*. Ed. by the Historische Reichskommission (Berlin, 1932–39), Vol. I (39 + 2); 2, part 1 (20 + 2); 2, part 2 (14 + 1); 3 (8 + 2); 5 (6)-6 (4 + 1); 8 (4 + 2); 10(0).

BD: *British Documents on the Origins of the War, 1898–1914*. Ed. by G. P. Gooch and H. W. V. Temperley 11 vols. London, 1926–38), Vols. 1 (6); 3 (4); 5 (8 + 2); 6 (17); 11 (11).

Beust: Beust, Friedrich Ferdinand Count, *Aus drei Viertel-Jahrhunderten. Erinnerungen und Aufzeichnungen* 2 vols. (Stuttgart, 1887), 1 (1); 2 (1).

BGW: Bismarck, Otto Fürst von. *Die gesammelten Werke*; 15 vols. in 19 parts (Berlin 1924–35). Vol. 1 (1); 2 (0); 3 (10, 1); 4 (1); 5 (2); 6a (4); 6b (6); 6c (2, 2); 7 (0); 10 (0); 11 (0); 15 (2).

Cavour-d'Azeglio: Cavour, Camillo Count. *Cavour e l'Inghilterra Carteggio con V. E. d'Azeglio* 3 vols. (Bologna, 1933). 1 (11 + 1).

Cavour-Nigra: Cavour, Camillo Count. *Il carteggio Cavour-Nigra da 1858 al 1861* 4 vols. (Bologna, 1926–29). 1 (1); 2 (1); 4 (1 + 1).

DDF: *Documents diplomatiques français (1871–1914)*. Published by the Ministère des Affaires Étrangères, Commission de publication de documents relatifs aux origines de la guerre de 1914 (3 ser.; Paris, 1929–46), ser. (1871–1900), Vol. 1

(10); 2 (8 + 1); 3 (1 + 4); 4(2 + 1); 5(2 + 1); 6(10 + 5); 7 (9 + 1); 8(9 + 1); 10 (6 + 1); 11 (0); 13 (2); 15 (8 + 1); 16 (5 + 1); ser. 2 (1901–11), 1 (1); 11 (1 + 1); 13 (4 + 1); ser. 3 (1911–14), 7 (18); 9(9); 10 (18 + 2).

DDI: I *documenti diplomatici italiani*. Commissione per la pubblicazione dei documenti diplomatici (Rome, 1952–70). ser. II, Vol. 1 (1870) (8 + 4); series III, 3 (5).

Gerlach: Gerlach, Ernst Ludwig von. *Von der Revolution zum Norddeutschen Bund; Politik und Ideengut der preussischen Hochkonservativen, 1848–1866*, ed. Hellmut Diwalt 2 vols. (Gottingen, 1970), Vol. 2 (0).

GP: *Die Grosse Politik der europdischen Kabinette*. Ed. by J. Lepsius, A. Mendelssohn Bartholdy, and Friedrich Thimme 40 vols. in 54 parts (Berlin, 1922–27), Vol. 1 (0); 2 (0); 3 (3); 4 (8 + 1); 5 (2); 6 (4 + 1); 7 (2); 8 (3 +1); 10 (0); 13 (0); 16 (4 + 2); 17 (4); 22 (2); 24 (5 + 1); 26, pt. 1 (3 + 3); 26, pt. 2 (7); 30, pt. 1 (4 + 2); 30, pt. 2 (0 + 1); 36, pt. 1 (2).

Guizot: Guizot, Francois. *Mémoires pour servir a l'histoire de mon temps* 8 vols. (Paris, 1858–67). 5 (14); 8 (5 + 1).

Hohenlohe: Hohenlohe-Schillingsfurst, Chlodwig Prince. *Denkwürdigkeiten des Fürsten Chlodwig zu Hohenlohe-Schillingsfürst* 2 vols. (Stuttgart, 1907), 1 (1); 2(0).

Holstein: Holstein, Friedrich von. *Die geheimen Papieren Friedrich von Holsteins*, ed. Norman Rich and M. H. Fisher. German edition by Werner Frauendienst 4 vols. (Gfittingen, 1956–63), 1 (0); 2 (0 + 1); 3 (3 + 3); 4 (3).

IB: Russia. Kommisiia po Izhdaniiu dokumentov epokhi imperialisma. *Die internationalen Beziehungen im Zeitalter des Imperialismus*. German edition by Otto Hoetzsch 9 vols. (Berlin, 1931–36), 2 (5 + 2).

Jelavich, Greece: Jelavich, Barbara, ed. *Russia and Greece during the Regency of King Othon, 1832–1835* (Thessaloniki, 1962), (1).

Jelavich, Russland: Jelavich, Barbara, ed. *Russland, 1852–1871; aus den Berichten der bayerischen Gesandtschaft in St. Petersburg* (Wiesbaden, 1963), (0).

Johann: Johann, King of Saxony. *Briefwechsel zwischen König Johann von Sachsen und den Königen Friedrich Wilhelm IV und Wilhelm I von Preussen* (Leipzig, 1911), (0).

Londonderry: Londonderry, Robert, 2nd Marquess of. *Memoirs and Correspondence of Viscount Castlereagh*, Ed. by his brother Charles Vane, Marquess of Londonderry 12 vols. (London, 1850–53), 10 (2).

PAP: Manteuffel, Otto Baron von. *Preussens A uswärtige Politik, 1850–1858. Unveröffentlichte Dokumente aus dem Nachlasse Manteuffels*, ed. by Heinrich von Poschinger 3 vols. (Berlin, 1902), Vol. 3 (1 + 2).

Metternich: Metternich-Winneburg, Clemens Lothar Furst von. *Aus Metternichs Nachgelassenen Papieren*, ed. by Prince Richard Metternich-Winneburg 8 vols. (Vienna, 1880–84), Vol. 1 (6); 2 (10 + 2); 3 (3); 4 (0).

Nesselrode: Nesselrode, Karl Robert Count. *Lettres et Papiers du Chancelier Comte de Nesselrode, 1760–1850*, Ed. by Count A. de Nesselrode 11 vols. (Paris, 1904–12 [?]), 5 (1 + 1); 9 (1).

Oncken: Oncken, Hermann, ed. *Die Rheinpolitik Kaiser Napoleons III. von 1863 bis 1870 und der Ursprung des Krieges von 1870/71* 3 vols. (Stuttgart, 1926), 1 (21 + 3); 2 (17); 3 (11).

OD: *Les origines diplomatiques de la guerre de 1870–1871*. Published by the Ministere des Affaires Étrangères 29 vols. (Paris, 1910–32). Vol. 1 (1); 4 (0 + 1); 7 (6); 10 (11 + 1); 11 (7 + 1); 12 (4); 15 (3); 18 (4); 21 (4 + 1); 24 (3); 27 (5); 28 (11 + 3); 29 (8 + 1).

Poincare: Poincaré, Raymond. *Au Service de la France—neuf Anneés de Souvenirs* 11 vols. (Paris, 1926–74), 2 (4 + 1).

Polovtsov: Polovtsov, A. A., ed. *Correspondance diplomatique des ambassadeurs et ministres de Russie en France et de France en Russie avec leur gouvernements de 1814 a 1830* 3 vols. (St. Petersburg, 1902–07), 1 (18 + 1); 2 (4).

Problema Veneto: Istituto Veneto di Scienze, Lettere, ed. Arti. *Il problema veneto e l'Europa, 1859–1866; raccolta di document i diplomatici,* 3 vols. (Venice, 1966–67), 3 (8).

QDPO: *Quellen zur deutschen Politik Österreichs, 1859–1866,* ed. by H. von Srbik 5 vols. in 6 parts (Oldenburg, 1934–38), Vol. 1 (3); 4 (6).

Raschdau: Raschdau, Ludwig, ed. *Die politischen Berichte des Fürsten Bismarcks aus Petersburg und Paris 1859–1862* 2 vols. (Berlin, 1920), Vol. 1 (4); 2 (0).

Rel. Dipl. Austria-Sardegna: Rome. Istituto storico per l'etá moderna e contemporanea. *Le relazione diplomatiche fra l "Austriaei" l Regno di Sardegna* 2nd ser. (Rome, 1972), 1 (0). *Le relazione diplomatiche fra l'Austria et il Regno di Sardegna,* 2nd ser. Rome, 1972. 1 (0).

Saitta: Saitta, Armando, ed. *Il problema italiano nel testi di una battaglia pubblicistica; gli opusculi del Visconte de la Gueronniere* 4 vols. in 5 (Rome, 1963–64), 1 (12); 2 (17 + 1).

Schweinitz: Schweinitz, Hans Lothar von. *Denkwürdigkeiten des Botschafters General v. Schweinitz* 2 vols. (Berlin, 1927), 1 (0); 2 (0).

Schwertfeger: Schwertfeger, Bernhard, ed. *Zur europäischen Politik, 1897–1914. Unveröffentlichte Dokumente im amtlichen Auftrage herausgegeben* 5 vols. (Berlin, 1919), 5 (6).

Talleyrand, Corr.: Talleyrand-Perigord, Charles Maurice de. *Correspondance Diplomatique* 3 vols. (Paris, 1889–91), 1 (4 + 1).

Thiers: Thiers, Louis Adolphe, *Discours parlementaires de M. Thiers,* publ. by M. Calmon 16 vols. (Paris, 1879–89), 10 (4); 11 (too many to count—most of Thiers's speeches in this volume were precisely on the subject of the balance of power).

VPR: Russia. *Ministerstvo inostrannykhdel. Vneshnaia Politika Rossii xixi nachala xx veka; dokumenti rossiiskogo Ministerstva inostrannykh del.* 1st ser., 1801–15; Vols. 1–8 (Moscow, 1960–67), 8 (12 + 2).

Wellington: Wellington, Arthur Wellesley, 1st Duke of. *Supplementary Despatches and Memoranda of Field Marshal Arthur, Duke of Wellington, K.G.* 15 vols. (London, 1858–72), 10 (0).

I have also gone through various treaty collections (Edward Hertslet's *Map of Europe by Treaty* [4 vols.; London, 1875–91], and some of the G. F. Martens and F. F. Martens collections) looking for balance language in the text of treaties and conventions, but found so very little that I decided not to include them in this compilation.

IV

TRENDS AND IMPLICATIONS

The Cold War and Its Ending in "Long-Duration" International History

This essay is a kind of flight forward (*fuite en avant*). Contributors to the Festschrift in which this was originally published were asked to discuss the most significant development in international relations in the twentieth century and its likely implications for the twenty first. My choice, an obvious one, was the end of the Cold War. Yet since my serious study of international history begins with the seventeenth century but hardly extends much beyond 1945 I am not well equipped to analyze the Cold War and its outcome. I could meet the problem by claiming, as historians often do, that only a long-range comparative historical perspective enables us to understand so recent a development, and then provide that perspective by comparing the end of the Cold War to supposedly analogous historical events or developments over several centuries (for example, the termination of other enduring rivalries). This essay may look like just such an exercise in historical comparison.

It is not, however, for two reasons. First, any such attempt faces grave epistemological and methodological problems in regard to its validity, intersubjective verifiability, and usefulness. Second and more immediate, it often receives from political scientists, international relations theorists, and policy experts a response of polite dismissal. They listen more or less attentively to the historical discussion, remark, "That's interesting," and then go back to analyzing the event by their own methods in line with their own concerns about its immediate origins, course, and present and future implications.

Therefore this essay attempts a bolder and more hazardous escape from the dilemma. Rather than try to draw analogies and lessons from the history of four centuries of European and world international politics to apply to the Cold War and its end, I propose instead to place the Cold War and its end into that long history, as an integral part of it, and to claim that such a placement can contribute to how we understand it.

Such a project requires showing (or rather, for reasons of space, asserting) two things. The first is that there is a history of the evolution of European and world international politics from the early seventeenth century that demonstrates certain distinct stages of development—in other words, that this history has gone somewhere, is in some sense directional, and is not simply a kaleidoscopic jumble of contingent events and merely cyclical change—"just one damned thing after another," as the historian Sir Richard Pares once said. The second assertion is that the Cold War and its termination fit into that general pattern and represent a particular stage in that long history. If these two points could be established, it would mean that though the Cold War began, ran its course, and came to an end because of particular historically unique late-twentieth-century events and developments and can be adequately accounted for in both historical and social science terms on the basis of these factors, nevertheless another kind of explanation and understanding of it is also possible and useful, achieved by situating the Cold War and its end within the long history of international politics and conceiving that history in a different way than most scholars have used.

The concept of a history of long duration (*"histoire de longue durée"*) comes, as many will recognize, from the so-called Annales school of historiography, which dominated historical writing in France and strongly influenced it elsewhere from the 1930s until recently. One of the principal Annales theses involved the concept of a history of long duration, of slow, almost glacially paced changes, underlying the more visible middle-range developments of history (*"conjunctures"*) and the kaleidoscopic surface changes of day-to-day and year-to-year events (event history, *"histoire événementielle"*). Annalistes typically found this fundamental history of long duration in the supposed deep structures of society—geography, climate, demography, socioeconomic structures, and certain aspects of collective mentalities—meanwhile consigning the history of politics, especially international politics, to the superficial, inferior category of event history.

Today Annales historiography no longer reigns supreme even in France, though like every other powerful school of historical interpretation it has left behind an important permanent legacy and influence. Two things, besides the normal shifts of fashion and interest among historians, helped end its reign. The first was the realization even among its ardent proponents that the concept of three different levels and paces of historical change—long-, middle-, and short-term, structural, conjunctural, and event—fit the ancient, medieval, and early modern worlds vastly better than the modern and postmodern ones. Science, technology, mass politics and society, and modern economics have rendered the old unchanging structures of society either obsolete and unimportant, or almost as subject to rapid change and deliberate manipulation as other aspects of society. To paraphrase the verdict of one leading exponent of Annales views, a history of long duration is no longer a history of this present world. The other realization was that certain vital arenas of human endeavor—among them, politics—were not well served or understood by Annales methods and presuppositions, and needed different ones.

In this essay, paradoxically, I as a non-Annaliste political historian will argue that this concept of a history of long duration, now considered inapplicable to the modern world, still applies to it, and applies, moreover, precisely to the sort of history, that of international politics, which Annales historians generally despised. I will offer (to repeat, by assertion more than argument and evidence) a broad scheme for a history of long duration discernible beneath the mid-range conjunctural level of international history and the kaleidoscopic event level of everyday international politics. The structure or pattern of long-range history proposed here is, I claim, different from the cyclical ones usually detected and described in histories of international politics (for example, the rise and fall of great powers, shifts in the balance of power, alternations between periods of stability and instability, cycles of war and peace). I will then attempt to show how the Cold War and its termination fit into this pattern, hoping thereby to shed light on the elements both of continuity and change, the familiar and the unprecedented, in them.

Since this statement of purpose is bound to arouse skepticism and seem to promise another grand scheme of history like those offered by philosophers and speculative world historians (Hegel, Toynbee, Spengler, and many more), some disclaimers and qualifications are called for. First, the argument, for reasons of time and space, will be extremely sketchy—hardly even a connected skeleton, more a collection of bones. The meager historical evidence cited is intended for illustration and explanation rather than proof. (Hence also the virtual absence of scholarly footnotes.) Second, though it may appear dogmatic or determinist, the scheme should be understood as provisional and open to change at many points. Obviously many details (dates of periodization, specific so-called turning points, particular alleged causes, facts and interpretations, and so on) are highly debatable.

Third and most important, to claim that a certain pattern can be discerned in international history over the last four centuries is not to claim that this must be the only pattern or perspective or necessarily the dominant one. A history of long duration, moreover, by definition underlies conjunctures and events; it does not cancel them out or render them unimportant. The putative pattern, moreover, should be seen as emergent rather than clear and dominant, as compatible with some other patterns while incompatible with others, clearer at some places than others. Finally, since an extended historical exposition, impossible here, would be needed to support this thesis and make it plausible, I expect no one to accept it on my word. I ask instead for a provisional suspension of disbelief in order to consider the question: Assuming that this scheme has a certain validity, what can it tell or suggest about the Cold War and its ending?

All that being understood, here in bare outline are the successive periods or stages of this putative international *histoire de longue durée* beginning early in the seventeenth century and going up to the beginning of the Cold War.

The periods and their content and character	Their dates
1. Emergence of a new order, conflict over its nature and rules, convergence on a concrete definition of peace	1643–1715, 1811–20
2. More or less stable operation of the new system	1715–39, 1820–48
3. Initial crisis, breakdown, and partial transformation of the new system, followed by apparent restabilization	1740–63, 1848–71
4. Normal operation of the revised system, marked by rising complications, tensions, and incipient breakdown	1763–87, 1871–1908
5. Final crisis and breakdown of the old order and pupal stage of the new	1609–43, 1787–1811, 1908–45

What follows is an attempt to indicate briefly the salient characteristics of each period or stage and to show that the scheme works historically (that is, broadly makes sense of the evidence and makes a difference in our overall conceptualization of international history). If it fails this prima facie test, it is useless for any other purpose. This is the reason for asking readers to follow what may seem to some a remote and irrelevant historical argument, in the hope that it will lead to ideas applicable to today's world.

Emergence of the New Order

This stage is the most difficult to explain and to defend historically; it therefore requires more exposition. It will help if three defining characteristics or elements of it are kept in mind. (1) A real, definitive break with the past occurs in both the 1643–1715 and 1811–20 periods. Not only later historians but also contemporaries sensed this, and they believed that the old order was no longer sustainable or tolerable and that something new and different had to replace it and was doing so. (2) At the same time, there was initially no agreement but instead widespread, deep uncertainty about the exact nature and rules of the new order. No one, including those most convinced that the old order must be supplanted, knew at first precisely what the new one would be, or how and whether it would work. This uncertainty helped generate and prolong a more or less protracted period of struggle over the new rules of the game—who would run it, how the costs and benefits would be distributed, how much of the old would be saved, restored, or transmuted in the new, and so on. (3) Out of this struggle, a new consensus or convergence on the rules of the game eventually emerged—enough agreement among enough key players to render the new system legitimate and more stable and enforceable than the old for a considerable period of time.

If we keep these defining characteristics in mind, it is easier to understand two peculiarities in the dates of this scheme of periodization. One is that two famous turning points in international history, 1648, the date of the Treaties of Westphalia and the birth of the so-called Westphalian system, and 1814–15, the date of the Vienna Congress and birthday of the Vienna system, become simply parts of longer periods. The other is that the first of these periods takes seven decades, so that the new order is supposedly emerging and crystallizing all the way from the final stage of the Thirty Years War through the wars of Louis XIV to 1715, while the same process takes less than a decade in 1811–20. These aspects of the scheme not only seem odd, but suggest, contrary to much historical scholarship and international relations theory, that the Treaties of Westphalia did not found a new international system, but only marked the beginnings of a process by which one finally emerged with the Treaties of Utrecht, Rastatt, and Baden in 1713–15, ending the War of the Spanish Succession.

Obviously this is not the place to quarrel over periodization in history, a theme of interest only to professional historians. What counts for our purposes, besides indicating how these apparent anomalies do fit the main historical facts, is to show how they reflect a fundamental characteristic of international history. The interpretive pattern presented here involves a basic assumption or premise: that change in the international system involves above all changes in the reigning assumptions, dominant understandings and conceptions, and collective mentalities of political leaders. In other words, it insists that international politics represents human conduct, not mere behavior. Systems do not change simply or mainly because power relationships change and leaders respond in more or less routine and predictable patterns of behavior to these changes, but because states, governments, leaders, and peoples react purposively, with conscious ideas and aims, to changes in power and to other concrete problems and circumstances. They act, moreover, within a generally shared understanding of the prevailing system, meaning thereby what some call political culture—the expectations, norms, and rules governing the common practice of international politics, and their understanding of the prevailing incentives or payoff structure. This understanding limits and to some extent governs what they attempt to do and their strategies and hopes for success. Systems change, then, when the reigning ideas about the system change fundamentally and durably.

It follows, then, that in this scheme the emergence of a new, more stable and durable international order (in other words, peace) involves and depends on a change in collective understandings, assumptions, and outlooks among leaders and governments. Peace further involves and requires a convergence or consensus among the major players on a new, concrete, practical definition of peace—something only possible through a process involving a long time and much struggle. It starts with an initial widespread recognition that the old system has hopelessly broken down and must be replaced with something new, and ends, if it comes to fruition, with a substantial working agreement on a new order with different rules, norms, and incentives. Peace treaties and settlements can play a role in creating this consensus, but do not do so always or even usually. The 1815 treaties, true, were exceptionally successful in turning an emerging consensus on a new order into a comprehensive, concrete peace settlement in a remarkably short time. Nevertheless it required a difficult, perilous process starting about 1811 and not completed until about 1820 to reach a common definition of peace, and even then there remained old dissents and new emerging rifts. Most peace settlements in European history, including some of the most important (1763, 1919, 1945), did not involve any such consensus or serve to create one.

Nor did the Westphalian treaties of 1648. Though they represent a vital turning point in international history, this is because they finally ended an old era, the long sixteenth century Habsburg–Valois/Bourbon contest for universal monarchy and undisputed leadership of a unified Christendom—a contest essentially ended or abandoned even before 1648—*without* founding a new system or consensus. The treaties did not even bring general European peace at that time. War between France and Spain lasted until 1659, war in northern Europe until 1660. Nor did the treaties settle all the vital issues, or try to. They deliberately omitted many vital aspects of an enduring settlement or left them vague and subject to dispute.[1]

More important is the widespread notion that the Treaties of Westphalia initiated a new brand of European international politics that was secular rather than religious in character, was played by absolutist princely states rather than feudal units with overlapping rights and jurisdictions, was based on state sovereignty and juridical equality, and operated on principles of raison d'état and balance of power. Although Westphalia undoubtedly represented an important stage in the long process producing these changes, these generalizations clash with so many realities of seventeenth- and even eighteenth-century politics that they should be used only with extreme care and qualification.

In fact, the Treaties of Westphalia, which replaced the fragile religious peace of 1555–1608 in Germany (the Holy Roman Empire) with a new, more solid one, thereby established rather than overthrew a pattern of politics based on religious confessions in Germany that lasted into the mid-nineteenth century. The granting of *ius foederis* (the right of making foreign alliances) to the estates of the Empire was not, as often supposed, decisive in establishing princely sovereignty and reducing the Empire to a hollow shell. It actually restored an earlier fifteenth and sixteenth century practice, and while it is true that many German princes tried to acquire full sovereignty over their territories and some succeeded, most units remained semifeudal, characterized by divided sovereignty and limited, overlapping jurisdictions. The Holy Roman Empire continued to exist and to operate on the basis of hierarchy, not autonomy, and the emperor at Vienna after 1648 regained much of his lost influence and authority over the estates. France's relations with its many allies were overwhelmingly those of patron and client rather than juridical equality. Seventeenth century rulers great and small continued to play both sacral and secular roles, seeking both real power and territory and traditional feudal rights, status, and glory (for example, Louis XIV, Emperor Leopold I, John Sobieski of Poland). The balance of power principle did not become clear or dominant until at least the early eighteenth century.

Though much more could be said on this theme, the point is that for our purposes it makes better sense to see the whole conflict-ridden period of

1643–1715 as one characterized by the kind of uncertainty and shakedown required before any general consensus on a definition of peace and on the nature and rules of politics under a new system could arise.

Even the narrow and fragile consensus reached after the long, exhausting War of the Spanish Succession (1702–13) emerged only late in the game. Once again a common generalization, that Britain and its European allies fought for decades against Louis XIV's hegemony in favor of a balance of power, and that they finally imposed peace on that basis on France in 1713–15, gravely oversimplifies and distorts both the process and the final outcome. To take just two of the problems: Although balance of power was a good slogan to use against Louis XIV's supposed attempt at "universal monarchy," it is easy to show that under the rubric of "balance of power" every power allied against France, as one would expect, fought for its individual aims, usually dynastic, religious, and territorial. Moreover, many princes were Louis's allies rather than opponents, or switched sides for their particular advantage, and all of his opponents, including the most important, the Dutch stadholder William of Orange who became Britain's King William III and led the various anti-French coalitions, made deals with Louis at various times that promoted his expansionist ambitions. As for Louis, though he certainly loved war, sought glory, and aspired for much of his reign to hegemony in Europe (that is, a recognized superior position, not unchallenged domination), by 1697 he had tacitly given this ambition up and by 1708 was desperate for peace at almost any price, while as late as 1710 the British and Austrians, if not the Dutch, still wanted all-out victory for the sake of empire ("no peace without Spain"). In the end, peace came when a new government in Britain worked out more moderate terms with the enemy, France, and helped impose these terms on its own allies, especially the Habsburg Empire.

What counts is that through this long messy process a change in collective outlook and a new understanding of international politics finally did develop and that it prevailed after 1715. A new system, based on a balance of power as Britain and France understood the term and enforced it, became accepted as the basis for peace in western and southern Europe, even though attempts to extend this system to northeastern Europe once again failed and peace would not come there under Russian domination until 1721. In operational terms, the system in the West depended on shared Anglo-French hegemony more than on balance of power. These two dominant powers set the rules of peace in the treaties and enforced them or supervised their revision thereafter.

In this respect and others, the Utrecht settlement, the first real peace system modern Europe enjoyed, shows a pale but recognizable resemblance to the Vienna settlement a century later. They both recognized some of the same basic international principles (such as the sovereignty, independence, and juridical equality of all units, and a distribution of power sufficient to prevent empire or "universal monarchy" in Europe), and used similar devices for enforcement and management of the system (a hegemonic partnership, dominant alliances, treaty revisions imposed by the great powers, and conferences and congresses to settle outstanding questions)—means strictly speaking more characteristic of concert and collective security than balance of power.

STABLE OPERATION OF THE SYSTEM

This stage requires less explanation. In both periods (1715–39 and 1820–48) the stability of the system or lack of it depended on how broad and deep the original consensus was on the definition and requirements of peace, how committed the victors were to maintaining and enforcing it, and how successful they were in repressing, channeling, or controlling ideological and power-political ambitions and rivalries so as to preserve the essential consensus. On all these counts the Vienna system proved superior to that of Utrecht. There was more peace and less conflict over a longer period, a broader and deeper original consensus, a more precise and comprehensive treaty settlement, less need or pressure for later revisions of the treaties, a greater will and capacity on the part of the managing powers to make the needed adjustments, more general cooperation and less defection and resistance, more success with international conferences and congresses, and more ideological conformity among the major powers and/or willingness to overlook and transcend their ideological differences in the interests of managing crises and solving problems.

The differences are stark enough to raise the question of whether the post-Utrecht period was comparable to the Vienna era at all. Yet the earlier era shows enough solid evidence of progress in peacemaking and peacekeeping, particularly when contrasted with the decades that preceded it, and includes enough examples of developments and ideas that would prove fruitful later, to justify including it.[2]

CRISIS, BREAKDOWN, TRANSFORMATION, AND RESTABILIZATION WITHOUT CONSENSUS

Most historians would probably accept the summary statement above as reasonably accurate for the international history of the 1740–63 and 1848–71 periods. Each began with a crisis in the old system. In 1740 it came suddenly and dramatically with a Prussian attack on Austria followed by a joint Franco-Bavarian assault on it, launching a general war and threatening to bring the Habsburg Monarchy down. In 1848 it came as a series of domestic revolutions and counterrevolutions leading to serious international crises and some armed conflict in Italy, Germany, and the Balkans. In both cases the initial crisis led to a further breakdown of the system. In 1740–63 the breakdown involved two long, exhausting general wars. In 1853–71 it involved five wars, none general and all less bloody and protracted than their eighteenth century counterparts, but even more important in transforming European power relations and the rules of the game. In both instances the wars seemed in the end to restabilize the system and allow international politics to resume its normal course. The only point some historians might object to is the phrase, "without consensus." In fact, they might claim, there was widespread agreement after both 1763 and 1871 as to who were the winners and losers, what was the new balance of power, and what were the new prevailing rules of the game.

This claim is true—and it shows how different an agreement on the outcome of a major conflict and new prevailing rules on the one hand is from consensus on a concrete, practical definition of peace on the other. After 1763 and 1871, what some governments saw as a concrete, practical definition of peace, a new status quo to be defended, represented for others latent war, a condition of insecurity, injustice, and threat to be radically changed or overturned. Still others seized on the split between defenders and opponents of the new status quo as an opportunity to exploit.[3] Moreover, in both cases the wars had proved that power was the final arbiter in international politics, meaning that the only serious way to change the system was not European Concert decision or great power cooperation but unilateral actions of a kind that risked or produced war. In other words, the agreement on the nature of the game and its recent results, current standings, and operating rules after both 1763 and 1871 not only failed to include a consensus on a definition of peace, but actually precluded a consensus on legitimate means of peaceful change and sanctioned violence.

In both periods both the crisis of the old system and the successful challenge to it reflected changes in collective attitudes. One such change is too obvious to need discussion: the growth of widespread dissatisfaction with the old system and its rules and restraints among many leaders and governments, derived from frustrated ambitions, demands, and pressures for change coming from those they governed, and their belief that the system was worn out and unjust.

The second source for the crisis and challenge is less obvious: optimism. A striking characteristic of 1740–63 and 1848–71 was that leaders in both periods were much more willing to gamble than their predecessors, deliberately risking or provoking war with bold initiatives in the sanguine expectation of short-term gains and long-term success. Sometimes the gambles paid off at least in the short term—witness the spectacular gains made by Frederick II of Prussia in 1740–45 or Cavour and Bismarck in the 1850s and 1860s. More often risky strategies failed even in the short term—witness the failures of French and Bavarian policy in the early 1740s, or Austria's in the Seven Years War, or those of Prussia and Sardinia-Piedmont in 1848–50, Russia and Britain in the Crimean War, and Napoleon III throughout the 1860s. Yet this widespread willingness of particular leaders and regimes to gamble for immediate gains is less remarkable than the optimistic belief (usually an unarticulated assumption) that these gambles, if they succeeded in the short term, could then readily be converted into stable long-term gains. The risk-takers in both periods assumed that the international system as a whole would survive the shocks and changes they administered to it and continue to function in their favor. After they had successfully broken the law and changed the rules, their gains would be accepted as legal, they themselves would be recognized as legitimate, respectable fellow statesmen, and a new consensus on the governing rules and norms of international practice would more or less automatically emerge.

After 1763, this clearly failed to happen. What developed instead was a quick revival of wars and crises, despite the general war-weariness, and a marked decline in international norms, demonstrated most clearly by the First Partition of Poland in 1772. After 1871, in contrast, Europe apparently regained stability under Bismarck's leadership, but that stability was always fragile and deceptive. The main source of instability in both eras was not, as sometimes believed, a missing or defective balance of power (supposedly consisting after 1763 in Britain's excessive colonial and naval domination combined with its isolation in Europe and Russia's power and invulnerability in eastern Europe; after 1871, in the dangerous growth in Germany's military power and its labile half-hegemony in Europe). Nor was the key weakness the fact that in both periods certain states became or remained dissatisfied and revisionist. Britain and Russia seemed invulnerable to any revisionist challenge in 1763, Britain and Germany equally so after 1871. The real Achilles heel in both systems lay in the absence of a real international consensus on a concrete definition of peace and on institutions and norms to embody and sustain it, and the illusory assumption by those in control of the system that it could work indefinitely even in the absence of such a consensus through manipulating the balance of power.

NORMAL OPERATION OF THE REVISED SYSTEM (1763–87, 1871–1908)

This section also needs little discussion. The two periods, as already indicated, differed significantly in certain ways. Major European wars occurred in the first but not in the second; the system was certainly better managed in 1871–90 than in either 1763–87 or 1890–1908. But the basic principles of operation were the same in both periods. Realpolitik prevailed; goals were pursued and crises managed primarily by means of shifting alliances and alignments. The overall trends over time were also similar in both—the rise of more complications, deeper tensions, balanced and unbalanced antagonisms, and threats of general breakdown and war. The fact that balance of power politics appeared to make Europe more peaceful and stable in the late nineteenth century than in the eighteenth is explained by three factors. The first of these was Bismarck's extraordinary ingenuity, skill, and restraint in managing crises in 1871–90. Second was the fact that in the late-nineteenth century European imperialism abroad served initially, until the 1890s, as an outlet for European energies that diverted them from Continental quarrels, whereas throughout the eighteenth century overseas imperialism, intensely competitive and directly connected to European power politics, helped promote war in Europe. Finally, nineteenth century industrialization and the rise of science and technology, particularly as applied to warfare, together with population growth, the rise of nationalism, and mass politics, all served sharply to increase the costs and risks of war for all major governments. It became much harder and politically riskier to go to war and easier to postpone the decision in each particular crisis, without, however, making leaders or peoples consider war less likely or necessary in the long run.

In other words, the greater peace and stability of the late nineteenth century came from temporary exogenous causes, not from a sounder system for solving problems and managing crises. The prevailing conviction in military and diplomatic circles for a decade or more before 1914 was that a great war was coming, that it would be terrible and costly, that it would decide the fate of nations for generations, but that it probably could not be avoided and must therefore be won. This was, in a tragic way, a realistic assessment of the situation.

In any case, in neither period did most governments, despite major crises and considerable fear of war, make serious efforts to revive the old consensus on a concrete definition of peace or develop a new one. That was left to fringe groups—peace advocates, women, and socialists.[4] This inaction on the part of leaders and governments does not indicate a survival of the earlier optimistic belief that the problems of preserving peace would somehow solve themselves or be solved by ordinary balance of power politics. Now the ruling elites increasingly rested their hope for peace on being militarily prepared for all contingencies (*"Si vis pacem, para bellum"*) and assumed that only fools and swindlers would believe or preach otherwise, or would pass up an opportunity to strengthen their relative position—another sign of the disappearance of any practical consensus on peace.

Exhaustion, Collapse, and Destruction of the Old System; Pupal Stage of the New

The statement that in 1609–43, 1787–1811, and 1908–45 the prevailing international systems became exhausted and collapsed into destruction seems a useless truism or cliché rather than a revelation or a thesis needing explanation and defense. Some discussion, however, will help show how despite obvious differences these three historic eras shared in the central characteristics of this stage, and why in each case the destruction of the old system made possible the emergence of a new one.

One common feature is that where *sacro egoismo* (sacred self-interest) had already become a leading principle of statecraft in the previous period, *va banque* (going for broke) took control in this one. Growing fear, greed, and opportunity, unchecked by consensual norms and reinforced by the phenomena known as the security dilemma, positive feedback, and escalation, turned the dominant strategy among the contending great powers into a quest for decisive victory, first in competitive high politics and ultimately in war—this despite the fact that no one really knew or could calculate what the final consequences of war, even victorious war, would be. The previous game of competition for security and advantage, increasingly tense but still confined within the bounds of a vague general agreement that the game was necessary for everyone's overall security and advantage and should continue indefinitely, gave way to a quest for victory regardless of its general consequences and of whether the game would survive.

This escalating, hypertrophic pursuit of victory, driven above all by fear of the intolerable consequences of defeat, caused governments to lose control first of the game of high politics and then of the wars that ensued. Despite slogans more or less genuinely believed and propagated justifying the quest for victory (defending the true religion, combatting revolution and lawlessness, preserving the social order, saving the nation, defeating tyranny, saving a people's culture and way of life, making world safe for democracy, ending war forever, and the like), the very concept of victory tended to become meaningless, self-encapsulated in the sense that no one could clearly and concretely define what victory would accomplish other than to defeat or destroy the foe and avoid defeat or destruction for oneself. Whatever precise definitions and programs were put forward tended to arouse serious opposition and divisions even among allies and to prolong the war more than end it.

A growing sense of the futility of war, heightened by the intolerable suffering its hyperbolic protraction produced, led in all three periods to a widespread, though not universal, revulsion against the old politics supposedly responsible for it and a broad and genuine, if vague, desire for a new politics of peace. This feeling, however, failed to produce agreement either on a concrete, practical definition of peace or on the specific means to achieve it. Ideas and proposals for a new structure of peace arose in each era, ranging widely in seriousness and practicality. None, however, produced consensus even among the ultimate winners. What prevailed in practical terms was a belief that victory was the prime essential and a hope that it would create and define the peace.

What follows is just enough history to indicate why in my view this description fits these three periods, despite their obvious differences, and also offers some new perspectives and insights.

The first point concerns the origins of the great systemic wars of these eras (the Thirty Years War, the revolutionary-Napoleonic wars, and both world wars). On each there has been endless dispute over what event triggered the final downward spiral, the positive feedback loop leading from tension and crisis into all-out war. These debates are not pointless, the narrow quarrels of academic scribes. The choice of one triggering event rather than another is always connected to larger questions—the nature and causes of the escalation of crises, the question of overall responsibilities for these wars, and even the general causes of war itself. Regardless of differences of opinion over what started the snowball rolling in each case, however, scholars basically agree that in each one of them a downward spiral developed. Key players became engaged in a series of defensive–offensive initiatives and responses taken not because their leaders were unaware of the risks or confident their moves would succeed, but because, knowing the risks, they considered these moves the only way to respond to others' actions and meet the general threat of defeat and destruction. This signals that at the beginning of all three periods the prevailing system went out of control, unable to correct itself or be corrected. *Va banque* was widely seen to be the only serious strategy for deterring an intolerable outcome and/or insuring a desirable one.

This pattern of self-reinforcing downward spiral is not a universal phenomenon in international history, or even a common one. It does not apply to most wars in these three centuries, including some very big and important ones, much less to periods of peace. Here is an indication that these particular periods represent systemic collapse rather than temporary outbreaks of violence or partial breakdown and revision.

An even more compelling indication is the way in which in all three instances general war turned into all-out hypertrophic war, war of unprecedented violence and extent in pursuit of unprecedentedly sweeping imperialist aims. Long before the Thirty Years War, Habsburg Spain and Valois-Bourbon France had been rivals over leadership of the Church and Spain's claim to world dominion, but they never fought with the commitment to these goals shown by Count-Duke Olivares and Philip IV in the Thirty Years War or the determined resistance and counteroffensive of Louis XIII, Richelieu, and Mazarin.[5] Protestants and Catholics had fought in Germany in the earlier sixteenth century, but no earlier Counter-Reformation prince or emperor had pursued the aim of restoring Catholic supremacy in the whole Empire to the lengths Ferdinand II did, in part because no earlier Protestants had presented so open and sweeping a challenge as the Protestant Union and the Bohemian nobility did from 1608 on, a response by the radical Calvinists among them to what they considered an intolerable menace from the Catholic League.[6] War and revolution broke out in Europe before the French Revolution—in fact, the first major clashes and territorial changes came in eastern and southeastern Europe—but nothing prepared Europe for the ferocious onslaught of revolutionary French imperialism from 1794 on, and still less for the boundless imperialism of Napoleon. To this onslaught France's most formidable foes, Britain and Russia, for most of the war responded by concocting their own revolutionary and imperialist programs for victory.[7] In World War I both sides, once engaged, developed sweeping imperialist war aims and sought a knockout victory; the democratic Allies on the whole did so more consistently than the authoritarian Central Powers.[8] In World War II both sides vastly outdid the belligerents in I in fighting the war in hypertrophic fashion and pursuing unlimited goals.

One cannot explain this hypertrophy of war simply as the result of accident, particular leaders or ideologies, changing technology, or the self-generating process by which war feeds on war. These all figure in. Yet most wars, including many big ones, have remained precariously under political control, limited by the politics of war (negotiations with allies and the enemy over war aims and goals, domestic pressures for peace, mutual exhaustion leading to changes in policy or governments, and so on). In other words, most wars fit Clausewitz's famous definition of war as politics pursued by other means. These systemic wars during most of their course did not.

In them, the politics of war as the art of limiting and ending war through negotiation, compromise, and consensus lost out, and politics was reduced mainly to serving the ends of more war for greater victory.

It is nonetheless significant that this kind of systemic breakdown, a constant potential danger in international relations, has happened only three times in four centuries. Only in these periods do we see a full descent into all-out pursuit of victory and hypertrophic war and imperialism, attended by horrors in each period analogous in character if not in scale; war has troubled peace within the international system many times in various degrees, but completely overwhelmed and destroyed it only in these eras. This fact is worth noting not only for purposes of balance and perspective, but also because it accounts for something detectable only in these three periods, especially toward their end. This is the early signs of a genuine break in the cycle, the emergence of a widespread conviction among the actors that the current game of international politics was no longer tolerable and that a new kind had to be discovered or invented, even if most contemporaries could not define the new kind precisely and many doubted its possibility.

These signs of a change in collective consciousness that emerged in each period cannot be described and compared here (for example, genuine and opportunistic conversions of former adherents and practitioners of the old politics to new ideas, rats leaving the sinking ship while true believers go down with it, ideas once discarded and derided as Utopian being revived, and so on). What matters is that the systemic breakdown at the end of these periods brought an opportunity for a breakthrough to a new system, though without assuring that breakthrough or making clear what it would be.

THE SIGNIFICANCE OF THIS SCHEME FOR THE LATE TWENTIETH CENTURY

Even readers willing to go along with this broad reading of the long history of international politics from 1609 to 1945 for the sake of argument may be asking the obvious question: What good is it? What does it do, besides dressing up old facts and conventional ideas in new clothing? What keeps it from being another example of the schemes of periodization, categorization, and narrative line historians like to concoct? In particular, how does it contribute to our understanding of the Cold War, its end, and its future implications?

These are legitimate questions. Admittedly the scheme, even if reasonably sound and useful as history, could be irrelevant to current concerns. The case for its relevance has to be made, and it is made more difficult by the fact that certain apparently plausible arguments for its relevance are invalid or insufficient.

One such argument would be that the scheme is useful in refuting or at least rendering more doubtful certain other broad interpretations of international history, in particular those of realists and neorealists, commonly used to explain the Cold War and its end. This could be true—certainly the emphasis here on systemic change and the decisive importance of shifts in collective mentality diverges from most realist positions—but even if that were true, the obvious way to refute these views in relation to the Cold War is by direct criticism, not by constructing an elaborate scheme like this. A similar claim, likewise possibly true but in any case inadequate, would be that setting twentieth century international politics, in particular the Cold War and its end, into a broad historical context like this one stimulates new ways of thinking about it that generate new insights. For example, it enables one to envision both world wars as a single conflict, a second Thirty Years War, which in destroying the nineteenth century system opened the way to something new. Once again the reply is that even if one accepts the notion that the two world wars constituted one long Thirty Years War (an old idea that the leading American historian of World War II, Gerhard Weinberg, flatly rejects), whatever value this concept supposedly had for understanding the Cold War would derive from the method rejected earlier, namely attempting to explain recent international developments by historical analogy and comparative history.

In other words, if this interpretation of centuries of earlier international history is genuinely to interest analysts of the Cold War, it must in some way show that the Cold War and its end fit into that long history as an integral component rather than by analogy, in such a way that our understanding of what happened in the Cold War and its outcome is significantly altered and enlarged. This is a tall order; whether the attempt succeeds, others more expert in the Cold War and its end must decide.

The specific claim I offer for consideration is that the Cold War and its end, placed within the long history of international politics, represent another breakthrough to a new system, like those of 1643–1715 and 1811–20. As in these two earlier eras, the most important thing that finally happened in and through the Cold War was that a transformed kind of international politics emerged and crystallized. The principles, rules, and constituent practices of a new system were worked out under competitive and dangerous conditions until in the end a consensus or at least convergence developed among most of the important players on a concrete, practical definition of peace. This view seems to me a defensible though controversial historical interpretation of the Cold War and a useful framework for analyzing the process and considering its implications.

It locates the roots and origins of the Cold War not primarily in a deliberate drive for empire by either side, or in a balance of power struggle for security and advantage, or even in a clash of rival ideologies and world views. True, the Cold War quickly became all these things. It started, however, with the parties as allies who intended to continue their cooperation and promote general peace and security but had not reached a basic agreement on a concrete, practical definition of peace (in fact, they had to an extent deliberately avoided doing so). The result of not working out what postwar "cooperation" and "peace" meant during the war in concrete detail was that each major player, when it began to implement its own concept of peace, viewed moves by others as direct threats and challenges to that concept, and considered them to be incompatible with real peace and intolerable in their long-range consequences.

No doubt these reactions resulted in part from misperceptions, latent suspicions, and hostility left over from prewar and wartime rivalry (among the Western allies, the United States, Britain, and France just as much as between them and the USSR). Yet misperception and the revival of old mistrust was not the main cause of this development, for it has to be recognized that even if the mutual accusations of deliberate hostility and breach of faith were often wrong, one-sided, or propagandistic, the judgments both sides made that the others' moves represented threats to their own interests were substantially correct. In other words, the wartime allies produced the Cold War precisely by trying to construct peace and a new order without first carefully defining what this project meant and what it required in individual and common action. As a result, the initial attempts at postwar cooperation for peace actually produced a Cold War by making the erstwhile allies face the fact that they were really opponents, possibly enemies.[9] In a still more remarkable paradox, that Cold War would lead first to limited cooperation among the rivals to keep it from turning hot, and finally and suddenly to a consensus on peace that would permit real cooperation.

This account of events makes 1945–91 resemble 1643–1715 as a breakthrough rather than 1811–20. In 1945–91, as in 1643–1715, it took decades of conflict and a decisive military–political outcome to establish the norms, rules, and conditions of the new system and arrive at a consensus definition of peace—which is what one would normally expect. Eighteen eleven–eighteen twenty was different because the final allied coalition against Napoleon in 1813–15 did something unique and astonishing in history. It abandoned the policy that previous anti-French coalitions had followed (also followed by the victors in the Thirty Years War and in both world wars) of concentrating mainly on military victory over the common foe and relying on that military victory and the spirit of wartime union to pave the way to peace and postwar cooperation. Instead, the powers in the last coalition in 1813–14, even before launching a new campaign against Napoleon, negotiated agreements among themselves on a comprehensive, concrete, practical definition of peace. They then fought the war to achieve that particular definition of peace, maintained this consensus on peace through the course of fighting, and made every effort to bring other parties, including their enemies, into it.

They thus put politics ahead of war, consciously fought for concrete, agreed political aims rather than mere military victory, and after victory translated this wartime consensus into a comprehensive network of treaties and a general alliance. Only because they did this *during* the war, drawing on lessons learned in a generation of earlier wars, could they produce solid peace through a single peace settlement at Vienna. The failure or inability to do this, as in the seventeenth century and the first half of the twentieth, insured that no matter how much states and peoples wanted peace and strove for it, it would come only out of further struggle.

According to this interpretation, the Cold War itself, like 1648–1713, was an era in which the wartime omission was made good. The terms, norms, principles, and rules were painfully worked out, first for a limited cold peace, then a wider, somewhat more positive cold peace (détente), and finally, as in 1713–15, with a decisive victory for one side, but also with most major players converging on a new concrete definition of peace and taking some major steps to implement it. This overall interpretation, though also controversial, is defensible. It does not denature or trivialize the Cold War, or downplay the fact that in the short and middle term, as event and conjuncture, it consisted of hostile confrontation, intense competition, and grave crises with potentially disastrous outcomes. Nor does it inflate the mutual restraint and sense of limits displayed by both sides during the Cold War and needed for averting war between the two sides into active cooperation and goodwill. It merely takes known facts about the Cold War and conceptualizes them differently within a *longue durée* view of international history. Just as a long-duration view lets one conceive the post-Westphalian era not simply as a contest between France's bid for hegemony and European efforts to maintain a balance of power, but also as a confused, conflicted process of working out how the new political principles and rules obscurely outlined and foreshadowed at Westphalia would really function in practice, so this view lets one understand the Cold War not simply as a struggle over who would rule the world, but also as a contest over what the rules, practices, and conditions of postwar peace would be and who would set them.

Peaceful coexistence, for example, did not develop simply out of balance of power competition and the fear of mutual assured destruction, nor as a slogan and policy the superpowers adopted in the course of the Cold War, after Stalin's death or the Cuban missile crisis. The idea and goal was there from the beginning. The conflicts and crises of the Cold War arose precisely from moves and countermoves on both sides to define the terms and conditions for peaceful coexistence in areas and over issues left dangerously undefined by the war and the failure to reach a real peace settlement (Berlin, Germany, Yugoslavia, Western and Eastern Europe, Japan, China, and Korea, Vietnam, the Middle East, much of the Third World).

At every point, moreover, the concern not to go too far, the desire to achieve one's own goals but at the same time to keep the outcome minimally tolerable to the other side, controlled the conflict on both sides and kept it from issuing in overt war, though the margin was sometimes dangerously thin. The Cold War competition was not a *va banque* struggle and spiral descent into the maelstrom like events before and during the Thirty Years War, the revolutionary-Napoleonic wars, or the two world wars. This fact is most strikingly apparent precisely in the most dangerous crises in 1948–49, 1956, 1958, 1961–62, and 1973. It does not really matter whether one attributes the restraint that repeatedly pulled both sides back from the brink solely to the nuclear stalemate or explains it more as a fundamental recognition that war among great powers for victory had ceased to be a viable goal. In either case, it meant a break with the politics of the previous era.

This view also integrates into the history of the Cold War another development of equal or even greater importance, too often seen simply as part of the Cold War or a kind of sideshow and byproduct of it—the permanent pacification and integration of Western Europe. While the terms of cold, peaceful coexistence between the two opposed blocs were being defined in competitive, conflictual fashion by the Cold War, the very concept of peace was being redefined, expanded, and transformed within one bloc in a different, essentially cooperative process. The political and economic integration of Western Europe, combined with its economic growth and the expansion of its economic and political ties to North America, the Pacific Rim, and much of the rest of the world, constituted nothing less than a new, concrete definition of peace. A large and growing number of important, highly developed countries redefined peace to mean not merely the elimination of hot war among themselves, but the joint advancement of economic development and prosperity, political and economic integration and interdependence, democratization, human rights, a market-oriented economy, liberal representative government, and a joint approach to common problems.

This new development coincided with the Cold War but was not simply a product of it. In fact, it affected the Cold War as profoundly as it was affected by it. Indirectly it promoted détente and the growth in trade and communication between the blocs; more directly it led to such things as the Helsinki Accords, the work of the Conference on Security and Cooperation in Europe (CSCE), and the encouragement of dissents in the Soviet bloc and the Soviet Union. It is not unreasonable to define the end of the Cold War as the adoption since 1985 of this new concept of peace developed above all in Western Europe by the countries of the former Soviet bloc and most of the USSR itself.

To repeat what was said at the beginning: No one should buy this interpretation of the Cold War and its end (as the sudden, unexpected climax of a long-developing subterranean convergence on a new concrete definition of peace) merely on the basis of this brief argument, much less accept the scheme of international history on which it rests. At most it is intended to be suggestive, and my further remarks on the implications this scheme and interpretation might have for the future are naturally even more tentative, speculative, and personal.

One obvious way to view what this scheme suggests about the future of world international relations is optimistic. On this reading, the end of the Cold War marks a real, meaningful convergence among many of the most important countries of the world on a concrete definition of peace—a consensus, moreover, potentially far more sustainable and defensible than earlier ones. The definition of peace now includes and is supported by values and principles that, unlike earlier ones, have a real future. That is, they are far more practical, desirable, adaptable, and widely applicable—liberal representative democracy, civil rights and the rule of law, the expansion of trade, interchange, and communication between open societies, market-based economies, governments responsible to their own citizens, and the development of institutions and norms to promote international cooperation in general and to act against at least the worst and most dangerous forms of international outlawry. In other words, this new phenomenon is not just a temporary and partial breakthrough to general world peace like earlier ones, but a real, permanent achievement, like that of manned heavier-than-air flight in 1903.

Another possible reading is pessimistic. Whatever else this history of long duration may indicate, it shows that breakthroughs of this sort do not last. The mood and spirit that inspired them and the circumstances that made them seem imperative change or disappear. The cycle of decay, crisis, partial overthrow, apparent but deceptive renewal, and further degeneration leading to another great systemic crisis takes over. Nothing suggests, much less proves, that the fate of this breakthrough will be different. The so-called consensus on a concrete definition of peace is anything but universal, and very thin and shaky where it exists. Commitment to its values and norms, even where they have taken root, will not survive any serious political or economic challenge, and many powerful enemies of these norms remain ready to challenge and defy them. Nor is there any guarantee or good reason to believe this breakthrough, even if it helps solve the problems that caused past wars, can master the new world problems looming in the future.

Both of these views and the outlooks they suggest are plausible; neither is necessarily true; and neither slant is particularly helpful. The only sensible attitude to take, if this scheme has merit, is a kind of sober realism, neither optimistic nor pessimistic. Something big and real has happened, both different from and analogous to major breakthroughs in the past. We do not know how well the emerging new system will work in an unknown future or how durably it will withstand the unpredictable but inevitable tests and shocks to come. We do know it is the only system for peace we have; that it is better (that is, both more effective and more solidly grounded) than anything that has gone before; and that it therefore makes sense to do everything possible to sustain it and make it work.

That general premise has two more specific implications. The first is that this scheme indicates how important ideas are in international relations (conceptions, visions of the future, understandings of what is possible and impossible, collective mentalities and outlooks, concrete formulations of aims and goals, attitudes about rules, norms, and expectations). Of course material realities influence these, possibly produce them. Nonetheless, ideas not only influence conduct in international affairs, but can also change material realities and what persons, societies, and governments do with them. Just as most of the great material improvements in the life of persons and societies, in this century as before, have come from ideas, mainly advances in science and technology, so the worst international crimes and horrors of the twentieth century (both world wars, Nazism, Communism, the Holocaust, other genocides, integral nationalism and tribal war, terrorism) have sprung above all from ideas and outlooks. So have the great advances (the liberation of conquered and oppressed peoples, an end to overt imperialism and colonialism, the rise of democracy and civil liberties, more open societies, the emancipation of women, the growth of international cooperation and the institutions to support it, the establishment of zones of peace replacing war).

The implications of this fairly banal point are less obvious. First, it places a high priority in international affairs, often treated as a theater of pure power politics, on the arena of ideas, collective mentalities. If, as claimed, a large section of the international community has now reached consensus on a new, concrete definition of peace, one which though fragile and incomplete is still more solid and hopeful than any earlier one, then the most important task becomes to maintain, strengthen, and broaden this consensus. Every action and every policy needs to be considered and decided finally in the light of whether it undergirds or undermines it, at home and abroad.

This consensus on a definition of peace certainly faces major external challenges, but my reading of history indicates that the greatest threats to it are likely to come from within, and that like the Vienna System it will fall to internal decay earlier than external assault. This fall will come about for some of the same reasons as in the nineteenth century, namely that some governments and elites benefiting from the peace settlement will try to preserve it unchanged and use it strictly for their own interests, adopting an ideology of the status quo, and that many of those who initially share the definition of peace will defect from its support because they have other interests or actively rebel against it, believing that it frustrates them while keeping one part of the international community permanently on top. Signs that this is happening or has already happened in the former Soviet Union, parts of Asia and Latin America, and elsewhere are easy to see and very disturbing.

Another argument made earlier, that a certain kind of optimism can threaten international consensus and cooperation, also applies here. Neither optimism nor pessimism is good or bad in itself, of course. The problem here lies in a particular form of optimism or simplistic thinking, the belief that a simple way or magic formula exists for achieving and maintaining peace. Let a certain formula be applied, a given principle be established, a mechanism be put into operation or a law obeyed, and peace will be secure. This kind of thinking has always been endemic in international affairs on all sides of the political spectrum from Right to Left, but though the tendency to rely on nostrums for peace is universal and timeless, the fashion in nostrums changes over time. Many of those common in history seem to be receding in appeal or least remain contested—peace through a balance of power or a preponderance of power in the right hands (the two phrases usually mean the same thing) or through the rule of law, national self-determination, the liberation of oppressed peoples, democracy, constitutional government, economic development, world federation or world government, international organizations and peacekeeping forces, universal disarmament, and so on.

One, however, seems to be gaining ground in the United States and part of the West, and to be reflected in certain of the contributions to this volume: a doctrine one might call economism. This is the belief not simply in the greater power and efficiency of free market–based economies in producing goods and services, but also in the ability of free-market economics to solve the major problems of world order, or at least to render them manageable and ultimately obsolete. Let the ideas of Adam Smith and J. S. Mill (which on examination turn out really to be more those of Bernard Mandeville and Herbert Spencer) be recognized as universally valid and given free rein; let governments concentrate on their legitimate tasks, which are to provide the institutional and legal frameworks under which the free market can operate, and otherwise get out of the way of market forces, freeing them to work across national and on global lines; let people and governments concentrate on the fundamental needs and requirements of society, promoting human welfare through the material wealth created by the free play of economic competition; and most of the sources of international conflict will decline or disappear. States, economies, even rival nationalities and religious groups will become too closely interdependent in economic activity to be able to fight on a large scale, or to want to.

Put aside all the challenges that could be made to these claims (here admittedly overdrawn and oversimplified) on various general grounds—economic, environmental, social, communitarian, and the like. Concentrate instead on the central issue of international order. Can one rely largely upon the free play of market forces to solve the kinds of problems, economic and other, that have caused international and civil wars in the past? If not, is it prudent to call for governments to abandon attempts to manage problems of trade, national production, unemployment, economic vulnerability, and general economic welfare through the instruments of international politics, all for the sake of the free market? Should one welcome the inability of governments to control the movement of capital internationally and applaud the signs of the putative obsolescence of the state and the takeover of many of its traditional functions by private groups, above all multinational corporations, when one at best does not know and cannot predict what the consequences may be in international politics?[10]

I do not think so. The marketplace is a valuable, in some respects indispensable, servant in the cause of world order. It can help make many problems soluble or manageable that would be insoluble without it.[11] Yet the unfettered marketplace is a bad, dangerous master in world affairs, mainly because there are many vital tasks it cannot touch and therefore many promises it cannot fulfill. It cannot defend national territory, or promote vital cultural and spiritual values, or insure the protection of rights and property abroad, or preserve the stability of government and law at home, or do a host of other things citizens everywhere naturally expect their governments to do for them in the international arena. And for many, a large majority in the world, the marketplace does not even produce a decent economic existence.

To suppose therefore that the movement toward greater world peace is essentially a shift from politics to economics is seriously mistaken. For one thing, it sets up a false dichotomy, like suggesting that the road to health lies in going from medical treatment to nutrition, whereas while any sensible program of medical treatment includes nutrition, nutrition can never constitute a full program of medical treatment or substitute for it. The more international relations comes to be concerned with international economics and tied to it, which is a long-standing, accelerating, and on the whole valuable trend, the more we need international politics in order to keep that trend from going beyond control. The suggestion that economics is the more vital, central, comprehensive sphere of activity in human society, and politics a narrower, less central, and more dispensable one, has things just backward. Politics, which comprises the organization and leadership of groups for collective enterprises and the processes whereby their decisions are made, is the most comprehensive, inclusive, and indispensable of social activities, in business and economics as everywhere else.

An even more fundamental conceptual error, however, is to conceive peace and order not as a path or process, but as a certain condition, a state of things brought about when the right policies and actions are followed, whether they be sound market economics or intelligent power politics backed by a good national defense, or strong political ties and friendships, or good treaties and international law well enforced, or democratic polity, or something else. The conceptual confusion shows up in the common phrase, "establishing a just and lasting peace." Peace and order are not a condition or set of conditions established by treaties, power politics, economics, or anything else, and then maintained or preserved. Peace and order must be conceived as organic, constantly changing, either growing or dying; something always becoming, being created and recreated.

A just peace can only mean one in which many diverse, conflicting aims, claims, rights, and calls for justice are creatively reconciled, compromised, or held in fruitful balance; a lasting peace can only be one that keeps changing and adapting to new demands for justice. The name for the only process and activity through which this job can be done is "politics." For this reason, the notion of another method or route to peace, economic or any other, is dangerous nonsense, and the widespread contempt for politics and politicians in the United States and elsewhere represents a pernicious trend. The British political writer Bernard Crick, correcting Thomas Jefferson's dictum about eternal vigilance being the price of liberty, has put it well: "Eternal politics is the price of liberty." This applies still more to the international arena. Eternal politics is the price of peace, and will remain so in the twenty-first century as in the past.

DOES THE HISTORY OF INTERNATIONAL POLITICS GO ANYWHERE?

The question in the title suggests a certain skepticism about the possibilities of development and progress in international history (diplomatic history, if you prefer). Such skepticism is not new or uncommon. Charles S. Maier's survey in 1980 of the previous decade of American work in this field clearly signaled by its title, "Marking Time," that he saw no new directions emerging in it.[1] The article, though it attracted considerable attention, was only a gust in a wind that has blown fairly steadily for decades. Since the late-nineteenth and early-twentieth centuries, international history has declined steeply and irreversibly from the position it had once held as king of the historiographical hill, and has also been specifically attacked and rejected, at least in anything like its traditional form, by some of the most influential currents of twentieth century historiography: by Marxists, because it supposedly ignored the real roots of international politics in socioeconomic structures, class struggle, and relations of production; by *Annalistes* because, like traditional political history in general, it was a history of mere short-term epiphenomenal events, ignoring the deeper rhythms and broader structures of total history or serial history; and by practitioners of *Gesellschaftgeschichte*, because it missed the driving force of history, the processes of industrialization and modernization, and their attendant consequences for society as a whole.

These criticisms, common in the 1950s and 1960s, were not new even then. Serious rebellions had arisen in Germany and elsewhere against the Rankean principle of the *Primat der Aussenpolitik* long before Fritz Fischer and his followers led their celebrated revolt against it a generation ago—for example, by Karl Lamprecht and his *Kulturgeschichte* at the turn of the century and by Eckhart Kehr with his insistence on the *Primat der Innenpolitik* in the 1920s and 1930s. Nor will the fact that the historiographical vogues of earlier decades have themselves become old orthodoxies and a bit passé cause international history no longer to be considered

David Wetzel and Theodore S. Hamerow, eds., *International Politics and German History*, 15–36. Copyright © (1997), by Praeger Publishers. Reproduced with permission of Greenwood Publishing Group, Inc., Westport, CT.

old-fashioned, shallow event history. Practitioners of currently fashionable brands of historiography (cultural history, gender history, new social history, history of everyday life, history from the bottom up) have their particular reasons for considering international history traditional, superficial, and not very useful, and might well add charges of sexism, elitism, and racism to the list. No field is more obviously open to the claim that it is a record of oppression, aggression, and exploitation by dead, white European males.

The current fate of international history in the United States, however, is probably not to be overtly criticized and rejected, but to be quietly ignored as not on the cutting edge of scholarship and unlikely ever to be.[2] This may sound like a querulous complaint about international history's being excluded from the spotlight and a call for other historians to give it more attention and respect, but it is not. If a certain imbalance can be detected here, it is only one indicator among several of a certain trendiness in American historiography, and as will be argued, this particular phenomenon is largely confined to the United States, probably transient, and not worth worrying about. Nor is this intended as a defense of international history against the usual criticisms—that it is superficial, that it deals with a kaleidoscopic jumble of events, that it tells us nothing new, that it records what one clerk said to another clerk, and so on. For one thing, this kind of defense has already been effectively made.[3] For another, the critics are open to counterattack. If, for example, it is true that the traditional diplomatic approach to international history often misses the forest for the trees, it is equally true that the Marxist at least as often misses the forest for the roots, the *Annaliste* misses the forest for the total global landscape, and *Gesellschaftsgeschichte* misses the forest for the lumber industry. Those who complain that international history is superficial and relies on a narrow range of questions and sources simply show thereby how little they understand the ways international history has changed since Leopold von Ranke's day—and Ranke was anything but a narrow historian. No international historian worth the name today contests the interdependence of foreign and domestic politics and the vital role of social and economic forces in international history, and all at least try to write international history accordingly. Neither do international historians still believe, as Ranke's principle of *Primat der Aussenpolitik* assumed, that the formation of nation-states and their quest for power and independence constituted the central theme of history and the driving force behind it. They only contend that this remains an important theme and driving force in history, and that many other historical themes and forces—social, cultural, economic, domestic-political—are inextricably tied up with international politics and vitally affected by it.

Neither this critique nor the defense of international history is very important, however, because the apparent decline of interest of American historians in European and world international history may not be a significant long-term phenomenon. It is certainly not worldwide; only France and the United States seem to show it and even in these countries the tide may be turning. If biography and political history can make a comeback in French historiography, as they have already done, can international history be far behind? In some countries, moreover, the study of international history has always flourished and continues to do so—Great Britain, the Netherlands, Austria, Canada, and Germany (of this, more later). The history of American foreign policy is highly organized, boasting its own society, SHAFR (the Society for the History of American Foreign Relations) and its special journal, *Diplomatic History*. Studies of the Cold War have shown a similar development. A journal founded in Canada in the late 1970s, the *International History Review*, has achieved a worldwide reputation as the leader in the field. Any survey of publishers' catalogues, moreover, will show that questions of international history, including especially the origins of both world wars, the Cold War, and various other crises and conflicts, perennially capture the attention not merely of professional historians but also of a broad public.

If some historians slight the history of international politics, moreover, the same certainly cannot be said of scholars in cognate fields. Scholars in such flourishing disciplines as international politics, strategy and security studies, studies on war and peace, and military history recognize the importance of international history for their work, and make more rigorous efforts to draw broad lessons and insights from it than historians often do. In fact, much of what political scientists write on international politics is quite simply international history, and historians who do not agree with the methods they use or the conclusions they reach should feel challenged to do it better.

It is ironic, moreover, to find international history relatively neglected in American historiography precisely at a time when both historians and other scholars have realized once more how central a role the state plays in society, and how vitally wars, military establishments, and international competition and conflict influence state development and the evolution and transformation of society. It is still more ironic that this should happen at a time when the relevance and importance of international history for current and future world developments becomes more obvious every day. The revolutionary transformation of the world scene and the international system occurring since World War II, especially in the last decade, far from ending international history, has revalidated it, and revalidated in particular the historical approach to understanding it. The current changes and upheavals in the former Soviet Union, the former Yugoslavia, the rest of Eastern Europe, Germany, and Western Europe, and the Near and Middle East, and the problems and challenges that these create, cry out for analysis in historic perspective, in terms of their historic roots. To solve or manage the problems they create also requires an understanding of the historic evolution of the international system and its current possibilities and limits. Though it would take too long to argue this point here, headlines serve to illustrate it almost every day.

In other words, the international historian should not waste his/her time worrying about the status of the field of international history, the attitudes of other historians toward it, or its place in the historiographical pecking order. It needs no defense in terms of its importance, its relevance to vital issues, or its intellectual depth and challenge; if some historians ignore or despise it, the more fools they.

However, the international historian, having stopped worrying about how much attention and prestige the field enjoys, might start worrying about something else: how the field of international history should be conceived and dealt with. Instead of asking the usual historian's question, "Is the history (meaning the historiography) of international politics going anywhere?" that is, "Are new methods being developed and exciting discoveries being made, putting it on the cutting edge of historical scholarship?" he or she might ask the question, "Does the *history* of international politics go anywhere?" That is, is there a direction to the history of international politics itself? Has international politics, considered as a historic practice, a societal institution, an organized, distinctive pattern of relationships within human society, moved in a particular direction over the course of time, developed in a particular way? The conventional criticisms of international history, as noted, are not very important or difficult to answer. The question of whether the history of international politics goes anywhere, in contrast, is important and challenging. It looks at the essential nature of international politics and asks whether it lends itself to useful historical treatment, whether its history can be written at all in the same way the history of other great themes is written. It addresses the possibility, assumed by some to be a fact, that international politics involves actions and principles that are inherently chaotic, irrational, and incalculable in any broad, encompassing sense, and that its history overall must therefore also be chaotic, kaleidoscopic, and irrational.

Why does this make a difference? History, according to Herbert Butterfield's well-known definition, is the study of the changes of things that change. It analyzes how human life and institutions have evolved, how this became that. Even an apparently static analysis of some historic phenomenon concentrating on a particular incident or place at a particular point serves to illuminate change over time, serves at least potentially as a single snapshot in an ongoing motion picture of evolution and change. If the history of international politics is not that of a developing, changing human practice or institution, but instead of a collection of many separate actions impinging on or colliding with each other; if that collection of actions and events we call for convenience's sake "international politics" remains unchanged in its essential nature and characteristic patterns over time, changing only in terms of instrumentalities and externalities; then one ought to doubt the centrality and importance of international politics in history. Then those political scientists may be right who claim that only the methods of social and behavioral science, not the "historiographical mode," can make the history of international politics produce useful generalizations. Then those historians may also be right who, while admitting that events in international politics, especially wars, have often made a major difference in history, see these events not as central factors in human development, but rather as contingent and accidental factors whose impact is similar to that of collisions with asteroids on the evolution of life on earth, or of epidemics on the history of medicine.

This point has been put simply and well by Sir Richard Pares, a distinguished historian whose work included considerable international history.

In a lecture in 1953 entitled "Human Nature in Politics," Pares argued that all politics could be rational only to a very limited degree, because politics consisted of the interplay of many conflicting ambitions, the simultaneous pursuit of many partial goods, and the overlapping and mutual interference of "many wills and reasons [which] bear, not on the same point, but on hundreds and thousands of different points." The nature of history, especially of politics, as "the product of thousands (perhaps, nowadays, millions) of different wills, none wholly dependent upon any other; of thousands or millions of different reasons, none wholly amenable to any other," explains "why conduct which is, in the main, reasonable so often brings about results which are not reasonable." The basic irrationality of politics, Pares continued,

> is truer of some kinds of activity than of others. Above all it is true of international relations, which are, by definition, the relations of independent wills, each one regarded by its subjects as embodying the highest and most general good which is practically conceivable; a good which is so general as to be self-subsistent. This is why diplomatic history, more than any other kind of history, is "one damned thing after another," from which one can deduce no laws or principles, but only generally applicable techniques.... If international relations could be abolished by the establishment of a world state, the greatest single impediment to the exercise of reason and foresight in domestic politics would be removed.[4]

This is a persuasive view of international politics and, by extension, of its history. It fits our intuitive impressions and appears supported by a good deal of social and psychological theory as well. The picture it draws of an international system inherently conflictual and incapable of durable rational control because the sovereign units that comprise it pursue independent, irreconcilable purposes is in accord with all realist international relations theory, including the neorealism or structural realism of Kenneth Waltz and his school.[5] This view also explains and justifies the way in which Pares, like many international historians, wrote the history of international politics—essentially as an irrational play of forces and wills, kaleidoscopic in its changes, without long-range direction, changing not in the nature of the game but only in the rise and fall of powers, the number and importance of the participants, and the level and character of the violence employed in playing it. It would explain equally well why even social and political scientists who take history seriously in trying to build and test their models and develop theories of international politics may use it as a quarry to be mined for useful examples and as a source of data for patterns of behavior remaining basically unchanged over time.

If Pares is right, the history of international politics does not and cannot go anywhere; it only turns faster and buzzes louder at some times than at others. He does not deny the possibility and reality of directional change and evolution in domestic politics or social institutions in general. Indirectly, at least, he affirms it, stressing only the limits of change and the factors that retard and distort it, chief among which is international politics. He knew,

for example, that between the late-seventeenth and early-twentieth centuries
the British domestic political system evolved from something close to abso-
lutism into full parliamentary democracy. But like many others, he denied
that international progress has gone anywhere in any similar fashion, or can.

International historians more than others should think about whether the
history of international politics goes somewhere, shows direction and development, or whether its pattern in history is essentially repetitive, cyclical, and
nondirectional. First, as already noted, this addresses assumptions central to
much of the study of international politics, both in history and social science,
especially those of realism: the structural anarchy of international politics, the
necessity and inevitability of a resort by actors to self-help, the inescapable
operation of balance of power. The question therefore goes to the intellectual heart of the issue.

It also addresses the more serious side of the criticism of international history as an easy, superficial, less useful kind of history. Pares's verdict on
diplomatic history as "just one damned thing after another," for example, is
not a confession that he found eighteenth century international history simple to research and write; his own work in the field is notable for its complexity and profundity. It rather expresses his conviction that it was
impervious to rational control, that international politics was, as he says,
though tactically complex, emotionally simple and unvarying. Like war, it
was about winning and losing and would always be so. If international politics remains an unchanging struggle for power and advantage, then the historian seeking to analyze and explain historic change ought to concentrate
on the things that do change—society, domestic politics, economic life, collective mentalities, ideologies, and so forth. These somehow must be the real
sources of change and development even within international politics. This
kind of thinking, to some extent, lies behind the constant search for the
domestic, economic, and political factors that supposedly determine foreign
policy, or current arguments that mature democracies do not fight each
other, or explanations of the long peace since World War II as the result of
the change in weapons' technology, which produced a nuclear stalemate
between the two superpowers. International politics, in other words, does
not change history; other things in history change international politics.

The assumption that the game of international politics does not change
must also deprive international history of much of the attraction of other
fields of history. New fields and varieties of history emerge and gain followers in good part by showing, or purporting to show, how various aspects of
human existence that were once deemed fixed by biology, physiology,
so-called human nature, or some other supposed unchanging structure can
better be seen as results of historical development, as products of change and
producers of it. This has happened in recent decades with psychohistory, the
history of gender, women, class, political culture, childhood, death, family,
sexual practices, and other important historical subjects. A view of international history as essentially unchanging deprives it of any such engaging
interest and emancipatory power.

The question of whether the history of international politics goes somewhere even reaches beyond the professional concerns of historians to wider ones for individuals and society as a whole. It has become a truism, even a cliché, to say that the survival of the world and its civilization depends upon bringing international politics and the international system under some better, more durable kind of rational control than in the past. Pares, speaking at the height of the Cold War, claimed that this could not be done. Rationality in international politics could be achieved only by its abolition through world government. Many others especially in his generation reached the same conclusion. Someone who (as I do) considers world government not an answer to this question but an impossible and horrible dream, yet who also does not believe that the indefinite continuation of "realist" power politics in the nuclear age is rational or tolerable, has a deeper reason to ask, "Does the history of international politics go anywhere?"

As a historian, I answer this question with an unequivocal "Yes." International politics has always gone somewhere in the past; its whole history is fundamentally one of systemic change. The structure of international politics, that is, its rules, practices, norms, aims, and constitutive procedures, are at once products of historical change and themselves produce change. Once we see where international politics has gone in the past, we can get some better idea of where it is going now and likely to go in the future. This gives us a certain amount of rational hope and emancipatory power in facing the future in international politics.

This essay cannot demonstrate this thesis, of course, or even make it convincing. The best it can do is to put down some earnest money for the undertaking, in the form of three propositions. They are, first, that the opposite view, that international politics has an unchanging power-political structure and core, is historically so inherently implausible, so out of line with our general knowledge of history, including international history, that it would require overwhelming proof to accept it, and this is not forthcoming. The second proposition is that besides detecting considerable gradual evolution and development in the nature and structure of international politics, we can show that at least one fundamental historic transformation occurred in this arena almost two centuries ago. The third proposition is that today we are experiencing an even more rapid and irreversible transformation of international politics.

To start with the first proposition: Of course one finds continuity in the history of international politics, as everywhere in history. No good historian, however, lets continuity blind him/her to the reality of change. The fact that Britain has had a representative parliament since the thirteenth century, or that capitalism in some clearly identifiable form has existed since the Medicis and Fuggers, or democracy since the ancient Greeks, does not lead one to deny ongoing, irreversible, directional change and development in the history of parliamentary government, capitalism, or democratic government. Why should one assume otherwise of international politics? No doubt some phenomena in it—war, diplomacy, struggles for power and resources, conflicts between governments and peoples—are as old as human society itself. But international politics, defined as an enduring system of political relations and transactions between more or less fixed, permanent, autonomous states in regular, more or less inescapable contact and communication with each other, is a fairly recent development in human history. Before about 1500 there was no international politics in Europe as a whole, only at most among the city-states of Italy, and for a long time thereafter the practice of international politics even among the more developed states of Europe was episodic and rudimentary. Before 1648 (and indeed for some time thereafter) there was no system of international politics in the sense of international relations conducted between juridically independent and supposedly equal states on the basis of accepted rules and treaties. Before the late-seventeenth and early-eighteenth centuries there was no working balance of power or even any clear, agreed concept of one, nor was there any considerable body of international law. Only in 1815 did a working Concert of Europe emerge, though the idea was much older. It was not until the late-nineteenth century that most of the world was included in a single international system. Before 1918 there was no global international organization. Only in recent decades since World War II has the entire world been organized in a system of formally recognized, juridically independent states. It is hard to see how even the most superficial glance at the history of international politics could support the notion of its having an unchanging, repetitive, power-political essence and character.

The second point: Besides all this evolution and development (uneven, spiral development, of course, marked by frequent breakdowns and reverses—but what great developments are not?), there has been at least one unmistakable revolution in international politics, occurring in 1813–15. Having published a good deal on this theme, I will say only enough here to make the claim of revolutionary change plausible, by comparing the historic eighteenth century (1700–89) and the historic nineteenth century (1815–1914). (The great world wars just before and after each of these dates are omitted, though including them would actually support the picture of drastic change.)

Compare them first on the incidence of general systemic wars and major wars (a general systemic war being defined as one involving all or most great powers, thereby constituting a systemic crisis or breakdown, and a major war as one involving at least two great powers, but not all or virtually all, and therefore not automatically threatening the system as a whole). By these definitions, admittedly debatable but not, I think, unreasonable, I count three general systemic wars during the eighteenth century, and seven additional major wars. In the nineteenth century, there were no general systemic wars and only four major European wars.

A similar comparison holds for battlefield deaths. My calculation, again challengeable in detail but not in terms of the broad picture, is that in relation to the population of Europe, the number of eighteenth century battlefield deaths in European wars exceeds that of the nineteenth century by a ratio of 7 or 8 to 1.[6]

Even more striking than the death rate on the battlefield is the death or murder rate among states. During the eighteenth century almost every European state, large and small alike, was the target at one time or another of planned partitions—"murders of states," one might call them. Some such murders were successful. Among states targeted for partition were: Spain, Russia, Sweden, Denmark, Poland, Prussia, the Ottoman Empire, Austria, Venetia, the Low Countries, and various smaller German and Italian states. During the nineteenth century, no great power planned or executed the partition of another state (though Prussia did absorb some German states and Sardinia-Piedmont a number of Italian ones in the process of German and Italian unification, and a number of smaller powers plotted and worked to partition the Ottoman and Austrian empires), and in a number of instances the powers cooperated to keep weak, threatened states considered important for the system (for example, the Ottoman Empire or the Papal State) in existence.

Equally impressive in the first half of the nineteenth century is the virtual absence of arms races. There were ideas for arms control in the eighteenth century, and a few half-hearted attempts were made to curb arms races, but none ever worked effectively or for long. Even major wars usually were followed fairly quickly by another arms race. The very exhausting Seven Years War (1756–63), for example, brought only a brief pause in Anglo-French rivalry at sea and Austro-Prussian or Russo-Turkish rivalry on land. In contrast, the long peace from 1815 to 1854 was not only marked by no major wars, but also by no arms race (with the possible exception of the renewal on a small scale of Anglo-French naval rivalry after the war scare of 1840). The fears that sometimes arose over one state's military might or dangerously aggressive intentions (fears, for example, of Russia's large army and military colonies after 1815, or of the French army in 1823 and in 1840) all proved baseless. One could almost argue that disarmament in the Vienna era went too far. When there was danger of war, as in 1830–32, 1840, and 1848–49, the states most threatened (usually the Low Countries, Germany, Prussia, Austria, and Northern Italy) were clearly unprepared militarily to meet them. The German Confederation, despite experiencing several such crises and developing a number of major proposals and initiatives for military reform, never succeeded in carrying through on it or gaining the defensive capacity intended and needed. This condition of relative disarmament persisted even after the European Concert broke down following the revolutions of 1848. The generally poor military performance of all the belligerent powers in both the Crimean War and the Italian war of 1859 demonstrates, among other things, their long neglect of military preparedness.

This general disarmament went beyond military unreadiness to include a widespread moral, psychological, and political reluctance to resort to the use of force. A reason why the revolutions of 1820–21, 1830–31, and 1848–49 brought down many established regimes, often with considerable ease, is that the armed forces in all these countries were generally weak and unprepared for action and that their rulers were reluctant to use the military force they had against their own people or other states. It is remarkable how frequently the standard historical treatments of this era turn things upside down on this score—emphasize, that is, how the Holy Alliance powers or others sometimes intervened to crush revolutions, but fail to discuss what is far more prominent and needs more explanation, namely why both conservative powers and other governments let revolutionary tinder pile up and be ignited before they resorted to force—why in a real sense they allowed revolutions to happen. Nor were the repressive measures the conservative powers ultimately took, even in 1848–49, nearly as harsh as those that regimes used in the age of liberalism and nationalism. This era saw the June Days, the crushing of south Italian resistance to unification, the Paris Commune, Bloody Sunday, the Easter Rising.

Along with a changed spirit in the international game in 1813–15 came changes in its fundamental rules. The seventeenth and eighteenth centuries formed the classic era of wars of succession; dynastic succession supplied both the main basis for the creation and preservation of states, and the primary structural cause of wars. The nineteenth century, at least in its first half, was as monarchical in spirit as the eighteenth. Kings and princes still ruled most states and were vitally concerned with establishing their succession, retaining and expanding their inherited patrimony, and other dynastic issues. Many dynastic questions arose, new and old, especially as revolutions and nationalism eliminated some independent states and created others. Bavaria, Baden, other princely houses in Germany, Greece, Belgium, France (Napoleon III in 1851, the Bourbons after 1870), Rumania, Serbia, Bulgaria, Spain, Schleswig-Holstein, and Albania were all involved. Yet no war arose over these succession questions. They still caused trouble and could be manipulated to create a crisis (for example, in Schleswig-Holstein in 1863, Spain in 1870, and Bulgaria in 1884–87) but they were never in themselves the real cause of war or even of the crisis.

Or look at the nature and purpose of alliances. Virtually every eighteenth century alliance was overwhelmingly, almost exclusively, an instrument for power politics, designed and used for capability aggregation and territorial aggrandizement. Virtually every nineteenth century alliance for the first forty years after 1815 was a restraining alliance used more to control one's allies and to preserve peace and manage international crises than to increase one's own capability, and all alliances specifically ruled out territorial aggrandizement.

Consider the causes and purposes of war. Every great European war in the later seventeenth and eighteenth centuries was also a world war, fought over extra-European, imperial rivalries and prizes as well as European issues. From the mid-seventeenth to the mid-eighteenth centuries war, both formal and informal, was one of the main ways of promoting a state's commerce, perhaps the main one. Frequently the destruction of the enemy's trade and the creation of a monopoly for one's own commerce was the avowed purpose of the war, sometimes the only one, and even where other causes predominated this one was seldom absent. The British, the French, the Dutch, the Spanish, and the Portuguese fought over prizes overseas; Swedes, Danes, Dutch,

Russians, Poles, Prussians, and other Germans contended for the *dominium maris Baltici*. Commerce and revenue played equally important roles in power struggles in the heart of the continent. Louis XIV coveted the Spanish inheritance partly for commercial reasons; Frederick the Great boasted that Silesia, which he stole from Austria by war, had brought him more treasure than all the silver mines of Peru.

As we know, 1815 did not bring an end to European colonial expansion. At most it slowed down a bit in the first half of the nineteenth century and then accelerated to its apogee in the latter half. Economic competition between European states was at least as important in nineteenth century international politics as in the eighteenth century. Yet no trade war or anything that could plausibly be called one ever occurred from 1815 to 1898, nor did a war or major threat of war between European powers over an extra-European, colonial issue.[7] Even after the Fashoda crisis of 1898 broke down the fence erected in 1815 to separate European and extra-European politics, colonial imperialism still involved as much cooperation as rivalry between the powers, and was not *per se* a major cause of war in 1914.

Many more fundamental changes in rules, norms, expectations, and collective assumptions could be added to this list of startling contrasts between eighteenth and nineteenth century international politics. These, however, ought to suffice to make the point. Historians readily recognize the impact revolutions had on domestic politics and society in late-eighteenth- and nineteenth-century Europe in Great Britain in 1789, 1830–32, and 1848. Yet none of these revolutions, including the French, can be shown to have produced such changes in fundamental relationships and patterns of conduct as those that differentiated international politics after 1815 from that which went before. Yet when historians discuss the Vienna System and the post-Vienna era, they typically speak of restoration, return to stability, reestablishment of the balance of power, and even of reaction and repression of revolution and change. This will not do. If any of the changes in this era deserve to be labeled "revolutionary," those of 1815 in international politics do. Leaving aside the question of whether 1815 does not deserve more than 1789 to be called the birth date of the modern world,[8] one can confidently claim that the one "revolution" of the period whose results were quickly apparent, effective, and clearly benign in terms of international peace and stability was the transformation of international politics.

This leads to the third point: The Vienna era pointed toward a future now being realized. We are presently living in an era of international politics dimly foreshadowed by it; experiencing fundamental changes in the international system, the seeds of which were sown and began to ripen then. Three major changes can be identified, products of a long historic evolution coming to fruition in our time. Once again they must be simply stated with little explanation and no proof, but prima facie evidence pointing to them lies all around.

They are, first, the rise of the trading state.[9] This refers not merely to the increasing importance of economic factors in international politics, but to a change in the main requirement for the survival and long-term prosperity of states. In the seventeenth and eighteenth centuries, the prime requirement was success at war. Commercial prosperity was important for supplying the resources vital for military establishments and war, but commercial prosperity not wedded to military power and success never insured a state's survival and security and often increased the danger from enemies. The fate of trading republics—the United Provinces, Venice, Genoa, Ragusa, and others—is eloquent witness to this. By the nineteenth and early-twentieth centuries and the development of the international system, it had become possible for some states to survive and succeed relatively well without great military power by taking refuge in neutrality—Switzerland, Scandinavia, the Low Countries. In great crises, however, the hiding places tended to break down, and for most actors success at war remained the key to survival and prosperity. Now, in the late-twentieth century, the main key to a state's success, both domestically and in the international arena, has increasingly become success at trade, the ability to compete in the international economic sphere and thereby to provide for the welfare of its citizens. A wide array of states has arisen both in the developed and the developing worlds that either have no significant military power or power far short of their economic strength and their defense requirements—Canada, Austria, Belgium, the Netherlands, Denmark, Norway, Sweden, Finland, Switzerland, Italy, Germany, Japan, Taiwan, South Korea, Singapore—states nonetheless successful because of their skill at commerce. In contrast, the USSR, the real military victor in World War II, a superpower that, unlike the United States and other major powers, had successfully maintained its empire against every military challenge from within and without for forty years after the war, stands revealed today as a colossal failure, simply because it failed as a trading state. The United States, now unrivalled in military power, recognizes that without success as a trading state its military power can only temporarily mask its decline. This insight, a cliché in current political discussion, marks a breakthrough in the long historic development of international politics.

A second change, closely associated with the first, is the declining utility of military power and military victory. War was once not only unavoidable in international politics, but also often necessary, useful, and even beneficial as a way of settling international disputes and achieving fundamental national aims. It is steadily becoming less so and being seen to be so. Military power *per se* has not become obsolescent or dispensable; but the range of tasks it can be expected to do in international politics, though still important, is clearly shrinking in relation to the ever-widening range of problems that need to be managed or solved in the international arena. Even where and when it must be used, military power serves best to check threats, not solve fundamental problems. The costs of its use, political and economic as well as military, are rising in comparison to its benefits; and for solving many urgent problems and advancing many interests it has no utility at all.

The third change, though harder to define, may be the most important. It is the rise of international integration and community, the growth of a consensus among governments and peoples on certain norms for conduct, both internal and international, which governments must meet to enjoy legitimacy, and a growing willingness among nations to cooperate to defend these norms and to promote conformity to minimal standards and bounds of law in international politics.

All these changes have deep historic roots. In terms of actions and institutions, we can see certain forerunners of them in the Vienna System and era; as ideas, many of the peace plans proposed by statesmen and writers since the late Middle Ages foreshadow them. Their role after World War II in the recovery, pacification, and economic and political integration of Western Europe is now clear. They were at work in the process of decolonization and disimperialism among the former great colonial powers, mainly voluntary and peaceful; so also in the admission of an astonishing number of new nations into the world community with at least juridical equality, and the gradual growth of the effectiveness and reach of the UN and other transnational bodies. The progress seems discouragingly slow and dangerously precarious—until we see in historical perspective how impossible all these accomplishments would have been in any earlier era.

Until a few years ago, it is true, one could not speak of a breakthrough. These trends were clearly detectable, but not clearly winning out in world politics as a whole; the possibility remained that all the progress could be wiped out in some international disaster. The events of 1985–90, in the Soviet Union, Eastern Europe, and South Africa, coming on top of what has been happening over recent decades in East Asia, the Pacific Rim, much of Central and South America, and the Mediterranean basin have surely done much to show what trends and principles are winning. One authoritarian, repressive regime after another came to terms with the primacy of economics over power politics; they faced up to the declining utility of the military force still at their command, as a means either of solving their internal problems, securing their position in the world, or enforcing their old policies at home. They reacted to economic, moral, and political pressure from their own peoples and the outside world by changing their policies and even surrendering power. Here was the most dramatic proof possible that old patterns and rules in international politics no longer held; that international politics was going somewhere.

If I may be pardoned a personal reference to show how startling a historic development this was, in early 1985 I published a brief essay entitled, "Does Murphy's Law Apply to History?"[10] arguing that Murphy's Law ("whatever can go wrong, will") need not apply to history, and that in particular the existence of great stocks of nuclear weapons did not mean that nuclear war was inevitable sooner or later. There had already been great progress toward durable peace in international politics, and more was possible. In another essay I had previously speculated tentatively about the possibility that the Soviet Union might some day recognize the futility of maintaining its current rigid system and might relax its grip on its own people and its East European empire.[11] This is not to claim that I was a prophet—rather the reverse. Instead, though I was already convinced by that time that the international system was changing and that change within the Soviet empire was possible, all the concrete predictions I would subsequently make to students and colleagues about Soviet policy after 1985 (fortunately for me, not in print) proved dead wrong. All my arguments, based on strong historical precedent, that the Soviet Union would not get out of Afghanistan, or allow its East European empire to disintegrate, or permit the reunification of Germany, or let a reunified Germany remain in NATO while the Warsaw Pact collapsed, or give up the Baltic states, or repudiate communism, or let the Soviet Union itself collapse, proved false. In other words, even while knowing that international politics was changing, going somewhere, I was myself too much caught in history to realize how far and how fast this change would go, unprepared for revolutionary changes with which scholars are still desperately trying to come to terms.[12]

There is, of course, an answer to the claim that in the last decade international politics has moved away from the old power politics and toward a new world order characterized by the primacy of commerce, the declining utility of military force as a solution to problems, and the rise of international consensus and cooperation. First of all, a critic might say, the aftermath of revolutions in the Soviet Union, Eastern Europe, and elsewhere gives us no good reason to believe that the next ten or twenty years will bring these areas a net increase of democracy, liberty, prosperity, integration into wider European and world communities, and general peace and cooperation. Many signs point to just the opposite—the breakdown of unstable regimes, economic decline, political instability, an explosive rise in political and economic nationalism and in ethnic, religious, and national conflict, serious new conflicts over borders, and in general far more danger of war and international instability than before.

Second, even if somehow these current and deepening problems in Eastern Europe, the former Soviet Union, the Middle East, and Africa are solved or managed without disaster, we have already had clear evidence that the basic power-political character of international politics has not changed, and that military power is still absolutely necessary both for deterrence and compellence to maintain any kind of tolerable world order, new or old. One dangerous dictator, Saddam Hussein, has already shown how he regards the preeminence of economics, the declining utility of military power and victory, and the importance of international consensus and legitimacy. Only massive military force stopped his aggression and reversed his gains, and even this still has not changed his mind or felled his regime. In the former Yugoslavia the Serbian government, its army, its militias, and apparently a majority of Serbs have demonstrated their belief in armed force to achieve their ends, and demonstrated it by horrors reminiscent of some aspects of World War II. The Croats are not much different or better. Similar terrible conflicts are possible or likely in many other areas; in some, like Tajikistan and Armenia and Georgia, they are already going on. Organized terrorism belongs as much to the new world order as cooperation. Nothing therefore is more naïve than supposing that the new world order, whatever it is, means less conflict, danger, and the need for vigilance, military power, and the willingness to use these elements if necessary.

Much of this argument is obviously true—that the road to liberal democracy, economic prosperity under a free market system, integration with the West, and stable constitutional government in Eastern Europe and the former Soviet Union will certainly be long and rocky, with some failures and disasters likely; that the same holds for South Africa, much of South and Central America, North Africa and the Middle East, and parts of Asia; and that the revolutionary developments of recent years have made more regional conflict, ethnic struggles, territorial disputes, civil war and struggles for power, and plain interstate war likely in the next decade or two. All this could well mean that some forms and uses of military power will become more necessary and frequent in coming decades rather than less.

Yet these facts and probabilities, far from proving that the international system is still essentially the same, show just the opposite. They prove that it has changed in the most basic sense: It no longer operates primarily on the basis of power politics or by the methods of a balance of power. The situation is parallel to that of the postrevolutionary and Napoleonic era. Just as in 1789–1815, the ultimate political, social, and economic results of the revolutions of the 1980s are not yet clear; what is clear is that the international system has been transformed.

To see this, one need only compare the international reaction today to developments in three prime trouble spots (the former Soviet Union, especially Russia; the rest of Eastern Europe; and the Balkans, especially former Yugoslavia) with the reactions of the international community in previous analogous eras. Nineteen eighty-nine was not the first time that Russians have made a revolutionary bid for liberal democracy. In 1905 liberal and democratic forces (the so-called Octobrist parties and Kadets) led the movement for constitutional democratic government. This revolution largely failed. When the tsarist regime was overthrown during World War I in March 1917, these same parties, though never in control of the revolution, headed the Provisional Government of Russia for a time, and until the Bolsheviks seized power in November 1917, various socialist parties and leaders in Russia tried to keep the revolution on a democratic path, if not a liberal or capitalist one. Both bids for constitutional democracy were thus defeated, the first by tsarist repression, the second by the war, Russia's collapse, and Lenin's strategy. The current third bid could also fail. The question here, however, concerns the international reaction to these developments. How did the other great powers react to these earlier Russian bids for democracy, and how are they reacting now?

The answer is well known and uncontroversial. Whatever other governments felt about the revolutions and democratic movements in 1905 and 1917 *per se*, whether they mainly inspired fear and dislike as in Germany and Austria–Hungary or approval and sympathy as in France and Great Britain, concern for the fate of the revolution and the democratic movement made little difference for the foreign policies of these countries. What counted was power politics, the balance of power. In 1905 Germany (or at least Kaiser Wilhelm II) tried to use the revolution to draw Tsar Nicholas and Russia away from France and over to Germany's side; Austria hoped the revolution would frighten the tsar into renewing the old Three Emperors' Alliance; while Britain and France, in order to prevent this, worked directly against the democratic revolution in Russia, granting the tsarist government large loans to enable it to govern without the Russian parliament (the Duma) and against it, using its police and army to restore semiautocratic rule. In 1917, power politics took primacy over the struggle for democracy in Russia even more clearly. Germany, then under the military dictatorship of a right-radical general, Erich von Ludendorff, deliberately promoted a Bolshevik revolution in Russia in order to overthrow the Provisional Government and the democratic socialists and thus to draw Russia out of the war. Meanwhile the Western powers persistently rejected the Provisional Government's pleas for a peace conference and frustrated its efforts at a negotiated peace, thereby destroying that government's only chance for survival, because all that counted for them was to keep Russia fighting on their side in the war.

There is nothing whatever surprising in these policies. The rules and stakes of the game of international politics as it was then played demanded that even liberal democratic regimes in the West sacrifice the liberal democratic cause in Russia and the chance to integrate Russia more closely into a peaceful Europe to the demands of national survival and victory in war and to balance of power politics.

The current internal situation in Russia does in some ways remind us disturbingly of those of 1906 or 1917–18. The decisive difference, however, lies in international politics. Once again the fate of Russia's liberal democratic revolution hangs in the balance, but the one thing missing from the picture is the factor that used to dominate it: power politics. Amid all the uncertainty and controversy in the West over how to aid the democratic forces in Russia, and the criticism levied against Western states, especially the United States, for doing too little too late to help them, no one doubts that American and other Western policy toward Russia should be to help the experiment in liberal democracy and a market economy to succeed. This goal, moreover, is not considered important primarily for strategic and economic reasons of power politics (for example, to gain Russia as a useful ally against some other enemy, or to prevent an undemocratic Russia from forming a hostile alliance with some other power or powers against the United States and its allies). One still encounters such notions, of course; the old atavistic power political thinking still survives in certain quarters. But surely today sensible persons recognize that the overriding reasons for wanting to see Russia free, democratic, and prosperous are intrinsic and systemic, not power-political. Russia is critically important not for its possible role in the balance of power but for its inescapable weight and influence in the whole emerging world order. A stable, free, and prosperous Russia will help promote a stable, secure world order; an unstable, unfree, and impoverished Russia will inevitably tend to destabilize and endanger it.

The same point holds for East Central Europe. Here also current internal developments may remind one ominously of what happened in the 1920s—how the initial gains in democracy and self-determination made by the new East European regimes after World War I were quickly blighted by economic troubles, ethnic struggles internally and externally, political instability and immaturity, and territorial conflicts between them. Much of this scenario could easily be repeated now. What is not recurring from the scenario of the 1920s to 1930s, and will not, is the *international* politics of that era, with the new smaller states seeking security through military power and rival alliances, and the great powers seriously interested in them only for their role in the balance of power. Instead, astonishing changes in the potential power balance of this region—the disappearance of East Germany, the independence of the Baltic states, Poland, Belarus, and Ukraine, the peaceful dissolution of Czechoslovakia, the unification of Germany, and the territorial withdrawal of Russia from this region, leaving behind a territorial enclave on the Baltic—has occurred not only without major fighting, but, so far at least, without any serious power-political crises or repercussions. What better proof can there be that the old power politics no longer rules?

One area, the Balkans, especially former Yugoslavia, seems at first glance to belie this and to prove that the old power politics is still alive and well. A closer look, however, reveals the same pattern: similarity in internal developments, but drastic change on the international front. True, the current struggles in Bosnia and those that threaten to erupt in Kosovo and Macedonia display some historical continuities that are striking and a bit frightening, evoking a sense of historical *déjà vu*. A common argument currently for intervening to stop the fighting in Bosnia is the reminder that World War I broke out precisely in this corner of the world, touched off by Great Serb nationalism and terrorism. But once again sound history can free us from the tyranny of a false historical analogy. Serbian and Croatian nationalism and South Slav and Balkan politics may not have changed much; the international system has. In every previous Near Eastern crisis or internecine Balkan conflict since the eighteenth century, no matter which side or faction the various great powers might favor or what they might try to do about the conflict itself, their policies always rested primarily on balance of power considerations. Today no major power cares much about its strategic position in the peninsula, the preservation of its alliances, or the enhancement of its great power influence there. Not even nationalist Russians think Serbia is vital as a power-political ally against some other state. They sympathize with the Serbs, or claim to, for reasons of historic tradition, religious and ethnic kinship, and Russian domestic politics and prestige. The very criticisms of West European states made by Americans and others for failing to get involved in Bosnia or to stop Serb aggression, even if they may be justified from the standpoint of crisis management or humanitarianism, prove that the international system is new. Imagine, if you will, Americans or Englishmen urging Germans, Austrians, or Italians to intervene forcefully in the Balkans in 1914 or 1941. Intervention today under the auspices of the

UN, whether or not it is effective, rests on a different set of motives than in the past, motives more commercial, humanitarian, and general-systemic than strategic and power-political. Intervention involves the recognition that territorial expansion and atrocities of the sort occurring in Bosnia are intrinsically dangerous and tend to undermine and destabilize the new international system even when, as here, they have no important power-political effects.

In short, it is time for historians, especially international historians, to recognize that the age of classic international politics, governed by the structural determinants of anarchy, self-help, and balance of power, is over, even if some leaders and states in some corners of the world do not yet recognize it and even if the exact dimensions and contours of the new system are not fully clear. What is clear is the duty and opportunity of international historians to join in the investigation, to help show how this decisive change came about, and to uncover its deeper roots—in short, to write the history of international politics as it is, the story of long-term structural change.

Any impression, however, that this is a new idea or new approach, much less something I have discovered or devised, would be wholly mistaken. Good diplomatic historians have been doing this, at least implicitly, for a long time. Moreover, in one country, Germany, this conscious, explicit approach to the history of international politics is already more or less standard procedure. This is not the place for a bibliographical essay, but one cannot read much German international history today without repeatedly encountering terms like "structural change" and "systemic development," and still more important, seeing the history of international politics increasingly conceived and written as the story of long-term structural change. The explanations and schemata vary considerably, of course, but the goal is basically the same. This purpose shows up clearly in the work (to name just a few leading figures) of Konrad Repgen, Fritz Dickmann, Wolfgang-Uwe Friedrich, and Klaus Malettke in the seventeenth century; Klaus Zernack, Johannes Kunisch, Heinz Duchhardt, and Michael G. Müller in the eighteenth; Wolf Gruner and Anselm Doering-Manteuffel in the nineteenth; Klaus Hildebrand and Peter Krüger in the earlier twentieth; and too many historians to mention in the period since 1945. A working group of historians and other scholars at the University of Marburg has made its program that of analyzing the history of international politics as an evolving system and has published a book of essays discussing and illustrating how it can be done.[13] It seems fitting to me that in a country where historians once almost unanimously promoted a view of international politics as an endless struggle for power, and where power was pursued to its most extreme and destructive ends, historians should now take the lead in a different approach.

13

International History: Why
Historians Do It Differently than
Political Scientists

An introductory note: this essay, originally published in a collection of essays on the relationship in international relations research between diplomatic and military historians and political scientists using qualitative methods, accompanied one by Robert Jervis[1] explaining the similarities and differences from a political scientist's point of view. Everyone interested in the theme should read it. My essay was supposed to develop the historian's standpoint on approach and methods independently, but there was so much agreement between us and Jervis's analyses of the similarities and differences was generally so sensible and perceptive that the best hope of adding something germane and useful appeared to be through comments on Jervis's arguments—comments that even where they demur generally say "Yes, but," and whose purpose is to develop some points he makes further, and to respond to certain questions he raises and possible answers he suggests with my own from a historian's point of view.

This essay therefore follows his themes fairly closely. To his initial arguments on what the differences are *not* between the international historian's and the political scientist's respective approaches to international politics, I have nothing to add or object; the analysis seems to me correct and pertinent. The same holds generally for most of his discussion of "environments," with only this marginal comment: I wish that his remark about American international historians being more international in outlook and conversant with scholarship being done in the rest of the world than American political scientists are strictly and universally true. My impression is that it usually holds for international historians doing European or world international history, but less so for those who work on U.S. foreign policy.[2]

Colin Elman and Miriam Fendius Elman, eds., *Bridges and Boundaries: Historians, Political Scientists, and the Study of International Relations*, 403–16. Copyright © (2001), MIT Press. All rights reserved. Printed by permission of the publisher.

A more important but still mild demurrer under "environments" concerns Jervis's explanation of the Leftward shift in recent decades in the study of history, a shift that has generally led, he writes, "to the marginalization of international, political, and military history, and to the growth of the study of non-elites and an anti-positivist methodology." Jervis attributes much of this to the impact of the Vietnam War and campus protests. I accept his description of the phenomenon and agree that these events played a role in it, but see more powerful causes of it in two areas: first, certain sociological changes in the country as a whole, in universities and colleges generally, and in the social makeup of the historical "profession"; and second, in the very nature of the historical enterprise, the kinds of material it uses, and its conception of its central task. On the sociological side, the rise of the feminist movement and similar movements among disadvantaged or marginalized groups in the country as a whole (gays and lesbians, various ethnic groups, etc.), combined with organized pressure on the universities to promote cultural and ethnic diversity, plus the greater entrance of women and members of ethnic and racial minorities into a profession previously dominated by white males, mainly accounts for this Leftward trend. The impact of the Vietnam War and the campus protests, initially important, has since receded.

More important still in accounting for these developments are certain features inherent in history as a discipline. First, the materials with which it works are almost infinite in their scope and variety and widely, though not infinitely, malleable in terms of their possible treatment, approach, and interpretation, so that new approaches are always possible and alluring. Second, since history became a serious scholarly discipline in the nineteenth century it has always been natural for it not to content itself with new discoveries and interpretations in historical fields as traditionally conceived and practiced, but constantly to try to discover (some would say, invent) new fields. Thus an essential task of history as it is now practiced is to show that areas of human life hitherto seen as timeless, permanent, and unchanging—part of "nature," so to speak—actually have a history and help shape history as a whole. This quest mainly accounts for the ongoing splintering of the historical profession into dozens of specialties, many of them new, and for the emergence in recent decades of such broad fields as psychohistory, gender history, history of everyday life, the history of memory, discourse, and representation, and even postmodernism and deconstruction.

Except for the very last, I consider all these to have been on balance valuable developments. For various reasons, however, some good, some bad, all normal, they have had the unfortunate side effect here in the United States (not everywhere and certainly not in some other parts of the Western world) of promoting the marginalization of more traditional fields of history such as the international history of Europe and the wider world. One can deplore this and see it as a serious loss without despairing of the future. These fields, I am confident, will eventually regain their due status and importance also in the United States (where US diplomatic history has always flourished); the beginnings of a recovery are already visible. In the meantime, to be sure, considerable short-range damage to these fields and imbalances within the discipline of history in the United States have occurred, and measures of fire-fighting and damage control are badly needed.

I also agree with Jervis's identification of parsimony as a prime source of difference between historians and political scientists, and his remarks on the inclination of the latter to seek and prize parsimony and of historians to be suspicious of it. His observations on how many historians conceive of the search for parsimony and react to it strike me as largely accurate. I contend, however, that the view commonly encountered among historians that the quest for parsimony is *per se* inappropriate for history because its true nature and genius lies in its complexity and richness of detail, and that the historian therefore should eschew parsimonious explanations for richer, more complex and ambiguous ones, is basically wrong, a misunderstanding of history's task. In fact, history as actually practiced and presented by good professional historians is full of parsimonious explanation, if not parsimonious theory, and historians should be as interested in achieving parsimony in their way and for their purposes as political scientists are in theirs.

How so? Every broad summary judgment, every conclusion of a major work that tries to sum up what the story finally amounts to, every insight or argument that says, "Here is the nub of the question, here lies the real answer," constitutes a parsimonious explanation. Works of history, especially good, important ones, are full of these.

To illustrate, one could point to the many widely-used collections of excerpts from the writings of historians designed to introduce students to major controversies and historical debates, often with titles like, "The Nazi Revolution: Germany's Guilt and Germany's Fate?" or "Britain and Appeasement: Guilty Men or Terrible Times?" These collections could, to be sure, be dismissed as mere pedagogical tools rather than serious history, whose intent and effect, moreover, in introducing students to the richness, indeterminacy, and ambiguity of the historical literature and encouraging them to read more deeply on their own, is to bring them to the realization that parsimonious explanations are impossible. Instead, all important developments have multiple causes or factors, these often contradict or work against each other, and no formula or thesis can do justice to this rich complexity. This may be what many historians would say—but again, they would be wrong. The very fact that these collections exist shows that good historians do offer explanations that are parsimonious, though not monocausal. They do say, "This in the final analysis is the central factor," or "This is the best way to understand this whole development and phenomenon, and to understand its component elements." Moreover, the competition and clash between such attempts at parsimonious explanations, far from being illegitimate and from distorting historical inquiry, drives it forward. Consider, for example, how much valuable research has been engendered by the clash in German historiography between the intentionalist and the functionalist views of the Nazi regime and its policies, including central ones like its foreign policy and the Holocaust. The fact that both broad views cannot be

equally sound and true does not mean that either is necessarily false or useless, and still less that no parsimonious explanations are possible at all. For
every James Joll, who in his classic study of the origins of World War I exam-
ines the major parsimonious explanations and finds them all wanting,[3] there
is an Ian Kershaw on Nazi Germany[4] or a Michael Marrus on the Holocaust[5]
who on reviewing and analyzing the literature comes to his or her own relatively parsimonious formulation of the best answer.

The reason for insisting on this point is not to contradict what Jervis says
on this score, but to prevent it from inadvertently strengthening a common
stereotype: that historians are mainly or solely interested in telling stories and
recounting developments in all their rich and fascinating detail, and that
political scientists are interested instead in explaining developments, categorizing them into classes, and determining their causes. Historians are just as
much interested in the latter pursuits and engage in them as much as political scientists—or at least they should be.

Why then do the differences Jervis points out on the score of parsimony
arise? Partly, as he says, they arise from the different subjects we typically
address. Political scientists typically, though not always, attempt to explain
classes of phenomena (wars, revolutions, international crises, foreign policy
decision-making in general, etc.). A normal, necessary question in political
science is, "Of what general phenomenon, development, pattern of behavior, etc. is this particular action an instance?" Historians more often (though
again far from always) propose to explain particular instances of these same
classes of phenomena, and are not satisfied to treat them simply or mainly as
examples of some general law or pattern. Partly they occur, as Jervis again
says, because the respective parsimonious explanations are arrived at by different routes—the political scientist's ideally by the hypothetico-deductive
method, the historian's by a more inductive method of process tracing. But
on a third aspect, what Jervis says is, I think, not wrong but needs further
development: his remarks on how political scientists are uncomfortable with
the phenomenon of inconsistency and apparent irrationality in behavior, and
dislike leaving cases of such apparent inconsistency (for example, in Soviet
behavior in the early Cold War, one of the examples he mentions) unresolved
and unexplained, while historians on the other hand are apt actually to
delight in the perverse, unpredictable nature of human conduct and are
comfortable with the bedrock fact of constant inconsistency. Perceptive as his
observations are, they do not quite get to the heart of the matter, especially
on the historian's side. The question has to do, I think, with why, despite the
fact that both groups prize parsimony (or should), historians are in fact often
suspicious of the parsimonious explanations actually arrived at by political
scientists; and most important, what each side tends to regard as satisfactory
explanation by cause.

Neither political scientists nor historians value parsimony for its own sake,
as a good and desirable in and of itself. Both desire it, as Jervis notes of political scientists, for the sake of robustness, explanatory power, effectiveness in
explaining as many phenomena as far as possible with as few explanatory

elements as possible. Historians, I insist again, are as much engaged in the business of providing robust explanations as political scientists and should recognize parsimony as one element or feature of it. They have no business ignoring Occam's razor and multiplying either entities or causes beyond necessity. The trouble is that the historian's experience often forces him or her to the conclusion that particular parsimonious explanations and theories, including those of political scientists, are not robust, do not integrate and accommodate the pertinent evidence but ignore or distort it. James Joll, to recur to the instance previously mentioned, did not reject all the parsimonious explanations of the origins of World War I out of a desire to see the phenomenon in the round and picture it in its richness of detail and great interest; he did so because he found them all not sufficiently robust, leaving too much relevant evidence unexplained or explained in an unacceptable way.

Both this reason for the historian's common skepticism about social scientific theories in his field—not their parsimony but their lack of effective explanatory power—and the historian's greater willingness to accept and live with inconsistency in human affairs, including international politics, point also to a major difference between historians and political scientists: how they conceive of causes in human affairs and deal with them. Presumptuous though it is of me as a historian to discuss the mindsets and assumptions of political and social scientists, my impression is that without being rigid about it they try to conform as closely as possible to a Humean concept of cause: an antecedent condition or set of conditions that regularly and predictably produces a particular result. Historians, without thinking much about the question (less than they should, in fact), almost automatically or unconsciously use the term "cause" in the far richer, more varied, but entirely legitimate human understanding of the term, learned from inside through life itself and merely refined and developed by many scholarly disciplines, scientific and humanist. In this definition, "cause" is anything that effectively prompts or influences human beings to do certain things, and therefore varies almost indefinitely in kind and is unpredictable in precise effect and outcome. Instinct, learning, socialization, custom, habit, rational conviction, irrational or nonrational belief, emotion, impulse, example, need, persuasion, influence of others, and so on can and do serve as "causes" for the historian, just as they are recognized by each of us as possible "causes" in our own lives and those of others. I would agree, even insist, that historians generally should be more aware of how they conceive of causality, more careful in how they use the term "cause" and its many synonyms, and more explicit in defining what they mean by it in particular instances. Doing this would at least help reduce the fog and smoke surrounding many historical controversies. I cannot agree, however, that history should forfeit its birthright by abandoning this wider, richer, and deeper concept of cause, with all its variety and the confusion it unquestionably introduces into every discussion, in exchange for the dubious pottage of social science rigor.

A further observation: Historians are less enamored of parsimony and more comfortable with inconsistency than political scientists in part because of a still more basic difference in their approaches: the tendency of political scientists to treat the common subject matter, international politics, as behavior, while historians insist on treating it as human conduct. This connects with observations by Jervis that I found intriguing, but also in need of further development—those on morality. Here my contribution can be more substantial and less parasitic than elsewhere. It consists of offering reasons why historians not only are more inclined to make moral judgments than political scientists, but why they must and should do so—why moral judgments are not superfluous and harmful addenda to historical investigation or mere appendages of it, but embedded, inescapable ingredients in it.

First, a mild objection to one of Jervis's propositions. Quoting Melvyn Leffler to the effect that the historian's scholarship and ethical values are closely tied to a commitment to history as a means to help achieve a more decent and humane world, Jervis writes: "I think that few historians would have trouble accepting this standard; many if not most political scientists would, arguing instead that the test is to attempt to do one's best to understand the world, not to change it." On this score, many if not most historians, including me, would agree with the political scientists, on precisely the same grounds. Scholarly history has traditionally conceived its task and goal predominantly in a Rankean sense, as that of portraying the past "wie es eigentlich gewesen," rather than the Marxian one of understanding the world in order to change it. There are, of course, serious scholars who consciously attempt to make history an instrument of social change. A good example is the program of doing history as critical historical science ("kritische Geschichtswissenschaft") directed toward emancipation and social progress, practiced by Hans-Ulrich Wehler and others in Germany, especially at the University of Bielefeld. These efforts, however, represent controversial protest movements against the mainstream, and the historical criticism they regularly face on evidential grounds often forces them in practice to subordinate their emancipationist-reformist goals to the general canons of historical investigation.[6] Moreover, while many historians, perhaps most, would deny that Ranke's ideal of an objective historical account corresponding to past reality is attainable (thereby incidentally misinterpreting what Ranke meant and intended by his aphorism), the claim that objective historical truth cannot be attained, which has now become the conventional wisdom, is not a denial that the proper goal of history is to improve our understanding of the historic past. The argument I will make here is that while a historian's scholarship and ethical values do involve a moral commitment and task, it is not the task of changing the world or providing the means for doing so. Instead, moral values and purposes are firmly embedded within the historian's task of understanding the past and are inseparable from it. The reasons can be discussed under three headings: narration, explanation, and vocation.

The first reason why doing history inescapably involves making moral judgments is the easiest to understand: the unavoidable moral content and dimension involved in the very language required if we wish, even in strictly

Rankean terms, to describe historical actions, to state what really happened. The subject matter of history is, as traditionally stated, all that humankind has done and suffered (in the sense of experienced, gone through). One cannot tell this story, or any substantial part of it, in value-free language devoid of reference to its moral dimension. One is forced, simply in order to give any sort of coherent narrative and analysis, to use adjectives such as good, bad, rational, irrational, harmful, beneficial, selfish, unselfish; verbs like kill, injure, massacre, slaughter, insult, wound, help, console, save, rescue, heal; nouns like courage, cowardice, honesty, lies, loyalty, betrayal, honor, dishonor, strength, weakness, and so on ad infinitum. Every attempt to construct an "objective" value-free language to tell the story of what human beings have done and suffered not only breaks down and denatures the narrative and analysis alike, but does so without really avoiding moral judgments, instead masking, blurring, and fudging them. To try, for example, to construct an objective, nonmoral standard for judging the German attacks on Poland in 1939 and on Russia in 1941 in terms of their motives, actions, and immediate and long-range consequences—to do so, say, in terms purely of their success or failure to advance Nazi goals, concluding that in the strictly immanent terms of Nazi aims the former was a success and the latter a failure, and to leave it there would not merely be extremely morally insensitive, but unhistorical, a failure to come to grips with the real, main story of what happened, what human beings here did and suffered. Apply this same sort of procedure to the Holocaust and it becomes wholly inhuman, obscene. The language of history, used to tell and analyze it, is inescapably moral in one of its essential dimensions, as is that of everyday life. That language can be used well or badly, sensitively or insensitively, subtly and by implication, or crudely and by imprecation, but it cannot be morally neutered without neutering history itself.

The second main reason why historians (as well as other social scientists, I believe) cannot escape making moral judgments is a bit less obvious: that any important theory or large-scale explanation as to why things happen in human affairs inevitably carries with it large-scale moral implications as well. Take, for example, the substantial literature, including recently David Landes' magnum opus on *The Wealth and Poverty of Nations*,[7] which argues that the main factors leading to prosperity or poverty are and always have been education and the development of human capital. An obvious implication of this theory or explanation is that if one wishes to promote economic well-being, one must not allow religious or ideological commitments and systems that stand in the way of education and the development of human capital to prevail. Similarly, if the theory of democratic peace is sound, the implication that one ought to promote liberal democracy and a market system for the sake of peace is unmistakable. One can leave these judgments implicit and unstated, or put them conditionally ("if you want peace or prefer prosperity, then combat religious fundamentalism and promote democracy," etc.), but this makes no difference; they remain implicit in the theory and explanation. Similarly, the fact that the moral implications may be unclear, contested, and ambiguous, and involve a clash of incompatible values (for example, "Is it right to destroy a traditional society and its culture for the sake of a highly unequal, consumption-oriented prosperity?") does not eliminate this moral dimension, but helps delineate it. To recognize moral ambiguity is to make a moral judgment.

There are even ways in which, in order to explain major events and to develop and test fairly broad theories or interpretations, one must make moral judgments on the nature of the actions involved. Let me illustrate this first from my own experience. Some years ago, in response to an important study of international crises by R. N. Lebow, I wrote an essay arguing that a major category of international crises was overlooked in his and other analyses in international relations theory, a category that I labeled the "failed bargain crisis."[8] My core argument was that many crises are caused by international bargains that fail after they have been successfully negotiated between the contending parties themselves, and that they principally fail because other parties not involved in the original bargain work deliberately or unwittingly to make them fail. I took as a major example of such a failed bargain crisis the Bosnian Crisis in 1908–09, principally involving Austria-Hungary and Russia. My interpretation was that a bargain had been made in good faith in September 1908 between the two foreign ministers, Baron Aehrenthal of Austria-Hungary and Count Izvolski of Russia, and that their bargain broke down when other leaders within the Russian government and among Russia's friends, France and Britain, acted to frustrate it. The British historian F. Roy Bridge later pointed out to me, however, that this explanation would not work and that the Bosnian Crisis could not be classed a failed bargain crisis because, according to Austrian and Russian documents he had discovered and published, there never had been a real good–faith bargain between Aehrenthal and Izvolski. Instead, the latter had always intended not to fulfill his end of the bargain, but instead to exploit Austria's actual annexation of Bosnia-Herzegovina, to which he had agreed, for purposes of embarrassing Austria, winning a diplomatic victory over it, and restoring Russia's sunken prestige in the Balkans.[9]

What does this have to do with the question of moral judgments in history? Simply this: I was forced to reclassify this crisis, removing it from the category of a failed bargain crisis, not simply because I learned facts hitherto unknown to me about Izvolski's actions and the hidden agenda he had pursued in the negotiations. Statesmen almost always have a hidden agenda, especially in foreign policy; prevailing conventions in diplomacy expect and allow for it.[10] Diplomats are supposed to conceal their own government's hidden purposes and to try to ferret out those of their counterparts. What compelled me to change my interpretation and categorization of this crisis was the meaning and significance of these facts, a meaning inescapably bound up with and deriving from a moral judgment—that Izvolski, unlike Aehrenthal, had gone over the line, broken the conventions of good–faith bargaining. The fact that he had not simply concealed his hidden purposes and tacitly deceived Aehrenthal, but had flatly lied and intended to betray the bargain, changed the whole character of the transaction and the explanation of the origins of the crisis, compelling me to blame Izvolski more and his Russian colleagues and British and French leaders less for it. (The story also illustrates one reason why historians may be less enamored of theory–building than political scientists—not necessarily because they have less interest in large-scale, idealized and stylized, more or less abstract explanations, but because they have repeatedly learned how easily such explanations, however neat and convincing, can be upset by inconvenient facts.)

This process by which moral judgments enter integrally into the explanation and categorization of major developments has wide application in international history. Repeatedly historians are compelled, in order to state what a statesman or country was doing, to judge the action or purpose morally in terms of the prevailing rules and norms of international politics, and thus to say what game was being played, and whether this actor or that was playing the game or wrecking it. Playing this "blame game" is not necessarily a needless distraction from the historian's real task of stating what the actors did, though it can become this; it is often an integral, necessary part of telling what they did and explaining it. For example, a key question in seventeenth century international history concerns how to interpret the policy of Cardinal Richelieu of France. Virtually all scholars have abandoned the old view (still held by Henry Kissinger[11]) of Richelieu as the founder of a new, rational, secular, egoistic politics of raison d'état. All would now agree, as Matthew Anderson says, that Richelieu did not distinguish between the needs of his king, Louis XIII, the French state, and those of the Catholic church and Christendom generally.[12] But major disagreement arises over how he conceived those interlocking interests and ends and tried to advance them, and the dispute involves differing judgments, essentially moral in character, made as to what Richelieu was really doing. Some leading historians (Fritz Dickmann, Emanuel Thau, William F. Church, Hermann Weber, Karl Otmar von Aretin, and Klaus Malettke) have argued that Richelieu's real goal was not conquest, expansion, and French domination of Europe, but rather the erection of a collective security system for lasting peace in Europe, led by France. According to this view, his successor Mazarin followed Richelieu's policy in its externals but without its European spirit, and Louis XIV distorted it into a quest for French domination, conquest, and glory. Others, however, notably Johannes Burkhardt and Derek Croxton, argue that Richelieu's actions in allegedly pursuing a French-led collective security system in Europe differed little in terms of tactics, claims, and strategies from the actions of Mazarin and Louis XIV later. Hence regardless of Richelieu's claimed motives and intentions, this was in effect the same policy of expansion and domination as that of his successors. Note that this is not a dispute about the moral character of Richelieu himself, or about the aims of his policy. It is a dispute essentially about the character, at once moral and practical, of his actions. The factual judgment as to what he was doing and how his policy should be understood cannot be separated from the moral one. Similar cases arise frequently.

The last reason (at least the last I will develop here) for the historian's being necessarily involved with moral judgments is the subtlest and trickiest to explain, but also (to me at least) the most central. It originated with the famous historian of the Renaissance Garrett Mattingly, was further developed by the historian of seventeenth century England J. H. Hexter,[13] and is here given a slight, further twist by me. It involves a proposition first stated by Mattingly: that the historian has the moral obligation to do justice to the past, not for the sake of the past but for his own. It is easy enough, I think, to say what the first part of this means, to do justice to the past. It means essentially the obligation to treat the whole past fairly and with integrity—to understand it on its own terms and not anachronistically, to let the other side be heard, to be sensitive to the unheard or neglected voices, not to employ an ethics of success but give a due respect and attention to lost causes, and the like. It may not be easy to give a precise, categorical, practical definition of "doing justice to the past," but the concept passes the Potter Stewart test on pornography—we recognize it when we see it or fail to see it, or at least are convinced that we do. Nor is it at all difficult to show that this desire to do justice to the past plays a large role in the actual investigation and writing of history, and a vital, beneficial one. It is impossible, for example, to imagine so distinguished a historian as J. H. Elliott spending great time and energy in researching the career of so unsympathetic a character as the seventeenth century Spanish statesman the Count-Duke of Olivares[14] had he not been convinced, as he tells us, that however unlikable Olivares was and however disastrous his policies turned out to be, history had not dealt justly with him. Not only are a great many individual works of history powerfully influenced by this feeling, but it also helps account for the emergence of new fields and emphases in history. The history of women, gender history, the history of everyday life, history from below, the history of various ignored or suppressed groups, and other such fields have arisen not just because their practitioners had career ambitions to pursue or ideological axes to grind, but because of a widespread conviction, often justified, that in these areas justice had not been done to the past.

It is harder to explain just what the second half of the axiom means: "not for the sake of the past, but for our own." The meaning of "not for the sake of the past" is clear enough: The past is not a sacred object of worship or veneration. Those in the past are beyond caring whether they receive justice from historians or not. But the second part, "for our own sake," admits of different meanings. Mattingly seems to have meant by it "our own sake as professional historians, in recognition of the high scholarly standards we have to live up to and the kind of history we want to deliver to our generation and future ones." Hexter takes it a bit further: "Our own sake as moral persons, recognizing that we owe the same fair treatment to historic personages as we do to living ones, and should accord them justice in response to the same general moral obligation."[15] Admitting both these as true and important, I would go one step further: "our own sake as human beings seeking self-knowledge." By doing justice to the past we go further and deeper in finding out important truths about ourselves as human beings. The most apt description of the historian's attitude toward his or her subject and work is, it seems to me, the statement of the Roman writer Quintilian (though I am told he meant it ironically): "To consider nothing human alien to myself." In doing justice to the past, we approach those goals that history has always acknowledged, if not always served—to make the strange familiar and the familiar strange, to expand the range and increase the depth of our understanding of what it means to be a human being.

This understanding of the Mattingly–Hexter formulation of the moral task of history appeals to me also as a further demonstration of how moral judgments in history are inescapable because they are embedded in it. The task of doing history does not merely contain a moral aspect or dimension but is intrinsically a moral pursuit, belonging to one of humankind's supreme moral obligations, "Know thyself." I am, of course, not saying or hinting that history is the only discipline with this lofty purpose and function. All the liberal arts and the sciences, including the social sciences, share it. Nor am I hinting that social scientists in abstaining from making moral judgments in order to achieve their purposes become thereby less moral or truth-seeking or profound than historians, and offer less self-knowledge. But I would say that a difference between the two fields and approaches stems from the same source as their different meanings and uses of cause and causality, namely the difference between treating human actions mainly as behavior or mainly as conduct. It is the latter emphasis that I think makes history especially valuable for self-knowledge, and it is a reluctance to abstract from it and the moral dimension it contains that makes me sure that I could never be a political scientist. However, as Jervis says, this is no reason why we cannot be friends and in many cases allies.

14

THE MIRAGE OF EMPIRE VERSUS THE PROMISE OF HEGEMONY

No one can doubt that the United States is currently the leading power in the world, and few at least in America would dispute that it needs to exercise world leadership in some fashion. The great debate is over what kind of leadership this should be and how it should be exercised. This essay offers only one idea, drawn primarily from the history of international politics: the United States has a choice between two modes of political leadership that, though they resemble each other and are often identified or considered interchangeable, nonetheless fundamentally differ in nature, practice, and effects. These are empire and hegemony. For purposes of world order and peace, the lure of empire, specious and inviting, is a mirage; the path of hegemony is genuinely possible and arguably necessary. The two, moreover, are not readily combined or compatible, but lead in contradictory directions. The current American pursuit of empire is undermining the chances for a useful, benign American hegemony, and if carried much further will end up promoting the very Hobbesian disorder it was supposed to prevent or overcome, one avoidable under a sane American hegemony.

To support these assertions with historically-based arguments would require at least three things:

(1) Establishing a clear conceptual distinction between empire and hegemony, terms often conflated and used as synonyms, and showing that the distinction is useful for analysis.
(2) Showing that this distinction is not merely useful for purposes of definition of terms, but that it represents a genuine choice or set of alternatives in history, and that the choice between policies of empire and policies of hegemony has made an important difference in historical outcomes.
(3) Showing historically why empire does not work within an international system of the kind first developed in Western Europe and now prevailing throughout the world, even though it can work outside that system and has done so in the past, while hegemony can work within an international system such as the current one, sometimes works well, and often is required for any such international system to function tolerably and to endure.

A serious exposition of these three points, amounting as they do to a theory of international politics and an interpretation of five centuries of world international history in a nutshell, obviously is impossible in a short essay. All that can be done is to assert and at some points illustrate the main lines of argument. The whole case, however, is likely to be dismissed at the outset by the advocates of American empire as something perhaps interesting to historians and antiquaries, but irrelevant in today's world because that was then and this is now. The world is different since 9/11; the current enemies and threats to the United States and the so-called free world in the form of international terrorist organizations and movements, hostile ideologies, rogue regimes, and proliferating weapons of mass destruction exist everywhere and must be fought everywhere and nowhere in particular, but always and necessarily proactively and preventively. Under these circumstances, the old international system simply gets in the way and must be discarded or replaced with something better. Furthermore, American power and supremacy today is so much greater than any other power's has ever been; the ability of the United States to project that power globally with great speed and devastating effect is so unprecedented, and America's economic global reach and the soft power it has through the influence of its material culture and its attractive political and social institutions and values is so effective in penetrating other countries and societies, that historical lessons and strictures drawn from the past do not apply.[1]

My response to this is a further, still stronger assertion: the current American bid for empire as a recipe for world order and peace not only will fail and prove counterproductive ultimately, at some time in the future, but at present, in early 2003, is already failing. This is not a prediction but an observation, based not on specialized historical research but on the kind of general historical knowledge that educated lay persons can be expected to command and understand. The only real question is how far the current administration will continue to push this venture, doubling and redoubling its bets and refusing either to fold on a bad hand or cash in its chips while it is still ahead, and how much damage will be done before its failure is acknowledged and the venture abandoned.

For reasons of space, the argument in support of this claim must be bareboned, apodictic, and apparently dogmatic. Clauses like "It seems to me" or "In my opinion" should be taken as read in much of what follows.

Both empire and hegemony are slippery terms, often defined in misleading or vague, excessively broad ways so that the difference between them becomes blurred or obliterated. Any sound definition of empire must include as one central element the exercise of political control by one organized community over another organized community different from and separate from it, giving the imperial power final decision-making power over essential political decisions affecting the community under its rule. Needless to say, many things contribute to the acquisition and exercise of that kind of imperial authority— military and economic power, scientific and technological prowess, culture, religion, ideology, ethnicity, and so on—but empire remains essentially the possession and exercise of political control over foreigners. Less obviously, empire need not mean *direct* political control and administration, and historically has not for the most part involved this. Most empire, ancient and modern, has existed and been exercised as informal empire, that is, indirect control through local authorities, recognized and acknowledged paramountcy in a particular region without direct administration of it.[2] Nonetheless, its essence remains intact, residing in the final authority and decision-making power in critical political matters resting with the imperial government.

The problem with the term hegemony as often applied to international politics is that a definition of it as cultural dominance serving as the tool of class rule, the concept promoted by the revisionist Marxist sociologist Antonio Gramsci, prevails in sociology and other social sciences[3] and has tended to dominate popular usage. For the history and theory of international politics, however, another meaning of the term is more appropriate. Hegemony in international history and politics means the possession and exercise of clear, acknowledged leadership and superior influence by one power within a community of units *not* under a single authority.[4] A hegemon is therefore in principle first among equals. An imperial power rules over subordinates. A hegemonic power is one without whom no final decision can be reached within the system, whose task and responsibility it is to see that necessary decisions are reached. An imperial power can impose its decision if it chooses.

This distinction like most such distinctions in social and political life is not airtight, but one of degree, like the differences between warm, hot, and boiling. As will be argued later, hegemonic powers can become empires and are regularly tempted to do so, and there are instances where empires attempt to devolve into hegemony (the British Empire into the Commonwealth, the French into the Union Française, the Soviet Union into the Commonwealth of Independent States). But the very fact that each can evolve into the other shows that the distinction is more than merely verbal or a matter of degree, and that it has important implications for the international system and its functions, perceptions, and practices.

As to system: in both theory and practice, hegemony as here defined is fully compatible with the modern international system composed of autonomous coordinate units (mainly states) juridically equal in status, rights, and obligations, though vastly unequal in power. Empire is not. Whatever they may claim, empires cancel out that essential juridical equality and the autonomy that goes with it.[5] The fundamental principles of empire and of a genuine international system of independent states are oil and water.

The difference extends to functions. Empires function to rule, to establish the final locus of authority in one center. Hegemony functions essentially to manage, to maintain some degree of order and decision-making capacity within a system of dispersed authority. Empire means the negation of balance within the system, both a sustainable balance of power and balance in elements equally important for a stable international system, namely equilibrium in terms of rights, status, privileges, duties, responsibilities, and honor. Hegemony in contrast is fully compatible with balance in both areas, and is often necessary to achieve and maintain it.[6] Empire tends by nature toward exclusive, final control and cannot be shared or exercised in common. Colonial territory can be parceled out and divided up among imperial powers, for example, but only if the respective parcels are clearly marked, each controls his own, and each honors the agreement.[7] Hegemony on the other hand can readily be shared and exercised in common, and often works better when shared either equally or unequally.[8]

Most important, this distinction between empire and hegemony is not an abstract academic one, but reflects perceived reality in history since the beginnings of the modern international system, and the difference between them has repeatedly made a critical difference in outcomes. Empires, both traditional and modern, can work for a considerable time, prove stable, and produce and maintain order in premodern, non-international settings. They produce such order essentially by imposing stable governance and law on areas either too little governed and organized or too mired in chronic, uncontrolled violence and war to enjoy peace and stability. However, once stable autonomous polities have developed and been organized within an international system such as the one that has evolved starting in Western Europe since the sixteenth century and now prevails worldwide, attempts to create order within that system or impose order upon it through empire invariably and inevitably produce disorder, instability, and war. Hegemony, on the other hand, can produce peace and systemic stability and sometimes does so, and the absence of hegemony or the failure to exercise it where it is needed can be and frequently is a cause of systemic breakdown and war.

This does not mean, of course, that the effects of hegemony are automatically good or those of empire always and everywhere bad. Austrian hegemony in Germany and Italy after 1815, for example, was undoubtedly repressive and regressive, even if stable and peaceful; Napoleonic empire in parts of Western Europe had some major stimulating and progressive aspects, even if its long-range tendency was toward ever greater tyranny, exploitation, and war. Other examples could be cited. The central point remains, however, that hegemony can exist and operate within an international system and help sustain it, and empire cannot.

These sweeping assertions can only be illustrated here, with references to a few of the leading authorities. First, one can point to crucial points in history at which leaders of states that were already potential or actual hegemons within the existing international system consciously or subconsciously chose empire rather than hegemony as their goal. These bids for empire did not necessarily involve attempts at direct rule, annexation, or conquest of their opponents—as noted before, most empire historically has not meant that— but simply an effort to secure final, undisputed authority for themselves over subjects and areas that those who felt targeted by these bids for empire regarded as critical for their independence and rights within the system. Whatever the reasons and motives behind these bids for empire, ranging from impulse to perceived unavoidable necessity, they not only ultimately failed but also wrecked whatever chances the empire-seekers had to enjoy a durable hegemony and promoted instability and war instead. Here is a list of some major instances in history where (as I see it) leaders who were hege-mons within a community of states or units and were arguably in a position to preserve and exercise hegemony for some time instead made bids for empire, with the results just described:

Charles V, Holy Roman Emperor, versus the German Lutheran princes in 1521–52[9]
Philip II of Spain and the magnates of the Netherlands in the 1560s[10]
Ferdinand II as Holy Roman Emperor and the German estates in the Thirty Years War, 1618–35[11]
Louis XIV of France in his (perceived and so-called) bid for "universal monarchy" from 1665 on[12]
Charles XII of Sweden in the Baltic after 1702[13]

Some obvious and conscious choices of empire over hegemony in more modern times hardly need mention, much less demonstration:

Napoleon in Europe on many occasions between 1801 and 1814
Hitler in Europe in 1938–39
Stalin in Eastern Europe at the end of World War II

One can find almost as many important instances in history where the fact that a particular leader or government pursued hegemony rather than empire (even if it was a choice forced on them by necessity or seemed the only rational one available) nonetheless enabled them to stabilize their positions and promote peace. Examples:

Charles V's successors as Holy Roman Emperor, especially Ferdinand I and Matthias[14]
Richelieu and Mazarin in France from 1624 to 1660[15]
Leopold I as Holy Roman Emperor 1658–1705[16]
Britain and France after the Peace of Utrecht in 1713[17]
Cardinal Fleury of France in the 1730s[18]
The victorious powers in the Napoleonic wars, who chose to settle for various kinds of hegemony rather than empire in the Vienna Settlement of 1814–15[19]
Bismarck and Germany's labile half-hegemony in Europe, 1871–90

Finally, the most obvious and impressive example is also the most recent: the American option for hegemony in Europe and the West during the Cold War, in contrast to the Soviet choice of empire in its sphere.

One might add to this major cases in history where an absence of hege-mony, that is, the refusal or inability of potential hegemons to exercise lead-ership and fulfill the needed hegemonic managerial functions, promoted systemic breakdown, disorder, and war. Two examples that seem undeniable to me (omitting others more debatable) are the era following the Seven Years War (1756–63) in which Britain's withdrawal from most European affairs and Russia's ruthless exploitation of its favored position in the east for imperialist expansion promoted wars, international crimes (the partitions of Poland), and revolutionary instability;[20] and still more obvious, the interwar era of 1919–33, when the victors in World War I, the United States, Britain, and France, either refused to fill the hegemonic roles required for general security at all, or in trying to do so contradicted and frustrated each other's efforts. The same picture holds for Britain and the United States in the economic arena.[21]

Obviously many of these individual historical instances are debatable, but the overall pattern can hardly be disputed or ignored. Its meaning and significance represent one of those truths that seem blindingly obvious, yet are often ignored, forgotten, never learned, or deliberately obscured and denied by persons with axes to grind and agendas to pursue. Empire can work outside a modern international system, even alongside it, but within a genuine international system it is incompatible with it and destructive of it, and along with creating great disorder, instability, and conflict ruins possibilities for useful hegemony within the system.

How relevant is this to the current world situation and American foreign policy? Besides replying to historical arguments like this one along the lines indicated earlier—"The world is new and different since 9/11; you talk of Old Europe and a bygone past in a world of new dangers from terrorists, rogue states, fanatical ideologies, and weapons of unbelievable destructive power, demanding new responses from a new America with unprecedented power"—some advocates of the present American policy (not all—a good many of its proponents are admirably frank in stating their imperialist aims) flatly deny that the current American course constitutes a bid for empire. A war on Iraq, they say, would be a justified war of liberation, fought to rescue Iraq from tyranny, defend the United States and other countries from international terrorism, eliminate a grave threat to the region, promote liberty, democracy, and a market economy, transform the Middle East, and promote other noble purposes. President Bush, Secretary of State Colin Powell, and others have repeatedly declared that the world knows that Americans do not fight to conquer, but to liberate. Leaving aside this historically challengeable statement, one must point out that the character of policies and wars is not determined by the declared motives of those who launch them and whether their declarations are sincere or not, but by what the actions taken in launching a policy and waging a war concretely represent within the system of international politics, and by what their immediate and longer-range impacts and results turn out to be. By that standard, when one country deliberately chooses to go to war with another for the purpose of invading and conquering it, overthrowing and replacing its government, and occupying it for an indefinite period in order to determine what sort of government, social system, and economic system that conquered country will have, who will govern it, who will control its natural resources, and what position in whose camp that government will take in the future on the vital regional and international questions confronting it, and when that invading country further insists in the international arena on acknowledged, unchallenged leadership and control in this process, that is a war for empire—informal empire, but empire nonetheless—no matter how one tries to dress it up with euphemisms and slogans.

But the ultimate critical question is not how to label this policy, or even whether if it must be considered a bid for empire it therefore stands automatically condemned or could still be defended on political and moral grounds. The final question is whether such a policy is suited to today's world, and whether it is now succeeding or will eventually do so if given a chance. Putting the question on this basis is more than fair to its defenders. This is the claim they make themselves for this policy against its critics, that it alone can provide peace and security for the United States and other decent members of the international community against undeterrable terrorists and rogue states.

A further concession: for this reason, arguments that contemporary evidence indicates that this bid for empire might already be breaking down in the international arena, regardless of the results of the coming military campaign, are worth noting but cannot be decisive. Those indications, to be sure, are significant: the huge expenditure in political, moral, and diplomatic capital required for the American effort to obtain the consent and support of the world community for a war with one small, weak, miserable, totally isolated state ruled by a universally despised and hated tyrant—an effort that nonetheless ended in unmistakable failure; the resulting sharp decline in world popularity and prestige for both the United States in general and the Bush administration in particular; the exiguous nature of the so-called coalition of the willing, one-third of whom are unwilling even to let their names be known, and many of the rest willing only to cheer softly from the sidelines; and the fact that other incipient crises and threats had to be put aside in order to meet this putative one. These must be seen as signs of danger and portents of failure, but not as clear proof that the policy is bound to fail.

Let me therefore argue as a historian rather than a current analyst or prophet, reversing the question from, "Does history show that this policy is bound to fail?" to the converse, "Does history shed any light on how it could conceivably succeed?" That is, could history indicate the conditions under which the United States might be able to conquer Iraq, set up a government it approves, restore order, and then leave the country to be governed by local administrators, keeping perhaps only a token military presence to ensure that the new government would not fall into dangerous hands and that American strategic interests in the region were protected? On the international front, could historical experience suggest circumstances under which the United States might persuade or compel the rest of the international community to accept this situation as permanent, come to terms with it, and even help America maintain its exclusive dominant position? Can history further indicate under what conditions the change in Iraq might help change the whole region in a way favorable to American interests? Are there historical instances in which the sort of project the United States is now undertaking in Iraq has enjoyed durable success?

Certainly there are. The best example among several possible is that offered by the British in Egypt in the late-nineteenth and twentieth centuries. The basic story, greatly oversimplified, can be sketched briefly. British military intervention in Egypt in 1882 came about in a far more hesitant, bumbling fashion, with much less deliberate intent at conquest, than the United States has shown with regard to Iraq. But when the Gladstone government finally decided to go in, they also like the Bush administration discovered a good moral reason for doing so, the need to liberate Egypt from the menace of a tyrant and terrorist, Colonel Urabi, blamed (falsely) for committing atrocities against Europeans and his own people. Though many in the British government understood that the critical issues were strategic (control of the Suez Canal and the routes to India and the maintenance of British prestige), Gladstone's long-standing slogan of "Egypt for the Egyptians" remained the official goal and justification for the venture. Military victory proved swift and easy, and superficial order was restored in Egypt relatively readily with the aid of a subservient head of state and an existing professional and commercial class willing to serve their new masters. The authorities through whom Britain then was able to govern by influence and advice proved dependent and compliant, the masses turned out to be inert rather than nationalist as feared, and the financial burdens of the British occupation and of protecting the British and European financial interests and the British imperial and strategic interests at stake could be imposed on a wretched but powerless Egyptian peasantry.

The internal problems of the takeover in Egypt were thus fairly easily managed. The international complications proved more difficult, but ultimately by showing enough resolve the British triumphed all along the line—first ignoring French pressure to restore Dual Control in Egypt, then ignoring and violating their own repeated promises to evacuate Egypt, next using Egypt to conquer the Sudan in 1898, facing the French down in a subsequent confrontation at Fashoda, and then making a deal in 1904 with France over Morocco enabling Britain to shake off the restrictions of the European bondholders and the Treasury of the Ottoman Debt in Egypt. Despite early signs of Egyptian restiveness in 1907, by 1914 Britain was not merely fully in charge of Egypt at very little or no cost to itself, but had brought most of East Africa under British control from Egypt outward—and made friends with France against Germany in the process. The fact that these great successes, achieved without provoking an international conflict, depended on a favorable international situation and system—in the 1880s, because Bismarck would not allow a European war to develop over this or other colonial questions, and after 1890 because the continental great powers became locked in a great competition for world power and continental security that Britain could exploit for its imperial purposes—meant nothing to the British. They ascribed their success to their unmatched power and wealth, their special virtue, and their indispensable role as leaders of the international system. Britain's imperial success in Egypt lasted into World War I and beyond, helping promote a great expansion of the British Empire in the Middle East in 1919–20.

The historical recipe therefore for a durable, successful American informal empire in Iraq and the Middle East is simple: restore the general conditions prevailing in the late-nineteenth and early-twentieth centuries. That is, eliminate Iraqi and Arab nationalism, or at least reduce it to an inchoate protonationalism; eliminate militant radical Islamist movements and regimes (which then existed only in the Sudan, where the British destroyed it in 1898); eliminate Iraq and the other states in the Middle East (with the exception of Israel) as independent states and members of an organized international system, returning them to the status of loosely-governed territories of decaying regimes (the Ottoman Empire and Persia), easy prey for Western imperialism; eliminate the UN, NATO, and all the other international and transnational institutions and organizations that now interfere with empire-building; eliminate radio, TV, the Internet, and other means of mass communications; reverse the globalization of industry, commerce, science and technology, and culture in the twentieth century; and restore the general international competition in alliances, arms, and imperialism of the late-nineteenth century— do these things, and the venture will probably succeed.

What this tells us about current American policy is that those who argue that our imperial strategy toward Iraq and the Middle East will succeed, despite historical arguments against the possibility of durable empire in today's world within the existing international system, on the grounds that all the historical evidence is essentially irrelevant because the world has changed since 1900 and especially since 9/11, and because the United States has such unprecedented power that it can do almost anything if it sets its mind to it, are themselves doing what they accuse critics like me of doing: living in the past. In concentrating on allegedly new threats and dangers (which are not really new) and boasting of America's new, unprecedented power and global reach, they ignore all the other old, standard dangers and threats that this policy will create and exacerbate and all the limits on American power and constraints on its employment and usefulness that the real new world of the late-twentieth and early-twenty-first centuries has actually promoted.

What they are now attempting therefore is not a bold, untried American experiment in creating a brave new world, but a revival of a type of nineteenth- and early-twentieth century imperialism that could succeed for a time then (with ultimately devastating consequences) only because of conditions long since vanished and now impossible even to imagine reproducing. Launched now, this venture will fail and is already failing. Its advocates illustrate the dictum that those unwilling to learn from history are doomed to repeat it. The sane course therefore for patriotic Americans and for friends and allies of the United States abroad is to work for its abandonment as quickly and with as little damage as possible, so that the United States might return to its previous position of benign or at least tolerable hegemony before it is too late.

PUBLICATIONS OF PAUL W. SCHROEDER

BOOKS

The Axis Alliance and Japanese-American Relations, 1941 (Ithaca, NY: Cornell University Press, 1958).

Metternich's Diplomacy at Its Zenith, 1820–1823 (Austin, TX.: University of Texas Press, 1962). Paperback reprint by University of Texas Press, 1976.

Austria, Great Britain, and the Crimean War: The Destruction of the European Concert (Ithaca, NY.: Cornell University Press, 1972).

The Transformation of European Politics, 1763–1848 (Oxford: Clarendon Press, 1994, 1996).

EDITED BOOK

Peter Krüger and Paul W. Schroeder, eds., *"The Transformation of European Politics, 1763–1848": Episode or Model in Modern History?* (Münster, Hamburg, London: LIT Verlag, 2002).

ARTICLES

"Metternich Studies since 1925," *Journal of Modern History*, 33 (September 1961), 237–66.

"Austrian Policy at the Congresses of Troppau and Laibach," *Journal of Central European Affairs*, 22, 2 (July 1962), 139–52.

"Austria as an Obstacle to Italian Unification and Freedom, 1814–1861," *Austrian History Newsletter* (1962), 1–32.

"American Books on Austria-Hungary," *Austrian History Yearbook*, 2 (1966), 1972–196.

"The Status of Habsburg Studies in the United States," *Austrian History Yearbook*, 3, pt. 3 (1967), 267–95.

"Bruck versus Buol: The Dispute over Austrian Eastern Policy, 1853–1855," *Journal of Modern History*, 40, 2 (June 1968), 193–217.

"Austria and the Danubian Principalities, 1853–1856," *Central European History*, 2, 3 (September 1969), 216–36.

"A Turning Point in Austrian Policy in the Crimean War: The Conferences of March, 1954," *Austrian History Yearbook*, 4–5 (1968–69), 159–202.

"World War I as Galloping Gertie: A Reply to Joachim Remak," *Journal of Modern History*, 44, no. 2 (September 1972), 319–44.

"The 'Balance of Power' System in Europe, 1815–1871," *Naval War College Review* (March–April 1975), 18–31.

"Rumania and the Great Powers before 1914," *Revue Roumaine d'Histoire*, 14, 1 (1975), 39–53.

"Munich and the British Tradition," *The Historical Journal*, 19, 1 (1976), 223–43.

"Alliances, 1815–1945: Weapons of Power and Tools of Management," in *Historical Problems of National Security*, ed. Klaus Knorr (Lawrence, KS.: University of Kansas Press, 1976), 247–86.

"Quantitative Studies in the Balance of Power: An Historian's Reaction," and "A Final Rejoinder," *Journal of Conflict Resolution*, 21, no. 1 (March 1977), 3–22, 57–74.

"Austro-German Relations: Divergent Views of the Disjoined Partnership," *Central European History*, 11, 3 (September 1978), 302–12.

"Gladstone as Bismarck," *Canadian Journal of History*, 15 (August 1980), 163–95.

"Containment Nineteenth Century Style: How Russia was Restrained," *South Atlantic Quarterly*, 82 (1983), 1–18.

"The Lost Intermediaries: The Impact of 1870 on the European System," *International History Review*, 6 (February 1984), 1–27.

"Österreich und die orientalische Frage, 1848–1883," in *Das Zeitalter Kaiser Franz Josephs von der Revolution zur Gruenderzeit* (Vienna, 1984), vol. 1, 324–28.

"Does Murphy's Law Apply to History?," *The Wilson Quarterly* (New Year, 1985), 84–93.

"The European International System, 1789–1848: Is There a Problem? An Answer?," Colloquium paper presented March 19, 1984 at the Woodrow Wilson International Center for Scholars, Smithsonian Institution, Washington, DC.

"The European International System, 1789–1848: Is There a Question? An Answer?," *Proceedings of the Consortium on Revolutionary Europe* (1985), 1–29.

"The 19th-Century International System: Changes in the Structure," *World Politics*, 39, 1 (October 1986), 1–26.

"Old Wine in Old Bottles: Recent Contributions to British Foreign Policy and European International Politics, 1789–1848," *Journal of British Studies*, 26, 1 (January 1987), 1–25.

"Once More, the German Question," *International History Review*, 9, 1 (February 1987), 96–107.

"The Collapse of the Second Coalition," *Journal of Modern History*, 59, 2 (June 1987), 244–90.

"An Unnatural 'Natural Alliance': Castlereagh, Metternich, and Aberdeen in 1813," *International History Review*, 10, no. 4 (November 1988), 522–40.

"The Nineteenth Century System: Balance of Power or Political Equilibrium?," *Review of International Studies* (Oxford), 15 (April 1989), 135–53.

"Failed Bargain Crises, Deterrence, and the International System," in *Perspectives on Deterrence*, ed. Paul C. Stern et al. (New York, 1989), 67–83.

"Germany and the Balance of Power: Past and Present Part I", in *Gleichgewicht in Geschichte und Gegenwart*, ed. Wolf Gruner (Hamburg, 1989), 134–39.

"Die Habsburger Monarchie und das europäische System im 19t. Jahrhundert," in *Die Herausforderung des europäischen Staatensystems*, ed. A. M. Birke and G. Heydemann (Göttingen: Vandenhoeck und Ruprecht, 1989), 178–82.

"Europe and the German Confederation in the 1860's," in *Deutscher Bund und Deutsche Frage 1815–1866*, ed. Helmut Rumpler (Vienna, 1990), 281–91.

"The Years 1848 and 1989: The Perils and Profits of Historical Comparisons," in *The Helsinki Process and the Future of Europe*, ed. Samuel F. Wells (Washington, DC, 1990), 15–21.

"Review Article. Napoleon Bonaparte," *International History Review*, 12 (May 1990), 324–29.

"Napoleon's Foreign Policy: A Criminal Enterprise," *Journal of Military History*, 54, no. 2 (April 1990), 147–61.

"Die Rolle der Vereinigten Staaten bei der Entfesselung des Zweiten Weltkrieges," in *1939: An der Schwelle zum Weltkrieg*, ed. Klaus Hildebrand et al. (Berlin: de Gruyter, 1990), 215–19.

"A Just, Unnecessary War: The Flawed American Strategy in the Persian Gulf," ACDIS Occasional Paper, March 1991.

"The Neo-Realist Theory of International Politics: A Historian's View," ACDIS Occasional Paper, April 1991.

"Did the Vienna Settlement Rest on a Balance of Power?," *American Historical Review*, 97, 2 (June 1992), 683–706, 733–35.

"The Transformation of Political Thinking, 1787–1848," in *Coping with Complexity in the International System*, ed. Jack Snyder and Robert Jervis (Boulder, CO.: Westview Press, 1993), 47–70.

" 'System' and Systemic Thinking in International History," *Journal of International History Review*, 15, 1 (February 1993), 116–34.

"Economic Integration and the European International System in the Era of World War I," *American Historical Review*, 94, 4 (October 1993), 1130–37.

"Historical Reality vs Neo-Realist Theory," *International Security*, 19, 2 (Summer 1994), 108–48.

"Britain, Russia, and the German Question, 1815–1848: Emerging Rivalry or Benign Neglect?," in *Germany and Russia in British Policy towards Europe since 1815*, ed. Adolf M. Birke and Hermann Wentker (Munich: K. G. Saur, 1994), 15–30.

"Balance of Power and Political Equilibrium: A Response," *International History Review*, 16, 4 (1994), 745–54 (the concluding essay in a number of the journal devoted to essays on "Paul W. Schroeder's International System").

"The New World Order: A Historical Perspective," *The Washington Quarterly*, 17, 2 (1994), 25–43. (Reprinted in Brad Roberts, ed., *Order and Disorder after the Cold War* [Cambridge, MA., 1995], pp. 367–86.)

"The Missing Dimension in the Manichaean Trap: A Comment," in *The Manichaean Trap. American Perceptions of the German Empire, 1871–1945*, ed. Detlef Junker (Washington, DC: German Historical Institute Occasional Paper No. 12, 1995), 37–47.

"The Historical Record on Peacekeeping: Grounds for Hope or Pessimism?" in *Regional Conflicts and Conflict Resolution*, ed. Roger E. Kanet (Urbana, IL: ACDIS, 1995), 149–66. (Also published in Roger E. Kanet, ed., *Resolving Regional Conflicts* [Urbana, IL., 1998], pp. 135–52.)

"Review Article: Can Diplomatic History Guide Foreign Policy?," in *International History Review*, 28, 2 (May 1996), 358–70.

"Austria and Prussia, 1813–1848: Pause in the Rivalry or Shift in the Paradigm?," in *Reich Oder Nation? Mitteleuropa 1780–1815*, ed. Heinz Duchhardt and Andreas Kunz (Mainz, 1996), 87–104.

"The Vienna System and Its Stability: The Problem of Stabilizing a State System In Transformation," in *Das Europäische Staatensystem Im Wandel*, ed. Peter Krüger (Munich, 1996), 107–22.

"History and International Relations Theory: Not Use or Abuse, but Fit or Misfit," *International Security*, 22, 1 (Summer 1997), 64–74.

"Making a Necessity of Virtue: The Smaller State as Intermediary Body," *Austrian History Yearbook*, 29, pt. 1 (1998), 1–18.

"Work with Emerging Forces in the International System," in *Just Peacemaking: Ten Practices for Abolishing War*, ed. Glen Stassen (Cleveland, OH., 1998), 133–45.

"A Pointless Enduring Rivalry: France and the Habsburg Monarchy, 1715–1918," in *Great Power Rivalries*, ed. William R. Thompson (Columbia, 1999), 60–85.

"International Politics, Peace, and War, 1815–1914," in *The Short Oxford History of Europe: The Nineteenth Century*, ed. T. C. W. Blanning (Oxford, 2000), 158–209.

"The Cold War and Its Ending in 'Long-Duration' International History," in *Peace, Prosperity and Politics*, ed. John Mueller (Boulder, CO., 2001), 257–82.

"A. J. P. Taylor's International System," *International History Review*, 28, 1 (March 2001), 3–27.

"The Luck of the House of Habsburg: Military Defeat and Political Survival," *Austrian History Yearbook*, 32 (2001), 215–24.

"Explaining Peace More than War," in *Nation und Europa. Studien zum Internationalen Staatensystem Im 19. und 20. Jahrhundert*, ed. Gabriele Clemens (Stuttgart, 2001), 271–84.

"The Risks of Victory: An Historian's Provocation," *The National Interest* (Winter 2001/02), 22–36.

"International History: Why Historians Do It Differently than Political Scientists," in *Bridges and Boundaries: Historians, Political Scientists, and the Study of International Relations*, ed. Colin Elman and Miriam Fendius Elman (Cambridge, MA., 2001), 403–16.

"Epilogue: Transformation or Evolution—Linear or Catastrophic?," in *"The Transformation of European Politics, 1763–1848": Episode or Model In Modern History?*, ed. Peter Krüger and Paul W. Schroeder (Münster, 2002), 323–32.

"Iraq: The Case Against Preemptive War," *The American Conservative* (October 2002), 8–20.

"A Papier-Maché Fortress," *The National Interest* (Winter 2002/03), 125–32. (This review of Philip Bobbitt's book *The Shield of Achilles* [New York: Knopf, 2002] was reprinted in French translation in *Commentaire* 26, no. 102 [Summer, 2003], 465–72.)

"Why Realism Does Not Work Well for International History (Whether or Not It Represents a Degenerate IR Research Strategy)," in *Realism and the Balancing of Power. A New Debate*, ed. John A. Vasquez and Colin Elman (Upper Saddle River, NJ, 2003), 114–27.

NOTES

INTRODUCTION

1. *The Axis Alliance and Japanese-American Relations 1941* (Ithaca, NY., 1958); *Metternich's Diplomacy at Its Zenith 1820–1823* (Austin, TX., 1962); *Austria, Great Britain, and the Crimean War: The Destruction of the European Concert* (Ithaca, NY., 1972); *The Transformation of European Politics 1763–1848* (Oxford, 1994).

2. For a discussion of how diplomatic historians and international relations theorists take different approaches in studying essentially the same phenomena, see Colin Elman and Miriam Fendius Elman, eds., *Bridges and Boundaries: Historians, Political Scientists, and the Study of International Relations* (Cambridge, 2001). Schroeder's contribution to this dialogue, pp. 403–16 in Elman and Elman, is reprinted in chapter 13 of this volume.

3. Martin Wight, *Power Politics*, ed. Hedley Bull and Carston Holbrand (London, 1978), 95.

4. Robert Aspery, *The Reign of Napoleon Bonaparte* (New York, 2001).

5. Quoted in James J. Sheehan, *German History 1770–1866* (Oxford, 1990), 395.

6. For an argument that Schroeder exaggerates the competitiveness of eighteenth century European politics and underestimates the restraining effects of the balance of power, see Charles Ingrao, "Paul W. Schroeder's Balance of Power: Stability or Anarchy," *International History Review*, 16, 4 (November 1994), 681–700.

7. T. C. W. Blanning, *The Origins of the French Revolutionary Wars* (London, 1986), 36–38.

8. A. J. P. Taylor, *The Struggle for Mastery in Europe* (Oxford, 1954), xix.

9. For a balance of power perspective that emphasizes the integral role of flanking powers, see Ludwig Dehio, *The Precarious Balance: Four Centuries of the European Power Struggle* (New York, 1962). For an argument that the dominance of Britain is in no way incompatible with a European balance of power system, see Jack S. Levy, "Balances and Balancing: Concepts, Propositions, and Research Design," in John A. Vasquez and Colin Elman, eds., *Realism and the Balancing of Power: A New Debate* (Englewood Cliffs, NJ., 2002), 128–53.

10. Alexander Hase, "Friedrich (v.) Gentz: Vom Übertritt nach Wien bis zu den 'Fragmenten des Gleichgewichts' (1802–1806)," *Historische Zeitschrift*, 211 (1970), 589–95.

11. Charles Kinglsey Webster, *The Foreign Policy of Castlereagh* (London, 1925); Heinrich von Srbik, *Metternich: der Staatsman und der Mensch*, 3 vols. (Graz, 1925–54). The last volume was largely a critique of the works that had appeared since 1925.

12. Henry A. Kissinger, *A World Restored: Metternich, Castlereagh, and the Problems of Peace 1812–1822* (Boston, 1957).

13. See also Paul W. Schroeder, "Balance of Power and Political Equilibrium," which responds to several assessments of his views of European history in a special issue of *International History Review*, 16, 4 (November 1994), 745–54.

14. Schroeder, "The Nineteenth Century System: Balance of Power or Political Equilibrium?" *Review of International Studies*, 15 (April 1989), 143. The transformation of political thinking included new conceptions of state interests and the informal norms and rules of the Concert system. Other components of the stability of the nineteenth century system, as Schroeder sees it, include the shared hegemony of Britain and Russia and the system of great power management based on restraining alliances. See Jack S. Levy, "The Theoretical Foundations of Paul W. Schroeder's International System," *International History Review*, 16, 4 (November 1994), 715–44.

15. George F. Kennan, *Realities of American Foreign Policy* (New York, 1954), 56.

16. In addition to the essays here, see "The Transformation of Political Thinking, 1787–1848," in Jack Snyder and Robert Jervis, eds., *Coping With Complexity in the International System* (Boulder, CO., 1993), 47–70; " 'System' and Systemic Thinking in International History," *International History Review*, 15 (February 1993), 116–34.

17. The defection of Rumania from the Triple Alliance to the Triple Entente in 1914, little noticed by historians (or by Great Britain at the time) greatly increased Austria-Hungary's vulnerability. See Schroeder's important but little-known essay, "Rumania and the Great Powers Before 1914," *Revue Roumaine d'Histoire*, 14, 1 (1975), 39–53.

18. Though the misguided application to Nazi Germany has discredited the term, appeasement often is appropriate, as Schroeder shows in "Munich and the British Tradition," *The Historical Journal*, 19 (March 1976), 223–43; also see Paul Kennedy, "The Tradition of Appeasement in British Foreign Policy, 1865–1939," in Kennedy, *Strategy and Diplomacy, 1870–1945* (London, 1983), chap. 1.

19. For a theoretical analysis of how political leaders learn from experience in international politics, see Robert Jervis, *Perception and Misperception in International Politics* (Princeton, 1976), chap. 6.

20. M. S. Anderson, *The Eastern Question* (London, 1966).

21. Paul W. Schroeder "Bruck vs. Buol," 19. See also David Wetzel, *The Crimean War: A Diplomatic History* (Boulder, CO., 1985), 82–85.

22. Norman Rich, *Why the Crimean War? A Cautionary Tale* (Hanover, NH, 1985), 206–07.

23. Paul W. Schroeder, "Europe and the German Confederation in the 1870s," in *Deutscher Bund und deutsche Frage 1815–16*, ed. Helmut Rumpler (Vienna, 1990), 291.

24. Paul W. Schroeder, "Lost Intermediaries," 6.

25. Ibid., 2.

26. Lothar Gall, "Bismarcks Süddeutsche Politik," in *Europa vor dem Krieg von 1870*, ed. Eberhard Kolb (Munich, 1987), 26–28.

27. This is (alas) true even of David Wetzel, *A Duel of Giants: Bismarck, Napoleon III and the Outbreak of the Franco-Prussian War* (Madison, WI, 2001).

28. Quoted in A. J. P. Taylor, *Bismarck: The Man and the Statesman* (New York, 1955), 135.

29. A good example of such an interpretation is Paul Knaplund, *Gladstone's Foreign Policy* (New York, 1935).

30. Paul Kennedy, *The Rise and Fall of the Great Powers, 1500–2000* (New York, 1988) 219, 571, n. 82.
31. Schroeder is reacting in particular to Lebow's argument that World War I was contingent upon the assassination of the Austrian archduke. Richard Ned Lebow, "Contingency, Catalysts, and International System Change," *Political Science Quarterly*, 115, 4 (Winter 2000–01), 591–616. For an argument that the German-backed Austro-Hungarian initiative was a necessary condition for war but that international structures and domestic pressures left political leaders very few choices and very little room to maneuver in 1914, see Jack S. Levy, "Preferences, Constraints, and Choices in July 1914," *International Security*, 15, 3 (Winter 1990–91), 151–86.
32. "Does the History of International Politics Go Anywhere," 22.
33. See David Wetzel and Diethelm Prowe, "Introduction," *International Politics and German History*, ed. David Wetzel and Theodore S. Hamerow (Westport, CT., 1997), 3–4.
34. Lynn Hunt, *Politics, Culture, and Class in the French Revolution* (Berkeley, 1984).
35. Harold Nicolson, *The Congress of Vienna: A Study in Allied Unity 1812–22* (London, 1945).
36. One of many important distinctions between Schroeder and the *Annales* school is that the former but not the latter emphasizes the primacy of politics.
37. Paul W. Schroeder, "History of International Politics," 27.
38. M. S. Anderson, *The Rise of Modern Diplomacy* (London, 1993).
39. Wetzel and Prowe, "Introduction," 5.
40. Robert Jervis, "Explaining the Bush Doctrine: Fear, Opportunity, and Expansion," *Political Science Quarterly*, 118 (Fall 2003).

CHAPTER 1   NAPOLEON'S FOREIGN POLICY: A CRIMINAL ENTERPRISE

The original version of this essay originated as comments on the preceding paper by Harold T. Parker presented in a session of the Bicentennial of the Consortium on Revolutionary Europe, September 28–30, 1989, and that version appeared in the Bicentennial Proceedings published by the Florida State University Press (1990).

1. Harold T. Parker, "Why Did Napoleon Invade Russia? A Study in Motivation and the Interrelations of Personality and Social Structure," *Journal of Military History*, 52, 2 (April 1990), 131–46.
2. Ernest L. Presseisen, *Amiens and Munich* (The Hague, 1978).
3. This is very apparent from Napoleon's published correspondence, but for more evidence of the deterioration, see E. A. Whitcomb, *Napoleon's Diplomatic Service* (Durham, NC., 1979).

CHAPTER 2   DID THE VIENNA SETTLEMENT REST ON A BALANCE OF POWER?

1. The standard work is still Karl Griewank, *Der Wiener Kongress und die europäische Restauration, 1814–1815*, 2nd edn. (Leipzig, 1954). Other important treatments include C. K. Webster, *The Foreign Policy of Castlereagh, 1812–1815* (London, 1931); E. V. Gulick, *Europe's Classical Balance of Power* (Ithaca, NY., 1955); H. A. Kissinger, *A World Restored* (Boston, 1957); Maurice Bourquin,

Histoire de la Sainte-Alliance (Geneva, 1954); and Enno E. Kraehe, *Metternich's German Policy*, Vol. 2, *The Congress of Vienna 1814–1815* (Princeton, NJ., 1983). See also Alan Sked, ed., *Europe's Balance of Power 1815–1848* (London, 1979), especially the essays by Douglas Dakin and F. Roy Bridge.

2. The main published documentary sources are Leonard J. B. Chodzko (pseudonym Comte d'Angeberg), ed., *Le Congrès de Vienne et les traités de 1815*, 4 vols. (Paris, 1863); Russia, Ministry of Foreign Affairs, *Vneshniaia politika Rossii xix i nachala xx veka: Dokumenty rossiiskogo Ministerstva inostrannykh del*, ser. 1: 1801–15, vol. 8 (Moscow, 1967); A. A. Polovtsov, ed., *Correspondance diplomatique des ambassadeurs et ministres de Russie en France et de France en Russie avec leuer gouvernements de 1814 à 1830*, vol. 1 (St. Petersburg, 1902); Klemens Lothar Wenzel Fürst von Metternich-Winneburg, *Aus Metternichs nachgelassenen Papieren*, Prince Richard Metternich, ed., 8 vols. (Vienna, 1880–84); Robert Stewart, 2nd Marquess of Londonderry, *Memoirs and Correspondence of Viscount Castlereagh*, Charles Vane Marquess of Londonderry, ed., 12 vols. (London, 1850–53); Charles Maurice de Talleyrand-Périgord, *Correspondance diplomatique*, 3 vols. (Paris, 1889–91); Talleyrand, *Mémoires du Prince de Talleyrand*, the Duc de Broglie, ed., 5 vols. (Paris, 1891–92); Arthur Wellesley, 1st Duke of Wellington, *Supplementary Despatches, Correspondence, and Memoranda*, 15 vols. (London, 1862–80); Karl Robert Count Nesselrode, *Lettres et papiers du Chancelier Comte de Nesselrode, 1760–1850*, Count A. de Nesselrode, ed., 11 vols. (Paris, 1904–12); Wilhelm Oncken, *Österreich und Preussen im Befreiungskriege*, 2 vols. (Berlin, 1876); and C. K. Webster, ed., *British Diplomacy, 1813–1815* (London, 1921).

3. This approach is quite common. Both Gulick's and Kissinger's works employ it, as does F. H. Hinsley, *Power and the Pursuit of Peace* (Cambridge, 1963); and Hedley Bull, *The Anarchical Society* (New York, 1977). Richard Little, "Deconstructing the Balance of Power: Two Traditions of Thought," *Review of International Studies*, 15 (1989), 87–100, contends that the concept of balance of power contains both an adversarial and an associative tradition, the 1815 settlement exemplifying the latter.

4. E. B. Haas, "The Balance of Power: Prescription, Concept, or Propaganda," *World Politics*, 5 (1953), 442–77; P. W. Schroeder, "The Nineteenth Century System: Balance of Power or Political Equilibrium?" *Review of International Studies*, 15 (1989), 136–37.

5. Morton Kaplan's attempt to define the working rules of a balance of power system in his *System and Process in International Politics* (New York, 1957) has been much discussed; see my "Nineteenth Century System," n. 4–5, as well as the entire April 1989 issue *of Review of International Studies*, 15; also Bull, *Anarchical Society*, chap. 6; and Barry Buzan, *People, States and Fear* (Brighton, Sussex, 1983), esp. 101–03.

6. Robert Jervis, "From Balance to Concert: A Study of International Security Cooperation," in Kenneth A. Oye, ed., *Cooperation under Anarchy* (Princeton, NJ., 1986), 60–61.

7. In addition to the works cited above in n. 1, see J.-H. Pirenne, *La Sainte-Alliance, organisation européenne de la paix mondiale: Les traités de paix 1814–1815*, 2 vols. (Neuchâtel, 1946–49).

8. In addition to Pirenne, *La Sainte-Alliance*, some major works on this period, all fitting the balance of power paradigm in different ways, are G. de Bertier de Sauvigny, *Metternich et la France après le Congrès de Vienne*, 3 vols. (Paris, 1968–71), and his

Metternich (Paris, 1986); C. K. Webster, *The Foreign Policy of Castlreagh, 1815–1822* (London, 1934), and his *Foreign Policy of Palmerston 1830–1841*, 2 vols. (London, 1951); Kenneth Bourne, *Palmerston: The Early Years 1784–1841* (New York, 1982); Roger Bullen, *Palmerston, Guizot and the Collapse of the Entente Cordiale* (London, 1974); and H. W. V. Temperley, *The Foreign Policy of Canning, 1822–1827* (London, 1925).

9. For a general discussion, see Buzan, *People, States and Fear*; for detailed analysis, Glenn H. Snyder and Paul Diesing, *Conflict among Nations* (Princeton, NJ., 1977).

10. Frank A. J. Szabo, "Prince Kaunitz and the Balance of Power," *International History Review*, 1 (1979), 399–408.

11. Wolfgang Stribrny, *Die Russland-Politik Friedrichs des Grossen 1764–1786* (Würzburg, 1966); Johannes Kunisch, *Das Mirakel des Hauses Brandenburg* (Berlin, 1978); Klaus Zernack, "Preussen—Frankreich—Polen: Revolution und Teilung," in Otto Büsch and Monika Neugebauer-Wölk, eds., *Preussen und die revolutionäre Herausforderung sei 1789* (Berlin, 1991).

12. Various efforts to measure power and power relationships quantitatively undertaken by political scientists, including such distinguished scholars as Robert North, Richard Rosecrance, A. F. K. Organski, J. David Singer and Melvin Small, and others, have encountered grave conceptual and methodological problems— e.g., how to quantify and weigh the impact of such factors as industry, natural resources, level of education, technological advancement, and national unity and morale on state power. William B. Moul, "Measuring the 'Balances of Power': A Look at Some Numbers," *Review of International Studies*, 15 (1989), 101–21, is both aware of the problems (Moul remarks, for example [p. 113], that "weighting each component equally is a *studied* confession of ignorance of the proper mixtures for each great power over a long period of time") and convincing as a rough approximation of capability ratios. What he shows is that two of the five great powers after 1815, Britain and Russia, always enjoyed a clear majority of the total capability (ranging from 55% to 70%) between 1815 and 1848. Even his study, moreover, cannot factor in their most decisive advantage, geographic invulnerability.

13. Edward Ingram, *The Beginning of the Great Game in Asia, 1828–1834* (London, 1979).

14. Irmline Veit-Brause, *Die deutsch-französische Krise von 1840* (Cologne, 1967).

15. Isabel de Madariaga, *Russia in the Reign of Catherine the Great* (New Haven, CT., 1982); Dietrich Gerhard, *England und der Aufstieg Russlands* (Munich, 1933).

16. See, for example, Carsten Holbraad, *The Concert of Europe: A Study in German and British International Theory 1815–1914* (London, 1970); Richard B. Elrod, "The Concert of Europe: A Fresh Look at an International System," *World Politics*, 28 (1976), 159–74.

17. Austria's relative weakness and overcommitment are often emphasized as strains on the 1815 system, e.g., by F. Roy Bridge and Roger Bullen, *The Great Powers and the European States System 1815–1914* (London, 1980), chap. 2.

18. John H. Herz, *International Politics in the Atomic Age* (New York, 1959); Robert Jervis, *Perception and Misperception in International Politics* (Princeton, NJ., 1976), chap. 3.

19. For the gradual revival of French interest in colonies, though without any desire to compete seriously with Britain, see Dieter Braunstein, *Französische Kolonialpolitik 1830–1852* (Wiesbaden, 1983).

20. Manfred Kossok, *Im Schatten der Heiligen Allianz* (Berlin, 1964), tries to show a growing German, especially Prussian, interest in Latin America but fails to convince. As for Austria, it is striking how little the government did to try to make itself even an Adriatic and Mediterranean commercial and naval power before 1848. See, e.g., Ronald E. Coons, *Seamen, Statesmen, and Bureaucrats* (Wiesbaden, 1985); and Lawrence Sondhaus, *The Habsburg Empire and the Sea* (West Lafayette, IN., 1989).

21. For an example of such rationalization, see Michael Sheehan, "The Place of the Balancer in Balance of Power Theory," *Review of International Studies*, 15 (1989), 123–34.

22. John Ehrman, *The Younger Pitt*, Vol. 1, *The Years of Acclaim* (New York, 1969); Paul L. C. Webb, "Sea Power in the Ochakov Affair of 1791," *International History Review*, 2 (1980), 13–33.

23. Orville T. Murphy, *Charles Gravier, Comte de Vergennes* (Albany, NY, 1982).

24. The French argued, among other things, that France's expansion merely restored the European balance destroyed by the partitions of Poland and the destruction or weakening of France's other traditional allies and intermediary bodies in Europe (the Ottoman Empire, the German empire, Sweden), and by Britain's colonial conquests, and that without some effective check on Britain's domination of the high seas and its ruthless use of its naval power in war there could be no real balance in Europe. The arguments were, of course, self-interested propaganda— but far more reasonable propaganda than the corresponding British and Russian ones. Leaving rhetoric and propaganda aside, it is impossible to conceive of any balance of power in Europe in the 1800s that did not recognize and accord to France the natural hegemony in Western Europe, that is, the Low Countries, western Germany, northern Italy, and Spain, that existing military, economic, political, and even cultural relationships accorded it. France repeatedly had this kind of leadership in its grasp under Napoleon; sensible Frenchmen (Talleyrand, Baron d'Hauterive, Joseph Fouché, the marquis de Caulaincourt, and others) urged Napoleon to accept and consolidate it; many Germans and other Europeans were willing or eager to go along with it; but Napoleon threw it away.

25. See especially the account in vol. 3 of Bertier de Sauvigny, *Metternich et la France;* also Temperley, *Foreign Policy of Canning;* and the standard accounts of the Greek War of Independence, including C. W. Crawley, *The Question of Greek Independence* (Cambridge, 1930); Douglas Dakin, *The Greek Struggle for Independence, 1821–1833* (Berkeley, CA., 1973); C. M. Woodhouse, *The Greek War of Independence* (London, 1952); and Richard Clogg, ed., *The Struggle for Greek Independence* (Hamden, CT., 1973).

26. Besides Webster and Bourne on Palmerston's policy (n. 8 above), see Charles H. Pouthas, "La politique de Thiers pendant la crise orientale de 1840," *Revue historique*, 182 (1938), 72–96; Afaf Lufti al-Sayyid Marsot, *Egypt in the Reign of Mehmet Ali* (New York, 1984); François Charles-Roux, *Thiers et Mehemet-Ali* (Paris, 1951); and J. P. T. Bury and R. T. Combs, *Thiers, 1797–1877* (London, 1986). A good overall interpretation is in H. A. C. Collingham, *The July Monarchy* (London, 1988). On the Franco-German confrontation of 1840 and its serious long-range results, see Veit-Brause, *Deutsch- Franösische Krise;* Raymond Poidevin and Heinz-Otto Sieburg, eds., *Aspects des relations franco-allemandes 1830–1848* (Metz, 1978); Anna Owsinka, *La politique de France envers l'Allemagne a l'époque de la Monarchie de juillet 1830—1848* (Wroclaw, 1974);

and Dieter Roghe, *Die französische Deutschland-Politik während der ersten zehn Jahre der Julimonarchie (1830–1840)* (Frankfurt, 1971).

27. Besides Ingram, *Great Game in Asia*, see G. D. Clayton, *Britain and the Eastern Question* (London, 1971); and David Gillard, *The Struggle for Asia, 1828–1914* (London, 1977). For evidence of how Russia exploited British collaboration for its own ends in 1826–1829, see Loyal Cowles, "The Failure to Restrain Russia: Canning, Nesselrode, and the Greek Question, 1825–1827," *International History Review*, 12 (1990), 688–720; on the late 1830s, see Harold N. Ingle, *Nesselrode and the Russian Rapprochement with Britain, 1836–1843* (Berkeley, CA., 1976).

28. Paul W. Schroeder, *Austria, Great Britain, and the Crimean War* (Ithaca, NY., 1972); Winfried Baumgart, *Der Friede von Paris 1856* (Munich, 1972); and Norman Rich, *Why the Crimean War?* (Hanover, NH., 1985).

29. Schroeder, "Nineteenth Century System."

30. For instances of Talleyrand's arguments, see Talleyrand, *Mémoires*, 2, 132–33, 226–27, 230–33, 236–41, 254–55, 294–95, 402–03, 452–53; Polovtsov, *Correspondance*, 1. nos. 35 and 87. Guglielmo Ferrero, *The Reconstruction of Europe* (New York, 1941), stresses this aspect of Talleyrand's thought.

31. I owe this phrase to a political science colleague, Professor Edward Kolodziej.

32. The concept of equilibrium as residing in a harmonious European family of states was of course not invented in 1813–15 but emerged gradually in the course of the wars. For some examples of how different statesmen and theorists developed it, see, for Prussia's Baron von Stein, Franz Herre, *Freiherr vom Stein* (Cologne, 1973), 87, 262–66; and Gerhard Ritter, *Stein* (Berlin, 1936), 374–75. For Spaniards during Spain's War of Independence (1808–14), see Rainer Wohlfeil, *Spanien und die deutsche Erhebung, 1808–1814* (Wiesbaden, 1965), 70–72, 88–89. For Metternich, his *Nachgelassene Papiere*, 1, 70–71. For Friedrich von Gentz, see Alexander Hase, "Friedrich (v.) Gentz: Vom Übertritt nach Wien, bis zu den 'Fragmenten des Gleichgewichts' (1802–1806)," *Historische Zeitschrift*, 211 (1970), 589–615. Immanuel Kant's doctrine of equilibrium in his *Idea of a Universal History from a Cosmopolitan Standpoint*, like that of Gentz, his pupil, was basically prescriptive and moral rather than political in character. See Lewis W. Beck, *On History* (New York, 1963), 11–26.

33. See, e.g., Paul C. Stern et al., eds., *Perspectives on Deterrence* (New York, 1989); Robert Jervis, Richard Ned Lebow, and Janice Gross Stein, eds., *Psychology and Deterrence* (Baltimore, MD., 1985); and Richard Ned Lebow and Janice Gross Stein, "When Does Deterrence Succeed and How Do We Know?" Occasional Papers, Canadian Institute for International Peace and Security, no. 8 (February 1990).

34. See especially Hans-Werner Hahn, *Die Geschichte des Deutschen Zollvereins* (Göttingen, 1984).

35. The best recent one is in Kraehe, *Metternich's German Policy*, chaps. 8–10; but see also Ulrike Eich, *Russland und Europa: Studien zur russischen Deutschland-Politik in der Zeit des Wiener Kongresses* (Cologne, 1986).

36. August Fournier, "Zur Geschichte der polnischen Frage 1814 und 1815," *Mitteilungen des Instituts für Österreichische Geschichtsforschung*, 20 (1899), 444–75; Fournier, "Londoner Präludien zum Wiener Kongress," *Deutsche Revue*, 43 (1918), 1: 125–36, 205–19; 2: 24–33; Nesselrode to Alexander I, September 25, 1814, *Vneshniaia politika Rossii*, ser. 1, vol. 8, no. 46.

37. Webster, *British Diplomacy*, 266–67, 277–80, 284–85.

38. Even a holistic critic of Kenneth N. Waltz and his structural realism (*Theory of International Politics* [New York, 1979]) such as Barry Buzan (*People, States and Fear*, 102–03), endorses Waltz's fundamental premise that balance of power is by definition a necessary result and reflection of state sovereignty and the resultant structural anarchy of international politics.

39. For example, Robert Gilpin, *The Political Economy of International Relations* (Princeton, NJ., 1987); and *War and Change in World Politics* (New York, 1981); Robert O. Keohane, *After Hegemony: Cooperation and Discord in the World Political Economy* (Princeton, 1984); Oye, *Cooperation under Anarchy*; Jervis, *Perception and Misperception*.

CHAPTER 3   BRUCK VERSUS BUOL: THE DISPUTE OVER AUSTRIAN EASTERN POLICY, 1853–55

* The archival research for this article was done chiefly in the summer of 1965 with the support of a grant-in-aid from the American Council of Learned Societies supplemented by a grant from the American Philosophical Society, whose aid is gratefully acknowledged. I should also like to express my appreciation to my assistant in Vienna, Miss Ursula Saudisch, who helped greatly in deciphering Bruck's often illegible scrawl.

1. Heinrich Benedikt, *Die wirtschaftliche Entwicklung Österreichs in der Franz-Joseph Zeit* (Vienna and Munich, 1958), 53.

2. On Bruck's ideas and actions as minister of trade in 1848–51, see Friedrich Walter, *Die österreichische Zentralverwaltung*, 3. Abteilung, 1 (Vienna, 1964) 239–40, 278–79, 394–97, 482–86. On Bruck's economic program and ideas, see Jacques Droz, *L'Europe centrale. Evolution historique de l'idée de "Mitteleuropa"* (Paris, 1960), 26–27, 92–97; Franz Josef Schoeningh, "Karl Ludwig Bruck und die Idee 'Mitteleuropa,'" *Historisches Jahrbuch*, 56 (1936), 1–14; Henry Cord Meyer, *Mitteleuropa in German Thought and Action* (The Hague, 1955), 16–18; H. Ritter von Srbik, *Deutsche Einheit: Idee und Wirklichkeit vom Heiligen Reich bis Königgrätz*, 4 vols. (Munich, 1936–42), 1, 281, 429; 2, 94–97; and Richard Charmatz, *Minister Freiherr von Bruck, der Vorkämpfer Mittel europas* (Leipzig, 1916), 22–25, 45–48, 55–57, 60–62.

3. Heinrich Friedjung, *Der Krimkrieg und die österreichische Politik* (Stuttgart and Berlin, 1907), 24.

4. A. J. P. Taylor considers Bruck the originator of the Mitteleuropa concept in the Schwarzenberg era (*The Habsburg Monarchy, 1809–1918* [New York, 1965], 86, 90–91). Srbik insists, however, that Schwarzenberg developed this as his own idea (*Deutsche Einheit*, 2, 94), a viewpoint backed by Eduard Heller, *Mitteleuropas Vorkämpfer: Fürst Felix zu Schwarzenberg* (Vienna, 1933); and Rudolf Kiszling, *Fürst Felix zu Schwarzenberg* (Graz-Cologne, 1952). See also Heinrich Friedjung, *Historische Aufsätze* (Stuttgart and Berlin, 1919), 64–89.

5. Angelo Filipuzzi, *La Pace di Milano* (Rome, 1955).

6. The two most important instances of favorable treatment are Friedjung, *Krimkrieg, passim*; and Charmatz, *Bruck*, 94–107.

7. Friedrich Walter ed., *Aus dem Nachlass des Freiherrn Carl Friedrich Kübeck von Kübau, Tagebücher, Briefe, Aktenstücke, 1841–1855* (Graz-Cologne, 1960), 109; Isidor Heller ed., *Memoiren des Baron Bruck aus der Zeit des Krimkrieges* (Vienna, 1877), 6.

8. The Austrian chargé d'affaires at Constantinople, Baron Klezl, to Buol, Constantinople, May 15, 19, 22, and 26, 1853 (nos. 38B, reserved, 40A, and 40B, 42, and 44C), Haus-Hof-und Staatsarchiv, Vienna, Politisches Archiv, sec. XII, *Türkei*, cart. 46; Buol to Klezl, Vienna, April 25 and May 2 (secret), ibid., cart. 48. (Since all the Buol-Bruck correspondence is in this section XII of the Politisches Archiv, and since virtually all Buol's letters were written from Vienna, and Bruck's from Constantinople or the suburbs of Pera and Buyukdère, their correspondence will hereafter be cited simply by date, number of the dispatch [if any], and number of the carton.)

9. "Politische Instruktion für Freiherr v. Bruck," May 31, 1853; and Buol to Bruck, June 9 and 13, private, cart. 48.

10. Bruck to Buol, June 23, 1853, private, cart. 48.

11. Walter, *Kübecks Tagebücher*, 115.

12. Bruck to Buol, June 28 and July 1, 1853, private, cart. 48. See also the liasse of correspondence in P.A., X, Russland, cart. 38, entitled "Affaire Koszta"; and *Recueil des traités de la Porte Ottomane avec les puissances étrangères*, ed. Baron I. de Testa (Paris, 1901), 10, 262–81. A detailed account of the affair is Audor Klay, *Daring Diplomacy* (Minneapolis, 1957).

13. French Foreign Minister Drouyn de Lhuys to Baron Bourqueney, ambassador at Vienna, Paris, July 16, 1853, no. 55, Archive du Ministère des Affaires étrangères, Correspondance politique; Autriche, 451. Buol's own policy was to liquidate the Koszta affair as quickly and quietly as possible; see his Vortrag of August 15 in P.A., XL: Interna, Vorträge, cart. 48.

14. Buol to Bruck, July 4 and 18, 1853, private, cart. 48.

15. Bruck to Buol, July 14, 1853, nos. 12A, 12B, and 12G, and a private letter, carts. 47 and 48.

16. Bruck to Buol, July 18 and 20, 1853, nos. 13 and 14, cart. 47.

17. Bruck to Buol, July 14, 1853, private, cart. 48.

18. Bruck to Buol, July 14 and 18, 1853, nos. 12A and 13, cart. 47.

19. Bruck to Buol, private, July 23, 1853, cart. 48.

20. Bruck to Buol, private, July 28, 1853, cart. 48.

21. At this time, Count Prokesch, Austrian delegate at Frankfurt, later to be an ardent exponent of an alliance with the West and even of open war against Russia, followed much the same line as Bruck (Prokesch to Buol, Frankfurt, June 17 and 23, 1853, in Anton von Prokesch [ed.], *Aus den Briefen des Grafen Prokesch von Osten*, 1849–55 [Vienna, 1896], 320).

22. Buol to Bruck, August l, 1853 (two regular dispatches and a private letter), cart. 48.

23. Bruck to Buol, August 11, 1853, nos. 22A and 22B (reserved), cart. 47; and private letter, August 11, cart. 48.

24. Bruck to Buol, August 15 and 17, 1853, nos. 23A, 23B, and 25A, cart. 47; and private letter, August 18, cart. 48; Buol to Bruck, August 29, private, cart. 48.

25. Bruck to Buol, September 9, 1853, no. 30, cart. 47, and September 5, private, cart. 48.

26. Bruck to Buol, September 19, 1853, no. 34A, cart. 47.

27. H. W. V. Temperley, *England and the Near East: The Crimea* (London, 1936), 355–56.

28. For Buol's reaction to the Anglo-French moves, see Buol to Bruck, Olmütz, September 26, 1853, no. 3; and two letters from Vienna on October 3, cart. 48.

29. Bruck to Buol, September 26, 1853, private, cart. 48.

30. Bruck to Buol, October 3, 1853, no. 38A, cart. 47; cf. also no. 39 of October 5, cart. 47.

31. Bruck to Buol, October 6, 1853, no. 40A, cart. 47; Buol to Bruck, October 10, 1853, no. 1, cart. 48.

32. Bruck to Buol, October 10 and 13, 1853, nos. 41 and 42A, cart. 47; October 13, private, cart. 48.

33. Bruck to Buol, October 24, November 7, and November 14, 1853, nos. 45A, 49, and 51, cart. 47.

34. Note, e.g., his protest against the "note-mania" ("*Notenwulh*") raging in England and France, and his refusal to go along with a new English proposal for conciliation, in Buol to Bruck, October 11, private, and October 31, no. 1, cart. 48.

35. On the painful negotiations involved in bringing the English to agree to any demarche at all, see Buol to Bruck, November 11, 1853, nos. 2 (reserved), 3 (reserved); and 4; Buol to Bruck, November 21, no. 1, (reserved), with copy attached of the dispatch of Foreign Secretary Lord Clarendon to Ambassador Lord Westmorland, London, November 16; and Buol to Bruck, December 5, no. 3, and a private letter, all in cart. 48.

36. Buol to Bruck, November 28, 1853 (reserved), cart. 48.

37. Their differences extended beyond the main issue to lesser points as well. Bruck, e.g., wanted to publish in Leipzig an anonymous article on Austrian policy which, he claimed, would give the public the right view of the Eastern question. Buol declined his permission on the ground that the source would become known, and the article would compromise Austria. Again, Bruck thought Russia entirely justified in her action at Sinope and was delighted at the victory; Buol was chagrined at the Turkish defeat (Bruck to Buol, December 8, 1853, private, cart. 48; and December 11, no. 58A, cart. 47; Buol to Bruck, December 14, no. 1, and December 26, private, cart. 48).

38. Bruck to Buol, November 21, 1853, private, cart. 48.

39. Bruck to Buol, December 12 and 15, 1853, nos. 59 and 60A, cart. 47.

40. Buol to Bruck, December 26, 1853, no. 1, cart. 48.

41. Bruck to Buol, December 19, 1853, no. 61, cart. 47; Redcliffe to Clarendon, private, Constantinople, December 24, 1853, Clarendon deposit, c. 10, Bodleian Library, Oxford (in which Redcliffe insists that Bruck fully supported the decision to suppress the note).

42. Buol to Bruck, January 2, 1853, no. 1, cart. 49.

43. Private letter, January 2, 1854, cart. 52.

44. Bruck to Buol, January 5, 1854, private, cart. 52.

45. Bruck to Buol, January 9 and 16, 1854, nos. 4 and 6B, cart. 50.

46. Bruck to Buol, January 16, 1854, private, cart. 52.

47. Bruck to Buol, December 8 and 29, 1853, nos. 57 and 64B, cart. 47; Bruck to Buol, January 30, 1854, no. 30, cart. 51; Buol to Bruck, January 2, 1854, no. 2, January 9, no. 1, and January 16, no. 2, cart. 49.

48. Buol to Bruck, January 16, 1854, no. 3, and a private letter, cart. 49; another private letter (but not in Buol's hand), January 16, 1854, cart. 52; Buol to Bruck, January 30, cart. 49.

49. Buol's Vortrag of January 16, 1854, P.A. XL: Interna, Vorträge, cart. 48.

50. Bruck to Buol, January 23, 1854, no. 8A, cart. 50.

51. Bruck to Buol, January 30, 1854, private, cart. 52.

52. Bruck to Buol, February 16 and March 16, 1854, private, cart. 52.

53. Buol to Bruck, March 6, 1854, no. 1, cart. 49.

54. Bruck to Buol, February 16, 1854, no. ISA, cart. 50.

55. Bruck's anglophobia was no secret to the other envoys at Constantinople. Baraguey d'Hilliers remarked in a private letter of February 2, 1854 to Drouyn on the intensity of Bruck's hatred for England (P. A., 9: Frankreich, cart. 49).

56. Bruck to Buol, February 9, February 13, February 23, and March 13, 1854, nos. 13B, 14A, 17A, and 22A, cart. 50.

57. Bruck to Buol, April 3, 1854, no. 28B, cart. 50.

58. Bruck to Buol, February 27 and March 27, 1854, nos. 18 and 26B, cart. 50.

59. Bruck to Buol, March 23, 1854, private, cart. 52.

60. Bruck to Buol, March 20, 1854, no. 24, cart. 52.

61. On these ministerial conferences, see Franz Eckhart, *Die deutsche Frage und der Krimkrieg* (Berlin and Königsberg, 1931), pp. 48–54; protocols of the conferences of March 22 and March 25, 1854, P.A., XL: Interna, Vorträge, cart. 48.

62. Vortrag by Hess, Vienna, April 28, 1854, Kriegsarchiv, Feldakten, 1854/13/210.

63. May 22, 1854, cart. 52. Buol also rejected repeated proposals by Bruck that he be empowered to cooperate with Baraguey in overthrowing Reshid and ousting Redcliffe (Bruck to Buol, March 23, April 27, and May 11, 1854, private, cart. 52).

64. Bruck to Buol, May 11, 1854, private, cart. 52.

65. Some of Bruck's charges against England—e.g., that she had revolutionary war aims—are without doubt entirely justified (cf. Bruck to Buol, May 22, and June 19, 1854, nos. 42A and 50A, cart. 50). In fact, my own verdict on English policy—reckless and irresponsible in general, brutal and treacherous toward Austria in particular—is nearly as severe as Bruck's, and one can well understand that a fiery Austrian patriot like Bruck would bitterly resent British actions and resist a policy of cooperation with the West. Nonetheless, the fundamental questions are whether Bruck's analysis of the main danger to Austria as that of an Anglo-French alliance with revolutionary forces to destroy Austria and Russia was sound, and whether his proposed Austro-German–Russian union against the West represented a viable answer (Bruck to Buol, June 22, no. 51C, cart. 50).

66. Buol to Bruck, April 24, 1854. no. 2, cart. 49; Bruck to Buol, May 4, 1854, no. 42A, cart. 50

67. Bruck to Buol, May 25, 1854, no. 43B, cart. 50.

68. Bruck to Buol, June 29, 1854, private, cart. 52.

69. In another instance of noncompliance with Buol's wishes, Bruck published a series of articles on Austrian foreign policy in Germany through his private secretary, Isidor Heller. Incensed, Buol told Bruck either to stop Heller from writing altogether or to bring him in line with Austrian policy, which he had entirely misrepresented (Buol to Bruck, April 24, 1854, no. 1, and May 1, no. 3 cart. 49).

70. It is in this sense, I believe, that Bruck's reply to Buol's private letter of May 22 (cited in n. 63 above) must be understood. Protesting that he fully agreed with the policy Buol had expounded (which was patently false), Bruck argued further that he merely wanted to see Austria as firm against the West as it was against Russia. "A purely German independent policy" was his ideal (June 1, 1854, private, cart. 52).

71. Buol to Bruck, July 17, 1854, cart. 49.

72. Buol to Bruck, May 8, May 15 (no. 2), and May 29 (no. 2), June 26, nos. 1 and 2 (reserved), and July 31, 1854, no. 1, cart. 49.

73. Bruck to Buol, July 20 and August 3, 1854, nos. 60B and 64B, cart. 50. L. Boicu discusses Bruck's general aims in the Principalities in his "Les Principautés roumaines dans les projets de Karl von Bruck et Lorenz von Stein pour la constitution de la 'Mitteleuropa' à l'époque de la guerre de Crimée," *Revue Roumaine d'Histoire*, 6 (1967), 233–56. Boicu, however, relies on newspapers and printed sources for Bruck's views, says nothing of the Buol–Bruck quarrel, and takes Bruck's plans for official government policy—which is very far from the truth.

74. Bruck to Buol, July 6 and 10, 1854, nos. 55B and 56B, cart. 50; private letter of July 20, cart. 52.

75. Buol to Bruck, July 31, 1854, no. 1, cart. 49; Bruck to Buol, August 10, no. 66C, cart. 50, and private letter, August 10, cart. 52.

76. Buol to Bruck, August 21, 1854, nos. 1 and 2, cart. 49, with a copy of Buol's letter of August 15 to Field Marshal Lieutenant Count Coronini instructing him on the correct policy of cooperation with Turkey and the Allies (Kriegsarchiv, *Feldakten, Serbisch-Banaler Armeecorps in den Donaufürstentümern*, 1854/326/8/37.

77. Bruck to Buol, August 10, 1854, no. 66B, cart. 50.

78. Bruck to Buol, August 28, August 31, September 7, September 11, September 14, September 21, and October 2, 1854, nos. 71, 72B, 75B, 76B, 77B, 80C, and 84C, cart. 50; Bruck to Buol, September 14, private, cart. 52.

79. Bruck to Buol, September 14, 1854, no. 77B, cart. 50.

80. Bruck to Buol, October 12, 1854, no. 90C, cart. 50.

81. Bruck to Buol, October 5, 1854, private, cart. 52; Buol to Bruck, September 25, 1854, no. 2, cart. 49; Hess to Buol, Jassy, October 7, 1854, and Coronini to Hess, with annexes, Bucharest, September 21, 1854, in P.A., XL: Interna, Korrespondenz, Innere Behörden, cart. 78; and Hess to Bruck, Kronstadt, September 20, 1854, in Kriegsarchiv, *Feldakten, III and IV Armee-Obercommando*, 1854/9.

82. Buol to Bruck, October 16, 1854, no. 1, cart. 49.

83. Buol to Bruck, September 25, 1854, no. 1, cart. 49.

84. Buol to Bruck, October 16, 1854, no. 1, and October 30, no. 1, cart. 49.

85. Buol to Coronini, October 16, 1854, *Kriegsarchiv, Feldakten, Serbisch-Banater Armeecorps*, 1854/327/X/85.

86. Buol to Bruck, October 23, 1854, no. 1, with copy of a "Minute d'une communication verbale faite à S. E. Mr le Cte Buol par l'Ambassadeur Ottoman," cart. 49.

87. Buol to Bruck, October 16, 1854, private, cart. 52.

88. Bruck to Buol, November 6, 1854, private, cart. 52.

89. See, e.g., Buol to Bruck, December 12, 1854, no. 3, cart. 49, and Buol to Bruck, January 8, 1855, no. 2, January 9 (cipher telegram), January 15, no. 1, and February 1, cart. 58. All deal with such relatively minor subjects as getting the Turks to send a plenipotentiary quickly to the impending Vienna Conferences and dealing with Turkish complaints about the Principalities. In several instances in this period, Buol warmly commended various actions of Bruck's.

90. Bruck to Buol, December 14, 1854, no. 109E, cart. 51; Bruck to Buol, January 18, January 22, January 25, and February 5, 1855, nos. 6B, 6C, 7B, 8A, 11B, 11D, cart. 53; Coronini to Bruck, Jassy, January 20, and Bucharest, March 19, 1855, private letters, cart. 57.

91. Buol to Bruck, December 4, 1854, no. 2, cart. 49; Bruck to Buol, December 21, 1854, no. 111B, cart. 50, and January 4, 1855, nos. 2C and 2E, cart. 53. In view of Bruck's bitter attack on the whole policy culminating in the December 2

treaty, the following statement by Coronini in a private letter to Bruck, Jassy, January 13, 1855, is worth citing: "If it proves possible to produce an honorable peace, this would justify the surprising treaty of December 2. Should Austria have tempered the immoderate demands of the one side [the Allies] and made an impression on the arrogance of the other [Russia], it will have completed a beautiful mission and celebrated a glorious triumph. Omnia ad maiorem Austriae et Cäsaris gloriam!" (cart. 57).

92. Bruck to Buol, January 18, 1855, private, cart. 57. Buol's reply congratulating Bruck on his new post is polite but colorless (February 7, 1855, private, cart. 58).

93. Srbik, *Deutsche Einheit*, 2, 252, 254, 272.

94. Ibid., 250; Charmatz, *Bruck*, 107; Friedjung, *Krimkrieg*, 25, 27, 42, 109–10; Viktor Bibl, *Der Zerfall Österreichs* 2 vols. (Vienna, 1922–24), 2, 243–46.

95. This view crops up even in such a well-informed study as Charles W. Hallberg's *Franz Joseph and Napoleon III, 1852–1864* (New York, 1955), 63.

96. "Considérations politiques," in Kriegsarchiv, *Feldakten, III and IV Armee-Obercommando*, 1855, 322/V/17 1/2. Friedjung, *Krimkrieg*, 164–66, links this *Denkschrift* to Bruck's influence, and all the internal evidence bears out this judgment.

97. As Srbik does in his *Deutsche Einheit*, 2, 230–31, and his *Metternich, der Staatsmann und der Mensch* 3 vols. (Munich, 1925–54), 2, 480–81.

98. In the best single source on Metternich's policy in 1853–56, *Briefe des Staatskanzlers Fürsten Melternich an ... Grafen Buol-Schauenstein aus den Jahren 1852–1859*, ed. Carl J. Burckhardt (Munich, 1934), various letters from 1853 and 1854 illustrate the points I have made (64, 81–83, 89–90, 93–94, 145, 156–57). One might add that there is far more similarity between Metternich's and Buol's views than is often supposed and that Metternich's criticisms of Buol's policy—that it was one of *va banque*, that it ignored the long-range consequences of Austria's actions, that it neglected moral factors essential for Austria's consideration—all apply far more strongly to Bruck's policy than to Buol's.

99. This view, repeated many times by Charmatz and Friedjung, can be found also in Josef Redlich, *Kaiser Franz Joseph von Österreich* (Berlin, 1929), 155; Srbik, *Deutsche Einheit*, 2, 230–31, 239; Eckhart, *Deutsche Frage*, 186–87; and Eugene Tarle, *Krymskaia Voina* 2 vols. (Moscow, 1950), 1, 242–43.

100. See, e.g., Nicholas's private letter to Franz Joseph, Tsarskoe-Selo, May 18/30, 1853, in P.A., X, Russland, cart. 38. In fact, both the Russian ambassador, Prince Meyendorff, and Count Orlov tried hard to persuade Austria to join Russia in a domination or partition of the Balkans.

101. Edurad Heller, "Aus den ersten zwei Jahrzehnten der Regierung Franz Josephs," in Eduard Ritter von Steinitz ed., *Erinnerungen an Franz Joseph* I (Berlin, 1931), 42–44.

102. On this point, see Eckhart, *Deutsche Politik*, 38–40, *passim*.

103. It is worth noting that Undersecretary of State Baron Werner, perhaps the only high official in the Ballhaus who was sympathetic to Prussia at this time, was equally clear in dismissing the idea of a great German bloc dictating the peace settlement to both sides as a Utopian dream (Werner to G. Esterhâzy, envoy to Prussia, September 10, 1855, Gesandtschaftsarchiv Berlin, cart. 113).

104. It was not only during the Crimean War that Bruck's actions and ideas on diplomacy and international relations were dangerous and impractical. Angelo

Filipuzzi, who is certainly not prejudiced against Austria, has nothing good to say in his *La Pace di Milano* (61–62, 64, 67, 73, *passim*) about the brutal and radical way Bruck handled the negotiations with Sardinia in 1849. Bruck, Filipuzzi argues, deliberately tried to blow up the negotiations and renew the war so as to take care of Sardinia once for all. In 1857 Bruck developed a fantastic scheme for Austrian imperialism in the Far East. Austria, allied with France, was to take over protection of the projected Suez Canal, build naval bases from the Red Sea through the Indian Ocean to China, and assume the protection of the Dutch, Portuguese, and Spanish East Indian possessions, together with founding a colony in New Guinea. The plan, Bruck argued, would help get Austria into the German Zollverein by tempting Prussia and Germany with a share in the Far Eastern trade. His final goal: "to gain some day the whole Dutch East Indies as one great colony for the one great Central Europe" (Benedikt, *Entwicklung Österreichs*, 84). One must agree with Friedjung that Bruck was indeed rich in ideas—but what ideas!

CHAPTER 4   THE LOST INTERMEDIARIES: THE IMPACT OF 1870 ON THE EUROPEAN SYSTEM

* *The International History Review*, 6 (February 1984), pp.1–27. Copyright © 1984, The International History Review. All rights reserved. Printed with permission of publisher.

1. Note the title of one of the major publications on Italian unification, Norbert Miko, *Das Ende des Kirchenstaats*, 4 vols. (Vienna-Munich, 1962–70).
2. There has been a considerable revival of interest in the Empire's downfall; see, e.g., Karl Otmar Freiherr v. Aretin, *Heiliges Römisches Reich 1776–1806*, 2 vols. (Wiesbaden, 1967), and John G. Gagliardo, *Reich and Nation. The Holy Roman Empire as Idea and Reality, 1763–1806* (Bloomington, IN., 1980).
3. This is especially evident in the spate of works produced in or around the centenary of the Reichsgründung, e.g., Josef Becker, "Zum Problem der Bismarckschen Politik in der spanischen Thronfrage 1870," *Historische Zeitschrift*, 222 (1971), 529–607; *Das Bismarck-Problem in der Geschichtsschreibung nach 1945*, ed. Lothar Gall (Cologne-Berlin, 1971); Eberhard Kolb, *Der Kriegsausbruch 1870* (Göttingen, 1970); *Entscheidung 1870. Der deutsch-französische Krieg* (Stuttgart, 1970); *Reichsgründung 1870/71*, ed. Theodor Schieder and Ernst Deuerlein (Stuttgart, 1970); Horst Bartel and Ernst Engelberg, *Die gross-preussisch militaristische Reichsgründung 1871*, 2 vols. (Berlin, 1971); *Probleme der Reichsgründungzeit 1848–1879*, ed. Helmut Böhme (Cologne-Berlin, 1968); *Europa und der Norddeutsche Bund*, ed. R. Ditrich (Berlin, 1968); and *Europa und die Einheit Deutschlands*, ed. Walter Hofer (Cologne, 1970).
4. The role of the South German states in the developments of 1866 to 1871 has not been neglected—far from it. Until well after World War II, however, it was regularly seen from the standpoint of Prusso-German nationalism. Works like Theodor Schieder, *Die kleindeutsche Partei in Bayern in den Kämpfen um die nationale Einheit 1863–1871* (Munich, 1936); Wilhelm Schüssler, *Bismarcks Kampf um Süddeutschland 1867* (Berlin, 1929); Michael Doeberl, *Bayern und die Bismarcksche Reichsgründung* (Munich, 1925); and Otto Becker, *Bismarcks Ringen um Deutschlands Gestaltung* (Heidelberg, 1958) belong to this tradition. In recent decades, along with a massive criticism of the character and policies of the Bismarckian Reich, historians have paid more attention to movements and forces

opposed to *kleindeutsch* nationalism. See, e.g., Karl Buchheim, *Ultramontanismus und Demokratie* (Munich, 1963); Willy Real, *Der deutsche Reformverein* (Lübeck, 1966); Martin Hope, *The Alternative to German Unification* (Wiesbaden, 1973); Rudolf Ullner, *Die Idee des Föderalismus im Jahrzehnt der deutschen Einigungskriege* (Lübeck, 1965); and Margaret L. Anderson, *Windhorst, a Political Biography* (New York, 1981). There are also excellent treatments of internal developments within the South German states up to the *Reichsgründung*—e.g., on Baden, Lothar Gall, *Der Liberalismus als regierende Partei* (Wiesbaden, 1968); and on Württemberg, Dieter Langewiesche, *Liberalismus und Demokratie in Württemberg zwischen Revolution und Reichsgründung* (Düsseldorf, 1974). None of these works, however, specifically discusses the demise of the South German states as a phenomenon in international politics. Perhaps this is because from a German standpoint these states continued their existence within the Reich.

5. The point is emphasized by both Aretin and Gagliardo (see n. 2 above).

6. A partial exception is Wolf D. Gruner's article, "Der deutsche Bund-Modell für eine Zwischenlösung?" *Politik und Kultur*, 9, Heft 5 (1982), 22–42. Oran R. Young, *The Intermediaries* (Princeton, NJ., 1967) deals only with international agencies and organizations since 1945. Theodor Schieder, "Die mittleren Staaten im System der grossen Mächte," *Historische Zeitschrift*, 232 (1981), 583–604, and Karl Bosl, "Das 'Dritte Deutschland' und die Lösung der deutschen Frage im 19. Jahrhundert," *Bohemia*, 11 (1970), 20–33, both offer stimulating ideas on the importance of the German middle states, but within a German rather than European framework.

7. Metternich gave clear expression to this idea in describing the Low Countries in 1815: "Placed between France and the Northern Powers, they belong to the peaceful and conservative line of central and intermediary powers, which lean on one side on Austria, to the other on England, and whose constant tendency must be to prevent France and Russia from weighing on the European center and destroying that equilibrium whose balance they hold in their hands." Quoted in Wolf D. Grüner, "Die belgisch-luxemburgische Frage im Spannungsfeld europäischer Politik 1830–1839," *Francia*, 5 (1977), 316. The idea that a stable peace required a system of intermediary states separating the great powers was commonplace in the late eighteenth and early nineteenth centuries, shared not only by many Austrian and German statesmen and publicists, but by Frenchmen as well— Talleyrand, Sieyès, even Napoleon. The common emphasis on the 1815 settlement as establishing a barrier against France has obscured the extent to which it really set up a system of intermediary states between all the great powers from the Arctic Circle to the Mediterranean and Levant.

8. As Metternich remarked to the French ambassador, Marshal Maison, during the Austro-French crisis over Central Italian revolutions in early 1831, since France and Austria had no common border, war could not occur unless the French succeeded in promoting revolution in one of Austria's neighbors. In a move typical of an intermediary state, Sardinia-Piedmont made Metternich's comment an argument in favor of Sardinian neutrality in case of an Austro-French war—a good example of the drag effect. *Le relazioni diplomatiche fra l'Austria e il Regno di Sardegna*, ed. Narcisco Nada, Ser. 2 (1830–48), Vol. 1 (Rome, 1972), 100–01, 163–65. For evidence of how Austro-French rivalry over Rome involved a good deal of cooperation as well, see Narcisco Nada, *L'Austria e la questione romana dalla rivoluzione di luglio alla fine della conferenza diplomatica romana (agosto 1830-luglio 1831)* (Turin, 1953).

9. Karl Otmar Freiherr v. Aretin, *Bayerns Weg zum souveränen Staat* (Munich, 1976); Wolfgang Quint, *Souveränitätsbegriff und Souveränitätspolitik in Bayern* (Berlin, 1971); Erwin Hölzle, *Württemberg im Zeitalter Napoleons und der deutschen Erhebung* (Stuttgart, 1937); Ernst R. Huber, *Deutsche Verfassungs geschichte seit 1789*, Vol. 1, 2nd ed. (Stuttgart, 1967).

10. Michael Doeberl, *Bayern und die wirtschaftliche Einigung Deutschlands* (Munich, 1915); W. O. Henderson, *The Zollverein* (Cambridge, 1939).

11. Lawrence J. Baack, *Christian Bernstorff and Prussia, 1818–1832* (New Brunswick, NJ., 1980); Robert D. Billinger Jr., "The War Scare of 1831 and Prussian-South German Plans for the End of Austrian Dominance in Germany," *Central European History*, 9 (1976), 203–19; Gustav Huber, *Kriegsgefahr über Europa* (1830–1832) (Berlin, 1932); Kurt M. Hoffmann, *Preussen und die Julimonarchie (1830–1834)* (Berlin, 1936).

12. Roy A. Austensen, "Austria and the 'Struggle for Supremacy in Germany,' 1848–1864," *Journal of Modern History*, 52 (1980), 195–225.

13. Carlo di Nola, *La situazione europea e la politico estera italiana dal 1867 al 1870* (Rome, 1956).

14. The basic work is now Heinrich Lutz, *Österreich-Ungarn und die Gründung des deutschen Reiches* (Frankfurt, 1979); but see also István Dioszegi, *Österreich-Ungarn und der französisch-preussische Krieg* (Budapest, 1974); F. Roy Bridge, *From Sadowa to Sarajevo* (London, 1972), 54ff.; and Helmut Rumpler, "Österreich-Ungarn und die Gründung des deutschen Reiches," in *Europa und die Reichsgründung*, ed. Eberhard Kolb (Munich, 1980), 136–69.

15. Heinrich Lutz, "Zur Wende der österreichisch-ungarischen Aussenpolitik 1871," *Mitteilungen des österreichischen Staatsarchivs*, 25 (1972), 169–84; Lutz, "Politik und militärische Planung in Österreich-Ungarn zu Beginn der Ära Andrássy," in *Geschichte und Gesellschaft. Festschrift für Karl R. Stadler* (Vienna, 1974), 23–44.

16. Bridge, *Sadowa to Sarajevo*, 49–51; Egon Cäsar Count Corti, *Mensch und Herrscher* (Graz, 1952), 436–37; H. Ritter von Srbik, "Erinnerungen des Generals Freiherrn v. John 1866 und 1870," in *Aus Österreichs Vergangenheit* (Salzburg, 1949), 147–9; Lutz, *Österreich-Ungarn*, 210–14. On the Austrian army's general situation, see Günther E. Rothenburg, *The Army of Francis Joseph* (West Lafayette, IN., 1975).

17. Harm-Hinrich Brandt, *Der österreichische Neoabsolutismus: Staatsfinanzen und Politik 1848–1860*, 2 vols. (Göttingen, 1978).

18. Lutz, *Österreich-Ungarn*, 416–83; Rumpler, "Österreich-Ungarn," 154–60; Ivan Pfaff, "Tschechische Politik und die Reichsgründung," *Jahrbücher fur die Geschichte Osteuropas*, 20 (1972), 492–515; Berthold Sutter, "Die politische und rechtliche Stellung der Deutschen in Österreich 1848 bis 1918," in *Die Habsburger Monarchie 1848–1918*, ed. Adam Wandruszka and Peter Urbanitsch, Vol. 3, Pt. 1 (Vienna, 1980), 154–339.

19. Allan Mitchell, *Bismarck and the French Nation, 1848–1890* (New York, 1971), 107, 112–13; George F. Kennan, *The Decline of Bismarck's European Order* (Princeton, NJ, 1979), 412–14; Raymond Poidevin and Jacques Bariéty, *Les Relations franco-allemandes 1815–1875* (Paris, 1977), 84–85, 94–115, 153–54.

20. Elisabeth Fehrenbach, "Preussen-Deutschland als Faktor der französischen Aussen-politik in der Reichsgründungszeit," in *Europa*, ed. Kolb, 126–36.

21. Two facts emerging clearly from the controversy over the origins of Germany's demand for Alsace-Lorraine are that popular pressure for it was strongest in

South Germany, especially Baden, and that Alsace-Lorraine served as a means for Bismarck both to lure the South German states into the Reich and to make them feel more secure in it. For an overview of the controversy and its literature, see Poidevin and Bariéty, *Relations franco-allemandes*, 84–85.

22. For evidence that France's main concern during the Old Regime had not been to reach the so-called natural frontiers, but to expand and consolidate her northern and northeastern frontiers, see various essays in *Louis XIV and Europe*, ed. Ragnhild Hatton (Columbus, OH., 1976); Jean-François Noël, "Les problèmes de frontières entre la France et l'Empire dans la seconde moitié du XVIIIe siècle," *Revue historique*, 208 (1966), 333–46; and Gaston Zeller, "La monarchie d'ancien régime et les frontières naturelles," *Revue d'histoire moderne*, 8 (1933), 305–33.

23. For an argument that Napoleon genuinely sought a Concert solution to European problems and would have preferred it even in 1870, see William E. Echard, *Napoleon III and the Concert of Europe* (Baton Rouge, LA., 1983), especially 295–308.

24. Outstanding on Russia's reactions to the Reichsgründung are two works by Dietrich Beyrau, *Russische Orientpolitik und die Entstehung des deutschen Kaiserreiches 1866–1870/71* (Wiesbaden, 1974), and "Der deutsche Komplex: Russland zur Zeit der Reichsgründung," in *Europa*, ed. Kolb, 63–108.

25. Beyrau, "Der deutsche Komplex," 80–90, 100–7; Charles and Barbara Jelavich, "Jomini and the Revival of the Dreikaiserbund," *Slavonic and East European Review*, 35 (1957), 523–50.

26. On the economic rivalry and partnership, see especially Dietrich Geyer, *Der russische Imperialismus* (Göttingen, 1977), 43–98; Horst Müller-Link, *Industrialisierung und Aussenpolitik. Preussen-Deutschland und das Zarenreich, 1860–1890* (Göttingen, 1977); Hans-Ulrich-Wehler, "Bismarcks späte Russland–politik 1879–1890," in his *Krisenherde des Kaiserreichs 1871–1918* (Göttingen, 1970), 163–80; and Sigrid Kumpf-Korfes, *Bismarcks Draht nach Russland* (Berlin, 1968). A balanced appraisal of political, cultural, and economic factors in the rivalry is in Beyrau, "Der deutsche Komplex."

27. The Russian nationalist historian S. S. Tatishchev made just this complaint about Russian policy—*Imperator Nikolai i inostrannye dvoryi: istoricheskie ocherki* (St. Petersburg, 1880). For details of Prussian policy, see Kurt Borries, *Preussen im Krimkrieg* (Stuttgart, 1930), and Paul W. Schroeder, *Austria, Great Britain and the Crimean War* (Ithaca, NY., 1972).

28. Schroeder, *Austria, Great Britain*, 252.

29. It is impossible here to review the immense, controversy-laden literature on Bismarck's policy in the Eastern crisis. Some recent contributions of varying merit are Bruce Waller, *Bismarck at the Crossroads* (London, 1974); Lothar Gall, *Bismarck der weisse Revolutionär* (Frankfurt, 1980), 511–25; Alexander Novotny, *Quellen und Studien zur Geschichte des Berliner Kongresses* (Vol. 1, Graz-Cologne, 1957); Nicholas Der Bagdasarian, *The Austro-German Rapprochement, 1870–1879* (Rutherford, NJ., 1976); and *Bismarcks Aussenpolitik und der Berliner Kongress*, ed. Karl Otmar Freiherr v. Aretin (Wiesbaden, 1978). The best overall interpretation of Bismarck's policy seems to me that of Andreas Hillgruber, given in his *Bismarcks Aussenpolitik* (Freiburg, 1972), 142–57, and in various articles.

30. Beyrau, *Russische Orientpolitik*, 72–75.

31. Martin Winckler, "Der Ausbruch der 'Krieg-in-Sicht' Krise vom Frühjahr 1875," *Zeitschrift für Ostforschung*, 14 (1965), 671–713; cf. also his *Bismarcks*

Bündnispolitik und das europäische Gleichgewicht (Stuttgart, 1964), and Juergen Doerr, "Germany, Russia and the *Kulturkampf*, 1870–75," *Canadian Journal of History*, 10 (1975), 51–72.

32. Wolfgang Zorn, "Die wirtschaftliche Integration Kleindeutschlands in den 1860er Jahren und die Reichsgründung," *Historische Zeitschrift*, 216 (1973), 304–34; Zorn, "Zwischenstaatliche wirtschaftliche Integration im Zollverein 1867–70," *Vierteljahrshefte für Sozial- und Wirtschaftsgeschichte*, 65 (1978), 38–76; Zorn, "Wirtschafts– und sozialgeschichtliche Zusammenhänge der deutschen Reichsgründungszeit (1850–1879)," *Historische Zeitschrift*, 197 (1963), 318–42.

33. As Dieter Langewiesche points out *(Liberalismus und Demokratie*, 438–39) the fact that the continuation of the Zollverein had been assured through Württemberg's ratification of the 1866 alliance with Prussia gave the Württemberg democrats the freedom to fight any use of the Zollverein for polit-ical ends at the Zollparlament. If Bismarck terminated the Zollverein, he would also risk losing the military and political ties to the South. However, Langewiesche does argue that long-term economic trends were pulling Württemberg toward further union (454–55).

34. The crash of 1873 actually sharply increased South German opposition to the free trade policy of the Zollverein. Helmut Böhme, *Deutschlands Weg zur Grossmacht*, 2nd ed. (Cologne, 1972), 369–70.

35. The main work is Richard Millman, *British Foreign Policy and the Coming of the Franco-Prussian War* (Oxford, 1965), but see also Klaus Hildebrand, "Grossbritannien und die deutsche Reichsgründung," in *Europa*, ed. Kolb, 9–62, and "Die deutsche Reichsgründung im Urteil der britischen Politik," *Francia*, 5 (1977), 399–424. Helmut Reinalter, "Norddeutscher Kaiser oder Kaiser von Deutschland?" *Zeitschrift für bayerische Landesgeschichte*, 33 (1976), 859–67, contains interesting information on the reaction of British Foreign Secretary Lord Clarendon to Bismarck's *Kaiser plan* of January 1870—among it, an expression of Clarendon's regrets that Bismarck had not solved the question by annexing South Germany in 1866, when it would have caused no trouble with France.

36. The claim that Napoleon made modern states in South and West Germany pos-sible, long common among French scholars (e.g., Marcel Dunan, *Napoléon et l'Allemagne* [Paris, 1942]), has been widely accepted by German historians (Elisabeth Fehrenbach, Karl-Georg Faber, Eberhard Weis, Kurt v. Raumer, Heinz-Otto Sieburg, Lothar Gall, and others)—even while they insist correctly on Napoleon's imperialist motives.

37. Wolf D. Gruner, "Frankreich und der deutsche Bund 1851–1866," in *Aspects des relations franco-allemandes a l'époque du Second Empire 1851–1866*, ed. Raymond Poidevin and Heinz-Otto Sieburg (Metz, 1982), 39–61.

38. This account of French policy for the period 1815–48 rests primarily upon: G. de Bertier de Sauvigny, *Metternich et la France après le Congrès de Vienne*, 3 vols. (Paris, 1968–71); Karl Hammer, *Die französische Diplomatie der Restauration und Deutschland, 1814–1830* (Stuttgart, 1963); Anna Owsinska, *La politique de la France envers l'Allemagne a l'époque de la Monarchie de juillet 1830–1848* (Wroclaw, 1974) ; Irmline Veit-Brause, *Die deutsch-französische Krise von 1840* (Cologne, 1967); Dieter Roghé, *Die französische Deutschlandpolitik während der ersten zehn Jahre der Julimonarchie (1830–1840)* (Frankfurt, 1971); Salvo Mastellone, *La politica estera del Guizot (1840 a 1847)* (Florence, 1957);

Ernst Birke, *Frankreich und Ostmitteleuropa im 19t. Jahrhundert* (Cologne, 1960); and *Aspects des relations franco-allemandes 1830–1848*, ed. Raymond Poidevin and Heinz-Otto Sieburg (Metz, 1978). An invaluable collection of documents is *Gesandtschaftsberichte aus München 1814–1848. Die Berichte des französischen Gesandten*, ed. Anton Chroust (*Schriftenreihe zur bayerischen Landesgeschichte*, vols. 39–43) 5 vols. (Munich, 1949–51). For 1848–66, besides older works, see *Aspects des relations franco-allemandes . . . 1851–1866*; Lawrence C. Jennings, *France and Europe in 1848* (Oxford, 1973); James Chastain, "Jules Bastide et l'unité allemande en 1848," *Revue historique*, 252 (1974), 51–72; Rudolf Buchner, *Die deutsch-französische Tragödie 1848–1864* (Würzburg, 1965); Helmut Burckhardt, *Deutschland, England, Frankreich* (Munich, 1970); André Armengaud, *L'opinion publique en France et la crise nationale allemande en 1866* (Paris, 1962); Herbert Geuss, *Bismarck und Napoleon III* (Cologne, 1959); and E. Ann Pottinger, *Napoleon III and the German Crisis, 1865–1866* (Cambridge, MA, 1966).

39. Douglas Johnson, *Guizot* (London, 1963), 317.

40. It is significant that two major works on Napoleon III's policy during this period, Pottinger, *Napoleon III and the German Crisis*, and Echard, *Napoleon III and the Concert of Europe*, barely mention the South German states and never discuss their role and importance in French policy. This is accurate; they had none, except as pawns in France's dealings with great powers.

41. Poidevin and Bariéty, *Relations franco-allemandes*, 78–79. Gall (*Liberalismus als regierende Partei*, 405–06) shows how French warnings to Baden against drawing closer to Prussia backfired, only encouraging the national movement there. Beust, the Austrian ambassador to France Prince Richard Metternich, and other Austrians were very critical of French tactics.

42. Max Spindler, *Handbuch der bayerischen Geschichte* (Munich, 1967), 4.1, 268–69: Langewiesche, *Liberalismus und Demokratie*, 420–03. For useful general accounts of Bavarian internal politics and German policies at this time, see Heinz W. Schlaich, "Bayern und Deutschland nach dem Prager Frieden," in *Gesellschaft und Herrschaft. Eine Festgabe für Karl Bosl*, ed. Richard van Dülmen (Munich, 1969), 301–38; Wolf D. Grüner, "Bayern, Preussen und die süddeutschen Staaten, 1866–1870," *Zeitschrift für bayerische Landesgeschichte*, 38 (1974), 799–827; William S. Trakas, "Particularism in Bavaria and Württemberg, 1866–70" (Ph.D., Wisconsin, 1979); and Frank D. Wright, "The Bavarian Patriotic Party 1868–1871" (Ph.D., Illinois, 1975). On Württemberg, E. Schneider, "Württembergs Beitritt zum deutschen Reich 1870," *Württembergische Vierteljahrshefte, neue Folge*, 29 (1920), 122–31; and Paul Sauer, *Das württembergische Heer in der Zeit des deutschen und des norddeutschen Bundes* (Stuttgart, 1958), 205–22, both show, despite their nationalist bias, how strong the resistance to military and political integration with Prussia was before and during 1870.

43. Gottfried Böhm, *Ludwig II* (Berlin, 1922), 209–10; Hans Rall, *König Ludwig II und Bismarcks Ringen um Bayern 1870/71* (Munich, 1973), 117–25; Doeberl, *Bayern und Reichsgründung*, 26–31, 220–21, 225–26, 231–33. On the policy of Bray-Steinburg in general, see Eberhard Weis, "Vom Kriegsausbruch zur Reichsgründung," *Zeitschrift für bayerische Landesgeschichte*, 33 (1970), 787–810.

44. Commenting on the irrelevance of the war guilt question in 1870, Lothar Gall remarks, "Neither side stumbled or, still less, was dragged into this war against its wishes (*innerlich widerstrebend*)" (*Bismarck*, 417). This is true of Prussia and

France—but clearly false of Bavaria and Württemberg, where both the governments and the majority parties stumbled and/or were dragged into the war
"*innerlich widerstrebend.*"

CHAPTER 5   GLADSTONE AS BISMARCK

The archival research for this essay was done in 1973 as part of a larger project
supported by a Fellowship of the National Endowment of the Humanities, whose
help is hereby gratefully acknowledged. I also wish to thank Professor Walter Arnstein
and Dr. Randall McGowan for their comments.

1. Program of the American Historical Association Meeting, St. Louis, MO.,
   December 28–30, 1962. I am relying on my memory for the remarks cited.
2. Philip Magnus, *Gladstone: A Biography* (New York, 1954), 401.
3. R. T. Shannon, *Gladstone and the Bulgarian Agitation 1876* (London, 1963),
   4–13, *et passim*.
4. P. A. Hanner, "The Irish Question and Liberal Politics, 1886–1894," *Historical
   Journal*, 12 (1969), 511–32; "Gladstone: The Making of a Political Myth,"
   Victorian Studies, 22 (Autumn 1978), 29–50.
5. John P. Rossi, *The Transformation of the British Liberal Party* (Philadelphia,
   1978), 99–103, 127.
6. Paul Knaplund, *Gladstone's Foreign Policy* (New York, 1935).
7. W. N. Medlicott, *Bismarck, Gladstone, and the Concert of Europe* (London,
   1956).
8. For example: Paul M. Kennedy in a recent review (*Guardian Weekly*, February 10,
   1980) makes it his strongest charge against Bismarck that he "did his utmost,
   often by very unsavory methods, to undermine an *alternative* European order,
   the Gladstonian Concert of Europe, which aimed at bringing nations together
   rather than playing them off against each other." (Italics in original.)
9. Theodor Schieder, "Bismarck—gestern und heute," in Lothar Gall, ed., *Das
   Bismarck-Problem in der Geschichtsschreibung nach 1945* (Cologne, 1971),
   368–69; S. A. Kaehler, "Bemerkungen zu einem Marginal Bismarcks von 1887,"
   in his *Studien zur deutschen Geschichte des 19. and 20.* Jahrhunderts (Göttingen,
   1961), 170–83, 388–89; Bismarck to Emperor William, October 22 1883, in
   Otto von Bismarck, *Die gesammelten Werke*, 15 vols. in 19 pts. (Berlin,
   1924–35), Vol. 6, Part C, 282–83.
10. Gladstone to Granville, August 22 1873, in Agatha Ramm, ed., *The Political
    Correspondence of Mr. Gladstone and Lord Granville, 1868–1876*, 2 vols. (London,
    1952), 2, 401. (Hereafter cited as *Glad. Corr. 1868–76.*)
11. Deryck Schreuder, "Gladstone as 'Troublemaker': Liberal Foreign Policy and the
    German Annexation of Alsace-Lorraine," *Journal of British Studies*, 18 (Spring
    1978), 106–35.
12. As Gladstone told Granville, "When he has supported & when he has opposed
    us he has been governed by one and the same principle all along." September 21,
    1884, in Agatha Ramm, ed., *The Political Correspondence of Mr. Gladstone and
    Lord Granville 1876–1886*, 2 vols. (Oxford, 1962), 2, 264. (Hereafter cited as
    Glad. Corr. 1876–86.)
13. Medlicott, *Bismarck, Gladstone*, 3–34, 314–35.
14. Ibid.; Schreuder, "Gladstone as 'Troublemaker,'" and "Gladstone and Italian
    Unification, 1848–70: The Making of a Liberal?" *English Historical Review*, 85
    (1970), 475–501. (However, Schreuder's book, *Gladstone and Kruger: Liberal*

Government and Colonial Home Rule, 1880–85 (London, 1969), reaches a less favorable verdict on Gladstone's handling of the South African problem). John Morley, *The Life of William Ewart Gladstone*, 3 vols. (New York, 1903), 2, 120–23, 150–53; J. L. Hammond, "Gladstone and the League of Nations Mind," in *Essays in Honour of Gilbert Murray*, ed. J. A. K. Thomson and A. J. Toynbee (London, 1936), 95–118; R. W. Seton-Watson, *Britain in Europe, 1789–1914* (New York, 1937), 546–48; Knaplund, *Gladstone's Foreign Policy*.

15. For example, Keneth Bourne, *The Foreign Policy of Victorian England, 1830–1902* (Oxford, 1970), 123–24, 138–40; Shannon, *Bulgarian Agitation*; Magnus, *Gladstone*, 191, 205, 239–41, 287–88; William L. Langer, *European Alliances and Alignments, 1871–1890* (New York, 1939), 12, 17, 202, 274–77, 317.

16. This is seen by critics who dwell on Gladstone's use of foreign policy for party and domestic policy ends. See, e.g., Shannon, *Bulgarian Agitation*, 90–93, 100–01, 110–11; Hamer, "Irish Question and Liberal Politics," 519.

17. Schreuder, "Gladstone and Italian Unification," sees the Italian question as decisive in forming his outlook, while the Crimean War seems even more important to me, and the letters Gladstone exchanged with Lord Aberdeen on the Eastern Question in 1856–57 particularly revealing (Aberdeen Papers, British Museum Add. Mss. 43071).

18. For a judicious recent appraisal of the relation between Gladstone's moral principles in politics and his personality, see Barbara C. Malament, "W. E. Gladstone: Another Victorian?" *British Studies Monitor*, 8 (Winter 1978), 22–38.

19. For convenience and in line with contemporary usage, the terms "Austria" and "Austrian" are here used in place of the more accurate but cumbersome "Austria–Hungary" and "Austro-Hungarian." Similarly "Turkish" and "Turkey" often substitute for "Ottoman" and "Ottoman Empire" and "England" occasionally for "Great Britain."

20. Brief treatments are in Medlicott, *Bismarck, Gladstone*, 59–62, and in F. R. Bridge, *From Sadowa to Sarajevo: The Foreign Policy of Austria–Hungary, 1866–1914* (London, 1972), 113. A thorough account is in Edith Partik, "Die Haltung Englands zu den Problemen Österreich-Ungarns in den Jahren 1878–1887," unpublished dissertation, University of Vienna, 1960, 130–44.

21. See, e.g., Sir William White, Ambassador to Turkey, to Lord Salisbury, October 22, 1879, and Sir Henry Elliot to Salisbury, January 5, 1880, Salisbury Papers, Christ Church, Oxford. A/13/28 and A/4/50.

22. Bridge, *Sadowa to Sarajevo*, 113–14.

23. Elliot to Salisbury, No. 13 Confidential, January 8, 1880, Public Record Office (PRO), FO7/988; same to same Nos. 139–42, March 22, 1880, FO/7/985.

24. Gladstone to the Duke of Argyll, March 26, 1880, Add. Mss. 44104.

25. Partik, "Haltung Englands," 130–44; speech of November 29, 1879, in W. E. Gladstone, *The Midlothian Campaign, 1879–80* (Edinburgh, 1880), 158–63. For instances of previous Gladstonian attacks upon Austria, see his "The Paths of Honour and of Shame," *19th Century*, 3 (March 1878), 600–03; "Liberty in East and West," ibid. (June 1878), 1170–74; speech of February 8, 1878 in the House of Commons, *Hansard's Parliamentary Debates*, 3rd ser., vol. 232, 1362–78.

26. The only important criticism came from Lord Spencer to Granville. March 28, 1880: "What an unnecessary mess the great W. E. G. has got into re Austria." Granville Papers, PRO 30/29/29A. Argyll mildly suggested to Gladstone that

his language had been somewhat strong (March 22, 1880, Add. Mss. 44104). On the other hand, some Liberals applauded the speech (Lord Bath to Granville, March 20, 1880, PRO 30/29/28A, and to Gladstone, April 4 and 11, 1880. Add. Mss. 44463; Lord Reay to Gladstone, April 12, ibid.), and in general the party seems to have ignored the incident.

27. Salisbury to Lord Balfour, private, March 18, 1880, Balfour Papers, Add. Mss. 49688; Salisbury to Elliot, private, March 22, 1880, Salisbury Papers, A/23/41.

28. Medlicott, *Bismarck, Gladstone*, 60–62; Karolyi to Gladstone, May 1, 1880, and Gladstone to Karolyi, May 5, FO 7/985; various letters, Karolyi to Granville, early May 1886, PRO 30/29/155; Gladstone to Granville, April 29, 1880. *Glad. Corr. 1876–86*, 1, 121–22.

29. Dudley W. R. Bahlman, ed., *The Diary of Sir Edward Walter Hamilton 1880–1885*, 2 vols. (Oxford, 1972), entries of May 15 and 18, 1880, 1, 13; memorandum by Gladstone, November 18, 1884, Add. Mss. 44547.

30. Gladstone to Granville, May 4, 1880, *Glad. Corr. 1876–86*, 1, 123.

31. Granville to Elliot. No. 221 A. May 11, 1880. FO 7/485; Karolyi to Granville, May 11, and Elliot to Granville, May 15. PRO 30/29/155.

32. Gladstone to Granville, May 8, 1880, *Glad. Corr. 1876–86*, 1, 125; Gladstone to Bath, May 7, 1880, Add. Mss. 44544. The consul, Evans, a traveler and publicist whose earlier pro-Slav writings had attracted Gladstone's attention, was later jailed and then expelled by Austria for his activities during the Bosnian insurrection of 1881. Granville to Gladstone, September 13, 1882, *Glad. Corr. 1876–86*, 1, 420.

33. Gladstone to Granville, May 11 and 28, 1880, *Glad. Corr. 1876–86*, 1, 125–26, 130; Argyll to Granville, May 4, 1880, PRO 30/29/29A. Gladstone also maintained contacts with a number of Balkan leaders, including the Croatian leader Bishop Strossmayer, an Austrian subject; the correspondence from this period is found in Add. Mss. 44463 and 44465. See also R. W. Seton-Watson, *The Southern Slav Question and the Habsburg Monarchy* (New York, 1969; original ed. 1911), 416–44; Joseph O. Baylen, "Bishop Strossmayer and Mme. Olga Novikov. Two Unpublished Letters," *Slavic Review*, 26 (1967), 468–73.

34. See Medlicott, *Bismarck, Gladstone*, 72–169.

35. See his "Montenegro a Sketch," *19th Century*, 3 (May 1877), 360–79. or "The Peace to Come." ibid. (February 1878), 209–26.

36. Medlicott, *Bismarck, Gladstone*, 170–95; Bridge, *Sadowa to Sarajevo*, 111–16 Outstanding in the vast German literature on Bismarck's policy during this period are Helmut Böhme, *Deutschlands Weg zur Grossmacht* (2nd ed., Cologne and Berlin, 1972) and Andreas Hillgruber, *Bismarcks Aussenpolitik* (Freiburg im Breisgau, 1972).

37. The best primary sources on Austrian policy are the memorials (*Vorträge*) of Haymerlé to the Emperor, February 21, May 30, September 9, and October 4, 6, and 7 1880, Staatsarchiv (Vienna), Kabinettsarchiv, Geheimakten, 18.

38. Salisbury to Elliot, January 14, 1880, and Elliot to Salisbury, January 23, Salisbury Papers, A/24/39 and A/4/49.

39. Elliot to Granville, May 27, July 4, 10. 22. 25, and 31, September 30, and October 5, 1880, PRO 30/29/155.

40. See Elliot's assurances to Granville, April 28, 1880, ibid.

41. Gladstone to Granville, May 11 and 12, 1880. and Granville to Gladstone, May 11, *Glad. Corr. 1876–86*, 1, 125–27. As a minute by Granville on May 11, makes clear (PRO 30/29/143), Gladstone's ideas about dealing with Russia met resistance within the cabinet.

42. Gladstone to Granville, 12, 2, 7, and July 1880, and Granville to Gladstone, July 7, *Glad. Corr. 1876–86*, 1, 142–45.

43. Entries of August 23 and 25, 1880, *Hamilton Diary*, 1, 36–37.

44. Gladstone to Granville, July 12, 14, and 23, August 20, 1880, *Glad. Corr. 1876–86*, 1, 145–46, 152, 162; undated memorandum by Gladstone entitled "The Concert," Add. Mss. 44764.

45. Gladstone to Granville, July 26, September 18 and 30, and October 4, 7, and 9 1880, *Glad. Corr. 1876–86*, 1, 153, 175–76, 189–91. 194; 196; entries of October 8 and 11 *Hamilton Diary*, 1, 63–64.

46. Gladstone to Granville, September 19, 22, and 23, 1880, *Glad. Corr. 1876–88*, 1, 178. 189–82; Gladstone to Lord Reay, September 16. Add. Mss. 44544. In view of Italian irredentist claims and Austro-Italian rivalry in the Adriatic, the idea of Italian armed action particularly frightened Austria. She protested to England against it at the beginning of the Montenegrin question, with no effect. Granville to Elliot, nos. 220–21, May 8 and 10, 1880, FO 7/985.

47. Gladstone to Granville, September 18 and 20, 1880. *Glad. Corr. 1876–86*, 1, 177, 180; Gladstone to Joseph Cowen, September 18, Add. Mss. 44544; entry of September 19 1880. *Hamilton Diary*, 1, 53.

48. For Gladstone's fear of its revival, see Gladstone to Argyll, October 14, 1880, Add. Mss. 44544.

49. Entries of September 19 and 21, 1880, *Hamilton Diary*, 1, 53–55.

50. Gladstone to Joseph Cowen, MP, September 19, 1880 and May 30, 1881, Add. Mss. 44544; Gladstone to Argyll, October 9, 1880, ibid.

51. Entry of February 9, 1885, *Hamilton Diary*, 2, 793.

52. Entry of November 7, 1880, *Hamilton Diary*, 1, 72–73.

53. Gladstone to Granville, October 15, and 20, and December 3, 1880, *Glad. Corr. 1876–86*, 1, 202, 204, 227; December 4, 1880, *Hamilton Diary*, 1, 84–85.

54. Gladstone to Granville, October 15, and December 3, 1880, April 15, 1881, *Glad. Corr. 1876–86*, 1, 202, 227. 257–58; November 10, *Hamilton Diary*, 1, 76.

55. Gladstone to Granville, October 28, 1880, *Glad. Corr. 1876–86*, 1, 210; Sir Charles Dilke to Granville, October 18, 1880, Dilke Papers, Add. Mss. 43878.

56. Gladstone to Granville, April 15, 1881, *Glad. Corr. 1876–86*, 1, 257; entry of February 27, 1881, *Hamilton Diary*, 1, 111.

57. Gladstone to Granville, December 17, and 20, 1880, and Granville to Gladstone, December 19, *Glad. Corr. 1876–86*, 1, 230–33.

58. See various notes from Cabinet ministers in late May and early June 1880 in the Granville Papers, PRO 30/22/143.

59. Granville to Gladstone, April 21, 1881 and Gladstone to Granville, April 22, *Glad. Corr. 1876–86*, 1, 262–63.

60. September 5, 1883, *Hamilton Diary*, 2, 480.

61. Gladstone to Granville, October 21, 1881, *Glad. Corr. 1876–86*, 1, 305.

62. Elliot to Granville, September 10 and December 6, 1883, PRO 30/29/155; Granville to Gladstone, October 5, 1883, *Glad. Corr. 1876–86*, 2, 94.

63. Gladstone to Granville, October 7, 1883, *Glad. Corr. 1876–86*, 2, 96; cf. also same to same, December 13, 1881 and September 1, 1883, ibid., 1, 318 and 2, 81, and entry of September 18, 1883, *Hamilton Diary*, 2, 483–84.

64. Gladstone to Granville, October 3, 1883, *Glad. Corr. 1876–86*, 2, 92.

65. On September 7 he had suggested to Granville that France might join Britain in encouraging a Balkan League of Serbia, Montenegro, Rumania, and Greece. Ibid., 84.

66. C. J. Lowe, *The Reluctant Imperialists.* Vol. 1: *British Foreign Policy 1878–1902* (London, 1967), 50–51; Ronald Robinson and John Gallagher with Alice Denny, *Africa and the Victorians: The Climax of Imperialism* (New York, 1968), 155–59.

67. Two excellent accounts are Robinson and Gallagher, *Africa and the Victorians*, 76–159, and Agatha Ramm, "Great Britain and France in Egypt, 1876–1882," in Prosser Gifford and William R. Louis, eds., *France and Britain in Africa* (New Haven, 1970), 73–119.

68. Ramm, "Britain and France in Egypt," 77–81.

69. Gladstone to Granville, January 4, 17, and 31, 1882, *Glad. Corr. 1876–86*, 1, 327, 330–31, and 337.

70. See various memoranda by Cabinet members dated January 28–February 1, 1882 in the Granville Papers. PRO 30/29/143.

71. Gladstone to Granville, December 23, 1881, *Glad. Corr. 1876–86*, 1, 322.

72. To Granville, January 19, 1882, ibid., 332–33.

73. To Granville, February 6, 1882, ibid., 340.

74. Gladstone to W. S. Blunt, January 20, 1882, Add. Mss. 44545; W. E. Gladstone, "Aggression on Egypt and Freedom in the East," *Nineteenth Century*, 2 (August–December 1877), 149–66.

75. Memorandum by Gladstone, July 5, 1882, *Glad. Corr. 1876–86*, 1, 385–86; entry of June 25, *Hamilton Diary*, 1, 292–94.

76. Entry of July 7, 1882, ibid., 298–99; Gladstone to Granville, June 27 and July 1, 1882, and Granville to Gladstone, July 9, *Glad. Corr. 1876–86*, 1, 382–83, 387–88; various documents on the Cabinet discussions of July 7–15 in the Granville Papers, PRO 30/29/143.

77. *Glad. Corr. 1876–86*, 1, 381.

78. Elliot to Granville, July 21, 1882. PRO 30/29/155; Gladstone to Bright, July 10, 12, 13, and 14, 1882, Add. Mss. 44545 (the last of these is published in Morley, *Gladstone*, 3, 84–85); Granville to Dilke, July 16 and 17, 1882; Dilke to Granville, July 17; and memorandum by Dilke, July 19, Dilke Papers, Add. Mss. 43880.

79. Gladstone to Granville, July 13, 14, and 21, 1882, *Glad. Corr. 1876–86*, 394–96, 400–01.

80. To Granville, July 22, 1882, ibid., 401–02.

81. Gladstone to Granville, July 23–26, 1882, *Glad. Corr. 1876–86*, 1, 402, 404–05 (nos. 780, 782, and 786–87).

82. Gladstone to his brother Thomas, July 23, 1882, Add. Mss. 44545.

83. Memorandum by Gladstone, July 29, 1882, Add. Mss. 44766.

84. Entry of August 25, 1882, *Hamilton Diary*, 1, 324–25.

85. Granville to Gladstone, August 21, 1882 and Gladstone to Granville, August 25, *Glad. Corr. 1876–86*, 1, 410–11.

86. Gladstone to Sir Henry Ponsonby, September 4, 1882, Add. Mss. 44545; entry of September 6, *Hamilton Diary*, 1, 334.

87. Granville to Gladstone, September 7, 1882, *Glad. Corr. 1876–86*, 1, 415; entries of September 5 and 7, *Hamilton Diary*, 1, 333, 335.

88. September 7, 1882, *Glad. Corr. 1876–86*, 1, 414–15.

89. Gladstone to Granville, September 9, 1882, ibid., 419.

90. Gladstone to Bishop Strossmayer, October 12, 1882, and to Madame Olga Novikov, September 15, Add. Mss. 44546 and 44545.

91. Gladstone to Granville, September 16, 19, 22, and 29, October 3 and 17, and December 21, 1882, and January 13, 1883, *Glad. Corr. 1876–86*, 1, 421–25,

429, 434, 440–41, 447–48, and 473; 2, 8. Cf. also entries of December 1, 1881 and September 10 and 15, 1882, *Hamilton Diary*, 1, 192, 337. 340; Gladstone to Lord Ripon, November 24, 1881, Add. Mss. 44545.

92. Gladstone to Granville, October 17, 1882, *Glad. Corr. 1876–86*, 1, 448; entry of October 30, *Hamilton Diary*, 1, 353.

93. Robinson and Gallagher, *Africa and the Victorians*, chap. 5.

94. My colleague, Professor Walter Arnstein, warns me against painting too apocalyptic a picture of Gladstone's second ministry, pointing out its impressive record of domestic reform and urging that the Irish question was not as paralyzing as it has often been portrayed. Granting this, it is hard to see the foreign policy record as anything but a failure, or to escape the impression that by early 1885 Gladstone felt he could not carry on much longer. See, e.g., the entries of February 15, 16, and 18, 1885, *Hamilton Diary*, 2, 796–97.

95. The following documents seem to me to illustrate best the points made: in *Glad. Corr. 1876–86*, nos. 1061, 1065, 1103, 1180, 1191, 1200, 1208, 1305, 1396, 1496, 1536, and 1545; in the *Hamilton Diary*, 2, 502–03, 754–57, 764–65, and 776–77; and in the Gladstone Papers, Gladstone to Childers, February 16, 1885, Add. Mss. 44547, and two memoranda, "Egyptian Finance," January 2, 1885, and "Policy in the Soudan," January 19, 1885, Add. Mss. 44769.

96. The old thesis is that of A. J. P. Taylor, *Germany's First Bid for Colonies, 1884–1885* (London, 1938). The most important work demolishing it is Henry Ashby Turner, "Bismarck's Imperial Venture: Anti-British in Origin?" in Prosser Gifford and William R. Louis, eds., *Britain and Germany in Africa* (New Haven, 1967), 47–82, and Hans-Ulrich Wehler, *Bismarck und der Imperialismus* (Cologne and Berlin, 1969). See also G. N. Sanderson, "The European Partition of Africa: Coincidence or Conjuncture?" *Journal of Imperial and Commonwealth History*, 3 (October 1974), 1–54; H. Pogge von Strandmann, "Germany Colonial Expansion under Bismarck," *Past and Present*, 33 (1969), 140–59; and H. P. Merritt. "Bismarck and the German Interest in East Africa, 1884–1885," *Historical Journal*, 21 (March 1978), 97–117.

97. Sanderson, "European Partition of Africa," 29.

98. See, e.g., Gladstone to Granville, August 22 and September 5 and 8, 1884, *Glad. Corr. 1876–86*, 2, 234, 248, and 250; memorandum by Gladstone entitled, "Commission on Suez Canal," February 26, 1885. PRO 30/29/145.

99. Gladstone to Granville, September 13, 1883, *Glad. Corr. 1876–86*, 2, 87; entries of September 10, 1883 and April 12, 1884 *Hamilton Diary*, 2, 481 and 594.

100. Entries of April 26 and July 28, 1884, *Hamilton Diary*, 2, 602–03, 661; Gladstone to Granville, December 7, 1884, *Glad. Corr. 1876–86*, 2, 291.

101. This is the consistent message of Elliot's private letters to Granville in 1882–83 (PRO 30/29/155). Cf. also Granville to Gladstone, September 16, 1884, *Glad. Corr. 1876–86*, 2, 258.

102. Granville to Gladstone, September 20, 1884, *Glad. Corr. 1876–86*, 2, 263; Granville to Lord Ampthill, June 14, 1884 in Winifred Taffs, *Ambassador to Bismarck: Lord Odo Russell, First Baron Ampthill* (London, 1938), 323; William R. Louis, "The Berlin Congo Conference," in Gifford and Louis, *France and Britain in Africa*, 167–220.

103. Medlicott, *Bismarck, Gladstone*, 117–19. At the time the British occupied Egypt, Bismarck not only was cordial and supportive, but also continued to urge Anglo-French cooperation and advised the British to pay attention to

French susceptibilities. See entries of September 11 and 12, 1882, *Hamilton Diary*, 1, 338; Taffs, *Odo Russell*, 310–15.

104. Sanderson, "European Partition of Africa," 28–32. There is considerable evidence of Derby's policy of preemptive imperialism, and the similar ideas of Kimberley, Chamberlain, and Selbourne, in the Granville Papers, PRO 30/29/120, and in Derby's correspondence with Gladstone, Add. Mss. 44142. Gladstone's attempt to curb Derby's annexationism is best reflected in his letter to Derby of December 30, 1884, Add. Mss. 44142.

105. The evidence on these points in the Gladstone–Granville correspondence is too massive to cite in detail. Good indications of Gladstone's basic attitudes are in *Hamilton Diary*, 2, 760–61 (January 1 and 2, 1885).

106. Entry of January 29, 1885, ibid., 784; Gladstone to Derby, December 21, 1884, Add. Mss. 44547.

107. A good illustration of how missionary ideals in foreign policy animated Gladstone to the end of his life is an undated and untitled memorandum he wrote in 1894 or 1895 (Add. Mss. 44776) which begins:

England is appointed to be a witness in Europe for great and salutary
  principles of liberty, against despotism
  law against arbitrary will
  disinterestedness, against intrigue, turbulence, and self aggrandisement.
In proportion to the prevalence of these principles, there will be peace; & in the train of peace there will be plenty.
  Selfishness in each particular State is the only danger of Europe, & the only enemy of England. It is a consolatory thought, amid the troubles of the time, that our cause, our interest, thus understood, are not our own cause & interest only but the cause, the interest of all. . . .

108. *Edinburgh Review*, October 1870.

109. October 2, 1884, *Hamilton Diary*, 2, 694–95.

110. Memorandum by Gladstone, April 8, 1895, Add. Mss. 44776.

111. Karl Otmar Freiherr von Aretin, *Heiliges Römisches Reich 1776–1806: Reichsverfassung und Staatssouveränität*, 2 vols. (Wiesbaden, 1967).

112. This is true also because Realpolitik in practice often becomes an ideology, making the service of state interest an ideological or moral principle. See Karl-Georg Faber, "Realpolitik als Ideologie," *Historische Zeitschrift*, 203 (1966), 1–45.

113. See, e.g., Otto Vossler, "Bismarcks Ethos," *Historische Zeitschrift*, 171 (1951), 263–92, and G. A. Rein, *Die Revolution in der Politik Bismarcks* (Göttingen, 1957).

114. A recent, convincing interpretation of Bismarck's policy as cynical and manipulative is given by Fritz Stern, *Gold and Iron: Bismarck, Bleichroeder, and the Building of the German Empire* (New York, 1977).

CHAPTER 7   WORLD WAR I AS GALLOPING GERTIE: A REPLY TO JOACHIM REMAK

1. Joachim Remak, "1914—The Third Balkan War: Origins Reconsidered," *Journal of Modern History*, 43 (September 1971), 353–66.

2. Nor will I attempt to "prove" my case with elaborate footnotes. The references will mainly serve to illustrate the kind of sources and literature I have used.

3. Fritz Fischer, *Griff nach der Weltmacht* (Düsseldorf, 1961), translated as *Germany's Aims in the First World War* (New York, 1967); "*Weltpolitik,*

Weltmachstreben und deutsche Kriegsziele," *Historische Zeitschrift*, 199 (1964), 265–346; and *Krieg der Illusionen* (Düsseldorf, 1969). The main rival work is Gerhard Ritter, *Staatskunst und Kriegshandwerk*, 4 vols. (Munich, 1954–68), now being translated as *The Sword and the Scepter* (Coral Gables, FL., 1969–). A good survey of the controversy is in Wolfgang J. Mommsen. "The Debate on German War Aims," *Journal of Contemporary History*, 1 (July 1966), 47–74; for citations of the literature, see James J. Sheehan, "Germany, 1890–1918: A Survey of Recent Research," *Central European History*, 1 (December 1968), 345–72.

4. Arno Mayer, "Domestic Causes of the First World War," in *The Responsibility of Power*, ed. Leonard Krieger and Fritz Stern (Garden City, NY., 1967), 286–300; "Internal Causes and Purposes of War in Europe, 1870–1956: A Research Assignment," *Journal of Modern History*, 41 (September 1969), 291–303.

5. Konrad Jarausch, "The Illusion of Limited War: Chancellor Bethmann Hollweg's Calculated Risk, July 1914," *Central European History*, 2 (March 1969), 48–76; Fritz Stern, "Bethmann Hollweg and the War: The Limits of Responsibility," in *The Responsibility of Power*, 252–85 (see n. 4 above).

6. Peter Loewenberg, "Arno Mayer's 'Internal Causes and Purposes of War in Europe, 1870–1956'—an Inadequate Model of Human Behavior, National Conflict, and Historical Change," *Journal of Modern History*, 42 (December 1970), 628–36.

7. See J. H. Hexter, *The History Primer* (New York, 1970), chap. 5; Gordon Leff, *History and Social Theory* (Garden City, NY., 1971), 48–90.

8. Hexter, *The History Primer*, 118–35. "Galloping Gertie" was the popular name for the Tacoma Narrows Bridge in Washington, which collapsed in 1940 when winds induced pressures on supporting members sufficient in turn to cause the supports to generate destructive forces within the bridge.

9. Hugo Hantsch, *Leopold Graf Berchtold, Grandseigneur und Staatsmann*, 2 vols. (Graz, 1963); Robert A. Kann, "Erzherzog Franz Ferdinand und Graf Berchtold als Aussenminister, 1912–1914," *Mitteilungen des österreichischen Staatsarchivs*, 22 (1969), 246–78.

10. A. V. Florovsky, "Russo-Austrian Conflicts in the Early 18th Century," *Slavonic and East European Review*, 47 (January 1969), 94–115.

11. As Norman Rich points out, the only way Germany could have avoided political defeat in 1905–06 was either by a more forceful diplomacy backed by the threat of war, or by war itself (*Friedrich von Holstein*, 2 vols. [Cambridge, 1965], 1, 742–45).

12. Kenneth Bourne, *Britain and the Balance of Power in North America, 1815–1908* (Berkeley, CA., 1967); Ian Nish, *The Anglo-Japanese Alliance* (London, 1966).

13. See, e.g., J. A. S. Grenville, *Lord Salisbury and Foreign Policy* (London, 1964); and Thomas M. Iiams, Jr., *Dreyfus, Diplomatists and the Dual Alliance* (Geneva and Paris, 1962).

14. Christopher Andrew, *Théophile Delcassé and the Making of the Entente Cordiale* (New York, 1968); Pierre Guillen, *L'Allemagne et le Maroc de 1870 à 1905* (Paris, 1967).

15. Firuz Kazemzadeh, *Russia and Britain in Persia, 1864–1914* (New Haven, CT., 1968); Horst Jaeckel, *Die Nordwestgrenze in der Verteidigung Indiens 1900–1908 und der Weg Englands zum russisch-britischen Abkommen von 1907* (Cologne, 1968).

16. A typical expression of this fear is Sir Edward Grey's remark in October 1905 that Britain "was running a real risk of losing France and not gaining Germany; who would want us, if she could detach France from us" (S. R. Williamson, Jr., *The Politics of the Grand Strategy* [Cambridge, MA., 1969], 60).

17. Gerhard Ritter, *Die Legende der verschmähten englischen Freundschaft 1898/1901* (Freiburg, 1929); H. W. Koch, "The Anglo-German Alliance Negotiations: Missed Opportunity or Myth?" *History*, 54 (1969), 378–92.

18. Curzon's argument is both typical and significant: "It [a German alliance] will mean the habitual and incessant surrendering to Germany on points where our commercial interests are concerned all over the world. What should we get from her in return? We do not want her army. Her navy is not sufficiently strong to be of much value. Austria can give us absolutely nothing and might entangle us in a fight over the Balkan Peninsula. Italy is too weak to be of any assistance" (Jaeckel, *Die Nordwestgrenze*, 152 [see n. 15 above]).

19. Minute of November 9, 1901, in *British Documents on the Origins of the War, 1898–1914*, 11 vols., ed. G. P. Gooch and H. W. V. Temperley (London, 1926–38), 2, 76 (hereafter cited as BD).

20. Jaeckel, *Die Nordwestgrenze*, 152.

21. G. N. Sanderson portrays well Salisbury's resentment at being forced by Bismarck to play a role in Europe: "He resented being forced to carry Bismarck's Austrian burden at the Straits; he resented still more the consequent deflection of Russian hostility from Berlin to London. But he made a shrewd bargain by committing the allies to the defence of Asia Minor as well as the Balkans; and as an interim defensive arrangement at the Straits the Agreement was at least as valuable to England as to Germany" (*Europe, England, and the Upper Nile, 1882–1899* [Edinburgh, 1965], 40–41). The agreement was really much more favorable to Britain than to Germany; as Paul Kluke points out, it marked the beginning of Salisbury's victory over Bismarck and the breakdown of Bismarck's system ("Bismarck und Salisbury. Ein diplomatisches Duell," *Historische Zeitschrift*, 175 [1953], 295–306). But Salisbury would already in 1887 have preferred a direct deal with France to having to rely on the Triple Alliance for support; the trouble was that France's price at this time, evacuation of Egypt, was too high.

22. On the general subject, C. J. Lowe, *Salisbury and the Mediterranean 1886–1896* (London, 1965). On the breakdown of the Second Mediterranean Agreement, I disagree with J. A. S. Grenville ("Goluchowski, Salisbury and the Mediterranean Agreements, 1895–1897," *Slavonic and East European Review*, 36 [1957–58], 340–69) and Margaret Jefferson ("Lord Salisbury and the Eastern Question, 1890–1898," *Slavonic and East European Review*, 39 [1960–61], 44–60, 216–21). The point is not, as both seem to feel, that Salisbury did not want to throw Austria over brusquely or act dishonestly toward her. It is that Salisbury saw absolutely no possibility of actively working with her or supporting her. He wanted an agreement with Russia and worked for it, knowing that Tsar Nicholas II was already very hostile toward Austria and looking forward to her demise; Salisbury merely hoped that such an Anglo-Russian agreement could be reached without the British acting basely toward Austria or undermining her essential position. Such scruples of conscience are seldom an effective barrier against reason of state; later British statesmen would easily get over them. See also C. J. Lowe, *The Reluctant Imperialists* (London, 1967), 1, 196–204.

23. L. K. Young, *British Policy in China 1895–1902* (Oxford, 1970).

24. Christopher Andrew, "German World Policy and the Reshaping of the Dual Allinace," *Journal of Contemporary History*, 1 (1966), 137–51.

25. Andrew, *Théophile Delcassé and the Making of the Entente Cordiale*; Howard Sieberg, *Eugène Etienne und die französische Kolonialpolitik (1887–1904)* (Cologne, 1968).

26. Max Beloff, *Imperial Sunset* (New York, 1970), 1, 102. British thinking is illustrated by Sir George Clarke's remark in 1905: "I believe that the defense of our Indian frontier against Russia is more a matter for the F. O. than for the Indian Army. When the war is over it may be possible to give way on the Dardanelles question in return for a binding agreement with Russia as regards Afghanistan" (Jaeckel, *Die Nordwestgrenze*, 84). Indeed, the main British worry was that concessions in the Near East would not be enough to appease Russia. "Whatever we do in the way of friendliness in South East Europe or elsewhere," argued Cecil Spring-Rice in 1903, "we shall never be forgiven the crime of possessing what Russia wants to have" (Jaeckel, *Die Nordwestgrenze*, 162).

27. In addition to the valuable older works of E. L. Woodward, A. J. Marder, Oron J. Hale, Eckhart Kehr, and others, see especially Jonathan Steinberg, *Yesterday's Deterrent* (New York, 1965), and Volcker R. Berghahn, "Zu den Zielen des deutschen Flottenbaus unter Wilhelm II," *Historische Zeitschrift*, 210 (1970), 34–100.

28. Zara S. Steiner, *The Foreign Office and Foreign Policy 1898–1914* (New York, 1970).

29. Beloff, *Imperial Sunset*, 1, 86–87, 103; David W. Sweet, "The Baltic in British Diplomacy before the First World War," *Historical Journal*, 13 (1970), 455–57; A. J. Morris, "The English Radicals' Campaign for Disarmament and the Hague Conference of 1907," *Journal of Modern History*, 43 (1971), 378–82.

30. Sweet, "The Baltic in British Diplomacy," 455–57, 482–84; Williamson, *passim* (see n. 16 above).

31. Jacques Willequet, *Le Congo belge et la Weltpolitik* (1894–1914) (Brussels, 1962); BD, vol. 10, pt. 2, docs. 266–69.

32. Hardinge to Nicolson, January 4, 1909, BD, 5, 550. (Also quoted in Steiner, *The Foreign Office*, 95, where it is dated March 26.)

33. Egmont Zechlin, "Deutschland zwischen Kabinettskrieg und Wirtschaftskrieg. Politik und Kriegführung in den ersten Monaten des Weltkrieges 1914," *Historische Zeitschrift*, 199 (1964), 347–55; "Die türkischen Meerengen-Brennpunkt der Weltgeschichte," *Geschichte in Wissenschaft und Unterricht*, 17 (1966), 9–15.

34. Sweet, "The Baltic in British Diplomacy," 284.

35. For example, Jonathan Steinberg, "Germany and the Russo-Japanese War," *American Historical Review*, 15 (1970), 1965–86.

36. "Germany has no friends in Europe," complained the Prussian diplomat Baron Bunsen in 1848. "No one grants aspiring Germany any favors" (Holger Hjelholt, *British Mediation in the Danish-German Conflict 1848–1850* [Copenhagen, 1966] pt. 2, 20). (Translation mine.)

37. See especially Fritz Fellner, *Der Dreibund* (Vienna, 1960).

38. What M. S. Anderson says of the balance of power in eighteenth-century British usage, that "very often it was no more than a phrase used to inhibit thought." seems to apply to the nineteenth and twentieth centuries as well (Ragnhild Hatton and M. S. Anderson, eds., *Studies in Diplomatic History* [Hamden, CT., 1970], 184).

39. Risto Ropponen, *Die Kraft Russlands* (Helsinki, 1968).

40. For example, in May 1914 the Russian Minister of War. General Suchomlinov, told the French Ambassador Paléologue that Russia meant to annex Galicia on Francis Joseph's death and the Tsar hoped that Germany would swallow this (F. N. Bradley, "Quelques aspects de la politique étrangère de Russie avant 1914 à travers les archives françaises," *Etudes slaves et est-européennes*, 1 [1967], 100–01).

41. Fischer's *Krieg der Illusionen* is riddled with this. See also the remarks of Fritz Fellner on the Ritter-Fischer debate, in Gerald D. Feldman, ed., *German Imperialism, 1914–1918* (New York, 1972), 193–95.

42. Howard S. Weinroth, "The British Radicals and the Balance of Power, 1902–1914," *Historical Journal*, 13 (1970), 653–82.

43. As Count Czernin wrote Berchtold on June 22, 1914: "Before our eyes, in broad day light, openly and obviously, as clear as the sun, with shameless impudence, the encirclement of the Monarchy is being completed; under Russian-French patronage a new Balkan League is being welded together, whose purpose, today still apparently complicated, will soon appear in astonishing simplicity—against the Monarchy" (Zechlin, "Die türkischen Meerengen," 14). (Translation mine.)

44. Andrew, *Théophile Délaissé and the Making of the Entente Cordiale*, 126–35.

45. Ljilana Aleksić-Pejković, "La Serbie et les rapports entre les puissances de l'Entente 1908–1913," *Balkan Studies*, 6 (1965), 325–44.

46. At the first signs of an Austro-Russian rift, Hardinge commented, "The struggle between Austria and Russia in the Balkans is evidently now beginning and we shall not be bothered by Russia in Asia" (Douglas Dakin, "British Sources Concerning the Greek Struggle in Macedonia, 1901–1909," *Balkan Studies*, 2 [1961], 76). His comments on British aims in regard to Macedonia are equally clear and revealing: "We are quite hopeful about Macedonian reforms, if we can only come to terms with Russia, we shall be able to secure the cooperation of France and Italy and although Austria and Germany will at first be obstructive we have reason to believe that Germany will so dislike to see a combination of four Powers in opposition to her and Austria that she will reluctantly follow us and thus force Austria to come in also" (Hardinge to Nicolson, April 13, 1908, BD, 5:236–37). See also Steiner, *The Foreign Office*, 95–97; and M. B. Cooper, "British Policy in the Balkans, 1908–9," *Historical Journal*, 1 (1964–65), 258–79.

47. Steiner, *The Foreign Office*, pp. 87–88.

48. Hardinge to Cartwright, October 4, 1909, BD 9 (1), 74.

49. Hardinge to Bax-Ironside, October 28, 1909, ibid., 80–81.

50. Steiner, *The Foreign Office*, 135, 146–47.

51. Ibid.

52. F. Roy Bridge, "Tarde venientibus ossa: Austro-Hungarian Colonial Aspirations in Asia Minor 1913–14", *Middle Eastern Studies*, 6 (1970), 319–30.

53. Steiner, *The Foreign Office*, pp. 134–37; see also n. 58 below.

54. F. Roy Bridge, "The British Declaration of War on Austria-Hungary in 1914," *Slavonic and East European Review*, 47 (1969), 401–22; Harry Hanak, "The Government, the Foreign Office and Austria-Hungary, 1914–1918," ibid., 162–67.

55. Hanak, 168–71; Beloff, *Imperial Sunset*, 1, 206–09. On the general subject of British aims toward the Continent, see Harold I. Nelson, *Land and Power* (London, 1963); Paul Guinn, *British Strategy and Politics, 1914 to 1918* (Oxford,

1965); and V. H. Rothwell, *British War Aims and Peace Diplomacy, 1914–1918* (Oxford, 1971).

56. For example, so brilliant a book as Zara Steiner's on the Foreign Office concentrates entirely on British attitudes toward Germany, virtually ignoring the impact of British policies on Austria. Beloff (*Imperial Sunset*) devotes 283 pages to an admirable discussion of British prewar and wartime policy, but mentions Austria only in passing. Only F. Roy Bridge's unpublished dissertation, "The Diplomatic Relations between Great Britain and Austria-Hungary, 1906–1912" (London, 1966) indicates the significance of British policy for Austria.

57. For example, see Rich, *Friedrich von Holstein*, 2, 215–20, 243–84.

58. In contrast, Grey's insistence in both the 1913 and 1914 crises that an Austro-Russian war over the Balkans, representing merely the struggle between Teuton and Slav for supremacy, as he put it, need not concern Britain or Europe unless Germany or France entered in, strikes one as remarkably insular and unrealistic (Grey to Buchanan, February 17, 1913, BD9 (2), doc. 626; Grey to Bertie, July 29, 1914, BD 11, doc. 283).

59. Although a number of Englishmen (Fairfax Cartwright at Vienna, Ralph Paget at Belgrade, Nicolson, and others) had long warned of the dangers involved in Austria's decline, only Francis Bertie at the last moment pleaded with Grey to put pressure on France to divert Russia from her absurd and dangerous policy of protecting her Balkan clients at all cost (Bertie to Grey, July 27, 1914, BD, doc. 192). By then it was too late, of course, and there is no chance Grey would have risked Britain's ententes by any such pressure.

60. Interestingly enough, as Egmont Zechlin repeatedly argues in criticism of Fischer, Germany (or at least Bethmann) tried to some extent early in the war to keep it a limited cabinet-style conflict. See his "Das 'schlesische' Angebot und die italienische Kriegsgefahr," *Geschichte in Wissenschaft und Unterricht*, 14 (1963), 533–56; and "Probleme des Kriegskalküls und Kriegsbeendigung im Ersten Weltkrieg," ibid., 16 (1965), 69–82. But Zechlin's evidence never indicates a real chance that the war could have been limited.

61. Wolfdieter Bihl, "Zur den österreichisch-ungarischen Kriegszielen 1914," *Jahrbücher für Geschichte Osteuropas*, 16 (1968), 505–30; Fritz Klein, "Die Rivalität zwischen Deutschland und Oesterreich-Ungarn in der Türkei am Vorabend des ersten Weltkrieges," in *Politik im Krieg 1914–1918*, ed. Fritz Klein (Berlin, 1964), 1–21.

CHAPTER 8   EMBEDDED COUNTERFACTUALS AND WORLD WAR I AS AN UNAVOIDABLE WAR

1. R. N. Lebow, "Franz Ferdinand Found Alive. World War I Unnecessary," unpublished paper presented at the Mershon Center, Ohio State University, Feb. 4–5, 2000.

2. Philip E. Tetlock and Aaron Belkin, eds., *Counterfactual Thought Experiments in World Politics* (Princeton, 1996), chap. 1.

3. An illustrative analogy: an attempt to drive an old automobile with faulty brakes and steering down a steep mountain road with no guard rails will not necessarily end in an accident. If the dangers of such an attempt are ignored and all the many decisions and moves necessary to avoid an accident are not taken, however, at some point a crash becomes inevitable. This kind of practical, commonsense reasoning is frequently used by historians. Orlando Figes, e.g., in his *A People's*

Tragedy: The Russian Revolution 1891–1924 (New York, 1997), repeatedly points to junctures where the revolution could have been avoided, but also shows why the necessary steps were not taken or contrary ones were, and ascribes this failure above all to the thought and actions of the conservative forces ruling Russia and to the personality, character, and beliefs of Tsar Nicholas II. These are contingent factors; so was the occasion of the revolution in March 1917—riots over bread shortages in St. Petersburg at a time when flour supplies were still available. Yet by this time a revolution had become inevitable.

4. Tetlock and Belkin, *Counterfactual Thought Experiments*, 4, 8; "Counterfactual Outline," Mershon Center, Ohio State University, February 24, 1997. The same assumptions seem to reign in Niall Ferguson, ed., *Virtual History: Alternatives and Counterfactuals* (New York, 1999).

5. One such illustration comes from the War of the Second Coalition (1798–1801) in Napoleon's era. Suppose that Napoleon had been killed or captured during this war, either in battle or at sea on returning from Egypt or by conspirators after he seized power—all easily imagined variants in history. No amount of historical research and reasoning could enable us to tell what the consequences of his death would have been. But suppose that he had lost the final major battle of that war at Marengo in June 1800—again something easily imagined, for it nearly happened and was only averted by the disobedience of his orders by a subordinate general. Here one can show by concrete evidence that reversing the outcome of this battle would not have changed the main outcome of the war, overthrown Napoleon's rule, or altered much the course of history much at all.

6. This argument agrees in part with Niall Ferguson's call (in his Introduction to Ferguson, ed., *Virtual History*, 86–87) for historians to consider only plausible unrealized alternatives and to examine these rigorously on the basis of valid evidence. He goes too far, however, in insisting that "We should consider as plausible or probable *only those alternatives which we can show on the basis of contemporary evidence that contemporaries actually considered*" (italics in original). This is too restrictive. As the discussion of World War I later will illustrate, the historian's purview includes both those possibilities and alternatives contemporaries saw and considered, and those they failed to see at all or to consider seriously.

7. Once again this general principle can be illustrated by an example from the Napoleonic era, the object of much counterfactual speculation, the Battle of Waterloo and the possible results of a Napoleonic victory rather than defeat there. I think it can easily be shown that a French victory in this battle could not possibly have changed the fundamental balance of military forces, overwhelmingly favorable to the allies, or their willingness to prosecute the war to victory, and therefore it could not have significantly altered the ultimate outcome of the war, as many have supposed. However, a Napoleonic victory, by prolonging the war and making victory more costly for the allies, would almost certainly have destroyed the Vienna peace settlement concluded just before Waterloo and have resulted in a far harsher, less stable peace settlement resembling that of 1919, with many of the latter's unfortunate consequences. In other words, Wellington's victory was not critical for the ultimate outcome of the war but it was vital for saving the peace. The evidence is too extensive to discuss here, but is summarized in Paul W. Schroeder, *The Transformation of European Politics, 1763–1848* (Oxford, 1994), 548–58.

8. This is my reason or excuse for the paucity of footnotes and the fact that many will be expository notes rather than references to the enormous scholarly literature

on this subject. Though I think I know the literature reasonably well (not exhaustively—no one does), this is not the place to prove it.

9. Some leading historians who maintain this are Martin Kitchen, A. J. P. Taylor, Volker Berghahn, and J. C. G. Röhl.

10. On the military situation, see David Stevenson, *Armaments and the Coming of War: Europe, 1904–1914* (Oxford, 1996); David G. Herrmann, *The Arming of Europe and the Making of the First World War* (Princeton, 1996); and Norman Stone, *The Eastern Front, 1914–1917* (New York, 1975). For more general depictions of Austria–Hungary's critical position, see F. R. Bridge, *The Habsburg Monarchy Among the Great Powers, 1815–1918* (New York, 1990), and Samuel R. Williamson Jr., *Austria-Hungary and the Origins of the First World War* (New York, 1991).

11. Examples of historians who argue along these lines are Solomon Wank, Vladimir Dedijer, Steven Beller, Alan Sked, and Leo Valiani.

12. This view is expressed most clearly by the authors mentioned in n. 10 and in general by Fritz Fischer and his school; it is more nuanced but still present in Wolfgang J. Mommsen, *Grossmachtstellung und Weltpolitik: die Aussenpolitik des Deutschen Reiches, 1871–1914* (Frankfurt am Main, 1993), and Klaus Hildebrand, *Das vergangene Reich: Deutsche Aussenpolitik von Bismarck zu Hitler, 1871–1945* (Stuttgart, 1995).

13. Besides the historians mentioned in n. 12, this view still dominates the nationalistic historiography of the successor states, Serbia, Czechoslovakia, Rumania, and to some extent Poland, as represented in Adam Wandruszka and Peter Urbanitsch, eds., *Die Habsburger-Monarchie 1848–1918*, Vol. VI: *Die Habsburgermonarchie im System der Internationalen Beziehungen*, Part 2 (Vienna, 1993).

14. An illustrative analogy, inevitably inexact, might help indicate where the argument is going. Suppose that one intends to challenge the verdict of an inquiry into a fatal accident in which an automobile carrying a number of passengers plunged off a cliff on a steep mountain road—that verdict being that the accident was caused by two passengers who had sent the car over the cliff in their efforts to seize the wheel by force. One might challenge that verdict in several ways: by arguing that the defects in the car's brakes and steering made it unlikely that it would make the trip safely in any case; by contending that the car was already out of control and heading toward the cliff when the two intervened; or by claiming that their attempt to seize the wheel was only part of an ongoing struggle over control of the car which made a crash likely at some point anyway. None of these claims, however, even if true, would prove that an accident was inevitable or disprove that their effort to seize the wheel was the proximate cause of the accident, and that they therefore bore the prime responsibility for it. If, however, one could do the following: first, show what kind of driving conduct would have been required for this car to make this trip without accident; second, show that none of the passengers who were struggling to control and steer the car displayed this kind of driving conduct; third, show that this was because for all of them the most important goal was not finishing the journey safely, but getting control of the car and determining its final destination against the wishes of some passengers; and finally, that the actual attempt to seize the wheel came when the two were convinced this was their last chance not to be kidnapped and possibly killed by the others; then, I think, one could argue that the verdict, even if technically correct, was substantively misleading, and moreover, that under these conditions an accident was unavoidable.

15. Good evidence for this is found in Harald Rosenbach, *Das Deutsche Reich, Grossbritannien und der Transvaal (1896–1902)* (Goöttingen, 1993), who shows that Germany's policy toward Britain on the important issue of South Africa regularly produced British hostility and counterproductive results no matter what the Germans were trying to do or how; and Konrad Canis, *Von Bismarck zur Weltpolitik: Deutsche Aussenpolitik 1890 bis 1902* (Berlin, 1997), who demonstrates the same point on a wide range of other issues. Other instances illustrate the point. German efforts to put pressure on France over Morocco or to work in partnership with France there both failed equally; so did German efforts to work with Britain in the Berlin to Baghdad railway scheme; so did Austro-Hungarian attempts either to conciliate and cooperate with Russia in the Balkans, or to put pressure on her.

16. For example, on British policy, David French, *British Strategy and War Aims, 1914–1916* (London, 1986); Keith M. Wilson, *The Policy of the Entente* (Cambridge, 1985); and Keith Neilson, *Britain and the Last Tsar: British Policy and Russia, 1894–1917* (Oxford, 1995). For France, see, e.g., J.C. Allain, *Agadir 1911: Une crise imperialiste en Europe pour la conquête du Maroc* (Paris, 1976); Raymond Poidevin, *Les relations économiques et financiers entre la France et l'Allemagne de 1898 à 1914* (Paris, 1969); Jean-Louis Miège, *Le Maroc et l'Europe (1830–1894)* (Paris, 1961) and J. F. V. Keiger, *France and the Origins of the First World War* (London, 1983).

17. It might well be that had Germany and Austria-Hungary been less constrained by prevailing circumstances, their prewar policies would have been more aggressive and dangerous than those of their opponents, at least Britain and France. I myself am inclined to believe this, given the German and Austro-Hungarian record during World War I, when some of the prewar restraints ceased to operate, and the joint German–Austrian record in 1933–45. But this does not apply to the period before 1914, when they were so constrained.

18. David Blackbourn and Geoff Eley, *The Peculiarities of German History: Bourgeois Politics and Society in Nineteenth Century Germany* (Oxford, 1984); Geoff Eley, *Reshaping the German Right: Radical Nationalism and Political Change after Bismarck* (New Haven, CT., 1980); Marilyn S. Coetzee, *The German Army League: Popular Nationalism in Wilhelmine Germany* (New York, 1990).

19. In Russia's case this was particularly true of its support of pro-Russian Ruthenian nationalism in East Galicia and the Bukovina and of some Russian official support and much public and press support of Czech and South Slav nationalism. On the Serbian anti-Habsburg program, see especially Wolf-Dieter Behschnitt, *Nationalismus unter Serben und Kroaten, 1830–1914* (Munich, 1980), and Katrin C. Boeckh, *Von den Balkankriegen zum Ersten Weltkrieg* (Munich, 1996).

20. Once again, in anticipation of a plausible objection, let me make clear that just as I am not arguing that Germany and Austria–Hungary, had they not been under severe pressures in international politics before 1914, would have pursued moderate, peaceful policies abroad (see n. 17), so also I do not claim that had there been no outside pressures on them or interference in their domestic problems, they would have solved or managed them more successfully. The opposite is more likely. But this also is irrelevant to what happened before and in 1914.

21. Richard J. Crampton, *The Hollow Détente: Anglo-German Relations in the Balkans, 1911–1914* (Atlantic Highlands, NJ., 1979).

22. Bruce Vandevort, *Wars of Imperial Conquest in Africa, 1830–1914* (Bloomington, IN., 1998); Thomas Pakenham, *The Scramble for Africa, 1876–1912* (London, 1991).

23. The examples are almost too numerous to mention. The numerous Anglo-French contests over West and East Africa always ended in deals; even their dangerous confrontation at Fashoda led eventually to their colonial bargain of 1904. Franco-German confrontations over Morocco eventually led to a colonial bargain, though it left behind hostility on both sides. The Anglo-German contest of 1884–85 over Southwest Africa ended similarly; so did later ones over South Africa, though the Germans ended up with worthless paper concessions. The Anglo-Russian conflict over Persia and Central Asia led to their Convention of 1907, though that did not end the rivalry; the Baghdad Railway dispute eventually led to an Anglo-German agreement. Even Russia and Japan ten years after going to war over East Asia came to an agreement for coordinating their imperialist aims in China.

24. It is somewhat surprising that historians and other international relations scholars, especially of the realist persuasion, do not automatically see this and apply it to the pre-1914 scenario, considering how commonly microeconomic competition between firms is used by realist theory as an analogy for the structure and operation of international politics.

25. Fritz Fischer's well-known thesis (*Griff nach der Weltmacht: Die Kriegszielpolitik des kaiserlichen Deutschland* 3rd ed. [Düesseldorf, 1964] and *Krieg der Illusionen: die deutsche Politik von 1911 bis 1914* [Düsseldorf, 1969]) of a continuity between Germany's prewar drive for world power and the imperialist war aims program it developed and pursued in 1914–18 may go too far in making Germany's wartime aims the actual motives for its prewar policy. Yet it is hard to deny that the aims Germany developed in wartime reflect what its elites were already thinking about before 1914 as to how Germany might solve its problems in case war arose. If we apply this same argument to the Allies, it tells us something important about their prewar attitudes toward Germany's economy. Prominent in the British, French, and Russian war aims programs were measures to break Germany's economic power while at the same time somehow preserving Germany as a market for their own economies. Along with the works of David French and Keith Neilson cited above (fn. 16), see especially G. H. Soutou, *L'Or et le Sang: Les buts de guerre économiques de la Première Guerre Mondiale* (Paris, 1989).

26. See the Forum in the *American Historical Review* 94, 3 (October 1993), 1106–42, an exchange between Carl Strikwerda and Paul W. Schroeder on the former's article, "The Troubled Origins of European Economic Integration: International Iron and Steel and Labor Migration in the Era of World War I."

27. The problems this causes are illustrated by Niall Ferguson's recent revisionist and controversial book on World War I, *The Pity of War* (New York, 1999). Ferguson actually makes some sound and important, if not really new, points about the origins of the war, mostly directed against the prevailing German-war-guilt thesis. The trouble is, however, that because like most other historians he virtually ignores Austria–Hungary and Eastern Europe, he not only misunderstands the origins of the war but advances an unsound counterfactual argument that a German victory would not have been so bad for Europe or the British Empire—indeed, that it might have averted later disasters—and that Britain would have done better to stay out of it. Critics have generally ignored the sound points in

his case and pounced on the unsound ones in reaffirming the conventional verdict about Germany as the main architect of the war.

28. As Geoffrey Hosking notes in his *Russia: People and Empire 1552–1917* (Cambridge, 1997), 397, Tsarist Russia tried to solve its nationalities problems before World War I by repression and Russification; Austria–Hungary tried to solve its by concessions. Neither policy worked, and the problem may simply be insoluble.

29. A good example of this is the Entente powers' reactions to the expansion of the Austro-Hungarian navy in the Adriatic before 1914. Entente leaders knew perfectly well that the Austrians were building solely against the Italians, their nominal ally, and had no thought of challenging Russia, France, or Britain on the sea. Never mind; Austria–Hungary was Germany's ally, and therefore its navy, like its army, must be regarded as simply part of the joint enemy forces in the coming war.

30. This is the point, in the analogy of the train wreck, of noting that the engineers of the three trains had been over this terrain previously and knew what caused wrecks and how to avoid them.

31. Lest one suppose that these historical examples counted for little in 1914, Johannes Burkhardt argues convincingly that analogies with Prussia's situation in 1756, 1813, and 1870 were very prominent in German thinking in 1914. "Kriegsgrund Geschichte? 1870, 1813, 1756—historische Argumente und Orientierungen bei Ausbruch des Ersten Weltkriegs," in Johannes Burkhardt et al., *Lange und Kurze Wege in den Ersten Weltkrieg* (Munich, 1996), 9–86.

32. For example, France was held back from war over the Near East in 1840 and Russia from war with the Ottoman Empire over Greece in 1821–23 and with Austria over Bulgaria in 1885–87 by just such collective pressure.

33. To be sure, there are historians, not merely Serb nationalists but others as well, who deny any Serbian responsibility for the assassination, arguing *inter alia* that Austria–Hungary had brought it on by the provocative character of the state visit to Sarajevo. Niall Ferguson (*Pity of War*, 146, n. 3) quotes A. J. P. Taylor's remark that if British royalty had chosen to visit Dublin on St. Patrick's Day during the Troubles, they could also have expected to be shot at. Let me amend Taylor's analogy to make it conform better to Austria–Hungary's position:

Suppose that the United Kingdom in 1914 was not separated from the continent by the English Channel, but had as its direct neighbor in the southeast, where the Low Countries are, an independent Kingdom of Ireland. This Kingdom of Ireland, though small and backward, was fiercely combative, violent, and conspiratorial in its politics, and committed to an ethnic integral-nationalist hegemonic state ideology calling for it to unite all Irishmen under its rule. Its definition of "Irish" included other Celts in the UK (Scots, Welshmen) on the grounds that they were really Irish corrupted by an alien regime and religion, and it taught its children in school that large parts of the UK really belonged to the Kingdom of Ireland and should be liberated. To this end its nationalist press waged a propaganda war against the UK calling for its overthrow and dissolution, and its military intelligence arm, operating secretly and without control of the government, supported dissidents and revolutionary organizations in the UK, and trained and armed terrorists to operate there. This Kingdom of Ireland was allied with and supported by Germany. When the decision to send the Prince of Wales on a state visit to UK Ireland was made in London, the Irish royal government, knowing that some form of Irish terrorist action was being planned and being unready for a war but not daring for internal reasons to act decisively to prevent one, gave a vague warning to London that the visit might have bad results. But London also knew that a cancellation of the planned state visit, designed as a measure to support and encourage UK loyalists in British-ruled Ireland, would be exploited by the royal Irish press and nationalist organizations as more proof of British cowardice and weakness and a further spur to Irish rebellion. Would the UK government under these circumstances have cancelled the visit? Or, when the Prince was assassinated by a UK Irishman who had contacts with the royal Irish military intelligence and when the entire royal Irish press and public hailed this act as a glorious patriotic deed, would British leaders have shrugged their shoulders and said, "Well, we asked for it?" One need not know the actual British response to Irish acts of rebellion like the Phoenix Park murders or the Easter Rising to guess the answer.

34. See J. F. V. Keiger, *France and the Origins of the First World War*, and Keiger, *Raymond Poincaré* (New York, 1997).
35. See the works cited above, n. 16, and also David French, *The Strategy of the Lloyd George Coalition, 1916–1918* (Oxford, 1995).
36. The history of the politics of World War I illustrates this dramatically. Imperial Germany was the great threat and object of hatred for the Allies, especially in the West; Austria–Hungary was taken much less seriously. Yet these same Allies never intended to eliminate Germany as a state, or even take away enough territory to cripple it as a major power. All, in fact, hoped to have Germany as a junior political and economic partner in the postwar era. In contrast, the territorial aims of the Allies were directed overwhelmingly against Austria–Hungary in the interest of gaining and keeping lesser allies—Serbia, Italy, Rumania, and ultimately the Czechs and the Poles. This went on until, in a marvelous instance of the irony of history, the western Allies decided in 1916–17, when faced with Russia's defeat and the possibility of a German victory, that it would be nice to get Austria–Hungary, by this time on its last legs and totally dependent on Germany, to defect, help defeat Germany now, and balance against Germany in the future. The only thing more astonishing than the notion that this absurd eighteenth-century-style volte-face was possible is the fact that some able historians take it seriously as evidence that Britain and France never meant real harm to Austria–Hungary and always wanted to preserve it. John Grigg, *Lloyd George, from Peace to War, 1912–1916* (London, 1983); French, *Strategy of Lloyd George Coalition*; Harry Hanak, *Great Britain and Austria-Hungary during the First World War* (New York, 1962).
37. The Matscheko memorandum of June 1914, changed after the assassination to be used against Serbia, called for joint Austro-German pressure on Rumania to commit itself publicly to the Austro-German alliance from which it had just defected. It has been interpreted by some, including F. R. Bridge, as showing that Austria–Hungary contemplated a political rather than military solution to its problems until after June 28 (see his *Habsburg Monarchy*, 334–35). My view is that the original plan, a proposal to force Rumania, now independent, to do what it was never willing to do even when it was a secret ally, would certainly not have solved Austria–Hungary's problem and was almost as likely to escalate into a general crisis as the actual Austro-German initiative did. Paul W. Schroeder, "Rumania and the Great Powers before 1914," *Revue Roumaine d'Histoire*, 14, 1 (1975), 39–53.
38. John Lloyd, "Österreich-Ungarn vor dem Kriegsausbruch," in Rupert Melville et al., eds., *Deutschland und Europa*, 2 vols. (Munich, 1993), 2, 661–83; Günther

Kronenbitter, " 'Nur los lassen'. Österreich-Ungarn und der Wille zum Krieg," in Burkhardt et al., eds., *Lange und kurze Wege in den Ersten Weltkrieg*, 159–87.

39. For a convincing argument that Russia had never had the kind of vital interest in the Balkans that its Orthodox and Pan-Slav publicists claimed, and that throughout the nineteenth century it had repeatedly become involved in costly complications there against its best interests, see Barbara Jelavich, *Russia's Balkan Entanglements 1806–1914* (New York, 1991).

Chapter 9   Alliances, 1815–1945: Weapons of Power and Tools of Management

1. This usage was particularly common among nineteenth-century European statesmen and publicists.
2. Académié Diplomatique Internationale, *Dictionnaire Diplomatique*, 7 vols. (Paris, 1933), 1, 109–12.
3. Julian R. Friedman, "Alliance in International Politics," in *Alliance in International Politics*, ed. Julian R. Friedman et al. (Boston, 1970), 10–11.
4. Wladyslaw W. Kulski, *International Politics in a Revolutionary Age* 2d rev. ed. (New York, 1968), 115.
5. Werner Levi, *International Politics: Foundations of the System* (Minneapolis, 1974), 164.
6. Hans J. Morgenthau, *Politics among Nations*, 3d ed. (New York, 1960), 181. Many other textbooks and treatises on international relations, too numerous to list here, use this definition of alliances, as do both the old *Encyclopedia of the Social Sciences* and the new *International Encyclopedia of the Social Sciences*. It seems safe to say that it is the reigning definition.
7. See Steven Rosen, "A Model of War and Alliance," in Friedman, *Alliance*, 215; and Christopher Bladen, "Alliance and Integration," in Friedman, *Alliance*, 121–22.
8. Bruce M. Russett, "Components of an Operational Theory of International Alliance Formation," in Friedman, *Alliance*, 238–40, 253–55; Ivo D. Duchacek, *Conflict and Cooperation among Nations* (New York, 1960), 372–73, 407–33.
9. For example, K. J. Holsti, *International Politics: A Framework for Analysis* (Englewood Cliffs, NJ., 1967), 110–20; Robert E. Osgood and Robert W. Tucker, *Force, Order, and Justice* (Baltimore, MD., 1967), 78–96.
10. For example Inis L. Claude, *Power and International Relations* (New York), 89, 115–16, 138–49.
11. See, e.g., John W. Burton, *International Relations: A General Theory* (Cambridge, UK, 1965), and *Systems, States, Diplomacy and Rules* (Cambridge, UK, 1968).
12. Raymond Aron, *Peace and War* (Garden City, NY., 1966), makes the point repeatedly. See also James N. Rosenau, *The Scientific Study of Foreign Policy* (New York, 1971), 197–237, in which Rosenau argues for "calculated control" as the central theme and analytic concept in foreign policy and (following Harold Sprout) lists eight means of control, ranging from diplomatic intercourse to total war. Alliance, however, is not among them.
13. For a discussion of various contradictory meanings of "balance of power," see Ernst B. Haas, "The Balance of Power: Prescription, Concept, or Propaganda," *World Politics*, 5 (1953), 442–77. The rules formulated by Morton Kaplan for a balance of power system (*System and Process in International Politics* [New York,

1957], 22–36, 52–53, 125–27) have been much debated as to their validity and internal consistency. See, e.g., Aron, *Peace and War*, 128–32, and Karl W. Deutsch, *The Analysis of International Relations* (Englewood Cliffs, NJ., 1968), 136–40.

14. William H. Riker, *The Theory of Political Coalitions* (New Haven, CT., 1962), 168–87. For a reply, see Dina A. Zinnes, "Coalition Theories and the Balance of Power," in *The Study of Coalition Behavior*, ed. Sven Groennings et al. (New York, 1970), 351–68.

15. For example, Richard A. Rosecrance, *Action and Reaction in World Politics* (Boston, 1963), arguing that the Concert of Europe, not a balance of power, stabilized the European system in the nineteenth century.

16. Ole R. Holsti and John D. Sullivan, "National-International Linkages: France and China as Nonconforming Alliance Members," in *Linkage Politics*, ed. James N. Rosenau (New York, 1969), 147–95.

17. Richard A. Falk, "Zone II as a World Order Construct," in *The Analysis of International Politics*, ed. James N. Rosenau et al. (New York, 1972), 187–206.

18. Robert E. Osgood, *Alliances and American Foreign Policy* (Baltimore, MD., 1968), 22 and 28.

19. George Liska, *Nations in Alliance: The Limits of Interdependence* (Baltimore, MD., 1962), 116, italics mine.

20. George Liska, *Imperial America: The International Politics of Primacy* (Baltimore, MD., 1967), 9–11, 20–21.

21. George Liska, *Alliances and the Third World* (Baltimore, MD., 1968), 24–35.

22. Limitations on space prevent any attempt to prove the case here, of course, and require me to omit many nuances and qualifications that should be included. The notes that follow are more suggestions for further reading than citations of the evidence on which this interpretation rests.

23. Edward V. Gulick, *Europe's Classical Balance of Power* (Ithaca, NY., 1955); Charles K. Webster, *The Foreign Policy of Castlereagh, 1815–1822*, 2 vols. (London, 1934).

24. Maurice Bourquin, *Histoire de la Sainte Alliance* (Geneva, 1954); Paul W. Schroeder, *Metternich's Diplomacy at Its Zenith, 1820–1823* (Austin, TX., 1962).

25. Enno E. Kraehe, *Metternich's German Policy* (Vol. 1; Princeton, NJ., 1963); Heinrich von Srbik, *Metternich, der Staatsmann und der Mensch*, 3 vols. (Munich, 1925–54).

26. Harold W. V. Temperley, *The Foreign Policy of Canning, 1822–1827* (London, 1925); Charles W. Crawley, *The Question of Greek Independence* (Cambridge, UK, 1930); Douglas Dakin, *The Greek Struggle for Independence, 1821–1833* (Berkeley, 1973).

27. Charles K. Webster, *The Foreign Policy of Palmerston, 1830–1841*, 2 vols. (London, 1951); Charles K. Webster, "Palmerston, Metternich, and the European System 1830–1841," *Proceedings of the British Academy*, 20 (1934), 125–58.

28. Christopher Howard, *Britain and the Casus Belli, 1822–1902* (London, 1974), 44–48.

29. Webster, *Palmerston*; Roger Bullen, *Palmerston, Guizot and the Collapse of the Entente Cordiale* (London, 1973); Douglas W. J. Johnson, *Guizot* (London, 1963).

30. Friedrich Meinecke, *Radowitz und die deutsche Revolution* (Berlin, 1913); Frank Eyck, *The Frankfurt Parliament, 1848–1849* (New York, 1969); Helmut Rumpler, *Die deutsche Politik des Freiherrn von Beust 1848 bis 1850* (Vienna, 1972); Rudolf Kiszling, *Fürst Felix zu Schwarzenberg* (Graz, 1952).

31. Waltraud Heindl, *Graf Buol-Schauenstein in St. Petersburg und London (1848–52)* (Vienna, 1970); Kiszling, *Schwarzenberg.*

32. Richard Blaas, ed., *Le relazioni diplomatiche fra l'Austria e le Stato Pontiffco* (3d ser. [1848–60], Vol. 1, Rome, *Istituto storico italiano per l'eta moderna e contemporanea*, 1973).

33. H. W. V. Temperley, *England and the Near East: The Crimea* (London, 1936); Paul W. Schroeder, *Austria, Great Britain and the Crimean War* (Ithaca, NY., 1972).

34. Ennio di Nolfo, *Europa e Italia nel 1855–1856* (Rome, 1967).

35. Schroeder, *Austria*; Winfried Baumgart, *Der Friede von Paris 1856* (Munich, 1972).

36. Denis Mack Smith, *Victor Emanuel, Cavour, and the Risorgimento* (London, 1971).

37. Derek Beales, *England and Italy, 1859–60* (London, 1961).

38. Stanislaw Bóbr-Tylingo, *Napoleon III, l'Europe et la Pologne en 1863–4* (Rome, 1963); Ragnhild Hatton, "Palmerston and 'Scandinavian Union,' " in *Studies in International History*, ed. K. Bourne and D. C. Watt (Hamden, CT., 1967), 119–44.

39. Helmut Burckhardt, *Deutschland, England, Frankreich* (Munich, 1970); Andreas Hillgruber, *Bismarcks Aussenpolitik* (Freiburg, 1972); Friedrich Engel-Jánosi, *Graf Rechberg* (Munich, 1927).

40. Rudolf Lill, "Die Vorgeschichte der preussisch-italienischen Allianz," *Quellen und Forschungen aus italienischen Archiven und Bibliotheken* 42/43 (1963), 505–70.

41. Since, in the peace treaty with Austria concluded at Prague later in August, Bismarck specifically conceded to the South German states the right to form their own confederation, a right that he had already frustrated through these alliances, he hereby managed, as his Saxon opponent Count Beust later remarked, to violate a treaty even before he had signed it.

42. Hillgruber, *Bismarcks Aussenpolitik.*

43. Heinrich Lutz, "Von Königgrätz zum Zweibund. Aspekte europäischer Entscheidungen," *Historische Zeitschrift*, 217 (1973), 347–80.

44. Martin Winckler, *Bismarcks Bündnispolitik und das europaische Gleichgewicht* (Stuttgart, 1964); Stephan Verosta, *Theorie und Realitätvon Bündnissen* (Vienna, 1971); Hillgruber, *Bismarcks Aussenpolitik.*

45. Besides the works cited in n. 44, see W. N. Medlicott, *Bismarck, Gladstone and the Concert of Europe* (London, 1956); and Bruce Waller, *Bismarck at the Crossroads* (London, 1974).

46. A. J. P. Taylor, *The Struggle for Mastery in Europe, 1848–1918* (Oxford, UK., 1954). A quotation from a private letter of Austrian foreign minister, Count Goluchowski, to the Austrian ambassador at St. Petersburg, Count Aehrenthal, on August 16, 1906, shows how clearly the partners understood the nature and purpose of the Austro-Italian alliance: "Now our position toward Italy is of such a nature, that our mutual relations must either assume the character of an alliance (even if not an entirely unreserved one), or the character of a latent enmity which then sooner or later leads to war. However few illusions one may have about the feelings in Italy toward us, the existing Triple Alliance nevertheless secures us

against surprises on our southern boundary." Quoted in Verosta, *Bündnisse*, 311 (translation mine).

47. Taylor, *Struggle for Mastery*; D. A. Farnie, *East and West of Suez* (Oxford, UK, 1969); Ronald Robinson and John Gallagher, *Africa and the Victorians* (New York, 1961); Cedric J. Lowe, *The Reluctant Imperialists* (London, 1967).

48. Hillgruber, *Bismarcks Aussenpolitik*; Paul Kluke, "Bismarck und Salisbury: Ein diplomatisches Duell," *Historische Zeitschrift*, 175 (1953), 285–306; Egmont Zechlin, *Staatsstreichpläne Bismarcks und Wilhelms II, 1890–1894* (Stuttgart, 1929). See also various essays, especially that by H. U. Wehler, in *Das kaiserliche Deutschland*, ed. Michael Sturmer (Düsseldorf, 1970).

49. Taylor, *Struggle for Mastery*; William L. Langer, *The Franco-Russian Alliance, 1890–1894* (Cambridge, MA., 1929), and *The Diplomacy of Imperialism, 1890–1902*, 2 vols., 2d ed. (New York, 1956).

50. Christopher Andrew, *Theophile Delcassé and the Making of the Entente Cordiale* (New York, 1968).

51. Fritz Fellner, *Der Dreibund* (Vienna, 1960); Norman Rich, *Friedrich von Holstein*, 2 vols. (Cambridge, UK, 1965); F. R. Bridge, *From Sadowa to Sarajevo* (London, 1972).

52. Max Beloff, *Imperial Sunset*, (Vol. 1, London, 1969); J. A. S. Grenville, *Lord Salisbury and Foreign Policy* (London, 1964); Ian H. Nish, *The Anglo-Japanese Alliance* (London, 1966); L. K. Young, *British Policy in China, 1895–1902* (Oxford, UK, 1970).

53. Nish, *Anglo-Japanese Alliance*; Firuz Kazemzadeh, *Russia and Britain in Persia, 1864–1914* (New Haven, CT., 1968); Briton C. Busch, *Britain and the Persian Gulf, 1894–1914* (Berkeley, 1967); M. B. Cooper, "British Policy in the Balkans, 1908–09," *Historical Journal*, 7 (1964–65), 258–79; Peter Lowe, *Great Britain and Japan, 1911–15* (New York, 1969).

54. Andrew, *Delcassé*; P. J. V. Rolo, *The Entente Cordiale* (London, 1969).

55. See, e.g., Jonathan Steinberg, *Yesterday's Deterrent* (New York, 1965), 20–21, 29, 205–06.

56. On Britain's use of the Entente in 1911, see Keith Wilson, "The Agadir Crisis, the Mansion House Speech, and the Double-Edgedness of Agreements," *Historical Journal*, 15 (1972), 513–32.

57. For a specific argument on this thesis, see Paul W. Schroeder, "World War I as Galloping Gertie: A Reply to Joachim Remak," *Journal of Modern History*, 44 (1972), 319–45. In general on British policy, see Zara S. Steiner, *The Foreign Office and Foreign Policy, 1898–1914* (New York, 1970); George W. Monger, *The End of Isolation* (London, 1963); and Samuel R. Williamson, Jr., *The Politics of Grand Strategy* (Cambridge, MA., 1969).

58. Ernst C. Helmreich, *The Diplomacy of the Balkan Wars, 1912–1913* (Cambridge, MA., 1938); Edward C. Thaden, *Russia and the Balkan Alliance of 1912* (University Park, PA., 1965).

59. Gerard E. Silberstein, *The Troubled Alliance* (Lexington, KY., 1970); Ulrich Trumpener, *Germany and the Ottoman Empire, 1914–1918* (Princeton, NJ., 1968); Frank G. Weber, *Eagles on the Crescent* (Ithaca, NY., 1970).

60. Clarence J. Smith, *The Russian Struggle for Power, 1914–1917* (New York, 1956); Wolfram W. Gottlieb, *Studies in Secret Diplomacy During the First World War* (London, 1957).

61. Jukka Nevakivi, *Britain, France and the Arab Middle East, 1914–1920* (London, 1969).

62. Jon Jacobson, *Locarno Diplomacy* (Princeton, NJ., 1972).

63. Piotr S. Wandycz, *France and Her Eastern Allies, 1919–1925* (Minneapolis, MN., 1962), and *Soviet-Polish Relations, 1917–1921* (Cambridge, MA., 1969); Marian Wojciechowski, *Die polnisch-deutschen Beziehungen, 1933–1938* (Leiden Netherlands, 1971).

64. Joel G. Colton, *Léon Blum* (New York, 1966); William E. Scott, *Alliance against Hitler* (Durham, NC., 1962).

65. Martin Gilbert, *The Roots of Appeasement* (New York, 1967).

66. Among many recent works using the cabinet papers to discuss British policy, the most important are Ian G. Colvin, *The Chamberlain Cabinet* (London, 1971), and Robert K. Middlemas, *Diplomacy of Illusion* (London, 1972).

67. Martin Gilbert and R. S. Gott, *The Appeasers* (Boston, 1963); Sidney Aster, *1939* (London, 1973).

68. George F. Kennan, *Russia and the West under Lenin and Stalin* (Boston, 1961); Adam B. Ulam, *Expansion and Coexistence,* 2d ed. (New York, 1974).

69. Elizabeth Wiskemann, *The Rome-Berlin Axis* (New York, 1949); Frederick W. Deakin, *The Brutal Friendship* (London, 1962); Norman Rich, *Hitler's War Aims,* Vol. 1 (New York, 1973).

70. Frel. W. Ikle, *German-Japanese Relations, 1936–1940* (New York, 1956); Paul W. Schroeder, *The Axis Alliance and Japanese-American Relations, 1941* (Ithaca, NY., 1958); Johanna M. Meskill, *Hitler and Japan* (New York, 1966).

71. John L. Snell, *Illusion and Necessity* (Boston, 1963).

72. Ernest L. Woodward, *British Foreign Policy in the Second World War* (London, 1962).

73. Ulam, *Expansion.*

74. The most important works on the orthodox side of the controversy are probably those of Herbert Feis, beginning with his *Churchill, Roosevelt, Stalin* (Princeton, NJ., 1957) and concluding with *From Trust to Terror* (New York, 1970), as well as John W. Wheeler-Bennett and Anthony Nicholls, *The Semblance of Peace* (New York, 1972). On the revisionist side, the most important are Gabriel Kolko, *The Politics of War* (New York, 1968), and Joyce Kolko and Gabriel Kolko, *The Limits of Power* (New York, 1972). A sensible survey is Gaddis Smith, *American Diplomacy During the Second World War, 1941–1945* (New York, 1965).

75. I refer especially to the various studies of J. David Singer and Melvin Small.

76. For evidence that the same realist vs. idealist debate long common in the West is also going on in postwar Japan, see Kei Wakaizumi, "Japan's Dilemma: To Act or Not to Act," *Foreign Policy,* 16 (Fall 1974), 33–35.

CHAPTER 10   THE NINETEENTH CENTURY SYSTEM: BALANCE OF POWER OR POLITICAL EQUILIBRIUM?

This essay is a revised version of a paper read at the American Political Science Association meeting in Washington, DC, in September 1977. Part of the research was supported by a fellowship from the American Council of Learned Societies, whose help is gratefully acknowledged.

1. See, e.g., the opening section of R. Rosecrance, A. Alexandroff, B. Healy, and A. Stein, *Power, Balance of Power, and Status in Nineteenth Century International Relations* (London, 1974).

2. For examples of historians' definitions, implicit and explicit, see R. Albrecht-Carrié, *A Diplomatic History of Europe since the Congress of Vienna* (New York,

1958); K. Bourne, *The Foreign Policy of Victorian England, 1830–1902* (Oxford, 1970), 10, and *Palmerston: The Early Years 1784–1841* (New York, 1984), 627–31; A. Cobban, *The Nation State and National Self-Determination*, rev. edn. (New York, 1970), 287–90; G. Davies, "English Foreign Policy," *Huntington Library Quarterly,* 5 (1942), 422–26, 470–71, and "The Pattern of British Foreign Policy, 1815–1914," *Huntington Library Quarterly* 6 (1943), 367–69; E. V. Gulick, *Europe's Classical Balance of Power* (Ithaca, NY., 1955); F. H. Hinsley, *Nationalism and the International System* (Dobbs Ferry, NY., 1973), 83–84; L. Lafore, *The Long Fuse: An Interpretation of the Origins of World War I,* 2nd edn. (Philadelphia, 1971), 33; L. C. B. Seaman, *From Vienna to Versailles,* pbk. edn. (New York, 1963), 130; W. Strang, *Britain in World Affairs* (New York, 1961), 17–18; C. K. Webster, *The Art and Practice of Diplomacy* (London, 1961), 23–27; Andreas Hillgruber, "Politische Geschichte in Moderner Sicht," *Historische Zeitschrift,* 226 (1973), 535–38; and R. W. Seton-Watson, "The Foundations of British Policy," *Transactions of the Royal Historical Society,* 29 (1947), 61–2. I have compiled an even longer list of discussions of the concept by political scientists which it seems pointless to produce; suffice it to say that the concept remains central despite various doubts about it, and that most political scientists, like historians, assume that a balance of power system prevailed in the nineteenth century.

3. E. B. Haas, "The Balance of Power: Prescription, Concept, or Propaganda," *World Politics,* 5 (1953), 442–77; M. Wight, "The Balance of Power," in *Diplomatic Investigations: Essays in the Theory of International Politics,* ed. H. Butterfield and M. Wight (London, 1966), 149–75. However, Professor Wight argues in his "The Balance of Power and International Order," in *The Bases of International Order,* ed. A. James (London, 1973), 85–115, that the multiplicity of meanings concealed a basic unity; he lists fifteen propositions on the balance of power on which he claims all balance thinkers agreed.

4. The best-known attempt is that of M. Kaplan, *Systems and Process in International Politics* (New York, 1957), 22–36, 52–53, and 125–27. For criticisms of Kaplan's systems approach, see R. Aron, *Peace and War: A Theory of International Relations* (Garden City, NY., 1966), 128–32, 146–47; A. L. Burns, *Of Powers and Their Politics* (Englewood Cliffs, NJ., 1968), 112–15, 248–51; W. H. Riker, *The Theory of Political Coalitions* (New Haven, 1962), 162–87; K. Deutsch, *The Analysis of International Relations* (Englewood Cliffs, NJ., 1968), 136–40; M. Kaplan, A. L. Burns, and R. M. Quandt, "Theoretical Analysis of the 'Balance of Power'," *Behavioral Science,* 5 (1960), 240–52; and D. Zinnes, "Coalition Theories and the Balance of Power," in *The Study of Coalition Behavior,* ed. S. Groenings et al. (New York, 1970), 351–68.

5. Some representative works are J. W. Burton, *International Relations: A General Theory* (Cambridge, 1965), and *Systems, States, Diplomacy and Rules* (London, 1968); I. L. Claude, Jr., *Power and International Relations* (New York, 1962); E. B. Haas, "The Balance of Power as a Guide to Policy-Making," *Journal of Politics,* 15 (1953), 370–98; Haas and A. Whiting, *Dynamics of International Relations* (New York, 1956); C. A. McClelland, *Theory and the International System* (New York, 1966); R. E. Osgood and R. W. Tucker, *Force, Order, and Justice* (Baltimore, 1967); Riker, *Political Coalitions;* and C. F. Doran, *The Politics of Assimilation: Hegemony and Its Aftermath* (Baltimore, 1971).

6. A. F. K. Organski, *World Politics* 2nd edn. (New York, 1968); R. Rosecrance, *Action and Reaction in World Politics* (Boston, 1963).

7. For example, C. Holbraad, *The Concert of Europe: A Study in German and British International Theory 1815–1914* (London, 1970); H. G. Schumann, *Edmund Burkes Anschauung vom Gleichgewicht im Staat und Staatensystem* (Meisenheim am Glan, 1964); P. Stauffer, *Die Idee des europäischen Gleichgewichts impolitischen Denken Johannes von Müllers* (Basel, 1960).

8. Essentially Gulick's approach in Europe's *Classical Balance*.

9. The best or worst example of this seems to me to be A. J. P. Taylor, *The Struggle for Mastery in Europe, 1848–1914* (Oxford, 1954), in most respects an outstanding book. He insists that the Balance of Power (which he often capitalizes) was the basis for European politics and operated in its purest form from 1848 to 1914. But he never defines it, and in his hands the term means variously an even distribution of power, a stable distribution of power, any distribution of power, an unequal distribution of power, hegemony, a struggle for power, the status quo, the European system, the opposite of moral principles and the European Concert, and other variant meanings. pbk. edn. (New York, 1971), 26, 30–32, 44, 61–62, 85, 99, 154–56, 159, 165, 168, 170, 173–74, 176–77, 199–200, 268, 283–84, 297, 303, 324–25, and *passim*.

10. See n. 5 above.

11. For a discussion of one such major effort, see the exchange in the *Journal of Conflict Resolution*, 21 (1977), 3–94.

12. See the appendix at the end of Chapter 10 for a summary of the evidence. To save space, all volumes of documents will hereafter be cited only by the abbreviations used there, and individual documents will be cited only by volume number and individual document number or page numbers.

13. Occasionally historians have noted this. F. R. Bridge and R. Bullen, e.g., write in *The Great Powers and the European States System 1815–1914* (London, 1980), 15: "The concept of the balance of power was hardly ever used except by British governments. The continental powers certainly did not consciously seek to uphold it." Bridge also remarks on "the fraudulent balance of 1815," which left Britain unchecked, in his "Allied Diplomacy in Peacetime: The Failure of the Congress System, 1815–1823," in *Europe's Balance of Power 1815–1848*, ed. A. Sked (London, 1979), 36. But this skepticism does not extend to rejecting balance of power as the operative basis of European politics.

14. Some examples to keep this from being a naked assertion: in *APP*, 6 (1865–66), one finds the following topics discussed, some at considerable length, without connecting them to the European balance: Prussian annexation of the Elbe Duchies, a war in Germany, the loss of Venetia by Austria, a coalition against France, a possible war against France, compensations to France for Prussian gains in Germany, a French or English war against the United States, a possible war in the Near East, a possible revolution in Hungary, and the possible breakup or partition of Belgium on the death of Leopold I. *OD*, 21 (March–August 1868) contains much evidence of French concern over Prussia's power and aggressive tendencies, but contains few references to the European equilibrium and these are contradictory in meaning and tendency (nos. 6603, 6752, and 6807). In *GP*, 7, the correspondence concerning the Russo-French alliance and Franco-German relations in the early 1890s contains nothing on the balance of power. *GP*, 26, pts. I and II, though full of the language of power politics and the clash of rival alliances in the Bosnian Crisis of 1908–09, contain virtually no references to the European balance. Further examples could be cited almost at will.

15. For example, the British, but not the Germans, made the naval race and a possible political agreement balance of power questions, but no other issue between the two countries counted as such. *BD*, 4, nos. 174, 182, 187, 200, 202, 442, and 462, and 310–13 and 626–29.

16. The British in 1900, e.g., claimed that the balance in China was a critical European concern. *BD*, 22, 24–25, and 31.

17. For samples of special balances, see *DDI*, ser. 2, 1, nos. 530 and 579; *QDPO*, 1, no. 93; *APP*, 2, pt. 2, p. 619. For local balances, see *DDI*, ser. 2, 1, no. 91; *GP*, 13, no. 3419; *DDF* ser. 1, 5, no. 273; 6, nos. 119 and 227; ser. 2, 11, nos. 86 and 95; and ser. 3, 9, nos. 77, 150, and 171.

18. For example, the frequent references to the Mediterranean equilibrium from the 1880s onward: *BD*, 1, no. 248; *DDF*, ser. 1, nos. 430 and 432; 4, no. 557; 6, nos. 311 and 325; 7, nos. 88, 102, and 212; 7, no. 420; 10, nos. 33, 408, and 433; and 15, no. 294; *DDF*, ser. 2, 11, no. 172; *GP*, 4, nos. 836, 838, and 843; 7, nos. 1426 and 1430; and 8, nos. 1714–15, 1768, and 1912.

19. Some examples: *DDF* ser. 1, 15, no. 83; ser. 2, 11, nos. 321, 403, and 414.

20. *OD*, 1, no. 47; *Cavour-Azeglio*, 1, no. 528; *DDF*, ser. 3, 10, no. 9. The opposite usage, in which "European order" or "European system" stand for "European equilibrium" is also common, e.g., *APP*, 8, no. 211; Guizot, *Mémoires*, 5, 43.

21. Some examples: *OD*, 21, no. 6752; *DDF*, ser. 1, 7, nos. 42, 43, and 383; *DDI*, ser. 2, 1, no. 538.

22. A good example is Italy's aspiration to hold the European balance while a member of the Triple Alliance (*DDF*, ser. 1, 8, no. 185; ser. 2, 11, no. 45; *BD*, 1, nos. 364 and 366; and *GP* 24, no. 8268). For other such ideas, see also *DDF*, ser. 1, 1, no. 40; *DDI*, ser. 2, 1, no. 523.

23. Tsar Alexander III hoped in the late 1880s to hold the balance as arbiter by staying out of any combinations and retaining a free hand (*DDF*, ser. 1, 6, nos. 441, 493, 552, and 665; 7, nos. 266 and 312; and 8, nos. 36 and 40). The British regularly believed that their insular position and lack of involvement on the Continent uniquely qualified them to hold the balance (see especially *BD*, 6).

24. Some apparent examples: *QDPO*, 1, no. 62; *BGW*, 3, no. 90; *APP*, 3, no. 715; Schwertfeger, *Zur europäischen politik*, 5, nos. 9 and 55; DDF, ser. 3, 10, no. 307; 1B, 2, no. 215.

25. While the clearest instances of the term "European equilibrium" being used to mean hegemony or control by a dominant coalition are the Entente powers' concept of a desirable European balance or Russia's of a Balkan balance just before World War I, proposals to establish equilibrium in Europe through a dominant alliance of the strongest continental powers (France, Russia, and Prussia), or the most progressive ones (France, Prussia, and Italy) were common in the 1860s.

26. Palmerston, e.g., believed that the liberal West should check the autocratic East, and Cavour suggested to Prussia that it ought to make Germany the European center of gravity between the Latins and Slavs (*APP*, 2, pt. 2, 47).

27. See Metternich, *Papiere*, 1, 33–35, 130 (note), and 330–31; 2, 26–27, 34–35, 289–90, 478–79, 486–87, 492–95, 502–03, and 510–11; 3, 166–69; Talleyrand, *Corr.*, 3, 4–7, 18, 49, 200–03, 206–09, 290–91, 376–77, 414; *GP*, 24, no. 8215.

28. BGW, 6, nos. 1344 and 1363. Bismarck also met Austrian or French complaints that Prussia's gains were threatening the equilibrium with a similar proposal

which had good eighteenth century credentials, viz. balanced compensations for the great powers at the expense of smaller ones. *APP*, 5, no. 436; *OD*, 7, nos. 1570 and 1574; *OD*, 11, no. 3143.

29. Even Bismarck, usually skeptical about balance of power arguments, insisted in his later years that Austria was essential to the European equilibrium (e.g., *GP*, 6, nos. 883, 889, 900, and 925). But one must keep in mind what kind of Austria Bismarck was willing to sustain, and how far. Austria was not allowed to ally with, or even lean toward, any other state but Germany. Bismarck reacted violently whenever he thought Austria was following too pro-Slav a domestic course of policy. More than once in the late 1880s, moreover, he seriously considered letting Austria go in favor of an understanding with Russia. Excellent discussions of Bismarck's policy are in A. Hillgruber, *Bismarcks Aussenpolitik* (Freiburg, 1972) and L. Gall, *Bismarck: Der Weisse Revolutionär* (Frankfurt, 1984).

30. P. W. Schroeder, *Austria, Great Britain and the Crimean War: The Destruction of the European Concert* (Ithaca, 1972); N. Rich, *Why the Crimean War? A Cautionary Tale* (Hanover, NH and London, 1985).

31. Saitta, *Il problema italiano* 1 and 2, contain many arguments on this score.

32. See, e.g., Oncken, *Rheinpolitik*, 3, nos. 661 and 666.

33. *GP*, 13, no. 350; xvii, nos. 5001, 5005–07, 5009–10; *DDF*, ser. 1, 15, nos. 48, 53, 72, 115, 255, and 258.

34. Gulick, *Europe's Classical Balance*, 30–31.

35. See, e.g., *BD*, 6, nos. 176–78, especially Sir Eyre Crowe's arguments.

36. For the documents, see above, no. 18.

37. If one asks why this has not been widely seen, at least in the English-speaking world, the answer seems to me to be that British statesmen never worried about any concept of European equilibrium other than their own; British scholars by and large have not challenged the reigning British-Whig interpretations of foreign policy, and Americans have adopted a balance of power ideology from the British.

38. The development can be easily traced in Metternich, *Papiere*, 1–3, Talleyrand, *Corr.*; and *Polovstov*, correspondance, 1–3. For general analyses of the period, see Gulick, *Europe's Classical Balance*; H. A. Kissinger, *A World Restored* (Boston, 1957); and Enno Kraehe, *Metternich's German Policy*, 2 vols. (Princeton, 1963, 1983).

39. I counted 37 references to the European equilibrium in the first half of *APP*, 1— an extremely high number. Their meaning was almost invariably conservative-equilibrist, calling for the maintenance of existing treaties, great power intervention to prevent a war or control its outcome, and the preservation of Austria's position in northern Italy as vital to the balance. After Solferino, there were only four references to equilibrium in the rest of the volume, three being colorless, and the other (680–83) advocating a new equilibrium in Europe to replace the 1815 system, based on satisfying the forces of nationalism, freeing Italy, and pushing Austria southeast to check Russia.

40. Count Albrecht von Bernstorff, ambassador to Britain who became Bismarck's predecessor as foreign minister, illustrates this well. In 1859 he attacked the British for refusing to help save the 1815 system in Italy (*APP*, 1, no. 395). In March 1860 he still agreed with the Austrian contention that it made no sense for Britain to attack France for upsetting the European balance by annexing Nice and Savoy while the British ignored Sardinia's far greater expansion and

wholesale violation of treaties (*APP*, 2, pt. 1, nos. 27 and 115). But by May 1861 he viewed a possible Austrian recovery of its place in the European balance as a grave threat to Prussian interests (*APP*, 2, pt. 2, no. 383), and by early 1862 he advocated a policy of pure state interests (ibid., no. 587). After Bismarck took office in September, Bernstorff urged him to wage war immediately on Denmark for Prussian gains (*APP*, 3, no. 45).

41. The evidence for this is too vast to summarize, much less cite in detail. The documentary sources are: *OD*, 1, 4, 6, 10–12, 25, 28, 31, 34, and 37; Oncken, *Rheinpolitik*, 1–3; *BGW*, 3–6; *Problema Veneto*, 3; *QDPO*, 1, 4, and 6; *APP*, 1–6, 8, and 10; and Thiers, 10–13. On Thiers, see J. P. T. Bury, *Thiers, 1797–1877* (London, 1986).

42. Some examples of the argument are in *Problema Veneto*, 3, nos. 141, 173, and 191; *APP*, 2, pt. 1, no. 2994; and *OD*, 11, nos. 2994, 3177, and 3195, and 12, no. 3409. See also Dietrich Beyrau, *Russische Orientpolitik und die Entstehung des deutschen Kaiserreiches 1865–1870/71* (Munich, 1974), 56–57 and 230–31, and Saitta, *Problema*, 2, 336–43 and 350–57.

43. *APP*, 2, pt. 1, nos. 9, 48, 81, 84, 89, 95–96, 111, 114, 175, and 268.

44. Guizot, *Mémoires*, 5, 34–35, 40–41, 70–71,224–25, 234–35, 242–43, 320–31, 336–37, 340–41, 368–69, 470–72, 487 ff., 502–05 and 506–09.

45. P. W. Schroeder, "Alliances, 1815–1945: Weapons of Power and Tools of Management," in *Historical Dimensions of National Security Problems*, ed. K. Knorr (Lawrence, KS., 1976), 227–56. For a concrete instance of a pact of restraint serving as guarantor of equilibrium, see *DDF*, ser. 1, 5, no. 225.

46. See, e.g., Cavour-Azeglio, *Carteggio*, 1, nos. 212, 234, 282, 337, 462, 502, and 553.

47. The clash between conceptions of equilibrium is brought out clearly in Saitta, *Problema*,—the pro-Italian view in 1, 27, 29, 50–51, 88–91, and 267; the anti-Italian in 2, 250 and 276–83.

48. Of 18 specific references to equilibrium in *DDF*, ser. 3, 7, 16 refer to the Balkan balance, and every one calls either for preventing Bulgaria from becoming too powerful, or, after its defeat and drastic weakening in the Second Balkan War, preventing its recovery. The same thing is true in vols. 9 and 10. For striking examples of what a Balkan "equilibrium" meant to French, Russian, and Serb statesmen, see ibid., 7, no. 319; 10, nos. 80 and 560; and *I*, 2, nos. 159 and 169 (annex).

49. *GP*, 23, chap. 159; Holstein, *Papiere*, 5, 401.

50. *DDF*, ser. 3, 10, nos. 20, 23–25, 101–02, and 155.

51. P. W. Schroeder, "World War I as Galloping Gertie," *Journal of Modern History*, 44 (1972), 319–45. For documentary evidence, see *DDF*, ser. 3, 7, nos. 41, 194, and 315; 9, nos. 281, 336, 355, 363, and 370–71; 10, Nos. 141, 173, 229, and 286; and *I*, 2, no. 146.

CHAPTER 11   THE COLD WAR AND ITS ENDING IN "LONG-DURATION" INTERNATIONAL HISTORY

1. Some examples: no peace was made between the two main combatants, France and Spain. There was no exact delimitation of territorial and sovereign rights in Alsace, a key area in dispute, between the king of France, the German emperor in both his imperial and Austrian Habsburg roles, and local princes, cities, and church authorities. The exact role and nature of France's and Sweden's new position as protectors of the constitution and liberties of the empire were not

delineated. The relation of former imperial territories and circles such as Burgundy and the Low Countries to the empire was not defined. Neither was the precise relation of the empire and imperial institutions and authorities to the imperial estates. War continued in the Baltic and northeastern Europe, and relations between Christian Europe and the still dangerous and aggressive Ottoman Empire in Southeastern Europe and the Mediterranean remained critical. All these issues and problems would continue to cause constant conflict and considerable war in the decades after Westphalia.

2. Some examples of progress are: cooperation between the hereditary enemies Britain and France to enforce and revise the settlement; their willingness to impose peace and compromise on former or current allies with relative success; the fact that international congresses and conferences were called to settle crises (even if they proved unsuccessful); and the persistent efforts for peace made by leading statesmen—Robert Walpole, the regent of France Philippe of Orleans, the abbé Dubois, and Cardinal Fleury. Perhaps the most striking evidence of change, though it ultimately backfired, was the long effort made by Emperor Charles VI of Austria to insure the most important goal of his reign, the peaceful and orderly sucession of his daughter Maria Theresia to all his domains, by means of a Pragmatic Sanction accepted by the various Habsburg estates and guaranteed by international treaties concluded with all the important powers of Europe. In other words, this was a major effort to solve the most critical problem of eighteenth-century international politics and main focal point of most of its wars, dynastic succession, through peaceful diplomacy and international law. True, the naked lawbreaking and aggression of Prussia under Frederick II in 1740, followed quickly by France and Bavaria, wrecked this attempt and nearly brought down the Habsburg Monarchy down. Nonetheless, the very attempt would have been unthinkable a century before.

3. The absence of any consensus on a definition of peace is evident in both cases. After 1763 France, though too exhausted to launch a new general war, remained bent on restoring the balance of power Britain had overturned, particularly on the high seas. Austria felt the same way about Prussia, Prussia was equally fearful of Austria, and both feared and resented their growing dependence on Russia. The Russian Empress Catherine II meanwhile exploited her position as arbiter to expand Russia's control of Poland, aggrandize Russia at the Ottoman Empire's expense, and intervene in German affairs. After 1871, France felt deeply threatened by Germany sought revision, while Austria found itself so dominated by the new German Reich and so dependent upon it that it bent its policy toward an alliance with Prussia–Germany directed squarely against Russia in the only area still left for Austria to play a role as a great power, the Balkans. Russia meanwhile was keenly aware of this danger, secretly worried by Germany's rise in power, and determined that Germany must prove itself Russia's friend or Russia would have to find ways to check it. The Italians meanwhile were simultaneously insecure, fearful, and greedy. Only the British at first were relatively satisfied with the outcome in 1871, as they had been in 1763, and in both instances that mood and optimistic appraisal did not last long.

4. Illustrating this inaction in the later eighteenth century was the failure of the French and Austrian efforts to get European cooperation to preserve Poland or the Ottoman Empire. In the late nineteenth century, examples are the failure of all attempts after 1887 to revive the Three Emperors' League and the inability of the Hague peace conferences to achieve practical progress on disarmament or arms control. On this last,

see Jost Dülffer, *Regeln gegen den Krieg? Die Friedenskonferenzen von 1899 und 1902 in der internationalen Politik* (Berlin, 1981).

5. J. H. Elliott, *The Count-Duke of Olivares* (New Haven, CT., 1986) and Elliott, *Richelieu and Olivares* (Cambridge, UK, 1984); R. A. Stradling, *Philip IV and the Government of Spain, 1621–1655* (Cambridge, UK, 1988); Lucien Bély, *Les relations internationales en Europe (XVIIè-XVIIIè siècles)* (Paris, 1992).

6. Robert Bireley, *Religion and Politics in the Age of the Counter-Reformation* (Chapel Hill, NC., 1981); Geoffrey Parker, *The Thirty Years War* (London, 1987); Johannes Burkhardt, *Der Dreissigjährige Krieg* (Frankfurt a M., 1992).

7. T. C. W. Blanning, *The Origins of the French Revolutionary Wars 1787–1802* (London, 1986); Paul W. Schroeder, *The Transformation of European Politics 1763–1848* (Oxford, 1994).

8. For a convincing exposition of this revisionist view, see G.-H. Soutou, *L'or et le sang: Les but de guerres économiques de la Première Guerre mondiale* (Paris, 1989).

9. This is not an original verdict of course but also not simply a conventional one. It seems to me, moreover, in line with the main outcome of the orthodox-revisionist debate in American foreign policy historiography, strengthened by work taking account of new material from the Soviet archives. See, e.g., Norman Naimark, *The Russians in Germany: A History of the Soviet Zone of Occupation, 1945–1949* (Cambridge, MA., 1995); Carolyn Eisenberg, *Drawing the Line: The American Decision to Divide Germany, 1944–1949* (New York, 1996); Vladislav Zubok and Constantine Pleshakov, *Inside the Kremlin's Cold War: From Stalin to Khrushchev* (Cambridge, MA., 1996), 276; Marc Trachtenberg, *A Constructed Peace: The Making of the European Settlement, 1945–1963* (Princeton, NJ., 1999). For an excellent survey and interpretation of the evidence, see Melvyn Leffler, "The Struggle for Germany and the Origins of the Cold War," Occasional Paper No. 16, German Historical Institute, Washington, DC (1996).

10. Some striking historical ironies are evident here—that anti-Marxists should develop a capitalist version of the Marxist–Leninist doctrine of the withering away of the state, or that strong hostility to big government and distrust of its power should coexist with a sanguine confidence about enormous concentrations of power and wealth in great corporations, mostly multinational, institutions generally more secretive and less transparent and accessible to the rule of law than democratic governments are.

11. For example, a functioning global market could help declining states incapable of sustaining their previous role as great powers accept their loss of great power status and security peacefully by holding out the prospect that this loss would not jeopardize their economic future. But even for this a working international market system is only a necessary and not a sufficient condition. Political action and commitment on the part of both victors and losers in the power-political game are needed to make it happen.

CHAPTER 12 DOES THE HISTORY OF INTERNATIONAL POLITICS GO ANYWHERE?

1. Charles S. Maier, "Marking Time: The Historiography of International Relations," in *The Past Before Us*, ed. Michael G. Kammen (Ithaca, 1980), 355–87.

2. Evidence of this, striking if impressionistic, can be seen in the questionnaire in which the American Historical Association in the 1990s asked its members to list

their fields of specialization. Sixty-five specific fields were included, categorized according to geography, chronology, and subject matter, including old standard fields like the history of ideas and newer ones like the history of women and gay/lesbian history. There were 19 separate fields for U.S. historians, including U.S. Diplomatic-International. But members of the AHA who specialized in the history of international politics in Europe and the wider world over the last five centuries had to write in this specialization in a sixty-sixth space, marked "Other."

3. For example, by Gordon A. Craig, in his AHA presidential address, "The Historian and the Study of International Relations," *American Historical Review*, 88 (1983), 1–11.

4. Richard Pares, "Human Nature in Politics," in *The Historian's Business and Other Essays*, ed. R. A. Humphreys and E. Humphreys (Oxford, 1961), 37–39.

5. Kenneth Waltz, *Theory of International Politics* (New York, 1979).

6. I base these estimates on the statistics supplied by Jack S. Levy, *War in the Modern Great Power System, 1495–1975* (Lexington, KY., 1975).

7. Some might dispute this, arguing that certain crises in the Anglo-Russian rivalry over Central Asia and the northwest frontier of India came close to causing war. My view is that these crises were local and overrated in nature, provoked by particular circumstances and the actions of men on the spot, and that the two governments actually never came close to war over them, as they did more than once over the Near East.

8. As Paul Johnson argues in *The Birth of the Modern World, 1815–1830* (New York, 1991).

9. Richard Rosecrance, *The Rise of the Trading State* (New York, 1987).

10. Paul W. Schroeder, "Does Murphy's Law Apply to History?" *The Wilson Quarterly* (New Year's, 1985), 84–93.

11. Paul W. Schroeder, "Containment Nineteenth Century Style: How Russia Was Restrained," *South Atlantic Quarterly*, 82 (1983), 1–18.

12. A few examples of attempts to do so are Rosecrance, *Rise of the Trading State* (New York, 1987); John Lewis Gaddis, *The Long Peace* (New York, 1987); and John E. Mueller, *Retreat from Doomsday* (New York, 1989). For a discussion of the impact of these developments on international relations see John Lewis Gaddis, "International Relations Theory and the End of the Cold War," *International Security*, 17, 3 (1992–93), 5–58.

13. Peter Krüger, ed., *Kontinuität und Wandel in der Staatenordnung der Neuzeit* (Marburg, 1991); see also his edited work, *Das europäische Staatensystem im Wandel* (Munich, 1996).

Chapter 13   International History: Why Historians Do It Differently than Political Scientists

1. "International History and International Politics: Why Are They Studied Differently?" in Colin Elman and Miriam Fendius Elman, eds., *Bridges and Boundaries: Historians, Political Scientists, and the Study of International Relations* (Cambridge, MA., 2001), 385–402.

2. This was illustrated by a recent interchange on the internet H-Diplo, whose contributors are primarily historians of U.S. foreign policy, in which various scholars

who usually disagreed on other issues agreed that the study of foreign languages and foreign language materials was sadly neglected in American historiography.

3. James Joll, *The Origins of the First World War*, 2nd ed. (New York, 1992). Joll's conclusion is not that no overall parsimonious explanation is possible—only that he finds no fully satisfying one among those he presents, and offers none himself.

4. Ian Kershaw, *The Nazi Dictatorship: Problems and Perpectives of Interpretation*, 2nd ed. (London, 1989).

5. Michael Marrus, *The Holocaust in History* (Hanover, NH., 1987).

6. An excellent example of this is Dietrich Geyer's *Der russische Imperialismus* (Göttingen, 1977), translated into English as *Russian Imperialism: The Interaction of Domestic and Foreign Policy, 1860–1914* (New Haven, CT., 1987). Geyer, a student of Hans-Ulrich Wehler, set out to test and substantiate Wehler's theory of imperialism as secondary integration. He did not end up rejecting or disproving it, but being a very good historian he did show that the interaction between domestic and foreign policy was more nuanced and complex than any theory of the primacy of domestic politics would allow—a finding that, while it made much sense historically, largely rendered the book useless for emancipationist-reformist purposes.

7. David S. Landes, *The Wealth and Poverty of Nations* (New York, 1998).

8. Richard Ned Lebow, *From Peace to War: The Nature of International Crisis* (Baltimore, MD., 1981); Paul W. Schroeder, "Failed Bargain Crises, Deterrence, and the International System," in *Perspectives on Deterrence*, ed. Paul C. Stern et al. (New York, 1989), 67–83.

9. F. R. Bridge, "Izvolsky, Aehrenthal, and the End of the Austro-Russian Entente, 1906–8," *Mitteilungen des Österreichischen Staatsarchivs, Sonderdruck*, 29 (1976), 316–62.

10. There are many anecdotes that illustrate this tendency of diplomats to see a hidden purpose behind everything their opponents do. My favorite is a remark attributed to Prince Metternich of Austria when he learned that an old rival, the Russian diplomat Pozzo di Borgo, had died: "Now why do you suppose he did that?"

11. *Diplomacy* (New York, 1994), 58–67.

12. M. S. Anderson, *The Rise of Modern European Diplomacy 1450–1919* (London, 1974) 161.

13. See the discussion of Mattingly in J. H. Hexter, *Doing History* (Bloomington, IN., 1974).

14. J. H. Elliott, *The Count-Duke of Olivares: The Statesman in an Age of Decline* (New Haven, CT., 1986). See also his *Richelieu and Olivares* (Cambridge: Cambridge University Press, 1984).

15. These are my formulations of Mattingly's and Hexter's positions, not quotations from them.

CHAPTER 14   THE MIRAGE OF EMPIRE VERSUS THE PROMISE OF HEGEMONY

This essay was presented at a conference on Systems of World Order at the School of Advanced International Studies, Johns Hopkins University in Washington, DC, March 28, 2003. Its main thesis was earlier advanced at a session on empire at the annual meeting of the American Historical Association in Chicago, IL, January 11,

2003. The text has been revised and expanded, but the arguments have deliberately been left unaltered so as not to reflect changes and developments since it was written in early 2003.

1. Some examples of arguments for unipolar American world supremacy are: C. Krauthammer, "The Unipolar Moment Revisited," *The National Interest* no. 70 (Winter 2002/03), 5–20; W. Kristol and L. F. Kaplan, *The War Over Iraq: Saddam's Tyranny and America's Mission* (New York, 2003); and R. Kagan, *Of Paradise and Power: America and Europe in the New World Order* (New York, 2003). A much more ambitious and outwardly impressive attempt to ground both America's world military and political supremacy and the emergence of what the author calls a "market state" in history is P. Bobbitt, *The Shield of Achilles: War, Peace and the Course of History* (New York, 2002). For a critique of the work as history, see P. W. Schroeder, "A Papier-Maché Fortress," *The National Interest*, no. 70 (Winter 2002/03), 125–32.

2. This was clearly the case with the second British Empire in the late eighteenth, nineteenth, and early twentieth centuries, e.g. The famous "imperialism of free trade" thesis of R. Robinson and J. Gallagher, *Africa and the Victorians: The Climax of Imperialism on the Dark Continent* (New York, 1961) was and remains controversial at many points, but the recognition that British ascendancy in Africa, India, and elsewhere at its height was mainly a matter of informal but recognized paramountcy and that the Empire actually passed its peak when competition compelled a change from informal paramountcy to formal rule has not been overturned. For an excellent analysis and survey of the controversy, see W. R. Louis, ed., *The Robinson and Gallagher Controversy* (New York, 1976). For the best introduction to the massive subject and its literature, see W. R. Louis, ed., *The Oxford History of the British Empire* 5 vols. (Oxford, 1998–99); on "informal empire" see especially vol. 3, *The Nineteenth Century*, ed. A. Porter, 8–9, 170–97, passim. For the relative decline of the British Empire in the era of New Imperialism as informal empire gave way to more formal rule, see M. Beloff, *Imperial Sunset* vol. 1, *Britain's Liberal Empire, 1897–1921* (New York, 1970); Ronald Hyam, *Britain's Imperial Century, 1815–1914* (New York, 1976).

3. For example, see N. J. Smelser and P. B. Baltes, eds., *International Encyclopedia of the Social Sciences*, vol. X (Amsterdam, 2001), 6642–50; A. G. Johnson, ed., *The Blackwell Dictionary of Sociology* 2nd ed. (Oxford, 2000), 141–42. C. J. Nolan, *The Enyclopedia of International Relations* 4 vols. (Westport, CT., Greenwood, 2002) is not very helpful on hegemony (vol. II, 699–700) but rightly stresses political control as the essence of imperialism. So does the famous authority on the structure of empires Shmuel N. Eisenstadt in D. N. Sills, ed., *International Encyclopedia of the Social Sciences*, vol. V (New York, 1968), 41.

4. The best discussions of hegemony within the modern international system have gained little attention in the Anglo-Saxon literature, perhaps because they come from German historians (Heinrich Triepel, E. R. Huber, and Rudolf Stadelmann) in the Nazi and immediate postwar era (though the basic ideas they present are much older). For a good brief discussion of the relation between hegemony and balance (*Gleichgewicht*) see O. Brunner, W. Conze, and R. Koselleck, eds., *Geschichtliche Grundbegriffe*, vol. II (Stuttgart: Klett, 1975), 968–69. For the importance and value of hegemony in political economy, see R. Gilpin, *The Political Economy of International Relations* (Princeton, NJ., 1987), and C. Kindleberger, *The World in Depression, 1929–1939* rev. ed., (Berkeley, CA., 1986).

5. Two examples: Following the British conquest and occupation of Egypt in 1882, Egypt remained technically an autonomous province of the Ottoman Empire with certain residual rights of suzerainty belonging to the Sultan. Officially the British were there only to advise the Egyptian government, and the British government even used the Egyptian government's claims to ownership of the Sudan to carry out a conquest of the Sudan in 1898 with the aid of Egyptian forces and resources (though subsequently denying the Egyptians any control over the Sudan). No one was fooled by this pattern, which also applied in various ways to other parts of the British Empire. Similarly, the Soviet Empire after 1945 included not merely ostensibly sovereign and independent Communist states behind the Iron Curtain, but supposedly independent republics within the Soviet Union itself, some of whom had seats in the UN. Once again, no one was fooled by this. Nor were many outside the United States deceived about the reality of American empire in much of Latin America, especially the Caribbean, in much of the nineteenth and twentieth centuries, by the absence of formal American rule.

6. R. Stadelmann's definition of hegemony as "guided balance" ("gelenktes Gleichgewicht"—see n. 4) often applies in history. For example, the relative stability and peace of the Bismarckian era in Europe (1871–90), frequently attributed simply to the operation of the balance of power, actually would have been impossible without what Andreas Hillgruber aptly described as a labile German half-hegemony and Bismarck's skillful use of that half-hegemony to devise and impose expedients for managing European crises (*Bismarcks Aussenpolitik* [Freiburg i. Breisgau, 1972]. Two excellent accounts of this are K. Hildebrand, *Das vergangene Reich: Deutsche Aussenpolitik von Bismarck bis Hitler* (Stuttgart, 1995) and G. F. Kennan, *The Decline of Bismarck's European Order: Franco-Russian Relations, 1875–1890* (Princeton, NJ., 1979).

7. Again examples are easy to find: the breakdown of Anglo-French Dual Control in Egypt, 1875–82, leading to heightened tension and imperial competition in Africa and elsewhere and a serious crisis in 1898, only healed by a clear delimitation of spheres in 1904; or the Anglo-Russian partition of Persia into spheres of influence in 1907, which worked badly and was breaking down by 1914 despite the two powers' shared interest in excluding and blocking Germany, because each side believed the other was interfering in its exclusive sphere and the intervening neutral zone or illegitimately expanding its control. For the Anglo-French contest, see G. N. Sanderson, *England, Europe and the Upper Nile, 1882–1899* (Edinburgh, 1965). For the Anglo-Russian one, F. Kazemzadeh, *Russia and Britain in Persia, 1864–1914: A Study in Imperialism* (New Haven, CT., 1964).

8. For example, as I argue in my book *The Transformation of European Politics 1763–1848* (Oxford, 1994, 1996), peace and stability in the Vienna era (1815–48) can best be explained by the existence and operation of an overall Anglo-Russian shared hegemony in Europe, Britain's in Western Europe, and Russia's in Eastern Europe, with each of them sharing their overall spheres of influence with junior great-power partners (Britain with France, Russia with Austria and Prussia). Where a great power felt shut out of its legitimate share of influence (e.g., France by Britain in Spain or by Austria in Italy), tension and crisis could easily result even if no tangible stakes were involved.

9. A. Kohler, *Karl V: 1500–1558: eine Biographie* (Munich, 1999).

10. G. Parker, *The Grand Strategy of Philip II* (New Haven, CT., 1998).

11. R. Bireley, *Religion and Politics in the Age of the Counterreformation* (Chapel Hill, NC., 1981); J. Burkhardt, *Der Dreissig jährige Krieg* (Frankfurt a. M., 1992).

12. F. Bosbach, *Monarchia Universalis: ein politischer Leitbegriff der frühen Neuzeit* (Göttingen, 1988); A. Lossky, *Louis XIV and the French Monarchy* (New Brunswick, NJ., 1994).

13. M. Roberts, *The Swedish Imperial Experience, 1560–1718* (New York, 1979).

14. A. Kohler, *Das Reich im Kampf um die Hegemonie in Europa, 1521–1648* (Munich, 1990).

15. K. Malettke, *Frankreich, Deutschland und Europa im 17. und 18. Jahrhundert* (Marburg, 1994); P. Goubert, *Mazarin* (Paris, 1990).

16. H. Duchhardt, *Altes Reich und Europäische Staatenwelt, 1648–1806* (Munich, 1988); A. Schindling, *Die Anfänge des immerwährenden Reichstags zu Regensburg* (Mainz, 1991); K. O. von Aretin, *Das alte Reich* Vol. I, *1648–1684* (Stuttgart, 1993).

17. D. McKay and H. M. Scott, *The Rise of the Great Powers, 1648–1815* (London, 1983); J. H. Plumb, *Sir Robert Walpole* 2 vols., (Boston, 1956–61); J. Black, *British Foreign Policy in the Age of Walpole* (Edinburgh, 1985); J. Black, *Natural and Necessary Enemies: Anglo-French Relations in the Eighteenth Century* (London, 1986).

18. P. Vaucher, *Robert Walpole et la politique de Fleury* (Paris, 1924).

19. See n. 8; also P. W. Schroeder, "Did the Vienna Settlement Rest on a Balance of Power?" *American Historical Review*, 97, 2 (June 1992), 683–706, 733–35.

20. H. M. Scott, *British Foreign Policy in the Age of the American Revolution* (Oxford, 1990); I. de Madariaga, *Russia in the Age of Catherine the Great* (New Haven, CT., 1982); M. G. Müller, *Die Teilungen Polens: 1772, 1793, 1795* (Munich, 1984).

21. S. Marks, *Illusion of Peace: International Relations in Europe, 1918–1933* (London, 1976); Kindleberger, *World in Depression*.

INDEX

Alexander I, 53, 55, 125–126, 128, 130, 199–200, 217

alliances, *see* Axis Alliance; Dual Alliance; Grand Alliance; Holy Alliance; Quadruple Alliance; Triple Alliance; Triple Entente

Alsace-Lorraine, 77, 85–86, 150–151, 174, 184, 211

Angell, Norman, 177

Annales school of historiography, 246–247

Annalistes, 17, 246, 267

appeasement, 27–28, 102, 145–146, 217, 287

Arabi, Colonel, 108

Austria, 2–4, 8–16, 48, 77, 116–117, 139–140, 178–181, 231, 233, 251–253, 275, 277, 292; alliances, 40–41, 199–217; Eastern policy, 59–75; hegemony, 45, 54, 236, 300; relations with Britain, 42, 99–105, 108–113, 142–143; relations with France, 26–34, 79–80, 105; relations with Germany, 42–45, 83–85, 88–89, 90–92; relations with Prussia, 11, 39, 43–45, 53–54, 73, 80–84, 203–205, 275; relations with Russia, 55–56, 86, 87–89, 122–125, 127–128, 131–132, 282; role in World War I, 147–155, 161–171, 173–175, 227–229, 236–239

Austria-Hungary, 2, 8, 15–16, 83, 85, 88, 102, 140, 147; and counter factual argument for World War I, 161–171, 178–181, 183–191; Torshluspanik in, 173–175, 209, 211–212; growing dependence on Germany, 215, 237–238, 292

Axis Alliance, 218

Baghdad Railway, 143, 145, 168, 175, 213, 341

balance of power, 39, 202, 207–208, 211, 213–214; an ambiguous concept, 4–5, 38, 126–127, 129–131, 146, 148–149; and the nineteenth century system, 221–234, 236–237; not important at Vienna, 37–52, 54–57, 74, 154, 171–172, 178, 188, 195–197; not same as political equilibrium, 239, 247, 250–251, 253–255, 259, 261, 264, 272, 277, 281–284, 300

Balkans, 2, 14–16, 29, 42, 60, 62, 66–67, 74, 100–113, 117, 122–129, 132, 137, 139, 142–154, 161, 163–164, 168–171, 175, 180, 184–191, 209–215, 219, 222, 227, 236–238, 252, 281, 283, 292

Balkan League, 149, 151, 163

Balkan policy, 105, 215

Balkan War, 137, 145, 163–164, 168, 171, 184

Bavarian Patriot Party, 91

Belgian question, 202

Belkin, Aaron, 157–158, 160 *see also* Tetlock, Philip

Berchtold Leopold Count, 139

Bethmann-Hollweg, Theopold von, 137

Beust, Friedrich Ferdinand Count, 84, 90–91, 94, 239

Bismarck, Otto von, 2, 7, 11–14; and 1870, 77, 83–85, 87–91, 93–94; as Gladstone, 97–98, 102, 104, 106, 108, 110–115, 117–119; alliances of, 125, 128, 132, 142, 146, 162, 174, 180, 187, 196, 203, 207–212, 214, 221, 228, 231–232, 234, 239, 241, 253–254, 301, 305

Boer War, 123, 141, 144

16600036R00214

Made in the USA
Middletown, DE
18 December 2014